Lancelot Andrewes
Selected Sermons and Lectures

Lancelot Andrewes

SELECTED SERMONS AND LECTURES

Edited with an Introduction
and Commentary by
PETER McCULLOUGH

OXFORD
UNIVERSITY PRESS

OXFORD
UNIVERSITY PRESS

Great Clarendon Street, Oxford OX2 6DP

Oxford University Press is a department of the University of Oxford.
It furthers the University's objective of excellence in research, scholarship,
and education by publishing worldwide in

Oxford New York

Auckland Cape Town Dar es Salaam Hong Kong Karachi
Kuala Lumpur Madrid Melbourne Mexico City Nairobi
New Delhi Shanghai Taipei Toronto

With offices in

Argentina Austria Brazil Chile Czech Republic France Greece
Guatemala Hungary Italy Japan Poland Portugal Singapore
South Korea Switzerland Thailand Turkey Ukraine Vietnam

Oxford is a registered trade mark of Oxford University Press
in the UK and in certain other countries

Published in the United States by Oxford University Press Inc., New York

© in the editorial matter and arrangement Peter McCullough 2005

The moral rights of the author have been asserted
Database right Oxford University Press (maker)

First published 2005

All rights reserved. No part of this publication may be reproduced,
stored in a retrieval system, or transmitted, in any form or by any means,
without the prior permission in writing of Oxford University Press,
or as expressly permitted by law, or under terms agreed with the appropriate
reprographics rights organization. Enquiries concerning reproduction
outside the scope of the above should be sent to the Rights Department,
Oxford University Press, at the address above

You must not circulate this book in any other binding or cover
and you must impose the same condition on any acquirer

British Library Cataloguing in Publication Data

Data available

Library of Congress Cataloging in Publication Data

Data available

Typeset by SPI Publisher Services, Pondicherry, India
Printed in Great Britain
on acid-free paper by
Biddles Ltd., King's Lynn, Norfolk

ISBN 0–19–818774–2   978–0–19–818774–5

1 3 5 7 9 10 8 6 4 2

In Memoriam
Gene and Lila McCullough
1935–2000

We shall then indeed receive the *fulnesse* of our redemption, not from the *Law* (that we have alreadie) but from *Corruption*, to which our bodies are yet subject; and receive the *full fruition* of the *Inheritance*, wherto we are heere but *adopted*. And then it will be perfect, compleat, absolute *fulnesse* indeed, when we shall all *be filled* with the *fulnesse of Him that filleth all in all*.

ACKNOWLEDGEMENTS

I wish to thank the Arts and Humanities Research Board for a Research Leave award, and Lincoln College and Oxford University for sabbatical leave and research grants which have all assisted me in bringing this edition to completion. Early work on the project was also made possible by a short-term fellowship at the Huntington Library, San Marino, California, sponsored by the Huntington and Lincoln College.

During my research, I have received the assistance of librarians and staff of the following institutions, and gratefully acknowledge their help: the Bodleian Library, the Music Faculty Library, and All Souls College Library, Oxford; Pembroke, Emmanuel, and Trinity College Libraries, and the University Library, Cambridge; St Paul's Cathedral Library, the Guildhall Library, and the Corporation of London Record Office, London; and the Huntington Library, San Marino. I must also record my special thanks to the Master and Fellows of Trinity College, Cambridge, and the Dean and Chapter of St Paul's Cathedral for granting permission to reproduce unique manuscript material held in their collections.

I owe a special debt of gratitude to Brian Vickers, Paul G. Stanwood, and W. Speed Hill, who took an encouraging interest in my early proposals for a new edition of Andrewes, and generously shared expertise and advice for editing early modern non-dramatic texts. Professor Vickers, together with Nicholas Tyacke, also provided invaluable support of my application for major research funding.

The daunting interdisciplinarity required to edit an author of such interest as Andrewes is to historians, theologians, and literary scholars was ameliorated by specialist knowledge shared by colleagues from Oxford and beyond. Since space does not allow due credit to be individually given in the commentary for the host of questions answered by them, I am particularly keen to record here my thanks to Margaret Aston, Margaret Bent, Kate Bennett, Robin Briggs, Andrew Gregory, Thomas Freeman, E. S. Leedham-Green, Peter Groves, Gareth Lloyd Jones, Morwenna Ludlow, Jayne Ringrose, David Skinner, Nigel Wilson, Jo Wisdom, and Hugh Wybrew.

Each text included in the edition, together with its annotations and apparatus, was scrutinized by other valued colleagues. This edition has thus benefited immeasurably from the scholarly acumen of Ian Archer, Susan Brigden, Kenneth Fincham, Felicity Heal, Erica Longfellow,

Diarmaid MacCulloch, Mary Morrissey, Isabel Rivers, David Harris Sacks, Johann Sommerville, Clare Tilbury, Philip West, and Henry Woudhuysen. The inevitable errors (whether of omission or commission) which remain are of course entirely my own.

In the final stages of preparation of the manuscript, I was blessed with the most expertly qualified research assistant imaginable in Ellie Bagley. Her training in textual criticism and bibliography was itself a godsend, but also came coupled with a command of the biblical languages and of the late sixteenth-century English Bible translation debates. In particular, I owe to her the notice given in the commentary of many of Andrewes's most surprising appropriations of Roman Catholic (Rheims) translations and glosses of scripture. Francis Whistler of Oxford University Press offered trenchant advice on textual matters, which was succeeded by the professionalism and enthusiasm of Tom Perridge and Andrew McNeillie.

Finally, work of this kind could not have been done without the less tangible, yet more important, moral support of friends. I would like to thank Stephen Gill, Clare Tilbury, Helen and Martin Foreman, Peter and Beatrice Groves, Paul Harper-Scott, Kate and Matt Peterson, John and Jan Logan, Lori Anne Ferrell, and Thomas P. Roche, Jr. for seeing me through the dark days that coincided with the genesis of this edition, and for sharing the happiness that has come since. My debt of gratitude to the source of that happiness—Thomas Knollys, his family, and Hugh and Eleanor McCullough—is immeasurable.

CONTENTS

Introduction	xi
Chronology	lviii

    I. Two most excellent Praiers, which the Preacher commonly used before his Exercises   1

  II. *from* The Pattern of Catechistical Doctrine   5
      1. Of the Interpretation of Scriptures   5
      2. Of Prayer and Thanksgiving   11
      3. Of outward reverence in God's worship   21
      4. The Sabbath not wholly ceremonial   33
      5. Of Places for publick Worship   38

  III. A Sermon Preached at Saint Maries Hospital, on the X. of April, being Wednesday in Easter-weeke, A.D. MDLXXXVIII   40

  IV. Sacrilege a Snare. A Sermon Preached *ad Clerum* In the University of Cambridg   82

  V. A Lecture on Genesis 2.18 (the Creation of Eve) Preached at St. Paul's Cathedral, 18 October 1591.   100

  VI. A Sermon Preached before Queene Elizabeth, at Hampton Court, on Wednesday, being the VI. of March, A.D. MDXCIIII.   108

  VII. A Sermon Preached at the Court, on the XXV. of March, A.D. MDXCVII. being Good-Friday.   122

  VIII. A Sermon on Isaiah 6.6–7, Preached at St. Giles Cripplegate, 1 October 1598.   138

  IX. A Sermon Preached before the King's Majestie, at White-Hall, on the V. of November. A.D. MDCVI.   146

  X. A Sermon Preached before the Kings Majestie at Whitehall, on Christmas Day. ANNO 1609.   162

	CONTENTS	
XI.	A Sermon Preached before His Majestie, on Sunday the fifth of August last, at Holdenbie... 1610	178
XII.	A Sermon Preached before the King's Majestie at Greenwich on the XXIV. of May, A.D. MDCXVIII. being Whit-Sunday.	207
XIII.	A Sermon Preached at White-Hall, on Easter day the 16. of April. 1620.	225
Appendix 1. A Sermon Preached at the Spittle by Master Andrewes... April. 10. 1588.		243
Appendix 2. Table of Correspondence: Sermon at St Mary's Hospital, 1588.		265
Explanatory Notes		267
Abbreviations		267
Other Works Frequently Cited		271
Notes		272
Index of Biblical Texts		467
General Index		479

INTRODUCTION

He was, as all our English world well knowes, a singular *Preacher*, and a most famous *Writer*. He was so singular a Preacher and so profound a Writer, that you will doubt in which he did excell.

(John Buckeridge, bishop of Rochester, 1626)

His sermons ... rank with the finest English prose of their time, of any time.

(T. S. Eliot, 1926)

I. REASSESSMENT

It is my hope that this edition will both confirm and complicate these judgements. Buckeridge (in Andrewes's funeral sermon) and Eliot (in a eulogistic appreciation on the tercentenary of Andrewes's death) wrote exactly 300 years apart.[1] But the Caroline bishop and the Modernist literary critic epitomize a literary-critical tradition which has insisted upon Andrewes's intellectual and literary brilliance, yet also limited the modern scholarly audience he deserves. Crucially, both did so through posthumous editions of Andrewes's works. These editions were primarily designed neither to commend his stunningly original English prose, nor to document the evolution of his thought across his long adult life, but rather to articulate their own ecclesiastical agendas. No editor—especially one who takes up the daunting task of presenting only selected works of an author—lacks an agenda. Mine here, unlike any previously, has been to attempt an annotated critical edition of selected prose works guided exclusively by neither literary nor religious principles, but rather by a desire for the most comprehensive possible range of date, occasion, place, and subject for the genre in which Andrewes excelled, the English sermon. That is, I hope to

---

[1] John Buckeridge, 'A Sermon Preached at the Funeral', appended to William Laud and John Buckeridge (eds.), *XCVI. Sermons by ... Lancelot Andrewes* (1629), 18; T. S. Eliot, 'Lancelot Andrewes', *TLS* 1286 (23 Sept. 1926), [621]–622; repr. in *For Lancelot Andrewes: Essays on Style and Order* (London, 1928; New York, 1929), and in *Selected Essays* (New York, 1932; new edn., 1960), 299–310; subsequent references are to the latter edition. The tercentenary allusion would have been clear to readers of the 23 Sept. 1926 *TLS* from the essay's opening sentence: 'The Right Reverend Father in God, Lancelot Bishop of Winchester, died on September 25, 1626.'

have assembled a group of texts that illustrates the origins and development, as well as the mature achievement, of Andrewes's prose style, theology, politics, and churchmanship—all of which deserve the epithet 'avant-garde'.[2] As that list suggests, I also hope that the fully annotated texts in this edition will serve the purposes of the wide interdisciplinary range of modern students of Andrewes in the allied fields of English literature, Reformation theology, and British ecclesiastical history. To do so has required the application of a sharp revisionist blade to the hitherto accepted canon of Andrewes's sermons, with the result that those familiar with the tradition begun by Buckeridge and celebrated by Eliot should be surprised, and that those approaching Andrewes for the first time can encounter him in a more fully historicized context than previous editions have allowed.

Most profoundly influential on the reception and study of Andrewes's sermons has been the first collected edition, *XCVI. Sermons*, a commemorative folio edited (not unlike the first folio of Shakespeare) by admiring colleagues: Buckeridge himself, and Buckeridge's pupil William Laud, then bishop of London and Andrewes's successor as dean of the Chapel Royal and, ultimately, executed archbishop of Canterbury.[3] *XCVI. Sermons* consciously presented Andrewes's writings as a Laudian manifesto. The overwhelming majority of sermons included in it were preached at court on high feast days after Andrewes's consecration as bishop under James I. And the editors' organizing principle for the sermons in their folio was not chronology or place of preaching (as was conventional), but the church's liturgical year. The resulting volume did not misrepresent what were undoubtedly Andrewes's own views late in his life, but *XCVI. Sermons* also articulated in the very contents and arrangement of the book itself Laud's (and of course Charles I's) vision of a ceremonial churchmanship defended by *jure divino* episcopacy and kingship, and committed to the forceful subjugation of preaching to the church's liturgy, especially the eucharist.[4]

No subsequent edition of Andrewes's sermons has scrutinized Laud's and Buckeridge's presentation of them. In fact, all have either preserved, or

---

[2] An apt term first applied by Peter Lake in 'Lancelot Andrewes, John Buckeridge, and Avant-Garde Conformity at the Court of James I', in Linda Levy Peck (ed.), *The Mental World of the Jacobean Court* (Cambridge, 1991), 113–33; cf. also Debora Shuger, *Habits of Thought in the English Renaissance* (Berkeley, 1990), 8, n. 25.

[3] *XCVI. Sermons by the Right Honorable and Reverend Father in God, Lancelot Andrewes, late Lord Bishop of Winchester. Published by His Majesties speciall Command*, ed. William Laud and John Buckeridge (London: George Miller for Richard Badger, 1629).

[4] See Peter McCullough, 'Making Dead Men Speak: Laudianism, Print, and the Works of Lancelot Andrewes, 1626–1642', *Historical Journal*, 41 (1998), 401–24.

even exaggerated, the Laudian gloss. The *Library of Anglo-Catholic Theology* (1841–54, hereafter *LACT*) reproduced the arrangement of *XCVI. Sermons* intact and was hailed in the unofficial journal of the Oxford Movement as 'one instance... which shows the steady progress we are making in shaking off the coldness and latitudinarianism of the last century'.[5] The only twentieth-century editor working to a scholarly standard, Graham Story, kept his selection of twelve sermons (all from *XCVI. Sermons*) in their liturgical order. A more recent student text edited by Paul Hewison presents both a short chronological sequence of sermons and a separate liturgical grouping of Christmas sermons. And Marianne Dorman's sanitized transcripts of the *LACT* texts, *The Liturgical Sermons of Lancelot Andrewes*, in its very title advertises her replication of the Laudian order.[6] Any reader of Andrewes's sermons since 1629 has therefore read an Andrewes bibliographically defined by William Laud and John Buckeridge. As a result, the relative unavailability of any of the sermons preached by Andrewes in parish churches, college chapels, and City and cathedral pulpits in the first twenty years after his ordination in 1580 has given the false impression that Andrewes was *tout court* a Jacobean 'court preacher', or even more anachronistically, a 'Caroline divine'. It also obscures the surprisingly early origins—which reach well back into the 1580s—of Andrewes's radical reassessment, indeed critique, of the English Reformation. Moreover, Andrewes did not express this in the form of usually leaden Elizabethan controversial writing, but through the brilliant exploitation, in sermons and lectures, of the whole armoury of Renaissance humanist literary art and scholarship that disguised frontal attacks on the dominant English Calvinist orthodoxy with deft literary wit and sophisticated rhetorical argument.

But the Laudian Andrewes has of course appealed to many, and most famously so to T. S. Eliot. Eliot is, in literary terms, the only begetter of modern interest in Andrewes, and, as will be discussed below, his landmark essay on Andrewes is so acute in its formal assessment of Andrewes's prose as almost to have frustrated attempts to take such criticism further. But he, like the Tractarian editors of the *LACT*, found in Andrewes a spokesman for the romantic fantasy of an 'English Catholic Church' who transcended

---

[5] James B. Mozley, review of *LACT*, vols. i–iv, in *The British Critic and Quarterly Theological Review*, 31 (1842), 169; *The British Critic* was edited by Mozley's intimate, J. H. Newman; for bibliographical details of *LACT*, see Abbreviations Used in Commentary.

[6] G. M. Story (ed.), *Lancelot Andrewes: Sermons* (Oxford, 1967); P. E. Hewison (ed.), *Lancelot Andrewes: Selected Writings* (Manchester, 1995); Marianne Dorman (ed.), *The Liturgical Sermons of Lancelot Andrewes*, 2 vols. (Edinburgh, Cambridge, and Durham, 1992–3); for a helpful review of the latter two editions, see P. J. Klemp, 'Editing Renaissance Sermons: The Construction of Lancelot Andrewes's Texts', *Review*, 20 (1998), 17–38.

period and history. Yet close scrutiny of Eliot's essay shows that he was not reading very widely in Andrewes, or even from the *LACT* edition. The Christmas day sermons occupied, by liturgical default, the opening section of *XCVI. Sermons*, and, correspondingly, the *LACT*'s first volume. They were therefore the first to be promulgated in the Tractarian appropriation of Andrewes. And in 1887, the heyday of late Victorian Anglo-Catholicism, they were published alone in a new edition as exemplars for parish priests preparing their own Christmas sermons. This was recommended by the anonymous (but obviously Anglo-Catholic) editor because in Andrewes's nativity sermons, he advised, 'the apprehension of [the Doctrine of the Incarnation], and the place in worship of the Blessed Eucharist, is particularly illustrated'.[7] And this is the volume which Eliot had to hand and recommends to his readers. In fact, the only quotations in his essay are from the Christmas sermons, and most of those are from only one, the 1622 sermon on Matthew 2: 1–2 from which he would also snip the opening lines of his haunting 1929 poem 'Journey of the Magi'. That poem itself uses Andrewes to ventriloquize an early stage on Eliot's own journey to the religious and political position he would finally declare under Andrewes's mitre in *For Lancelot Andrewes*: 'The general point of view may be described as classicist in literature, royalist in politics, and anglo-catholic in religion.'[8]

II. ANDREWES'S LIFE AND WORKS, AND THE SELECTIONS FOR THIS EDITION

My attempt to enlarge the study of Andrewes from outside the limits of the Buckeridge, Laud, and Eliot tradition, then, has been defined by attention to Andrewes's biography. The rationale for the texts included in this edition is thus best cast in those terms.[9]

---

[7] [Ed. anon.], *Seventeen Sermons on the Nativity... by Lancelot Andrewes... A New Edition* (London, [1887]), p. vii.

[8] Eliot, 'Lancelot Andrewes', in *Collected Essays*, 304–8; T. S. Eliot, 'The Journey of the Magi', in *The Complete Poems and Plays* (New York, 1950), 68; T. S. Eliot, preface to *For Lancelot Andrewes* (London, [1928]), p. ix.

[9] Andrewes awaits a complete scholarly biography, forthcoming in the present editor's *Lancelot Andrewes: A Life* (Oxford); the most up-to-date published survey is P. E. McCullough, 'Andrewes, Lancelot', in the *Oxford Dictionary of National Biography* (Oxford, 2004), the source for the account which follows, as well as the Chronology in this edition; see also Paul A. Welsby, *Lancelot Andrewes* (1958); for biographical documents, including correspondence and Andrewes's will, see *LACT*, vol. xi.

Andrewes was the product of the burgeoning early Tudor mercantile class, the eldest child of a prosperous Essex mariner who, with his wife, settled in London in the shadow of the Tower where they raised the six of their thirteen children who survived to adulthood. Born in 1555 under the Catholic Queen Mary, Lancelot was 5 years old when his family's parish church, All-Hallows-by-the-Tower, was stripped of its rood, altars, and images under the reformed Royal Injunctions of 1559. He seems to have been destined, like his younger brothers, to an apprenticeship in trade. But his prodigious academic talent caught the eye of his first schoolmaster, and, more crucially, that of All Hallows's most prominent parishioner, Sir Francis Walsingham, who contributed toward the fees required to send Andrewes to the pace-setting new Merchant Taylors' School. Here Andrewes was taught by the leading Elizabethan humanist Richard Mulcaster in the company of contemporaries such as Edmund Spenser, Thomas Kyd, Thomas Lodge, and Edwin Sandys. The hallmarks of Mulcaster's curriculum—not only Latin grammar and Greek, but also Hebrew; high esteem for modern languages, including English; liberal use of drama and public speaking; the study of music—are all prominent in Andrewes's sermons.

With Spenser, Andrewes proceeded in 1571 to Pembroke Hall, Cambridge, where, with what by then was legendary academic talent, he proceeded through the usual course of degrees, winning a fellowship in 1575, and taking holy orders in 1580. With ordination began Andrewes's career as an esteemed preacher. He had been appointed his college's catechist in 1578, responsible for weekly lectures on fundamentals of the faith, and by the mid-1580s his reputation stretched far beyond the college gates. It is from this period that Andrewes's earliest work survives—notes from his catechetical lectures on the Ten Commandments, delivered *c.*1585 in Pembroke Hall chapel. Laud and Buckeridge professed in their preface to *XCVI. Sermons* that 'there came to our hands a world of Sermon notes', but that they had printed only those which 'came perfect', that is, which had been fully drafted in final form by Andrewes.[10] Presumably on these grounds alone they ignored the early Cambridge lecture notes. But even had they survived 'perfect', the college lectures would have sat oddly in generic terms with the solemn court sermons which Laud and Buckeridge preferred to showcase. The textual history of these notes (detailed in the headnote to the selections) is very complex, since several textual traditions derive from notes taken by hearers, and only the very late *Pattern of Catechistical Doctrine* (1650) can claim to be based on authorial manuscripts.

[10] *XCVI*, sig. A2^r.

But that complicated textual history should not, as it long has, obscure the signal importance of these texts to understanding the evolution of Andrewes's thought.[11] The selections presented here from the 1650 *Pattern* are chosen to illustrate two things: first, statements by Andrewes on biblical interpretation and prayer; and second, his very early departure from conformist English orthodoxy on matters of public worship. The former summarize the exegetical principles that Andrewes applied to scripture as a preacher, and the great importance he attached to both private and public prayer. These are conventional in the Reformed tradition, but are a useful starting point for any serious student of Andrewes, either as a preacher or as the author of the posthumously famous book of private devotions, the *Preces Privatæ*.[12] The selections from lectures on outward ceremony in worship, on the moral obligation to observe the sabbath, and on the sacrality of churches, however, are anything but conventional for their time. In them is found categorical proof that Andrewes was venturing criticisms of mainstream moderate puritanism at least a decade before Hooker's *Laws of Ecclesiastical Polity* (1593, 1597). With pronouncements against tawdry communion tables, against the failure to observe ceremonial gestures in worship, against the overemphasis on preaching at the expense of liturgy, and a high view of Sunday religious observance (which would in the next century be wilfully mistaken as an endorsement of puritan sabbatarianism), Andrewes was by the mid-1580s edging out onto the same limb only firmly occupied by the likes of Richard Hooker and Richard Bancroft in the late 1590s.

The Armada year of 1588 was as auspicious for Andrewes as it was for the nation. Having proceeded bachelor of divinity in 1585 and served as a chaplain to the Earl of Huntington in 1586, in February 1588 Andrewes's reputation as a rising star in the national church secured him an invitation from the Mayor and Court of Aldermen to preach in one of London's most famous pulpits, in its most prominent sermon series, the Easter sermons at

---

[11] A crucial first step in this direction has been taken by Nicholas Tyacke, 'Lancelot Andrewes and the Myth of Anglicanism', in Peter Lake and Michael Questier (eds.), *Conformity and Orthodoxy in the English Church c.1560–1660* (2000), 5–33.

[12] I acknowledge what may be a lacuna in this edition, that is, the lack of selections from the *Preces*. Strictly speaking, these prayers should be studied in the original languages of their composition (Latin, Greek, and Hebrew). Although both seventeenth- and twentieth-century translations could have been used, space did not allow what I deemed to be the amount of text necessary to represent the *Preces* properly. Moreover, it would have been difficult to add anything sufficiently significant to the magisterial translation and edition by F. E. Brightman, *The Preces Privatæ of Lancelot Andrewes* (1903). In my judgement, editing the lecture on prayer from the *Pattern* provided a more helpful new contribution to the subject. The *Preces* are used liberally here in my annotations to the sermons; several of the private devotions are included in Hewison's anthology, pp. 133–58.

St Mary's Hospital, Spitalfields (the 'Spital Sermons'). The text of this sermon (one of only three non-court sermons included in the 1629 folio) is the earliest surviving authorial text by Andrewes. On these grounds alone it merits inclusion here as witness to how early in his career his grand sermon style had been formed, and how the salient features of that style were not reserved only for court auditories. But in content, too, it is a highly significant example of how far Andrewes was willing to distance himself from Calvinist orthodoxy (here on the disputed point of the efficacy of works for salvation) and as an early essay in his lifelong insistence upon almsgiving. But even more important is the recently discovered independent manuscript witness of the Spital sermon, transcribed here as Appendix 1. This allows for the first time the study of what differences could exist between a sermon text as Andrewes prepared it and how he actually delivered it (see part V of this Introduction, and the headnotes to the two versions of the sermon).

The Spital sermon was probably also an audition for higher preferment in London. For within a matter of months, Andrewes was appointed, allegedly on the motions of his patron Walsingham, to the large extramural parish of St Giles Cripplegate (burial place of John Foxe and, later, John Milton). In the very next year Walsingham secured him a prebend in St Paul's Cathedral, and he was also elected master of Pembroke. Although Andrewes was an exemplary governor of his college (he completely overhauled its beleaguered finances), he chose to reside in his native city, repairing at his own expense a prebendal house in Creed Lane, immediately south of St Paul's churchyard and in the heart of the London book trade. Over the next decade, Andrewes preached so conscientiously at both St Giles and St Paul's that, according to his first biographer, 'he became so infirme, that his friends despaired of his life'.[13] Yet only two sermons included in *XCVI. Sermons* represent this huge body of preaching.[14] Given the disproportionate number of Jacobean court sermons in the folio, it has been far too easy to assume that Andrewes was a court prelate of the most sybaritic sort, who used high office to avoid hard graft, and preached only for the nice ears of royalty.[15] But it was at St Giles and St Paul's—in the years largely passed over by Laud and Buckeridge—that Andrewes earned a deserved reputation as a conscientious pastor.[16] In the

---

[13] Henry Isaacson, *The Life and Death... of Lancelot Andrewes* (1651), sig. *2ᵛ.
[14] Sermons on the second and third Commandments preached at St Giles in 1592; *XCVI*, pt. 2, pp. 25–48.
[15] Cf. Hugh Trevor Roper, 'King James and his Bishops', *History Today*, 5 (1955), 571–81.
[16] My point here is not that Buckeridge and Laud wished to suppress this achievement, but that it was not a priority in their polemical design for *XCVI*. Cf. their acknowledgement in the preface

parish Andrewes composed his own manual for ministration to the sick and dying, instituted monthly communions, and re-edified the chancel; at the cathedral he was admired for his regular divinity lectures, and for reviving the pre-Reformation custom of hearing confession in Lent. But perhaps more to the point for our purposes here, it was in these years that he became famous, especially among London's literati, as a dazzling preacher. Thomas Nashe proclaimed in 1596 that by the playwright John Lyly's 'immoderate commending him [Andrewes], by little and little I was drawne on to bee an Auditor of his: since when, whensoever I heard him, I thought it was but hard and scant allowance that was giv'n him, in comparison of the incomparable gifts that were in him.'[17] That Andrewes found such an admirer in the socially conservative but literarily radical Nashe tells us much about both men.

And that we can sample what 'fare' Nashe and Lyly found so delicious is due not to Laud and Buckeridge's *XCVI. Sermons*, but to the mixed financial and ideological motives of a consortium of royalist printers who published those notes in 1657 as *ΑΠΟΣΠΑΣΜΑΤΙΑ SACRA: or A Collection of Posthumous and Orphan Lectures... Never before extant* (the Graeco-Latin main title means 'Holy Fragments'). Part of a growing stream of royalist and episcopalian printing in the waning days of the Protectorate, and with a preface by the strident Laudian Thomas Pierce, this folio reprinted the impressively full notes of over 100 sermons preached by Andrewes at St Giles and St Paul's between 1590 and 1601. These include systematic lectures on the first four chapters of Genesis and occasional sermons for Sundays and feast days.[18] They not only double the size of the *XCVI. Sermons* canon, but give an invaluable picture of Andrewes as a parochial preacher. He clearly excelled at the genre of the lecture—sermons on a large tract of biblical text delivered in a continuous pedagogical series in the afternoon over a course of months (almost entirely absent from *XCVI. Sermons*; see n. 14)—as well as in the Sunday or feast day sermon

---

to *XCVI*, 'And he was not a *greater Preacher* in his age, then he was both *great* and *frequent*, in his younger and stronger time' (sig. A3ʳ), though Buckeridge did retail the anecdote that Andrewes 'ever misliked often and loose preaching... and he would be bold with himself, and say, *when he preached twice a day at Saint Giles, he prated once*' ('Sermon... at the Funerall', 21).

[17] Thomas Nashe, *Have With You to Saffron Walden*, in *The Works of Thomas Nashe*, ed. R. B. McKerrow, rev. ed. F. P. Wilson, 5 vols. (London, 1958), iii. 105, 107.

[18] Pierce's prefatory claim that these texts derive from notes taken by contemporary hearers has been disproven. After I submitted this edition, Prof. Graham Parry and Prof. Paul G. Stanwood informed me of a hitherto unknown manuscript, still in private hands, of the Genesis lectures. These appear to be in the hand of Andrewes's Elizabethan amanuensis, Henry Isaacson, with emendations by Andrewes himself. It is at present unclear whether the occasional sermons not on Genesis found in the printed edition of 1657 are also in the manuscript. We await Prof. Stanwood's assessment of this important discovery.

preached in the context of a prayer book liturgy (predominant in *XCVI. Sermons*). So here we find Andrewes offering the kind of practical divinity that was the staple fare of early modern Londoners—a vital counterbalance to the court sermons of the Laud and Buckeridge edition. The lectures on Genesis afforded treatment of conventional social matters like trade, labour and harvest, marriage and children, and magistracy, and of fundamental moral issues such as temptation, sin, revenge, and murder. They are also interlaced with the sophisticated handling of doctrinal points like creation *ex nihilo*, and election and reprobation.[19]

The first text from *ΑΠΟΣΠΑΣΜΑΤΙΑ* included in this edition, a lecture on the creation of Eve (Gen. 2: 18), shows Andrewes entering the lists in contemporary debates about the nature of woman. In it he sharply condemns contemporary misogynist satire, and exemplifies the more positive view of human nature in general, and of women in particular, that sets him apart from Calvinism's total depravity of fallen men and women. Andrewes's civil politics may have been more conservative than Milton's, but his gender politics were decidedly more liberal. The lecture also anticipates the sympathy for Christian women exemplified in the final text in this edition, the exquisite 1620 Easter sermon on Mary Magdalen.

One of *ΑΠΟΣΠΑΣΜΑΤΙΑ*'s several sermons preached at the monthly Sunday communions instituted by Andrewes at St Giles, on Isaiah 6: 6–7, is, in theological terms, perhaps the most important in this edition. Safe from the fierce scrutiny of court or university audiences, at St Giles Andrewes expounded in detail a eucharistic theology far more radical for its English context than has ever been appreciated. Scholars have always acknowledged Andrewes's high view of the sacrament as expressed in the poignant but fleeting calls to receive communion which conclude most of the court feast day sermons. But the exact doctrine of the eucharist hinted at there has never been satisfactorily explained, nor its sources understood.[20] In the St Giles Isaiah sermon, however, Andrewes pulled no punches by asserting emphatically that the consecrated eucharistic elements themselves remit sins. In doing so, Andrewes was promulgating

---

[19] Professor Tyacke, 'Lancelot Andrewes and the Myth of Anglicanism', has again been the first to call necessary attention to these texts. In my estimate, the lectures on Cain and Abel (Gen. 4; *ΑΠΟΣΠΑΣΜΑΤΙΑ*, 363–499) demand careful study for their avant-garde negotiation of predestination and reprobation; it also seems urgent for Milton scholars to add the lectures on Gen. 1–3 to the body of hexameral literature that should be considered as a source for *Paradise Lost*.

[20] See Lake, 'Lancelot Andrewes, John Buckeridge', in Peck, *Mental World of the Jacobean Court*, and Tyacke, 'Lancelot Andrewes', in Lake and Questier (eds.), *Conformity and Orthodoxy*. The best treatment of the eucharistic theology contained in *XCVI* is to be gleaned from Nicholas Lossky, *Lancelot Andrewes the Preacher*, trans. Andrew Louth (Oxford, 1991), *passim*.

the eucharistic theology of the late sixteenth-century Lutheran Martin Chemnitz (also Kemnitius or Kemnisius), which was equally condemned by both Roman Catholics and Calvinists. This and similar work on other sermons in this edition reveals that Luther and Chemnitz are the contemporary theologians to whom Andrewes owes the greatest debt. That much of Lutheran theology, especially of the eucharist, was treated with suspicion by the late Elizabethan Calvinist mainstream explains why Andrewes was so careful never to acknowledge this debt openly, and why it has eluded scholars for so long. It is perhaps the most important vein for students of Andrewes's theology to mine in future.

While still new in his posts at St Giles and St Paul's, Andrewes had proceeded doctor of divinity at Cambridge in the summer of 1590. By this time, he had been appointed chaplain to archbishop John Whitgift, and was known throughout the university as an opponent of the presbyterian and puritan cells led there by Thomas Cartwright, around which Whitgift was beginning to draw a fatal noose. Andrewes used his divinity lecture to the heads and fellows of the university—a compulsory part of taking his degree—for a swingeing but erudite attack not just on emergent puritanism, but also on the very Edwardian reformation which, in his judgement, had spawned it. Delivered in the required Latin, Andrewes's dissertation argued that the system of church tithes was warranted by scripture and tradition. It was first published as 'Concio ad clerum pro gradu doctoris' in *Reverendi in Christo Patris, Lanceloti, Episcopi Wintoniensis, Opuscula Quædam Posthuma* (1629), a quarto volume of Latin and miscellaneous English works edited by Laud and Buckeridge as a companion to *XCVI. Sermons*. The text presented here is an English translation published as *Sacrilege a Snare* in 1649. I have included it for several important reasons. First, it illustrates yet another genre of sermon absent from *XCVI. Sermons*, the formal academic lecture. As Andrewes admits in it, he says things in that rarefied context that he would not dare broach before a more popular audience, and his style and use of sources is far more flamboyant and eclectic than in even the court sermons. Its assault on the erastian anti-clericalism influential at Elizabeth's court, its condemnation of the crown's and laity's appropriation of clerical livings, and its open nostalgia for pre-Reformation liturgies show just how avant-garde Andrewes could dare to be in public. And the 1649 translation epitomizes another crucial aspect of the textual and political history of Andrewes's works—the fierce attempts by almost every party in the Civil War period to appropriate Andrewes's legacy for their own purposes. The historical irony in this case is particularly salty: the sermon was promulgated by the parliamentary Presbyterian faction—Andrewes's *bêtes noires* in 1590—to press their *own* case in 1649 for the retention of clerical tithes against the now more radical congregationalism of the Independents.[21]

At the same time as his appointment as chaplain to Whitgift (*c*.1590), Andrewes was also appointed one of the twelve chaplains to queen Elizabeth herself. And so began the court career for which Andrewes is now perhaps disproportionately famous. Royal chaplains were required to attend (presumably to reside) at court in pairs for one month of the year in order to share the duties of preaching and leading the daily liturgies in the chapel royal.[22] Two sermons were to be preached each Sunday, one to the below-stairs household servants, and one to the queen's own entourage. From the pattern of Elizabethan court sermons preserved in *XCVI. Sermons* it is clear that Andrewes's 'month of waiting' at court was November. In addition, he, like other royal chaplains, was appointed in the rota of preachers for the great court Lent sermon series, a pre-Reformation tradition reinvigorated by Protestantism's emphasis on preaching. In it, sermons were preached either from the great outdoor pulpit in the former Privy Garden at Whitehall, or inside one of the chapels royal, thrice weekly between Ash Wednesday and Good Friday. The Elizabethan court sermons presented here are both from this series, which Elizabeth herself assiduously attended, dressed in Lenten black. The literary structure of Andrewes's sermons will be considered in a following section, but it is important to stress here that with the exception of the Christmas, Easter, and Whitsunday sermons, court sermons (like most others elsewhere) were not preached as part of a liturgical service. The Lent sermons in particular were, like sermons at London's Paul's Cross, free-standing events in themselves. If preached inside a chapel royal, they may have been preceded and followed by a choral anthem. But otherwise, a court sermon consisted of the solemn procession of the sovereign to the elevated royal closet (if delivered in a chapel) or council chamber window (if delivered in the outdoor Whitehall Preaching Place), followed by the preacher ascending the pulpit, making three low bows to the monarch, pronouncing a long statutory prayer, declaring his biblical text, and then delivering his entire sermon from memory. The court Lent sermons attracted thousands and were followed by Londoners as well as courtiers with the keen interest reserved at other times of the year for theatregoing and blood sports (pastimes outlawed during Lent).

---

[21] For sectarian battles over Andrewes's literary legacy in the 1630s and 1640s, see McCullough, 'Making Dead Men Speak'.
[22] This survey of the practices and institution of preaching at court is based on Peter E. McCullough, *Sermons at Court: Politics and Religion in Elizabethan and Jacobean Preaching* (Cambridge, 1998).

Precisely this attitude of attending sermons as a form of entertainment exercised Andrewes throughout his life. Paradoxically, the greatest preacher of the age was thus also the greatest critic of the age of preaching. Andrewes's version of the statutory prayer-before-sermon (pp. 1–4) opened with a petition for God's grace to keep listeners from hearing 'without care of conscience to become the better therby'. Much of the intensity of Andrewes's sermons (both in style and content) comes from his straining of every nerve to make hearing his sermons more than a pastime—not only for him to teach through them, but to insist that the listener turn his words into actions. And here lies one of those great confluences of classical humanism and Christianity so often encountered in Andrewes: Cicero's insistence that the orator's *lexis* must become the auditor's *praxis*, joined with the apostolic injunction, 'And be ye doers of the word, and not hearers only, deceiving your own selves' (James 1: 22). Human doing—active participation, effort, works—is paramount to Andrewes's entire conception of the Christian faith. Whether scripture, sermon, or sacraments, Andrewes warns that the elements of religion (especially preaching) are nothing but Falstaff's catechism of words as 'air' unless those signs are—on the model of the Word, Christ himself—incarnated in actual human lives and bodies. As he put it in a startling beatitude of his own composition in a sermon on James 1: 22, '*Blessed are they, that so incarnate the written word, by doing it*, as the *Blessed Virgin* gave *flesh*, to the *æternall word*, by *bearing it*.'[23] Although Andrewes sees such incarnation as enabled by the grace of God, he does not, like early modern Calvinists, rule out the possibility of the efficacious participation with it by the believer. Instead, he demands it. As Lossky has observed on Andrewes and the believer's participation in the eucharist, 'this participation implies an effort, a collaboration on man's part, who is himself also dispenser, disposer, in so far as he is responsible for the gift of faith which must bear fruit'.[24]

Precisely such participatory effort was the insistent theme of the remarkable 1594 Lent sermon on the 'recidivation', or relapse, of Lot's wife. No other Elizabethan sermon so sabotaged the twin Calvinist totems of predestination and eternal security of the elect. Like his arguments about Cain in the St Giles lectures of 1598, Andrewes insists here that only the failure of Lot's wife's own moral will—not God's predestinating will—led to her destruction. Effort, the exercise of a moral strength that is almost physical, is the obligatory human involvement in the economy of salvation. In the sermon's conclusion, such daring theological revisionism was, in a final

---

[23] 'A Sermon...at Greenwich, *Anno D.* MDCVII', *XCVI*, pt. 2, p. 137.
[24] Lossky, *Lancelot Andrewes*, 97.

stroke of genius, made politically safer by ascribing the virtues lacking in Lot's wife to the queen who was watching the whole performance. In a remarkable twist to conventional praise of the redoubtable Elizabeth, she was held up not as one saved by God's providence, but as one who had persevered, and thus preserved her self and nation, through sheer moral fortitude. Another act of human will animated Andrewes's revolutionary Good Friday court sermon of 1597, where, in terms not used since the Reformation, the auditory was repeatedly called to the main verb of the text, 'And they shall looke upon Me, whom they have pierced' (Zech. 12: 10). Active 'looking upon' the crucified Christ—long a taboo in a reformed church that had pulled down roods and crucifixes—was for Andrewes yet another obligatory action on the part of any believer who hoped to lay hold of the salvation purchased on that cross.

Elizabeth returned Andrewes's many compliments, and rewarded his daring sermons, with further preferment. In 1597 she appointed him a canon of Westminster and offered him two bishoprics, the latter of which he refused on the ground that those offers came only with the unacceptable alienation of church lands to the crown (a position consistent with his 1590 doctoral oration). In 1601 Andrewes did accept Elizabeth's appointment of him to the deanery of Westminster, where he took an active role not only in abbey administration, but also in teaching at its school where he earned the admiration of, among others, George Herbert. The accession of James VI and I in March 1603 brought the further preferment that no doubt would also have come from Elizabeth. By this time in his late forties, Andrewes was a prime candidate for elevation to the bench of bishops, which duly occurred in November 1605 when he was consecrated bishop of Chichester on the day before the discovery of the Gunpowder Plot. James's delight in Andrewes's erudition and eloquence also saw that he was appointed at the same time as the king's lord high almoner. The incumbent of this post was charged with the distribution of royal alms to the poor, but also by tradition preached before the sovereign on the highest feast days of the church's year.[25] This is the institutional explanation for the remarkable course of sermons preached by Andrewes at court after 1605 on Christmas, Easter, Whitsunday, and the anniversaries of the Gowrie Conspiracy (5 August) and the Gunpowder Plot (5 November) which compose the bulk of *XCVI. Sermons*.

Those sermons will always be regarded justifiably as Andrewes's finest, and selecting from among them has been my most difficult task. Thanks

---

[25] For preaching at James's court, and Andrewes's prominence there, see McCullough, *Sermons at Court*, ch. 3.

largely to Eliot, the nativity sermons are Andrewes's most known and loved, in particular those on the annunciation of the angels to the shepherds, and of course on the coming of the Magi.[26] Modern criticism has also singled out for particular praise Easter sermons on Mary Magdalen and the triumphant treatment of the *Christus Victor* in 'Who is this that commeth from Edom?'[27] But it has not been my aim to key this edition to twentieth-century literary assessments of Andrewes, but rather to represent the Andrewes known to his contemporaries. Hence I have in the first instance tried to include from *XCVI. Sermons* texts preached on each of the major holy days represented there. Within that initial limit, I have then chosen sermons on the grounds of not only their literary merit, but also their contemporary popularity (as evidenced by royal favour, popular commendation, or print runs), their political and theological significance, a desire for an even chronological range, and the limited duplication of texts edited by Story. And finally, I was keen to include, for bibliographical reasons, representatives of the ten sermons printed in quarto by royal command during Andrewes's lifetime. The competing claims of these different criteria have inevitably led to compromises of almost all of them. Most significant is the absence of an Ash Wednesday sermon, of which *XCVI. Sermons* contains three before Elizabeth and five before James (pp. 173–262). I felt, however, that inclusion of any of these would repeat themes found in the Elizabethan Spital, Lent, and Good Friday sermons already included.[28] The luxury of more space should have also allowed inclusion of a sermon from the last four years of Andrewes's life. But again, fears of repetition, and a desire to give more space to the hitherto neglected Elizabethan career has meant stopping with Easter 1620. Of the texts included here, one—that for Easter 1620—is also found in Story (pp. 192–217). I have freshly edited it not only on the grounds of its sheer excellence, but also because Story strangely chose not to collate its rare surviving authorial manuscript.

Some may be dismayed not to find Eliot's beloved Magi representing Andrewes's efforts for Christmas in this edition. But to have done so would

---

[26] On Luke 2: 12–14, Matt. 2: 1–2, preached 1618, 1619, 1620, and 1622, respectively (*XCVI*, 108–47); cf. Story (ed.), *Lancelot Andrewes: Sermons*, pp. xxxviii–xliii.

[27] On John 20: 11–17 and Isaiah 43: 1–3, preached 1620, 1621, and 1623, respectively (*XCVI*, 531–76; the first of these is included in this edition); cf. Stanley Fish, 'Structuralist Homiletics', *Modern Language Notes*, 91 (1976), 1208–21; and Brian Vickers (ed.), *Seventeenth Century Prose* (1969), 70–92.

[28] The Jacobean Ash Wednesday sermons are of particular biographical, literary, and theological interest, as they were written at the end of Andrewes's career (1619–24) and contain some of his most strident statements on the efficacy of good works. That for 1619 is included in Story (ed.), *Sermons*, 119–42.

have been to replicate a more modern Andrewes—not just because those sermons were so important to Eliot and approached by him through a Victorian anthology, but because evidence suggests that they were not the Christmas sermons which made the greatest impression on contemporaries. That award goes instead to the Christmas sermon I have chosen, preached before James in 1609 on Galatians 4: 4–5 ('When the fulnesse of time was come, God sent his Son ... '). John Chamberlain immediately reported to Dudley Carleton that Andrewes had 'preached at court on Christmas day with great applause, being not only *sui similis* ["like himself"], but more then himself by the report of the King and all his auditors'. He then enthused to another correspondent that 'I hope we shall have [Andrewes's] sermon ... preached on Christmas day last with great applause: the King with much importunitie had the copie delivered him on Tewsday last before his going toward Roiston, and sayes he will lay yt still under his pillow'.[29] 'The copie' may have been a manuscript from the author, but given Chamberlain's anticipation of print publication, might also have been an advance copy of the quarto about to appear by royal command from the King's Printer.[30] Choosing this to represent Andrewes's eighteen surviving Christmas sermons is not without risk, because it is a challenging text. The reasons for King James's enthusiasm for the sermon, and for the relative neglect of it in modern times, may be the same, for stylistically Andrewes's prose here is at its most clipped and compressed. But the cumulative achievement of precisely that style is a *tour de force* that, although it lacks the discursive narrative or the pictorial imagery of the Magi sermons, is in its very form imitative of its subject: the miraculous 'fulness' that is to be found in the Word. Characteristically, Andrewes concluded the sermon by calling the court to a bodily participation in the 'fulness' of the Incarnation not just in its ensuing Christmas revels, but also through incorporation into the eucharistic and ecclesiastical body of Christ. And the sermon's themes of sonship, adoption, inheritance, and investiture from the second verse of the text ('that we might receive the adoption of sonnes') would have had rich contemporary resonance as the court prepared for Prince Henry's imminent investiture as Prince of Wales (May 1610).

My selections from *XCVI. Sermons* also deliberately showcase a group of texts the popularity of which not even Laud and Buckeridge's edition has

---

[29] John Chamberlain, *The Letters of John Chamberlain*, ed. N. E. McClure, 2 vols. (Philadelphia, 1939), i. 292, 295.

[30] The Magi sermons appeared only posthumously in *XCVI. Sermons*. James I ordered twenty-five court sermons to be printed during his reign, and ten of these were by Andrewes. In addition to that for 1609, the Christmas sermon for 1610 (on the angels' annunciation to the shepherds, Luke 2: 10–11) was commanded into print (1611; repr. in *XCVI*, 33–43). See McCullough, *Sermons at Court*, 210–12.

secured—the sermons for those peculiarly Jacobean holy days, the Gowrie and Gunpowder anniversaries. For the editors and royal patron of *XCVI. Sermons* in 1629 they were of course pristine defences of Stuart absolutism. The early Victorian editors of *LACT* could still manage to commend them for their exhibition of 'the sacredness of the persons of princes' and 'the extreme and desperate wickedness of those who presume ... to rise up in rebellion against their authority', adding that, 'as they are conversant with principles of scriptural and therefore unchanging truth, they are not of mere temporary interest'. But subsequent generations have been even less indulgent.[31] Eliot does not mention them. Hewison omits them on the grounds that they are 'more political than theological'. Story bars them from his edition by claiming that in them Andrewes 'write[s] flatly' and adding that 'to read them is a task for Embertide, though they were admired by judicious contemporaries'.[32]

Readers may judge for themselves from the Gunpowder and Gowrie sermons included in this edition. But I would defy any to describe the passion of the sermon on the first anniversary of the Gunpowder Plot, or the indignation in that for the tenth anniversary of the Gowrie Plot (itself also a response to the recent assassination of Henry IV of France) as 'flat'. In any historical approach to Andrewes, these sermons which distil not just James's views on the sacrality of kings, but also on the royal prerogative over non-doctrinal church matters, and his disputes with Rome over papal powers, demand a generous place. This is a place which scholars have begun to recognize. Lori Anne Ferrell has judiciously argued for the significance of Andrewes's and other preachers' plot sermons in the religio-political fabric of James's regime. Nicholas Lossky has shown how Andrewes's sermons for these 'political festivals' reach beyond the 'material, physical, human level' of their occasions to offer profound studies of the theology of 'deliverance'. In expositions of liturgical time entirely 'complementary' to the great soteriological sermons for Christmas and Easter, he argues that Andrewes 'give[s] the character of properly religious feasts to these official manifestations of the State and to festivities that seem otherwise to have been rather profane'. And in a welcome (though brief) view quite independent from the dominant literary critical tradition, Trevor Owen has acknowledged that 'some of Andrewes's most excellent work lies buried' in the Gunpowder sermons.[33]

---

[31] J. P. Wilson (ed.), preface to *LACT*, iv. pp. v–vi; Mozley (see n. 5 above) only discusses the sermons for 'the four great ecclesiastical seasons, Christmas, Lent, Easter, and Whitsuntide'.

[32] Hewison (ed.), *Lancelot Andrewes*, p. xi; Story (ed.), *Lancelot Andrewes*, p. xxxiii.

[33] Lori Anne Ferrell, *Government by Polemic: James I, the King's Preachers, and the Rhetorics of Conformity* (Stanford, Calif., 1998), ch. 2; Lossky, *Lancelot Andrewes*, ch. 7; Trevor Owen, *Lancelot Andrewes* (Boston, 1981), ch. 9.

Finally, the Gowrie and Gunpowder sermons allow me to stress that a historical approach to Andrewes only intensifies an appreciation of his literary skill, and vice versa. Andrewes is an author who exemplifies (perhaps even better than more conventionally 'literary' authors like Shakespeare) the symbiotic relationship between literary form and historical context. But students and scholars have for too long studied Andrewes for only one or the other. Sermons like those for the Gunpowder or Gowrie anniversaries have been shunned by literary scholars because of their overtly political subjects, yet used by historians as glosses on historical events. But reading them with an eye to how Andrewes uses artful 'literary' methods of exegesis *and* addresses matters of significant contemporary political argument offers both fields a sum total of interpretative richness greater than their individual disciplinary parts. Take, for example, the exfoliation of the meanings of the single verb '*tangere*' ('to touch') or the epithet '*Christus domini*' ('the Lord's anointed') in the 1610 Gowrie sermon. For literary scholars, reading a sermon on 'anointing' against the backdrop of James's revival of that custom at his own coronation (with its attendant claims that kings are, etymologically at least, 'christs'), and controversies over making the sign of the cross at baptism (before the Reformation, 'chrismation'), makes Andrewes's fugue on the etymology and derivatives of '*christus*' much more than clever wordplay. And by the same token, if historians can learn to accept exegesis as historical evidence, they will find in Andrewes's sermon on 'not touching' kings a theological defence of patriarchal absolutism perhaps more rich and sophisticated than any contemporary tract written on the subject.[34]

The Gunpowder, Christmas, and Gowrie sermons presented here, which span the first decade of James's reign, represent Andrewes at what was probably the most productive stage of his Jacobean career. He had been translated to the diocese of Ely in September 1609, and continued as James's almoner. But even beyond his routine court sermon duties, much of his literary productivity during these years was imposed upon him by James, rather than sought by Andrewes himself. In 1604 the king had appointed him one of the principal translators of the Bible which would appear as the Authorized Version in 1611. Andrewes's involvement, like the project itself, is largely shrouded in undocumented mystery, but he gathered in his translation committee at Westminster like-minded men who combined scholarly erudition with a deep distrust of puritanism. And he

---

[34] For an excellent review of the disciplinary challenges presented by sermons, see Mary Morrissey, 'Interdisciplinarity and the Study of Early Modern Sermons', *Historical Journal*, 42.4 (1999), 1111–23.

may himself have been almost independently responsible for translating Genesis–2 Kings, inclusive.[35] Andrewes had succeeded as master of Pembroke William Fulke (d. 1589), the chief published critic of the Roman Catholic ('Rheims') New Testament, and must have been intimately familiar with Fulke's voluminous debates with the Catholic translator, Gregory Martin. But the work of annotating even the small selection here of Andrewes's surviving works from the 1580s and 1590s shows that before Fulke was very cold in his grave, Andrewes was happily, though tacitly, accepting a host of Rheimist readings which Fulke had vehemently rejected. Further work along these lines may be the most productive way to reveal the as yet little understood contribution of Andrewes to English Bible translation.

A no doubt less welcome assignment from James was the command for Andrewes to respond to the Jesuit Cardinal Robert Bellarmine's attacks on James's Oath of Allegiance, his attempt to separate subversive from loyal English Catholics after the Gunpowder Plot. Chamberlain candidly observed that it was a task 'I doubt how [Andrewes] will undertake and performe, beeing so contrarie to his disposition and course to meddle with controversies'; he later conceded that '[Andrewes] were like to performe well . . . yf he might take his owne time, and not be troubeld nor intangled with arguments obtruded to him continually by the Kinge' (*Letters*, i. 264, 270). The result was two years' hard work (1608–10) on two lengthy Latin defences of James's church and crown from papal claims to authority over foreign princes. Many of Andrewes's most salient points are summarized in his sermon for the Gowrie Anniversary 1610 (pp. 178–206), preached only months before the publication of the final response to Bellarmine. Although doing his royal master's work, these treatises bear the hallmarks of their author's lifelong attitude to Rome—scathingly critical of its political ambitions as embodied in the papacy and the Jesuit mission, but unwilling to accuse it of not being a true church, and willing to entertain some of its doctrines and practices (like prayers to saints and transubsantiation) as valid points for theological debate, but not as matters of faith.

Upon Archbishop of Canterbury Richard Bancroft's death in November 1610 many expected (or perhaps only hoped) that Andrewes would succeed him. Passed over for George Abbot, Andrewes continued his pattern of court service, oversight of Ely diocese, and the cultivation of academic associations and friendships with Francis Bacon, the émigré Isaac Casaubon, and (less comfortably) the Dutch theologian Hugo Grotius. In 1616 he was sworn of the privy council, and in 1617 was a prominent member of the

---

[35] The facts as they survive receive a lively retelling in Adam Nicolson, *Power and Glory: Jacobean England and the Making of the King James Bible* (2003), 93–102, 192–5.

ecclesiastical entourage which accompanied James on his homecoming tour of Scotland, a progress largely designed to impress upon the Scottish kirk James's determination to impose upon it the English liturgies and ceremonies so long endorsed by Andrewes. This was the only known occasion on which Andrewes left England, and he preached forcefully against presbyterian scruples in the chapel royal of Holyrood House itself. But like James, Andrewes saw Scottish presbyterianism as only English puritanism writ large, and he reprised many of his anti-Scottish arguments, adapted for the English context, one year later at Whitehall on Whitsunday 1618 (pp. 207–24).

1618 saw a major shift in Andrewes's career, as it did in James's reign, and for related reasons. The death of several leading Calvinist bishops with strong court connections had opened the way for James to appoint men like Andrewes, Laud, and Buckeridge to more prominent posts where their liberal theology and views on European politics could be of advantage in his attempts to secure the marriage of Prince Charles to the Spanish Infanta.[36] Andrewes was duly promised the deanery of the Chapel Royal and translation to the prestigious diocese of Winchester in the summer of 1618. He eventually took up these positions at Christmas 1618 and in June 1619, respectively. The delay over Winchester was due to squabbles with his predecessor's heirs over episcopal property. But he seems to have baulked at the Chapel deanery for reasons directly related to his preaching, for to accept it required his relinquishing the lord almonership along with its holy day sermons before the king. The Chapel dean preached before the monarch only on Ash Wednesday; on the other feast days his auditory was the royal household. Andrewes finally relented—'against his Will', according to William Camden—but only after clinging to his sermons *coram rege* until Whitsunday 1620. In exchange, as dean Andrewes presided over the refitting of the chapels royal along lines which anticipated Laud's altar policy and campaign for the 'beauty of holiness' in the 1630s, and he also used his new powers to purge the household of the Prince of Wales of its puritan chaplains.[37] Although his presence as a preacher at court was waning, this was not the high-water mark of Andrewes's political influence, which arguably only increased as the anti-Calvinist faction of which he was the grandfather consolidated its hold not just on James, but also on Charles.

The court sermons Andrewes preached after laying down the almonership were not inferior to those written before. But ill-health began to dog him persistently from 1621, and many of his court sermons were assigned

---

[36] Kenneth Fincham and Peter Lake, 'The Ecclesiastical Policies of James I and Charles I', in Kenneth Fincham (ed.), *The Early Stuart Church* (Basingstoke, 1993), 33–6.

[37] McCullough, *Sermons at Court*, 150–4, 204–6.

to substitutes, with those written by him sometimes left perfect, but undelivered.[38] With the exception of Easter 1623 (on Isaiah 43: 1–3), there is also a palpable sense not exactly of exhaustion, but perhaps of resignation and even some bitterness in the remaining sermons, epitomized by the choice of Matthew 3: 8 ('O generations of vipers... Bring forth therefore fruits worthy amendment of life') as his Ash Wednesday text for 1623 and 1624. Calls to good works, cast in strong condemnations of moral hypocrisy, predominate in these sermons, extending even to the choice of Hebrews 8: 20–1 ('The God of peace... make you perfect in all good workes') for an Easter text in 1624. Freed from the reticence on anti-Calvinist points that had been imposed on him by James's pre-1618 attempts to hold factions in tactful balance, the outspoken forthrightness of the Elizabethan Andrewes reappears after 1618, but tinged with even greater amounts of sarcasm, satire, and irony. One reason for sacrificing the post-1620 sermons to the pressures of space in this edition has been that they do not contain new themes, but just familiar ones (anti-puritanism, ceremonialism, calls for good works, satires on excessive preaching) more archly expressed. Easter 1620 is arguably his most formally sophisticated and emotionally compelling sermon and is in my judgement an apt finale to this selection of his works.

Andrewes did survive more than a year into Charles's new reign, his life an arch flung from the reign of the penultimate Tudor to that of the second Stuart. But after a last lingering illness he died in his sleep at Winchester House, his episcopal residence in Southwark only metres from the Globe Theatre, on 25 September 1626. In a state funeral marshalled by the College of Heralds, he was interred in November in an apsidal chapel at the east end of St Saviour's parish church (since 1905 Southwark Cathedral) where his restored effigy tomb now stands in a position of honour beside the high altar.

III. THE LITERARY ACHIEVEMENT OF ANDREWES'S SERMONS

About the salient qualities of Andrewes's prose there has been a remarkable critical consensus since his own lifetime. As surprising is the fact that his style has for just as long been acknowledged as unique, even *sui generis*. Most modern assessments of Andrewes owe a singular debt to Eliot's 1925

---

[38] Surviving court sermons written but not delivered are Whitsunday 1622; Gowrie Anniversary 1623; Ash Wednesday and Easter 1624; see *XCVI*, 249, 577, 755, 876.

essay; like the authors of those, I find Eliot's judgements difficult to transcend, so will attempt to open up new critical space by at first setting aside his and other modern criticism to turn instead first to Andrewes's texts themselves and the qualities that to me are the most important for students and scholars.

Like most early modern preachers' works, Andrewes's sermons are first and foremost the exposition of a chosen scriptural text for the instruction and edification of a Christian auditory.[39] But these compositions follow structural conventions which derive ultimately from the classical rules for orations set down by Aristotle, Cicero, and Quintilian. The latter had been adapted over more than a millennium by theologians (most influentially Augustine in Book IV of *De Doctrina Christiana*) and in later preachers' manuals. They thus employ the same rhetorical devices designed to teach (Lat., 'docere') by moving the emotions (Lat., 'movere'), with the overriding aim of prompting action on the part of the listener. And as such, they are just as much examples of epideictic rhetoric (eloquent praise or blame) as any of the now more familiar Renaissance literary genres, ranging from the anatomies of vice and virtue in Ben Jonson's terse epigrams and Shakespeare's polished sonnets, to Spenser's epic, *The Faerie Queene* or Sir Philip Sidney's romances, *The Arcadia*'s. For students unfamiliar with early modern sermons' religious purpose or generic form, rhetorical analysis should be the first means of approach.[40]

Structurally, Andrewes's sermons show the conventional outlines of the parts of the classical oration found in most sermons of the period. The opening declamation of the chosen scriptural text itself defines the subject of the ensuing sermon. Then follows a short introduction ('exordium'), which justifies the sermon in the terms of its occasion. In the best sermons these one or two opening paragraphs use considerable wit to arrest the listener's attention while also explaining the preacher's choice of text. This included why the text was to be judged fitting for the day (for Andrewes's holy day sermons this is usually liturgical), and why it was appropriate for

---

[39] The now more familiar term 'congregation', although occasionally used in Andrewes's time for an audience gathered for service or sermon, then carried more non-conformist connotations; 'auditory' was the conventional term in conformist parlance until the eighteenth century.

[40] For a seminal outline of classical rhetoric and the importance of its expressive functions, see Brian Vickers, *In Defence of Rhetoric* (Oxford, 1988); for its application to sermons, see Peter McCullough, 'John Donne as Preacher', in Achsah Guibbory (ed.), *The Cambridge Companion to John Donne* (Cambridge, 2005); and Peter Mack, *Elizabethan Rhetoric: Theory and Practice* (Cambridge, 2002), ch. 8. Mary Morrissey offers a salutary caution against emphasizing the debt to classical rhetoric at the expense of what early moderns believed to be the unique task of preaching as a means for the receipt of grace in 'Scripture, Style and Persuasion in Seventeenth-Century English Theories of Preaching', *Journal of Ecclesiastical History*, 53.4 (Oct. 2002), 686–706.

the particular auditory addressed. As Andrewes himself explained in the exordium of his 1588 Spital sermon,

> Every Scripture is profitable: yet, not every Scripture, in every place alike. For, the Place and Auditorie have great interest in some Scripture; and a fitt Scripture hath a greater and fuller force, in his [its] owne Auditorie.

So, with an auditory at the Spital composed of the leading merchants and governors of the City of London, the text *'Charge them that are rich in this world ... that they trust not in the uncertenty of riches'* (1 Tim. 6: 17) is unambiguously applied:

> So, of this, it may be rightly said, that it is *Scriptura Divitum*, The *Rich mans Scripture*. And, if this be the *Scripture* for *rich men*; this place, is the *place* of *rich men*: and therefore, if this Scripture have his place, no where so fitt, as in this place. (p. 40)

Next comes a brief elaboration of the themes and even key words from the text which will define the argument, known in the period as the preacher's 'sum' ('summary') of his text. This then leads to the division (in Latin, 'divisio') of that text into the component parts which will make up the body of the sermon. Here Andrewes can be much more elaborate than some of his contemporaries, breaking down the syntax and even diction of his scriptural text to compose an often diagrammatic outline of his whole sermon by using strict methods of both logical and grammatical analysis. The stark enumeration of the many sequential points in the division (a particularly good example is again that for the Spital sermon, p. 41) can be off-putting to a modern reader keen for a discursive narrative. However, one must keep in mind not only how important the logical development of argument is for Andrewes, but also how important in much more pragmatic terms the division was for both preacher and auditory. For the latter, who experienced sermons first and foremost as a spoken (not written) text, these outlines were a crucial 'road map' to help one follow the extensive ensuing arguments, and a very deliberate means for aiding either note-taking during the sermon, or the recapitulation of the sermon from memory in a commonplace book later. And for the preacher himself, the 'divisio' was also a crucial aide-mémoire for keeping the parts of the sermon in their correct order during delivery.[41] After the division, the body of the sermon then progresses through the points announced in it, culminating (in classical terms) in an emotive summary 'peroratio' which concludes the whole either with a specially composed prayer (cf. pp. 81, 161),

---

[41] Stanley Fish suggests an intriguing alternative to how readers might respond to Andrewes's divisions in 'Structuralist Homiletics', 1208–21.

or some adaptation of the *Gloria Patri*.[42] Even within this broadly conventional structure, Andrewes's sermons are defined by a rigid attention to the parts of the scriptural text unsurpassed in those by any of his contemporaries. Rather than using the text as a foundation upon which to erect a sermon, Andrewes works in the opposite direction, almost like an archaeologist revealing by painstaking excavation what unseen structures lie beneath the visible surface of that foundation.

In addition to using the classical parts of the oration as adapted for sermons, Andrewes, like any verbal artist trained up on a humanist curriculum, also exploits the whole range of accepted rules for the actual composition of an oration or argument: 'inventio' (the 'discovery', or research and selection of arguments and examples), 'dispositio' (the strategic arrangement of those things into their most persuasive order), 'elocutio' (the figures of speech used to express them), and—unique to oral genres like speech-making, preaching, and acting—'pronuntiatio et actio' (the actual delivery, or performance, of the sermon). The third of these, 'elocutio', which in modern terms would be called prose style, is that in which Andrewes is most distinctive. He had an almost obsessive fondness for curt, short syntactical units that were shorn of connectives (asyndeton) and void of the often expansive prose periphrasis achieved by the extended proliferation of subordinate clauses. To that extent, his prose does bear some comparison with Francis Bacon's in its wary avoidance of decadent Ciceronianism, and in the prominence given by its small, chiselled units to the expressive functions of both syntactical symmetry and thematic imagery or metaphor. But a crucial difference lies in the influence of genre on the otherwise similar styles of the two men. Although he was many things, Bacon was never a preacher. Had he been, he and his friend Andrewes might have composed a pulpit school, whereas Andrewes alone is an isolated monument. In all of Bacon's many chosen genres, he wrote about ideas from a sociological, or even psychological perspective.[43] In sermons, however, Andrewes wrote resolutely and exclusively from a textual perspective; that is, one always mediated by the scriptural text he interprets. To import an anachronistic nineteenth-century term, Andrewes's prose is first and foremost 'exegesis', or, 'the interpretation of

---

[42] The traditional ascription of praise to the Trinity—'Glory be to the Father, and to the Son, and to the Holy Ghost, as it was in the beginning, is now and ever shall be, Amen', or with the variant ending, 'to whom be all honour and glory, now and forever, Amen'—was so conventional as to be usually abbreviated in the printed texts, sometimes as severely as with a simple '&c.' (p. 224) or 'To whom, &c.' (p. 177).

[43] I am here indebted to the revisionist appreciation of Bacon's prose consolidated in the introduction and annotations of Brian Vickers (ed.), *Francis Bacon: A Critical Edition of the Major Works* (Oxford, 1988); for more detail, see Vickers, *Francis Bacon and Renaissance Prose* (Cambridge, 1968).

Scripture' (*OED*). Put in modern secular terms, Andrewes's sermons might be thought of as exercises in literary criticism.[44]

The unique prose style which Andrewes adopts for the analysis of scripture springs from his view of the ability of single words, indeed of even the component syllables of single words, to contain vast amounts of meaning.[45] As the words which are the subject of his analysis demand microscopic treatment to reveal all that is contained in them, so his own prose honours its subject with similarly microscopic syntax. The opening of his 1594 sermon on Luke 17: 32 ('*Remember* LOT'*s Wife*', p. 108) is thus simultaneously a statement of Andrewes's belief that even a tiny sample of scriptural words contains worlds within it, a description of his own ideals for exegetical prose, and a manifestation or example of the same:

> The words are few, and the sentence short; no one in Scripture so short. But it fareth with *Sentences* as with *coynes*: In coines, they that in smallest compasse conteine greatest value, are best esteemed: and, in sentences, those that in fewest words comprise most matter, are most praised. Which, as of all sentences it is true; so specially of those that are marked with *Memento*. In them, the shorter, the better; the better, and the better caried away, and the better kept; and the better called for when we need it. And such is this heere; of rich contents, and with all exceeding compendious: So that, we must needs be without all excuse, it being but three words, and but five syllables, if we doe not remember it.

On display here, in addition to his love for meaningful brevity (note the opening repetition of the key concept, 'short'), are several other hallmarks of Andrewes's prose at its best. First is the introduction of a colloquial, homely simile ('with *Sentences* as with *coynes*'). Then that simile is elaborated by the use of short syntactical units to build symmetries that are all the more apparent—and thus meaningful—for their skeletal appearance, which needs little typographical manipulation to emphasize it:

> in coines,
> they   that in smallest compass   conteine greatest value,   are best esteemed:

and,

> in sentences,
> those that in fewest words   comprise most matter,   are most praised

---

[44] It is one of the disciplinary blind spots of a profession ostensibly committed to understanding texts and how they were interpreted that the vast body of sermon literature has not been more fully explored as paradigms of how a culture—here the Renaissance—interpreted texts. Cf. the absence of any exegetical works in Brian Vickers (ed.), *English Renaissance Literary Criticism* (Oxford, 1999). Calvinism (mostly its influence in France) gets a brief treatment in Catherine Randall's essay in Glyn P. Norton, *The Cambridge History of Literary Criticism*, iii: *The Renaissance* (Cambridge, 1999), 466–74.

[45] See Joan Webber, 'Celebration of Word and World in Lancelot Andrewes' Style', *Journal of English and Germanic Philology*, 64 (1965), 255–69.

The simile then grows with the brief intensifying addition of 'so specially those that are marked with *Memento*'. The preacher imagines coins which are literally stamped ('marked') with the imperative motto '*Memento*' ('Remember'), which heightens what had been a simple comparison to a conceit worthy of Donne's most 'metaphysical' poetry.[46] But it also linguistically ties even this preliminary passage to the exegetical work of interpreting the set text, which Andrewes always declaimed in Latin as well as English: '*Memore* estote Uxoris LOT' (emphasis added). Although obviously clever, this is more than the witty deployment of metaphor for pleasure's sake. Through it, the key word of the text has been made real— as real as a valuable coin that is to be 'the better caried away' in the listener's pocket so that it can be 'the better called for when we need it'. The careful use of the plural first person in that last phrase is also anything but incidental. The business of interpreting the text and its key word 'remember' will, as always for Andrewes, be a joint enterprise requiring not only his own skill, but also the cooperation of the listener's intellect and subsequent action. Similarly, Andrewes will require a feat of memory himself to deliver the ensuing oration, and he would expect his audience to remember his arguments as well. And so, with amazing economy, Andrewes reveals in only a few lines something 'exceeding compendious', charging both himself and his listeners that they are 'without all excuse... if we doe not remember it'.

With those last words, 'remember it', Andrewes puts in motion one of the other most striking features of his style, the urgent focus on one single word as the interpretative key or leitmotif for the entire oration. This is usually an imperative verb or verb phrase, which in itself is further evidence of his insistence that words be turned into actions. And one of the ways Andrewes gets as much out of single words as possible is to double his interpretative options by treating these key words in both English and Latin (and sometimes also Greek or Hebrew). Almost every Andrewes sermon, especially those for the major feasts, can be epitomized by the single word with which he so memorably defines it.[47] So in this sermon, not only is the whole short text repeatedly used as a refrain, and the imperative 'Remember' deployed in a climactic litany of moral injunctions (pp. 119–20). But also, repetition of a host of derivatives of the English 'Remember' and Latin 'Memores' keeps the fingers of the preacher and the listener on that

---

[46] For coins as a metaphor for anti-Ciceronianism popular in the 1590s, see George Williamson, *The Senecan Amble: Prose from Bacon to Collier* (Chicago, 1951), 104.

[47] Randomly taking some of those in this edition, Lent 1594 is 'remember' ('memores'), Good Friday 1597 is 'look upon' ('respicient'), Christmas 1609 is 'sent' ('misit'), Gowry 1610 is 'touch not' ('nolite tangere'), Whitsunday 1618 is 'pour out' ('effundam').

coin stamped *'Memento'*: 'call to mind', 'remind', 'memorie', 'memorial', *'memorandum'*, *'Remembrancers'*. And of course, as the key root word evolves, so do the moral and theological ideas of the sermon, in a process like that of the coin image in the opening paragraph, but on a larger scale. Hence 'remembering' is applied not just to the example of Lot's wife's sin, but also to her 'memorial' pillar of salt, to our own sins, to the example of 'CHRIST too, that gave the *Memento*', to preachers as those who 'remember' ('remind of' in modern English) these duties, and (climactically) to the 'full *Memento, Remember the Reward*'—'Eternity it selfe' (p. 120).

It is not an exaggeration to say that Andrewes has a sacramental understanding of language, indeed of words themselves.[48] When a person—whether a preacher or a listener—finds the meaning (or often, meanings) in a word and acts upon it accordingly, that person incarnates that word and participates bodily in its efficaciousness. (There is only a very small step between Andrewes's understanding of words and of the eucharist.) So, to quote again from the 1607 sermon on James 1: 22, 'unto the *word*, that we *heare*, let there be joyned the *Element* of the *Worke* ... and so shall you have the great Mysterie or *Sacrament* of *Godlinesse*. ... Which very *Sacrament of godlinesse* is there [in scripture] said to be *the manifesting of the word in the flesh*' (xcvi, pt.2, p. 137). And 'works' for Andrewes are not only physical acts. They also include acts of understanding and of interpretation. Works and words are thus in some sense inseparable for Andrewes; both have real presence, both are substantive things. They are also thus to be in a sense consecrated. Wilful acts of *mis*interpretion desecrate words in a way analogous to how acts of sin violate the temple of the body. Andrewes's use of 'Touch not mine Anointed' (1 Chron. 16: 22) to defend divine right monarchy in the 1610 Gowrie sermon is unsurprising. But very surprising indeed is his assertion that the text itself, like a king, is something that needs protection from the violent 'touch' of Roman Catholics. In Andrewes's view, their interpretation of the verse (which claimed that it did not apply to kings) was an attack on a text every bit as real as the assassination of a king:

And so, see we the summe of the Text, which is sufficient enough to keepe Kings from *touching*, if it selfe might be kept untouched: but as the times are, the Text it selfe is touched, there needes a second *Nolite tangere* for it. To that end then, to see the Text safe and well kept, the three persons in it, all to joyne together: *Kings*, touching whom; and *Subjects*, to whom; and *GOD* himselfe, by whom it is given in charge. (pp. 180–1)

---

[48] Peter E. McCullough, 'Lancelot Andrewes and Language', *Anglican Theological Review*, 74 (1992), 304–16; Noam Reisner, 'Sacramental Prose: Tracing and Submitting the Divine in the Sermons of Lancelot Andrewes' (Oxford, unpublished M.Phil. thesis, 2002).

It is this drive to find meaning in words, a sort of chronic logophilia, that, even if one does not share Andrewes's theological assumptions, makes him the most literary of literary artists. Ambiguity, paradox, and multiple meanings are a thing of delight for Andrewes. Preaching on the 'signe' of Christ in the manger (for Andrewes of course a metonym for all words) he exclaims, 'Well may this be said a *Signe . . . to wonder at*: If it be well looked into, it is hable to strike any man into an extasie.'[49] Verbal ecstasy is the reward for those that attend closely to Andrewes's own words.

For all his sermons' erudition, and his insistently elitist views about the scholarship required to preach well ('God hath bestowed this gift upon the learned, and to those of the learned which have the guift of interpretation', p. 6), his English is predominantly colloquial and monosyllabic. Against this coarse native ground his multilingual flourishes sparkle even more strikingly. Andrewes is also capable of a surprising degree of humour, albeit dry, and usually sarcastic. His paraphrase of Acts 2: 13, the crowd's reaction to the apostles' speaking in tongues at Pentecost ('And others mocked, and saide, They are full of newe wine', Geneva), could be lines written for a group of witty gallants mocking a bad sermon in a City comedy (the paraphrase is even introduced and punctuated as dialogue):

Ye may heare them speake (at the thirteenth verse:) *Well fare this same good new wine; these good fellowes have been at it, and now they can speake nothing but outlandish: some little broken Greek or Latin they had, and now out it comes.*

But after that colloquialism ('Well fare', 'good fellowes', 'outlandish', 'out it comes') immediately come Latin epithets, the very contrasting linguistic register of which recapitulate Andrewes's point about the scandal of mistaking 'a great miracle' for 'a big game': 'Thus, that which was indeed *grande Miraculum*, they turned into *grande ludibrium*.' The Latin internal rhyme ('*grande Miraculum*' . . . '*grande ludibrium*') is then turned back into an English parallelism made more trenchant by its native alliteration, 'Of the great Mysterie of this day, they made a meer mockerie.' He then concludes with a summary so contemporary in its wry diction, that the Holy Ghost is as much brought into the world of a Whitsunday at the court of James I as it was into that of the first Pentecost in Jerusalem: 'Those, that were *baptized with the Holy Ghost*, they traduced, as if they had soused themselves in *new wine*. Heer is the *Holy Ghost's* welcome into the world' (p. 208).

How lines like these were actually spoken would obviously influence the degree to which Andrewes intended a contemporary satire. Even a slight

---

[49] Christmas 1618 (Luke 2: 12), *XCVI*, 113.

emphasis on 'Heer' could force the king and court to ask whether their often bacchanalian holiday feasting after sermon and communion 'made a meer mockerie' of Whitsun. Surely consideration of performance, though almost completely absent from the study of early modern sermons, is one of the most important ways available to carry such study forward. Sermons, although avidly consumed by Elizabethan and Jacobean readers, were first and foremost live, theatrical events. As Vickers has said of classical oratory, they are 'performance-art'.[50] Andrewes was famously reluctant to publish (either in manuscript or print) his sermons, doing so only when commanded by the king. His sermons were composed for hearing, not reading. Attention to this fact can be justified not only in historicist terms, but also pragmatic ones, for Andrewes's prose is decidedly easier to understand in the ear than the eye. The heavily punctuated and italicized appearance of Andrewes's prose in print can impede the eye of a modern reader, as in the exordium of Christmas 1609:

If, *when the fulnesse of time commeth*, God *sent his Sonne*: then, When *God sent his Sonne, is the fulnesse of time come*. And as this day, *God sent his Sonne*. This day therfore, (so oft as by the revolution of the yeere it commeth about) is to us a yeerely representation of *the fulnesse of time*. So it is: and a speciall honour it is to the *Feast*, that so it is. And we our selves seeme so to esteeme of it. For we allow for every *month* a *day*, (Looke how many *months* so many *dayes*) to this *Feast*; as if it were, and we so thought it to be, the *full* recapitulation of the whole yere. (p. 162)

Andrewes's punctuation and his use of italics seem to me designed to highlight rhetorical structures of composition more than they call for their vocal exaggeration in delivery. Italics are the less ambiguous case here. They are used not for vocal emphasis, but in the first instance simply for quotations—usually biblical, patristic, or classical, where we would use quotation marks or inverted commas—hence in this passage the italicization of his opening recapitulation of the text. Andrewes will then also italicize the derivatives of key words from his main text ('the *full* recapitulation'), and parts of speech which are reiterated in parallel constructions ('*month* a *day*... *months* so many *dayes*').[51] Such conventions intensify our sense of Andrewes's esteem for words since they highlight special categories of words (scripture, names, key thematic concepts) and the almost

---

[50] Vickers, *Defence of Rhetoric*, 65.

[51] Also routinely italicized are proper nouns, which in this passage I think Andrewes takes '*Feast*', i.e. Whitsunday, to be (cf. more clearly, 'writers of the *Latin* Church, *Tertullian*, and *Cyprian*', p. 162). This discussion of course only applies to authorially prepared texts (viz., the quartos published in Andrewes's lifetime, and works in *XCVI* and the *Opuscula Posthuma*). That even the minutiae of such typography, spelling, and punctuation is authorial is proven by the Trinity Manuscript sermons corrected in Andrewes's own hand (see section V, below).

tactile manipulation of words into meaningful patterns. Because of this, to modernize spelling or typography would obliterate a signifying system as integral to Andrewes's verbal texture as it is to Spenser's. But having acknowledged that, I am not convinced that oral delivery of this same prose did not (or at least can not) smooth some of the otherwise very rough edges presented on the page.[52] A modern spelling and punctuation of the same passage might indeed come closer to what Jacobeans actually heard Andrewes say:

> If 'when the fulness of time commeth, God sent his son', then when 'God sent his son is the fulness of time come'. And as this day 'God sent his son', this day therefore (so oft as by the revolution of the year it commeth about) is to us a yearly representation of 'the fulness of time'. So it is, and a special honour it is to the feast that so it is. And we ourselves seem so to esteem of it, for we allow every month a day (look—how many months, so many days) to this feast, as if it were, and so thought it to be, the 'full' recapitulation of the whole year.

There are undoubtedly losses as well as gains here. But the losses may be of things that tell us more about how Andrewes composed than how he necessarily spoke.

Even if one does not take Andrewes's punctuation (especially his semicolons and commas) literally in modern terms of vocal articulation, one of the most striking effects of hearing one of his sermons delivered is the unrelenting intensity and urgency of tone required by the speaker.[53] There are no emotional peaks and troughs in an Andrewes sermon: no digressions or subsidiary passages of reflection, no purple passages which ask for dramatic contrasts in the pace of delivery or pitch of the voice. Instead, an Andrewes sermon is a relentless, ever-increasingly pitched ascent, or carefully calibrated crescendo. To venture a further musical analogy, an Andrewes sermon is like a complex canonic fugue by Bach—a contrapuntal composition that begins firmly and simply with the statement of the subject or canon (here, the scriptural text); then gradually overlays with literally mathematical precision the same subject in other voices; then counterpoints increasingly complex variations on that original theme (the repeated interlacing of the sermon's key words and ideas) until it gathers them all up in a

---

[52] But compare the observation of Aubrey's 'Scotish Lord', section IV, below.

[53] Cf. F. E. Brightman's observation that 'it is clear from what was said of [Andrewes] as a preacher, that his delivery was a very real part of the charm of his sermons; and perhaps no one could read them aloud with effect who did not possess a considerable faculty of dramatic interpretation' (*Preces*, p. xl). The following remarks are based on my delivery of sermons by both Andrewes and John Donne in performance reconstructions of choral mattins with sermon, following early modern Chapel Royal practice, at Lincoln College, Oxford (16 Feb. 2002), Trinity College, Cambridge (17 May 2003), and the Chapel Royal, Hampton Court Palace (20 Nov. 2004).

final, resounding cadence. Like such a musical composition, it is almost impossible to excerpt any passage from the middle of it because all has been built on what has come before. By the same token, the preacher's voice can never drop when delivering an Andrewes sermon; once it begins, the sermon spins on and on, with the preacher progressing from one terrific act of intellectual and syntactical will to another. There are no stops for breath, no cæsurae, no aposiopeses. And there are certainly no excess words—every syllable contributes to the driving forward of the continually elaborated subject.

It was this kind of verbal intensity, fully appreciable only in delivery, that delighted Nashe and Lyly, and stunned generations of courtiers. About court sermon auditories Sir John Harington observed that 'Courtiers eares are commonly so open as it goes in at one eare and out at the other'. But Andrewes's sermons, he said, 'left an aculeus behinde in manie of all sorts'. An 'aculeus' (diminutive of Latin, 'acus', 'a needle', or 'bodkin') is a 'sting', as from a nettle, a bee, or a pin, or (transferatively) from cutting remarks. Andrewes's prose, especially when animated by an incisive delivery, was designed to achieve precisely the result observed by Harington.[54] To prove his point, he added the exemplum of the courtier-poet Henry Noel (d. 1597), who, in spite of being 'one of the great gallants of those times', upon hearing Andrewes preach, 'sware as he was a gentleman he never heard man speake with such a spirit'.[55] We are left with textual remains of Andrewes which preserve much of that 'spirit'. But our appreciation and understanding of those remains will be enriched if we attempt too to hear him 'speake'.

IV. CRITICAL RECEPTION

Harington's appreciation of Andrewes's preaching—in his quite subjective biographical directory of Elizabethan and early Jacobean bishops—is, after Nashe's, one of the earliest to survive. Andrewes plays a starring role in Harington's ideological project of steering the young Prince Henry away from moderate puritanism and toward liturgical conservatives like

---

[54] 'Aculeate' was an adjectival form used by Bacon to criticize the potential excesses of the style; cf. 'Of Anger' (1625), with its 'special caution' against 'extreme bitterness of words, especially if they be aculeate' (Vickers (ed.), *Francis Bacon*, 450); cf. also Bacon, *De Augmentis Scientiarum*, 'the labour here is altogether, *That words may be aculeate, sentences concise, and the whole contexture of the speech and discourse, rather rounding into it selfe*' (trans. Gilbert Wats), quoted in Williams, *Senecan Amble*, 112.

[55] Sir John Harington, *An Addicion or Supplie to the Catalogue of Bishops to the Yeare 1608*, ed. R. H. Miller (Potomac, Md., 1979), 141.

Andrewes. Still, it captures the outlines of Andrewes's life and pulpit achievement that are in every point verifiable from other sources, while anticipating (in its focus on Andrewes's avant-garde conformity) the image of the man and preacher later promulgated by Laud and Buckeridge. The 'two speciall things' singled out for praise by Harington are Andrewes's politics ('to raise a joynt reverence to God and the Prince... by uniting and not severing them'), and the persistence in his sermons 'to leade to amendment of life and good works', aspects well represented in this edition.[56]

One of the only negative remarks about Andrewes's style to date from his lifetime is probably contemporary with Harington's, but it too is at least partially motivated by ideology as much as aesthetic judgement. In the conclusion of his vignette on Andrewes, John Aubrey observed (after the Restoration),

> he had not that smooth way of Oratory, as now. It was a shrewd and severe animadversion of a Scotish Lord, who, when K. James asked him how he liked B^p A. sermon. he comp ^said^ that he was learned, but he did play wth his Text, as a Jack-an-apes, does, who takes-up a thing and tosses and plays with it, & then he takes up another, & playes a little with it: here's a pretty thing, and there's a pretty thing[57]

King James was an exception to his countrymen's preference for the unadorned style of preaching of the Scottish kirk which, like much godly preaching in England, focused upon clear moral 'doctrines and uses' from scripture rather than the filigreed academic exegesis of a preacher like Andrewes. Moreover, if this anecdote dates (as it very likely does) from James's tour of Scotland in 1617—when Andrewes and the rising Laud were his right-hand men for 'reducing' the Scots to ceremonial and episcopal conformity with England—there lies behind this judgement as much criticism of churchmanship as of prose style. But that does not compromise this as a perceptive characterization of what I have already described as Andrewes's logophilia and his resulting habit of 'playing' with words.

Moreover, this was a judgement levelled against close exegetical preaching by a man irreproachably devoted not only to the English Church, but also to Andrewes himself—George Herbert. In his priestly conduct book, *A Priest to the Temple or, The Country Parson* (written *c.*1630?, printed 1652), Herbert recommended as 'the Parsons Method' in preaching, 'a plain and evident declaration of the meaning of the text', and added that

---

[56] Harington, *An Addicion*, 138–42; see Jason Scott Warren, *Sir John Harington and the Book as Gift* (Oxford, 2001), ch. 7.

[57] John Aubrey, *Brief Lives*, ed. Kate Bennett (forthcoming, Oxford); I am very grateful to Dr Bennett for sharing with me her new text based on Aubrey's manuscripts.

'the other way of crumbling a text into small parts... hath neither in it sweetnesse, nor gravity, nor variety, since the words apart are not Scripture, but a dictionary, and may be considered alike in all the Scripture.'[58] This has often been interpreted as a condemnation of Andrewes.[59] But I find it hard to believe that Herbert had Andrewes in mind. The first point of rebuttal to make is a contextual one—that Herbert was writing a manual for country parsons whose parishioners ('Countrey people') 'live hardly' and whose level of education demanded 'a slighter forme of Catechizing, fitter for country people' (pp. 227, 230). If he condemns preaching like that which Andrewes offered to university, City, and court auditories, it is only to warn that it is not fitting in a rural parish where the parson must exercise a careful 'particularizing of his speech' to his auditory.[60] Second, Herbert openly idolized Andrewes from the time he first encountered him when a new boy at Westminster, aged 11. But more to our point here, there is evidence of Herbert's approbation of Andrewes's prose style itself. In a Latin letter of 1619 which hailed Andrewes as 'Heros illustrissime' ('illustrious hero'), Herbert added in a self-conscious postscript,

> I could have filled line upon line with your titles and obsequious forms of address, but, in my view, Roman style and its traditional 'periodic' rhythm (*Romana elegantia, periodique vetus rotunditas*) forbids that. It is for that reason that I preferred to defer to the way that you like to hear prose—concise and well polished (*creberrimâ Antiquitatis lectione tersis atque expolitis*)...[61]

Here Herbert anticipates George Williamson's thesis that Andrewes self-consciously shunned the flowing periods of Ciceronian Latin ('*Romana elegantia*'), and offers, in his own terse Latin, a richly suggestive piece of literary criticism. He sees Andrewes as having rejected the dominant style of his own age, and instead self-consciously imitating that of a distant 'former age' ('*Antiquitatis*'), most likely the prose style of Seneca and Tacitus. Even the word translated here as 'prose' (*lectione*) suggests further qualities of Andrewes style: 'lectio' (fr. *lego*, 'to read') literally means a 'picking out' or 'selecting', or a 'reading out', which captures not just

---

[58] *The Works of George Herbert*, ed. F. E. Hutchinson (Oxford, 1941), 234–5.

[59] W. Fraser Mitchell, *English Pulpit Oratory from Andrewes to Tillotson* (1932), 362–3; Williamson, *Senecan Amble*, 248–9; Owen, *Lancelot Andrewes*, 145.

[60] *Works*, ed. Hutchinson, p. 235. More work needs to be done on whether Herbert had in mind bad imitations of Andrewes's preaching, rather than Andrewes's own. Many preachers, beginning with Laud himself, attempted it, usually with disastrous results. See Chamberlain, *Letters*, ii. 391; Owen, *Lancelot Andrewes*, 145–6; and the examples collected in Mitchell, *English Pulpit Oratory*, 157, 174–5, 308, 355.

[61] The free English trans. is by Christopher Turner, in David Scott, *Sacred Tongues: The Golden Age of Spiritual Writing* (2001), 46; Latin supplied here from *Works*, ed. Hutchinson, p. 473.

Andrewes's scrupulous economy with words, but also the possibility that Herbert had in mind hearing Andrewes's prose, not reading it. And the adjectives *creberrimâ* ('most tightly packed', 'crowded'), *tersis* (lit., 'scoured', 'neat'), and *expolitis* ('polished') could hardly have been better chosen to compliment—and complement—Andrewes's style.

The triumph of Royal Society plain-style prose after the Restoration marked a summary end to Andrewes's popularity as anything but the author of the *Preces Privatæ* in the 'long' eighteenth century. Chief among the Augustans' charges against Andrewes was his love of what they called 'punning'. As the important new work of Sophie Read shows, the term 'pun' (according to the *OED*, first coined by Dryden in 1662) is an anachronism when applied to Andrewes's wordplay. Moreover, the eighteenth century's disgust for such displays of wit led to charges of superficiality that were entirely blind to the deep seriousness of such 'play' in the Renaissance.[62] Addison condemned Andrewes and Shakespeare together for it: 'The sermons of Bishop *Andrews*, and the Tragedies of *Shakespear*, are full of [puns]. The Sinner was Punned into Repentance by the former, as in the Latter nothing is more usual than to see a Hero weeping and quibbling for a dozen lines together.'[63] Even though bound in a pejorative judgement, to find these authors so linked is in itself testament to how Andrewes deserves scholarly consideration as serious as that given the playwright. In fact, Shakespeare's puns might even be deemed more superficial—more for the sake of comic sound than intellectual sense—than Andrewes's. As Read observes, 'the aim of [Andrewes's] wordplay is not simply to demonstrate a heard similarity, but to argue for a necessary congruence which can be felt and thought.' That is, Andrewes's wordplay, in keeping with his stylistic ideals of efficiency and economy, always performs important interpretative work. To take even a relatively simple example, consider his parody of papal claims to authority over kings in the 1610 Gowrie sermon: 'The *Pope*, he was *Gods*, and they [kings] were *his* [the Pope's] *anointed*, and of him had their *dependence*, and he to *depose* them and to *dispose* of them' (p. 185). The aural play on '*depose*' and '*dispose*' is funny, but deadly funny. Its arch 'paranomasia' (as early moderns would have called it) epitomizes, with cutting efficiency, the twin papal claims to be able to excommunicate and dethrone kings, and then to endorse the killing of them. More positively, after summing the text of his Spital sermon, Andrewes appeals to the auditory, 'Beloved in the Lord,

---

[62] I am gratefully indebted here to Ms Read for allowing me to draw on her brilliant essay 'Lancelot Andrewes and Puns', chapter 1 of her Cambridge Ph.D. thesis, 'The Rhetoric of Real Presence in the Seventeenth Century' (2005).

[63] *The Spectator* (no. 61; 10 May, 1711), ed. Donald F. Bond, 5 vols. (Oxford, 1965), i. 260.

I beseech you weigh but the place; weigh it, and have pitie on us' (p. 44). The 'place' is primarily the 'place' or verses of scripture he asks his listeners to consider with him; but 'place' also refers to the physical place and occasion of his sermon, that is, the Spital sermon series sponsored by the governors of the City of London to raise charitable donations for the poor; and finally, there is Andrewes's own 'place', in terms of his office or profession as a preacher. So with one 'pun', he gathers his text, his auditory, and himself into one collective unit for which he asks 'pitie'.

Andrewes's most sophisticated wordplay, however, flows from his sensitivity to the etymological roots of English words. Here is found the best evidence that Andrewes's deployment of his legendary multilingualism was not mere decoration or display. The grammatical treatment of 'God sent his sonne' (Gal. 4: 4) in the exordium for Christmas 1609 achieves nothing less than a crafty *apologia* for the word 'Christmas' itself, a word then spurned by the godly for its etymological derivation from 'Christ's mass':

This honour it hath, from *Christ*, who is the *substance* of this, and all other *Solemnities*. Peculiarly, *à Christi missâ*, from *Christs sending*. (For, they that read the ancient writers of the *Latin* Church, *Tertullian*, and *Cyprian*, know that *Missa*, and *Missio*, and *Remissa*, and *Remissio*, with them are taken for one. So that *Christi missa* is the *sending of Christ*.) And when then hath this Text place so fit, as Now? Or what time so seasonable to entreat of it, as This? Of *the sending of his Sonne*; as, *when God sent his Sonne*: (p. 162)

Here Andrewes cleverly goes behind late-medieval Latin usage to find a prior patristic justification for the English word 'mass'. As ever, Andrewes begins with his text, but from the Vulgate: '*misit Deus Filium suum*' cleverly turned here into its more suggestive phrase, '*Christi missa*' ('*sending of Christ*'). Andrewes of course would have known that 'Christmas' was unambiguously 'Christ's mass', from the sixth-century transferative sense in the Roman Catholic dismissal '*ite missa est*' ('a sending out', fr. Lat., 'mittio', 'to send') pronounced at the end of the eucharist. To avoid this, Andrewes needs to reclaim its literal sense, as in '*God sent his Sonne*'. He achieves this with the historical-linguistic note that in pre-sixth-century Latin, 'missa' and 'remissa' were accepted gerundive forms of 'missio' and 'remissio' (for 'a sending' and 'a remitting') which had subsequently passed out of use. Hence, Tertullian and Cyprian exemplify early church writing that used those words literally, without any transferative application to the eucharist or 'mass'. This grammatical 'punning' therefore reforms the word 'Christmas', freeing it from association with the Catholic mass, and allows Andrewes to conclude the sermon with a resounding affirmation of the joy felt 'to have held such a *Feast*, to have kept a *Christmasse*' (p. 176).

As discussed at the beginning of this introduction, the nineteenth century, in particular the Oxford Movement, saw the birth of modern interest in Andrewes. Like the Laudians, the Tractarians found in Andrewes an important vehicle for their particular version of Anglicanism. The Tractarians not only produced the first new edition of Andrewes since *XCVI. Sermons*, but also an important early piece of criticism that deserves more attention than it has hitherto received. J. B. Mozley's review for the *British Critic*, in addition to expressing quite openly a Tractarian religious agenda, anticipated by almost a century major points of literary analysis too often attributed only to Eliot. Mozley observed perceptively that Andrewes's prose style was the product not of quaint Jacobean fashion, but of his philosophy of language and principles of exegesis: 'his style, which though partly that of the age in which he lived, is at the same time obviously a natural style and expresses the working of his own mind' (p. 173). In a metaphor which recalls that of Andrewes's Lenten coin, Mozley observed that 'he seems always on his guard, either against losing sight of his text himself, or allowing his hearer to do so; and so he takes it about with him wherever he goes' (p. 175). He appreciated, too, Andrewes's habit of productive reiteration of key words and terms, noting that 'he is never tired of using the same word: it meets us again and again in every shape and connexion, and pierces and perforates the whole sermon' (p. 193). He was also frank about the challenges of appreciating Andrewes. He called for a historically sensitive approach to what was even in the nineteenth century an alien mode of writing, acknowledged how resistant Andrewes's prose is to brief quoted excerpts, and admitted that Andrewes's greatest strengths lie in precisely the qualities that modern readers can find most off-putting:

Accuracy and system are the greatest of all obstacles to an easy flowing style; they are the most difficult elements to subdue and accommodate to a good construction. This is one great cause of Bishop Andrewes' peculiarities; his *irregularity* of style proceeds very commonly only from his *regularity* of plan, a regularity of a much minuter and more precise kind than would be thought expedient at the present day. (p. 203)

Finally, Mozley wrote with eloquence of the 'beauty' that can be found in Andrewes by an attentive reader. Perhaps surprisingly for our post-Eliotan generation—which often assumes that Andrewes could only be the darling of Romanticism's discontents—Mozley actually compared any rash dismissal of Andrewes's sermons 'as so much simple pedantry' to the dismissal of 'Mr. Wordsworth's poetry as so much simple mawkishness'. 'In our humble opinion', he intoned, 'both censures would involve the very extreme of dulness and narrowmindedness' (p. 202). And his peroration on the beauty of Andrewes was even cast in the famous terms of Wordsworth's 'Preface' to *Lyrical Ballads*: 'The characteristic of *beauty* appears in the constant risings and spontaneous overflowings of feeling whenever anything comes up, that naturally elicits feeling—overflowings, commonly sudden and short ... which one unacquainted with his style might easily overlook.'[64]

Regaining a sense of the beauty and feeling in Andrewes may be the best direction for literary appreciation of Andrewes to take in this century. It would certainly be a departure from the dominant terms of the last century. And those terms were T. S. Eliot's. For Eliot, the only passion in Andrewes is 'his passion for order in religion ... reflected in his passion for order in prose'. Add to this Eliot's other back-handed compliment—that 'the sermons of Andrewes are not easy reading. They are only for the reader who can elevate himself to the subject' (p. 304)—and one may be forgiven for thinking that like the Andrewesian Magi Eliot so admired, readers of Andrewes are supposed to have 'a cold coming of it'. Eliot has certainly given us some analyses of Andrewes that are so apt, so accurate, that they come as naturally as breathing to anyone who has read them even once and then tries to write about the bishop:

no one is more master of the short sentence than Andrewes (p. 306)

there are often flashing phrases which never desert the memory (p. 307)

Andrewes takes a word and derives the world from it; squeezing and squeezing the word until it yields a full juice of meaning which we should never have supposed any word to possess (p. 305).

But, like so much of his work, Eliot's essay on Andrewes might say more about Eliot himself than anyone else. What Eliot craved in literature was an escape from authorial personality, and in Lancelot Andrewes he thought that he had found an author who had achieved this: 'Andrewes's emotion is purely contemplative; it is not personal, it is wholly evoked by the object of contemplation, to which it is adequate; his emotions wholly contained in and explained by its object' (pp. 308–9). Andrewes is, as I hope to have shown, almost unsurpassed in his ability to inhabit a scriptural text and to carve out of it works of exegetical art remarkable for their precision, focus, and intensity. But Andrewes was decidedly not the disembodied, atemporal, contemplative mind of Eliot's vision. And by this I do not only mean the obvious point that Andrewes was a very real political animal—leading

---

[64] p. 204. Mozley, later a distinguished theologian, was at this time a Fellow of Magdalen College, Oxford, and an intimate of Newman, Pusey, and Keble; his appeal to William Wordsworth is probably best seen as part of the Oxford Movement's keen, though unsuccessful, attempt to enlist the Laureate in its cause. See Stephen Gill, *Wordsworth and the Victorians* (Oxford, 1998), 64–6.

in the last twenty years of Elizabeth's reign the rearguard action to arrest any further reformation of the Church of England, and in James's reign laying the foundation of William Laud's and Charles I's disastrous attempt to reform it in another way. But I mean too that Andrewes in his sermons engages human passions, both his own and those of all who then heard and now read him. In his quest to praise Andrewes as passionless and 'pure' (p. 309) Eliot also visited upon Andrewes scholarship what at best could be called the mixed blessing, at worst the curse, of comparison with John Donne.[65] Eliot's 'Lancelot Andrewes' is in fact a double portrait: of the impersonal, 'pure' Andrewes all in white, and the self-advertising, 'impure' Donne painted in lurid blacks and reds. Very close to the surface of Eliot's characterization of Donne is the critic's palpable fear of sex. Donne is 'the sorcerer of emotional orgy' whose 'experience was not perfectly controlled', who 'lacked spiritual discipline', who reminds Eliot of the decadence of Huysmans, and who 'is dangerous' for those who read him for 'indulgence of their sensibilities' (pp. 302, 309–10). But to escape from this Donne ('We emphasize', he admitted, 'this aspect to the point of the grotesque', p. 302), Eliot created an Andrewes that was just as much a caricature.

Andrewes does speak with passion and with personality. Only a writer keenly aware not only of his own self, body, and emotions, but also those of all listening to him—women and men—could compose something as beautiful as his account of Christ's revelation of himself to the grieving Mary Magdalen in the garden (p. 241). This is a passage that deserves to stand with any of Shakespeare's great recognition scenes, not least the vivification of Hermione's statue in *The Winter's Tale*. Andrewes of course lights upon the fact that it is a word, and at that a special category of word, a name, that opens Mary's eyes to Christ: 'this one word, these two syllables [*Mary*] from *His* mouth, scatters it, all. No sooner had *His* voice sounded in her eares, but it drives away all the mist, dries up her tears.' Soon after comes the surprising comfort of proverbial wisdom, 'Well now, He that was thought lost, is found

---

[65] Comparison of the two men and their very different preaching styles has become a *de rigeur* set piece for Andrewes criticism; at the risk of censure, I do not wish to perpetuate it. There is obvious worth in comparing the two, especially for undergraduates developing a sense of the differences in early modern prose. But in scholarly work this has too often been carried out under the tacit assumption that Donne is superior. I do not think that this would be possible if Donne did not bask in the glow of modern admiration for his poetry. See Peter McCullough, 'Andrewes and Donne', *John Donne Journal* (2005); Owen, *Lancelot Andrewes*, 139–44; John Carey, 'Prose', in Christopher Ricks (ed.), *English Poetry and Prose 1540–1674* (1970); Story (ed.), *Sermons*, p. xxix; W. Fraser Mitchell, *English Pulpit Oratory from Andrewes to Tillotson* (1932, repr. 1962), 160, 183–95; Horton Davies, *Like Angels from a Cloud: English Metaphysical Preachers 1588–1645* (San Marino, Calif., 1986), *passim*, esp. pp. 195–9; Daniel Doerkson, 'Preaching Pastor versus Custodian of Order: Donne, Andrewes, and the Jacobean Church', *Philological Quarterly*, 73 (1994), 417–29.

againe', followed by the delight of a paradox: 'and found, not, as He was sought for, not as a dead body, but a living soule, nay, *a quickening Spirit*, then.' But the emphasis does not, as one might expect, stay on Christ, but on the person there so affected by his resurrection: 'And that might *Marie Magdalen* well say. Hee shewed it, for He quickened her Spirits, that were as good as dead.' Then Andrewes immediately makes an electrifying direct address to the auditory in front of him, saying, 'You thought you should have come to *Christs* Resurrection to day, and so you doe. But, not to His alone, but even to *Marie Magdalens* resurrection, too.' Andrewes is here staging a play, surprising his audience with the entrance of a character they had not expected, driving home the fact that the main action, the resurrection of Christ, is re-enacted in Mary, and, by implication, in everyone watching. 'For, in very deed, a kind of resurrection it was, was wrought in her, revived, as it were, and raised from a dead & drowping, to a lively and cheerfull estate.' And then, in a line that is almost heart-breaking in its humble but evocative summing up of so many poignant themes and images, he concludes, 'The *Gardiner* had done his part, made her all greene, on the soddaine.'

Since Eliot there has been some fine criticism of Andrewes, yet it has almost all recapitulated (often quite eloquently and insightfully) his compelling descriptions of the style, rather than analysed it or put it into its historical context. As Elizabeth McCutcheon observed decades ago,

> if Andrewes is ever to emerge in his own right as a creative religious artist, scholars and critics need to get beyond this fatigued general question to provide sustained and probing assessments of his rhetoric, poetics, intellectual attitudes, religious beliefs, spirituality, and polemics in the light of newer developments in the many relevant disciplines and with a fresher sense of his historical situation.[66]

It is hoped that this edition will encourage precisely these things.

V. ANDREWES'S TEXTS

As I have argued earlier, Laud and Buckeridge's *XCVI. Sermons* has largely defined the Andrewes canon since 1629. A principal aim of this edition has been to demonstrate the greater variety of sources for Andrewes's texts, and

---

[66] Elizabeth McCutcheon, 'Recent Studies in Andrewes', *English Literary Renaissance*, 11 (1981), 102. Since McCutcheon's bibliography, the most significant steps in the direction she has called for are Shuger, *Habits of Thought*, ch. 1; Lossky, *Lancelot Andrewes*; the ongoing work on Andrewes's manuscripts by Klemp, and the historical work of Lake, Tyacke, Fincham, MacCulloch, and McCullough (see Works Frequently Cited).

the different manners and contexts of the production and circulation of those texts in the sixteenth and early seventeenth centuries. What follows is a brief description of the bibliographical complexities of Andrewes's texts as witnessed by the texts in this edition; it could be expanded by subsequent work on others. Much greater detail on individual texts will be found in the textual headnote to each selection.

Story's ground-breaking editorial work on Andrewes produced not only his selected edition, but also a separately published outline of the major print traditions of Andrewes's work, the principal conclusions of which I accept.[67] First, those texts collected in *XCVI. Sermons* represent authorially perfected copies found by Laud and Buckeridge. To this point I would only add that it must also be at least entertained that these complete texts were entrusted to them by Andrewes himself during his long last illness; although there is no evidence for this, it seems unlikely that a man so cautious about the publication of his works during his lifetime would have left his textual posterity to chance. An important subcategory within *XCVI. Sermons* are the ten texts which had already appeared by royal command during Andrewes's lifetime. Story limited his comment on these to their first quartos, correctly judging that the absence of substantive variants between them and their folio incarnations (in *XCVI. Sermons*) means that they, as the earliest surviving texts, 'will, in each case, possess the highest authority' (p. 20). But some of these quartos in fact appeared in several editions before *XCVI. Sermons*. These texts are far more important to the task of finding the best copy than has previously been appreciated. For when resetting the quarto sermons for the folio, the editors or compositors did not always use as copy either the first or the best anterior printing. For example, Christmas 1609 (pp. 162–77) appeared in two quarto settings in 1610; my collation shows that the second is an improved new edition which corrects several of the first quarto's most egregious typesetting errors. *XCVI. Sermons*, however, used the inferior first quarto as copy. In 1620 there appeared a rather haphazard collected edition of Andrewes: eleven sermons preached between 1604 and 1620 which had already appeared separately. There was no general title-page. The first eight sermons were reprinted with continuous signatures; the final three were reissues which retained their original title-pages. The eight reprinted sermons are typographically some of the sloppiest work an authorized text of Andrewes ever received. But again collation shows that for the 1610 Gowrie sermon (this edn., pp. 178–206), *XCVI. Sermons* took as its copy

---

[67] G. M. Story, 'The Text of Lancelot Andrewes's Sermons', in D. I. B. Smith (ed.), *Editing Seventeenth Century Prose* (Toronto, 1972), 11–23.

text the inferior 1620 edition, not one of the two anterior quartos of 1610 from which 1620 was itself badly set.[68] But the status of the quartos themselves is complicated even further by scrutiny of those for the same 1610 Gowrie sermon. Printed either simultaneously or in very close proximity to one another, all ten of the copies examined for this edition are composed of sheets mixed (differently in each case) from the two settings. This has required here my own reconstruction of a text from sheets of the superior of these (the second) found in several different copies. All authorized editions of Andrewes during his lifetime appeared from the King's Printing House of Robert Barker; clearly, unsold copies and loose sheets were retained by the printer and used, as demand required, either as copy for subsequent settings, or sheets for reissue.[69]

Story only grudgingly acknowledges the possible importance of the surviving printed texts which derive from notes taken by hearers: 'An age which treasures its literary scrap heaps, and elevates to a fine art the reconstruction of each stage or state in the genesis of a literary work, will be more curious about, and reverend towards, such unperfected, or even reported, compositions than Laud or Buckeridge—or Andrewes.'[70]

These are the words of an editor who preferred his Andrewes in a New Critical 'well-wrought urn'. The *LACT* had been far more generous by including texts of the unauthorized printings of notes from lectures on the Temptation in the Wilderness, the Lord's Prayer, and the Ten Commandments; but even it ignored the treasure trove that is *ΑΠΟΣΠΑΣΜΑΤΙΑ SACRA*. The texts presented here from the latter, and from the authorially derived *Pattern of Catechistical Doctrine*, are indisputably genuine, and, though uneven, they capture Andrewes's distinctive idiom and argumentative structures as well as his independent thought. The latter texts of course cannot sustain the close literary analysis of the authorially polished sermons. But if scholars applied the same strict textual standards imposed on the study of Andrewes by Buckeridge and Laud in rejecting those texts that survive in note form by the author or his hearers, the canon of theologians as diverse and important as Chrysostom and Luther would be infinitely

---

[68] Story ('The Text', in Smith (ed.), *Editing*, 19–20, n. 21), evidently unaware of the intervening 1620 setting, mistakenly attributes its errors to the typesetters of *XCVI. Sermons*.

[69] Andrewes was on intimate terms with Barker; one of the largest cash bequests to an individual in Andrewes's will was to 'Mr Robert Barker (latelie the Kings Printer) the some of one hundred pounds'; he also forgave Barker the debt of 'several somes wherein he stands bound to my Brother Thomas deceased', and left to Barker's 'two Sonnes Robert and Charles my Godsonnes, to either of them ten pounds' (*LACT*, vol. xi, p. cii). Also employed in the King's Printing House late in Andrewes's life was Richard Badger, later Master Printer and printer-publisher for Laud and Buckeridge of *XCVI. Sermons*.

[70] Story, 'The Text', in Smith (ed.), *Editing*, 18.

impoverished. The same is true of Andrewes. It is long past time that they were lifted from the 'scrap heap'.

One final and very important category of texts remains to be addressed—manuscripts. Precious little holograph material by Andrewes survives. The copy texts for *XCVI. Sermons* must be assumed lost, and only a handful of his letters survive.[71] And on inspection a disappointing majority of the manuscripts of Andrewes sermons listed in Peter Beal's exhaustive *Index* prove to be notes taken from printed editions, mostly *XCVI. Sermons*.[72] A dramatic exception is Beal's 'AndL12', or Trinity College Cambridge MS B.14.22, which contains fair copies of the court Easter sermons for 1618 and 1620.[73] These are written in the exquisite secretary and italic hands of Andrewes's amanuensis, Samuel Wright, and contain corrections by him and in Andrewes's own hand. They provide the best surviving proof that the distinctive presentation of Andrewes's texts in the authorial quartos and *XCVI. Sermons*—carefully chosen distinctions between italic and roman type, small and large capitals, drop-capitals, punctuation, rules between sections, and systems of marginalia—are indeed Andrewes's own, and not imposed either by a printing house style or (in the case of *XCVI. Sermons*) posthumous editors. As Klemp has argued, and as the collation of the MS with both the quarto and folio texts of the 1620 sermon in this edition shows, the Trinity witness preserves invaluable evidence of Andrewes's composition techniques. The minute refinements—of word order, punctuation, citation of sources—bear out Buckeridge's funeral sermon claim that 'of his Solemne Sermons he was most carefull of, and exact; I dare say, few of them, but they passed his hand, and were thrice revised, before they were preached'. Similarly, the manuscript reveals an intimate working relationship between Andrewes and his trusted secretary, Wright, a relationship hinted at in Buckeridge's testimony that, although Andrewes's Roman Catholic opponents 'imploy[ed] whole *Colledges* and *Societies* to study and read for them, and so furnish them; he onely used an *Amanuensis*, to transcribe that, which himselfe had first written with his own hand.'[74] Having chosen to base his edition only on 'the earliest printed edition of each sermon', Story cited the existence of this manuscript, but did not collate it.[75]

---

[71] The majority of surviving letters are reprinted in *LACT*, xi. pp. xxxix–l.

[72] Peter Beal, *Index of English Literary Manuscripts*, vol. i, pt. 1 (1980).

[73] fos. 15^r–47^v; for a full description, and an efficient summary of Andrewes's other surviving manuscripts, see P. J. Klemp, ' "Betwixt the Hammer and the Anvill": Lancelot Andrewes's Revision Techniques in the Manuscript of His 1620 Easter Sermon', *Papers of the Bibliographical Society of America*, 89 (1995), 149–82.

[74] Buckeridge, 'A Sermon... at the Funeral', *XCVI*, 19, 21.

[75] Story (ed.), *Lancelot Andrewes*, p. xlix, n. 1.

Study of sermons, like the study of early modern drama, will always be vexed by questions of what relationship written or printed texts have to what was performed in the pulpit or on stage. Practices varied between preachers, but even in Andrewes's individual case this matter requires space not available for detailed discussion here. Broadly speaking, on the evidence already quoted, it seems undeniable that Andrewes almost obsessively perfected his sermons in writing before memorizing them and then delivering them to a degree we would call *verbatim*. But even in the case of the 1620 Easter sermon it remains debatable whether the surviving manuscript version came before or after delivery (see headnote). But the final text included in this edition underscores the unavoidable fact that any sermon, however carefully prepared and memorized, could for any number of reasons require *extempore* alteration in the pulpit. Mary Morrissey's 2004 discovery of a hitherto unknown manuscript version of Andrewes's 1588 Spital sermon (Appendix 1) provides the best evidence of this for Andrewes, or indeed, for any contemporary preacher. Pressures of time obviously required Andrewes to radically truncate his planned oration on the spot. Comparison of the two texts (summarized in Appendix 2) shows exactly how Andrewes edited (or perhaps even censored) himself while in full oratorical flow.

Of previous editions of Andrewes, only the *LACT* can claim to be close to a 'complete works', and it is an impressive monument of Victorian scholarship. It will no doubt continue to be useful to students of Andrewes as the easiest way to access in one place the bulk of his writing. Its final volume (xi, ed. James Bliss) compiles a host of helpful, well-annotated biographical documents, and includes still invaluable indices of scripture, sources, and general topics.[76] The volumes containing Andrewes's Latin writings against Bellarmine (vols. vii and viii, ed. Bliss) are annotated to a far higher scholarly standard than the English sermons (vols. i–iv, ed. J. P. Wilson). But the *LACT* is not without serious shortcomings. Foremost among these was the editors' decision to modernize not just Andrewes's spelling, but also (quite ruthlessly) his punctuation, which runs rough-shod over precisely the verbal and syntactical detail that was of such paramount importance to Andrewes himself. In addition, Wilson used as his copy text the decidedly inferior second edition of *XCVI. Sermons* (see below).

---

[76] Users should beware, however, that the general 'Index to Bishop Andrews' Sermons' (vol. xi, pp. 393–456) is based on the index of the third edition of *XCVI. Sermons* (1635), itself an ideologically subjective guide to what Laud thought important; to this is added the Tractarian concerns of the *LACT* editors themselves.

The increasing availability of the original seventeenth-century editions in electronic format makes it almost inexcusable to quote Andrewes's texts from *LACT* for work of any scholarly seriousness.

Story's edition of twelve complete sermons from *XCVI. Sermons* is an elegant volume, reliably edited, although Story regrettably eradicated Andrewes's sensitive system of marginal citations and numbering, moving them either into the main text or placing them in distracting numbered footnotes. It is also a disappointment that for texts so carefully edited Story offers no annotations or commentary.

VI. THE PRESENTATION OF TEXTS IN THIS EDITION

This critical edition presents texts of twelve complete sermons, two prayers before sermon, and five excerpts from Andrewes's Cambridge catechetical lectures. The copy texts chosen are in my judgement those closest to their lost authorial originals. For reasons explained in section V (above) these are not necessarily always the earliest surviving witnesses. Because of the variety of copy texts, it is not possible to generalize about them, nor about the other witnesses chosen for collation with each; for detailed discussion of these decisions, see the headnote 'Text' for each selection.

But because a majority of the selections presented here are found in *XCVI. Sermons* (nos. III, VI, VII, and IX–XII), some general remarks about that source should be made. The first folio was followed by a second edition of 1631 with two variant reissues in 1632 (*STC* 606, 607, 607.5, and 608, respectively); a third edition, with index, appeared in 1635 (*STC* 609); a fourth edition, with an additional sermon on the Gowrie Conspiracy, appeared in 1641 (Wing A3142); the last early modern edition appeared in two variant states in 1661 (Wing A3142B, A3142C). As Story has shown, the first edition, printed by George Miller for Richard Badger, 'inspires considerable confidence' as an attractive and reliably composed piece of workmanship. Although the second edition (printed, like the third and fourth, by Richard Badger) corrects many small typographical errors, it and the subsequent editions chart a consistent progress of textual deterioration.[77]

---

[77] Story (ed.), *Lancelot Andrewes*, l; Story, 'Texts', in Smith (ed.), *Editing*, 22–3.

This is not only in the inevitable appearance of new compositors' errors, but in the surprisingly thoroughgoing modernization of spelling that begins with the second edition's eradication of many of what must have been Andrewes's own mid-Tudor spellings.[78] For these reasons, for texts which appear in *XCVI. Sermons* I have taken the first edition as copy, collating it with the second and third editions. Those texts having an earlier quarto as copy (nos. X, XI, XIII) are also collated with their witnesses in the first three editions of *XCVI. Sermons*. I have also made occasional recourse to *LACT*, particularly its settings and corrections of marginalia. The present editor's copy of the 1629 first edition used here was that formerly owned and used by Story.

Textual variants appear at the bottom of each page, keyed to line numbers, and record only substantial variants. Most spelling variants are judged incidental and thus not recorded unless the rejected reading can assist a modern reader with the sense of the passage (e.g. 'than' for earlier 'then', or 'counted' for earlier 'compted'). Given Andrewes's care with punctuation, I have recorded all such variants when they could possibly be judged to change either the sense or the vocal inflection of a passage. Marginal apparatuses have been faithfully reproduced from all chosen copy texts. As was often the case in early modern printing, these contain the largest number of errors, and many of the recorded variants relate to them. Any variant supplied by the editor is cited as '*ed.*'

Throughout the edition I have preserved all accidentals of spelling, punctuation, italics, and capitalization of the copy texts. In the titles of texts set from *XCVI. Sermons* I have slightly simplified their more flamboyant use of varied large type sizes; I have also not reproduced *XCVI. Sermons*' use of rows of type-ornaments for rules, nor its occasional patterned settings of final paragraphs (centre-justified lines of gradually reduced length). The only silent alterations are as follows: short 's' for long 's'; 'ss' for 'ß'; modernization of 'i', 'j', 'u', and 'v'; expansion of conventional early modern contractions of Greek letter combinations; substitution of Arabic for Roman numerals in books of the Bible ('1 Sam.' for 'I Sam.'), and in outline and division numbers where the main sequence is Arabic ('1. 2. 3.', for 'I. 2. 3.'). These alterations have *not* been followed in title-page transcriptions or in the text of the Spital sermon manuscript (Appendix 1) where all incidentals and contractions have been retained.

---

[78] Taking examples from just one paragraph of the Spital sermon, cf. 'seely flies'/'silly flies', 'whither'/'whether', 'Counsaile'/'Councell', 'then'/'than', and 'hastie'/'hasty' (p. 43).

VII. COMMENTARY

This is the first fully annotated edition of works by Andrewes. For each selection, readers will find a five-part system of commentary composed of a textual essay, an introductory headnote, a summary of the most prominent or significant sources, and suggestions for further reading, followed by exhaustive annotations on specific words and passages in the text itself. I have endeavoured to annotate these texts in a way useful for students and scholars of literature, history, and theology. Glosses therefore fall into the following major types of matter: difficult or obsolete English words and syntax; allusions to contemporary social, political, and religious matters; documentation of sources for every identifiable quotation or allusion to other authors or works; and the translation of all words and phrases not in English. I have also been as liberal as space allowed with cross-references and quotations from other works by Andrewes.

Documenting Andrewes's sources has proved a mammoth task for two main reasons. First, Andrewes's own system of marginal citation is not complete. But unlike Bliss and Wilson (*LACT*) and Story, I have decided against supplying further citations in the margins, preferring to retain intact Andrewes's own system of annotation as a valuable record of his thought and practice. Instead, all references and citations for matter not found in the copy text margins are placed in my own commentary. Second (and presumably related to the first), Andrewes seems to quote largely from memory, resulting in quotations that are almost never exact, often indeed extremely faint, and quite frequently (especially with patristic sources) incorrectly attributed. Like many humanists trained up on the ideals of classical *imitatio*, with its free, creative use of sources, he is not concerned with the kind of exact citation of sources modern scholars expect.[79] *LACT* did invaluable work supplying additional documentation of sources, in particular biblical references, and, to a lesser extent, patristic sources. I have been able to take even further the range of documentation in this edition largely because of the availability of searchable electronic databases, most crucially the *Patrologia Latina Database*, *The Bible in English Database*, and *Early English Books Online* (*EEBO*), all generously supported at Oxford by the Bodleian Library. This edition could not have been done without them. Finally, the three main documentary and imaginative sources for Andrewes require separate comment.

---

[79] Points lamented by previous editors; see Story (ed.), *Lancelot Andrewes*, p. lii; *LACT*, i. p. vii; and vol. vi, 'Notice' (n.p.).

The Bible

Andrewes's knowledge of the Bible—in every ancient biblical language, as well as most modern ones—probably surpassed that of any Englishman of his age. But the English Bible from which he consistently quoted throughout his lifetime was always the Geneva (even after the 1611 publication of the Authorized Version to which he had contributed). Therefore all biblical references and quotations in my notes and commentary, unless otherwise cited, are from the Geneva Bible (in the 'Tomson' revision, Christopher Barker, 1587; *The Bible in English Database*). The second most important biblical text for Andrewes is the Vulgate. Suggestively, he makes very little use of the Protestant Latin Bible of Tremellius. When I quote from the Vulgate, it is always followed by an English translation; this is usually Geneva, but if (as is often the case) it is closer to the Vulgate, I use the Roman Catholic Douai-Rheims (Douai, 1609/10; *The Bible in English Database*). Those who use this edition should be reminded not only of the different names of books of the Bible in its different versions and translations, but the fact that the numeration of both chapters and verses can vary, even in earlier English translations, from the Authorized Version. Similarly, the force and sense of many of Andrewes's allusions depend on the unique diction found only in Geneva.

The Church Fathers

Like many theologians of his age, Andrewes was steeped in the patristic writings of both the Eastern and Western churches of the first six centuries after Christ. But his engagement with them takes to a new creative height the return to these authors which had first been prompted by the Reformation, when both sides scrambled to find ancient authorities for their arguments. Of all the Fathers, Augustine is by far the most frequently cited. Of the other Latin Fathers, Andrewes makes most frequent appeal to Gregory the Great, Ambrose, and Jerome, as well as Tertullian and Irenaeus. Of the Eastern Fathers he cites predominantly Chrysostom and Basil, occasionally in Greek, but often in Latin translation. Origen (who wrote in Greek, but whose works were known predominantly in Latin) is an important source for the 1620 Easter sermon. Of later theologians Andrewes owes a singular debt to Bernard of Clairvaux, and occasionally appeals to Aquinas. The inaccuracy of Andrewes's quotations from these writers frustrates almost any attempt to determine which early modern editions he might have been using. The catalogue of books which he left in his will to Pembroke College Cambridge Library does capture the range of his learning, but notably absent from it are many standard works Andrewes is known to have used.[80] I have therefore, unless otherwise stated, cited patristic authors from J. P. Migne's encyclopedic *Patrologia Latina* and *Patrologia Graecae*, always giving English translations for quotations from them (my own unless otherwise cited). Finally, evidence perhaps of his reputation for eschewing open controversy is the almost complete avoidance by him of even naming, much less openly engaging, contemporary continental scholars, whether Protestant or Catholic (notable exceptions are the *vituperatio* reserved for the Jesuit Mariana in the 1610 Gowrie sermon, and the highly unusual hat-tipping to Calvin and Musculus for the benefit of the godly London aldermen at the Spital). Instead, and probably more effectively, he usually refutes some (like Calvin) only by implication, and employs others (Luther, Chemnitz, the Rheims New Testament) only tacitly.

Classical Texts

Obviously unmoved by puritan criticisms of the use of secular or 'pagan' learning in preaching, Andrewes drew unapologetically upon moral, historical, and poetic classical texts.[81] In this edition, these are most prominent in the university oration *Sacrilege a Snare*, but also appear in the solemn holy day sermons. Cicero ('the Heathen') and Seneca take pride of place, but Andrewes was also fond of quoting Homer ('the Poet'), Horace, Juvenal, Ovid, and the historians Herodotus and Josephus, and the philosophy of Aristotle. All quotations and translations from these authors, unless otherwise cited, are from the editions in the Loeb Library. Very useful for tracing many of these allusions has been the *Bibliotheca Teubneriana Latina* database of Latin literature.

---

[80] D. D. C. Chambers, 'A Catalogue of the Library of Bishop Lancelot Andrewes', *Transactions of the Cambridge Bibliographical Society*, v (1972), 99–121. It has always been assumed that this benefaction represents Andrewes's whole library at his death; the gaps in it, however, suggest to me that many select works from it must have been given to friends and associates before his death.

[81] Andrewes's strongest defence of the use of classical learning in sermons is in his 1592/3 St Giles's sermon on Acts 2: 42 (*XCVI*, pt. ii, 31–2).

CHRONOLOGY

1555 Month and day unknown: born in parish of All Hallows' Barking (All Hallows-by-the-Tower), London, eldest child of Thomas Andrewes (d. 1593), mariner, and his wife Joan (d. 1595).

1563 Goes to Cooper's Free School, Ratcliffe, a charity school for '60 poore mens Children'.

1565 Proceeds to Merchant Taylors' School through benevolence of Sir Francis Walsingham, where, under Richard Mulcaster, he masters Latin, Greek, and Hebrew.

1571 Proceeds to Pembroke Hall, Cambridge, as a scholar on the foundation of Thomas Watts; appointed fellow of Jesus College, Oxford (honorific).

1575 Graduates BA, and elected fellow of Pembroke.

1578 Proceeds MA, appointed college catechist, focuses academic work on the acquisition of further languages (Chaldee, Syriac, Arabic).

1580 11 June: ordained deacon and priest by William Chaderton, bishop of Chester, and appointed senior college treasurer under its head, William Fulke.

1585 June: proceeds BD with a degree exercise against usury.

1586 Appointed chaplain to Henry Hastings, 3rd Earl of Huntingdon, Lord President of the North, and earns reputation for converting recusant Catholics to Protestantism.

1588 February: appointed by the London Court of Aldermen to preach one of the Easter Spital sermons; preferred (allegedly on Walsingham's recommendation) to the extra-mural London parish of St Giles, Cripplegate, where he preaches routinely in term time, institutes monthly communions at a railed altar, and composes for his own pastoral use a manual of devotions and prayers for the sick and dying.

1589 May: granted the prebend of St Pancratius in St Paul's, at the hands of Walsingham and Lettice (*née* Knollys), Countess of Leicester, and a prebend in Southwell Minster. September: elected master of Pembroke. At St Paul's he delivers regular lectures in divinity and revives the custom of hearing confession during Lent.

1590 March–April: participates in conferences with the imprisoned separatist, Henry Barrow. June: proceeds DD with an avant-garde defence of clerical tithes. Chaplain to Archbishop John Whitgift and Queen Elizabeth, attending court in the latter capacity each November and preaching there routinely in Lent. Begins intimacy with Richard Bancroft, John Buckeridge, and Richard Hooker.

1597 Appointed to twelfth prebend of Westminster Abbey. Declines offers of bishoprics of Ely and then Salisbury because of proposals to detain episcopal property from both.

1600 November: involved in attempts to protect and preserve the private papers of Richard Hooker, including the three final books of *The Lawes of Ecclesiastical Polity*.

1601 July: appointed by the queen, on the recommendation of Sir Fulke Greville and formal nomination by Sir Robert Cecil, to deanery of Westminster Abbey, retaining his other benefices, and taking an active interest in the education of the school's boys, among them John Hacket (later bishop of Coventry), Brian Duppa (later bishop of Winchester), and George Herbert.

1603 July 25: participates intimately as 'abbot of Westminster' in the coronation of James VI & I.

1604 January: attends Hampton Court Conference. Good Friday, 6 April: first known sermon before King James. July: appointed one of the translator's of the Bible, as chairman of 'Westminster' committee charged with Genesis–2 Kings (inclusive).

1605 3 November: consecrated bishop of Chichester, resigns from Westminster, St Giles, and Pembroke Hall, and appointed Lord High Almoner, in which capacity he preaches before the king on all major feast days.

1608 February: involved by James in controversy with Cardinal Robert Bellarmine over papal vs. royal authority and the Oath of Allegiance.

1609 June: *Tortura Torti*, Andrewes's first refutation of Bellarmine, published. September: translated to diocese of Ely.

1610 Publishes *Responsio ad 'Apologiam' Card. Bellarmine*, his most systematic statement of the English Church's differences with Rome. June: assists in the consecration of Scottish bishops at Lambeth Palace.

1613 August–September: joins slim majority voting in favour of the divorce of the third Earl of Essex and Lady Frances Howard. Andrewes had baptized the future earl, grandchild of Andrewes's patron Walsingham, at Walsingham House in 1591.

1616 September: sworn of the Privy Council, participating assiduously only when church matters were discussed.

1617 March–September: prominent in James's progress to Scotland, preaches forcefully at Holyrood in defence of episcopacy and English prayer book liturgies. Sworn of the Privy Council for Scotland.

1618 August: translated to diocese of Winchester. December: sworn dean of the Chapel Royal.

1619 May: reluctantly surrenders Lord Almonership. Henceforth as dean of Chapel Royal preaches to the king only on Ash Wednesday, and to the royal household (vs. the king himself) on other major festivals.

1621 First signs of failing health. October: instrumental in securing royal pardon of Archbishop George Abbot for manslaughter.

1622 Probably assists in drafting James's orders for decent order and deportment in the Chapel Royal, oversees redecoration of the chapels at Greenwich and Whitehall, including painted images of saints, silver altar crucifixes, and altar rails.

1623 April: intervenes to prevent the puritan Henry Burton attending Prince Charles to Spain, replacing him with his own anti-Calvinist clients Leonard Mawe (master of Peterhouse) and Matthew Wren (master of Pembroke). July: presides over ratification ceremony for the Spanish Match in the Whitehall chapel royal.

1624 Christmas Day: last known sermon at court.

1625 March: too ill to heed James's call to attend him on his deathbed.

1626 January: heads committee which absolves Richard Montagu of anti-Calvinist heterodoxy, crypto-popery and exaggeration of royal prerogative in his sermons and pamphlets. February: participates in coronation of Charles I at Westminster. Bedridden from spring until death on 25 September at Winchester House, Southwark. Buried 11 November in St Saviour's, Southwark (now Southwark Cathedral). In his will, leaves library to Pembroke, and majority of sizeable fortune to charitable foundations.

I

Two most excellent Praiers, which the Preacher commonly used before his Exercises

That the name of God may be glorified by this our assembly, and his holie Woord blessed, to the end he hath ordained it: let us in all humblenes, present our selves before the mercie seat of God the father, in the name & mediation of Christ Jesus his deer sonne, through the sanctifying of his holy spirit, with an unfained humble acknowledgement, both of our owne unworthines, to receive anie of his graces, and unablenes when we have received them, to make right use of them. And both these, by reason of our manifolde sundry sinnes and offences, among the rest, of this one (as the chiefe one) that wee divers times have bin hearers of his divine and precious woord, without care or conscience to become the better therby: let us beseech him in the obedience of the life, & sacrifice of the death of Christ Jesus his deer sonne to receive both us & this our humble confession: to pardon both this and the rest of our sinnes, and to turne from us the punishments deservedly due unto them all; especially that punishment, which most usualy he doth exercise at such meetings as this is, which is, the receiving of his sacred word into a dead & dull hart: & so departing with no more delight to heare, nor desire to practise, than we came with. That so, throgh the gracious assistance of his good Spirite inward, adjoined to the outward ministerie of his word at this present: the thinges which shall bee spoken and heard, may redound to some glorie of his everlasting blessed name, and to some Christian instruction & comfort of our owne soules, thorow Jesus Christ our onely Lord and Saviour.

*This praier ended, hee proceedeth
againe in this manner.*

And as the Church of Christ, wheresoever it is at this present assembled, & met together, is mindfull of us that be here, so is it our parts and duties, in our praiers to remember it, recommending unto the Majestie of Almightie God, the prosperous and florishing Estate thereof: beseeching God the Father, for Christ Jesus hys sonnes sake, to bee mercifull to all his servaunts, even his whole Militant Church, scattred farre and wide over the face of the whole earth: both preserving it in those truethes that it hath recovered, from the sundrie grose and superstitious errors of the former age, and restoring it also unto that unitie (in his good time) which it hath almost lost, and daily looseth, through the unchristian and unhappy contentions of these dayes of ours.

And in this Church, let us be mindfull of that part thereof, which most especially & principally needeth our remembrance: that is, the poore afflicted members of Christ Jesus, in what place, for what cause, or with what crosse soever: that it would please God to minister into our hearts the same spirit of compassion and fervencie, now in the time of their need, that we would wish should be ministred into theirs, in the time of our need, for them to become suters for us. And let us wish them al from the Lord (in his good time) the same joyfull deliverance; and till his good time bee, the same measure of patience, that wee would wish unto our owne soules, or would have them intreate and praye for at his hands for us, if ever our case shall be as theirs is at this present.

And forasmuch as those Churches or members of Churches, which enjoy the outward benefits of the Lord; as of health, plentie, peace, and quyetnesse: doo manie times as much, and (for the most part) much more neede the prayers of Christ his faithfull Congregation, than those that are under his hande in the House of affliction: Let us beseech him for them also, that he will give unto each and everie of them, a thankfull receiving of those his benefites, a sober using of them, and a Christian employing of them, to his glorie that hath sent them.

And in these our prayers, let us be mindfull also of the Churche and Countrey wherein we live, yeelding first and formost ever-more, our unfained and hartie thankes-givings, for all his mercies and gracious favours vouchsafed this Land of ours: and namely for our last, no lesse gracious than mervailous deliverance from our enemies, and for all those good signes and tokens of his loving favour which ever since, and daylie he sheweth towards us.

And together (withall) let us beseech him, that while these dayes of our peace doo last, hee will open our eies to see, & encline our harts to seek after those things, which maye make for the continuance, and establishing of this peace long amongst us.

And (as by especiall dutie we all stand bound) let us commend unto his Majestie, his chosen servaunt *Elizabeth* our Soveraigne, by his grace, of *England, France, & Ireland* Queene, Defendresse of the faith, and over all estates and persons within these her Dominions, (next and immediatelie under God) supreame Governesse: let us beseech God (daylie more and more) to perswade her Highnes hart, that the advauncement and flourishing of this Kingdome of hers, consisteth in the advancement and flourishing of the Kingdome of his Sonne Christ within it: that it may be therefore her Majesties speciall care and studie, that both her Highnes in that great place wherein GOD hath set her, and everie one of us in the severall degrees wherein we stand, may be as carefull to testifie unto the whole world, a speciall care and endevour that we have, for the propagation of the Gospell of his sonne: as Christ Jesus hath shewen himselfe, by many arguments both of olde and of late, (and that of weight) that he hath caried & still carieth a speciall care of the preservation and welfare of us all.

Let us commend also unto God, the severall Estates of the Land, for the right honorable of the Nobilitie, and of her Highnes privie Councell; that they may be carefull (from the spirite of the Lord) to derive al their Councells; that so God, which sendeth the Councell, may send it good and happie successe also, and maie confound & cast out the councels of the enemy.

For the estate of the Cleargie, the right reverend Fathers in GOD, in whose hand the government of the Church is, and all other inferior Ministers; that he will give unto each and everie of them, sufficie[n]t graces for the discharge of their functions, & together (with the graces) both a faithfull and fruitful employing of them.

For the Estate of Magistracie, and namely for the Governors of this honorable Citie: that they together with the rest, according to the trust that is reposed in them, may be no lesse carefull speedely, without delay; than incorruptly, without partialitie, to administer justice to the people of God.

For the Estate of the Commons, that they all in a Christian obedience, towardes each and everie of their superiors, and in a godly love, with the frutes and duties thereof one towards another, maye walke worthie of that glorious calling whereunto they are called. And that the blessings of the Lord may not only be with us for our times, but successively also be delivered to our posterity: let us beseech God, that he will visit with the spirite of his grace, the two Universities, *Cambridge* and *Oxford*, all Schooles of learning, and places of education of youth: that they being watered with the deaw of his blessing, maye yeeld foorth such plants, as may both serve for a present supply of the Churches need: and also in such sort furnish the generations that are to come, that our posteritie also may bee counted unto the Lord, for a holy seede, and a Christian generation, as we our selves are.

And thus recommending our selves unto the praiers of Christ his Church, as wee have commended Christ his whole Church by our praiers unto the Majestie of Almightie God, reposing our trust and confidence, neyther in our owne prayers, nor in the Churches prayers, but in the alone mediation of Christ Jesus our Advocate: Let us unto him, (as unto our sole Intercessor) offer up these our supplications, that hee maye present them to God his Father, for the effectuall obtayning of these and whatsoever graces else he knoweth needfull for his whole Church, and for us, calling uppon him, as himselfe in his Gospell hath taught us.

Our Father, &c.

II

from The Pattern of Catechistical Doctrine at Large: or A Learned and Pious Exposition of the Ten Commandments

INTRODUCTION
CHAP. XIII

And now having found out the true way, and being thus far entred into it, we are come where it is divided into two. For there are two sorts of Christians that lay claim to the true way, and each party pleads possession of it, each thinking the other to tread in a by-path, and to be out of the right way. We will therefore examine, which of the two are in the right.

Christian Religion, as it now stands in these parts of the World, consists of Papists and Protestants. It will not be amisse therefore, because the Papists build upon the Word of GOD as do the Protestants, to examine the main point between them in difference, which is about the interpretation of it: and to whom this interpretation belongeth properly.

[Addition 1]

The Papists hold that the Scriptures are to be interpreted by one of these four wayes. 1. Either by the Fathers. 2. Or Councels. 3. Or the Church. 4. Or the Pope, whom they call the chief Father of the Church. Concerning which we do partly agree, and partly differ from them.

1. We hold that there is a certain and infallible rule, *viz.* the Word of God, whereupon a man may relye, else we may begin to build, but not upon a Rock, and then our building will be subject to be overthrown and beaten down with every blast of false doctrine.

2. That the Scriptures (as Saint *Peter* tells us) not being of any private interpretation, we are to beware that every man interpret it not after his own fancy, because (as the same Apostle speaks elsewhere of Saint *Pauls* epistles) some things are hard in them to be understood, which they which

2 Pet. 2.20.

3.19.

are unlearned and unstable may wrest, which ought not to be: but we are (as *Hilary* saith) *referre sensum Scripturis, non auferre*, to give to the Scripture its proper sence, not take it away, or devise one for it.

1 Cor. 12.10.

3. We hold, that God hath given the gift of interpretation to some (as Saint *Paul* affirms) and they are such to whom God (as he saith) hath revealed it by his Spirit; that is, a naturall man cannot interpret them aright; nor yet the vulgar or common sort, whom (as Saint *Augustine* saith) *non vivacitas intelligendi, sed simplicitas credendi salvos reddit*, rather their simplicity in beleeving, then vivacity or quicknesse of apprehension and understanding bringeth to salvation. And if the Eunuch a man of great place, were not able to interpret without Saint *Philip*, much lesse the vulgar sort. But God hath bestowed this gift upon the learned, and to those of the learned which have the guift of interpretation.

12.10–14.

[Addition 2]

1 Cor. 12.11.

4. Now forasmuch as God (according to Saint *Paul*) divides his gifts *singulis prout vult*, to every one according to his good pleasure, it were hard to restrain it to any one Order (as to that of Bishops) as some of the more rigid Papists would have it. And *Stapleton* (one of them) when he had done all he could to maintain his tenet, in the end was forced to confesse that God gives these guifts extraordinary, as well to others, as to them: as well to *Amos* a Herdsman, called and gifted extraordinarily, as to *Jeremie* a Priest. Yet *Andradius*, and others of them hold, that the interpretation of Bishops assembled together, may be taken howsoever.

Lib. 10. c. 7.

5. Now concerning the sense of the Scriptures. As it is well said by the Lawyers, that *Apices juris non sunt jus*, so is it in the Scriptures, not the letters or words, but the meaning is that which is Scripture indeed. To finde out which *Aquinas* gives these rules.

1. In matters of faith and manners, *nullus sensus sumendus nisi literalis*, none but the literal sense is to be taken.

2. In point of exhortation or instruction, *uti licet sensu tropologico, uti patres ubique*, it is lawful for us to use a figurative sense, as the fathers often did.

3. Albeit a man may draw sundry consequences *a contrariis, similibus, &c.* by contraries, similies, and the like, by the rules of Logique, yet the literal sense, can be but one, in one place.

4. That is to be taken for the literal sense of every place, which the construction will beare, if it lead not into an absurdity, and then it must needs be a trope.

Now seeing there must be an Interpretation, and it must be that which is literal, unlesse it draw an absurdity with it: we are now to come to the examination of this sense; and because we must never looke to stop the mouthes of sectaries and hereticks, but they will still finde an occasion or place to wrangle upon, we must therefore bring them to one of these two inconveniences.

1. Either to drive them to condemn themselves in their own hearts. *Tit. 3.11.*

2. Or because the Devil doth so much blinde the understanding of some, that they will not understand reason, we may argue so long with them, till their folly be made manifest to all men, as the Apostle speaks. *2 Tim. 3.9.*

We are to know that as in all other Sciences, so in Divinity, the judgement of every thing is to be taken *ex principiis* from the principles. And concerning the principles in Divinity, which are the Scriptures, S. *Augustine* saith, *In eis quæ sunt aperte apposita, inveniuntur omnia quæ pertinent ad fidem moresque vivendi,* in those things which are plainly set before us, we may finde all things belonging to faith and good life. And Saint *Chrysostome, Manifesta sunt quæ sunt ad mores & fidem necessaria, &c.* those things are apparent, which are necessary to faith and manners: and *Melchior Canus* saith, that there are diverse places, of which none can give any other then the literal sense, or can wrest them, except he have a minde to wrangle. And *Ireneus* saith, that the plain places make the principles, by which all other of dubious understanding must be judged. *lib. 2 de doct. Christ.* *homil. 3 in 2 Thess.* *c. 3 de locis Theolog.* *l. 2 heres. c. 46, 47.*

Now the means to finde out the true sense of the Scriptures are many, but may be reduced to six.

1. Some means there are wherein all agree, as namely, there is, *pietas & diligentia adhibenda,* goodnesse and diligence must be used. And in the first place, Prayer. S. *Augustine* saith, *Oratio postulet, lectio inquirat, meditatio inveniat, contemplatio degustet & digerat,* let us ask by prayer, seek by reading, finde out by meditation, tast and digest it by contemplation. *de doct. Christ. l. 2 c. 8.*

2. The second means is by conference of places. Saint *Augustine* saith, that the lesse plain place in Scriptures, is to be referred to that which is more plain, and the lesse in number to the more in number.

3. The third seemeth to be according to the counsel of the holy Ghost, *Inspectu fontium,* the better to discern the signification of the words to consult with the Original tongues; with the Hebrew for the Old Testament, and with the Greek for the New.

4. To be acquainted with the phrase of the holy Ghost, and this is to be gotten by the knowledge of the Dialect, Idiome or Stile of the holy Spirit, as the Apostle speaks, by use to discerne it, as the crucifying of the flesh, *Heb. 5.14.*

39 *in marg.* Heb. 5. 14] *ed.*; Heb. 5.10 P

mortifying the concupiscence, &c. for sometimes the holy Ghost in Greek, sends us to the holy Ghost in Hebrew. And these three last are for understanding of words, the two next are for understanding of sentences and chapters.

5. The fifth is that which the fathers call *Oculus ad scopum*, to have an eye to the intent: as what was the intent of giving the law, in setting down such a prophecy, doing such a miracle, and the like: as Saint *Paul to Timothie* reasoneth from the end of the law, against those that made evil use of the law. So saith *Hilary*, *Ex causis dicendi, habemus intelligentiam Doctorum*, we finde out the meaning of the learned, by finding out the cause why a thing was spoken.

6. The last is that which the wise men among the Jewes say, we must look round about us, behinde and before us, that is, we must well weigh the Antecedents, and Consequents, and every Circumstance, to understand any sentence and chapters, whereof we doubt.

To these may be added those of *Ireneus* and *Augustine*, That every one of these rules serve not for every thing, but to diverse things, diverse wayes and means may be applyed for the true understanding of words and sentences in the Scripture. And therefore *Stapleton* committed an errour.

1. Because he perceiving that some of these rules were not necessary to all, concluded that it was not necessary at all.

2. Because we attribute not the interpretation of the true sense of every place, to each one of these, but to all together, he therefore concludeth that they were not sufficient at all.

Now besides these means, and those of prayer and diligent study wherein they agree with us, they propound these four following (as is before said) and hold them infallible.

1. The interpretation of Scriptures by the fathers.
2. The exposition of them by Councils.
3. The practise of the Church.
4. The definitive sentence of the Pope.

Concerning the first and second of these in general we say, that as there may arise some doubt or scruple in some places of Scripture, so may there also in their expositions. And for the two last a question may be made, whether the Church they mean be a true Church, and whether the Pope may not erre in his sentence.

Again, as we unfeignedly hold and acknowledge, that some of their means are commendable, yet we say that they are not allowable, where they are evidently contrary to our rules or without them. And if ever they took the right course, it was by using our means, and if they erred, it was by relying wholly on theirs, and excluding ours. But take their means without or against ours, and they may erre.

[Addition 3]

Now come to the particulars.

1. For the fathers, It is a vain speculation, to beleeve that the fathers concurre all in one exposition of all places of Scripture. And if we must take them where they all agree, we shall finde many places which they do not expound alike[.]

[Addition 4]

2. In their expositions, they did not usually keep the literal sense, except in point of controversies which fell in their times: for in their Homilies they followed the tropological or figurative sense, drawing from thence diverse necessary doctrins, and applications necessary and tending to good life and manners. So saith S. *August. contra Julian*, that in controversies which fell not in their times they spake more carelessely.

3. Again, *Basile* saith of *Dionysius* a Father, that he spake many things ἀγωνιστικῶς *disputationis gratia* by way of disputation, not δογματικῶς *definitive* positively against the Heretiques of his time: and therefore in many things the fathers must be taken to have spoken *per modum contradicendi, non docendi*, by way of contradiction, and not positively.

4. *Cardinal Cajetan* affirmed in the Councel of Trent, that if he knew a true and sound exposition upon any place of Scripture, not used by the fathers, he would hold, and maintain it *contra torrentem omnium Doctorum & Episcoporum* against the current of all Doctors and bishops. And *Andrad.* saith as much, and all of them use to deny the fathers in their schools. And now in regard that the fathers often dissent, they lean to that which the greatest part of the fathers say.

5. There was a controversy between Saint *Augustine* and Saint *Jerome*, whether Saint *Pauls* reproof of Saint *Peter* were real or not? *Jerome* maintaining that Saint *Paul* did it onely *pro forma formally*, and *Augustine* that he did it simply, and from his heart. And though *Jerome* quoted the opinions of divers fathers to strengthen his, yet *Augustine* would not alter, holding this among other rules, that we are not to regard *quis*, but *quid*, not who, but what any man speaketh. And *Jerome* himself in his own exposition of the Psalms, saith, that he had delivered diverse things, contrary to the tenet of those times: *that is, in matters præterfundamental, wherein liberty of dissenting may be indulged*.

6. Lastly, the Papists themselves reject the exposition of many of the Fathers upon this text, [*Tu es Petrus, &c.* Thou art *Peter* and upon this rock I will build my Church.] many of the Fathers holding, that it was meant of Saint *Peters* faith, not his person. As also they leave all the rest of the

1.

Epl. 4.

Epl. 11.
Gal. 2.10.

Matth. 16.18.

Fathers, and adhere to Saint *Aug.* onely in the division of the commandments: for the current of the Fathers divide them as we do, but they following Saint *Augustine* make but one Commandment of the first two, and divide the last into two: *but these were not matters of faith.* But S.*Augustine* was carried away in this, by a conceit of having but three commandments in the first Table in reference to the Trinity, as may be seen in his division of the Decalogue.

2.   For the Councils which are divided into Action or Agitation of a point, and Canon.

1. In the Action commonly is such errour, that they are forced to lay all upon the Canon, and say, that it matters not what the premises be, so the Conclusion be good.

2. And for the Canon, we may finde in some Councils, that the Canons of one are flat and direct against another, as in the case of marriages of Priests, some for them, some against them. We see the two Councils of Constance and Basile, both general, and both confirmed, one by Pope *Martin* the fifth, and the other by *Eugenius* the fourth. The Bulls of which (though the Canons agree) be opposite to each other. The one holding, *Concilium posse errare, non Papam*, that the Council may, but the *Pope* cannot erre: the other, *Papam errare posse, non Concilium*, that the Pope may erre, but the Council cannot. And the Canon of the Council of Ferrara holding against that of the Council of Florence, one, that the Pope is above the Council, and the other that the Council is above the Pope.

[Addition 5]

3.   For the Church and the practise thereof. This is as uncertain as the other. For the Churches of the East and West agree not in diverse points, and among other, in the case of the Popes supremacy, the Eastern Church totally opposing it. And if we urge the practise of the Church, it will be found, that at some time most of the Bishops were Arrians. So that in this there's both ambiguity and peril. And *Basile* saith, that in the case of Baptism, the Children at the first were dipped but once, and afterwards thrice, and we know at this day, they are but once dipped.

De spiritu sancto. c.27. de trina mersione.

[Addition 6]

4.   4. The last way they prescribe is that of the Popes. And that they may erre in their interpretation may appear in that many of them were not found in the faith. Saint *Jerome* saith that *Damasus* Pope, did consent *ad subscriptionem hereseos* to the subscription of heresy: and *Ambrose* reporteth that *Liberius* the Pope, though for a while he was orthodox, and for not

subscribing to the condemnation of *Athanasius* he was banished into Thrace, but shortly after he became an Arrian, and at one of their Councels subscribed to heresy. *Honorius* the first, after his death was accursed and condemned, in the thirteenth Action of the sixth general Council of Constantinople, held *anno* 680. under *Constantinus Pogonatus* the Emperour, *quia impia dogmata confirmavit*, for confirming wicked opinions: which were those of the Monothelites. But to shift off these things, they have nothing to say, but that the Councils were corrupt, and not onely they but the writings of *Beda* shall be corrupt. So that we see that none of these rules severally are infallible, Let us see them a little together.

In the administration of the Sacrament of the Lords supper to infants, we may see they fail: for S. *Paul* saith, Let a man examine himself, and so eat, &c. which a Childe cannot do, And in this and other things wherein they fail, they are forced to say, We beleeve not the Fathers, because they say it, but because they say it according to rules. And if they beleeve it in respect of the person that speaketh, not the *quid*, the reality of the thing, they erre much, though *Stapleton* say, that the interpretation of a Bishop, though unlearned, is to be prefer'd before that of a learned Divine, because of his office and authority. *Andradius* yet saith, The Fathers are to be beleeved, not in whatsoever they say, but in whatsoever they say according to their rules; and so say we. And thus much for the Preface.

1 Cor. 11.28.

THE EXPOSITION OF THE FIRST COMMANDEMENT.
CHAP. XI.

* * *

This duty of Invocation here commanded contains in it two things.

1. A lifting up of our soul, a fixing of the minde upon God, as the Authour and giver of all good.

Psalm 25.1.
62.8.

2. A pouring out of our soul, a full declaration of our desires, and meditations, or what it is we require of God.

142.2.

Invocation or prayer is divided into

1. Petition, and that
 - either for our selves, which also is subdivided into
   - Deprecation δέησις, for the removal of some evil.
   - Precation, for the obtaining of some good, προσευχή
 - or for others which we call Intercession, ἔντευξις

2. Thanksgiving, εὐχαριστία

1. The first part of Petition is Deprecation, that evil felt or feared may be removed; and this is most properly and usually the matter of our prayer. Is any man afflicted (saith *S. James*) let him pray; and though hope apprehends nothing but good, yet the removal of evil hath *rationem boni*, and so may be the object of hope, and the subject of prayer. And this consists in three points.

_{Jac. 5.13.}

1. *Ut malum avertatur*, that evil may be turned away before it come, I beseech thee, O Lord, (saith the Prophet) let thine anger and fury be turned away. That Gods wrath may be turned away, before it come upon us.

_{Dan. 9.16.}

2. *Ut malum auferatur*, that evil may be taken away after it hath seized upon us. Deliver Israel, O Lord, out of all his troubles. That being in trouble we may be delivered out of it: and this is called *liberatio*, deliverance.

_{Psal. 25.21.}

3. *Ut malum minuatur*, that evil may be lessened. Let thine anger cease from us (saith the Psalmist) *mitiga iram tuam*; when we pray for a diminution, that so we may be able to bear it.

_{85.4. 3.}

But as a necessary preparative to this, the Saints have ever used Confession and acknowledgement of sins. The Prophet in sundry Psalms runneth first over all his sins, sins of omission and commission, of thought, word, and deed, against God, his brethren, or himself, by instigation of others, or of his own accord. For *Prov.* 28.13. He that covereth his sins shal not prosper; that's a dangerous saying: and in *Psal.* 32.3,4. there's a dangerous example; till he had opened his sins, his bones consumed, and his moysture was turned into the drought of summer. So likewise did *Daniel* make confession before he comes to petition.

1. The chief thing to be prayed against, *maxime deprecandum*, is to be kept from falling into sin by temptation. That we may not be winnowed by *Sathan*. Not to wish as commonly we do, I would I were out of the world, but as our Saviours prayer for his Disciples, I pray not that thou shouldest take them out of the world, but that thou shouldest keep them from the evil. And we desiring but thus, certainly Gods promise will not be unperformed, for he is faithful who will not suffer us to be tempted above that we are able. And either our strength shall encrease with the strength of our crosse, or, as our strength, so our crosse shall diminish. The enemy shall not be able to do us violence.

_{Luke 22.31.}

_{John 17.15.}

_{1 Cor. 10.13.}

_{Psalm 89.23.}

2. We are to deprecate temporal dangers, as *Jehoshaphat* did. We know not what to do, *hoc solum restat, ut ad te oculos dirigamus Domine*, Our eyes

_{2 Chro. 20.12.}

---

27 *in marg.* Luke 22.31] *ed.*; Luke 22.32 P

are upon thee, O God. And then in our trouble and distresse *Nomen Domini* shall be *turris fortissima*, The Name of the Lord will be a strong tower to us. But yet concerning temporal evil, we must stand affected as the three children were, who answer'd K. *Nebuchadnezzar*, our God whom we serve is able to deliver us from the burning fiery fornace; but if not (because the promise and covenant is conditionall) we will not serve thy God &c.

And thus far and no farther went our Saviour when he used deprecation, Father if it be possible, let this cup passe from me: neverthelesse not my will, but thine be done.

The second branch of Invocation is προσευχὴ, Precation, which is the desiring of some thing that is good. There is no one thing more common in the Psalms then this; as, 1. Give me understanding. So 2. Establish the thing that thou hast wrought in us, &c. As the first prayer is to give what we want; so the second is, establish and confirm it in us when we have it. 3. The third is that of the Apostles, to our Saviour, Lord increase our faith in us. We must not keep at a stand in grace, but desire an increment, that we may grow in grace, as the Apostle counselleth us.

Concerning that part of prayer, petition of the good we want, It is true, our desires are not always granted; for as Christ answered the sons of *Zebedee*, ye ask ye know not what; so it may be said to us, we often desire rather that which is agreeable to our own humours then to Gods will; as *Chrysostome* reports of a Thief, who purposing to continue in his sin, *orabat Deum ut non caperetur, & eo citius capiebatur*, he prayed that he might not be taken, and was taken so much the sooner, because he so prayed.

Therefore the rule we must follow, and whereon we must ground our prayer is that promise, *Quicquid secundum voluntatem eius petimus*, whatsoever we ask according to his will, he will grant us: such are the graces of his spirit, and whatsoever is necessary to salvation, as the Word, Sacraments, publique Worship, &c. These are that *unum necessarium*, which the Psalmist so earnestly begged, *unum petii a Jehovah*, One thing have I desired of the Lord. He desired many things, but one thing especially, κατ' ἐξοχὴν, to dwell in the house of God all the dayes of his life, to continue in the Church of God all his life, where he might glorifie God, and work out his own salvation. Whatsoever is absolutely necessary to these ends, we may safely ask, and be sure God will grant, and therefore our Saviour tells us, that God grants his Spirit to those that ask him, this is one thing which he will not deny us.

Now with these, or after these, we may pray for temporal things, that is, we may pray, first, for a competency, not for superfluity. The Patriarch *Jacob* prayed onely for food and raiment, and *Agur* the son of *Jakeh* prayes, Give me neither poverty nor riches, but *sufficientiam victus*, a sufficiency

Prov. 18.10.

Dan. 3.17.18.

Matth. 26.39.
Luk. 22.42.

2.
Psal. 119.73.
125.
68.28.

Luke 17.5.

2 Pet. 3.18.

Matth. 20.22.

1 John 5.14.

Psalm 27.4.

Gen. 28.20.

Prov. 30.8.

onely, whereupon *S. Augustine* saith, *non indecenter petit, quia hoc petit, & non amplius*, it is no unbeseeming prayer, because he asks onely so much, and no more. 2. We must desire them with condition, if God see it expedient, submitting to his will; as Christ, If it be possible, and if it be thy will: so did *David* praying for restitution to his kingdom. If I have found favour in the eyes of the Lord, he will bring me again, &c. if not, here I am, let him do what seemeth good to him. He resignes all to Gods will, and there is no more compendious way to obtain what we need, then to resigne all to Gods pleasure, whatsoever means we use, or however we struggle, nothing will avail without this.

_{2 Sam. 15.25.}

Now that which was mentioned before, concerning *omnis & omnia*, falls in best to be expounded here. It seems strange that every one that asks shall have, and that whatsoever he asks he shall have, seeing it is certain that many ask and have not.

1. We must remember that of *S. Augustine*, that our duty is to pray however; for as he saith, *Jubet ut petas, & si non petis displicet, & non negabit quod petis; & tu non petes?* doth God command thee to pray, and is he displeased if thou prayest not, and will he not deny thee what thou prayest for, and yet dost thou not pray?

2. We must know that the cause why we receive not, is not in his promise, but in our asking. Ye ask and receive not, because ye ask amisse, saith *S. James*. For it is not a demonstrative signe of Gods favour to us, to have all we desire granted; for we see that the Israelites desired flesh, and flesh God sent them, but it was with displeasure: for while the meat was yet in their mouthes, the wrath of God came upon them, and slew the mightiest of them, and smote down the chosen men of Israel. And upon the peoples violent desire to have a king, God gave them one, but in displeasure. Nay it is so far from a favour, that God sometimes grants the Devils (whom he favours not) their requests; as in the case of *Job* and the Swyne.

_{Jac. 4.3.}
_{Psal. 78.18.}
_{27.}
_{30.}
_{31.}
_{1 Sam. 8.22.}
_{Job 1.&2.}
_{Mark 5.13.}

1. And as this is not an absolute signe of favour, so Gods denying of our requests, is not always a signe of his displeasure. This we may see in *S. Paul*, who obtained not that he desired concerning the prick in the flesh. 1. One reason *S. Isidore* and *S. Aug.* give; *Sæpe multos Deus non exaudit ad voluntatem, ut exaudiat ad salutem*, God oft-times hears not many as they desire, that he may hear them to their good. 2. Another reason is given by *S. Aug.*, God denies not, but only defers to grant, that we might by his deferring them, ask and esteem of them more highly. *Desideria dilatione crescunt, & cito data vilescunt*, desire encreaseth by delay, and things soon given are of light esteem: and therefore he adds, *Servat tibi Deus quod non vult cito dare, ut & tu discas magna magis desiderare*, God keeps for thee, that he will not give thee quickly, that thou mayest learn with more affection to desire great things. 3. A third

_{2 Cor. 12.8.}

_{De summo bono lib. 3. cap. 1.}

_{De verb Dom. cap. 1.}

reason is, that we might the more earnestly ask for them; which our Saviour intimates in two parables to us; one of the unjust judge, and the importunate widow: and the other of the friend that called up his neighbor at midnight; by both telling us, how much importunity prevails with God. 4. A fourth is; God, though he gives not *quod petimus*, what we ask, yet he will give *quod novit utilius*, what he knows to be more profitable for us: as in the case of *S. Paul*, My grace shall be sufficient for thee. 5. Some things we pray for may be hurtful to us, (as knives for children) so as that *non accipiendo accepimus*, we are better by wanting then possessing them. *Chrysostome* calls prayers for such things, childish and aguish prayers; as *S. Aug. male usurus eo quod vult accipere, Deo potius miserante non accepit*, God in compassion lets not him receive, that which he meant to use ill. And therefore sometime to misse that which we conceive to be a benefit, is a blessing. And therfore we wil conclude this point with a saying of *S. Aug. fideliter supplicans Deo pro necessitatibus hujus vitæ, & misericorditer auditur, & misericorditer non auditur: quid enim infirmo sit utilius, magis novit medicus quam ægrotus*, God in mercy hears, and in mercy hears not a faithful suppliant for the necessities of this life; for the Physitian knows what is profitable for the sick man better then himself. These reasons are from the matter of our prayers, others taken from the manner of our asking may be mentioned hereafter.

Luke 18.2.
Luke 11.8.

2 Cor. 12.8.

In Johan.14.

In lib. sent. Prosperi.

The third part of Invocation is Interpellation or Intercession, which is prayer either for the prosperity or against the crosses of others. The Fathers seldome quote the Fathers: but in this *S. Aug.* cites *S. Ambrose. Frater mi, si pro te rogas tantum, pro te unus orabit, si autem pro omnibus rogas, omnes pro te rogabunt*, My brother, if thou only pray for they self, one shall pray alone for thy self, but if thou pray for all men, all men will pray for thee. And *S. Gregory* saith, *Quisquis pro aliis intercedere nititur, sibi potius ex charitate suffragat, & pro semet ipso tanto citius audiri meretur, quanto magis devote pro aliis intercedit*, whosoever prayes for others, doth the rather pray for himself, and by so much the sooner deserves to be heard for himself, by how much the more devoutly he intercedes for others. *S. Chrysostome* hath an excellent speech to this purpose. *Pro se orare necessitas cogit, pro aliis charitas fraternitatis hortatur: dulcior autem ante Deum est oratio, non quam necessitas transmittit, sed quam charitas fraternitatis commendat*: it is meere necessity that compels a man to pray for himself, but it is a brotherly affection that draws a man to pray for others: and that prayer is more acceptable to God, which is caused by love then necessity.

3.

Hexam. lib. 1.

In Moral.

In Matth.

This part of invocation hath divers branches. As we are to pray for all men. 1. For sinners, that have not sinned unto death, and there is a promise that prayer shall be heard. In which respect there is a prayer in our Liturgie, first for them that are without the Church, for their conversion, as

1 John 5.16.
James 5.15.

Heathens, Jews, Turks, Hereticks, Schismaticks: then for those that are in the Church; which are with us, and yet not of us, but are still in blindnesse and ignorance, or know but practise not. 2. We are to pray for them, that not onely are oppressed with outward affliction, but inward temptations, and the burthen of their sins. 3. For those that stand, that they fall not, but persevere. 4. For them that are our enemies and persecute us. And for this we have not onely our Saviours precept, but the practise of holy men. Saint *Gregory Hom.* 27. *in Evang.* upon that place in *Jeremiah* 15.1. where God saith, though *Moses* and *Samuel* stood before me, yet my heart could not be towards this people, &c. asks the question, why *Moses* and *Samuel* are especially named; and gives this reason, Because the prayers of such are most powerful with God, who having received an injury, can presently pray for those that wronged them. Now such are *Moses* and *Samuel*. For *Moses* when the people were ready to stone him, presently prayeth for them. *Samuel* though the people desired to cast off his government, yet saith, God forbid that I should cease to pray for you. And of these prayers it is said, that they shall return into our own bosome. They are very effectuall, for in these cases, *Qui pro aliis orat, pro se laborat,* he that prayes for others, labours for himself. 5. For Kings and Magistrates, as the Apostle adviseth. 6. Lastly, but most especially for the peace and good of the Church. O pray for the peace of Jerusalem, saith the Psalmist, who also wished, that his tonge might cleave to the roof of his mouth, if he forgate to pray for it.

4. The fourth branch of Invocation is Thanksgiving. Invocation is for that we want and desire. Thanksgiving is for that we have received. So that whether we be answered before we call, as the Prophet speaks, when God gives before we ask; or whether it be given us when we ask, in both cases we have cause to enter into this consideration, *Quid retribuam Domino*, what shall I render unto the Lord for all his benefits. And indeed the chief end of all should be the glory of God. For, for his glory all things that are made were created: the seventh day when he had finished his work of creation was instituted for his praise and glory. And for this purpose man was placed in Paradise to praise him, and after his fall mankinde had perished, and all things had been again reduced to nothing, but that God might have some to glorifie him. Now it is plain that God takes and accepts of thanks as a great part of his glory. And therefore were the thank-offerings among other sacrifices for Gods service and glory instituted of old; and he that offereth me thanks (saith God by the Prophet) giveth me glory: and the Apostle, All things are for your sakes, that the aboundant grace might, through the thanksgiving of many, redound to the glory of God.

That which the Heathen said is true, *Gratus animus est meta benignitatis,* gratitude is the end of bounty. And it is the condition of our obligation to

God, and of Gods to us. Call upon me in time of trouble, and I will hear you, there is Gods, and thou shalt glorifie me, there is ours. — Psalm 50.15.

The Hebrews make Thanksgiving to consist of four parts, according to the four words used by thankful persons in Scripture.

1. Confession or acknowledgement, *Confitebor*, I will confesse, that we have nothing but that we have received from God. That our help cometh from the hills from no inferiour creature, from above ἄνωθεν from the Father of lights. Nor must we conceal what we have received. Saint *Augustine* saith, that as he *Qui putat se habere quod non habet temerarius est*, he is rash that thinks he hath that he hath not, so he *qui non confitetur quod habet ingratus est*, that confesseth not what he hath is unthankful. And therefore we must acknowledge them, as *data* not *innata*, as of Gods gift, not of our own acquiring. — 1 Cor. 4.7. Psalm 121.1. James 1.17.

2. The second is contentment and complacency in Gods gifts by a gratefull acceptation of what it pleaseth God to bestow upon us, *complacui*, I am well pleased. King *David* may be a pattern to us in this point. The Lot is fallen to me in a fair ground, yea I have a goodly heritage, it liked him well, he desired no more. For as Saint *Bernard* saith *Spiritui gratiæ contumelium facit, qui beneficium dantis grata mente non suscipit*, The undervaluing of gods blessings by not being content with what he sends us is a reproach to the spirit of grace. And it was the disease of the Israelites fourty years together. Of which Saint *Augustine* saith, *De nulla magis Deum offendisse ille populus Judaicus dicitur, quam contra Deum murmurando*, The Jews offended God in nothing more then in murmuring against him. Saint *Paul* learned better that is, to be content in whatsoever estate he was. And his counsel was, be content with that ye have. — Psal. 16.6. In Eph. In Johan. Philip. 4.11. Heb. 13.5.

3. The next is Promulgation or publishing to others the benefits we receive *Anuntiabo*, I will declare. I will tell you (saith the Psalmist) what God hath done to my soul; and in another place he saith, he will not onely tell it in private, but publickly in the congregation, and in *magna Congregatione*, in the great congregation: and (that being not enough) to all the people and among all nations. And yet higher, to his seed and posterity, and beyond that, to all generations to come. Which he hath done, we see it. For as Saint *Chrysostom* saith well, *Optima beneficiorum custos est ipsa memoria beneficiorum, et perpetua confessio gratiarum*, The best preserver of benefits is the memory for them, and perpetual thankfulnesse of them. — Psal. 66.14. 111.1. 40.9. 35.14. 57.10. 71.16. 40.9. Hom. 25. in Math.

4. The fourth and last is *Incitatio*, a stirring up or provocation of others to do the like. *Venite*, O come let us sing unto the Lord &c. Saith the Psalmist. And praise the Lord O Jerusalem, praise thy God O Sion. And again praise ye the Lord, Sing unto the Lord a new song, and his praise in — Psal. 95.1. 147.12. 149.1.

---

40 *in marg.* 149.1] *ed.*; 148.1 P

the congregation of Saints. And his last Psalm is all incitation, not onely to men, but to the creatures, to perform this duty.

Now as there is Deprecation, or intercession, for others so this duty of thanksgiving is to be performed not onely for our selves, but also for others; in which the first example we have in Scripture is *Abrahams* servant, after he had found a wife for his masters son, Gen. 2.27. So did *Daniel* for the secret revealed, Dan. 2.20. *Moses* composed a song for the deliverance out of Egypt, Exod. 15.1. *Deborah* and *Barak* for the victory over *Sisera*, Judg. 5. and so Saint *Paul* usually begins his Epistles with thanksgiving for others, as Rom. 1.8. 1 Cor. 1.4. and 2 Cor. 1. Ephes. 1.3.

To stir us up to this duty of praise, King *David* hath the commendation above all other of the Patriarches for his exact performance of it, in all the parts above mentioned and in this respect was called a man after Gods own heart, as *Samuel* told *Saul*. S. *Chrysostom* examining why he was so stiled rather then *Abraham* and *Moses* and the rest, saith, he could finde no other reason for it but this, because (God desires that his name should be exalted and praised above all) he laboured more plenteously in this point then any other, and in that respect deserved that title better then any other. In the 55. Psalm he professeth that he will keep his hours for prayer. In the Evening and morning and at noon day will I pray. But for praises in the 119 Psalm, Thrice a day shall not serve, but seven times a day do I praise thee. Yea he would praise God at midnight, Psalm 119.62 Psal. 6.7. and Psal 118.17. and Psal. 39.15. And the desire he had to have his life prolonged was, to praise God, O let me live (saith he, and wherefore) and I shall praise thee, and this the rather, because he knew that it was not onely the end of mans creation, but of Angels also whom he desired to imitate, who continualy praise God. It was & is their song, Glory be to God on high: and in the Revelation, Blessing, glory, and wisdom, and thanksgiving, and honour, and power, be unto our God for ever and ever. And in this respect it was that *David* accounted his tongue the best member he had and called it his glory because he employed it to the glory and praise of God: which was the end why God created both it and all the other members.

And as it was the cause why God created man, so was it also of all the creatures; and they (as the Psalmist saith) perform their duty herein. The Heavens (saith he) declare the glory of God, and the firmament sheweth his handy work &c. Insomuch as we see that he calleth upon the very worms to performe this duty; upon which Saint *Chrysostoms* note is, that they were in worse estate then worms that neglect it.

34 *in marg.* Psal. 19.1] *ed.*; Psal. 19.1 P

But for the Church there it is the most natural duty that can be performed; In thy Temple every man speaketh of thy praise: what is preaching: *predicare*, but to declare to all the world, his benefits of creation, redemption by Christ, and other benefits we have by him, in publishing whereof we praise and honour God, and therefore the conclusion of all sermons is with a Doxology, To whom with the Father &c. be all honour &c. As was usual with the Fathers. For the Sacraments, that great mystery which is the complement and perfection of all our service on earth, is called εὐχαριστία a thanksgiving; for what is it but a solemne commemoration of that grand mercy and benefit of our redemption by Christs sacrifice upon the crosse, and therefore it ends with *a gloria*, Glory be to God on high &c. and for prayer, we pray, that we may have matter of praise, yea praise for benefits received must be joyned and goe along with our prayers, els they are not acceptable, so that we in all our church exercises tend to this.   Psal. 29.9.

The Psalmist saith of unity, that it is good and pleasant. The Fathers observe from hence, the excellency of unity; for that some things are good, but not pleasant, others pleasant, but not good, but this is both. The same may be said of praises, the Psalmist tells us, that it is both good and pleasant, and addes a third thing, for whereas some thinge may be both good and pleasant, but not comely, he therefore saith, that it is both good and pleasant, and a comely thing to praise the Lord, and to be thankfull.   Psal. 133.1. Psal. 147.1.

Besides this, let's consider, that this is a profitable and an excellent service, profit is a great mover, and all excellency without this is contemned. Here is excellency and honour for *beatius est dare quam accipere*, It is more blessed to give then to receive. Now here we give some thing to God, and there is nothing els we can give or return to him for his benefits, *quid retribuam*, saith *David*, I will take the cup of salvation &c. that is, offer the sacrifice of praise. That's all I can return. God esteems it an addition to his honour, and therefore it is called magnifying, glorifying and sanctifying of his name, as if we made him hereby more great and glorious and holy then he is. And as the duty is thus excellent, so it is profitable; for we never give praise and thanks, but we receive some thing: *Deus vult nos gratos esse ut capaces simus majorum benificiorum*, by gratitude for benefits received, we are fitted for greater benefits. Ten lepers were cleansed, and onely one returns back to give thanks, who hereby became capable of a greater mercy; Christ tells him, his faith had saved him. Our gratitude is never done *gratis*, but gets a reward; as there is first *ascensus orationis*, the ascent of prayer, and then *descensus gratiæ*, a descending of grace.   Act. 20.35.

So as *Bernard* saith, when there is *recursus gratiarum*, a sending back of thanks, then there is a new *decursus gratiæ*, a descending of benefits, and *si esset recursus gratiarum, cessat decursus gratiæ*, if thanks be not returned, there will be noe more return of grace and other benefits: that grace we have received, if it stand still, and be not in *recursu*, in perpetual succession by returns, then like water (to which its oft compared) it stands still, and putrifies: and rots all the gifts and graces bestowed formerly. The same Father on Act. 7. makes a question, why those excellent and rare examples of grace and vertue, which were so common in the primitive times, are not now seen; we have the same beginnings they had, and we admire those that continue, as they begun in grace, but they not onely continued, but increased, and went forward, and had their gifts increased, which is, as he saith, because Gods hand is not shortned, or his good will altered, but our thanksgivings are scant and thinn sowen, and therefore our harvest must be scanty and thinn too, and therefore he saith *væ ætati nostræ propter ingratitudinem*, wo to our age for unthankfulnesse; this is the reason why there is not the same progresse of grace in us as was in them. For as *Prosper* saith, *Gratiæ nullum certius est signum quam gratiæ*, there is no surer signe of grace then thanksgiving. Nay we see that we are tied to it, though we should be prohibited from it. It must needs be an excellent duty which must not be omitted, though forbidden by God. Our Saviour when he had healed the leper, inhibited him from telling any body what he had done unto him: yet we see he proclaymed it, and it is recorded to us for his great praise, and this was a godly disobedience, for it was onely a commandment of trial, as some think.

Luc. 5.14.
Mar. 5.20.

* * *

Now because prayer is the means to obtain all other graces, it cannot properly be said to have means to obtain it. Yet are there diverse helps to it.

1. There is no greater help or spur to prayer, then the consideration of our own wants, and imperfections, by taking a view of our soules, and frequent examining our own hearts, whereby we come to see the evils we are most inclinable to, and the good things wee want. This knowledge and sense of his own wants made *David* thirst after God, and powre out his soule before him, Psalm 42.1.2.4.5.

2. Another help is the remembrance of God's benefits to us. King *David* was so well versed in this duty that there is not a benefit he received, or that we may, but that there is a Psalm for it Psal. 40.3. He had still *canticum novum* for *beneficium novum*, when he wants any singular benefit, then he reckons up the lesser, which Saint *Augustine*, calls, *colligere fragmenta*, the gathering up the fragments, and these he made great account of, and as the woman of Canaan was thankful for the crums, Mat. 15.27. so was he for

the least mercies: when he had no new benefits then he takes up old benefits and makes of them a new song, as Psal. 38. and 70. and rather then fail he remembers to God and gives thanks for his wonderfull forming in his mothers womb Psal. 139. and sometimes enlargeth himself to those benefits that are common to all the world, as Psal. 8. 19. 104. yea to the very wild asses quenching their thirst in the wildernes.

3. Another is fasting and alms, which the Fathers call the wings of prayer. *S. Augustine* saith, *Jejunium orationis robur, oratio vis jejunii,* fasting is the strength of prayer, and prayer the like of fasting. And *jejunia & elemosynæ orationem juvant,* fasting and alms are assistants to prayer. These both are the wings that prayer mounts up by. *Illud hanc corroborat, hæc illud sanctificat,* as fasting strengthens our prayers, and prayer sanctifies our fast, so alms. *Ep.* 121.
1 Cor. 7.5.
Dan. 4.24.

4. If our own prayers be weak, then are we to desire the prayers of the Church, according to *S. James*'s direction. *Si oratio tua fulmen sit* (saith one) *ascendat ad cœlum sola per se*: otherwise *esto gutta in nube grandinis,* if thy prayer be fervent, or as a thunderbolt, it may ascend to heaven by it self, but if it be as a drop in a cloud, it will need the help of others. James 5.15.

5. If none of all these help, yet there is *oratio fidei,* as well as *oratio sensus,* though I cannot have the prayer of feeling, yet I may have the prayer of hope. For spiritual duties are likened to seed, of which harvest comes not presently, but lie in the bosome of the earth till the time that the Lord fructifie.

***

SECOND COMMANDEMENT.
CHAP. VII.

We are now to take a view of the affirmative part of this precept that is, how we are to behave our selves in the external worship of God. The worship enjoyned in the first Commandment (as hath bin said) is internal; this in the second is outward or external honour or worship. Honour being a testimony of excellency given by outward signe or deed, and praise by word. The honour of the signe, is expressed by the word *Tishtacaveh,* in bowing down, and of the deed by the word *Tagnabod,* in serving. For the first, as the negative was, thou shalt not bow down to them, the affirmative is, thou shalt bow down to me. And for the other as in the Negative, thou shalt not worship or serve them, the affirmative is, thou shalt serve me. *Honor signi et facti*

1. For the outward worship first in general. Christ tells us, that a candle is not lighted to be put under a bushel: upon which, the fathers have raised this note or Maxime, that *Bono debetur manifestatio,* our good must be made Mat. 5.15.

manifest, and therefore, candles that have *bonum lucis*, the goodnesse of light, must not be thrust *sub malo tenebrarum*, under the evil of darknesse. So then, if the candle of light be in our soules, that is, if we inwardly worship God, we must set it upon a candlestick: our inward religion, must appear in our outward worship, and it must not be onely in a Chamber, as our private Religion, a close godlinesse that cannot be seen.

1 Cor. 6.20. 2. The next reason for this point, the Apostle gives. Ye are bought with a price, therefore glorifie God in your body and spirit, glory being nothing else, but an effect of conspicuousnesse, the fair spreading and enlarging of honour and praise: and therefore containeth honour in it. Now in conjunctions copulative, the rule is *In copulativis non sufficit alterum*, In things that are coupled, one is not sufficient, but *utrumque faciendum*, both are to be performed. And the Apostles conjunction [καὶ] [in body and spirit] sheweth, that this honour must be done in both. The devil knoweth this, that

Mat. 4.9. God requireth both, and therefore asked of our Saviour but one, a little glorifying of him, but the bowing of the body, because he knew that if God have not the copulative, body and spirit both, he will have neither, God will have all or none.

Exo. 3.5. The third thing is, that seeing God every where almost through the Scripture, hath put a distinction and difference between his house and private houses, as being in more special manner there, then in other places, and that as the psalmist speaketh holines becometh Gods house for ever, therefore he will not onely have a manifestation of our worship towards him, and that to be in body as well as Spirit, but he assignes his house for the place, where he will have this honour exhibited to him. You shall keep

Levit. 19.30. 26.2. my sabbaths (saith God) and reverence my sanctuary. And therefore it is, that the preacher gives us this rule when thou goest into the house of God,

Eccles. 5.1. *observa pedem utrunque*. Look to thy foot, and if God have a care how we serve him in our inferior members in that place, no question but he hath much more, how we imploy our eyes, ears, and hearts there, our external worship must be apparent, and it must not be by halves, and it must be in the house of God, in the midst of the congregation.

1. The outward worship of God (according to the former division)

Honor signi. consists 1. In Signe 2. In deed. And this *Honor signi* is twofold, which the

Phil. 2.7. 8. Apostle setts down in the example of Christ 1. *Exinanivit se*. He emptied himself, or made himself of no reputation. 2. *Humiliavit se*. He humbled himself.

1. The emptying of ones self is that, which is called *deponere magnificen-*

Job 19.9. *tiam*, to lay a side all titles of honour, which holy *Job* expounds, and calls

Rev. 4.10. *spoliavit me honore* a stripping one of glory, it is that, which the Elders did,

2 Sam. 6.22. cast down their crowns before God. King *David* laid aside his robes, and

made himself vile before the Lord, in his service. The Apostle tels us, there must be *Nudatio capitis*, our heads must be uncovered. The wearing of a cap, *pileo donari*, among the Romans, was peculiar to free men onely, and an Hieroglyphick of honour, for once if a man *cepisset pileum*, he was free, and when he laid aside his cap, he was said *deponere magnificentiam*, to lay aside his honour and priviledge, whereby he was distinguished from a servant. So then, as servants are to be uncovered in their masters service, so are we to be in Gods: and therefore Saint *Paul* (in the place before cited) tells us, that it is a shame for a man to have his head covered at that time. That's the first signe. 1 Cor. 11.4.

1 Cor. 11.4.

2. The other signe is *humiliare nos metipsos* to humble our selves, which is nothing else, but to make a man neerer the ground, to bow himself as low as he can: and this was it, which the devill required of Christ: and it is a posture which God expects at our hands and was used from the beginning. We may see it, by that which God said to *Elias*. I have yet left me 7000. in Israel, all the knees which have not bowed to *Baal*, by which he signified, that bowing was a signe of them, that worshipped him aright: and it was his quarrel against them, that bowed themselves to Idols for which he would not forgive them. Mat. 4.9.

1 Kin. 19.18.

Esa. 2.9.

2. But *Honor signi* is not enough, there must be *Honor facti* too. The first was Reverence, this is service and worship, which we call properly devotion, or the devoutnes and readines of the will to serve God. And this *Honor exhibitus facto*, hath also two parts. 1. To come and go at Gods command. 2. To do his worke. *Honor facti*.

1. Both of these we have in the Centurions servant, approved by Christ himself. 1. In going and coming when he is bidden. I say go and he goeth, come and he cometh. 2. In doing his Masters will or service. Do this and he doeth it. And in these two respects it is that Christ will say to some *Nescio vos*, I know you not. 1. Either for not comming at all to his house, so that he cannot take notice of them for his servants. 2. Or for coming unwillingly, with an ill will to do his work, and so they do not perform service to him, and in this respect are not known to him neither. Mat. 8.9.

We see that Gods servants did both. *Abraham* was no sooner spoken to by God but he was presently at his call and answered, *Ecce ego*, behold, here I am. The kingly Prophet before he was called, had a longing desire to go into Gods house but when he was called, he presently answered, Lo I come. It is Gods threat—Because I called and ye refused &c. I will laugh at your calamity. And in the Gospel, they which were invited to the Supper and came not; were thought unworthy; none of them shall tast of it. And as we are to come, so in our coming two things are required to make us welcome. Gen. 22.1.
Psal. 84.2.
40.9.
Prov. 1.24.
Esa. 65.12.
Luc. 14.24.

1. The first is, we must come *mature* betimes they that seek me early shall Pro. 8.17.

finde me; and secondly we must come *quotidie* daily. Blessed is the man that heareth me, watching daily at my gates. We must wait and be desirous to be called.

2. The second is the Act. [Service,] to do his will. It is the property of a good servant to do his masters work, and to preferr it before his own. We see the practize of it, in *Abrahams* servant, he refused to eat before his masters work was done and here falls under this, the commandment of the great service, the service of the altar which that we may think it no dishonour to be Gods servants we finde that he chose the Tribe of Levi, to serve him at the altar, so that this service is the service of choice and howsoever some account but lightly of it, yet it was the greatest honour, to be chosen to perform this service.

Now to apply these things to the point in hand. There is in the 95. Psalm, which is used as an antipsalm or Introduction (as it were) to the service of God by our Church, 1. A coming, 2. A worshipping. 3. A falling down and 4. a kneeling before the Lord, whereby we may see, that in the precept of worship, in the substantial parts of the service of God prayer, preaching, the Sacraments, and discipline (especially in the former) there is a due gesture and behaviour required. And in this we are to follow the rule prescribed by Saint *James* which is, to take the Patriarchs and prophets for our guides and directors, and it is Saint *Peters* rule too for women, to follow the steps of holy women of old. So that laying this for our ground, and withal taking the approved practise of the Church with it, we cannot go amisse. Now we shall finde (in this outward worship of God) that they never came together to serve the Lord nor departed from it, without exhibiting some reverend external worship, and behaviour, both *in accessu & recessu*, in coming in and going out.

In accessu, in their coming together, it is plaine, *Solomon* in the consecration of his Temple, at the beginning, before his prayer kneeled upon his knees. And in *recessu*, we see, that when *Hezekiah* and his people had ended their service, they bowed their heads and worshipped. We have seen what our gesture must be in *accessu* and *recessu*. Let us now see, what it must be while we are present at Gods service, in the particulars of it.

1. First for our outward gesture in prayer, which is either publick or private. And in both these, since we are to remember, that they are to proceed partly from Humility, partly from hope, our external signes must be answerable to both these.

1. In publick prayer, the signes are first, that which we called before *depositionem magnificentiæ*, with our heads uncovered. 2. The other which we called Humiliation, by bowing our selves to the ground or kneeling as *Abraham* did, and his servant too, bowed, and worshipped the Lord. So did

the people at the institution of the passeover. So did king *Solomon*, praying upon his knees. The Prophets, *Daniel* 6.10. After the first temple *Ezra* 9.6. Our Saviour himself upon the mount of Olives kneeled down and prayed: lastly, Saint *Paul*, and the whole Church prayed kneeling Saint *Peter* Act. 9.40.

1 Kin. 8.54.
Luk. 22.41.
Act. 20.36.

Thus we see our pattern, if we look at the Patriarchs, or Prophets, at Christ or his Apostles, or at the whole church.

True it is, because we onely kneeling, but also standing before another is a signe of service and reverence, therefore we read in many places that the gesture in prayer was standing, and that some prayed standing, as *Gehezi* stood before his master *Elisha*. So *Abraham* stood before the Lord, and *Abrahams* servant stood by the well of water when he prayed. The people rose up and worshipped every man in his tent door. *Balaam* said to *Balack*, stand by thy burnt offering and I will go &c. Thus *Samuel* stood before the Lord, and the Psalmist saith. Ye that stand in the house of the Lord &c. The king stood by his pillar at the entring &c. And thus standing may be a reverend gesture, when kneeling or some other gesture in publick worship is not prescribed by the church in which case we must conforme to what is injoyned, for that which is indifferent in it self, in the gesture, is not indifferent to us, or in the practise of it, when it is commanded by lawfull authority.

Gen. 19.27.
Gen. 24.13.
Exod. 33.10.
Numb. 23.10.
Psal. 135.2.
2 Chr. 23.13.

2. In private prayer, we shall see it to be a familiar thing sometimes to fall down prostrate, as *Moses* and *Aaron* did. This gesture of prostration was used by *Moses*, as he testifies of himself. And the Evangelist reports of our Saviour, that he used it. So likewise was kneeling a custome of the holy men of God in their private prayers. *Ezra* fell upon his knees, and spread out his hands. And *S. Paul* in his private devotions, bowed his knees, as he sayes of himself. In private devotions liberty and freedome of gesture may be used, so it be reverent and humble, which sitting at prayer cannot be: *Balaam* willed *Balak* to stand by his burnt-offering, *Numb.* 23.15. and being set he bids him rise up.

Deut. 9.18.
Matth. 26.39.
Ezra 9.5.
Eph. 3.14.

2. The exterior signes in respect of hope, are *oculi elevati, & manus extense*, eyes lifted up, and hands stretched out. And these are to be used in that part of prayer, which is called Petition, (for in deprecation the Publicans posture is fittest, which is, *oculis dejectis*, with eyes cast down) for the other we finde King *David* lifting up his eyes. And in *S. Johns* gospel it appears, that our Saviour did the like. For the other, the lifting up of hands, we see that in the battail with the Amalekites, *Moses* practised it. *Ezra* (in the place before cited) spread out his hands to God. The Prophet *David* tells us, that he stretched out his hands to God, Let the offering up of my hands, be an evening sacrifice. And it is the Apostles counsel to use this

Luk. 18.13.
Psalm 123.1.
Psalm 121.1.
John 11.41.
17.1.
Exod. 17.11.
Psalm 88.9.
141.2.
1 Tim. 2.8.

gesture, I will that every man pray, lifting up holy hands. For as *oculus elevatus expectat*, the eye lifted up expects, so *manu extensa petit*, the stretched out hand begs and asketh.

But in this point corruption is crept into our Church. Instead of humbling ourselves by prostration and kneeling, we are pleased to sit at our ease, and that in a proud manner: instead of the *depositio magnificentiæ, & nudatio capitis*, kneeling and uncovering our heads, we sit, and with our heads covered too; this is not to enquire, at least not to imitate, the dayes of old. *Balaam* would not suffer *Balac*, though a King, to sit down, but to stand at his burnt-offering, and when he was set, he bade him arise. This sedentary prayer, and proud fashion of covering the head, cannot be warranted by any text in Scripture.

2. Secondly, the outward gesture at the word preached, or read in the old Testament, was usually sitting, as we may see in *Ezekiel*. They sit before thee, and they hear thee, &c. saith the Lord by the Prophet. And so in the new, The multitude sate about our *Saviour*, while he was preaching: and the Pharisees, and Doctors of the Law sate by him, as he was teaching. So *Mary* sate at Jesus feet, and heard his word. *Eutychus* also sate to hear *S. Paul* preach. Sometime the word preached was heard standing: as when *Ezra* opened the book, standing in a pulpit of wood, all the people stood up. And these two gestures have ever been indifferently permitted and used.

3. In the administration and receiving the Sacraments, the nature and dignity of them, with the prayer for the preservation both of our bodies and soul unto eternal life (to say no more) may easily direct us, with what exteriour reverend behaviour we are to carry our selves, *viz.* that the gesture of kneeling and humble adoration is most fit, and that such a gesture, as doth not signifie our humble reverence, as sitting, is utterly unlawful.

4. In point of discipline the gesture is evident, the Judge sits, and the party accused, or that hath any cause depending before him stands.

So that the end of all this is 1. That God may be glorified, as well by the body, which is the external worship, as by the soul and spirit, which is for the internal. 2. That our outward gesture may stir up our souls to their duty, as clothes increase the heat of the body, though they receive their heat at first from the body. Lastly, as to stir up our selves, so to stir up others by our example, that they seeing our reverend behaviour, may fall down with us, and be moved to do that which they see us do, and to glorifie God on our behalf.

Thus as we have shewed what we are to learn out of the affirmative part, *viz.* what duties to perform, so out of the Negative part, we must learne, what sinnes we must avoid: and to finde out this, we shall need to go no further, then by opposing the contraries to that, which hath been delivered in the affirmative part.

1. To Humility, and *depositio magnificentiæ*] he is opposite that carries himself proudly in Gods service. The Wise man tells us, a proud eye is an abomination to the Lord, and if at all times much more at that time. It is the Prophets counsel to decline this behaviour, especially in Gods service. Hear ye, give ear, (saith he) be not proud, for the Lord hath spoken. Prov. 6.17.

2. To *Humiliare*] He is averse, that is stiffe necked, not willing to bow, and that hath knees like an Elephant, that cannot bend, when we give him not the reverence, of the knee, head, and of our whole body.

3. To Coming] Our absenting our selves from Gods service and worship, *S. Chrysostome* saith, *Ludus jubet & facis, vocat aurea tuba, & venis: Cultus Dei jubet, & non facis, vocat & non venis*; pleasure commands thee, and thou obeyest; the golden trumpet calls thee, and thou comest. Gods worship commandeth, and thou obeyest not; it calls thee, and thou comest not. Whose servant then thou art, thou mayest judge by the Centurions words, even his at whose command thou comest and goest. Matth. 8.9.

4. Lastly, to the doing of his work; the neglect of it is opposed, and the neglecters out of Gods favour: for *neglectus præcepti, præcipientis injuria est*, the neglect of a command, is an injury to him that commandeth. He that knoweth his Masters will, and doth it not, shall be severely punished. Hier. in Epist.
Luke 12.47.

But in the manner of doing Gods work and his will, in his service and publique Liturgy, there are five things required of us: of which though something hath been formerly spoken, yet considering the great neglect and contempt of this work by many, more is here to be said of them.

1. The first is, Unanimity and uniformity, to come together at the same time, and to joyn together in the same worship, that there be no disagreement in our behavior in Gods service, one to do one thing, and another to do another, some come into the Church at prayer, some not till the sermon begin. But, as the Apostle enjoyns, tarry one for another: that is, all praise God together. Inward unanimity, and outward uniformity being a delight to God. It was *Davids* joy, I was glad when they said to me, Let us go into the house of the Lord: and soon after he addeth, Jerusalem is as a City, that is compact together, or (as some translation) at unity in it self. And this spiritual union, is without question, a great strengthening to the Church, for when, either one comes after another, or if in time of Gods service, some sing not, nor pray with the other, this must needs make a breach in the fabrick of it. *In Discordia* (saith *Augustine*) *nemo benedicit Dominum*, God is never truely or well served, where there is discord or separation. The Prophets earnest desire is, O magnifie the Lord with me, and let us exalt his name together: And therefore it is, that the holy Ghost mentioneth so *Unanimitas.*

1 Cor. 11.33.

Psalm 122.1.

In Ps.
Psalm 34.3.

often this unanimity to be in the infancy of the Church, as being one of the chief causes of the growth and enlarging of it. The Spirit came upon them when they were all together with one accord in one place, as if the whole Church were one person, and had but one tongue, and one lip. And in prayer it is said, They lift up their voice with one accord. And they heard so too. The people with one accord gave heed to the things which *Philip* spake. So in the point of uniformity; we see, that he was punished, that was not like the rest of the guests, that had not a wedding garment. And as the separation and division of tongues was a curse, that the earth was no more *unius labii*, of one speech or language, so it is a great part of the blessednesse of the heavenly Jerusalem, that the Elders sing with one voice unto the Lord. The Fathers beat much upon this: and Saint *Chrysostome* extolleth it highly, and saith, that it falleth upon God like a showre of hailstones: and Saint *Augustine* saith, of singing of prayses, that it sounds in Gods eares, *tanquam resonantia maris*, as the voice of many waters, which he seemeth to take from that place in the Revelation.

2. The second is fear, ἐν παντὶ φόβῳ, in all fear, saith S. *Peter*; with fear and trembling, saith S. *Paul*; for if the service of men (according to the rule of S. *Paul* and Saint *Peter*) must be so, much more the service of God. But in our exteriour service of God, there is commonly so little fear, or rather such want of fear, that commonly we sleep in it, like the Apostles, who could not hold open their eyes, being *in horto*, in the garden with their Master, they could not watch one hour, and therefore that judgement befell them, that they all forsook Christ and fled. And there is little fear in sleep. When *Jacob* was afraid of his brother *Esau*, he slept not all that night. The Example of the Christians in the Primitive Church, is left upon record for our observation, That they heard S. *Paul* preaching till midnight. Upon which place *Chrysostome* saith, *Ad hoc commemoravit eos, qui media nocte vigilabant, ut pudeat eos, qui media die dormiunt*, the Evangelist recordeth those that watch till midnight to this end, that they may be ashamed, that sleep at mid-day.

Now because the actions of a natural man, are eating, drinking, and sleeping, the same reason which condemneth the using of the two former in the Church, must needs be of force to condemn sleeping too. Have ye not houses to eat and drink in, saith the Apostle; thereby condemning those that used to eat and drink in the Church. So if he could have supposed that the Corinthians would have slept there, he would have asked the same question concerning sleeping.

And as he reasons from the place, so we may reason from the time, out of another place of the same Apostle, *Vigilate, nam qui dormiunt, nocte dormiunt*, watch, for they that sleep, sleep in the night. But with us, we may say, They that sleep, sleep in the day. And so, whereas the place of sleeping should be our houses, and the time of sleeping the night; we, (because we will be crosse) in the day-time sleep at Church.

Natural reason tells us, that *Actio vestita indebitis circumstantiis illicita est*, every action cloathed with undue circumstances, is unlawful. The Prophet (as his manner is) after he had denounced a curse upon a carelesse people, falleth to blessing the Church of God; in which he saith, *Non dormiet quisquam, neque dormitabit*, none shall slumber, nor sleep among them. And our Saviour gives this caveat; Beware, that the Lord when he cometh, find you not sleeping, which though it have a spiritual understanding, yet there follows a temporal punishment. _{Esay 5.27.} _{Mark 13.36.}

In prima pœna est estimatio peccati, we may consider of the sin, by the first punishment; and so we may weigh every sin *in prima pœna*. God usually punisheth sin in its own kinde. We see it from the beginning, *Cains* murder God threatneth with blood. Sodoms heat of lust punished with fire, &c. *Eutychus* sleep (in this case) with a dead sleep. This carelesnesse in Gods service, is the onely way to bring us, first to profanenesse; and then to Apostacy, and no religion at all. We finde it punished in the Church, she slept and awoke, but found not her beloved. And this judgement followed the Apostles themselves; because they could not watch one hour, they all forsook our Saviour, and *Peter* forsware him. _{Acts 20.9.} _{Cant. 3.1.} _{Matth. 26.40.}

But howsoever it stands in respect of Gods punishments or mercies, yet the former reasons condemn it: and we may adde, that the heart truely and rightly affected in Gods service, is *ardens cor*, (as the Disciples were that talked with our Saviour going to Emaus, their heart burned) and a Father saith, that it is impossible to have *cor ardens sub oculo gravi*, a burning heart, and a heavy eye, are not compatible. _{Luke 24.32.}

3. There must be with these, *Cordis præsentia*, our heart must be present, and watchful too: for though we watch outwardly, yet there may be such extravagant and wandering thoughts in the heart, that we may be said to be *præsentes absentes*, absent, though present. And where the heart is absent, the other members will discover it. The note of *Cor fatui*, a fools heart, is to be *in domo lætitiæ*, it turneth that way, where the sport lyeth, whereas *cor prudens*, the heart of him that hath understanding, *quærit scientiam*, seeketh to get knowledge. The inner parts of a fool are like a broken vessel, he will hold no knowledge; so long as he liveth, it runneth out as fast as it is poured in, but the wise inquire at the mouth of the wise, in the Congregation, and ponder his words in their heart. _{Eccles. 7.4.} _{Prov. 15.14.} _{Eccus. 21.14.} _{17.}

---

7 *in marg*. Esay 5.27] *ed*.; Esay 5.26 *P*   9 *in marg*. Mark 13.36] *ed*.; Mark 13.27 *P*
20 *in marg*. Matth. 26.40] *ed*.; Matth. 36.40 *P*

And these are testified by some signes. A fools eye is in all places, but the eyes of the wise are (as theirs were that heard Christ in the Synagogue) fastned on the Preacher. The fools eyes, hands, and feet, all speak, and will tell you that he is not present with his heart, and when they are reproved, all is but *risus*, they make but a mock at it. Therefore it is nothing to hear, except we take heed how we heare, and be affected with *Lydia* to attend to that which is spoken; for it is the wise ear that getteth knowledge. And as it is a curse to speake to an eare that heareth not, so it is a blessing to speake to a hearing eare.

The place before named is terrible, mentioned by *Esay* against foolish hearers, Hear ye, but understand not, and it is often repeated in other places of Scripture, as *Matth.* 13.15. *Mark* 4.12. *Luke* 8.10. *John* 12.40. *Acts* 28.26. and *Rom.* 11.8. It is the extremity of Gods wrath, and a heavy curse, and so to be accompted, to be given up to this spiritual judgement: and we are to take heed, that by our own carelessnesse it be not laid upon us. If it be true which the Heathen said, that *pietas non est vultu lædenda, sive serio sive simulato*, then surely we ought to have a special care of our looks and gesture, when this part of piety, Gods worship is performed.

4. The fourth is *silentium*, silence; we must not talk while we are in the service of God. The Preachers counsel is against it, for talking is flatly opposite to hearing the Word. Be more ready to hear (saith he) then to give the Sacrifice of fools, whose heart (as he saith in another place) proclaims folly, they cannot be silent. *Job* reckoned it as one of the honours done unto him, while he was in prosperity, That men gave ear to him, and kept silence. If a man should turn from us, and talk with another, while we are speaking to him, we would think he little regards us, or what we speak. The Prophets command was, The Lord is in his holy Temple, let all the earth keep silence before him. And, Hold thy peace at the presence of the Lord, that is, when the Lord speaketh: and he speaketh when his Messenger speaks. *Qui vos audit, me audit*, saith Christ, he that heareth you, heareth me. In the Primitive Church the first word, was σίγα λαὸς, Be still and silent ye people, which had its original, from that place in the *Acts*, where S. *Paul* being to preach to the Antiochans, beckoned with his hand for silence, and said, Men of Israel, and ye that fear God give audience.

5. The last is, *constantia in cultu divino*, we must tarry while Gods service is done, and not depart till it be ended. It was *Joshuahs* commendation, that he departed not out of the Tabernacle. The offending herein is that which the Prophet calls, *discedere a lege*, which relates, to depart out of the Congregation, while the Law was reading. For as by preaching, God speaks to us, so by Prayer we speak to God: and it is but *lex Talionis*, the law is equal. As we deal with God, so will God deal with us. If we stay to hear

him, he will stay to hear us: and when we say, *Quare dereliquisti me, Domine?* Lord, why hast thou left me? he will answer, *Quare dereliquisti me, serve?* Servant, why hast thou left me? And that speech of his at the last day, *Discedite a me*, depart from me, will be a just punishment for them, that depart from him here in this kingdom of grace. Matth. 25.41.

In the Primitive Church, from the first words σίγα λαὸs, let the people be silent, to the last words λαὸς ἄφεσο, let the people depart, none might go out from the Congregation upon pain of Excommunication, as appears by the fourth Council of Carthage. If we would well consider this, this fault would not be so common among us. Canon 24.

Now the means to perform this outward worship are these. 1. If we follow the Preachers counsel in taking heed to our feet, when we go into Gods house. 2. If we consider, that it is a more fearful thing to come to the Church, then it was to touch the Mount, and in respect of Gods presence, we must not refuse him that speaketh. 3. That the Angels are present among us, though we see them not, and that the doctrine of the new Testament is such, *in quam desiderant Angeli prospicere*, which the Angels desire to behold, therefore if they shall see any not to esteem that, which they make such accompt of, shall not they be Ministers of Gods wrath? 4. That the end of our Creation is to glorifie God; now glorification comes from instruction, and instruction from hearing; so then as our hearing is, our doing shall be. *Ut audies ita facies*, if you hear not well, you can never do well; a carelesse hearing ever begets a carelesse doing, it cannot go *ultra speciem*. 5. If we put to it, *ut audies, ita audieris*, as you hear, so shall you be heard of God, and men. If we be carelesse of him, he will be carelesse of us likewise, and more then that, our very Prayers shall be an abomination to him. He that turneth away his ear from hearing the law, even his prayer shall be an abomination, saith *Solomon*. And this may be a punishment upon some Preachers, who have had dull ears themselves, that they shall speak to a dull people, that will not hear. The means.
Eccles. 5.1.

Heb. 12.22.
25.

1 Pet. 1.12.
1 Cor. 11.10.

Prov. 28.9.

1. That which God saith in the Prophet, there is a very low, and as *Augustine* saith, an unlawful comparison, God compares himself to an earthly King, I am a great King saith the Lord of hosts &c. and with all, how he reasons in the Chapter against the carelesse in his service. Offer this to your governour will he be pleased with thee? As if he should say, do such service as this to your Prince, would he take it well at your hands? and do you think that I that am King of Kings, will not look for such observance in my service as an earthly Prince will looke for? so if we say with our selves, this service which I offer in praying, hearing &c. would I offer no better to a great king this is a good signe. The signes.
Mal. 1.14.
8.

If as *David* was to *Saul*, we be to God, be careful, that we be not missing from his house, for else as *Jonathan* said to *David*, Tomorrow is the feast, and you will be looked for, and if my father finde your place empty, he will be angry. So will God look for us, and if he finde us not at his service, he will be angry too, unlesse he have just cause of absence. Now there are some causes wherein a man may be excused for absenting himself, such as these.

_{1. Sam. 20.18.}

1. The first is sicknesse. *Michol* excused *David* from coming to *Saul*, by saying that he was sick, and it had been barbarous in *Saul* to urge a sick man to come.

_{1. Sam. 19.14}

2. Secondly. Sacrificing our selves, is a sufficient cause. *Jonathan* excused *David* likewise, from coming to *Sauls* sacrifice, because he was gone to Bethlem, to offer sacrifice for himself.

_{20.29.}

3. Lastly, *Misericordiam volo, non Sacrificium*. I will have mercy, and not sacrifice; works of mercy, as visiting the sick, and the like, are lawfull excuses.

_{Mat. 9.13.}

2. The second signe is, if upon the meditation of *Lex Talionis*, as you hear you shall be heard. We can truly say, Even as I hear, so hear me O Lord. This is a good *signe*.

_{Judg. 4.7.}

3. The third is. If we be companions of them that fear God and love them that are Gods servants; because they be reverend and zealous in his service, for he that loveth God, loveth them that worship him, with fear and reverence.

_{Accessory Psal. 119.63, 79. 15.4}

The last thing (according to the sixth rule) is, that we procure this outward worship to be performed by others. *Hierome* saith *Quilibet verus Christianus est cortina fratris*, every good Christian is a Curtein to his brother, for every curtein must have a hook, and a catch to draw his brother to Gods service. King *David* drew the multitude to the house of God. *Andrew* brought his brother *Simon* to Christ, so *Philip* called *Nathaneal*. We must tarry one for another, according to the Apostles rule. For they that desert others, and disswade them from this outward worship and service of God, shall be accursed and stricken with blindenes of body and soul, as *Elimas* the Sorcerer was for dehorting *Sergius Paulus* the Governour, and seeking to turne him away from the faith.

_{in Num. 3.26.}

_{Psal. 42.4.}
_{John 1.42, 45.}
_{1 Cor. 11.33.}

_{Act. 13.8}

And thus much for the first part of this Commandment which as we said in our division of it, was an expresse Prohibition, in these words. Thou shalt not make to thy self any graven image &c. And an included affirmative precept, thou shalt worship me in such manners as I do command thee.

FOURTH COMMANDEMENT.
CHAP. II.

Now here are two things, and both commanded, but not alike or equally, but the one for the other. 1. The first is *Sanctification* which is the last end and drift of God in this commandment, and that which is required for it self. 2. The other which is the means subordinate to it is *Rest* without which, sanctification of the day cannot be had, as God requireth. *Of the rest required not for it self.*

To make it plain. The heathen by the light of nature could see, that every thing is then best ordered, when it hath but one Office, and is ordained to do but one thing at once, for whatsoever would be throughly done would be done alone: the reason is, because we are *res finitae, finite creatures*, and if two things be done at once, and together, one will be done imperfectly, because our thoughts will be distracted between both, for part of our thought, will be taken of, when they are set upon several objects, so that we cannot wholly intend two things at once. It was *Adams* case in the state of Innocency: for he having a natural soul and finite, was not able to intend the dressing of the garden commanded him, and the sanctification of the sabbath together, and therefore God would have him imploy six dayes upon the first, and *blessed the seventh day* to be bestowed in his worship. And this was the end why God instituted, blessed, and sanctified the seventh day, for a remedy against distraction, especially in the solemne worship of God, which is enough to take up the whole man, and ought to be without all distractions and therefore permitteth none to be intent to any other thing during the performance of it. Gen. 2.15. Gen. 2.3.

Now if *Adam* in that estate could not be free from distraction, much more have we need of remedy against it. And therefore is this rest and ceasing from servile work commanded, to free us from it, and to further our sanctification: and thus cometh in this rest, because this total sanctification cannot be performed without ceasing from labour and doing our own works: for without rest we cannot sanctifie: and if our rest should hinder our sanctification it ought to be taken away and omitted.

And indeed our Saviour Christ acknowledgeth, that *man was not made for the rest*, but for *sanctification*. Sanctification was his end, and man was created and made for that. Rest is but a subordinate end, and man was not made for it, but rather rest was made for man. Rest is but the means to attain to sanctification which is mans end, and that for which he was made. For as the Apostle saith of *bodily exercise, it profiteth little*, so it may be said of bodily rest, that bodily rest profiteth little, or indeed nothing at all, except it be applied to sanctification which is the end: nor doth God approve of it without this but wholly disliketh it. Mat. 2.27. 1 Tim. 4.8.

[Addition 7]

There is here besides in the Commandment another word [*Remember*] which because it is properly of a thing past, it referreth us to some time or place before: and there is no mention of the sabbath but in two places before: the one of them is in *Exodus*, but that is not the place here meant: for God in the end of the Commandment adding [*God blessed it, &c.*] referreth us to that other place where those words are; namely to, *Genesis* 2.3.

And by this occasion falleth in that first question about the morality of the day: many think the sabbath is meerly a ceremony, and are perswaded that it is so, and therefore hold, that men are not bound to sanctifie it since Christs time, it being abrogated by him. In answer whereto we are to follow our Saviours rule, who in the case of Polygamie, bids us inquire how it was *ab initio*, from the beginning, to call it to the first institution: for the first institution is that which will inform our judgements best, and the first end which appears by the institution is the true end.

A thing is not said to be meerly ceremonial, if a ceremonial use or end be annexed to it, for then scarce any of the ten Commandments but should be ceremonial, for they have many of them some ceremony annexed to them.

But that is to be accounted ceremonial whose first and principal end is to be a ceremony, and to type out something, which this day of rest cannot be said to do. The reason is, because Paradise and mans perfection cannot consist with ceremonies, a ceremony cannot agree to the state of mans innocency.

[Addition 8]

And the reason of that is, because that before there was a Saviour, there could not be a type of a Saviour, as ceremonies were; and before there was sin, there needed no Saviour: and so consequently needing no Saviour, there needed no ceremony, and needing no Saviour, nor ceremony, it could not be ceremonial.

But this was it, that *Adam* (having in the six dayes a natural use in his body of the creatures) should for the glory of God on the seventh day have a spiritual use and consideration of them in a more special manner. And although there might be a worship performed to God on other dayes, yet that it might be more solemn, publick, and universal, and the heart of man more free from distraction, and wordly avocations, God therefore would have a special day dedicated to his honour and service, wherein the Creature should solemnly performe his homage to the Creator, and this was the first generall end, though other ends were after added: as in *Deuteronomie* it pleased God to adde this reason, that the People should remember their Delivery out of Egypt, but this was but *finis posterior*, a particular and after end, and accessory. And it were well if we might adde to our dayes of rest the memory of benefits received. And in *Exodus* God yieldeth a reason taken from a politick end, that our family and cattel may rest, and return more fresh to their labour.

And if any will say, that besides these ends, there was prefigured by this rest, that rest we shall have from sin; It's true, but yet that is but an accessory end. As in the Sacraments of Circumcision and Passeover, besides the general ends of their institution, which were to seal and signify Gods preventing and following grace, there were other ends typical and accessory: as that of Circumcision did signifie the Circumcision of the heart, and the Passover the sacrifice of Christ offered upon the cross. In which respects, though those two Sacraments are abolist, yet the Sacrament of initiation, and another of our confirmation in grace are still continued, to wit, Baptism and the Lords supper, according to the general ends of the two former Sacraments, which ends do still remain. So though the Sabbath or seventh day from the Creation be ceased, yet there is another day still remaining, because the end of keeping a day is immutable from the beginning, to wit, that God might be honoured by a solemne and publick worship.

This reason of it self is so forcible and plain, that without bringing in a manifest absurdity it cannot be denied and avoided. When they see these ends carry us to the Institution, and that in Paradise where no type or Ceremony was, they seek to avoid it by saying, It's true, *that God sanctified it in Paradise*, but *Adam* never kept it, neither was it kept till immediately before the Law was given: which may seem to be a very absurd thing, that God should sanctifie a thing two thousand years before it was to be put in practise. This is like to that assertion of those Hereticks, that held, the *materia prima* to be made by God many years before the world it self, and that it abode by him, till the world was made. But they are confuted by the Fathers thus, That no wise man will make any thing to be many years by him, before he shall have occasion to put it to any use. And therefore much lesse would God bless this day before there should be any use of it: to make *rem ante usum*.

1. We must understand, that God in *Deuteronomy* seemeth to make a distinction between Ceremonies and the Moral Law, *Deuteronomy* 4.13, 14 as, that the one proceeded from himself immediately: the other by the ministery of *Moses*, so also *Deuteronomie* 5.31.

2. Again it breeds confusion, and breaks order (a thing which God misliketh) if any thing meerly ceremonial and not in some sort moral should be placed among the ten Commandments. One of the Fathers upon the

words [*Nunquid & Saul est inter Prophetas? Is Saul also among the Prophets?*] saith, that *Saul* being no Prophet by profession, *est heterogeneus*, of another kinde, and an irregular person among the Prophets: so it will fall out to be against order, for a meer ceremonial Precept, to stand in the midst of moral Commandments. For every ceremony or type of the Law, is as it was a foretelling of something in the Gospel; so it must be referred to the Gospel, as the shadow to the body. And indeed no typical ceremonies are in their own nature, for the type or ceremony is to cease when the substance comes, as the shadow when the body appears. But this Commandment for the substance of it, continues in the time of the Gospel.

3. Thirdly, this being a principle, that the Law of *Moses* (expressed in the Decalogue) is nothing but the Law of nature revived, and the Law of nature being a resemblance of God's image. If we say this precept is in its substance ceremonial, then we must also say, that in the image of God something is ceremonial, not to abide, but for a time onely: but all things in him, and in his image are eternal according to his Nature.

4. In the Law of grace, Christ delivering the sum of the ten Commandments to the Scribes and Pharisees, *Thou shalt love the Lord, &c.* there's no question, but that it is the sum of the Decalogue, and therefore therein is included the religious observation of the Sabbath, and so it will be for the substance moral, as the love of God is, in which it is contained, or else our Saviour had delivered an imperfect sum.

5. Again, it is dangerous to hold, that any precept in the Decalogue is ceremonial: for by this the Papists (as *Parisius* and *Politianus*) will bring another of them to be so, and will say, that the second Commandment concerning images is ceremonial, and then why not three as well as two, and so four and five, and all. The best way therefore to hold the duties eternall, and to keep them without blemish is to deny that any of these ten precepts is ceremonial in the substance or nature of the Commandment, but that they are plainly moral.

6. To come to the time of the Gospel. We hold that all typical ceremonies of the law are ended and abrogated by Christs death. Then if the day of rest be not abrogated by his death, it is not a meer Ceremony or ceremonial. And that it is not, is plain by our Saviour himself for his denouncing the destruction of Jerusalem bids them pray that their calamity fall not in the winter, nor on the Sabbath day: Now we know that Jerusalem was destroyed many years after Christs death, when all ceremonies were ended. Therefore if Christ knew that the Sabbath as a ceremony should be wholly abrogated by his death, his counsel might well have bin spared, that they should pray that their flight might not be on the Sabbath day, *Matth.* 24.20 which if it had been quite abolished, should have been no day.

Again in things meerly ceremonial, there is not *commutatio*, a change, but *abrogatio*, an abrogating of them wholly: but we see in this matter of the Sabbath, there is *commutatio*, not *abrogatio*, the Lords day is appointed instead of the Sabbath; but no total abrogation of the Sabbath. Thus the seals of the Covenant though they had something typical, yet being in their general nature moral, therefore they are changed, but not quite abrogated, whereas in things meerly typical, there's no maner of commutation, but they are clean taken away: for Christ having broken down the partition wall, *Ephes.* 2.14,15. hath wholly taken away the law of ordinances, &c. But it is manifest, that instead of the Jews seventh day, another seventh day was ordained in the Apostles dayes; therefore as the ministery and seals of the Covenant, and the chief place of it, to wit the Temple, were not abolished but changed, as having a moral reason in them; so also was the day of the Covenant; for we read *Acts* 20.7. that the Apostles and Disciples came together on the first day of the week, to hear the word, and to break bread, and in 1 *Corin.* 16.2. the Apostle wills them in their meetings on the first day of the week to lay aside for the poor, and *Revel.* 1.10. it is plainly called, ἡμέρᾳ κυριακῇ, the Lord's day.

So that we see in the whole time of the Apostles it was not taken away, but changed by them, and therefore cannot be a meere ceremonie, nor of the nature of the types of the Law. But when the old Covenant ceased, then ceased the Ministery thereof: the Priesthood of *Levi* was changed, and given to choice men of all Tribes, and instead of it is our Ministery. And as the seals of the Covenant ceased as of Circumcision and the Paschal lamb, and in place thereof came our Sacraments of Baptism and the Lords supper: so the day of the old Covenant is taken away, and instead thereof is put the Lords day, none of them in the first end being ceremonial, but having a continual use, and to last as long as the Church militant.

The reasons which might seem to have moved the Apostles to change this day may be fitly taken from the Institution of the Sabbath in the time of the law. For as then nothing was more memorable then the day of the creation: so when it pleased God that old things should cease, and that there should be a new creation, and that there was a benefit, that did overshadow the former, the benefit of redemption; therefore when that was accomplished by Christs resurrection, from that day we celebrate the memorial of it on the first day of the week, and whereas that other great work of the sending the holy Ghost, which was fifty dayes after, concurd on the same day, whereby that inestimable benefit of sanctification and speaking with strange tongues was conferred upon the Church, and because the memory of the benefit of the creation may also be kept on the first day of the week, as well as on the last. Hence we may see upon what great reasons this day is establisht, wherein do concur the three special works and benefits of the three persons to be forever thankfully remembred, *viz.* that of Creation by the Father, Redemption by the Son, and Sanctification by the holy Ghost. And so much for the clearing of that point.

FOURTH COMMANDEMENT.
CHAP. IX.

4. Rule.
The Meanes.

In the next place (according to the former rules of exposition) we are to proceed to those things which help and conduce to the keeping of this Commandment, which we usually call the means; for where the end is commanded, there those things are also Commanded, whithout which the end cannot be attained.

* * *

Places of
publick worship.
Levit. 19.30.
26.2.

1. For the place, we finde it joyned with the day in several places, *Ye shall keep my Sabbaths, and reverence my sanctuarie.* Where the observation of the day is joyned with reverence of the place in one verse making them thereby to be of one Nature. This should be observed by those men among us, who are so strict and punctual about the day, urging it even to Jewish superstition, and yet are wholly negligent of the place, and prophane it most of all: when as it is most certain, that the time and place do *pari passu ambulare*; and that there is no more ceremony in the one, then in the other: but that both are of the like moral use, and both alike capable of sanctification; and the place the more capable of the two as a thing permanent, whereas the time is transient.

Psalm 132.14.

The day is the day of rest, and when we hallow it, it is called the Lords rest; and the same name is given by God himself to the place, when it is consecrated to him, *This is my rest for ever, here will I dwell, for I have a delight therein,* saith God of Sion: concerning which, as the Apostles took order, that the exteriour part of Gods worship should be performed decently and in order, so also that the place of worship should not be prophaned, but decently kept, and reverently esteemed, and therefore the Apostle reproves the Corinthians for their irreverent carriage in the place,

1 Cor. 11.22.

whereby they despised the Church of God,* Have ye not houses to eat and drink in? or despise ye the Church of God? But if he had lived in these times, what would he have said, to see the houses of God, and places of worship so highly prophaned and abused, and so homely and poorly kept, that the

---

27 *in marg.* Psalm 132.14] *ed.*; Psalm 133.14 P

Table of the Lord, where (as *S. Chrysostome* saith) *Tremenda Dei mysteria*, the dreadful mysteries of God are celebrated, looks more like an oyster board, or a table to eat oysters on, then the holy Table fit for Gods Sanctuary. This is so far from *Pompa* outward pomp (which is the extream that some men pretend to be against) that it comes far short of ευσχημοσυνη, that decency which is required in Gods house. This is a thing to be thought on, and though it may seem to some not to be *inter graviora legis*, yet I am sure it is not to be neglected, as we see it is now adayes: for as by travelling, working, &c. we shew that we esteem not the day, so the very walls and windows, and other parts neglected, shew we esteem not Gods sanctuary.

[Addition 9]

Thus briefly for the Places: now for the Person.

III

A Sermon Preached at Saint Maries Hospital, on the X. of April, being Wednesday in Easter-weeke, A.D. MDLXXXVIII

I. TIM. CHAP. VI. VER. XVII. XVIII. XIX

Charge them that are rich in this world, that they be not high-minded, that they trust not in the uncertenty of riches, but in the living GOD, *which giveth us all things to enjoy, plenteously;*
That they do good, be rich in good workes, ready to distribute and to communicate:
Laying up in store, for themselves, a good foundation, against the time to come, that they may lay hold of æternall life.

2. Tim. 3.16.

THE commendation of the Word of GOD is, that *Every Scripture is profitable for our instruction*. Every Scripture is profitable: yet, not every Scripture, in every place alike. For, the Place and Auditorie have great interest in some Scripture; and a fitt Scripture hath a greater and fuller force, in his owne Auditorie. And GOD, in so excellent a manner hath sorted His Scriptures, as there ly dispersed in them, several Texts, seasonable for each time, and pertinent to each place and degree; for *Prince*, for *people*; for *rich*, for *poore*; for each, his peculiar Scripture, in due time and place, to be reached them. This Scripture which I have read, whose it is, and to whom it speaketh, is at the very reading streightway evident: as one saith of the XLI. *Psalme (Blessed is he that judgeth rightly of the poor)* that it is *Scriptura Pauperum*, the *Poore man's Scripture*; So, of this, it may be rightly said, that it is *Scriptura Divitum*, The *Rich mans Scripture*. And, if this be the *Scripture* for *rich men*; this place, is the *place* of *rich men*: and therefore, if this Scripture have his place, no where so fitt, as in this place.

a Esa. 23.3.

For, no where is there such store of *riches*, by the ^a*Harvest of the water*, which farre surpasseth the harvest of the ground; No where are the like

b Ezek. 28.12.
c Deut. 33.19.
d Esay 23.8.

^b*Summes sealed*; No where doe they ^c*sucke the abundance of the Sea* and *the treasures hid in the sand*, in like measure: No where are the ^d*Merchants*

Noblemen's fellowes and *able to lend the Princes of the earth,* so much, as heer. Therefore when as I gave all diligence to speake, not onely true things but also seasonable, both for this time and this place, I was directed to this Scripture. I need not to say much in this point; to shew, it concerneth this Audience. I will say, as the Fathers say, upon the like occasion; *Faxit Deus tam commoda, quàm est accommoda.* I pray GOD make it as *profitable,* as it is *pertinent*; as *fruitfull* to you, as it is fitt for you.

The Division.

1. This whole Scripture hath his name given it even in the first word: *Charge* (saith he) *the rich &c* It is a *Charge.*

I.

2. It is directed to certaine men; namely, to *the Rich of this world.*

II.

3. It consisteth of foure branches: Whereof Two are *negative,* for the removing of two abuses.

III.

  1. The first, *Charge them, that they be not high minded.*
  2. The second, *Charge them, that they trust not in their riches.*

The reason is added (which is a *Maxime* and a *Ground* in the *Law* of *Nature,* That we must trust to no uncertaine thing:) *Trust not in the uncertaintie of riches.*

The other two are *affirmative,* concerning the true use of riches.

  1. The first: *Charge them that they trust in* GOD. The reason: Because, *He giveth them all things to enjoy plenteously.*
  2. The second: *Charge them that they do good*; that, is the *substance*: The *quantitie,* that *they be rich in good workes*: the *qualitie,* That *they be ready to part with* (and a speciall kind of doing good) to *communicate,* to benefit the *publique.*

And all these are one *Charge.* The *reason* of them all doth follow: Because by this meanes they shall *lay up in store,* and that *for themselves, a good foundation, against the time to come.* The end: *that they may obtaine eternall life.*

Præcipe divitibus: *Charge* the *rich* of this world, &c. Beloved, heer is a *Charge,* a *Præcipe,* a *Precept,* or a *Writt,* directed unto *Timothie,* and to those of his Commission to the world's end, to convent and call before him; He, the *rich men* of *Ephesus*; and we, the *rich men* of this *Citie,* and others of other places of the earth, and to give them a charge.

I.
A Charge.

Charges (as you know) use to be given at *Assises* in *Courts* from the *Bench.* From thence is taken this judicial term παράγγελλε, as it appeareth, *Act.*5.28. *Did not we* charge *you streightly?* saith the *Bench* in the *Consistorie* judicially assembled. Whereby, we are given to understand, that in such Assemblies as this is, the *Lord* of *Heaven* doth hold His *Court,* whereunto all men, and (they that of all men seeme least) the *rich* and *mighty* of the world owe both

1 things] things, F_2 15 not] F_3; not, F_1, F_2

suit and service. For, as earthly Princes have their *Lawes*, their *Commissioners*, their *Ministers* of the Law, their *Courts* and *Court-daies*, for the maintenance of their peace: So hath the *King* of *Kings* His *Lawes* and *Statutes*, His *Precepts* and *Commissions* by authority delegate, *Ite prædicate*, Go preach the *Gospel*; His *Counsailors at Law*, whom *Augustine* calleth *Divini Juris Consultos*; His *Courts In occulto conscientiæ*, in the hid and *secret part* of the *heart* and *conscience*, for the preservation of His peace, which the world can neither give nor take away; to the end, that none may offend or be offended at it.

<small>Rom. 7.</small>
<small>Matth. 28.19.</small>
<small>Psal. 7.8.</small>
<small>Psal. 119.165.</small>

This we learne. And with this we learne, all of us, so to conceive of, and to dispose our selves to such Meetings as this, as men that are to *appeare* in *Court*, before the *Lord*, there to receive a *charge*, which when the *Court* is broken up, we must think of how to discharge.

In which point, great is the occasion of complaint, which we might take up. For, who is there, that with that awe and reverence standeth before the *Lord*, at His *charge-giving*, that he receiveth a *charge* with, at an earthly Barre? Or with that care remembreth the *Lord* and his *charge*, wherewith he continually thinketh upon the *Iudge* and his *charge*? Truly, the *Lord's Commission* is worthy to have as great reverence and regard attending on it, as the *charge* of any *Prince*; truly, it is. Weigh with your selfe; is not GOD's *charge* with as much heed and reverence to be received, as an earthly *Iudge's*? *Absit ut sic* (saith *Saint Augustine*) *sed utinam vel sic* : GOD forbid, but with more heed and reverence; well, I would it had so much, in the meane time: And (which to our shame we must speak) I would we could do as much for the *Bible* as for the *Statute-Books*; for *heaven* as for the *earth*; for the Immortall GOD, as for mortall man. But whither we doe or no, yet as our SAVIOUR CHRIST said of *Saint John Baptist, If ye will receive, this is that Eliah which was to come*; so say I of this *Precept, If ye will receive it, this is the* Charge *the Lord hath laid on you*. And this let me tell you farther; that it is such a *Charge*, as toucheth your estate in *everlasting life*, the very last words of my Text. That is, the well or evill hearing of this *Charge*, is as much worth as your *æternall life* is worth. And therefore, *He that hath eares to heare, let him heare*.

<small>Matt. 11.14.</small>
<small>Matt. 11.15.</small>

<small>2</small>
<small>To the *Rich*.</small>

It is a *Charge* then, and consequently to be discharged. To be discharged? where? *Charge* (saith he) *the rich*. He speaketh to the *Rich*: you know your owne names; you know best, what those *rich men* are. Shall I tell you? You are the *rich*; he speaketh unto you. It is the fashion and the fault of this world, to exercise their authority on them most, that need it least: For *rich men*, to feast them that least need it; for mighty men, to preferre them that

<small>32 *in marg*. Matt. 11.15] *LACT*; Matt. 11.14 F_1</small>

least deserve it. It is an old *Simile*, we have oft heard it; that The *Lawes* are like *Cobwebbs:* that they hold fast the seely *flies*, but the great *Hornetts* breake through them, as oft as they list. And as there are *cobwebb-Lawes*, which exempt mighty men; So, the same Corruption, that was the cause thereof, would also make *Cobwebb-Divinitie*. For, notwithstanding the *Commission* runneth expresly to the *Rich, Charge &c:* notwithstanding they be in great danger, and that of *many snares* (as the *Apostle* saith in this *Chapter*) and therefore need it greatly: Yet (I know not how) it comes to passe, whither, because they thinke themselves too wise to receive a *charge*, any *charge* at all; or because they thinke themselves too good to receive it, at the hands of such meane men, as we be (and, if they must needs be charged, they could be charged from the *Counsaile*, from men more Noble and Honorable then themselves) they would not gladly heare it, surely they would not; and because they would not gladly heare it, we are not hasty they should heare it. And great reason, why (as we thinke:) for, as it is true which is in the *Psal.* 49.18. *So long as they do good to themselves, men will speake good of them*: So, it is true backward too; *So long as we speake well of them*, spare them, call not on them, *they will do good to us*. And otherwise, if we spare them not but prosecute our charge, then commeth *Odi Michæam filium Jimlæ*, I hate *Michea* the Sonne of *Jimlah*. And who would willingly live in disgrace, and susteine, I say not the fierce wrath, but the heavie looke of a man in authoritie? That, makes this Office of giving a *charge*, a cold Office, and therefore to decay, and be shunned of all hands: that, makes us, if we cannot of the *Eunuch* learne to *speake good to the King*; yet, to follow *Balack's* counsaile at the least, *neither to blesse nor curse*: That makes, that though for shame of the world, we will not sett up for *Upholsters*, and stuffe *cushions* and *pillows*, to lay them under their *elbowes*; yet, for feare of men, we shunne the Prophet *Esay's* occupation to take *the trumpet* and disease them, lest we lose *Balack's promotion*, or *Ahab's friendship, Esau's portion*, or I wote not what els, which we will not be without. In a word: this maketh, that *Jonah* was never more unwilling to deliver his message at *Ninive*, then is *Timothee*, to give his *Charge* at *Ephesus*.

The *Apostle* saw this, and what it would come to; and that you may see, that he saw it, you shall understand, he hath besides this of yours, directed another Writ to us, Verse 13. *I charge thee &c* running in very rigorous and peremptorie termes, hable to make any that shall consider them aright, to tremble. Streightly commanding us, *in the name of* God *the Father and of the Lord* Jesus Christ; laying before us the *Passion* of Christ, *If there be any grace*, and the day of judgement, *and there be any feare*, that we fulfill every

Verse 9.

2. Reg. 22.8.

Ibidem.
Num. 23.25.

Esay 58.1.

Verse 13.

Verse 14.

19 not but] not, but F_2

44   A SERMON PREACHED AT SAINT MARIES HOSPITAL

<small>Verse 14.</small> part of our *charge*; and immediately after nameth this your *charge* for one. And knowing that we are given to feare *Princes* and *Lords*, he telleth us of <small>Verse 15.</small> the *Prince of all Princes*, and *Lord of all Lords*: Knowing, that we are given to feare and be dazeled with the *glittering* of their *pompe* (which yet a man may <small>Verse 16.</small> abide to looke on) he telleth us of him, *whose brightnesse no eye may once abide*: Knowing, that we feare honour and power, though it last but for a <small>Ibidem.</small> small time, he feareth us with one, whose *honour* and *power lasteth for ever*.

Beloved in the Lord, I beseech you weigh but the place; weigh it, and have pitie on us. For, *Nunquid nos recipimus, nunquid nos delere possumus? Si delemus, timemus deleri* (saith *Saint Augustine*.) We writt not this *charge*, our pennes dealt not in it; it was not we that writt it, and it is not we that can blott it out, unlesse we our selves will be *blotted out of the booke of life*.

Such is our *charge* as you see, to *charge* you: and, but for this charge, but that we are commanded, but that we are threatned, and that in so fearefull manner threatned, we should never do it; of all men, we should never deale with the *Rich*. For, who would not choose to hold his peace and to seeke his owne ease from this *charge*, many times *changeable*, sometimes *dangerous*, evermore *unsavory*, but for this Processe that is out against us? For my selfe, I professe, and that in the same words that *Saint Augustine* did sometime: *Ad istam otiosissimam securitatem nemo me vinceret*: In this *discreet* kind of *idlenesse*, no man should go beyond me, if *Saint Paul* would be content; if order might be taken, to have these Verses cancelled; if we could *deliver* (I say not yours, but) *our owne soules* with silence. But, this standing in force, *Cogit nos Paulus iste*, we are enforced by this *Paul*; His *Pæcipio tibi*, I *charge* you, drives us to our *Præcipe illis*, to charge them: We charge not you, but when we are charged our selves: we terrifie not you, but when we are first terrified our selves. And I would to GOD we *knowing this terror* might both *feare* together this day, at the *charge-giving*, that so we might both *rejoice* together in the great Day, at the *charge-answering*. This may serve; and I beseech you, let it serve to stand betweene us and your displeasure in this behalfe: and seeing the Commission is penned to our hand, and that *Rich men* are in it *nominatim* (except the levin of affection shew it selfe too evidently in us) to thinke, we cannot otherwise do; and that therefore it is, because the commandement of <small>II.</small> our GOD is upon us, is heavie upon us. The *Charge* it selfe followeth.

<small>1.
The first
point of the
Charge:
Not to be
High-minded.</small> *Charge the Rich &c.* This is the first point of the charge, *that they be not high minded*. 1. First, against that, which if it come with all the *riches*, yea all the *vertues* in the world, it spoileth them all; that is, against *Pride*. 2. Secondly, against that which is the root of this bitter branch, and the prop and stay of a high raised minde, namely, a vaine *trust in our riches*. Both these forbidden, by meanes of their *uncertaintie*, ἀδηλότης: such, as a man

cannot tell where to have them, therefore not to be *boasted of*, therfore not to be *trusted in*.

Ever since our first Fathers, by infection took this *morbum Sathanicum*, this Divelish disease (*Pride*) of the *Devill*; such tinder is in our nature, that every little sparke setts us on fire: our nature hath growen so light, that every little thing *puffeth* us up, and setts us aloft in our altitudes presently. Yea indeed, so light we are, that many times, when the *gifts* are low, yet for all that, the *mind* is as high, as the *bramble*: low in qualities (GOD knoweth) yet had his mind higher then the highest *Cedar* in *Libanon*. But if we be but of meane stature once, but a thought higher then others our fellowes, if never so little more in us, then is in our neighbours, presently we fall into *Simon's* case, we seeme to ourselves as he did, to be τις μέγας, no doubt *some goodly great thing*. But if we come once to any growth indeed, then presently our case is *Haman's* case: Who but he? *Who was he, that the King would honour* more then him? Nay, *who was there*, that the King could honour, *but he?* He, and none but he. Through this aptnesse in us that we have to learne the Devill's lesson, the Devill's *Discite à me*, for *I am proud*; (for so it is, by opposition of CHRIST's lesson, which is *Discite à me; quia mitis sum*, because I am *meek* and *gentle*;) we are ready to corrupt our selves in every good gift of GOD; in *Wisdome*, in *Manhood*, in *Law*, in *Divinitie*, in *Learning* or *Eloquence*, every and each of these serveth for a stirrup to mount us aloft in our own conceipts. For, where each of the former hath (as it were) his owne circuite (as *Wisdome* ruleth in *Counsaile*; *Manhood* in the *Field*; *Law* in the *Iudgement-seat*; *Divinitie* in the *Pulpitt*; *Learning* in the *Schooles*; and *Eloquence* in *Perswasion*:) onely *Riches* ruleth without limitation: *Riches* ruleth with them all, ruleth them all, and over-ruleth them all: his Circuit is the whole world. For which cause, some think, when he saith *Charge the rich*, he presently addeth, *of this world*, because *this world* standeth altogether at the devotion of *Riches*; and he may do what he wil in this world, that is *rich in this world*. So said the Wiseman long agoe, *Pecuniæ obediunt omnia*: all things answer Money; Money mastereth all things; they all answer at his call, and they all obey at his commandement. Let us go lightly over them all; you shall see, that they all els have their severall predicaments to bound them, and that *Riches* is onely the transcendent of this world.

Wisdome ruleth in *Counsaile*; so do *Riches*: for we see, in the Court of the great King *Artaxerxes*, there were *Counsailors*, whose *wisdome* was to be commanded by *riches*, even to hinder a publique benefit, the building of the Temple. *Manhood* ruleth in *warre*; so do *riches*: Experience teacheth us, it is so: It is said, it was they, that wan *Deventer*; and that it was they, and none but they, that drave the *Switzers* out of *France*, and that without stroke strooken. *Law* governeth in the *Seat* of *Justice*; so do *Riches*: and oftentimes

Jud. 9.15.

Acts 8.9.

Ester 6.6.

Matt. 11.29.

Eccles. 10.19.

Ezra 4.5.

they turne justice it selfe into *wormewood*, by a corrupt Sentence; but more often doth it turne Justice into *vineger*, by long standing, and infinite delayes, yer Sentence will come forth. *Divinitie* ruleth in the *Church* and *Pulpit*; so do *Riches*: For, with a sett of *silver peeces* (saith *Augustine*) they brought *Concionatorem mundi* the Preacher of the world JESUS CHRIST to the Barre, and *the Disciple is not above this Master*. *Learning* ruleth in the *Schooles*; so do *Riches*: And indeed, there, *Money* setteth us all to schoole. For (to say the truth) *Riches* have so ordered the matter there, as *Learning* is now but the *Usher*; *Money* he is the *Master*: the *Chaire* it self and the disposing of the Chaire, is his too. *Eloquence* ruleth in *perswasion*; and so do *Riches:* when *Tertullus* had laboured a goodly flowing oration against *Paul*, *Fælix* looked, that another, a greater Orator should have spoken for him, namely that *Something should have been given him*: and if that Orator had spoken his short pithy sentence *Tantum dabo*, *Tertullus* his oration had been cleane dasht. *Tantum dabo* is a strange peece of Rhetorique: Devise as cunningly, pen as curiously as you can, it overthrowes all. *Tantùm valent quatuor syllabæ*, such force is there in foure syllables. Though indeed, some think (it being so unreasonable short as it is, but two words) that it cannot be the Rhetorique of it, that worketh these strange effects, but that there is some *sorcerie* or *witchcraft* in them, in *Tantum dabo*. And surely a great *Sorcerer (Simon Magus)* used them to *Peter*: and it may well be so, for all estates are *shrewdly bewitched* by them. I must end: for it is a worlde to thinke and tell, what the *Riche of the world*, may do in the world.

So then, *Riches* seeing they may do so much, it is no marvell though they be much sett by. *Et divites cum habeant quæ magni sunt ab omnibus, quid mirum, si ab omnibus ipsi magni fiant; & cum magni fiant ab omnibus, quid mirum si & à se?* Rich men having that which is much sett by, no marvell though of all men they be much sett by; and if all other men sett much by them, no marvell, if they sett much by themselves; and to sett much by a mans selfe, that is to be *high-minded*. It is our owne Proverb in our owne tongue: *As riseth our good, so riseth our blood.* And *Saint Augustine* saith, that Each *fruit*, by kind hath his *worme* breeding in it: as the *Peare*, his; the *Nutt*, his; and the *Beane*, his: So, *Riches* have their worme, *Et vermis divitiarum, Superbia*; and the *worme* of *riches*, is *Pride*. Whereof we see a plaine proofe in *Saul*: Who, while he was in a poore estate, that his boy & he could not make *five pence* between them, was as the Scripture saith, *low in his owne eyes*: after, when the *wealth* and pleasant things of *Israël* were his, he grew so sterne, as he forgatt himselfe, his friends, and GOD too: and at every word that liked him not, was ready to runne *David*, *Jonathan*, and

---

11 in marg. Acts 24.26] *LACT*; Acts 24.27 F_1

every one through *with his javeline*. It is very certaine; where *riches* are, there is great danger of *pride*. I desire you to thinke, there is so, and not to putt me to justifie GOD's *wisedome* heerein, in perswading and proving, that this charge is needfull for you that be *rich*; that it was needfull for the *Prophet*, to preach under the Law, *If riches encrease, sett not your heart on the top of them,* Let not that rise as they rise: Nor for the other *Prophet, Give me not riches, lest I wax proud*: Nor for the *Apostle Paul* under the Gospell, to say: *Charge them that be rich in this world, that they be not high-minded*. I beseech you, Honour GOD, and ease me so much as to thinke, there was high cause, it should be in charge; and that, if a more principall sinne had been reigning in the *rich*, this sinne should not have had the principall place, as it hath.

Psal. 62.10.
Pro. 30.9.

How then? what, are you hable to charge any heere? will some say: It is not the manner of our *Court*, nor of any *Court*, that I know. To us it belongeth, onely to deliver the *Charge*, and to exhort, that if none be *proud*, none would be; and if any be, they would be lesse: and, if any be not humble, they would be; and if any be humble, they would be more. You that are the *Court*, your part is to enquire, and to present, and to endite; and that, every one in his owne conscience, as in the presence of GOD, unto Him to approve your innocencie, or of Him to sue for your pardon. You find none (you will say): I would to GOD you might not.

When a *Judge* at an *Assize*, giveth his charge concerning treason and such like offenses, I dare say, he would with all his heart, that his *charge* might be in vaine, rather then any Traitor or Offender should be found. A Physitian, when he hath tempered and prepared his potion, if there be in him the heart of a true Physitian, desireth (I know) that the potion might be cast downe the kennell, so that the patient might recover without it: So, truly, it is the desire of my heart (CHRIST he knoweth) that this *charge* may not find one man guilty amongst all these hearers; amongst so many men, not one *high-minded* man. I wish, it might be in vaine. The best *Sessions*, and *Potions*, and *Sermons* are those, which are in vaine: I say not, in vaine, if there be cause of reproofe and no amends. But, if there be no cause, and so it be in vaine, *I joy therein and will joy*. But, if it be farre unlikely, amongst so great *riches* as is heere, to finde no *pride* at all; very unlikely: then, hear the *charge* and present yourselves and find your selves guilty heere in our Office, this day, while you may find grace, lest you be tried and found so, in that day, when there shall be no hope of grace, but onely a *fearefull expectation of judgement*.

Which that you may do the better, so many as GOD shall make willing (as, some (I hope) He doth) I will enforme you, how to trie your selves; referring you, to the severall branches, in our Statutes, in the *High Court* of

14 belongeth,] belongeth F_3

Parliament in Heaven: laying them out unto you, as I find them in the *Records* of the *Holy Ghost*.

The points are three in number. First, if the mind of any man be so exalted, that he looketh downe on his brethren, as if he stood on the top of a *Leades*, and not on the same ground they do, that man is *high-minded*. Saint *Augustine* said well: *Excipe pompatica hæc & volatica*, they are the same that you are. They have not *vestem communem*, the same *coat*; but they have *cutem communem*, the same *skinne*: and within a few yeares, when you die, if a man come with a *Joyner* and measure all that you carrie with you, they shall carrie away with them as much: and within a few yeares after, a man shall not be hable to discern, between the sholder-blade of one of them and one of you. Therefore, no cause, why you should *incedere inflati, insericati*, and from a *high mind* bewraying it selfe by a *high looke*, contemne them, as many of you do. I say then, if any of you be a child of *Anak*, and looke downe so upon another, as in his sight his brethren *seeme as Grashoppers*; [1]Wither it appear in the *countenance*, in drawing up his ey-browes, in a *disdainefull* and *scornefull eye*; such a one as *David* (though he found no pœnal statute to punish it) could never *abide* (and *David* was a man *after* GOD*'s owne heart*, and therefore neither can GOD abide it:) [2]Or whither it appeare, in a proud kind of *Dialect* of speech, as was that of *Saul's; Ubi nunc est iste filius Ishai?* Where is this Sonne of *Ishai*? that he come to the Pharisee's *Non sum sicut*: [3]Or whether it be in the course of their life, that they be like to the great *fishes* (to *Pikes*) that think, all the little fishes in the streame were *made for them to feed on*. So that, it appeareth, they care not, what miserie, what beggerie, what slaverie they bring all men to, so they may *soak in the broth of the cauldron*, and welter in their wealth and pleasure: who are in their streets and parishes as *Lyons*, a great deale more feared then beloved; as implacable as *Lamech* to beare any injurie, and will have for one drop of bloud, no lesse then a man's life: what speake I of bearing injurie? which will do injurie, and that for no other reason but this, thus it must be, for *Hophni will have* it *thus but thus*; and except they may do thus (what they will, to whom they will, when and how they will) forsooth they do not *governe*, their autority is nothing: in this sort, overbearing all things with their countenance and wealth, and whosoever standeth but up, *drawing him before the Judgement-seats, and wearying him out with Law*. These men who do thus, from a high *in-bearing* of the *head*, in phrase of *speech*, and in the order, or rather disorder of their *dealing*: over-looke, over-crow and over-beare their brethren of mean estate, it is certaine, they be *high-minded*: Enquire and look, whither any be so.

---

15 *in marg.* Num. 13.34] *LACT*; Num. 33.34 F_1 23 *in marg.* Hab. 1.14] *LACT*; Hab. 2.14 F_1

Margin references:
Num. 13.34.
Pro. 30.13.
Psal. 101.5.
1. Sam. 20.27.
Hab. 1.14.
Eze. 11.3.
Zeph. 3.3.
1 Sam. 2.15.
1. Reg. 21.7.
Jac. 2.6.

Secondly, if any mind *clime so high*, that the boughes will beare him no longer, by *exalting* himselfe above either his *abilitie, condition* or *calling* (a fault, which hath like to cost our times deare;) that man's footing will faile him, he will downe; he and his mind are too high a great deale. The late *treasons* and *conspiracies* came from such kind of minds. For, when the minds of men will over-reach their abilities, what must be the end, but (as we have seen of late) to prove *Traitors?* Why? because they have *swolne themselves out of their skinne.* Why so? because they had *lashed on more on their pleasure then they had.* For, so doing, when they had over-reached themselves, they became προπετεῖς, they must take some headdy enterprise in hand. What is that? to become προδόται; that, seeing their credit is decaied in this State, they may set up a new; and that is by over-turning the old.

And not only this passing the ability is dangerous to the over-turning of a Common-wealth; but the passing of a man's condition too: and tendeth to the impoverishing and at last to the overthrow of the Estate also. ¹Whither it be excesse of *diet*: as when being no Magistrate, but plaine *Master Nabal*, his *dinner* must be *like to the feast of a King.* ²Or whither it be in excesse of *apparell*, wherein the pride of *England* now, as the pride of *Ephraim* in times past, ᵃ*testifieth against her to her face.* ³Or whither it be in ᵇ*lifting up the gate too high*, that is, in excesse of *building.* ⁴Or whither it be in keeping too great a *traine* (*Esau's* case) that he go with ᶜ*foure hundred* men at his taile, wheras the fourth part of the fourth part would have served his father well enough. ⁵Or whither it be in perking too high in their alliance, the *Bramble's sonne in Lebanon, must match with the Cedar's daughter.* These are *evidences* and *signes* set downe to prove a *high mind:* see and search into your selves, whither you find them or no.

There is yet of this feather another kind of *exalting* our selves above that we ought, much to be complained of in these dayes. Saint *Paul* calleth it a *stretching of our selves beyond measure.* Thus, if a man be atteined to any high skill in *law*, which is the gift of GOD; or if a man be growne wise, and experienced well in the *affaires* of this *world*, which is also his good blessing: presently by vertue of this, they take themselves to be so qualified, as they be hable to over-rule our matters in *Divinitie*, able to prescribe *Bishops* how to *governe*, and *Divines* how to *preach*; so to determine our cases, as if they were professed with us: and that many times, ᵈ*affirming things they know not*, and ᵉ*censuring things they have little skill of.* Now seeing we take not upon us to deale in cases of your *Law*, or in matters of your *Trade*, we take, this is a

2.

2. Tim. 3.4.

1. Sam. 25.36.
a Hos. 5.5.
b Pro. 17.19.
c Gen. 32.6.

2. Reg. 14.9.

1.Cor. 10.14.

d 1 Tim. 1.7.
e Jude 10.

20 in marg. Pro. 17.19] *LACT*; Pro. 17.16 *F₁*   22 in marg. Gen. 32.6] *LACT*; Gen. 32.16 *F₁*   36 in marg. d 1 Tim. 1.7] *LACT*; d Tim. 1.7 *F₁*

<small>f Hos. 4.4.</small>
<small>g 1. Thes. 5.12.</small>
<small>h Rom. 12.3.</small>

stretching beyond your line. That in so doing you are ^f*a people that controll the Priest*: that you are too high, when you ^g*set your selves over them that are over you in the Lord*: and that this is no part of that ^h*sober wisdome*, which S *Paul* commendeth to you; but of that *cup-shotten wisdome* which he condemneth. Which breaking compasse and outreaching is (no doubt) the cause of these lamentable rents and ruptures in the *Lord's Nett*, in our dayes. For, *Only by pride commeth contention,* saith the Wise man. Which point I wish might be looked upon and amended. Sure, it will marre all in the end.

3.

<small>i Hos. 6.5.</small>
<small>k 2. Cor. 10.5.</small>

Thirdly, if any man *lift up* himselfe *too high*, any of both these wayes, GOD hath taken order to abate him and take him downe: for, He hath appointed his Prophetts, to ⁱ*prune those that are too high*; and he hath ordeined his word, to ^k*bring downe every imagination that shalbe exalted against it.* Now then, if there be any man, that shall seek to set himselfe without the shot of it, and is so high minded, as that he cannot *suffer the words of exhortation*; and where GOD hath said, *Charge them that be rich*, he cannot bide to heare any *Charge* (and such there be:) sure, that man without all question is very *high-minded*; and if he durst, he would teare out this leafe, of all other, where like *charge* is given through the *Bible.* Of *Naball* it

<small>l 1 Sam. 25.17.</small>
<small>m 2 Sam. 3.7.</small>

is recorded, ^l*He was so surly, a man might not speake to him*: Of ^m*Abner* (a great man, and a speciall stay of the house of *Saul*) that upon a word spoken, of his adulterous life with one of *Saul's* minions, he grew to such choler, that he forgat all, and laid the plot that cost his Master *Ishbosheth* his kingdome. *Micheah* prophesied *good things*, that is to say, *profitable* to *Ahab*, the event shewed it: yet because he did not prophesie *good things*, that is, such as *Ahab would heare*, he spared not openly to professe, *he hated him*: and wheras the *false Prophets* were *fedd at his owne table*, and fared no worse then he and the Queen, he tooke order for *Micheah*-his diet, that it should

<small>1 Kings 22.27.</small>

be the *bread of affliction* and the *water of trouble*; and all for a *charge*-giving. These were (I dare boldly affirme) *high-minded* men in their generations: If any be like these, they know what they are. If then there be any that refuse to be pruned and trimmed by the *word* of GOD, Who either when he heareth

<small>*Deut. 29.19.</small>

the words of the charge, [*]*blesseth himselfe in his heart and saith, Tush he doth but prate; these things shall not come upon me, though I walk still according to the stubornesse of mine owne heart:* ²Either in hearing the word of GOD, takes upon him (his *flesh and bloud, and he*) to *sitt on it*, and *censure it*: and say to himselfe one while, this is well spoken, while his humor is served; another while, this is foolishly spoken, now he *babbleth*, because the *Charge* sitts

---

3 *in marg.* h Rom. 12.3] *LACT*; h Rom. 12.4 *F*₁   11 *in marg.* i Hos. 6.5] *LACT*; i Hos. 6.6 *F*₁   12 *in marg.* k 2. Cor. 10.5] *LACT*; k 2. Cor. 10.4 *F*₁   28 *in marg.* 1 Kings. 22.27] *LACT*; 1 King. 22 *F*₁   32 *in marg.* *Deut. 29.19] *F*₃; m Deut. 29.19 *F*₁, *F*₂

somwhat neer him: ³Either is in the *Pharisee's* case, which after they have heard the *Charge*, do (as they did at CHRIST) ⁿἐκμυκτηρίζειν, *jest* and *scoffe*, and make themselves *merry* with it, and wash it downe with a cup of sack, and that °*because they were covetous*: If in very deed ᵖ*the word of god be to them a reproch*, and they take like delight in both, and well were they if they might never heare it; and to testifie their good conceipt of the word, shew it in the account of the *Ephod*, which is a *base & contemptible garment in their eyes*, and the *word* in it and with it (this is *Micholl's* case.) Whosoever is in any of these men's cases, is in the case of a *high-minded man*; and that of the highest degree: for they *lift* themselves *up*, not against earth and man, but against heaven and GOD himself. O beloved, you that be in *wealth* and authoritie, love and reverence the word of GOD. It is the *root* that doth beare you; It is the Majestie thereof that keepeth you in your thrones, and maketh you be, that you are: But for *Ego dixi Dii estis* (a parcell commission out of this commission of ours) the *madnesse of the people* would beare no government, but runne headlong, and overthrow all chaires of estate, and breake in peeces all the *swords* and *scepters* in the world; which you of this Citie had a strange experience of in *Jack Straw*, and his meiny, and keepe a memoriall of it in your *Citie scotcheon*, how all had gone downe if this *Word* had not held all up. And therefore, honour it I beseech you; I say, honour it. For, when the highest of you your selves, which are but *grasse*, and your Lordship's *glory* and *Worship*, which is the *flower of this grasse*, shall *perish and passe away*, this Word shall continue for ever. And if you receive it now, with due regard and reverence, it will make you also to *continue for ever*.

This is your *Charge*, touching the first branch. I beseech you, enquire of it, whither there be any guilty in these points: And if there be, suffer us to doe our Office, that is to humble you; or els sure, the *Lord* will do His, that is pull downe *riches* and *mind* and *man* and all, *Patimini falcem occantem, ne patiamini securim extirpantem*. GOD will not suffer it certenly: He would not suffer it in a ᑫ*King*; He would not suffer it in an ʳ*Angel*; He cannot beare it, to rise, in an ˢ*Apostle, for the greatnesse of revelations*; therefore, He will not beare it in any man for any cause whatsoever. Let this be the conclusion of this point.

We shall never have *pride* well pluckt up, so long as the *rest* of it sticks still; that is, a *Vaine confidence in riches*. For if we doubted them, we would not *trust* in them, we would not *boast* of them. But, we *trust* in them, and that inordinately, as *countermeanes* against GOD: not subordinately, as *under-meanes* unto GOD: and in so doing, we translate GOD's Office unto us, and our *homage* unto Him, to a plate of silver or a wedge of Gold. And

n Gal. 1.16.

o Luke 16.14.
p Jer. 6.10.

Psal. 82.5.

Esay 40.8.

q Deut. 17.20.
r Jude 6.
s 1. Cor.12.7.

2.
The second Point: *Not to trust in uncertaine riches.*

27 is to] is, to F_2 27 sure,] sure F_3 27 is] is, F_3

Col. 3.5.
Psal. 135.15.

that is (*Saint Paul* saith) *the worldly man's idolatrie*. And indeed there is little difference: It is but turning the sentence of the Prophet *David*; of *Idolaters*, to say thus, *their Idols are silver and gold*; and of the *Worldly men*, thus, *Silver and Gold are their Idols*.

Prov. 11.28.

We may examine our selves, in this point of the charge; namely, whither our *trust be in our riches*, by two waies. For it being a received ground, that our *strength* is our *confidence*; where we take our chiefe *Strength* to lie, that is it certainly, which we *trust* to. Now, what that is, we shall soone finde. [1]If we can certifie our selves, in our *need*, among all meanes, what doth first offer it selfe in our intention; [2]And againe, when all meanes forsake us and faile us, what is our last succour in execution.

1.

By course of nature, every thing, when it is assalted, ever rouseth that part first, wherin his principall strength lieth: if it be in his *tuskes*, them; or in his *hornes*, or whatsoever it is, that. To a *poore* man (if he have a cause in hand) there is nothing commeth to mind but GOD and *innocencie*, and the goodnesse of his cause: there is his *strength*, and that is the *Horne of his salvation*. But, the *rich* (saith *Amos*) hath *gotten him Hornes in his owne strength*; and not *iron-hornes*, as were *Zidkiah's*, but *golden hornes*, with which he is hable to push any *cause*, till he have *consumed* it. For indeed, if he be to undertake ought, the first thing that commeth to his head is, *Thus much will dispatch it*: Such a gift will assure such a man, and such a gift will stop such a mans mouth, and so it is done: *Neither is* GOD *in all his thoughts*.

Amos 6.13.

Tell me then, in your affaires, what commeth first to mind? nay, tell your selves what it is. *Aures omnium pulso* (saith *Saint Augustine*) *conscientias singulorum convenio*. Tell your selves, what it is; and by this, trie and know, wherein your *trust* is; whither this charge meet with you or no, whither your *riches* be the strength of your *confidence*.

2.
Pro. 18.11.

Now lightly, what we first thinke of, that we last flie to. It is so. *Salomon* saw it in his time and said, *The rich mans wealth is his castle*: that, even as men, when they are foiled in the *field*, and beaten from the Citie walls, flie last of all into the *Castle*, and there thinke themselves safe, as in their place of chiefe strength; So, it falleth out with the *rich of this world*, in many of their causes, when Justice and æquitie and truth, and right, and GOD, and goodmen, and a good conscience and all forsake them (and yet yield they will not, in the *pride* of a *high minde*) they know, when all other have forsaken them, their *purse* will stand to them: and thither, as to their *strongest salvation* they flie, when nothing els comforts them. So that, when they cannot in heart, say to GOD, *Thou art my hope*, their matter is so bad

A SERMON PREACHED AT SAINT MARIES HOSPITAL 53

they do say ('tis he, in *Job*) *to their Wedge of Gold*, Well yet, *thou art my confidence*. And surely, he that deviseth or pursueth an unrighteous cause, *because his hand hath strength*, that man may be arreigned of the point. As againe if any say, and say within truly *(dic, dic, sed intus dic*, saith *Augustine*) with all my *riches*, with all my friends and all the meanes I can make, I can do nothing against the truth: when a man is so *rich* that he is poore to doe evill; so *wise*, that he is a foole to do evill; so *trusteth* in his *riches*, that he dare not take an evill cause in hand, no more then the poorest commoner in the citie; I dare discharge that man the *Court* for this point. Oh beloved, thinke of these things; and secretly betwixt GOD and you, use your selves to this examination: Sure, if GOD be GOD, and if there be any truth in Him, you shall find great peace and comfort in it at the last.

Job 31.24.

Mic. 2.1.

The Reason,

Charge the rich, that they be not high-minded, nor trust &c. And, why *not high-minded?* and why *not trust?* Inclusively the reason is added in these words, because of the *uncertainty* of *riches*. It is *Paul's* reason; and it is *Salomon's* too, who knew better what belonged to *riches*, then *Paul* or any other. *Travaile not too greedily for them, bestow not all thy wisedome upon them* (saith he:) *for they have the wings of an eagle, and will take their flight of a sodein.* Such is *Saint Paul's* word heere, the very same. We behold them, we hold them, they are heer with us; let us but turne our selves aside a little, and looke for them, and they are gone. It is, as if he should say; Indeed if we could *pinion the wings of our riches*, if we could *naile them downe fast to us*, then were there some shew or shadow, why we should repose *trust* in them: but it is otherwise; they are exceeding *uncertaine*; even the *harvest of the water* much above all *trades*. Yea, I take it, the *Merchants* confesse so much, before they be aware: For, by this, he claimeth to be allowed an extraordinarie gaine, because he *ventureth* his traffique as *uncertaine*, and that he is driven to *hazard* and putt in a *venture* his *goods* continually, and many times his *person*, and (to make him a right *venturer*) many times his *soule* too. And, if they be not *uncertaine*, how commeth it then to passe, that *rich men* themselves are so *uncertaine?* that is, that they that were but the other day even a little before, of principall *credit*, within a while after, and a very short while after, their *bills* will not be taken? And if *riches* be not *uncertaine*, what need they upon a night of foule weather, any *Assurances* upon the *Exchange?* What need the *Merchants* have *securitie* one of another? What need they, to have their estates *sure*, and so *good?* such *assurances* and *conveyances*, so strong, yea more strong then the wit of man can devise, if both *riches* and *men* be not *uncertaine?* I know, they pretend the *mans mortalitie*:

The *Uncertaintie of Riches.*

Pro. 23.4,5.

Pro. 27.24.

---

9 citie] Citie F_3 16 *in marg.* Pro. 23.4,5] *LACT*; Prov. 23.5 F_1

but, they know, they meane many times, the mortalitie of his *riches* rather then himselfe; or at the least, of the one as of the other. I will be judged by themselves.

I would have you marke *Saint Paul's* manner of speech. Before, he called them, not *rich*, barely; but, with an addition, the *rich of this world*. Sure, it is thought of diverse of the best Writers both old and new (I name, of the new, *Master Calvin*; and of the old, *Saint Augustine*) that this addition is a diminution; and that it is (as it were) a *barre*, in the *armes* of all *rich men*; and that, even by that word, he meanes to enthwite them, and (as I may say) to crie them down; so, to make an entrance to his charge, that men should not be too *proud* of them. For, being *of this world*, they must needs savour of the *soile*; be as this *world* is (that is) *transitorie, fickle* and *deceitfull*. And now, he comes in with *riches* againe; and will not put it alone, but calleth it the *uncertainty of riches*. And I see, it is the *Holy Ghost's* fashion, not in this place onely, but all along the Scriptures, to speake nothing magnifically of them, as the manner of the world is to do. *Saint Paul* calleth them not *rich*, but the *rich of this world: Saint John* likewise calleth them not *goods* simply, but *this world's goods*. *Saint Paul* calleth them not *riches*, but the *uncertainty of riches*: Our Saviour Christ calleth them not *riches*, but the *deceitfullnesse of riches*. So *David*: the *plate* and *arras* and *rich furniture* of a wealthy man, calleth it of purpose, *the glory of mans house*; not *his glory*, but the glorie of *his house*; (that is *Saint Chrysostome's* note.) And *Salomon* calleth them (as they be indeed) God's *blessings of his left hand*. For, *immortalitie, æternall life*, that onely is the *blessing of His right hand*. All, to learne us, not to *boast* our selves, or *stay* our selves, or (as Christ calleth it) to *rejoice* (I say not, as He to his *Disciples*, that a few *devills*, but) *that a few mineralls be subject unto us*; but that, by our *humblenesse* of mind, *trust* in God, dealing truly with all, and mercifully with our poore brethren, we are assured, that *our names are written in the booke of life*. This then is the *uncertainty* of our *riches*; because, they are the *riches of this world* (the *world*, and they, are all within the compasse of our Text) that is, you must leave them to the *world*, they are none of yours. *Denique si vestra sint* (saith *Gregorie*) *tollite ea vobiscum*, If they be yours, why do you not take them with you, when you go? By leaving them behind you to the *world*, you confesse, they are not *yours*, but the *world's*. But, indeed, they are the *riches of this world; Hic enim acquiruntur, hic vel amittuntur, vel dimittuntur*: heere you *get* them, and heere you may *lose* them; heer you get them, and heere you must *leave* them. And in this disjunctive, you have the certainty of *riches:* the very certainty is *losing* or *leaving*, that is, *forgoing*; so, the very certainty is an *uncertainty*. Leave them, or lose them we must: *leave* them when we die, or *lose* them while we live. You must either leave them when you die, or they will leave you while you

I. John. 3.17
Matt. 13.22.

Psal. 49.16.

live, this is certaine; but, wither you, them; or, they you; this is uncertaine. *Job* tarried himselfe, his *riches* went: The *Rich mans riches* tarried, but he himselfe went. One of these shall be, we know; but which of them shall be, or when, or how, or how soone it shall be, that we know not.   Luk. 12.

Let us briefly consider this double *uncertaintie:*
1. Of our *riches staying with us* first.
2. And then, of *our staying with them.*

1. In 2. *Cor.* 11.26. when as he would glorie, he saith, *He will glorie in his infirmitie:* which when he would recount, as a principall part of it, he reckoneth, that he *had beene in perills of waters, in perills of robbers, of his owne nation, among the Gentiles, in the citie, in the wildernesse, in the sea, and amongst false brethren.* If this were *frailtie*, then (sure) *fraile* and weake are *riches.* And sure, if the *rich* will glorie, they must glorie with *Saint Paul*: for, they are in all, and in more and greater then the *Apostle* ever was. He was in perills of *water*; they in perill both of *water* and *fire*: He was in perill of *robbers*, they in perill of *Rovers by Sea*, and *Robbers by land*: He in perill of his *owne nation*; they are in perill of *our owne* nation, and *of other nations*; both removed as the *Moore* and *Spaniard*, and neere home, as the *Dunkerker*: He in perill of strangers; they, not of strangers onely, but of their *owne houshold*, their *servants* and *factours*: He in perill of the *Sea*; they, both of the tempest at the *Sea*, and the *Publican* on *land:* He in perill of the *wildernesse*, that is, of *wild beasts*; they, not onely of the wild beast called the *Sycophant*, but of the tame beast too, called the *flatterer*: He in danger of *false brethren*; and so are they in perill of certaine *false brethren* called *wilfull Bankrupts*, and of certaine other called *deceitfull Lawyers*; for the one, their *debts*; for the other, their *estates* and *deeds* can have no *certainty.*

Musculus on that place (where CHRIST willeth *Our treasure to be laid, where no mothes come*) saith, his Auditors did laugh in conceipt, at CHRIST, that frayed them with *moths*, their maids should deale with the *mothes* well enough: (Saith he) you think, he meant the seely poore *flies*: Tush you are deceived, what say you to *Tineæ urbanæ, evill Creditors*? You must needs *creditt*, you can have no *vent* for your merchandizes: and what say you to a second kind of *mothes*, called *Tineæ forenses, Westminster-Hall-mothes*? (for I trust, I may speake of the *corrupt Lawyer*, with the favour of the better sort) you must needs credit them with your *evidences* and *estates*; it is not certaine what wealth these two *mothes* do wast, and in what *uncertaintie* mens *riches* are, by their meanes.   Matt. 6.

8 2. *Cor.* 11.26] 2. *Cor.* 11.30 *LACT*;   33 merchandizes] merchandize *F*₂

These are out of *Saint Paul's* perills; he was free from these *mothes*. But many *rich men* might be brought forth in a faire day and shewed, whose substance hath by these *moathes* been fretted to peeces. Thus little certainty have we, of their *staying with us*.

2. But grant, Let it be that they were *certaine*: yet, except we our selves were sure to stay with them also, it is good as nothing. That there may be certaintie between two things (as a *man*, and his *wealth*) to continue together, they must either of them be *sure*: els, if the one faile, where is the other's assurance? Grant then, we were certaine of them, we are not certaine of our selves; and in very deed, we are no more certaine of them, then they of us. *Leases* of them we have for *sixtie yeares*; but they have no leases of us for *three houres*: If they might take *leases* of us too, it were somewhat. Now, when the *Lease* is taken, nay when the *Fee simple* is bought, and the *house*, and the *ware-house* filled, and the purse too, if GOD say but *Hâc nocte*, it dashes all. For which cause, I thinke, Saint *James* (speaking in two severall places of our *life* and our *riches*;) our *riches* he compareth to the *grasse*, of no certentie; it will either *wither*, or be *pluckt up* shortly: but this is a great certaintie in respect of that of our *life*, which he resembleth to a *vapour*, which we see now, and by and by we turne us to looke for it, and it is *vanished* away. To us then that are uncertaine of our selves, they cannot be but *riches* of *uncertaintie*.

But, let us admitt, we were sure of both these, what is it to have *riches* and not to enjoy them? And the enjoying or *riches* dependeth upon two *uncertainties* more.

1. First, a mans *uncertaintie*, which hangeth upon the *favour* of a *Prince*; which is many times wavering and uncertaine. I know not, whether I shall make you understand it, because of the want of examples in our time, by meanes of the mild and blessed governement we live in. For, a practise it hath been, and many *Records* do our *Chronicles* affoord, in the daies of some Princes of this Realme, when a man was growen to wealth, to picke holes, and make quarrells against him, and so seaze his goods into the Prince's hand; to use wealthy Citizens as *spunges*, to roule them up and downe in moisture till they be full, and then to wring all out of them againe. GOD wot, an easy matter it is, if a *Prince* stand so minded, to find matter of disgrace against a subject of some wealth; and then he might fare never a whit the better for his wealth, for fine and forfeiture whereof, rather then any fault els, the businesse it selfe was made against him. We cannot tell, what this meaneth; we may thanke the gracious government, we live under; so that,

Luk. 12.20.

James 1.11.

14 *in marg.* Luk. 12.20] *LACT*; Luk. 12 F_1

I thinke, I do scarse speake so that I am understood. But, such a thing there is, such an *uncertaintie* belonging to riches, whither we conceive it or no.

2. Againe, if the times which we live in, happen to prove *unquiet* and troublesome, then againe comes another *uncertaintie*. For, the daies being evill and dangerous, a man can have joy, and indeed no certaintie neither of *riches*. For, if there fall an invasion, or garboile into the State by forren or Civill *warre*, then (if ever) is *Job's simile* verified, that *Riches are like a Cobwebb*; that which a man shall be weaving all his life long, with great adoe and much travaile, ther comes me a souldier, a barbarous souldier, with his broome, and in the turning of a hand sweeps it cleane away. How many in our neighbour countries, during their miserie have tasted this *uncertaintie*? Great troubles are looked for, and great troubles there must be and will be, doubtlesse. The world now *knoweth his Master's will and doth it not, it must therefore* certainely *be beaten with many stripes*, with many more then the ignorant world was. And therefore this word [*of this world*] in this Text, we may with an *Emphasis* pronounce and say, Charge them that are rich in this world, *that they trust not in the uncertaintie of riches*. Job. 8.14.

There are but three things in *riches*. ¹The *possessing*, ²the *enjoying* ³and last the *conveighing* of them. Little assurance is there in the two former, and what shall we say of the *conveighance*? If our pompe cannot descend with us; well yet, if we were certaine to whom we should leave them, somewhat it were for the certainty of them. These considerations oft had in mind would loosen both our *assurance in*, and our liking of them.

What for the *conveighance*? do we not see daily that *men* make *heritages*, but GOD makes *heires*; that *many sonnes rost not that, their fathers gett in hunting*? that they that have been in chiefe accompt for their wealth, their sonnes should be driven even *to flatter the poore, and have nothing in their hands, no not bread*? that, never snow in the Sunne melted faster, then doe some mens riches as soone as they be gone? Job 20.10.

These things are in the eyes of the whole world. O Beloved, these are the judgements of GOD. Deceive not your selves with vaine words: say not in your hearts, this is the *way of the world*, some must gett and some must lose. No, no: it is not the way of the world, it is the way of GOD's *judgement*. For, to the reason of man nothing can be alledged, but that considering the infinite number of infinite *rich men* in this place, the posteritie of them these many yeares should by this time have filled the whole land, were it much bigger then it is, with their progenie, even with diverse both *Worshipfull* and *Honourable Families* from them descended: and it is well knowen it is otherwise, that there is scarse a handfull in comparison. This is not *the way of the world*, for we see diverse Houses of diverse lines remaine to this day in continuance of the same wealth and worship which they had five hundred yeares since. It is not therefore the *way* of the *world*; say not it is so; but it is a heavy *judgement* from the *Lord*. And these *uncertainties*, namely this last, came upon some of them for their *wicked* and *deceitfull getting* of them: upon some of them, for their *proud* and *riotous abusing* them: upon some of them for their *wretched* and *covetous reteining* them. And, except ye now heare this the *Lord's Charge*, looke unto it, howsoever you wrastle out with the *uncertainties* your selves; assuredly this last *uncertaintie* remaineth for your children. *The Lord's hand is not shortened.* I shall never get out of this point, if I breake not from it.

<small>Esay 59.1.</small>

There are but three fruits of all your getting ¹the *tenure*: ²the *fruition*: ³the *parting* with. See, whither the *Lord* hath not laid one *uncertaintie* on them all. ¹*Uncertaintie*, in their *tarrying with us*; and *uncertaintie*, in our tarrying *with them*. ²Uncerteintie of *enjoying*, by reason of the danger of the time; ³Uncertaintie of our *leaving them*, by reason of the danger of our children's scattering. The estate in them, the enjoying of them, the departing with them, all being *uncertaine*, so many uncertainties, might not *Saint Paul* truly say, the *uncertaintie of riches*?

There is yet one behind, worse then them all. I will add no more but that: and that is, that our *riches* and our worship they shall leave us, because they be *uncertaine*; but the *pride* of our *minds*, and the *vaine trust* in them, them we shall be certaine of, they shall not leave us. And this is *grave jugum*, a heavie miserie upon mankind: The *Goods*, the *Lordships*, the *Offices* that they gott, them they shall leave heere: the *sinne*, that they commit in getting and enjoying them, they shall not leave behind them for their hearts, but that shall cleave fast unto them. This is a *certaintie* you will say: it is indeed a certaintie of sinne, but therefore an *uncertaintie* of the soule: so doth *Job* reckon it amongst *the uncertainties* of *riches*. For, *what hope hath the hypocrite when he hath heaped up riches, if* GOD *take away his soule?* where is his hope or his trust then? Never will they shew themselves in their own kind, to be a *staffe of reed*, as then: both deceiving them *which leane on them*, and besides *going into* their soules *and piercing them*. For very sure it is, many of that calling die in great *uncertainty* this way; wishing, they had never seene that *wealth* which they have seen, that so they might not see that *sinne* which they then see. Yea some of them (I speake it of mine owne knowledge abroad) wish, they had never come further then the *shovell* and the *Spade*: crying out at the houre of death, both of the *uncertainty* of their *riches*, & of the *uncertainty* of the estate of their *soules* too.

<small>Job 27.8.</small>

<small>Esay 36.6.</small>

This point, this, is a point of speciall importance, to be spoken of by me, and to be thought of by you. I would GOD, you would take it many times (when GOD shall move you) into sad consideration. With a great affection, and no lesse great truth (said *Chrysostom*) that heaven and earth, and all the creatures in them, if they had teares, they would shedd them in great abundance, to see a great many of us, so carelesse in this point as we be. It is the hand of the LORD, and it is His gracious hand, (if we could see it) that He in this manner, maketh the world to *totter* and *reele* under us, that we might not *stay* and *rest* upon it, where *certainty* and *stedfastnesse* we shall never find; but in Him above, where onely they are to be found. For, if *riches*, being so brittle and unsteady as they be, men are so mad upon them; if GOD had setled them in any *certenty*, what would they have done? what *poore man's right*, what *widowe's copie*, or what *Orphans legacie* should have been free from us?

Well then: if *riches* be *uncertaine*, whereto shall we *trust*? If not in them, where then? It is the third point: *Charge them that be rich in this world, that they be not high-minded, neither trust in the uncertenty of riches: but that they trust in* GOD. It is the third point of the *Charge*, in generall; and the first of the *affirmative* part: and conteineth, Partly a *Homage* to be done for our riches, to GOD, and that is, *trust in Him:* and partly a rent charge layd upon our *riches*, which is *doing good*. And indeed no other then *David* had said before, *Trust in the Lord and be doing good*. The III. Point, Trust in God.

Psal. 37.5.

Saint *Paul* will batter down, and lay flat our Castle, but he will erect us another, wherein we may *trust*. Yea indeed, so as *Salomon* did before, setteth up a tower against a tower, the *Tower of the righteous, which is the Name of the* LORD, against the *Rich-man's tower*, which is as you have heard before, *his riches*. In stead of the *Worldling's* faith, which is to make *money* an article of faith; teacheth us the faith of a Christian, which is, to vouchsafe none but GOD that honour. Even so doth the Apostle heer; and that, for great reason: *Nam qui vult securus sperare, speret in Eo qui non potest perire,* He that will *trust*, and be *secure* in his trust, let him trust in *Him*, who himselfe never failed, and never faileth those, that put their trust in him: in whom is *no uncertainty*, no not so much as *any shadow of uncertainty*.

Pro. 18.10.

Jam. 1.17.

Trust in him, by looking to Him first, yer we admitt any els into our conceipt: and by looking to Him last, and not looking beyond him to any, as if we had a safer or trustier then He.

And that, because he is the *living* GOD: as if he should say, that you phansie to yourselves, to trust in, is a *dead idoll*, and not a *living* GOD; and if ever you come to any dangerous disease, you shall find, it is an *idoll*, dead in it self, not hable to give it selfe life; much lesse to another: not hable to ransome the *bodie* from the *death*, much lesse the *soule* from hers; not hable to recover life when it is gone, nay not hable to preserve life when it is present; not to remove *death*, nay not to remove *sicknesse*, not any sicknesse, not the *gout* from your feet, not the *palsie* from your hands, nay not so much as the *ache* from your *teeth*: not hable to add one haire to your head, nor one hair's bredth to your stature, nor one houre to your dayes, nor one minute to the houres of your life. This *moath-eaten God*, as our Saviour CHRIST calleth it, this *canker-eaten God*, this *God*, that must be kept under locke and key from a thiefe, *trust* not in it for shame. O let it be never said, the *living trust in the dead. Trust* in the *living* GOD, that *liveth* himselfe, nay that is *life himselfe*; in His Sonne, that was hable to *quicken himselfe*, and *is hable to quicken you*; of whose gift and inspiration you have already this life; by whose daily *spirit* and *visitation* your soule is preserved in this life, in this mortall and corruptible life; and of whose grace and mercie we looke for our other immortall and æternall life.

Who not onely liveth, but also *giveth you*, &c:] A *living* and a *giving God*; that is, that *liveth*, and that *giveth*; of whose *gift* you have not onely your life and terme of yeares, but even also your *riches* themselves; the very hornes that you lift so high, and wherwith unnaturally many times you push against Him that gave them. *He giveth* for the *earth* was the *Lord's and all that therein is*; till *the earth he gave unto the children of men*: And *silver* and *Gold* were the *Lord's*, till, not by a casuall *scattering*, but by his appointed *giving*; not by *chance*, but by *gift*, He made them thine. He *gave* them: *thou broughtest none of them with thee into the world, thou camest naked*. He *gave* them; and when He gave them, He might have given them to thy brother of low estate, and made thee stand and ask at his door, as He hath made him now stand and ask at thine. He *giveth* you *riches*; you *get* them not; it is not your own wisdome or travaile that getteth them, but His grace and goodnesse that *giveth* them. For, you see many men of as great understanding and foresight as yourselves, want not onely *riches*, but even *bread*. It is not your travaile; *except the Lord had given them, all the early up-rising, and late downe-lying had been in vaine*. It is GOD that *giveth*: make your recognisance it is so, for feare lest if you denie *Dominus dedit*, you come to affirme *Dominus abstulit*. GOD teacheth, it was He that *gave* them, by *taking* them away.

This is *Saint Paul's* reason: let us see how it serves his conclusion to the overthrow of our vaine *pride* and foolish *trust* in them. If it be *gift, Si accepisti quid gloriaris?* be not *proud* of it: And if it be *gift*, He that sent it, can call for it again; *trust* not in it.

Who giveth us all things &c] *All things*, spirituall or corporall, temporall or æternall, little or great, from the least and so upward; from the greatest and so downward: from *panem quotidianum*, a morsell of bread, to *Regnum cælorum*, the Kingdome of heaven. He giveth us all even unto Himselfe: yea He *giveth us himselfe* and all, and more we cannot desire.

Why then, if He give all, all are *Donatives*; all that we hold, we hold in *franck almoigne*; and no other tenure is there, at GOD's hands, or in our *Law*.

Psal. 24.1.
115.16.
Ag. 2.9.

Eccl. 9.11.

Job 1.21.

1. Cor. 4.7.

For, *quid habes quod non accepisti?* What is there: that is to say, name one 1. Cor. 4.7.
thing, thou hast, that thou hast not *received*; and if there be any one thing,
boast of that and spare not. But if that be nothing, then let *Cyprian's*
sentence take place (so much commended and so often cited by *Saint*
Augustine) *De nullo gloriandum est, quia nullum est nostrum*: and add unto
it, *De nullo fidendum est, quia nullum est nostrum:* we must *glorie* of nothing,
for that we have nothing *of our owne*; neither must we *trust* any thing, for
that we have *nothing of our owne*.

That giveth us all things to enjoy:] Not onely to *have*, but to *enjoy*. For, so
to have them, that we have no *joy* of them; so to get all things, that we can
take no part of them, when we have gotten them; so to possesse the labours
of our hands, that we cannot eat the labours of our hands, as good be
without them: *This is a great vanitie and vexation*; and indeed (as *Salomon* Eccles. 6.2,3.
saith) *an untimely birth* were *better*, then so to be. But blessed be *God*, that
besides these *blessings* to be *enjoyed*, giveth us *healthful bodies* to enjoy them
with, the *favor* of our *Prince* to enjoy them under, the dayes of *peace* to enjoy
them in; whereby our soules may be satisfied with good things, and every
one may eat his portion with joy of heart.

That giveth all things to enjoy:] that is, dealeth not with you as he hath
dealt with the *poore*; hath given you things not onely of *use* and *necessitie*, but
things also of *fruition* and *pleasure*: hath given you not onely *Manna* for your
need, but also *Quailes for your lust*: Hath given you out of *Ophir* not onely Psal. 78.29.
linnen cloth, and *Horses* for service, but also, *Apes, Ivorie*, and *Peacockes*, for
your delight. Unto them he giveth *indumenta*, covering for their naked-
nesse; but unto you *ornamenta*, clothing for your comlinesse. Unto them he
giveth *alimenta*, nourishment for their emptinesse; unto you *delectamenta*,
delicious fare for daintinesse. Therfore you above all men, are to rejoyce in
Him, there is great cause: that he may rejoyce over you, unto whom He
hath given so many wayes, so great cause of rejoycing.

That giveth us all things to enjoy plenteously:] *Plenteously*, indeed, *may* Psal. 147.20.
Israël now say, (said the Prophet;) may *England* now say (say I) and I am
sure upon as great cause. *He hath not dealt so with every Nation*, nay He hath
not dealt so with *any Nation*. And *plenteously* may *England now say*; for it
could not alwayes: Nay it could not ever have said the like. *Plenteously*
indeed, for He hath not *sprinkled*, but *powred* His benefitts upon us. Not
onely *Blessed be the People whose God is the Lord* (that blessing which is Psal. 144.15.
highly to be esteemed, if we had none besides it,) but *Blessed be the People* *Ibid.*
that are in such a case. That *blessing* He hath given us, *all things to enjoy*
plenteously; we cannot, nay our enemies cannot but confesse it. O that our
thankfulnesse to Him, and our bounty to Him, might be as *plenteous*, as His
gifts and goodnesse have beene *plenteous* to us!

To move us from the two evills before, the *Apostle* used their *uncertaintie*, which is a reason from *Law* and the course thereof. So he might now have told us, if we *trusted* not *in God*, we should have the table turned, and his *giving* changed to *taking away*; and *all things*, into *want of many things*, and having nothing neer all; our *plenty* into *penurie*; and our *enjoying more then we need*, into *no more then needs*, nor so much neither. Thus he might have dealt: but He is now in a point of *Ghospell*, and therefore taketh his perswasion from thence. For, this indeed, is the *Evangelicall argument* of *God's* goodnesse; and there is no goodnesse to that, which the consideration of *God's* goodnesse worketh in us.

The arguement is forcible; and so forcible, as that choose whither this will move us or no: Sure, if this will not prevaile with us, we shall not need *Moses* nor CHRIST, to sit and give sentence upon us; the Devill himself will do it. For, as wicked as he is, and as wretched a *spirit*, yet thus he reasoneth upon *Job: Doth Job feare Thee for nought?* As if he should say: seeing thou hast dealt so *plenteously*, yea so bounteously with him, if he should not serve thee, if he should so farre forget himselfe, it were a fault past all excuse, a fault well worthy to be condemned. A bad fault it must be, that the *Devill* doth abhorre: yet so bad a fault it is (you see) that the Devill doth abhorr it. When men receive blessings *plenteously* from *God*, and returne not their *homage* back againe, *unthankfull rich men* shall need no other judge but the *Devill*, and then, as you see, they are sure to be condemned. For, if *God* will not do it, the *Devill* will.

Let me then recommend this third part of the *Charge* to your carefull remembrance and regard. It concerneth your *homage*, which is your *trust in him*, that you *trust in him* with your service of body and soule, who hath trusted you with his plenty and store, and hath made you in that estate, that you are trusted with matters of high importance both at home and abroad. For, it is the argument of all arguments to the true Christian, because GOD hath given him (saith Saint *James*) without *exprobation*; and given *all things*, without *exception* of any; and that *to enjoy which is more then competencie; and that* plenteously, which is more then sufficiencie; therefore, even therefore, to *trust in Him* onely. If ther be in us the hearts of true *Christians*, this will shew it; for it will move us: and so let it I beseech you. Let us not, as men under the *Law*, be tired with the *uncertainty* of the creatures; but as men under *grace*, have our hearts broken with the goodnesse of our GOD. In that GOD to place our *trust*, who beyond all our deserts *giveth*: if we respect the quantitie, *all things*; if the manner, very *plenteously*; if the end, to *joy* in

Job 1.9.

Jam. 1.5.

37 deserts] desires F_3

them; yet so, that our joy and repose end in Him: a very blessed and heavenly condition.

Trust in the Lord and *be doing good*, said *David*: Saint *Paul* saith the same, *Charge the rich of this world, that they do good.* The last was a very plausible point, which we have dwelt in with great delight. What? *the plentie of all things*; that we *enjoy*, and long may *enjoy* I beseech GOD: who is not mooved with *joy* to heare it reported?

But little know they, what a consequent Saint *Paul* will inferr upon this antecedent. For, thus doth *Paul* argue. GOD hath done good to you by *giving you*; you also are bound to do good to others, by *giving them*. If he hath given you *all things*, you ought to part with something: (and the more you part with, the liker ye become to Him, that *giveth all things*.) If he have given you to *enjoy*, you ought to receive others into the fellowship of the same *joy*: and not to think, that *to do others good*, is *to do your selves hurt*. If *plenteously* He have given you, you ought to be plenteous in giving; and, not when the *Lord* hath the *Epha* great, wherein He hath mete to you, to make your *Hin* small, whereby you measure to the *poore*, turning the plentie of heaven into the scarsitie of earth.

Thus doth the *Apostle* fetch the matter about, and thus doth he inferre your *doing good* to these little lambes and such like, out of GOD's *doing good* unto you.

And that which he inferreth, he doth exceeding fitly and sheweth great art and learning in it. For, speaking of *enjoying* (his very last word) he is carried in a very good zeale and affection to the *rich* of this world, to desire of GOD, and to entreat of them that they may not have onely πρόσκαιρον ἀπόλαυσιν of them (that is) *enjoy them for a season*, (we cannot tell well which) but from everlasting to everlasting: And that is, by *doing good*. So *enjoy* that we may *do good* too.

To say truth: *Saint Paul* could not better devise, then heere to place it. For, our too much *enjoying* eateth up our *well doing*, cleane. Our too much lashing on in *doing our selves good*, maketh that we can *do good* to none but *our selves*. Our present *enjoying* destroyeth our *well doing* utterly, and consequently the *æternall enjoying* we should have of our *riches*. As *Pharo's leane kine devoured the fatt, and it was not seene on them*, so doth (saith *Basil*) our ἐφ' ἃ μὴ δεῖ, our riotous *mispending* (where we should not) eat up our ἐφ' ἃ δεῖ, our *Christian bestowing* where we should: and a man cannot tell, what is become of it. Very well and wisely said that Father, Ἀκόνη γὰρ τῆς ἀσωτίας ἡ φιλοτιμία, *Pride is prodigalitie's whetstone*, and it setts such an *edge* upon it, in our *enjoying*, that it cutts so deepe into our wealth;

The IIII. Part.
That they do good.
Psal. 37.3.

Heb. 11.25

Gen. 41.4.

34 up our] F_2; up out F_1

and shares so much for our vaine and riotous *enjoying*, that it leaves but little for our *well-doing*.

Looke how the *trust in* GOD, and the *trust in riches* are sett one against another, heere by the *Apostle*; so are our *high minds*, and our *doing good*. One would not thinke it at the first, but (sure) so it is; we must have *lower minds* and lesse *pride*, if we will have more *good works* and greater plenty of *well-doing*. You may therefore *enjoy* your wealth, that is true: but you must also take this with you, you must *do good* with it, and learne of the *Apostle*, there be two uses of your *riches*, and that therefore GOD hath given them, ¹*To enjoy*, ²*To do good*: not, to *enjoy* only; but, to *enjoy* and to *do good*.

Enjoying, is *doing good*: But, not to our selves onely; but, by *doing good*, heere, *Saint Paul* meaneth, to do it to others, that they may be the better for us. The very same two doth *Salomon* in very fitt termes sett downe: that *Water is given into* our *cisterne*, ¹*that we may drinke of it our selves*, ²*that our fountaines may flow out*, and they that dwell about us fare the better for them. The very same two doth a *greater then Salomon*, our SAVIOUR himselfe compt of too: for, of his purse, we read He had these two uses, to *buy that He had need of himself*, and *to give something to the poore*. It is good reason, that man consisting of two parts, the *soule* and *body*, the *body* only should not take up all; but, the *soule* should be remembred too. *Enjoying* is the bodie's part; and *well-doing* is the soule's: your soules are suiters to you to remember them, that is, to remember *well-doing*, which is the soule's portion.

Remember this second: the other (I doubt not) but you will remember fast enough. This was the use of our SAVIOUR CHRIST'*s* purse, and if yours be like His, this must be the use of yours also. For surely, it is greatly to be feared, that many *rich* at this day, know not both these: indeed know no other use of their wealth then an *Oxe* or an *Asse*, or other brute beasts would know; to have their *crib* well served, sweet and cleane *provender* of the best in the *manger*, and their *furniture* and *trappings* fitt and of the finest fashion: No other, then the *Glutton* did, to go in *soft linen* and *rich silke* and to *fare decliciously every day*. Or then the other, his pew-fellow that professed, it was all the use he compted of; and therefore we see he saith to his soule, *Eat thy fill (soule)* and *drink thy fill*; fill and *fatt thy selfe*, and enjoy this life; never looke to enjoy any other.

We must learne one use more, one more out of our *charge*, and consequently. When we looke upon our sealed summes, our heapes of treasure, and continuall commings in, thus to thinke with our selves: This that I see heere, hath GOD *given* me *to enjoy*, but not onely for that, but, to *do good*

Pro. 5.15.

Matt. 12.42.
Joh. 13.29.

Luk. 16.19.

Luk. 12.19.

33 compted] counted F_2

with, also. The former use of my *riches* I have had long and daily still have, but what have I done in the other? The *rich men* in the *Gospel*, they had the same; they did *enjoy* theirs; but now (it is sure) little joy they have of them: why? for want of this other. *Abraham* he did both; he *enjoyed* his *riches* heere, and now another, an *æternall joy* of them. Yea he received *Lazarus* into his bosome. Why? he received him into his bosome, and cherished him, and *did good* heere on earth. And so did *Job*, and so did *Zachæus*. Now good *Lord*, so give me grace, so to *enjoy* heere, that I lose not my endlesse joy in thy heavenly kingdome. Let me follow their stepps in my life, with whom I wish my soule after death. These things are good and profitable for the *rich*, oft to thinke on.

Well then, if to *do good* be a part of the *Charge*, what is it to *do good?* It is a *positive* thing (*good;*) not a *privative*, to do *no harme*. Yet, as the world goeth now, we are faine so to commend men; He is an honest man, *he doth no hurt*: of which praise any wicked man, that keepes himselfe to himselfe, may be partaker. But, it is to doe some *good thing*: what *good thing?* I will not answer, as in the *Schooles*; I feare, I should not be understood; I will go grossely to worke. These that you see heere before your eyes, to do them good, to part with that, that may do them good; use the goods that you have, to do but that, which sundry that have heertofore occupied those roomes where you now sitt (whose *remembrance* is therefore *in blessing* upon earth, and whose *names* are in the *booke of life* in heaven) have done before you in diverse *workes* of *charitie*, to to the maintenance of the *Church*, the benefit of *Learning*, and the reliefe of the *Poore* of the land. This is to *do good*. This, I trust, you understand.

This know; that GOD hath not given sight to the eye, to *enjoy*, but to *lighten* the members; nor *wisedome* to the *honourable* man, but for us men of simple shallow forecast; nor *learning* to the *divine* but for the ignorant: so, neither *riches* to the *wealthy*, but for those that want reliefe. Thinke you *Timothee* hath his *depositum*, and we ours, and you have none? it is sure, you have. We, ours, in inward graces and *treasures* of *knowledge*: You yours, in outward blessings and *treasures* of *wealth*. But, both are *deposita*, and we both are *feoffees of trust*. I see, there is a strange hatred, and a bitter gainsaying every where stirred up against *unpreaching Prelates* (as you terme them) and Pastors that feed themselves onely; and they are well worthy: If I might see the same hatred begoon among your selves, I would thinke it sincere. But, that, I cannot see. For, that which a slothfull *Divine* is, in things spirituall; that is, a *Rich man for himselfe and no body els*, in things carnall, and they are not pointed at. But sure, you have your harvest as well, as we ours; and that a great harvest. Lift up your eyes and see the streets round about you, *the harvest is verily great and the Labourers few*: Let

Matt. 9.37.

us pray (both) that the *Lord* would thrust out *Labourers* into both these *harvests*, that the treasures of *knowledge* being opened, they may have the *bread* of *æternall life*: and the treasures of *well-doing* being opened, they may have the *bread* of *this life*, and so they may want neither.

I will tell you it, another as easie a way: *Saint Augustine* making it plaine to his auditorie (somewhat backward as it should seeme) was faine to tell them thus, thus to define *doing good: Quod non vultis facere, hoc bonum est.* (said he:) that that you will not doe, that that I cannot get you to do, that is to *doe good*. Shall I say so to you? No indeed, I will not; *I hope better things*, and partly I know them. But, this I will say: that which the *Papists* with open mouth, in all their books, to the slander of the *Gospell*; that which they say, you doe not; nay, you will not doe; that is, to *doe good*.

One of them saith, that our Religion hath comforted your force *attractive* so much, and made it so strong, that nothing can be wroong from you. Another, he saith, that our Religion hath brought an hardnesse into the bowells of our *Professors*, that they pitie little, and the cramp or *chiragra* into their hands, that they *give* lesse. Another, that our preaching hath bredd you minds full of *Salomon's* horseleches, that cry *bring in, bring in* and nothing els. All of them say, that your good workes come so from you, as if indeed your religion were, to be saved *by faith onely*. Thus through you, and through want of your doing good, the *Gospell of* CHRIST *is evill spoken of among them that are without*. They say, we call not to you for them: that we preach not this point, that we leave them out of our *Charges. Libero animam meam*, I deliver heere mine owne soule: I do now call for them; I have done it else where yer now. Heere, I call for them now, I take witnesse, I call you to record, I call heaven to record, *Domine scis quia dixi, scis quia locutus sum scis quia clamavi: Lord*, thou knowest, I have *spoken* for them, I have *called* for them, I have *cried* for them, I have made them a part of my *charge*, and the most earnest and vehement part of my *charge*, even the *charge* of *doing good*.

Unto you therfore that be *rich* be it spoken; heare your *charge* I pray you. There is no avoiding, you must needs *seale* this fruit of *well-doing*, you must needs do it. For, having *wealth* and wherewithall to *do good*, if you do it not;

1. Imprimis, talke not of *faith*, for you have no faith in you; if you have wherewith to *shew* it, and shew it not, *Saint James* saith, you have none to shew. Nor, tell me not of your *religion*, there is no *religion* in you: *Pure religion is this*: (as to very good purpose was shewed yesterday) *To visite the fatherlesse & widowes*: and you never learned other religion of us.

Jam. 1.27.

34 Imprimis] F_3; Inprimis F_1, F_2

Secondly, if you do it not, I warne you of it, now; you shall then find it, when you shall never be hable to answer the exacting of this *charge*, in the great Day: where, the question shall not be of the *highnesse* or lownesse of your *mindes*, nor of your *trust* and confidence, or any other vertues, though they be excellent, but of your *feeding, clothing, visiting, harbouring, succouring*, and in a word, of your *well-doing* onely. This I say to you; beare witnesse I say it.

Now to Them, in your just defense I say: (for, GOD forbidd, but while I live, I should alway defend this Honourable Citie in all truth:) to them whom the mist of envie hath so blinded, that they can see no good at all done, but by themselves. I forbidd them, the best of them, to shew me in *Rhemes* or in *Rome* or any popish Citie Christen, such a shew, as we have seene heer these two daies. Today, but a handfull of the heape, but Yesterday and on Moonday, the whole heape; even a mightie armie of so many *good workes* as there were relieved *Orphans*, and the *Chariotts* of this Citie, I doubt not, and the *horsemen* thereof.

They will say, it is but one; so they say: Be it so, yet it is a matchlesse one. I will go further with them; Spoken be it to GOD's glorie *Non nobis Domine non nobis, sed Nomini Tuo da gloriam. Not unto us, not unto us O Lord, but unto Thy Name give the praise, for thy loving mercie and for thy truthes sake which we professe.* I will be able to prove, that *Learning*, in the foundation of *Schooles* and encrease of revenues within *Colledges*; and the *Poore*, in foundation of *Almes-houses*, and encrease of perpetuities to them, have received greater helpe in this Realme within these *forty yeares* last past, since (not, the starting up of our Church, as they fondly use to speake, but since) the reforming ours from the error of theirs, then it hath, I say, in any realme Christen, not onely within the selfe same *fortie yeares* (which were enough to stop their mouthes) but also then it hath in any *fortie yeares* upward, during all the time of *Poperie*: which I speake, partly of mine owne knowledge, and partly by sufficient grave information to this behalfe. This may be said and said truly.

And when we have said this, what great thing have we said? that, time for time, so many yeares for so many; *thirtie yeares* of *light* have made comparison with *thirtie yeares* of *trouble*. But, this is not as we would have it: We would have it out of all comparison. This, that hath been said, is strange to them (I know) and more, then they reckoned of. But I would have you in these times of peace and truth, so farre beyond them, as that you might φιμοῦν *snaffle* them in this. So, that they durst not once offer to enter into

2.

2. King. 2.12.

Psal. 115.1.

1. Pet. 2.15.

15 in marg. 2. King. 2.12] 2 Kings 13.14 *LACT*   20 *thy loving* F_2; *the loving* F_1

this theme with us, or once to mention it more. So it should be, I am sure; so the *Gospel* deserves to have it.

You have the *substance* of that you must do, to *do good*. Now heer is the quantitie: *Be rich in good workes*: that seeing you are *rich* indeed, you would not be poore men but *rich in good works*.

Good works (*Saint Paul* saith) not *good words*. *Good*, with the goodnesse of the *hand*, not with the goodnesse of the *tongue*, and tongue onely; as many now are, (well therefore resembled to the tree that *Plinie* speaketh of, the *leaves* of it as broad as any *targett*, but the *fruict* is no bigger then a *bean*:) to *talke targetts*, and to *do beanes*. It were better reversed, if we were (as Saint *Paul* saith) *perfect in all good workes*, then perfect in certaine curious and *queint termes*, and *sett phrases*, wherein a great part of many men's religions do now adayes consist: plaine speech and sound dealing; plaine speech and *good works*, best.

And *rich in them*. The *Rich man* in the *Gospell*, would (as he said) *build his barnes bigger* to put in them πάντα ἀγαθὰ, *all his goods he had*: no good out of his *barne*. Yes yes, some in *good workes* too. *Saint Paul* hath heere within the compasse of this Text two *rich men*; his desire is, they may both meet together in every *rich* man. *Rich*, ἐν τῷ νῦν αἰῶνι in the world that now is; so, ye are: *Rich*, in the world that shalbe after this; be that too. *Rich* in *cofer*; so ye are: *Rich* in *conscience*; be so too. Your *consciences* you shall cary with you: your *cofers* you shall not. Thus you are valued in the *Queene's bookes*: what are you in GOD's bookes? So much worth in this land of the *dying*: how much worth in the *land of the living*? Saint *Paul's* advise is, that you strive for both: which you shalbe, if ye be *rich in good workes*. The true *riches* are the *riches* of *His glorious enheritance*. They be the true *riches*, which except a man can assure himselfe of, after the lease of his life is out, he shalbe in a mervailous poor case, as was the *Rich man*; and begg of *Lazarus* there, that begged of him heer. Those *riches* must be thought of, mary then you must be *rich in good workes*. Not to give something, to sombody, at some time: Why? Who doth not so? That is not to be *rich*. To give φειδομένως, *sparingly*; a peece of bread, or a draught of drink, and that onely; that belongeth to him whom GOD hath *sparingly* blessed, to the brother of low estate: it is not your worke.

In the *Law*, to the building of the *Tabernacle*, the poore gave *Goate's haire*, and *Badger's skinns*; that was for them, and that was accepted: the rich they gave *purple, gold* and *Jewells* to the *Tabernacle*; they were *rich in good works*. And in the *Gospell, to whom much is given, of him* proportionally *much shalbe required*: That is, in a word, as you are sessed in the *Queene's bookes*,

11 in marg. 2. Tim. 3.17] *LACT*; 2 Tim. 3.16 F₁

so are you in GOD's *bookes*, each one according to his abilitie. And GOD will looke, that according to that sessement they should be done: that you should περισσεῦσαι abound in *good works*, as you do in *wealth*, that you should προίστασθαι *Go before* and *sit highest*, and have a *precedence* in *works*, as you have in your *places*. And in a word, that you should be Lords, Knights, Aldermen, Masters, Wardens, and of the *Livery* in *good works*, as you be in your severall *Wards* and *Companies*. And indeed to say the truth, to commit so many sinnes, as no *Auditor* can number them, and to affoord so few *good workes*, as a child may tell them: to receive such *profitts* as great compt-bookes will not hold them; and to yeeld so small of *good workes*, as a little paper not so broad as my hand may conteine them: To lash out at a *banquet*, you know what; and to cast to a *Captive's redemption* all the world knowes what: To cast your *pride* with pounds, and your *good works* with *pense*; what cohærence is there in these? This is not to be *rich*: But that, is a part of the *charge* too. I pray you remember it; Remember to be *rich*: not onely to *do good*, but to be *rich in doing good*. That, will make you in case well to die, as now (GOD be thanked) you are well to live.

Col. 1.10.
2. Cor. 9.8.

And with the *quantitie*, take the *qualitie* too, I pray you; for the quantitie, *richly*; for the qualitie, *readily*. Ἐξ ἀνάγκης, *with compulsion*, not *willingly*; and ἐκ λύπης, *with grudging*, not *cheerfully*, these are the faults contrary to this vertue. GOD must have it done with a facilitie, with a *readinesse*, *easily*. And good reason, *easily*; for easily you may. We that want, cannot without difficultie; we would and we cannot: we have a heart without a hand: though we be willing, nothing is done; why? we are not hable. You are well hable (GOD be thanked) if you be well willing, there is no more to do; it is done. This *readinesse* is a necessary vertue in our dayes: where, yer a *benefitt* come (nay many times, yer a *debt*) so much ingenuitie is spent, so many *Rogo's* such a *Vade & redi*, go and come such a time; such a *dauncing on the threshold*, such a *failing of the eyes*, yer it can be seene; such a cleaving to the fingers, yet it will come off, such instillation by now a dropp and then a dropp: as to a liberall nature, when it commeth, it is like to bread full of gravell; for hunger a man must needs have it, and but for needs must, a man, had as leef be without it. O beloved, marr not all you do before GOD and man for want of this one thing. You love a faire seed-time, all of you: *Hilaris datio, serena satio*; cheerfull giving is like a faire *seed-time*. As you, for your seed, to burie it, wish a seasonable time; so and no lesse GOD desireth for His; that His *seed* may not be sowen with an *overcast mind*, but with gladnesse of heart and *cheerfulnesse of countenance*. Even as He doth

3. The *Qualitie:* Ready to distribute.

Pro. 3.28.

10 compt-bookes] count-bookes F_2 30 off] F_2; of F_1 38 gladnesse]thegladnesse F_2

himselfe; who what He bestoweth, bestoweth so, as He taketh as much, yea more delight in *giving*, then we in *receiving*. So do, and then this *Charge* is at an end: *Be ready to communicate.*

There is of this word, some difference among Writers; but such, as you may easily reconcile. Some think, the *Apostle* would have rich men to be εὐπροσόδους, easie to be spoken with, and to be spoken to. Some, that he would not onely have them *give readily*, but *lend freely*, and not practise the *Devill's Alchimistry* (as they do) by *multiplication* in *lending*. Some, that they should not think their beneficence to be a *taking from* them without *receiving back*, inasmuch as there is an entercourse of the giver's grace, and the receiver's praier. Some, that his mind is, that they should not do good to some few, but even to a *multitude*. All are good and godly, and agreeable to the *analogie of faith*: and you by doing all, may verifie and agree all, and make of a discord in opinions, an harmonie in practise. Saint *Heirome* (me thinketh) saith best, that *Communicare est communitati dare, aut ad aliquid commune*, to be beneficiall to a *Societie*, or to bestow to some *common use*.

2. Cor. 4.15.

This is the perfection or pitch of *well doing*, that *most plenteous grace by the thanksgiving of many, may redound to the glorie of God*. The *Apostle* therefore is a further suitor to you that be *rich*, and will not end his *Charge*, till he hath laid this on you too, to do good to *Societies* and *Foundations*, either necessarie to be erected, or more then necessarie to be maintained, lest through *our evill doing*, our father's *well doing* perish. It is not for every man to reach unto them; there is no hope to have them upholden but by you: that you would therefore have them in remembrance, and thinke upon them to do them *good*.

But alas, what hope is there to heare, that *good* wilbe this way done, since it is thought, that many may be endicted for seeking to eat up *Companies*, and to convert that which was the good and making of many, into their owne *singulare commodo*, by *out-buying* and *out-bidding* all besides themselves, that they alone may appropriate civil livings, turne common into private, the whole bodie's nourishment into one forgrowen member, and in the end *dwell alone upon the earth*.

Jer. 49.31.

That the world is toward an end, other men may be perswaded by other reasons; none more effectuall to perswade me, then this one, that every man doeth what in him lieth to *discommon communities*, and to bring all to the first privation. For the world being it selfe a maine *Society*; these men, by dismembring *under-societies*, seeke and do what they can to dissolve the whole. So that GOD must needs come to make an end of the world, or els, if this hold on, we should shortly make an end of it our selves.

29 *commodo*] F_2; *commodum* F_1

It is further complained, that whereas there hath been and is given charitably to the poore and their maintenance, that the *poore* themselves want, and they that have the *receiving* of the profitts doe yet encrease mightily, Had not these things need to be put in the *Charge?* Are they not in the eares of the *Lord?* Is it not a *sinne crying to* heaven? *Shall he not visit for these things?* for this discredit of His *Gospell*, for this unexcusable, unfaithfull dealing, in the eares of *Jew* and *Gentile*, of *Turke* and *Christian*, of God and *man?* I beseech you still, *suffer the words of exhortation:* it is good for you to know, what things are said abroad. For my part, in God's presence I protest, I know none; and if there be none, present none. It is that I desire; the *charge* is now given, may be given in vaine.

Now, if you enquire, to whom your *doing good* should stretch it selfe? Saint *Paul* himselfe will tell you. To them that instruct you, they are to [a]*communicate with you in all your goods*, that is, the *Church*: and to the necessitie of the Saints, or to the [b]*Saints that be in necessitie*, that is, to the *Poore*.
[1] *To the Church.*
a Gal. 6.6.
b Rom. 12.13.

The Church first: [c]*For this end*, came *Ester* to the *Kingdome*, and [d]*Nehemiah* to his *great favour with the Prince*, even to do good to the Church: And for this end hath [e]*Tyrus* that *rich Citie*, that abundance bestowed on her, even to be a *covering Cherub* to the *Church* of God, and to *stretch her wings over it*. The *Prophet's* meaning was, that *rich men* must be a shadow of maintenance and defense to the *Arke*, to *Divinitie*, their *riches* must serve them as *wings* to that end; they must be *covering Cherubs* on earth to the *Church militant*, if ever they wilbe *singing Cherubs* in heaven with the *Church triumphant*.
c Est. 4.14.
d Neh. 1.11.
e Ezek. 28.14.

And much good might be done, and is not, in this behalfe: and that many wayes. I will name but one, that is, that with their *wings* stretched out, they would keep the filth and pollution of the sinne of sinnes (whereof you heard so bitter complaint both these dayes) of *Simonie* and *Sacriledge*, from falling on the *Arke*, and corrupting and putrifying it, which it hath almost already done. That seeing the *Pope* do that he doth (howsoever some have alledged the Papist's great detestation of this sinne, and of us for this sinne, for a motive; it is all but dissembling, their hand is as deep in this sinn as any man's:) I say, seeing the *Pope* doth as he doth, that is, as he hath dispensed with the *oath* and *duety* of *Subjects* to their *Prince*, against the *fift Commandement*: with the *murder*, both *violent* with *daggs*, and *secret* with *poyson* of the Sacred Persons of *Princes*, against the *sixt*: with the uncleannesse of the *stewes*, and with *incestuous marriages*, against the *seventh*: So, now of late, with the abomination of *Simonie*, against the *eighth*; having lately (as it is knowne by the voluntarie confession of their owne Priests) by speciall and expresse warrant of the See Apostolique sent hither into this Land his

Licence dispensative to all *Patrons of his marke* to set up *Simonie*, and to mart & make sale of all *Spirituall livings* which they have or can get, to the uttermost penny, even (if it were possible) by the sound of the *drumme*; and that with a very cleare conscience (so that some portion therof be sent over to the relief of his *Seminaries*, which by such honest meanes as this, come to be now maintained.) Seeing thus do the *Papists*, and we (loth to be behind them in this gain of bloud) make such merchandise with this sinne, of the poore Church and her patrimonie, as all the world crieth shame of it: To redeeme the orderly disposing them to the *Churche's* good, were a speciall way for you *rich men* to *do good* in these dayes. Neither as these times are, do I know a better service, nor which (I am perswaded) will please GOD better, then this, or be better accepted at His hands.

This for the *Church*: you must have a wing stretched abroad to cover it. And for the *poore*, you must have a bosome wide open to receive them. *Lazarus* in a *rich man's bosome*, is a goodly sight in heaven; and no lesse goodly in earth. And there shalbe never a *rich man* with *Lazarus* in his bosome, in heaven, unlesse he have had a *Lazarus* in his bosome heer on earth.

[²To the Poore.]

[Joh. 12.8.] The poore are of two sorts: Such as *shalbe with us alwayes* (as CHRIST saith) to whom we must do good by relieving them: such is the comfortlesse estate of *poore Captives*; the succorlesse estate of poore *Orphanes*; the desolate estate of the poore *Widowes*; the distressed estate of poore *Strangers*; the discontented estate of poore *Scholars*: all which must be suffered and succoured too.

There are others, such as should not be suffered to be in *Israël*, whereof *Israël* is full: I meane, *beggers*, and *vagabonds*, able to worke; to whom *good* must be done, by not suffering them to be as they are, but to employ them in such sort, as they may do good. This is a *good deed* no doubt; and there being, as I heare, an honourable good purpose in hand for the redresse of it, GOD send it good successe. I am as one, in part of my *charge*, to exhort you by all good meanes to helpe and further it.

Me thinketh it is strange, that the exiled Churches of *Strangers* which are harboured heer with us, should be hable in this kind to do such good, as not one of their poor is seene to aske about the streets; and this Citie, the harborer and maintainer of them, should not be able to do the same good. Hable it is no doubt, but men would have *doing good* too good cheape. I know, the charges will be great: but, it will quitt the charges, the *good* done will be so *great*. Great good to their *bodies*, in redeeming them from diverse corrupt and noysome *diseases*, and this Citie from danger of infection. Great good to their *soules*, in redeeming them from *idlenesse*, and the fruit of idlenesse, which is all naughtinesse, no where so rife as among them; and this Citie from much *pilfering*, and losse that way. Great good to the *Common-wealth*, in redeeming unto it many rotten members, and making them men of service, which may heereafter do good in it, to the publique benefit, and redeeme this Citie from the blood of many soules which perish in it for want of good order. Last of all, great good to the whole *Estate*, in bringing the blessing of GOD upon it; even that blessing, that there shall not be *a begger in all Israël*. So much for *doing good*. Deut. 15.4.

Laying up in store, &c.] That is, your worke shall not be in vaine in the end, but receive a recompense of reward: which is a prerogative, the which GOD's *Charges* have above all other. In mans, there is death to the Offender; but if any have kept his charge, he may claime nothing but that, he hath. Onely the *Lord's Charges* are *rewarded*. The last point: The *Reason*.

So that, besides the two reasons which may be drawn out of the former, ¹one of the *uncertaintie*, ²the other of GOD's *bounty*: 1. Of the *Uncertainty*, *Da quod non potes retinere:* That we would part with that, that we cannot keepe long; that we must part with yer long, whither we will or no: 2. Of the *Bounty* of GOD, *De meo peto, dicit* CHRISTUS; That GOD which gave, asketh but his owne; but of that, He gave us, a part to be given Him, and we (if there be in us, the heart of *David*) will say, *quod de manu tuâ accepimus*. 3. Besides these, a third; Though GOD might justly challenge a *free gift* without any hope of receiving againe, He will not; but tells us, His meaning is, not to empoverish or undoe us, but to receive these, which he gave us and came from him every one, and those that within a while forgoe we must, to give us that, we shall never forgoe. That is that, he teacheth us: commandeth not our losse, but commendeth to us a way to *lay up for our selves*, if we could see it; not, to leese and leave all, we know not to whom. 1. Chro. 29.14.

Well said *Augustine*, preaching on these very words: At the very hearing these words [*Part with* and *distribute*] the covetous man shrinkes in himselfe; at the very sound of *parting with*; as if one should poure a bason of cold water upon him, so doth he chill and draw himselfe together, and say *Non perdo*: he saith not, I will not *part with*, but, I will not *lose*; for he counteth all *parting with* to be *losing*. And will ye not *lose* saith *Saint Augustine*? yet, use the matter how you can, *lose* you shall: for, when you can cary nothing away of all you have, do you not lose it? But, goe to (saith he) be not troubled, hear what followes, shut not they heart against it.

Laying up for your selves.] I know, *Judas* was of the mind, that all that went besides the *bagg*, was *Utquid perditio*? and so be all they that be of his *Laying up for your selves.*

19 *in marg.* 1. Chro. 29.14] *LACT*; 1 Chro. 29.40 F_1

spirit. But, *Saint Paul* is of that mind, that ἀγαθοεργεῖν, to *lay out to good uses*, is to *lay up to our owne uses*: that, in parting thus with it, we do not *dimittere* but *præmittere*; not *lose* it, by leaving it heer from whence we are going, but *store* it up, by sending it thither before, whither we are going. And indeed, one of the two, we must needs, either leave it behind and lose it for ever; or send it before and have it our owne for ever. Now choose whither you will hold of *Judas's*, or *Paul's*.

For indeed, it is not *laying up*, *Saint Paul* findeth fault with; but the *place* where: not *building* or *obteining*, or *purchasing*; all which three are specified, and the *Apostle* speaketh in your owne termes, and the things you chiefly delight in: but, the *laying up* in the *flesh*, which will rott, and with it whatsoever is laid up with it; or in the *world*, which is so variable now, and will be consumed all to nought, and with it, whatsoever is laid up in in. But, he would have us to lay it up in *heaven*; which (besides that it is our owne countrey, and this but a strange land) is the place, whither we passe leaving this place behind; and from whence we must never passe, but stay heer, and either for ever want, or have use for ever of that, we part with heere. And to say truth, *Utquid respicimus?* With what face can we look up and look upon heaven, where we have *laid up* nothing? or what entertainment can we hope for there, whither he have sent no part of our provision; but for ought of our sending, the place is cleane empty?

You will say; how can one reach *heaven* to *lay* any thing there? I will aske you also another question: How can a man being in *France*, reach into *England* to lay any thing there? By *exchange*. And did you never hear of our exchange, *Cambium cæleste*? You know, that to avoid the danger of *Pirates*, and the inconvenience of forein Coine, not currant at home, it is the use of Merchants to pay it ther, to receive it heer. Such a thing is there in this *laying up*. We are heere as *strangers*: the place where we wish our selves, is our Countrey, even *Paradise* (if so be, we send our carriage thither before; if not, I feare, we intend some other place: it is not our country.) When we shall take our way thither, through the way of all flesh, through death, certainely we lose all; he stripps every one, he laies hold of: and put case, we could get through with all our baggs; heer it is currant (for it is the coine of the world;) but, there it is base, and goeth for nought; what shall we then do? *Quare non facis?* why deale you not with *exchange*, paying heer so much, to have so much repaid you there. *Adires trapezitas*, you should go to the *Bankers*: who be those? *Cum quæsiveris*, when you have sought all, *Pauperes sunt campsores*, they be the poore: *Da pauperibus & accipies thesaurum*. Where is our bill? *Quod, vel quantum uni*. Who will repay it? *Ego resolvam: Nec repetit mercedem sed dat mercedem*. What? refuse you to take CHRIST's bill? If you dare trust your servants without feare of losing; if you trust your

Lord, feare you to lose? If them, of whom you receive nothing, but, they of you; what, not him of whom earst you professed to receive all things? If CHRIST be of credit, and heaven be not *Utopia*; if we thinke there is such a life after this, we shall ever have to doe there, *Lay up* heere. Thinke, it is a *laying up*. Upon the beleeving of this one word, the weight of doing and not doing, all the Text lyeth.

When we recount our good deeds, we commonly say, For him, and for him, we have done this and that; It is true, saith *Saint Paul*. That good you doe, you do for them, and *for your selves too*: but more, *for your selves* then *for them*. To *lay up*, and to *do good*; yea, to others; nay to do your selves good, to *lay up for your selves*. Before, you thought it scattering, it was indeed *laying up*: Now, you thinke, it is for them; it is, *for you, and your sakes*, GOD commandeth it.

GOD hath no need of you to feed the poore; No need of the *Widow* to feed *Elias*, he could still have fedd him by *ravens*: and as he fed *Elias* by one; so could he them, by others, or other meanes, and never send them to *Sarepta* among you. He could have created sufficient for all men; or so few men, as all should have been sufficient for them. He would not: He ordered, there should ever be *poore in the land*: Why? To *prove them*; and to *prove you by them*: that, He which feedeth you, might feed them by you; that your *superfluities* might be their *necessaries*: that they of their *patience*, in *wanting*; and you, of your *liberalitie* in *supporting*, might both together, of Him that made you both, *receive reward*. They with you, in your bosomes there, as heere: a good sight in heaven, and a good sight in earth. For sure, there shall never be a *rich man* in heaven, without a *Lazarus* in his bosome. Therefore, we have need of them, as they have need of us; yet, that, we make theirs, remaineth ours still. Deut. 15.11.

It liketh the *Holy Ghost*, as to terme our *preaching* our *seed*, so to terme your *wealth*, your *seed*. The *seed*, the husbandman casts it, the *ground* receives it: Whose is it? the *ground's*? No, the husbandman's. And, though it be cast out of his hands and rott in the bowells of the earth, and come to nothing, and there becomes of it, no man can tell what, yet, this compt he maketh, it is his still; and that every graine will bring him an *eare*, at time of the yeare; and so, that he hath, in casting it from him, stored it up for himselfe. Whereas, in foolishly loving it (as many do their wealth) he might have stored it up for wormes and mustinesse, and by that meanes indeed have lost it for altogether. The *seed* is your *almes*: The *ground* is the *poore*: You are the *Sowers*. When it is therefore sowen among them, how it is spent, or what becomes of it, you know not: yet, this you know, and may 2. Cor. 9.6.

32 compt] count F_2

reckon; that at the fulnesse of time, at the *harvest of the end of the world*, for everie graine of temporall contribution, you shall receive an eare of æternall retribution. Whereas, storing it up heer, it may after your decease be stored for *harlotts* and *gamesters* and *rioters*, in whose hands it shall corrupt and putrifie, and your selves lose the fruit thereof for ever. By this comparison you may know, that when you are dealing for the *poore*, it is your owne business, you entend: that, not forgetting them, you remember *your selves*; pittying them you have *pitie on your owne soules*, and that *your labour* shall not be *in vaine in the Lord*.

1. Cor. 15.58.

Men use to reason with themselves; it will not alwaies be health, let us lay up for sicknesse; it will not alway be youth, for age: and why not (saith *Saint Paul*) it will not alway be this life, not alway present life, *lay up for your selves against the life to come*. In this place, heere, we shall not be alwaies, but in another of our æternall abode. This time, that is, will not be alwaies; but such a time will come, as in which, that we call a *thousand yeares*, shall be no more then *a day*, now. That place and time would be thought of: and good wisedome it will be, for a man to forget what he is, and to weigh what he shall be. Surely for any present matter GOD did not make us; *Sed ad nescio quid aliud*, to some further matter yet to come. Not yet present: as yet, in *promise*, not yet in performance; as yet in *hope*, not in possession. I know, that even in this place the *Lord* doth reward, and sheweth us plainely that *Date* and *Dabitur* are two *twinnes*: We our selves have by good tryall found it true; when our carefull *Date* and provision for the poore last yeare save one, was requited *in presenti* with a great *Dabitur* of the last yeare's encrease. But this is but an *Et cætera*, making nothing to the maine promise which is to come, which our SAVIOUR would never have out of our eye; *Habetis hic*, heere you have your comfort, *Habete illic* have it there too, for heere you cannot ever have it. For the present time, you have officers and servants to wait on you; in the time to come, none will accompanie you, all will leave you, when to the grave they have brought you, save *mercie* onely; none will wait or make roome, but *opera eorum*, your workes which you have heere *layd up for the time to come*.

Psal. 90.4.

Luk. 6.24.

The Scripture speaketh of this life, and all the fælicitie therein, as of a *tent* or *booth*, spread for a day and taken downe at night. Even like *Jona's gourd* for all the world; fresh in the morning and starke withered yer evening. But, of the life to come, as of a *ground-worke*, never to remove it selfe, or we from it; but to abide therein, ἐν τῇ φυλακῇ or ἐν τῇ βασιλικῇ in the *prison* or the *palace* for evermore. We shall not therefore *lose* but *lay up in store*: not for others, but for *our selves*: Not, for a few daies now, but for *heereafter*: Not a tent to be taken downe, but a foundation never to be removed.

Heb. 11.9.
2. Cor. 5.1.

Of all the words in the Text, not one was meet for the teeth of the *Rhemists*, save this onely: heere you have a perillous note close in the margent: *Good workes are a foundation*. A *foundation*, very true: who denies it? but whither a *foundation* in our graces, as CHRIST is without us, that is the point. The ground whereon every building is raised, is termed *fundamentum*. The lowest part of the building immediately lying on it, it so termed too. In the first sense, CHRIST is said to be the onely *foundation*: Yet the *Apostles*, because they are the lowest row of stones, are said to be *foundations*, in the second. So, among the *graces* within us, *faith* is properly in the first sense, said to be the *foundation*: yet, in the second, do we not denie, but as the *Apostle* calleth them, as the lowest row, next to *Faith*, *Charitie*, and the *workes of charitie* may be called *foundations* too. Albeit the margent might well have beene spared at this place: for, the note is heere, all out of place. For, being so great Schoolemen as they would seeme, they must needs know, It is not the drift of the *Apostle* heere, in calling them a *foundation*, to carry our considerations into the matter of *justifying*, but onely to presse his former reason of *uncertaintie* there, by a contrarie weight of certaine *stabilitie* heere; and so, their note comes in like *Magnificat* at *Matins*.

1. Cor. 3.11.
Eph. 2.20.
Col. 1.23.

Eph. 3.18.

Thus reasoneth, *Saint Paul*: This world is *uncertaine*, of a *sandy* nature; you may reare upon it, but it is so bad a soile, as whatsoever you raise, will never be well settled, and therefore ever tottering; and when the *raine*, and *wind*, and the *waves beat against* it, it commeth downe on your heads. Therefore to make choise of a faster soile, build upon GOD's ground, not upon the world's ground: for, πάντα ἐκεῖνα βέβαια, μεταβολὴ οὐδεμία (saith *Chrysostom*;) there all is firme, there you may build and be sure, fall the *raine* upon the top of it, blow the *wind* against the side of it, rise the *waves* against the foot of it, it stands irremovable. Wherein the *Apostle* (saith *Chrysostome*) doth teach a very goodly and excellent art, how to make of our *fugitive riches* a trusty and *fast friend*; how to make *Gold* of our *Quicksilver*, and of the *uncertaintie of riches*, a sure and *certaine groundworke*.

Mat. 7.27.

Chrys. in locum
Hom. 18.

Assurance and *securitie* are two things (we know) that *rich men* many times buy deare: heere they may be had; not for thus much, or thus long, but for as much as you list, and as long as *æternitie* is long, that never shall have end. The meaning is; that if you lay out, or lay on that you have, on these earthly things (the plott, which the world would faine commend unto you) with this life, or at the furthest, with this world they shall be shaken in peeces and come to nought; and you possibly in the houre of death, but most certainely in the day of judgement, shall shake, when the world your

22 *in marg*. Mat. 7.27] *LACT*; Mat. 7.16 F_1

ground-worke shakes, and be in trembling feare and perplexed agonie touching the estate of your soule: knowing, there is nothing comming to you but the fruit of this *world*, which is ruine; or the fruit of the *flesh*, which is corruption. But, if you shall have grace to make choise of GOD's *plot*, which He hath heere leveled for you to raise upon, *O quanto dignum pretio!* that will be worth all the world in that day: the perfect certaintie, sound knowledge, and pretious assurance, you shall then have, whereby you shall be assured to be received, because you are sure you are CHRIST's, because you are sure you have true *faith*, because you are sure you have framed it up into *good workes*. And so shall they be a *foundation* to you-ward, by making evident the assurance of salvation: not, *naturá*, to *God-ward*, in bringing forth the essence of your salvation.

Looke you, how excellent a *ground worke* heere is! (not for a cotage;) whereon you may raise your frame to so notable a height, as standing on it, you may lay hand on and lay hold of *eternall life*. O that you would minde once these high things, that you would be in this sense *high-minded*! Saint Paul's meaning is to take nothing from you, but give you a better to requite it by farre. He would have you part, with part of your wealth to *do good*; he will lay you up for it, *treasure in heaven* for your owne use. He would have you forsake the world's sand and *uncertaintie*, wherein you cannot *trust*; but therefore, he markes you out a plott out of the *rock* whereto you may trust. He would not have you *high-minded* in consideration or comparison of ought on this earth; but he would have your *mindes* truely *exalted* to reach up to heavenly things higher then the earth. And last, instead of *this world*, the lusts and *riches* thereof, to match that, if you will lay hold of it, he holdeth out *æternall life* and the glorie thereof.

To take a short prospect into *æternall life*. Life it selfe first (you know) is such a thing, as were it to be sold, would be staple ware; if it stood where hold might be laid on it, some would thrust their shoulders out of joint, but they would reach it. It was a great truth out of a great lier's mouth, *Skinne and all*. And I meane not *æternall*, but this life; and therefore some readings have, *to lay hold of true life*; as if, in this, were little truth. Indeed *Saint Augustine* saith, it is nothing but a disease: We say of dangerous sicknesses, he hath the *plague*, he is in a *consumption*, sure he will die; and yet it failes; diverse die not: whereas (saith he) of life it selfe, it may be said, and never failes: *He lives, therefore he will certainly die*.

Well yet, this life, such as it is, yet we love it, and loth we are to end it: and, if it be in hazard by the *Law*, what running, riding, posting, suing, bribing, and if all will not serve, breaking prison is there for it! Or, if it be in danger of disease, what adoe is there kept, what ill favoured druggs taken!

Job 2.4.

what scarifying, cutting, searing and when all comes to all, it is but a few yeares more added; and when they are done, we are where we should have been before; and then, that which is now life shall be then no life. And then, what is it the neerer? What if *Adam* had lived till this morning, what were he now the neerer? Yet, for all that, as short and fraile as it is, we do, what possibly man can do, to eeke it still; and think our selves jolly wisemen when we have done, though we die next yeare after for all that. If then with so great labour, diligence, earnestnesse, endeavour, care and cost, we busy our selves sometimes to live for a while, how ought we to desire to *live for ever*? if for a time to put death away, how to take death away cleane? You desire *life* I am sure, and *long life*; and therefore a long life, because it is *long*, that is, commeth somewhat neerer in some degree to *æternall life*: If you desire a *long lasting life*, why doe you not desire an *everlasting life*? If a life of *many yeares, which yet in the end shall faile*; why not that life, *whose yeares shall never faile*? If we say, it is lack of witt or grace when any man runnes in danger of the law of man, whereby haply he abridges himselfe of halfe a douzen yeares of his life; what wit or grace is there, wilfully to incurre the losse of *æternall life*? For indeed, as in the beginning we sett downe, it is a matter touching the losse of *æternall life*, we have in hand; and withall touching the paine of æternall death. It is not a losse onely, for we cannot lose life, and become as a stone, free from either: if we leese our hold of this life, *æternall death* taketh hold upon us: If we heape not up the *treasure of immortalitie*, we heape up the treasure of *wrath against the day of wrath*. If your wealth be not with us to life, *pecunia vestra vobiscum est in perditionem*. We have not farre to seeke for this. For, if now we turne our deafe eare to this *Charge*, you shall *fall into tentations*: fear ye not that? *Into many foolish and noisome lusts*; not feare ye that neither? yet feare whither these lead; *which drowne men in perdition and destruction of body and soule*. Feare ye not these? doth the *Lord* thunder thus and are ye not moved? *Quibus verbis te curabo?* I know not how to do you good. But, let *æternall life* prevail. Sure, if *life* come not, *death* comes. There is as much said, now (not as I have to say, but) as the time would suffer: Onely let me in a few words deliver the charge concerning this, and so I will breake up the Court for this time.

    And now *(Right Honourable, beloved, &c.)* albeit that according to the power that the *Lord* hath given us, I might testifie and charge you *in the presence of* GOD *the Father, who quickeneth all things; and of the Lord Jesus, who shall shew himselfe from heaven with His mighty Angells in flaming fire, rendring vengeance to them, not onely that know not* GOD, *but to them also that obey not the Gospell of our Lord* JESUS CHRIST, *that ye thinke upon these*

Psal. 91.16.

Rom. 2.5.
Act. 8.20.

Verse 9.

11 *in marg.* Psal. 91.16] *LACT*; Psal. 101.28 F_1

things which you have heard, to do them: yet *humanum dico*, for your infirmitie, I will speake *after the manner of men*, the nature of a man best loveth to be dealt withall, and even beseech you *by the mercies of* GOD, even of GOD *the Father, who hath loved you, and given you an everlasting consolation, and a good hope through grace, and by the comming of our Lord* JESUS CHRIST *and our assembling unto Him*, that you receive not this *Charge* in vaine; that ye account it His charge, and not mine; received of Him, to deliver to you. Looke not to me I beseech you: in whom, whatsoever you regard (countenance or learning, years or autoritie) I do most willingly acknowledge my selfe farr unmeet to deliver any; more meet a great deale, to receive one my selfe, save that *I have obteined fellowship in this businesse*, in dispensing the *Mysteries*, and delivering the *Charges* of the *Lord*. Looke not on me, looke on your owne soules, and have pitie on them: Looke upon heaven, and the *Lord* of heaven and earth, from whom it commeth, and of whom it will be one day called for againe. Surely there is a *heaven*; Surely there is a *hell*: Surely there will be a day, when enquirie shall be made, how we have discharged that we have received of the *Lord*; and how you have discharged that, you have received of us in the *Lord's Name*. Against which day, your consciences stand charged with many things, at many times heard. *O seeke not death in the error of your life*, deceive not your selves; think not, that when my words shall be at an end, both they shall vanish in the aire, and you never heare of them againe. Surely you shall; the day is comming, when it shall be required againe at your hands. A fearefull day for all those, that for a little *riches*, thinke basely of others; upon all those that *repose* in these *vaine riches* (as they shall see then) a vaine *confidence*; upon all those, that *enjoy* onely with the *belly* and the *backe*, and doe either no *good*, or miserable *sparing good* with their *riches*: whose *riches* shall be with them to their *destruction*. Beloved, when your life shall have an end (as an end it shall have) when the terror of death shall be upon you; when your soule shall be cited to appeare before GOD, *in novissimo*; I know and am perfectly assured, all these things will come to mind againe, you will perceive and feele that, which possibly now you do not. The *devill's charge* commeth then, who will presse these points in another manner, then we can: then, it will be too late. Prevent his charge, I beseech you, by regarding and remembring this, now. Now is the time, while you may and have time wherein, and abilitie wherewith; thinke upon it, and provide for *æternall life*; you shall never in your life stand in so great need of your *riches*, as in that day; provide for that day and provide for *æternall life*. It will not come yet, it is true; it will be long in comming: but when it comes, it will never have an end.

Wisd. 1.12.

6 *assembling*] *assembly* F_2

This end is so good, that I will end with *æternall life*, which (you see) is *Saint Paule's* end. It is his, and the same shall be my end, and I beseech GOD, it may be all our ends. *To* GOD *immortal, invisible*, and *onely wise*; GOD, who hath prepared this *eternall life* for us; who hath taught us this day, how to come unto it; whose grace be ever with us and leave us not, till it have thereto brought us; the *Father*, the *Sonne*, and the *Holy Ghost*, be all glorie, praise, and thanksgiving, now and forever, *AMEN*.

IV

Sacrilege a Snare. A Sermon Preached *ad Clerum* in the University of Cambridg

PROV. XX. XXV.
It is a snare to the Man who devoureth that which is HOLY.

IT is commonly received, among *Divines*, that *The Proverbs*, which we read scattered and in parcels, from the Xth. *Chap*. are without Method, not written in a constant tenor, as the former *Nine*, by *Solomon*; But some at one time, some at another, as the matter and occasion afforded, were uttered by the *King*, observed by standers by; and, afterwards, not without great benefit, though without order, committed to Writing.

And other occasions there were for uttering others (for, so wise a man spake nothing rashly or unseasonably;) but, for this *Proverbe* now in hand, what hint was given, to what it was an answer, upon what occasion it was propounded, is not so evident. For what? *Solomon* was no Grater on the *Laity*, much lesse (which is as infamous) on the *Clergy*. None more bountifull then Hee, towards *Holy things*; none farther from *Alienating*. Whence then, or what had He to do with *Sacrilegious persons*, or *Vow-breakers*, whom this Verse points at? Was there any in *Solomons* time, of so cursed a stomach, that *Consecrated Things* must be his Morsels? Any, in that age, such an enemy to *Holy Things*, as to *Devour* them? Of *Vowes*, as to breake them? So it should seeme: And indeed to this passe it came, that *Interpreters*, of no small account with mee, are of opinion it was so; and that there were some such in those dayes, of whom there are not a few, now. And that this pious and wise answer, was given by that Wise and Pious *Prince* to those *Counsellors*, who laboured to perswade him, that those things, which were given and designed by His *Father*, by *Saul* and *Samuel*, and reserved in the *Threasury* for the building of the *Temple*, might be *Alienated*, and spent upon *Court* Vanities.

I shall diduce this a little higher.

To *David* (whom the Holy Scriptures call a *Man after Gods heart*) God gave such a mind, being a man to *His* mind, that he judged it unseemly, the storm of War being now blown over, that He himselfe should dwell in *Kedar*, and the *Ark of GOD* lodg between *Curtaines*: And truly it is an unjust demand of certaine men, that the *Church* should be in no better condition, now flourishing with Peace, then formerly she was, when groaning under the Crosse; never *Abound*, ever in *Need*. The *Temple* must have its share in *Prosperity*; so thought *David*, so with *David* all the Saints. In times of War and distractions the *Church* must be content with Goat-skins; In Peace, and setled times, she requireth Carved works and *Cedar*. To this therefore *David* wholly gives and applyes Himselfe; and, besides much formerly dedicated and stored up to this purpose, by *Saul, Abner, Samuel*, and by Him piously and faithfully conserved, he bestowed further at his own charge, both *Cedar* and *Marble, Precious stones* and *Metals*: And that not sparingly or grudgingly, and with an evill eye: For he expended 3000 *Talents* of *Gold*, 7000 of *Silver*. And besides not content with that, partly by his example, partly by his perswasion, he wrought so far upon his *Nobles*, that they likewise ingaged themselves in the like vow and promise: By whose bounty there was an accession, of 5000 *Talents* of *Gold*, 10000 *Talents* of *Silver*, of *Brasse* 18000 *Talents*, and 100000 *Talents* of *Iron*; so great an accession, say I, that, which hapned in our memory in the taking from the *Church*, did then in the addition to it, there was need of a *Court of Augmentations*, over which, the *Chronicles* testifie, one *Jehiel* was President.

This so great weight of *Gold* and *Silver*, when *David*, at the point of his death, delivered to *Solomon* his Sonne, for the building of the *Temple*, it being as yet in the *Threasury*, and not brought into the *Temple*; that there was certaine *Court-Ratts* (haply *Jeroboam* and others of the same stamp,) who would perswade the *King*, as they in the Prophet, *That the House of GOD needed no sieling*; as He in the Gospel, *That CHRISTS head might be well enough without Ointment; To what purpose is this waste?* That therefore He should apply it to his *Threasury*, for which it was much fitter then the *Temple*; and that they, to this end, were ready to make inquisition into *Sauls* and *Abners Vowes*, and (which is easily done) pick out some holes, find out some tricks, to make those *Vowes null and invalid*. These Counsellers were not effectuall with the True-hearted *King*, but such Counsellers there were; and it seemes probable to mee, that this was the occasion of this Verse, and that the *Rabbies*

2 Sam. 7.2.

Philip. 4.12.

1 Chro. 26.27. 28.

1 Chro. 26.4.

1 Chro. 29.7.

1 Chro. 29.8.

P. Hag. 1.4.
St. Mark 14.4.

were not much out in their conjecture. That these Counsellers were not effectuall, this Verse declares; which, with *Solomon* and the like godly *Princes*, will for ever stop the mouths of such Petitions. And also, why they were not. For, it would be a certaine *Snare* to Himselfe, and the *Ruin* of his Kingdome, if he should permit so great a wickednesse. It is indeed a bait, sufficiently inticing, but wrapt about with a *Snare* not to be avoyded.

You see whether the Words tend (and at the first view deliver themselves) *Viz.* to the conservation of the Sacred *Patrimony*, to the repelling of *Sacrilegious* hands from it, and stupifying or deading their *Teeth* who do *Devoure it*. Which I would to GOD this our Age could be perswaded of; in which a wicked custome, hath prevailed, and growes dayly more and more, of *Laying hands upon HOLY Things*; in which, there are no improvements to the *Clergy*, (would that were all?) there are frequent impairings; I say, frequent impairings; and I wish it might only be said, there are; and that there might never be cause of using the *Future tense*. But, I shall speak freely; what for that *Unholy hunger after Gold*, there is nothing esteemed *HOLY*; and the restitution of *Holy Things* is the pretence for *SACRILEGE*.

Adde to this humour of the present Age, another Errour; That those Worthies, not to be named without all honorable respect, whose help *GOD* made use of for the *Reformation* of *Religion*, were very sollicitous for the *Reformation* of *Doctrine*, but lesse attended the *Churches Patrimony*; and almost said, what the *King* of *Sodom* did to *Abraham*, though in another sense, *Give us the Soules, and take the rest to You*. But as they, who thought they should find the *Baptist* in Kings Courts, so they, that think they shall find *ABRAHAM* there, are both deceived.

Which Errour, though a small one (and a small one indeed it is, if we compare it with those great and famous acts performed by them) yet, we may justly feare, if not seasonably withstood, will lie heavy upon succeeding Ages: in which true-hearted honest men (from that of *Solomon, Pro.* 14.4. *Where no Oxen are, the crib is cleane*) presage Barbarisme, or somewhat worse, which I will not speake of; falsly perchance, and I pray *GOD* it prove so, but not rashly, I am sure, not without cause. So that, in very truth, unlesse we would have the *Universities* to be broken up, the *Clergy* to be trampled on, and all that is called *HOLY* come to ruin, there lyes a necessity upon us to plead for the *Churches Patrimony:* That, which is left of it, let us aneil and rub over with this bitter juice; let us shew them the *Snare* in which they take paines to trap themselves; and, that it is not lawfull for them to do what dayly they attempt, unlesse it be lawfull for them to blot this Verse out of the *Holy Scriptures*.

And indeed to confesse the truth, this blur upon *our Age*, that *Holy Things* are so *Devoured*, much troubles me, (though there were, there were indeed, in *Solomons time*, such, whose teeth itched to be at them.) But this troubles me more, that we *Divines* see these things, and are lukewarme, nay silent; that we *put up* and *Devoure these Devourings*; that (which the *Apostle* complaines of, 2. *Cor.* 11.20.) *We suffer if a man devoure us, if a man bring us into beggery.* But this most of all, that *we our selves*, (so it is) dayly expose *our selves* to be eat and drunk up, as I may so say, by *these Devourers of the Clergy.* This is not the way, believe me, to effect what we desire.'Tis the wish of many, and mine among the rest, that we may have a *Learned* and a *Teaching Clergy*: Grant it Lord *JESUS*, grant it speedily; It is a *Holy* and a *wholsome wish*: But, if wee suffer the *Churches Meanes* to be thus gnaw'd and shav'd, eaten, and devoured, a *Vaine wish*. This was one piece of *Pharaohs* madnesse; He would have them sacrifice to the *Lord*; but not a Sheepe or Oxe to be allowed. *Exod.* 10. 24. And this is our *Errour*, our *Madnesse* rather. Commanders of Armys are a great deal wiser: first, they take care for *Victuals*, then for *Souldiers*. But we dayly list many strong, good *Souldiers*; we bring them in no *Provision*, nay wee suffer that they have to be taken from them. And (which I have not seldome wondred at in these men) wee are ever talking of *increasing the Light*, seldome or never of *allowing Oyle*. But we must preach for one, as well as the other, the *Oyle* as well as the *Light*. We must often and vehemently call upon men to remember the *Threasury of GOD*: Wee must labour to bring them to that passe *Solomon* brought his, to esteeme it a part of *Religion*, not to touch any thing *set apart for Religion*; to fast, rather then make their meales upon *Holy Things*: to give themselves for choaked, and strangled, if they should, even unwittingly, swallow down that which is *Holy*: This if accomplished, I shall hope for dayes as good as *SOLOMONS*. If not———But I will not presage any thing grievous. I goe on to my purpose.

The Verse I shall divide, as it divides it selfe, into 2. Parts. The One, concerning *Holy Things not to be Devour'd*. 2. The Other, concerning *Vowes not anxiously to be inquir'd into*.

The First, for my more distinct progresse, I shall part into 3. Members.

1. What Things those are which *Solomon* calls *HOLY*.

2. Who they are that *Devoure* them.

3. They, that do, ingage themselves in *a great sin*, catch themselves in a Snare.

1. Of the first. By *Solomon* in this Chapter, that part of our *substance* is called *Holy*, wherewith (chap. 3. ver. 9.) Hee told us, God ought to be honoured. For not *Augustus* alone hath power to *tax the world*, God hath also His power of *Taxing*; and that out of His full right over our Goods. Of which to take away all obscurity or doubt from any; Under the *Law* He

I
What things are called Holy.

commanded two diverse *Coines of money.* ¹One stamped with the *Sword, and Scepter of the Prince.* ²The other with the *Pot, and Rod of Aaron.* By the *One* allotting to the *Prince his Tribute*, for his Protection of us; by *his Scepter*, against *Injustice and Contention*; by *his Sword*, against *Hostility*. By the *Other* allowing the *Priest* his due; by whose labour it is *Gods* pleasure of dry Trees to make us live and flourish; and, living to *Feed* Us with Heavenly *Manna* to Eternall life. *God* the *Father* commanded both; *God* the *Son* paid both: *Doves to the Temple, Tribute* to the *Prince.* That First is the *sacred Tribute.*

Of which to take a little more exact knowledge. Four things there are, which in *Holy Scripture* are called *Holy.*

1. Among them that is the first and principall, for which the other are sanctified: I meane, the *first Fruits* of the *Spirit*; namely *Holinesse* it selfe, with which they must bee adorned, who looke to enter into that *holy and heavenly Hierusalem.* It is the Encomium given to *God* by the *Holy Angells* (so by *them*, so by *us*,) P. Esay 6.3. *Holy, Holy, Holy*: So hath *God* commanded us under the *Law. Be yee holy, for I am holy.* So *under the Gospell*, 1 Thess. 4.3. *This is the will of God even your holinesse: This is the will of God*, ought to be *ours*. Since ᵃ*God* the *Father* hath chosen his *Church* (which we are) *before the world.* ᵇ*God the Son Redeemed from the world*: and ᶜ*God the Spirit annointed in the world.* You have the first, our *Sanctification.*

Levit. 20.7.

ᵃ Eph. 1.4.
ᵇ Eph. 5.26.
ᶜ 1 St Joh. 2.20.

2. But, for the begetting of *Holinesse*, first, and then increasing it, in us, Hee hath sanctified a second sort of *Holy things.* To wit, Foure *Meanes*: ¹*The Word.* ²*Prayer.* ³*Sacraments.* ⁴*Censures.* 1. The *Word*, principally; ᵈ*Sanctifie them by thy Truth, thy Word is Truth.* 2. To which *Prayer* is coupled. ᵉ*Sanctified by the Word of GOD and Prayer.* 3. Then the *Holy Sacraments.* ¹Of *Baptisme*, Ephes. 5. ²Of the *Eucharist*, Hebr. 13.4. Lastly, *Censures.* These *Christ* calleth ᶠ*Holy*, *not to be cast to dogs*; Sanctified by himselfe, both to retain us in, and recall us to our duty. This the Second. *Holy Meanes.*

ᵈ St. Joh. 17.17.
ᵉ 1. Tim. 4.5.
ᶠ S. Matth. 7.6.

3. Further, for the exercising of these *Meanes*, and applying them to that use to which he hath ordained them, Hee hath *sanctified* a third sort of *Holy things*: Which is threefold. ¹Of the *Place, where.* ²Of the *Time, when.* ³Of the *Persons, by whom*, they ought to be administered.

1. Of the *Place*; Which He therefore calleth *Holy*, and the *Sanctuary*, S. Matth. 24.15.

2. Of the *Time*; Which He calleth the *Holy day of the Lord*, P. Esay 58.13.

3. Of the *Person*; Whom He therefore calleth his *Holy One*, Deut. 33.8. You have the *Third.*

4. But to these *persons* thus imploy'd in Divine Offices, and making little account of their own in respect of *Holy things*, a fourth kinde, *viz.* of *Holy*

Tribute was appointed for their *maintenance and lively-hood*. *Ezechias*, the best *of Kings*, hath very well comprised the whole businesse, appointing a fit *portion* to the *Priests & Levites*, that they might more couragiously attend the study of the *Law*. Which *portion* that it should be deemed *Holy*, there was an expresse command by GOD Himselfe: Both under the *Law*, where the People was taught to say; *I have brought away the hallowed things out of my house*; which was, to acknowledge that which was payd to the *Levite* as a *Holy Tribute*: and also under the *Gospell*; where, not only those things we are exercised in, but, those also which we live upon, are termed by *Saint Paul, the Holy things of the Temple*.

 So you have a fourefold sort of *Holy things*, one issuing from another, and appointed for the conservation each of other. ¹*Holy Manners*. ²*Holy Meanes*. ³*Holy Persons*. ⁴*Holy Revenues*. Our busines is about this fourth. For no man gapes after, or fastens his teeth upon those three: This last, this, this it is, upon which they set their teeth and stomack. Though indeed, as I shall shew anon, there is but one bit, one draught of all. Truly, they are ty'd in a close and strong knot together, *Holy Revenues, Holy Persons, Holy Meanes, Holy Manners*. Nor shall we be ever able to keep up *Holy Manners* without due *Meanes*; nor due *Meanes* without fit *Persons*; nor fit *Persons* without ample *Revenues and comings in*.

 This therefore which *Solomon* calleth *Holy*, is the *Tribute of the Sanctuary*. But what is that, or how so called? I shall tell you that, too. The *Holy Scripture* is plentifull about it; but it may be reduced to two heads. ¹*Of Oblation*. ²*Of Indiction*.

 1. Of *Oblation*; either by *Vow*, or *Freewill*; that the *Hebrews* call ᵃ*Neder*, this ᵇ*Nedabah*. These will fall into the second member, I will not prosecute it. Only this I say; The *Church* had a *Patent* granted her, by vertue wherof every one had leave to *alienate and set apart* what he would of his own *to holy uses*, and that either by way of *Freewill offering*, or by *Vow*; whether it were *Person*; or *Beast*, Cleane or uncleane, of the Flock, or of the Herd; whether *Houses* or *Lands*, of inheritance or purchase. The same gracious Licence remained under the *Gospell*, for any to lay downe, what, how much hee would, of his own, at the *Apostles* feet, that is, to give, bestow, dedicate, consecrate his Goods to God.

 2. I come to the *Indiction*, that which is set and determined. And sure there was a necessity for this, lest, if those *Freewill offerings* should come in coldly, and the *Threasury of the Church* should be, as it is often, empty for want of a constant showre of *Manna*, the Priests should well nigh starve. I am to treat of a hard point, and (that, which grieves mee most) but briefly. It is certain that in every ones *estate* there is a *sacred part*. This is more obscure, *what* that is, or *how much*. Abraham the father of the Faithfull

2 Chro. 31.4.

Deut. 26.13.

1 Cor. 9.13.

ᵃ a Vow, simply. vid. Gen. 28.20.
ᵇ a free-wil Offering. vid. Levit. 7.16.
Deut. 16.10. joyned with *Missah*.
Levit. 27.
Acts 4.35.

Gen. 14.20.

(wholly to bee imitated by his Children for the *Place* and *Measure* of their donation) layd upon himselfe the *Tith*, the *Leviticall Law* being not then written. How so, who declared to him the *measure of the Divine portion?* no doubt but the *Holy Spirit* to so *holy a man.* That same *Spirit*, who before had tacitely dictated it to *Abraham*, did afterward by an expresse Law take order for that and no other *portion*, to bee payd to *Persons consecrated* by Him. Indeed to some this seemes wholly *ceremonial*, as all things doe now a dayes that touch the *purse.* Others will not allow any portion to be *by Natural Right*, nor *so great* by *Positive*. That GOD was indeed as carefull for our sustenance, as He was for the *Levites.* That there was nothing then reserved to the *Positive Law*, nor therefore now: and to this purpose they urge that in the 23. of *St. Matth. Ye ought not to leave the other undone.* I came hither to Preach, not to dispute: and therefore betake my self to the more received opinion, that *Tithes* have their force from the *Imposition of the Church*: For the same power which the *Church* had of old to make *Ordinances*, and to charg it self with a *Shekel* or the third part of a *Shekel* for the *Service of the House of God* remaineth still the same under the *Gospel*, in which you shall meet with ὁρισμοὺς and διαταγὰς, *Decrees* and *Ordinances*; and those, not only, as *St. Paul* testifieth, for *Almes* to the Poore, but also, for *Offerings.* When therefore the *Primitive Church* would take order for a *set allowance* for *such as attended the Divine Service*, turning her selfe on all sides, and casting up her thoughts, she found out no equaler *Portion* which she could ordaine, then that known old one and appointed by the Law, *Viz.* the *Tith of the yeerly comings in*; the most equal in respect of GOD and Man. In respect of *GOD*, so *St. Augustine* in the person of *GOD. Thou art mine, ô man; this Earth, which thou tillest, is mine; these Seeds, which thou sowest, are mine; these Beasts, which thou imployest, mine; the Raine and Showers, mine; the Sun and heat, mine; all, mine; thou which lendest only thy hand, deservest only the Tithe; but I grant Nine to thee, give me the Tithe.* Could a more reasonable speech possibly be made?

In respect of *Man*, that must needs be most equal, which is not *too loose* for one, *too strait* for another. By *this*, there is a most exact equality: the *Rich* are not spared, the *Poore* are not opprest: which is the common complaint of the *Edicts* of *Princes*; the *Crow*, better then the *Dove.*

This *Portion* therefore the *Church* hath hallowed, and given that honor to God the *author of this Imposition*, to believe that He best knew the *Measure of His own Tribute*; and that no *Councils of the Church*, no *Assemblies of the Kingdome* could settle that affaire more wisely, then it was of old provided for by the *Sacred Law*; then *the Lawyer himselfe* (so absolute, that *Justinian* is no body to him) had proclaimed many ages since. But then, you'l say, She who imposed it, may, when She will, forbid it. I think not, but, however,

Marginal notes:
Numb. 18.21.
II. Nehe. 10.33.
Acts 11.29.
1 Cor. 16.1.
Acts 24.17.

would not perswade her to it; and that upon this ground; both, because a dangerous custome might thence arise, to hold for *Sacred* what we list, how much we list, as long as we list, if we grant that: and also, because the *rights of inheritances* ought to be *most holy*: and *God* calleth His *Covenants,* *Covenants of salt,* therefore not to be made and unmade, incroach'd upon, exchang'd, or repealed at our pleasure: Againe, because an *ancient Law* ought not to be *antiquated,* saving for its (ἀσθενές or ἀνωφελές) *weaknesse* or *unprofitablenesse.* Heer's neither. For I see its *strength* from the *Author, Consent, Custome, Multitude*; and not the *mute* or *silent,* but the *expresse* and *clear approbation* of all ages. And its *use,* as manifestly: for it hath a long time been imployed, without complaint of any, to that *use* to which it was appointed: and, unlesse the sinewes of it had been cut by certaine *Improper Proprietaries,* it had been better imployed, neither would the *Church* have ever complained in that point. And then, lastly, because, where by crafty counsell the *Tithe* hath beene chang'd into a *stipend,* they wish it undone: thence many *errors, deceipts, difficulties, complaints* have risen. There was a complaint of the *Church of Scotland exhibited to the Parliament at Edinburgh,* A.D. MDLXV, when I read the eighth Leafe of it, it pities me for them: I say no more, but what the Boys use to sing, *Felix quem faciunt, &c.* Happy they, whom other mens harms make to beware.

Let this *custome* then stand inviolable; and so I shut up this first part, with telling you, that whatsoever is either *dedicated by Vow,* or *imposed by Law* is *Holy*; and (in the language of the *Twelve Tables*) *Qui clepserit repseritue, Sacrilegus esto*: whosoever diminisheth or devoureth it, is guilty of Sacrilege.

You know now what are *Holy things*. What it is *to devoure Holy things,* which I promised to shew in the second place, now learne: The *Prophet Malachy,* for the *Old Testament* calls it [a]*to rob*; Saint *Luke*, for the *New*, [b]νοσφίξεσθαι to *defraud,* or *divert*. In which point *Solomon* seemes to mee to have used a most fit word, when he called that *devoured,* which was most properly to be said to be *alienated*.

1. For, when we eate of *our owne,* we eate, as mannerly people doe, by morsells, well chewed and ground: if it be *Anothers,* we snatch at it, and, lest the true owner of it should come upon us and take the bit out of our mouthes, we swallow it down suddenly and all together. In that respect, first, properly said to devoure, because not *our own*.

2. Secondly in this, because *Greedily*. Look me upon *Seneca's Mastiffe,* or rather the *P. Esays Dog,* gaping at the table, never stirring his eyes, but wagging his tayle, and fawning upon you, while you sling him somewhat. And then shew me one of our *Clergy-Devourers* stretching his chops and soul upon the *Church Meanes,* gaping, and his teeth itching to beat them,

[2] What it is to devoure Holy things.
[a] P. Mal. 3.8. קבע
[b] Acts 5.3.

P. Isai. 56.11

ever and anon up with, *Give me those grounds, give me that superfluous farme, that decayed Church*. I pray what difference? In that respect, secondly, because *Greedily taken*.

3. Againe, mark that *Dog* well, you shall see him not only *Greedy*, but *one that cannot be satisfied, never having enough*. If a bone be flung to him,'tis down in an instant, and he's gaping againe, no lesse then afore. In like manner, you may observe these to be ever craving, *sick of a dropsie*; their thirst increaseth with their drink; you may know them to be a kin to the Horseleach, whose daughters are ever crying, Give, Give.

<small>Pro. 30.15.
חבחב</small>

4. Lastly, what usually falls out to such devouring and ravenous creatures, as Kites, Wolves, Locusts, that they are ever *starvlings*, none of them growes the *fatter*, or in *better case*; even so to these. Just as *Pharaohs leane kine* eat up the fat ones, and yet were ill favoured as before; so these are ever snatching, and ever in want, GOD blowing upon their goods thus gotten, that we may even wonder what is become of that masse of treasure which, not many yeares since, went into the *stomach of the Common-wealth*. Let this tell us what it is to *Devoure*: Namely, [1]*Greedily to swallow down*, [2]*What is not ours but Gods*, [3]*With which we shall not be nourished*, [4]*nor satisfied*. I have done with the *Thing*: now briefly of the *Persons*.

<small>Gen. 41.4.</small>

There is a twofold sort of men. [1]Such as have *no Right* at all. [2]Such as indeed have a *Right*, but shamefully and wickedly abuse it.

<small>Who the Persons that Devoure.
I. Such as have no Right.</small>

1. Such as have no *Right*: Their sin is a hundred times more heinous, though both's be heinous. For if hee sinneth, who flingeth away that which is *his owne*; how great a sinner is hee, who taketh away that which is *anothers*, to which he hath *no Right*, no nor any *capacity of Right* (as they say) and that with injury to *God*; and that not to *any God*, but the *living God*. *Every one his owne*; so *Justice* wills: This is their *owne*; but so *Theirs*, that, first, *Gods*: and these men sin, first, against *Heaven*, then against *Us*: for *His primary Right God* reserveth to *Himselfe*. If *every ones owne to the true owner*, then, what is *Gods, to God*. But these are *Gods*, if we will believe *God*. *Gods*, twice, indeed. First, by *His Creation*; so that wee must all necessarily say with *David*, *These things which wee give are all thine owne: we give thee but thine owne*. By *His Creation*, first; by *our Dedication*, secondly. Which *God* by a *secondary Right* hath made over to *Us*, as most just that *We*, who are constituted *for men* in the things which appertain to *God*, should be constituted for *God* in those things which appertain to *Men*; that *We*, who reach to *Men* the things which are *Gods*, should receive, the things which are *Gods*, from *Men*. GOD hath made over to us this *Right*, and that so strictly, that it is lawfull, not only not to take any thing away, no not by *Ignorance*; But (which is lawfull in *Civill* matters) not to *sell*; I say not, not all, but not *a part*. Not to *sell*; I say not *not all*, but not *a part*. Not to *sell*,

<small>Rom. 13.7.
Numb. 18.
St. Matth. 22.</small>

<small>1 Chro. 29.14.</small>

<small>Levit. 5.</small>

<small>P. Eze. 48.14.</small>

not to *buy*? much lesse then to *devoure*. And truly this is not his fault alone who extorts it, but the *Magistrates* too who permits it: Whereupon that *good Prince Nehemiah* protesteth, not only that He did not take away the *Holy things*, but, that He was absent from the *City*, when they were taken away. And that if he had beene present, rather than have suffered it, hee would (with *Artaxerxes*) have bestowed somewhat from his own *Exchequer*, or (with *Pharaoh*) from his own *Table*. I say therefore, that they, who cut the *Levites* short of what they ought to receive, offend against *God*, whether they do it by *force* or by *fraud*; whether they imploy it *to pay Souldiers*, or build *Houses*; whether they do it for *profit*, or *pleasure*; whether they invert *all*, or but *a part*. By *Force* wicked *Athalia* breaking into the *House of God*, and taking away all that was therein: by *Fraud* wicked *Achan* privily digging in his Tent, added the *Sacred spoyles* to his own household stuffe: *Joas* pretended to provide for the *Publique Good*; for with the Threasurie of the *House of God* He procured conditions of Peace, but a slippery Peace; for He *Devoured the Holy things*. *Jeroboam* seemed to intend the *Publique Honor*; for He built *Shechem*, and *Phenuel*; but in *blood*; for it was with the spoile of the *Temple*, and the alienating of the *Tithes*: *Tobias* furnished himselfe a chamber in the *Porch of God*, for his *Profit* and *Convenience*: *Baltazar* for His *Pleasure* drank out of the *Vessels of the Sanctuary*: all of them were *Sacrilegious*. Finally, not only that *EPIMANES* who ransackt *All*; but *Judas* also, who was so bold as to thrust his *Sacrilegious* fingers into *Christs bag*, though content with a *Part*, was guilty of the same crime: as was likewise that *Sacrilegious Couple*, who durst invade the *Church Threasure*, and detein but a part of that which had touch'd the feet of the *Apostles*. Every one of these was guilty of *Sacrilege*.

H. Nehe. 13.6.

2. Now we must speak concerning the second Sort. A kind of men there is indeed, who have a *Right*, but they wickedly abuse that *Right*. You think, perhaps, I will go far hence to seeke; I stir not a foote, I move not hence; We are the Men; and even amongst us, there are many, too too many, who *Devoure Holy things*. For (which, it is to be feared, some of us do) by sloth and Idlenesse, to tarry here like *Drones*, to fling away our precious houres, to flow in Luxury, to be at leasure for feasts, and playes, and vanities, to do these things, and yet to fatten our selves with those things which are consecrated to *Holy* uses, this is, in our *Saviours* judgment, to *Devoure*, and *spend* our Fathers goods in riotous Living.

2 Such as have right, but abuse it.

S. Luk. 15.13.

I will come nearer yet. A great part of that former *Devouring* came from our selves: and therefore are *Holy things Devoured* by *others*, because they are *Devoured* by *Our selves*: And indeed as lawfull (think some) for *them*, to gather the *Holy Tithes*, and to neglect the *Holy Duties*, as for *Us*. And truly (to tell you my feares) they who now sheere the fleece, will one day pull off skin and fleece together; they who are now gnawing at *Church Meanes*, will consume *them* at last with open mouth, unlesse GOD change *our* minds and manners. For sure there is no throat so *Holy*, that it can be lawfull for *it to consume the things that are Holy*; it is lawfull to *eat*, to *feed upon them*: but to *Devoure them* is, not only unlawfull, but, a high wickednes, not only for those *Locusts*, but even for us too. May there be heapes, heapes of provision, but for them that *war the Holy warfare*; let them that *partake* of the *Altar, wait at the Altar*. 1 *Cor*. 9. 13. But to him that partakes and waits not, that spends the Meanes, and attends not the work, to him it is sin.

[margin: 2 Chron. 31.4.6.]

I speak not this that the people may purloin the (*Priests*) wages: they may no more take from the *Shekel* of *Caiphas* an evill *Priest*, then from the *tribute* of *Tiberius* a wicked *Prince*; to both they must give their *due*, though *they* do not performe their *duty*; both of them are the *Ministers* of *God*, and stand or fall to *Him*. Both take that, which belongs to God, if they take it with *Sacrilegious* hands, and must give an account to GOD. I speak it to this end, as wishing Both in a better mind, *Laity* and *Clergy*. *Them*, that, for the future, they would be *quiet* and forbear to *Devoure Holy things*, by *unjust detention* and *alienation*; *These*, that, for the future, they would *labour* and forbear to *Devoure Holy things*, by *idlenesse, and misimploying*.

[margin: S. Matth. 22.21. Rom. 13.7.]

What it is, who they are that *Devoure Holy things*, is now clear, I would it were not so clear.

[margin: 3 Their punishment who Devoure.]

Him, that shall, what is like to befall, (which was my third Proposall,) now hearken: *It is a snare*. That some such there should be, who would do it, *Solomon* foresaw; and future ages have prov'd too true. In truth there is such a *cursed holy hunger*, that there will be *Theft*, there will bee *Sacrilege*, there will be a *totall overthrow* of all that is called *Holy*, unlesse *God* Himselfe take order, to the contrary, by immediate command, countermand, nay by thunder and lightning, and so provide that they be untouch'd: 'Tis so *sweet a bit*, so pleasant to the *Palat*, so full of *delights*, that you may rend their chops, and breake their jawes, yer you shall get it from them. This is not as it should be; *Solomon* therefore adds, Let them eat and drink *Holy things*, if they like them so well: perhaps the *bait* may please, but under the *bait* there lyes a *hook*, which they swallow with it. Let them take heed of the *bait*, there is a *net* not far off: let them not meddle with the *Field*, it is an *Acheldama*, *a field of bloud*. Let them not take away *the gifts of the Temple*, for *they are* wrapt about with the *Anathema of Heaven*, a curse for the spoylers. By which word *Solomon* very aptly, and elegantly compareth the whole matter, whereof he treateth, to *Fowling*, wherein *Satan* the great *hunter of soules*, (for so H. *David*, Psalm 91.3. so Saint *Paul* calls him, 2 Tim. 2.26.) *waiting for his prey*, layeth out, *for his bait, Church Lands* and *Revenues*, but covered over with the *Crime of Sacrilege*, as with a *gin* or *snare*.

There you may see our *Clergy-eaters*, who (as *Pharaoh* thought, when he opprest the *Church, Come let us deale wisely*) take themselves to be very wise, having made a *gaine of holy things*, hasten to *the snare with those foolish birds*, (Prov. 7.23.) not knowing that it is for their life: *Fly as soone as they see the prey*, to *take*, but *are taken*, and *devouring the prey*, are made *his prey*, who *goes about*, day and night, *seeking whom he may devoure*. It is a most true saying, that in every *sin* there is a *bait* and a *snare*, a *bait* pretended, *a snare* which lyeth hid. The *bait*, some *little profit* of iniquity, or *some small trifling pleasure* of sin; the *snare*, the *sin*, with its *sting*, viz. the *fearefull curse of the Law*. I will not go far hence; chap. 5. v. 3.4. In wandring *Lust*: the *bait*, the *lips of the Harlot*, distilling nothing but hony; the *snare*, the *reliques* of sin more bitter than *wormwood*, more sharp then a sword. Chap. 23. v. 31. 32. In *luxury* and *drunkennes*; the *bait*, the *colour of the Wine* in the Glasse, the *tast* in the Palat; the *snare*, the biting as of the *Serpent* or *Basilisk*, which with its sting brings certaine death.

    In this very chap. ver. 17. In *stealth*; the *bait, Bread of deceipt*, stollen, got without *sweat*; the *snare, sin* filling the mouth with *gravell*, whence necessarily followeth *the gnashing of the teeth*. Every *sin*, I say, hath its *bait*, and its *snare*: but this *sin of Sacrilege*, more and above all other. The *bait*, I take for granted: the *snare* I shall shew, if you please, even in *Prophane stories*. *Cambyses*, who rifled the *Temple* of *Jupiter Hammon*, found it destructive to *himselfe*: *Brennus*, who robbed the *Delphick*, found it destructive to *himselfe* and *his*. *Crassus* who did as much to the *Temple* at *Hierusalem*, was forced to swallow downe melted Gold with the same chaps, which he had before devoured the *Holy things* with. Had you rather have *Sacred stories*? I follow your desires in that too. *Dathan*, who had but a mind to *devoure Holy things*, was himselfe *devoured* of the Earth. *Achan*, who was the first that adventured to add the *Sacred* Wedge of Gold to his owne housholdstuffe, was *devoured* of a heap of stones in the Valley of *Achor*. *Baltazar*, when he held the *sacred* Vessells betwixt his fingers, saw, over against him on a Wall, fingers, which proved fatall to his life and Kingdom. *Athalia*, slaine with a sword within the close of the *Temple*, of that very *Temple*, whose *Threasure*, it is not long since, she tooke away. But because 'tis an easie matter to find the just vengeance upon *Sacrilege*, under the *Law*, and the credit of the *Old Testament* is in this point suspected, I had rather shew it from the *New*. There, *Judas* who first filch'd from his *Masters* baggs, afterwards betrayed his *Master* himselfe, and, as a just punishment of his former sins, taught us by his miserable example, that there is an *halter*, a *snare*, which lyeth hid in these *Holy things*. This befell him who theiv'd from *Christ*. But they, who first dared to make an inrode upon the *Church stock*, (though it be all one) I say not to take it away being given, but

Exod. 1.10.

Numb. 16.31.
H. Jos. 7.26.

P. Dan. 5.24.25.

2 Kings 11.16.

Act. 5.10.

only to detein it, before it was given, (the *Gospel* it selfe making no plea, nor interceding for the fact) were choaked with a sudden and most horrid death, upon a word of the *Apostle*. Upon which place I will stand a little more: For it is, as the fairest, so the most apposite and full in this point.

First, then, it is evident that *things may be consecrated to Holy use*, even under the *Gospel*.

Secondly, That *being so consecrated*, they are no longer *ours*.

Thirdly, that, since they are not *ours*, they cannot be deteined without great *sin*, not *taken away* without greater.

Fourthly, That whosoever doth one or t'other, doth it therefore, because *Satan hath filled his heart.* (*Sacrilegious Persons*, then, are filled with *Satan*.)

Fifthly, That this kind of men is to be punished with *death*, not only with *censures*.

Sixthly, And that *death sudden*, that there should be no space for the *expiating of so great a sin.* And,

Seventhly, with *death immediately from Heaven*, wherby *God* declared, as it were from Heaven, that he himselfe was the *avenger of so great a wickednesse*.

These examples, *Fathers* and *Brethren*, are from the *Gospel*. The *Gospel* is no milder against these men then is the *Law*. And even the *Gospel* itselfe, the Minister of life, hath its *snare, a snare of death*, for that man, for that Conscience, which makes no *Conscience or Religion* of *devouring* what belongs to *Religion*.

Yes, but how many *Sacrilegious persons* hath no such thing befallen? For it is not usuall or perpetuall which is inflicted on *a growing mischiefe*: Neither doth *Solomon* say it is; that they shall be taken in the *very act*. But what he saith, is *usual*, neither do examples fail us; for, though they may escape the *light* and *day* for a while, they shal not escape so; *Solomons snare* will take them by the *heele*. For the *snare* he speakes of, is the *Snare of a Fowler*; in which perhaps the *bird*, that is taken, is not presently strangled, but tangled by the *foot* or *neck*, oftimes till the evening, and oftimes longer, till the return of the *Fowler*. Many times the destruction is slow, but ever sure.

I believe you have observed, that the *Holy Scriptures* speak not of the *punishment of wicked men*, alwayes, after the same manner. The Wrath of *God* is sometimes as a *storme* suddenly rushing down all before it; sometimes as a *Net* taking for the present, and after a while slaying. In P. *Esay*, (*Chap.* 51. v. 8.) it is an *Axe* suddenly cutting down: and it is a *Moth* consuming by piecemeale. In P. *Hosea*, (*Chap.* 5. *v.* 12.) He saith, he will be a *Lyon* to some, to others *rottennesse* and a *Moth*: a *Lyon*, which teareth in a moment; a *Moth*, which weareth out insensibly and by degrees. The

Apoplexie killeth one way, the *Hectik* another, but both kill. A *Ship* perisheth one while by *neglecting the Pump*: another while by the *Overflowing of the Billowes*; but both wayes it perisheth. That *Thunderbolt* of St. *Peter* effected the businesse sooner; this *Snare* of *Solomon*, slower: but both this and that bring the same businesse about, have the same issue.

This is the fruit of *Sacrilege*. Men fly upon the *bait*, nay into the *net* too, but being wholly intent and set upon the *prey*, they tast its *sweetnes*, but take no heed to the *danger*, with which they intangle and snare both Soul and Conscience. Not so indeed, that they come suddenly to ruin, but, feast upon this *Worme*, while they have devoured all; but when they would get loose, they shall find that they are held with the *cords* of sin, *Pro.* 5. 22. with the *snares* of death, *Psal.* 18. and that the *judgment*, which, perchance, rusheth not suddenly upon them, but waiteth at the doore, is not to be made slight of. That the *Fowler* will come at last, will certainly come, and the *Soule* so *insnared* shall be *his* prey; a prey, I say, to the *Devill*, (*GOD* and what belongs to *God*, having been formerly *his* prey) by that most just sentence, P. *Jer.* 30.16. *They that devoure thee shall be devoured.*

I have shewed you the *Snare*. And that is layd for *Man. Both *Him* that sins, and *others* for his sake. For such is the nature of this *sin*, that it reacheth all the Camp over, that it makes the whole *Common-wealth* a valley of *Achor*. Touching the *Sacrilegious Person* himselfe, we have told you, that he provides very il for *his own private fortune*, into which he bringeth this *cursed* gain, as a pledg or earnest of misfortune. These *Holy things* will eat out the bottom of his bags, in which they are crowded, and will make them full of holes and rents. *This field* will blast and burn up all his other *fields: This stuffe* will bring a consumption upon all the *rest*; the punishment, this, denounced by the P. *Haggai*. Worse, then so, betides their *Souls*, which they fill with *Satan*, who catcheth them in an inexplicable *Snare*, and reserveth them to that *Judgment* which is insufferable.

I will speake breifly, both of the *Common-wealth*, and of the *Church*.

When this *sin* is once admitted, GOD sendeth a *Devourer* upon the *State*, for the *Devouring of his Holy things*. Either the *Catterpiller*, P. *Malachy* 3. 11. or *Men* worse then the *Catterpiller*. The *Kings of Israel*, when they once plundred *Holy things*, had no peace, but much trouble and vexation, going out or comming in; what they took from the *Temple*, they were forc'd to fling away upon the *Souldiers*, the *Camp-Locusts*. In S. *Augustin's* time, when the *President of the Provinces* rifled the *Sanctuaries*, that people was not inriched by it. What they tooke from the *Temple*, they were forc'd to fling away upon the *Lawyers, the Bar-Locusts.* Because *Devotion* to *God* decreased, the commings in to the *Exchequer* increased. *One devourer*

*לאדם

P. Hag. 1.6.

2.16.17.
Acts 5.3.

follows *another*, either a Brigade of *Souldiers*, or a swarm of *Lawyers*. There will be a *Snare* for certain; or a *Snare* of *Law*, or a *Snare* of *Taxes*, or a *Snare* of *War*: doubtlesse, *God* will raine down *Snares* upon such a Nation.

Now briefly, touching the *Church*. But, there, when the *Holy Portion* is *devour'd*, all that is *Holy* is *devoured* with it. For by weakning the hands of the present *Clergy*, and alienating the minds of others for the future, either there will be no *Prophet* at all, or he, that shall be, will himselfe be a *Snare* in the *waies of Israel*. The *People* will become the prey of the *Dragon*: of that *Dragon* who standeth before the *woman now ready to bring forth*, that, when she hath brought forth, he may *Devour* it. For certainely a greater *sin* then *Sacrilege* lyes under this; and (what I admonished at the first) these men are, not only *Sacrilegious*, but, to be taken for Enemies to all that is called *Holy*.

For whereas these foure kinds of *Holy* cleave, and are, as it were, bound up together, [1] *Holy Manners*. [2] *Meanes*. [3] *Persons*. [4] *Revenues*. There is but one bit of all; and, it cannot be but, he, that shall swallow *one*, must needs swallow *all* the rest, at the same draught. [1] Let there be no *Revenue*, there wil be no *Levite*. H. *Nehe*. 13.10. Do you see al this great Assembly? Every one of them will betake himselfe to the Country, and give over the *House of God*, unlesse order be taken for their sufficient maintenance. [2] Let there be no *Prophet*, there will be no *Prophecy*, no *Law*. If those be but once gone, there will be no learned *Priest*, to teach the people. The *Holy Spirit* joynes these two together. 2 *Chro*. 15.3. *Without* [1]*a Teaching Priest, and without the* [2] *Law*. [3] Let there be no *Prophesy*, and there shall be no *People*. K. *Solomons* word for it. *Prov*. 29.18. The issue of all is; those men, who *Devoure Holy things*, *Devoure* also the *Prophets*, as they did their *Judges*. But they, who *devoure* the *Prophets*, *devoure Soules*. They, that *devoure Soules*, *devoure the People of GOD* as it were *bread*. Whosoever then swallow down *Holy things*, are the gulfs not only of *Revenues* and *Maintenance*, but also of the *Prophets*, of *Sermons*, of *Soules*, of *Kingdoms*. Let no man deceive you with cunning words; as *salvation* is not without the *Word*, nor the *Word* without a *Prophet*; so, most certain it is, that, there will be neither *Prophets* nor *Schooles* for the PROPHETS, long, without liberall maintenance.

Say I these things after the manner of men? Say not the *Holy Scriptures* the same also? What all *Heathen* writers inculcate, that, *Honour is the Nurse of the Arts*, the same doth St. *Paul*, thrice in a verse, affirme to be the *Nurse* of *Divinity*. That we must plow, sowe, thresh, *in Hope*: that without this *Hope of Carnal things*, we may bid adieu to the harvest of *Spiritual*. K. *SOLOMON* said, *where the Crib is empty, the Oxen faile*: He said it for us: who in vaine expect well manag'd *Oxen*, unlesse we store up *Provender* for them. A wiser then K. *Solomon* said, though not of this matter, yet not beside it, unlesse there be a *Carcass* there will be no *Eagles*. He said it to us, who in vaine expect *Eagles*, if we take away the *Carcass*. The *study of Divinity* must have its incouragements. For *CHRIST* and his *College* were not *begging Fryers*, as some have determined. No, but He had a bag, and that so larg, that He could buy with it not only what was needfull, but also give unto the *Poore*. And *St. PAUL* wills that there be an *abundance*, not only in *Almes*, but much more in *Offerings*; (for we must understand him to speak of both, as I formerly acquainted you.) *bountifully*, not *sparingly*, not only *supplying want*, but also *abundant*. Besides, he that will have a *Bishop* to be given to *Hospitality*, as well as *apt to teach* (and indeed if there be any prejudice against it, he puts, in the first place, *given to Hospitality*) would have him to be not only well furnished from his *Study*, for *Doctrine*; but also from his *Chest*, for *Hospitality*. And, lastly, he is of opinion that they wither in the *Faith*, who are so tenacious, such holdfasts. And that, if at any time *their Faith* increase, *our condition* and *fortune* will be mended. The *condition* of the *Clergy* ought to be, such as should be, nearer *Envy*, then *Mercy*. S. Joh. 13.29.
2 Cor. 8.20.
2 Cor. 9.6,12.
1 Tim. 3.2.
Philip. 4.10.

Look upon the *Old Canon*. One part of *Consecration* was *Annointing*; another, *Filling of the hand*; and, where the last failes, the first is also wanting. So under H. *Moses*; *Dathan* envyed at it. The Levites must have, *Asuppim*, their gatherings, and, *Parbar*, their store. So under K. *David*. There must be *heapes*, great *heapes*, enough to eate, plenty, great store. So under K. *Hezechiah*. Nor was there ever a merrier world, then under those *Kings*, who have been *bountifull to the Levites*. Nor ever a more dismall face of the *State*, then under those *Kings*, who look'd with a Malignant, envious eye upon the *Levites*. 1 Chro. 26.15,18.
2 Chro. 31.10.

Look upon that *Anarchy* of the *Judges*; See the *Levites* wandring up and downe: the *Reason*: why, their *wages* were *Ten Shekels*. Look on *Saul's* time; the *Ark* was not sought to in those dayes: the *Reason*: why, their fortune was to bow themselves for a *piece of silver*, and *a bit of bread*. *Doeg* was in more esteem then was *Ahimelech*. Look on *Jeroboam's*. Whosoever would was *consecrated Priest*, even of the *lowest of the people*: the *Reason*: why, the *lowest* are fit enough for the *lowest condition*. And, with *Us*, (Fathers and Brethren) if we would fling away our paines at so *low a price*, as some, now they have bras'd their foreheads, sticke not to say; any, that can but *weare a long Gowne*, and *prate by the houre-glasse, and huddle out much, no matter what, to the purpose or beside*, shall bee a fit *PROPHET* for Us. Judg. 17.7,8,10.
1 Sam. 2.36.
1 Sam. 22.9.
1 Kings 12.31.

What remaineth, I shall give you in a word. Consider wee how *GOD*, in the *Prophet Zachary*, Chap. 11. v.12 when hee had thoughts of forsaking *Israel*, forsooke them upon this very point, because they requited His paines with too cold and beggerly a *reward*. Doe you heare? quoth He; if you think good, give mee my price: and, if not, forbear. When they had weighed him some money, *viz. Thirty pieces*, He, in indignation, flyes out into these words; surely, a glorious *Reward*, a goodly *price* that I am prised at of you. And he broke the *Staff* of the *Pastorall* Office, and made voyd whatsoever good he had purposed to *that* people. This example was not given in vaine. Believe me, this happens dayly to Excellent Spirits, and full of *GOD*, (unlesse there be perchance one or two, an *Eldad* or *Medad*) who sometimes have these thoughts, and tacitly speake thus to themselves: Alas, this of its owne nature is *a weighty burthen*; but, by the *Pharisaicall* laying on of load, (which yet they touch not with the little finger) is now made *infinite*; the place is *slippery*, and full of *Cares* and *Troubles*: Will there be any *Reward?* When they see that men are cold in that point, that they must take *pains* at a *low price*, that *infinite labour* is required, and *Thirty pieces* shall be payd for all; many who otherwise incline to the study of *Divinity*, break their *Staves*, betake themselves to other Studies, and fall off from their purpose of consecrating themselves to these Studies, and to this *sacred* work.

Which that it may not come to passe, (*Fathers* and *Brethren*) that there may be no more breaking of these *staves*, apply early remedies to this disease. Free the *Church* from that *taile* of *Prophets*, which is otherwise likely to happen; free the *Common-wealth* from these *snares* of troubles; free your selves from the bloud of so many soules, which daily perish by *SACRILEGE*. Often urge this Text, and others like it.

<small>P. Isai. 9.15.</small>

<small>P. Eze. 3.18.20.</small>

I take it for granted, and confessed by all, that a Learned *Clergy* would be an excellent and most desired thing, so we might see grounds how it may be effected. Which that it may be, it seemes to me to be the better course to inculcate *this point* in our Sermons, then (what we have long done with lamentable successe) to bite and teare one another, while at length we be consumed one of another.

<small>Gal. 5.15.</small>

Unlesse this be done, truly the *wasts* and *ruins* of the *Church* are manifest: but the *buildings* or *materials* of the building appeare not. I see the *decaies, and dilapidations*, but, how they should be *repared* or *made up*, I see not. I cannot *hope* that things will be *better* then they are: that they will be *worse* then they are, I can *feare*.

I have treated of a Subject, as I often think with my selfe, necessary to be treated of and thought upon. My judgement concerning it, and myselfe too, I, a *Prophet* of the same *Order*, though not of the same *Worth*, submit to you who are the *Prophets, and Fathers of the English Prophets*.

The true *Light* of the world inlighten our minds with his light, that we may not only see the vices and corruptions of the present times, and search out the causes of them; but also that we may dislodg them out of those things which are of greatest moment, and apply our selves with all our might to remove them. Let us, what lyeth in us, make the *Church* to flourish, and keep it so being made. Finally, let us reflect upon *Hiersalem*, as the chief of all our joyes, through *JESUS CHRIST our LORD Amen.*

$$\left(\begin{smallmatrix}&*&\\ *&&*\end{smallmatrix}\right)$$

5   *Some believed the things which were spoken, and some believed not.* Acts. 28.24

FINIS.

Octob. the 29th. 1646.
Imprimatur
JOHN DOWNAME.

V

A Lecture on Genesis 2.18 (The Creation of Eve) Preached at St. Paul's Cathedral, 18 October 1591

Gen. 2.18.   *Dixerat autem Jehovah Deus, non est bonum esse hominem solum: faciam ei auxilium commodum ipsi.*

Octob. 18.
1591.

THE Prophet *Esay* 51.1 exhorteth the Church of God after this manner, *Look back* (saith he) *unto the stone out of which yee were hewn, and to the pit out of which you were digged*; By which he certifieth the Church of God, that there is a very necessary and profitable consideration to be made out of the historie of *Abraham* and *Sara*, and their lives, as it is expressed in the Scriptures. So may we say of the historie of *Adam* and *Eve* our first Grandfather and Mother; for they are more properly indeed to be termed the first stone, out of whom all mankinde were hewn, and the pit, out of whose womb we all were digged and taken: And so much more profitable is this historie and the explication thereof, because *St. Paul* saith, *Ephes.* 5.25. that the creation of *Eve* and her marriage, is *magnum Sacramentum*, shewing us the mysterie of Christ, the second *Adam*, and his espousage to the Church, which was his *Eve* taken out of his side. I told you that from the 6. verse of this Chapter to the end of it, is conteined a Commentary upon the 27. verse of the first Chapter, where *Moses* in one word dispatcheth the Creation of Man and Woman, saying *Marem & fœminam creavit eum*, which he so briefly passed over there, because he purposed in this Chapter to retorn to a more large and ample discourse thereof.

We have heard of the Creation of *Adam* in the former part of this Chapter hitherto, which is nothing else but a glosse upon these words of the first Chapter *Marem creavit*: Now therefore we come to the explaning of the other part, which is *Fœminam creavit eum*, which he performeth from this verse to the end of the Chapter. In all which verses, the Fathers say,

Two principall points.

that there are but two principall points to be considered, the first is, The

1–3 *A Lecture ... 1591.*] ed.

creation of the woman, the other, The espousall and marriage of her to the Man.

Touching the creation and framing of *Eve*, it conteineth partly a deliberation, and then the work of creation it self; the deliberation is in these words, *non est bonum homini esse solum, ei faciamus, &c.* which containeth also two parts, first the consultation in this 18. verse, and then the occasion of it, in the verse following, 19. 20.

But before we speak of the consultation, let us first consider what coherence with that which went before, which is thus sorted.

After the Almighty God had framed the estate Ecclesiasticall, which is his Church, by the Covenant made between God and man. Now in this next place he proceedeth to the ordering of the estate œconomicall, which is of particular Families, by the duty of Man and Wife in Mariage: By which God would have us learn to know, that by his will and ordinance all men (next after our duty to Almighty God, which is first) are bound to have a most speciall care and regard of their duties in that other society, which is this, If they be Husbands, their next care must be of their duty to their Wives; if Children, of their duty to their Parents; if Servants, of their duty to their Masters; for these duties of the private Families in the Commonwealth, are next in honour and reverence to the divine duties which we own in the houshold of Faith, which is in the Church unto God; for this society is *lege ipsa antiqua*, as one saith, and therefore we must give more honour and reverence unto it.

Now for the summe and scope of this verse, we will divide it into two parts, first into Gods *Dixit*, and secondly into the tenor of his speech, which is, *Non est bonum, &c.* and first briefly of *dixit Deus*, because we often heard of it before, we must note, that *qui dicendo facit, verbo facit*, which teacheth us to give honour to Christ the second person in Trinity, who is *the word of God, of whom all things are made and ordained, John* 1.3. Secondly, touching this *Dixit*, which we see by it and other singular prerogatives herein given to Mankinde, which we may add to all the former.

For in the creation of other Creatures, God used only the word of authority *fiat*, but here he useth the word of his good will and pleasure which is *faciam*.

Before he ever directed his speech to that which was not, *Gen.* 1.3. saying *fiat lux*, when there was then no light but all darknesse; But now he reflecteth his speech to himself, as it were, consulting with deliberation about this work, in that the Contents of his speech, in touching the good and happinesse of Man, in foreseeing what is not good for him, in providing

5 *ei*] *ed*.; *i*. AS

that which is best for him, we doe not only see his care over us above other Creatures, but also we are taught to acknowledge how well and reverendly we ought to esteem this ordinance of marriage, for God knew that many speeches and reproaches would arise among men against this work which God had in hand, of making Woman. Some by way of jest and merriment to disgrace that sex, and others in contempt to dispraise them, calling them necessarie evills; &c. therefore God saw it needfull to expresse the absolute good which cometh to Man by Woman, as being so necessarie that we cannot be well without them; for seeing we cannot deny, but that God that doth best know what we want and what is good, doth affirm that it is good for us to have *Eve* made, and that it were evill for us to be alone without her; therefore that we presume not foolishly in jest nor earnest to contradict and crosse Gods will.

The tenor or content of the Consultation standeth upon two parts, The first is a reason or cause which moved God to make *Eve* in the words, *Non est bonum, &c.* The other is his purpose and Decree to make him a help; the form of both which standeth thus, *I will make her to be a help to him, because it was not good for him to be without help.*

Touching which the Fathers doe say, That now a pawse is to be made, because this form of speech which is first used, is to set down the true and right use of Logick; which is the art of right reasoning, or cause which moveth God to make *Eve* in these words, *Non est bonum, &c.* the other is his purpose by argumentall conclusion; for they observe well, that all the speeches which hitherto have been used, have been imperative, absolutely commanding things to be done: So that Gods authority and will is the only reason of all that hath been done: But now at the making of Woman God useth a speech of argument and reason, concluding and informing the absolute necessitie of this work; which also must teach us, to be a rule to direct us in the immortality of our actions, namely, to consider, as here God doth, what is good touching our actions, and what evil may come by doing and not doing it: if we in sound judgment can say *bonum est*, then we are to conclude this, *ergo faciendum est*: If right reason telleth us this *malum est*, we are taught to resolve upon this conclusion *ergo non faciam*: So that the rule of reason is in all things to consider, whether it be good or bad. Again, He saith not *Non est bonum mihi, sed non est bonum domino*, that is, he respecteth more the good of others, than of himself; this is Christs reason which he used and moved in all his actions, *expedit vobis ut hinc abeam, John* 16.7. which is to teach us to doe the like, for it is *q.d.* all one because it shall be better for his, and the perfecting of his estate; therefore for his sake I will make him a meet help, which example must teach superiors how to frame all their reasons and actions, alwaies respecting the common good of their inferiors more than their own private commoditie, for we shall see it both here and elsewhere, that God maketh the good and welfare of his people the ground of his Decrees; so may we observe the like in the reversing that which he had decreed, to punish them and destroy them for sin, yet if they repent of their evill, God will reverse his Decree for their good, which *Jonas* knowing *Jon*.4.7. saith, that God doth oftentimes by this means seem to make his Prophets lyars, because that for the good of mankinde he doth often reverse and revoke the sentence denounced by them against wicked men; wherefore we may well say, that Gods goodnesse is as much seen in caring for the good of man, being made, as in creating man, which was nothing before: All which he doth that the consideration of his love and goodness to us might be, as it were, *cords & links of love to tie us unto him in all duty and obedience, Ose* 11.4. and to teach us to frame all our thoughts words and deeds to the augmenting of the glorie of God; As to say, Because it is good and acceptable to his glorie I will doe this, *& è contra*.

I come now to the reason, and first to the antecedent thereof, in which we see that God doth set his heart upon Man, being made, that now he taketh a speciall view to see whether he can espie any good thing to be wanting about him which he might supply. We read in the end of the first Chapter, *that God*, looking upon man, *saw all to be very good*, yet here he that thought man by creation *to be very good*, saw a defect of one good thing yet, which might make much for his perfection: And therefore he taketh order here to furnish him with it, that nothing might be wanting to those that he loveth.

By this therefore it appeareth that solitarinesse is counted an imperfection in Mankinde, but not in God; for he being most perfect, yea, the perfection of all things, needeth not any other thing to be adjoyned to him as a companion or help meet for him.

Therefore he is and ever will be set alone, and will be called *solus sapiens Deus*, as the Psalmist saith, *Thou art God alone*: But among the Creatures this sheweth all things to be imperfect, in that it is not well with them, if they be alone; For the perfection of Angells is in multitude; being an Host: The perfection of Mankinde, touching the civill perfection, is in societies, by which Families, Cities, and Common-wealths are made; so we may mark that solitarinesse: God in the Creation doth at least double every thing, that it might not be alone. In the firmament he made great lights and lesser lights: The waters were made double, the upper and nether waters: The Earth had herbs and trees: And as for Fish, Fowl, and Beasts, he made all things in aboundance. *Salomon* sheweth, in the 4. *Eccles*. 9, 10, 11. that above all other Creatures it is most meet and convenient for man, in divers respects, not to be alone, and concludeth the point with *væ Soli*, because it is not good for man especially to be alone: And therefore when our Saviour Christ calleth his

Disciples, it is said, *he sent them out by pairs, two and two*, because he would not alwaies they should be solitary and alone, *Matth.* 10.4. *Luke* 10.1. But there is no rule so general, but that hath his particular exceptions in some special causes, unlesse it be in moral rules, of good things commanded by God, for against such there is no exceptions to be taken. But in the rules of naturall goodnesse touching conveniency, we may ever in some instance make an exception, As (*Husay* 2 *Sam.* 17.7) *this counsell is good, but not at this time*: So we may say, the light is good for all, yet it is evill and hurtfull to ill eyes: So may we say of solitarinesse, that sometimes it is most good & meet for a man to be alone in solitariness; so it is good and most meet for some man to be alone without companie; for so *Moses* said *Leprosus habitabit solus*, that is to avoid infection. God saith of his Schollars *Ducam eos in solitudinem & docebo eos*, shewing oftentimes solitarinesse is best for Students, and so our Saviour Christ often frequented solitarie places for private prayer, as most fit for it. Thus we see generally how this is to be taken, but more particularly we must consider of it in the speciall case of Marriage, to see how this is verified in a single and unmarried life, whether (in that respect) it be not good for all men to be alone.

It is not good for man to be alone.

Object. *A question may be made here of the truth and true meaning of the word of God in*
Resp. *this speech?* In resolving of which we must make a concordance and agreement, between these two verses of the old Testament, and that of *St. Paul* in the new Testament, 1 *Cor.* 7.1. which saith contrary to this, *non est bonum mulierem tangere*.

For reconciling of which we must remember, that in the 17. and 18. verses of this Chapter is offered to our consideration a double kind of good, in the 17. verse is spoken of *bonum morale*, to which is opposed the evill of sinne and transgression, but in this 18. verse is spoken of *bonum naturale*, which is the good of conveniency either for our profit or pleasure, to which is opposed not the evill of sinners, but of inconveniency and indecency, by reason of the want of something which is requisite and meet, and of such a good is here spoken: For *St. Paul* saying, it is not good to touch a woman, doth not mean that it were a sinne to marry, for 1 *Cor.* 7.36. he saith, if a man doth marry he doth not sinne therein, for Christ saith of the Angells, they neither marry nor are given to be married, and yet they are holy, they sinne not, because they doe not marry, yea their estate is better without marriage, than *Adams* was in Paradise being married; *St. Paul* telleth us, *Gal.* 3.28. That in Christ all the faithfull shall be, as the Angells without Sexes of male and female, and so without marriage, wherefore the inconvenience for which it is not good to be alone here on earth is in respect of circumstances, places, times, and persons, of which *Augustine* saith well, *Distingue circumstantias &*

concordant, to be understood, *q.d.* It is not good for man to be alone without a wife while he liveth on the earth, for we have seen that in Heaven this is not verefiable, because it shall be (there) best for man to be unmarried, and as the Angels are. In regard of the circumstance of time, we must understand this *q.d.* it is not good now at the beginning of the World, that man should live and continue alone, for if he had been alwayes alone and without a wife, the world had been as a waste wildernesse without inhabitants to dwell on it, and in this respect it had not been good in regard of the purpose and decree of almighty God, who as it is in the *Epistle to the Hebrews*, purposed to bring many children unto glory, and had said, *Gen.* 1. That mankinde should so multiply as to fill the earth, which had not been done but by means of marriage of male and female, so that we say, in respect of the circumstance of persons, that though it is true, that it is not good for such a man to live unmarried, which cannot abstain in raging lust from burning, yet if a man hath received the gift of continency and chastity, then it is good and best for such a man to be alone; But this end was accessory and came after the fall, for in the state of innocency there was no danger of such lust and uncleannesse, and, as *propter fornicationem*, did not concern *Adam* in Paradise; so the other end which was to encrease and fill the earth, respecteth not us now, for we see the earth is so full of people and so mightily replenished, that it may seem in this respect, more convenient now to restrain the liberty of marriage in some, that fewer families might be: We see then in what respect *Moses (bonum)* must take place, and *St. Pauls (bonum non)* must give place and yeeld to it; To conclude for the full resolution of this point, we must know that the principall good of man is *Adhærere Deo Psal.* 37.6. Which cleaving fast to the Lord as *St. Paul* saith, 1 *Cor.* 7.35. must be our rule to know, whether it be good for us, not to marry or to marry at all, for though it be a good and lawfull thing to have a wife, yet we must know it to be so farre forth good, as it will further us in cleaving fast to the Lord.

For rather than marrying a wife, should be a means to divert and separate us from God, which is our first conjunction by religion, we must never marry, nor be married, but count it evill and hurtfull to us in this case to take a wife: Again if a single life be found in us an occasion of fleshly lust and temptations, by which we are plucked further from God, and are lesse able to be neer unto him in Christian duties, then if we were married; in this case we know that it is good for us to marry, and it is not good for us to be alone any longer. If we finde that the cares and troubles of this life, which the estate of marriage bringeth with it, will be a means to keep and separate us from God, then saith *St. Paul*, in that respect a single life is better, 1 *Cor.* 7.28. For Christ telleth us, that many are separated and plucked away from God, by marrying a wife, by attending to their Farms and Oxen, &c.

The question then standeth *inter solicitudinem & solitudinem*, for that estate which we finde doth least trouble our mindes with the cares of this world, must be thought best and fittest for us.

And thus *Moses* and *St. Paul* may be reconciled, if we shall advisedly consider it will be a means to keep us from the two extremes which are in the world, and make us keep the middle way wherein it is best to walk; For being grounded in this we shall not be moved by *St. Pauls* words, to condemn and contemn marriage as the Papists doe: Nor yet on the other side shall we give ourselves to that licentiousnesse and liberty of the flesh, of which *St. Paul* speaketh, 1 *Tim.* 3.7. When men and women of wantonnesse doe marry for filthy lust, and as the superstition of Papists, and lasciviousnesse of wantonnesse will be avoided; so by this means marriage and a single life shall be well used of all, as shall be best for their good and the glory of God.

Object. There is also a second objection made against this saying of almighty God, the occasion is, *Seeing he saith it is best for man to cut away all occasion and alurement of evill. Therefore it may seem that God might better have said, it were good for man to remain alone without a wife, &c.* But they which object this, doe but cavell with the word of God and crosse that which is here said, God saith, that a wife is good for man, but they say she is evill for him, and God saith she is a meet help, but they say she was a hurt and hindrance to him, and a help in nothing but this, to help forward to a further misery. Therefore (say they) it had been better for *Adam* to have remained alone still in happinesse, than to have such a companion which would bring him to misery.

For answer to which it was not, *causa sine qua non*, as they would make it, for though *Adam* had been alone without *Eve*, yet (no doubt) he might and would have fallen as he did now: For as the Angells which though they were unmarried, yet notwithstanding did fall and not keep their first estate: So (no doubt) the Divell would have been as strong in his delusions to have made him to fall, as he was in deceiving his wife; we may therefore lay the fault of this sinne upon *Eve* or the Divell; for as *St James* saith, *Jam.* 1.14. It was not so much any outward occasion as his inward and corrupt concupiscence which made him to sinne; But be it that she was the cause of fall, yet from whence then came that occasion of evill to him, *Non e, e latere viri*, why then, out of himself came all this cause of sinne.

But if any shall complain yet further of the womans hurt and fault; let us know that this woman was made by the counsell of God, the means and occasion by which amends was made, and that with advantage for the evil, for all the evill which she had first done, for as she brought forth sinne and death, so she was a means to bring forth a holy seed, which should bring eternall righteousnesse and life unto all, for as the Serpent should deceive the woman: So it was Gods purpose, that the seed of woman should destroy the Serpent and his works; wherefore we must not so much with grief marvail that the womans sinne was made the occasion of all our misery, as with joy and comfort to wonder, that God made the seed of the woman to save us from sinne, and to bring us to felicity. And thus much for the resolution of these two doubts.

Now for the second part, we see that after deliberation, God cometh to this determination and saith, *Faciam adjutricem,* where we may mark that God saith not *fiat*, as when he made other Creatures, but *faciam* which is a word of advisement and wise deliberation, whereas *fiat* is a word of haste, and expedition to be presently done without delay, which almighty God doth, to put us in minde, that when we goe about to get our selves wives, or to give our children in marriage, that we must not goe about it rashly or suddenly, to post up such matters on the sudden, but with great discretion, wise advice, and consultation, to attempt so weighty a matter, that is, first by considering whether it be good or no for us that a match should be made; Again, seeing it is plain that God only is the giver of good and meet marriages and wives, we learn, that therefore it is our duty when we lack this help, to pray earnestly unto God, that it would please him to say unto us, as he said unto *Adam, I will make a meet help for thee,* For want of observing which rules in wedlock, it often cometh to passe, that very unmeet matches and marriages hath been in the world, and foul corruptions and abhominable abuses, have crept into this holy ordinance to the slander and disgrace thereof, for this is set down as the chiefest cause of all the monstrous sinnes of the first age of the world *Gen. 6.2. Because the sonnes of God looking upon the daughters of men, took them wives according to their own fancies,* that is, rashly and headily without advice and deliberation, and they took them at the first sight as pleased themselves, and did not crave of God to give them such as might please him, *Micholl, Davids* wife, is said to be a wife of *Saules* making and giving, and therefore because God made not the match and marriage between them, she was not a meet help, but a snare to intangle him: And so God doth threaten, *Joshua* 23.12,13. *verses,* that if the Israelites doe after their own wills take unto them heathenish woman to be their wives, which he had forbid, they should be no helps to them but hurts, namely, *They should be thorns to their eyes, whips to their sides, and snares to their feet,* because they doe not take wives at Gods hands, that is, such as he alloweth and willeth them to take.

VI

A Sermon Preached before Queene Elizabeth, at Hampton Court, on Wednesday, being the VI. of March,

A.D. MDXCIIII

LUKE CHAP. XVII. VER.XXXII.
Memores estote Uxoris LOT.
Remember LOT'*s Wife.*

A Part of the Chapter read this Morning, by order of the Church, for II. *Lesson.*

The words are few, and the sentence short; no one in Scripture so short. But it fareth with *Sentences* as with *coynes*: In coines, they that in smallest compasse conteine greatest value, are best esteemed: and, in sentences, those that in fewest words comprise most matter, are most praised. Which, as of all sentences it is true; so specially of those that are marked with *Memento*. In them, the shorter, the better; the better, and the better caried away, and the better kept; and the better called for when we need it. And such is this heere; of rich contents, and with all exceeding compendious: So that, we must needs be without all excuse, it being but three words, and but five syllables, if we doe not remember it.

The Sentence is our SAVIOUR'*s,* uttered by Him upon this occasion. Before, (in *Verse* 18.) He had said: that the dayes of the *Sonne of man should be as the dayes of* LOT, in two respects. [1]In respect of the sodeinesse of the destruction that should come: [2]and in respect of the securitie of the people, on whom it should come. For, the *Sodomites* laughed at it; and *Lot*'s wife (it should seeme) but slightly regarded it. Being then in *Lot*'s storie, verie fitly, and by good consequence, out of that storie, He leaveth us a *Memento*, before He leaveth it.

17 with all] withall F_2

There are in *Lot*'s storie, two very notable monuments of GOD's judgement, ¹The *Lake of Sodome*, ²and LOT's *Wive's Piller*. The one, the punishment of *resolute sinne*; the other, of *faint vertue*. For, the *Sodomites* are an example of impenitent wilfull Sinners: and *Lot's wife* of imperseverant and relapsing righteous persons.

Both these are in it: but CHRIST, of both these, taketh the latter onely. For, two sorts of men there are, for which these two *Items* are to be fitted. ¹To those in state of Sinne that are wrong, the *Lake of Sodome*: ²To those in state of Grace, that are well (if so they can keepe them) *Lot's wive's Piller*. To the first in state of Sinne, *Moses* propoundeth the Vine of *Sodome* and grapes of *Gomorra, quæ contacta cinerescunt*, that if ye but touch them, turne to *ashes*. To the other in state of grace, CHRIST heere, *Lot's wive's Piller*. To the one, *Jeremie* crieth, *Qui cecidit, adjiciat ut resurgat*. To the other, Saint Paul: *Qui stat videat ne cadat*. *Agar*, that is departed from *Abraham*'s house, with her face toward *Aegypt*, the Angel calleth to returne, and not to persevere: *Lot's* wife, that is gone out of *Sodome*, and in the right way to ZOAR, the Angell willeth to persevere and not to returne. So that, to them this *Memento* is by CHRIST directed, that being departed from the errors of Ur, are gone out from the Sinnes of *Sodome*, are entered into the profession of truth, or into the course of a vertuous life. So that, if we lay it to our selves we shall lay it aright; that *Lot's Wife* be our example, and that we sprinkle our selves with the salt of her *Piller, ne putescamus*, that we turne not againe to folly, or fall away from our owne stedfastnesse. And, if it be meant to us, needfull it is, that we receive it. A point (no doubt) of important *consideration* and necessitie, as well for *Religion*, to call on; as for our *Nature* to heare of. First, for *Religion*: her glorie it is, no lesse, to be hable to shew *antiquos Discipulos*, old *Professors*, as *Mnason* was, then daily to convert and make new *Proselytes*. And therefore, with CHRIST, we must not ever be dealing with *Venite ad me*; but sometimes too, with *Manete in me*; That, hath his place: Not ever with *stimuli*, goades to incite men to; but, otherwhile, with *Clavi*, neyles to fasten them in. For, as *Nature* hath thought requisite as well the *Brests* to bring up, as the *Womb* to bring forth: and *Philosophie* holdeth *tueri* of no less regard then *quærere*: And with the *Lawyers, Habendum* is not the onely thing, but *Tenendum* needfull too: And the *Physitian* as carefull of the *regiment*, and fearefull of the *recidivation*, as of the *disease* and *cure*: So *Divinitie* is respective to both; both, to lay the groundworke surely *Ne corruat*, that it shake not with *Esay's Nisi credideritis*; and, to roofe it carefully, *Ne perpluat*, that it rain not through and rott the principalls, with *Paul's, Si permanseris, alioquin excidéris & tu.*

Deut. 32.32.

Jer. 8.4.
1 Cor. 10.12.
Gen. 19.17.

Matt. 11.28.
John 15.4.

Esay 7.9.

Rom. 11.22.

7 fitted.] fitted: F_2 14 *stat*] *stat*, F_2 22 selves] selves, F_2 27 then] than F_3

Needfull then for *Religion*, to call on this vertue: and, as for *Religion*, to call on; so, for our *Nature* to be called on: Wherein, as there is *tenellum quid*, a tender part not hable to endure the crosse, for which we need the vertue of *Patience*: So is there also ἀψίκορόν τὶ, a *flitting humor*, not hable to endure the *tædiousnesse* of any thing long; for which we no lesse need the vertue of *Perseverance*. The *Prophet* (in the 78. *Psal.*) saith, our Nature is as a *Bow*, which when it is bent to his full, except it be followed hard, till it be sure and fast, starts back againe, and is as farr off as ever it was. The *Apostle* compareth it to *flesh* (as it is) which will *sine sale putescere*, and if it be not *corned*, of it selfe bring forth *corruption*. And to help this our evill inclinaton forward, there be in all Ages dangerous examples, to draw us on. The *Israëlites*, after they had passed the red Sea and all the perills of the desert, & were now come even to the borders of *Canaan*, even there, say *Benè nobis erat in Ægypto*, we were better in *Ægypt: Let us make a Captaine and returne thither*. The *Romanes* (in the *New*) at the first, so glorious Professors, that Saint Pauls saith, *All the world spake of their faith*: After, when trouble arose, and *Saint Paul* was called *coram*, of the same *Romanes* he saith, *Nemo mihi adfuit, sed omnes deseruerunt*, None stood by me, All shrunke away. And in these dangerous dayes of ours, The falling away quite of diverse, and some such, as have said of themselves (with *Peter*) *Etsi omnes, non ego*; and others have sayd of them, *Etsi omnes non ille*: The declining of others, which (as *Daniels image*) decay by degrees; from a *head* of fine *Gold* fall to a *silver brest*, and from thence to *loines of brasse*, and thence to *Leggs of iron*, and last to *feete of clay*: The wavering and *amaze* of others that stand in the Plaine (with *Lot's* wife) looking about, and cannot tell, whither to go forward to little *Zoar*, or back to the ease of *Sodom*; shew plainly that *Lot's wife* is forgotten, and this is a needfull *Memento, Remember Lot's wife*. If then it be ours, and so nerely concerne us, let us see, *quantum valent hæ quinque Syllabæ*.

The Division

I. 1. First, CHRIST sending our memorie to a storie past; of the use of *remembering stories* in generall.

II. 2. Secondly, Of this particular of *Lot's wife*, and the Points to be remembred in it.

III. 3. Thirdly, How to apply those points, that (as *Saint Augustine* saith) *Condiant nos, & Sal Statuæ sit nobis condimentum vitæ*, that the *Salt* of this *Piller* may be the *Season* of our lives.

I. _____

8 off] F_2; of F_1 *in marg*: Rom. 7.18] *LACT*; Rom. 7.1 F_1, F_2, F_3

A SERMON PREACHED THE VI. OF MARCH MDXCIIII

The Prophet *Esai* doth call us, that stand in this place, the *Lord's Remembrancers*: As to GOD, *for the People*, by the office of *Prayers*; so from GOD, *to the People*, by the office of *Preaching*. In which office of *Preaching*, we are imployed as much about *Recognosce*, as about *cognosce*; as much in calling to their mindes the things they know and have forgott, as in teaching them the things they know not, or never learnt. The things are many, we have Commission to putt men in mind of. Some touching themselves: For, it is, many times, too true, which the Philosopher saith: *Nihil tam longè abest a nobis quam ipsi nos*, Nothing is so farr from our minds, as we our selves. For, naturally (as saith the *Apostle*) we do παραρρυέιν *leake*, and *runne out*; and when we have looked *in the glasse*, we streight *forgett our fashion againe*. Therefore we have in charge to put men in minde of many things, and to call upon them with diverse *Memento's*. *Memento quia sicut lutum tu*, Remember the basenesse of our mold what it is: *Memento quia vita ventus*, Remember the frailnesse of our life how short it is. *Memento tenebrosi temporis*, Remember, the *dayes of darkenesse* are comming, and *they be many*. All which we know well enough, and yet need to be put in mind of them.

But, the *store-house*, and the very *life* of *memorie*, is the *Historie* of time; and a speciall charge have we, all along the Scriptures, to call upon men to looke to that. For, all our wisedome consisting either in *Experience* or *Memorie*; Experience *of our owne*, or Memorie *of others*; Our daies are so short, that our *Experience* can be but slender, *Tantùm hesterni sumus* (saith *Job*;) and our own time cannot affoord us observations enough, for so many cases, as we need direction in. Needs must we then (as he heer adviseth) *interrogate generationem pristinam*, aske the *former Age*, what they did in like case: search the *Records* of former times; wherein, our cases we shal be hable to match, and to paterne them all. *Salomon* saith excellently, *Quid est quod fuit? Quod futurum est*; What is that that *hath been*? That that *shalbe*: and back againe, What is that that *shal be*: That that *hath been*: *Et nihil novum est sub Sole*, and there is nothing under the Sunne of which it may be said, *it is new*, but it hath been already in the former generations. So that, it is but turning the wheele, and setting before us some case of *Antiquitie*, which may sample ours, and either *remembring to follow* it, if it fell out well; or *to eschew* it, if the successe were therafter. For example, By *Abimelech's* storie, King *David* reproveth his Captaines, for *pursuing the enemie too neer the wall*, seeing *Abimelech* mis-caried by like adventure; and so maketh use of remembring *Abimelech*. And by *David's* example (that, in want of all other

Esa. 62.6.
The use of Stories in generall.

Heb. 2.1.
Jam. 1.23,24.

Job 10.9.
Job 7.7.
Eccles. 11.8.

Job 8.9.

Job 8.8.

Eccles. 1.9.

2. Sam. 11.21.

Mat. 2.25.

---

12 *in marg.* Jam. 1.23, 24] *LACT*; Jam. 1.23 F_1, F_2, F_3 26 *in marg.* Job 8.8] *LACT*; 8. F_1, F_2, F_3 31 Sunne] F_2; Snn F_1

bread, refused not the *Shew-bread*) CHRIST our SAVIOUR defendeth His Disciples in like distresse, and sheweth, that, upon such extremitie, *Necessitas* doth even *legem Legi dicere*, give a Law, even to the Law it selfe.

[1] Deut. 32.7.
[2] Esay 46.9.
[3] Jer. 6.16.
[4] Job 8.8.
[5] Jam. 5.10.
[6] Heb. 10.32.

Seven severall times we are called upon to doe it: [1]*Memento dierum antiquorum* (saith *Moses*:) [2]*Recordamini prioris Seculi (Esai:)* [3]*State super vias antiquas, (Jeremie:)* [4]*Investiga patrum memoriam (Job:)* [5]*Exemplum sumite Prophetas, (James:)* [6]*Rememoramini dies priscos, (Paul:)* [7]*Remember Lot's wife*, CHRIST, heer; that is, To lay our actions to those, we finde there, and of like doings, to looke for like ends. So read stories past, as we make not our selves matter for storie to come.

II.
Of this of *Lots Wife*.

Now, of and among them all, our SAVIOUR CHRIST after a speciall manner commendeth unto us, this of *Lot's wife*. Of which thus much we may say, That it is the onely one storie, which, of all the stories of the Old Testament, He maketh His choise of, to putt in His *Memento*; which He would have them, which have forgotten, to *remember*, and those that remember, never to forget. Oft to repaire to this *storie*, and to fetch *salt* from this *Piller*: that they lose not that they have done, and so perish in the *recidivation* of *Lot's wife*.

Then to descend into the particulars: I find, in *stories*, two sorts of *Memento*: 1. *Memento & fac*, Remember *to follow*: 2. *Memento & fuge*, Remember *to flie* the like. *Marie Magdalen's ointment*, an example of one; *Lot's wife's Salt Stone*, an example of the other. Or (to keepe us, to this storie) *Lot looked not back*, till he came safe to *Zoar: memento, & fac. Lot's wife* did, and died for it: *memento & fuge*.

The verse before sheweth, why CHRIST layd the *memento* upon her. Μὴ καταβάτω μὴ ἐπιστρεψάτω, that we should not turne or returne back, as she did: that we should not follow her, but, when we come at this *Piller*, turne at it and take another way. That is, we should *remember Lot's wife*, but *follow Lot*; remember her, but follow him.

Now, in either of both *memento's*, to *follow*, or to *fly*, we alway enquire of two points (and so, heer) [1]*quid fecit*, [2]*quid passa est*: *what they did*, whose storie we read; and, *how they spedd*: The *Fact* and the *Effect*. The *Fact*, *Vice* or *Vertue*: the *Effect*, *Reward* or *Punishment*.

Gen. 19.26.

Both which, concerning this unfortunate woman, we find sett downe in one verse (in the XIX *of Gen.*) what She *did*; that *She drew back or looked back*: this was her *Sinne*. The *effect*, that *She was turned into a Salt stone*: this was her *Punishment*. And these two, are the two *Memorandum's* concerning her, to be *remembred*. First of her *fault*.

4 *in marg.* Deut. 32.7.] *LACT*; Deut. 33.7. F_1, F_2, F_3 35 Gen.] Genesis F_2 38 First] First, F_2

The *Angell* had given charge to *Lot* and his companie (in the seventeenth of that Chapter) *Scape for thy life: Stay not in the plaine: Looke not once behind thee lest thou perish. Scape for thy life:* She trifled for all that, as if no perill were. *Stay not in the plaine*, yet stayed she behind. *Looke not back lest thou dye*; she would, and did looke back, to dye for it. So that, she did all that, she was forbidd, and regarded none of the *angels* words, but *despised the counsell of* GOD *against her owne soule*. This was her sinne, the sinne of *disobedience*; but consisteth of sundry *degrees* by which she fell: Needfull, all, to be *remembred*.

^{1.} Her *fault*.

1. The first was: That she did not *Severè custodire mandatum Dei*, strictly keepe her to the *Angells* charge, but, dallied with it, and regarded it by halves; that is, say what he would, she might use the matter as she would; goe, or stay and looke about as she list. Such light regard is like enough to have growen of a wandring *distrust*; lest happly, she had left *Sodome* in vaine, and the *Angell* feared them, with that which never should be. The *Sunne rose* so *cleer*, and it was so goodly a morning, she repented, she came away. Reckoning her *Sonnes in Law* more wise in staying still, then *Lot* and herselfe, in so unwisely departing. Which is the sinne of *unbelief*, the bane both of *Constancie* and *Perseverance*. Constancie, in the *purpose of our mind*; and Perseverance in the *tenor of our life*.

¹*Wavering*.

2. From this grew the second, That she begann to *tire*, and *draw behind*, and kept not pace with *Lot* and the *Angells*. An evill signe. For (ever) *fainting* is next step to *forsaking*; and *Sequebantur a longè*, a preparative to a giving cleane over: *Occasionem quærit* (saith *Salomon*) *qui vult discedere ab amico*, He that hath no list to *follow*, will pick some quarrell or other *to be cast behind*.

²*Fainting*.

Pro. 18.1.

3. This *tiring* had it growen of weaknesse, or wearinesse, or want of breath, might have been borne with; but, it came of another cause, which is the third degree. It was (saith the text) at least to *looke back* and to cast her eye to the place, her soule longed after. Which sheweth, that the love of *Sodom* sticketh in her still: that though her feet were come from thence, her heart stayed there behind: and that, in looke and thought she returned thither, whither in body she might not; but (possibly) would in body too, if, as NINEVE did, so SODOM had still remained.

³*Looking back*

4. *Looking back* might proceed of diverse causes; So might this of hers, but that CHRIST's application directs us. The verse before saith, *Somewhat in the house*, somthing left behind affected her: Of which He giveth us warning. She grew weary of trouble, and of shifting so oft: From *Ur* to *Haran*; thence, to *Canaan*; thence, to *Egypt*; thence to *Canaan* againe; then

⁴*Preferring Sodom* to *Zoar*

6 that,] that F_3

to *Sodom*; and now to *Zoar*; and that, in her old daies, when she would fainest have been at rest. Therefore, in this wearisome conceit of new trouble now to beginn; and withall remembring the convenient seat, she had in *Sodome*, she even desired to *die by her flesh-pots*, and to be buried in *the graves of lust*: wished them at *Zoar*, that would, and her selfe at *Sodom* againe: desiring rather to end her life with ease in that *Stately city*, then to remove, and be safe perhapps, and perhapps not, in the *desolate mountaines*. And this was the sinne of restinesse of soule, which affected her eyes and knees, and was the cause of all the former. When men weary of a good course, which long they have holden, for a little ease or wealth, or (I wote not what) other secular respect, fall away in the end: so losing the praise and fruict of their former perseverance, and relapsing into the danger and destruction, from which they had so neer escaped.

Behold, these were the sinnes of *Lot's wife*; A wavering of mind: Slow stepps: the convulsion of her neck: all these caused her wearinesse and feare of new trouble, she preferring SODOM's *ease* before ZOAR's *safety*. Remember Lot's wife.

The Aggravation of her fall. This was her sinne: and this her sinne was, in her, made much more heynous by a double circumstance, well worth the remembring: as (ever) weighty circumstances are matter of speciall regard, in a *storie* specially. ¹One, that she *fell*, after she had *stood long*. ²The other, that she fell, even then, when GOD, by all meanes offered her safety, and so *forsooke her owne mercie*.

¹*After so long standing.*
ᵃJob 6.15.
ᵇAm. 8.12.
ᶜHos. 6.4.
ᵈMat. 13.20.
ᵉExod. 8.

Touching the first. These ᵃ*winter brookes* (as *Job* termeth flitting desultorie Christians) if they *drie*; these ᵇ*Summer fruicts* (as *Amos*) if they *putrifie*; these ᶜ*morning clouds* (as *Hosea*) if they *scatter*; these ᵈ*shallow rooted corne*, if they *wither* and come to nothing, it is the lesse grief. No man looked for other. ᵉ*Pharao* with his *fitts*; that at every plague sent upon him, is godly on a sodeine, and *O pray for me now*; and when it is gone, as prophane as ever he was; beginning nine times, and nine times breaking of againe; he moves not much. To go further: *Saul*, that for *two* yeare; *Judas*, that for *three*; *Nero*, that for *five* kept well, and then fell away, though it be much, yet may it be borne. But, this woman had continued now *thirty* yeare (for, so they reckon from *Abraham's* going out of *Ur*, to the destruction of *Sodom*:) This, this is the grief, that she should *persist* all this time, and after all this time fall away. The rather, if we consider yet further, that not onely she *continued many yeares*, but *susteined many things* in her continuance, as being companion of *Abraham* and *Lot*, in their exile, their travaile, and all their affliction. This is the griefe, that after all these stormes in the broad *Sea*

7 perhapps, and] om. F_3 9 weary] F_2; wery F_1

well past, she should in this pitifull manner, be wracked in the *haven*. And when she had been in *Egypt*, & not poisoned with the *superstitions* of *Egypt*; when lived in *Sodom*, and not defiled with the *sinnes* of *Sodom*; Not fallen away for the *famine* of *Canaan*, nor taken harme by the *fullnesse* of *the Cities of the Plaine*; after all this she should lose the fruit of all this, and doe and suffer so many things all in vaine: This is the first: *Remember* it.

The second is no whit inferiour: That, at that instant she wofully perished, when GOD's speciall favour was profered to preserve her: and that, when, of all other times she had meanes and cause to stand; then, of all other times, she fell away. Many were the mercies she found and felt at GOD's hands, by this very title, that she was *Lot's Wife*. For, by it, she was incorporated into the House and familie, and made partaker of the blessings of the *faithfull Abraham*. It was a mercie, to be delivered from the errors of *Ur*; a mercy, to be kept safe in *Egypt*; a mercy, to be preserved from the *sinne of Sodome*; a mercy, to be delivered from the *Captivitie of the five Kings*; and this the last and greatest mercy, that she was sought to be delivered from the *perishing of the five Cities*. This (no doubt) doth mightily aggravate the offense, that, so many waies before remembred by GOD in trouble, she so coldly remembred Him: and that now presently, being offered grace, she *knoweth not* the *day of her visitation*: But, being brought out of *Sodom*, and warned of the danger that might ensue; having the *Angells* to goe before her, *Lot* to beare her companie, her daughters to attend her, and being now at the entrance of *Zoar*, the haven of her rest; this very time, place and presence, she maketh choise of, to perish in, and to cast away that, which GOD would have saved; in respect of her selfe, *desperately*; of the Angells, *contemptuously*; of her husband and daughters, *scandalously*; of GOD and His favours, *unthankfully*; forsaking her owne mercie, and perishing in the sinne of willfull defection.

Remember Lot's wife, and these *Two*, [1]That she *looked back*, after so *long time*, and so many sufferings: [2]That she *looked back*, after so many, so mercifull, and so *mighty protections*. And remember this withall, That she *lookt back* onely, and *went not* back: Would, it may be, but that, it was all on fire. But, whither she would or no, or whither we do or no, this forethinking our selves, we be gone out this faint proceeding, this staying in the plaine, this convulsion of the neck, and writhing the eyes back; this irresolute wavering whither we should choose, either bodily *pleasures* in perishing *Sodom*, or the *safety of our soules* in little *Zoar*, was her sinne; And this is the sinne of many as *stand* as she stood, and *looke* as she looked, though they goe not back: but, if they goe back too, they shall justifie her, and heape upon

[2]Now, *when best meanes of standing*.

5 Plaine] Plaines F_2 32 that, it] that it F_2 33 whither...whither] whether... whether F_2 36 whither] whether F_2

themselves a more heavy condemnation. So much for the sinne, which we should *remember*, to *avoid*.

¹Her *Punishment*.

Now for her punishment, which we must *remember*, to *escape*.

This relapse in this manner, that the world might know it to be a sinne highly displeasing his Majestie, GOD hath not onely marked it for a *sinne*, but *salted* it too, that it might never be forgotten.

Death.
Rom. 6.23.

The wages and punishment of this sinne of hers, was it, which is *the wages of all sinne*, that is, *Death*. Death, in her (sure) worthily, that refused life with so easy conditions, as the holding of her head still, and would needs *looke back* and dye.

The sound of *death* is a fearefull, what death soever: yet it is made more fearfull foure waies; which all be in this of hers.

¹*Sodein.*

1. We desire to die with respite; and *sodeine death*, we feare and pray against. Her death was sodein, back she looked, and never looked forward more. It was her last looke.

²*In the act of sinne.*

2. We desire to have *remorse of sinne* yer we be taken away; and death, in the very act of sinne, is most dangerous. Her death was so. She died in the very *convulsion*; She died, with her *face* to *Sodome*.

³*Unusuall.*

3. We would die the *common* death of mankind, and be visited *after the visitation of other men*: and an unusuall strange death is full of terror. Hers was so. GOD's own hand from heaven, by a strange and fearefull visitation.

⁴*Without buryall.*

4. Our wish is, to dye, and to be *buried*, and not remaine a spectacle above ground which Nature abhorreth: She so died, as she remained a spectacle of GOD's wrath and a By-word to posteritie, and as many as passed by. For, untill CHRIST's time, and after, this monument was still extant and remained undefaced so many hundred yeares. *Josephus* (a Writer of good accompt, which lived after this) saith ἱστόρηκα αὐτήν, ἔτι γὰρ καὶ νῦν διαμένει: I my selfe have seene and beholden it, for it stands to be seene to this day. A *reed* she was, a *Piller* she is; which she seemed to be, but was not. She was *melting water*: She is congeled to *salt*. Thus have we, both her *fault* and *punishment*: Let us *remember* both: To shun the fault, that the penalty light not on us.

III.
Our *Lesson from this.*

Now, this *Piller* was erected, and this verdure given it, for our sakes. For, among the many waies that the wisedome of GOD useth to dispose of the sinne of man, and out of evill to draw good, this is one, and a chiefe one, that he suffereth not their evill examples to vanish as a shadow, but maketh them to stand as *Pillers* for Ages to come, with the Heathen mans inscription,

16 yer] ere F_2 32 erected,] F_2; erected; F_1

Ἐς ἐμὲ τις ὁρέων εὐσεβὴς ἔστω, *Looke on me, and learne by me, to serve* GOD *better*.

And, a high benefit it is for us, that he not onely embalmeth the memorie of the *Just*, for our *imitation*; but also powdreth and maketh brine of the *Evill, for our admonition*: that, as a *Sent*, from *Marie Magdalen's ointment*; So, a *relish*, from *Lot's wive's piller*, should remaine to all posterity.

Prophane persons, in their perishing, GOD could dash to peeces, and root out their remembrance from the off the earth. He doth not, but suffereth their *Quarters* (as it were) to be *sett up* in stories, *Ut pœna Impii sit eruditio Justi*, that their punishment may be our advertisement. Powreth not out their blood, nor casts it away, but saves it, for a *Bath*, *Ut lavet Justus pedes in sanguine peccatoris*, that the *Righteous* may *wash their footstepps in the blood of the ungodly*: that *all* (even the *ruine of the wicked*) may *co-operate to the good of them that feare* GOD. This woman, in her inconstancie, could He have sunke into the earth, or blowen up as *salt-petre*, that no remembrance should have remained of her: He doth not; but, for us, and for our sakes, he erecteth a *Piller*: And not a *Piller* onely, to point and gaze at; but a *Piller* or *rock of salt*, whence we may and must fetch, wherewith to season whatsoever is unsavorie in our lives. And this, this, is the life and soule of memorie: this is wisedome, The art of *extracting salt*, out of the *wicked*; *Triacle*, out of vipers; our own happinesse out of *aliena pericula*: and to make those that were unprofitable to themselves, profitable to us. For (sure) though *Lot's wife* were evill, her *salt* is good. Let us see then, how to make her evill, our good; see, if we can draw any savory thing from this example.

1. That which we should draw out, is Perseverance, *Muria virtutum* (as *Gregorie* calleth it) the Preserver of vertues, without which (as Summer fruits) they will perish and putrifie: The *Salt of the Covenant*; without which, the flesh of our Sacrifice will take winde and corrupt. But *Saint Augustine* (better) *Regina virtutum*, the Queene of vertues; for that, how ever the rest runne and strive, and doe masteries, yet *Perseverantia sola coronatur*, Perseverance is the onely *crowned vertue*.

2. Now Perseverance we shall attaine, if we can possess our soules with due care and ridd them of *securitie*. Of *Lot's Wive's* securitie, as of water, was this *Salt* heer made. And, if *securitie* (as water) doe but touch it, it melts away presently. But *Care* will make us fix our eye, and gather up our feet, and, forgetting that which is behind, *tendere in anteriora*, to follow hard toward the prize of our high calling.

3. And, to avoid *Securitie*, and to breed in us due care, *Saint Bernard* saith, Feare will do it: *Vis in timore securus esse? securitatem time*; The only

[1] *Perseverance.*

Psal. 58.10.
Rom. 8.21.

[2] *Care.*

Phil. 3.13.

[3] *Feare.*

8 off] F₂; of F₁

way to be *secure in feare*, is to *feare securitie*. *Saint Paul* had given the same
counsell before; that, to preserve *Si permanseris*, no better advise, then *Noli altum sapere, sed time*.

Rom. 11.22.

Considerations out of her fault.

1.

Now, from her Storie, these considerations are yeelded, each one as an handfull of *salt*, to keepe us, and to make us *keepe*.

First, that we see; as of Christ's *twelve*, which He had sorted and selected from the rest, one miscaried; *Et illum gregem non timuit lupus intrare*, and that the Woolfe feared not to seise, no, not upon that Flock: and as of *Noah's eight* that were saved from the flood, one fell away too; So, that of *Lot's* foure, heere, and but foure in all, all came not to *Zoar*, one came short. So that, of *twelve*, of *eight*, of *foure*; yea, a little after (*verse* 35.) of *two*, one is *refused*: that we may remember, few there be that scape from *Sodome* in the *Angels* companie; and of those (few though they be) all are not safe neither: Who would not feare, if one may perish in the companie of *Angells*?

2.

Secondly, that as one miscarieth; so, not every one, but one that had continued so long, and suffered so many things, and after all this continuance, and all these sufferings, falls from her estate, and turnes all out and in; and, by the inconstancie of one houre, maketh void the Perseverance of so many yeares, and (as *Ezekiel* saith) *in the day, they turne away to iniquitie, all the former righteousnesse they have done, shall not be remembred*.

Ezek. 18.24.

3.

Thirdly, that, as she perisheth; So, at the same time, that *Sodome*: She, by it; and it, by her. That, one end commeth to the sinner without *repentance*, and to the just without *perseverance*. One end, to the abomination of *Sodome*, and to the recidivation of *Lot's Wife*; *Et non egredientes, & egredientes respicientes*: They that *goe not out* of her, perish; and they that goe out of her, perish too, if they *looke backe*. *Lacus Asphaltites*, is a monument of the one; *Lot's Wive's salt stone*, a memoriall of the other.

4.

Lastly, that as one perisheth, and that *such a one*; So, that she perisheth at the *gates*, even hard at the entry of *Zoar*: which of all other, is most fearefull; So neere her safety, so hard at the gates of her deliverance. *Remember*, that neere to *Zoar gates*, there stands a *stands* stone.

These very thoughts, what her case was, these four waies; and what ours may be (who are no better then she was) will search us like *salt*, and teach us, if we remember, what we have been, we may (saith *Saint Bernard*) *erubescere*; so, if we remember what we may be, we may *contremiscere*: that, we see our beginnings, but see not our ending: we see our *Stadium*, not our *dolichum*. And that, as we have great need to pray (with the *Prophet*)

Thou hast taught me from my youth up, untill now, forsake me not in mine old age, now when I am gray headed; So, we had need stirr up our care of *continuing*, seeing we see, it is nothing to beginne, except we continue; nor to continue, except we doe it, to the end.   Psal. 71.18.

Remember, we make not light accompt of the Angel's *Serva animam tuam*: blessing our selves in our hearts and saying, *Non fecit tibi hoc*; we shall come safe, goe we never so soft: *Zoar* will not runne away.   Matt. 16.22.

Remember, we be not weary to goe wither God would have us; not to *Zoar*, though a *little one*, if our *soule* may there *live*: and never buy the ease of our body, with the hazard of our soule, or a few daies of vanitie with the losse of æternitie.

Remember, we slacke not our pace, nor *stand still* on the Plaine. For, if we stand still, by still standing, we are meet to be made a *Piller*, ever to stand still, and never to remove.

Remember, we *looke* not *back*, either with her, on the vaine delights of *Sodome* left; or with *Peter* or *Saint John* behind us, to say, *Domine, Quid iste*? both, will make us forget our *following*. None that casteth his eye th'other way, is εὔθετος, meete as he should be, *meet for the Kingdome of* God.   Joh. 21.20. Luk. 9.62.

But specially *remember*, we *leave not our heart behind us*, but that we take that with us, when we goe out of *Sodome*: for if that stay, it will stay the feet, and writhe the eye, and neither the one nor the other will doe their duty. *Remember*, that our *heart* wander not, that our heart long not. This *Care*, if it be fervent, will bring us *Perseverance*.

Now, that we may the better learne somewhat out of her *punishment* too: Let us *remember* also, that as to her, so to us, God may send some *un-usuall visitation*, and take us sodenly away, and in the act of sinne too.   Out of her punishment.

Remember the danger and damage: It is no lesse matter, we are about, then *perdet animam*. Which if we doe, we frustrate and forfeit all the fruit of our former well continued course; all we have done, is vaine. Yea, all that Christ hath done for us is in vaine; whose paines and sufferings we ought specially to tender, knowing that *Supra omnem laborem labor irritus*, No labour to lost labour; and Christ then hath *lost His labour* for us.

Remember the folly: that *beginning in the Spirit* we *end in the flesh*: turning our backs to *Zoar*, we turne our face to *Sodome*: joyning to a *head* of fine gold, *feet* of *clay*; and to a precious foundation, a covering of thatch.   Gal. 3.3.

Remember the *Disgrace*: that we shall lose our credit and accompt, while we live, and shall heare that of Christ, *Hic homo*; and that other, *Quid existis in desertum videre? A reed shaken with the winde*.   Luk. 14.30. Matt. 11.7.

       8 weary] F_2; wery F_1 13 ever] even F_2

Remember the *Scandall*: That, falling our selves we shall be a blocke for to make other fall: a sinne no lighter; nor lesse, nor lighter then a *mill-stone*.

Remember the *Infamie*: That we shall leave our memorie remaining in stories, among *Lot's Wife*, and *Job's Wife*, *Demas* and *Ecebolius* and the number of *Relapsed*; there to stand to be pointed at; no lesse then this heape of *Salt*.

Remember the *Judgement* that is upon them after their relapse, though they live, that they doe even (with her heer) *obrigescere*, wax hard and numme, and serve others for a *caveat*, wholy unprofitable for themselves.

Remember the *difficultie* of *reclaiming* to good: *Seven evill spirits* entering insteed of one, that their *last state is worse then the first*.

And lastly, *Remember* that we shall justifie *Sodome* by so doing; and her *frozen sinne*, shall condemne our *melting vertue*. For, they in the wilfullnesse of their wickednesse persisted till fire from heaven consumed them: And, they being thus obdurate in sinne, ought not she (and we much more) to be constant in vertue? And, if the drunkard hold out, till he have lost his *eyes*; the uncleane person, till he have wasted his *loines*; the contentious, till he have consumed his *wealth*, *Quis pudor quòd infœlix populus Dei non habet tantam in bono perseverantiam, quantam mali in malo!* What shame is it, that GOD's unhappy people should not be as constant in vertue, as these miscreants *have beene*, and be in vice!

Each of these by it selfe; all these putt together, will make a full *Memento*: which if she had *remembred*, she had beene a *Piller* of *light* in heaven, not of *salt* in earth. It is too late, for her: we, in due time yet, may *remember* it.

And, when we have *remembred* these, *Remember* CHRIST too, that gave the *Memento*: that He calleth himselfe *Alpha* and *Omega*; not only *Alpha* for his *happy beginning*; but *Omega*, for His *thrise happy ending*. For that He left us not, nor gave over the worke of our redemption, till He had brought it to *Consummatum est*: And that, on our part, *Summa Religionis est, imitari quem colis*, The highest act of Religion, is, for the Christian to conforme himselfe, not to *Lot's Wife*, but to CHRIST, whose name he weareth. And though *Verus amor non sumit vires de spe*, True *love* (indeed) receiveth no manner strength from *hope*, but, though it hope for nothing, loveth neverthelesse; yet, to quicken our love, which oft is but faint, and, for a full *Memento, Remember the Reward*. *Remember*, how CHRIST will *remember* us for it; which shall not be the wages of an hireling, or (*lease-wise*) for time, and terme of yeares, but αἰῶνες αἰώνων, Eternity it selfe, never to expire, end, or determine, but to last and endure for ever and ever.

But this *reward* (saith *Ezekiel*) is for those, whose foreheads are marked with *Tau*, which (as *Omega* in *Greek*) is the last letter in the *Hebrew*

1 selves] selves, F_2 11 insteed] in stead F_2

Alphabet, and the mark of *consummatum est*, among them: They onely shall escape the *wrath to come*. And this crowne is laid up for them, not of whom it may be said, *Currebatis benè* Ye *did runne* well; but, for those that can say (with Saint *Paul*) *Cursum consummavi*, I have *finished* my course well. Gal. 5.7.
2. Tim. 4.7.

And (thanks be to GOD) we have not hitherto wanted this *salt*, but *remembred Lot's wife* well. So that, this exhortation, because we have prevented and done that which it calleth for, changeth his nature and becommeth a *commendation*, as all others do. A commendation (I say:) yet not so much of the people (whose onely fælicitie is to serve and be subject to one that is constant; for otherwise, we know how wavering a thing the multitude is) as of the *Prince*, whose constant standing giveth strength to many a weake knee otherwise. And *Blessed be* GOD *and the Father of our* LORD JESUS CHRIST, that we stand in the presence of such a *Prince*: who hath ever accompted of *Perseverance*, not onely as of *Regina virtutum*, the Queen of vertues; but, as of *virtus Reginarum* the vertue of a *Queen*. Who (like *Zorobabel*) first, by *Princely magnanimitie*, layd the *Corner-stone*, in a troublesome time: and since, by *Heroicall constancie*, through many both alluring proffers and threatning dangers, hath brought forth the *head stone* also, with the Prophett's acclamation, *Grace, grace, unto it*: *Grace*, for so happy a *beginning*; and *Grace*, for so thrice happy an *ending*. No terrors, no enticement, no care of her safety hath removed her from her stedfastnesse: but, with a fixed eye with streight stepps, with a resolute mind, hath entred her selfe, and brought us into *Zoar*. *It is a little one*, but therein *our soules shall live*; and we are in safety, all the Cities of the *Plaine* being in *combustion* round about us. Of whom it shalbe *remembred*, to her high praise, not onely that of the Heathen *Illaque virgo viri*; but, that of *David*, that, all her dayes she served GOD, with the covenant of *Salt*, and with her *Israël*, from the first day untill now. And of this be we perswaded, that *He which begann this good worke in her, will performe it unto the day of* JESUS CHRIST, to her everlasting praise comfort and joy; and, in her, to the comfort, joy and happinesse of us all. 2. Chro. 13.5.

Yet it is not needlesse, but right requisite, that we which are the LORD's *Remembrancers* put you in mind, that as *Perseverance* is the Queen of vertues, *quia ea sola coronatur*; so is it also, *quia Satanas ei soli insidiatur*, for that, all *Satan's* malice, and all his practises are against it: The more carefull need we to be, to cary in our eye this example. Which GOD graunt we may, and that our hearts may seriously regard, and our memories carefully keepe it, *Ut hæc columna fulciat nos, et hic sal condiat nos*, that this *Piller* may *prop* our weaknesse, and this *salt season* our sacrifice; that it may be remembred, and accepted, and rewarded in the day of the LORD. Which, &c.

VII

A Sermon Preached at the Court, on the XXV. of March, A.D. MDXCVII. Being Good-Friday

ZACH. CHAP. XII. VER. X.
Respicient in Me, quem transfixerunt.
And they shall looke upon Me, whom they have pierced.

Act. 8.34.

That great and honourable Person the *Eunuch* sitting in his Chariot, and reading a like place of the Prophet *Esai*, asketh S. *Philip: I pray thee, Of whom speaketh the Prophet this? of himselfe, or some other?* A question verie materiall, and to great good purpose; and to be asked by us, in all *Prophecies*. For, knowing who the Partie is, we shall not wander in the *Prophet's* meaning.

Now, if the *Eunuch* had been reading this of *Zacharie* (as then he was, that of *Esai*) and had asked the same question of S. *Philip*, he would have made the same answere. And as he, out of those words tooke occasion; so may we, out of these, take the like, *to preach* JESUS unto them. For neither of himselfe, nor of any other, but of JESUS, speaketh the Prophet this: and the *testimonie of* JESUS *is the Spirit of this Prophecie.*

Apoc. 19.10.

That so it is, the *Holy Ghost* is our warrant; who, in S. *John's Gospell* reporting the Passion, and the last act of the Passion (this opening of the side, and piercing the heart of our *Saviour* CHRIST) saith plainly, that in the piercing, *the very words of the Prophecie were fulfilled, Respicient in me quem transfixerunt.*

Joh. 19.37.

Which terme of *piercing* we shall the more clearely conceive, if with the ancient Writers, we sort it with the beginning of *Psalme* 22, the Psalme of the Passion. For, in the verie front or inscription of this Psalme, our Saviour CHRIST is compared *Cervo matutino*, to the *morning Hart*: that is, a Hart rowsed early in the morning, (as from his very birth he was by *Herod*) hunted and chased all his life long, and this day brought to his end, and (as the poore Deere) stricken and pierced thorough side, heart and all: which is it, we are here willed to *behold*.

There is no part of the whole course of our Saviour CHRIST's life or death, but it is well worthy our *looking on*; and from each part in it, there goeth vertue to do us good: But, of all other parts, and above them all, this last part of his piercing, is here commended unto our view. Indeed, how could the Prophet commend it more, then in avowing it to be *an act of grace*, as in the fore-part of this Verse, he doth: *Effundam super eos spiritum Gratiæ, & respicient, &c* as if he should say: If there be any *grace* in us, we will thinke it worth the *looking on*.

Neither doth the *Prophet* onely, but the *Apostle* also, call us unto it, and willeth us ἀφορᾶν to *looke unto* and regard JESUS *the Author and Finisher of our faith*. Then specially, and in that act, when for the *Joy of our Salvation set before Him, He endured the Crosse, and despised the shame*; that is, in this spectacle, when He was *pierced*.   Heb. 12.2.

Which (surely) is continually, all our life long, to be done by us; and at all times, some time to be spared unto it: But, if at other times, most requisite at this time; this very day, which we hold holy to the memorie of his Passion, and the *piercing* of His precious side. That, though on other dayes, we employ our eyes otherwise, this day at least, we fix them on this object, *Respicientes in Eum*. This day (I say) which is dedicated to none other end, but even to *lift up the Sonne of man, as Moses* did *the serpent in the wildernesse, that we may looke upon Him and live*: When every Scripture that is read soundeth nothing but this unto us: when by the office of preaching, JESUS CHRIST is lively described in our sight, and (as the *Apostle* speaketh) is *visibly crucified among us*: when in the memoriall of the holy Sacrament, *His death is shewed forth untill He come*, and the mysterie of this *His piercing*, so many waies, so effectually represented before us. This Prophecie therefore, if at any time, at this time to take place, *Respicient in Me, &c*.   Joh. 3.14.   Gal. 3.1. 1. Cor. 11.26.

The principall words are but two, and set downe unto us, in two points. ¹The *sight* it selfe, that is, the thing *to be seene*: ²and the *sight* of it; that is, the act of *seeing* or *looking*. *Quem transfixerunt* is the Object, or spectacle propounded. *Respicient in Eum*, is the Act, or duety enjoined.   The Division.

Of which, the *Object* though in place latter, in nature is the former, and first to be handled: for that, there must be a thing first set up, before we can set our eyes to looke upon it.

OF the Object, *generally* first. Certaine it is, that CHRIST is here meant: Saint *John* hath put us out of doubt for that point. And *Zacharie* (here) could have set downe His name, and said, *Respice in Christum*: for, *Daniel* (before) had named his name, *Occidetur* MESSIAS; and *Zacharie* being after   I. The *sight* or *object* generally. 1. CHRIST. Dan. 9.26.

10 ἀφορᾶν]F_3; ἀρορᾶνF_1, F_2; om. *LACT*   20 did *the*] F_2; did, *the* F_1 29 ²] om. F_1

him in time, might have easily repeated it. But, it seemed good to the *Holy Ghost* and to Him, rather to use a circumlocution; and suppressing His name of CHRIST, to expresse Him by the stile or terme, *Quem transfixerunt*. Which being done by choise, must needes have a reason of the doing, and so it hath.

First, the better to specifie and particularize the *Person* of CHRIST, by the kind, and most peculiar circumstance of his death. *Esay* had said, *Morietur, Dye He shall,* and *lay downe His soule an offering for sinne*. ²Die, but what Death? a naturall, or a violent? *Daniel* tells us, *Occidetur*: He shall die, not a *naturall*, but a *violent* death. ³But many are slaine after many sorts; and divers kinds there be of violent deaths: The *Psalmist* the more particularly to set it downe, describeth it thus: *They pierced my hands and my feet*: which is onely proper to the death of the Crosse. ⁴*Die*, and be *slaine*, and be *crucified*: But, sundry els were crucified; and therefore, the *Prophet* (heere) to make up all, addeth, that he should not onely be *crucifixus*, but *transfixus*; not onely have his *hands* and his feet, but even his *heart pierced* too. Which very note severs Him from all the rest, with as great a particularitie as may be: for that, though many besides at other times, and some at the same time with Him were *crucified*; yet, the *side* and the *heart* of none was *opened*, but *His*, and His onely.

Esa. 53.10.

Dan. 9.26.

Psal. 22.16.

2. CHRIST *pierced*.

2. Secondly, as to specifie CHRIST himselfe in person, and to sever him from the rest; so in CHRIST himselfe, and in his Person, to sever from the rest of his *doings* and *sufferings*, what that is, that chiefly concerneth us, and we specially are to *looke to*: and that, is this daies worke, CHRIST PIERCED. S. *Paul* doth best express this: *I esteemed* (saith he) *to know nothing among you, save* JESUS CHRIST, *and Him crucified*: That is, the perfection of our knowledge, is CHRIST: The perfection of our knowledge in, or touching CHRIST, is the knowledge of *Christ's piercing*. This, is the chiefe *Sight*; Nay (as it shall after appeare) in this sight, are all sights: So that, know this and know all. This generally.

1. Cor. 2.2.

2. The *Object* specially.
1. The *Passion* it selfe *Quid*.

Now, *specially*: In the *Object*, two things offer themselves. ¹The *Passion*, or suffering it selfe; which was, *to be pierced*. ²And the *Persons*, by whom. For, if the *Prophet* had not intended, the *Persons* should have had their respect too: he might have said *Respicient in Eum qui transfixus est*, (which *Passive* would have carried the *Passion* it selfe full enough:) but, so, he would not; but rather chose to say, *Quem transfixerunt*; which doth necessarily imply the *Piercers* themselves too. So that we must needs have an eye in the handling, both to the *fact*, and to the *persons*; ¹*Quid*, and ²*quibus*, both what, and of whom.

1. The *Degree* thereof: *Trans-fixerunt*.

In the *Passion*, we first consider the degree: for *transfixerunt*, is a word of gradation: more then *fixerunt*, or *suffixerunt*, or *confixerunt*, either. Expressing unto us the piercing, not with *whipps* and *scourges*; nor of the *neiles* and *thornes*; but, of the *speare-point*. Not, the *whipps* and *scourges*, wherwith His skin and flesh were *pierced*; nor the *nailes* and *thorns*, wherewith his feet, hands and head were *pierced*; but, the *Speare-point*, which *pierced* and went through his very *heart* it selfe: for, of that wound, of the wound in his *heart*, is this spoken (*Jo.* 19.34.) Therefore *trans*, is heer a *transcendent*; through and through: through skin and flesh; through hands and feet; through side and heart and all: the deadliest and deepest wound, and of highest gradation.

Secondly, as the Preposition (*Trans*) hath his gradation and divers degrees; so, the *Pronoune* (*Me*) hath his generality of divers parts; best expressed in the *Originall*. *Upon Me*: not, upon my body and soule: *Upon Me*, whose Person, not whose parts, either *body* without, or *soule* within; but *Upon Me*, whom wholly, body and soule, quicke and dead, they have *pierced*. 2. The Extent, *Me*

Of the *bodie's piercing*, there can be no question; since, no part of it was left unpierced. Our senses certifie us of that, what need we further witnesse? 1. His *Bodie*.

Of the *Soule*'s too, it is as certaine; and there can be no doubt of it neither: that we truly may affirme, CHRIST, not in part, but wholly was *pierced*. For, we should do injury to the sufferings of our *Saviour*, if we should conceive by this *piercing*, none other but that of the *Speare*. 2. His *Soule*.

And may a *soule* then be *pierced*? Can any *Speare*-point go through it? Truly *Simeon* saith to the *Blessed Virgin*, by way of prophecie, that *the sword should go through her soule*, at the time of His *Passion*. And as the sword through *her*'s; so, I make no question, but the *Speare* through *His*. And, if through *her*'s, which was but *anima compatientis*; through His, much more, which was *anima patientis*; since *Compassion*, is but *Passion* at *rebound*. Howbeit, it is not a *sword* of *steele*, or a *Speare*-head of *iron*, that entreth the soule, but a metall of another temper: the dint whereof no lesse goreth and woundeth the soule in proportion, then those doe the body. So that, we extend this *piercing* of CHRIST further, then to the visible gash in His side, even to a *piercing* of another nature, whereby, not His *heart* onely was stabbed, but his very *spirit* wounded too. Luc. 2.55.

The Scripture recounteth two: and of them both, expressly saith, that they both *pierce the soule*. The *Apostle* saith it, by *Sorrow*: *And pierced themselves through with many sorrowes*: The *Prophet*, of *Reproach*: *There are, whose words are like the pricking of a sword*: and that, to the *soule* both: for, the *body* feeles neither. With these, even with both these, was the Soule of CHRIST JESUS wounded. 1. Tim. 6.10. Psal. 64.3, 4

For *sorrow*: it is plaine through all foure *Evangelists*; *undique tristis est anima mea usque ad mortem; My *soule* is invironed on every side with *sorrow*, With *Sorrow*. *Matt. 26.38 Mar. 14.34.

37 undique] LACT; undiq; F₁, F₂   38 usque] LACT; usq; F₁,F₂

126   A SERMON PREACHED GOOD-FRIDAY

^aMar. 14.33. *even to the death*: ^a*Cœpit* JESUS *tædere & pavere*, JESUS began to be *distressed*
^bLuc. 22.44. and in great anguish. ^b*Factus in agoniâ*, being cast into an *agonie*. ^c*Iam*
^cJoh. 12.27. *turbata est anima mea*; Now is my *soule troubled*: Avowed by them
all; Confest by Himselfe. Yea, that His strange and never els heard of
sweat; dropps of bloud plenteously issuing from Him all over his body, what
time, no manner of violence was offered to his body, no man then touching
him, none being neere him; that bloud came certainly from some great
sorrow, wherewith his *soule* was *pierced*. And, that his most dreadfull crie,
Matt. 27.46. which at once moved all the powers of heaven and earth, *My God, My God,*
&c was the voice of some mighty *Anguish*, wherewith His *soule* was smitten;
and that in other sort, then with any materiall *speare*. For, *Derelinqui à Deo*,
the body cannot feele it, or tell what it meaneth. It is the *soule's* complaint;
and therefore without all doubt, His *soule* within him was *pierced*, and
suffered, though not that, which (except charity be allowed to expound
it) cannot be spoken without blasphemy; Not so much (GOD forbid:) yet
much, and very much; and much more then others seeme to allow; or how
much, it is dangerous to define.

With *Reproach*   To this *edge* of *sorrow*, if the other of *piercing despight*, be added as a point
(as, added it was) it will strike deepe into any *heart*; especially, being
wounded with so many sorrowes before. But, the more noble the *heart*,
the deeper; Who beareth any *griefe* more easily then this griefe, the griefe of
Psal. 69.26. a contumelious *reproach*. *To persecute a poore distressed soule, and to seeke to*
vexe him that is already wounded at the heart, why it is the verie pitch of all
wickednesse; the verie extremity that malice can doe, or affliction can suffer.
And to this pitch were they come, when after all their wretched *villanies* and
spitting, and all their savage indignities in *reviling* Him most opprobriously,
he being in the depth of all his distresse, and for verie anguish of soule
crying *Eli, Eli &c*: they stayed those that would have relieved Him; and
Matt. 27.49. (void of all humanity) then scorned, saying: *Stay, let alone, let us see, if*
ELIAS *will now come & take him downe*. This barbarous and brutish
inhumanitie of theirs, must needs *pierce* deeper into his *soule*, then ever
did the *iron* into his *side*.

To all which if we yet add, not onely that horrible ingratitude of theirs,
there by him seen; but ours also no less then theirs by him foreseen at the
same time; (Who make so slender reckoning of these his *piercings*, and (as
they were a matter not worth the *looking on*) vouchsafe not so much as to
spend an houre in the due regard and meditation of them: Nay, not that
onely, but further, by uncessant *sinning*, and that without *remorse*, do most
unkindly requite those His bitter *Paines*, and as much as in us lies, even

28 *&c*:] F_2; *&c* F_1 29 *Stay*] F_2; *stay* F_1 33 yet] it F_2, F_3, LACT

crucifie afresh the SONNE OF GOD, *making a mocke of Him and His piercings.*)   Heb. 6.6.
These, I say (for, these all and every of them in that instant were before his eyes) must of force enter into, and go thorow and thorow his *Soule* and *Spirit*; that, what with those former sorrowes, and what with these after indignities, the *Prophet* might truly say of Him, and he of himselfe, *In Me, Upon Me*; not whose *body*, or whose *soule*; but, whom entirely and *wholly* both in body and soule, alive and dead, they have *pierced* and *passioned* this day on the *Crosse*.

Of the *Persons*: which as it is necessarily implied in the word, is very properly incident to the matter it selfe. For, it is usuall, when one is found slaine (as heere) to make inquirie, *by whom* he came by his death. Which so much the rather is to be done by us, because there is commonly an error in the world, touching the *Parties* that were the causes of CHRIST'S death. Our manner is, either to lay it on the *Souldiers*, that were the Instruments; Or if not upon them, upon *Pilate* the *Judge* that gave sentence; Or, if not upon him, upon the *people* that importuned the Judge; Or lastly, if not upon them, upon the *Elders of the Jewes* that animated the People: And this is all to be found by our *Quest* of *Inquirie*.   2. The *Person, à quibus*

But the *Prophet* heere inditeth others. For, by saying, *They shall looke &c*, whom *They have pierced*, he entendeth by very construction, that the first and second [*They,*] are not two, but one and the *same Parties*: And that *they* that are here willed to *looke upon him*, are *they*, and none other, that were the authors of this fact, even of the murther of JESUS CHRIST. And (to say truth) the Prophet's entent is no other but to bring the malefactors themselves that *pierced Him*, to view the body and the wounded *heart* of *Him, whom they have so pierced*.

In the course of Justice, we say and say truly; when a party is put to death, that the *Executioner* cannot be said to be the cause of his death; nor the *Sherif*, by whose commandement he doth it; neither yet the *Judge* by whose sentence; nor the *Twelve men*, by whose verdict; nor the Lawe it selfe, by whose authoritie it is proceeded in. (For, GOD forbid we should endite these, or any of these, of murther:) *Solum peccatum homicida*: Sinne, and Sinne onely is the murtherer. Sinne (I say) either of the Party that suffereth: or of some other, by whose meanes, or for whose cause he, is put to death.

Now, CHRIST'S owne sinne it was not, that he died for. That is most evident. Not so much by His owne challenge, *Quis ex vobis arguit me de peccato?* as by the report of his *Judge*, who openly professed, that he had examined Him, *and found no fault in Him: No nor yet* Herod, *for, being sent to him, and examined by him also, nothing worthy death was found in Him*: And therefore, calling for *water*, and *washing his hands*, he protesteth his owne   Joh. 8.46.

Luc. 23.14, 15.

Matt. 27.24. *innocencie of the bloud of this* JUST MAN: Thereby pronouncing him *Just*, and void of any cause, in himselfe, of his owne death.

It must then necessarily be the sinne of some others, for whose sake CHRIST JESUS was thus *pierced*. And if we aske, who those *others* be? or whose sinnes they were? the Prophet *Esai* tells us, *Posuit super Eum iniquitates omnium nostrûm*, He laid upon Him the transgressions of *us all*; who should (even for those our many, great, and grievous transgressions) have eternally been *pierced*, in *bodie* and *soule*, with torment and sorrowes of a never dying death, had not he stept between us and the blow, and receiv'd it in his owne body; even the dint of the wrath of GOD to come upon us. So that it was the sinne of our *polluted hands*, that *pierced* his *hands*: the *swiftnesse of our feet to do evill*, that *nailed His feet*: the wicked *devises* of our *Heads*, that gored his *head*: and the wretched *desires* of our *hearts*, that *pierced* his heart. We that *looke upon*, it is we that *pierced Him*: and it is we that *pierced Him*, that are willed *to looke upon Him*. Which bringeth it home to us; to me my selfe that speake, and to you your selves that heare; and applieth it most effectually to every one of us, who evidently seeing, that we were the cause of this his *piercing*, if our hearts be not too too hard, ought to have remorse, to be pierced with it.

Esa. 53.6.

When for delivering to DAVID a few loaves, *Ahimelech* and the Priests were by *Saul* put to the sword, if *David* did then acknowledge with griefe of heart, and say, *I, even I am the cause of the death of thy Father and all his house*, (when he was but onely the occasion of it, and not that direct neither:) may not we (nay, ought not we) much more justly and deservedly say of this *piercing* of CHRIST *our Saviour*, that we verily, even we, are the cause thereof: as verily we are, even the *principalls* in this *murther*; and the *Jewes* and others, on whom we seeke to derive it, but onely *accessaries* and instrumentall causes thereof. Which point, we ought, as continually, so, seriously to think of; and that no lesse then the former. The former, to stirre up compassion in our selves, over him that thus was *pierced*: the latter, to worke deepe remorse in our hearts for being authors of it. That he was *pierced*, will make our bowels melt with compassion, over CHRIST. That he was *pierced* by *us, that looke on Him*, if our hearts be not *flint* (as *Job* saith) or as the *nether mil-stone*, will breed remorse over our selves, wretched sinners as we are.

1. Sam. 22.22.

Job. 41.24.

II.
The *Act*.
To *looke upon Him*.

The *Act* followeth these words: *Respiciet in Eum*. A request most reasonable, to *looke upon Him*; but *to looke upon Him*; to bestow but a *looke* and nothing else; which even of common humanitie we cannot denie, *Quia non aspicere, despicere est*. It argueth great *contempt*, not to vouchsafe it the cast of our *eye*; as if it were an *Object* utterly unworthy the *looking* toward. Truely, if we marke it well, nature it selfe, of it selfe enclineth to this act.

32 *in marg*. Job. 41.24] *LACT*; Job. 41.15 F_1, F_2, F_3 37 vouchsafe it] $F_1, F_3, LACT$; vouchsafe in F_2

When *Amasa* treacherously was slaine by *Joab*, and lay weltring in his blood by the waies side, the storie saith, that not one of the whole Armie, then marching by, but when he came at him, *stood still and looked on him.*   2. Sam. 20.12.

In the Gospell, the party that going from *Jerusalem* to *Jericho* was *spoiled and wounded* and lay drawing on, though the *Priest* and *Levite* that passed nere the place relieved him not, as the *Samaritan* after did: yet it is said of them, they *went neere* and *looked on*, and then passed on their way. Which   Luc. 10.32. desire is even naturall in us: so that even *Nature* it selfe enclineth us to satisfie the *Prophet.*

Nature doth; and so doth *Grace* too. For, generally we are bound to regard the *worke of the* LORD, and to *consider the operations of His hands*: and   Psal. 28.5. specially this work; in comparison whereof GOD himselfe saith, the former workes of His, *shall not be remembred*, nor *the things done of old once regarded.*   Esa. 43.18.

Yea CHRIST himselfe, *pierced* as he is, inviteth us to it. For, in the *Prophet* heere, it is not *In eum*; but *In me*: not, *on Him*; but, *on Me*, *whom they have pierced.* But more fully in *Jeremy*: for, to CHRIST himselfe do all the ancient Writers apply (and that, most properly) those words of the *Lamentation: Have ye regard all ye that passe by this way? Behold and see, if there be any*   Lam. 1.12. *sorrow like my sorrow, which is done unto me, wherewith the* LORD *hath afflicted me, in the day of His fierce wrath.*

Our owne profit (which is wont to perswade well) inviteth us: for that, as from the *brazen Serpent* no vertue issued to heale, but unto them that   Num. 21.8, 9. steddily *beheld it*; so neither doth there, from CHRIST, but upon those, that with the eye of faith have their contemplation on this object: who thereby drawe life from him; and without it may and do perish, for all CHRIST and his passion.

And, if nothing els move us, this last may: even our danger. For, the time will come, when we our selves shall desire, that GOD looking with an angry countenance upon our sinnes, would turne his face from them and us, and looke upon the face of his CHRIST, that is, *respicere in Eum*: which shall justly be then denied us, if we our selves could never be gotten to do this duty, *respicere in Eum*, when it was called for of us. GOD shall not looke upon him, at ours; whom we would not *looke upon*, at his request.

In the *Act* it selfe are enjoined three things. 1. That we do it with *attention*: for, it is not Me, but *in Me*: Not onely *Upon* Him, but *Into* Him. 2. That we doe it oft, againe and againe; with *iteration*: for, *Respicient*, is *re-aspicient*. Not a *single act*, but an *act iterated*. 3. That we cause our nature to do it, as it were, by vertue of an *Injunction, per actum elicitum*, as the *Schoolmen* call it. For, in the *Originall*, it is in the *commending Conjugation*, that signifieth, *facient se respicere*, rather then *Respicient*.

        2 waies side] way side F_2

First then, not slightly, superficially or perfunctorily, but stedfastly, and with due attention, to *looke upon Him*. And, not to look upon the out-side alone; but, to looke *into* the verie entrailes; and with our eye to *pierce* him that was thus *pierced*. *In Eum* beareth both.

<small>I
With *Attention*.
Respicient In Eum.</small>

1. *Upon* him, if we *looke*, we shall see so much, as *Pilate* shewed of him, *Ecce Homo*, that *He* is a *Man*. And, if he were not a *man*, but some other *unreasonable creature*, it were great ruth to see him so handled.

2. Among men we lesse pitie *Malefactors*, and have most compassion on them that be *innocent*. And, he was innocent, and deserved it not (as you have heard) his enemies themselves being his Judges.

3. Among those that be innocent, the more *noble* the person, the greater the griefe, and the more heavy ever is the spectacle. Now, if we consider the Verse of this Text well, we shall see, it is GOD himselfe, and no man that here speaketh (for, to GOD onely it belongeth, to *poure out the Spirit of grace*; it passeth mans reach, to do it:) so that, if we *looke* better *upon* him, we shall see as much as the *Centurion* saw, that *this partie* thus *pierced is the* SONNE *of* GOD. The *Sonne* of GOD slaine! Surely, he that hath done this deed *is the Child of death*, would every one of us say: *Et tu es homo, Thou art the man*, would the *Prophet* answere us: You are they, for whose sinns the SONNE *of* GOD hath his very heart-bloud shed forth. Which must needs strike into us remorse of a deeper degree then before: That, not onely, it is we that have *pierced* the Partie thus found slaine; but, that this Partie, whom we have thus *pierced*, is not a principall person among the children of men, but even the *Onely begotten* SONNE *of the most High* GOD: which will make us crie out (with S. *Augustine*) *O amaritudo peccati mei, ad quam tollendam necessaria sumit amaritudo tanta!* Now sure, deadly was the bitternesse of our sinnes, that might not be cured, but by the bitter death and blood-shedding passion of the *Sonne* of GOD. And this may we see *looking upon Him*.

<small>Matt. 27.54.
2. Sam. 12.5, 7.</small>

But now then, if we looke *in Eum, into* Him, we shall see yet a greater thing, which may raise us in comfort, as farre as the other cast us downe. Even the bowels of *compassion* and tender *love*, whereby he would and was content to suffer all this for our sakes. For that, whereas [a]*no man had power to take His life from Him*, (for he had power to have commanded [b]*twelve Legions of Angells*, in his just defense: and, without any *Angell* at all, power enough of himselfe, with his [c]*Ego sum, to strike them all to the ground*.) He was content notwithstanding all this, to *lay downe His life for us sinners*. The greatnesse of which love passeth the greatest love that man hath: for [d]*greater love then this, hath no man, but to bestow his life for his friends*; wheras, He condescended to lay it downe for *His enemies*. Even for them that sought his death, to lay downe his life, and to have his blood shed for them that did shed it; to be *pierced* for his Piercers. Look how the former *In Eum* worketh

<small>[a]Joh. 10.18.
[b]Matt. 26.53.

[c]Joh. 18.6.

[d]Joh. 15.13.</small>

griefe, considering the great *injuries* offered to so great a *Personage*; So, to temper the griefe of it, this latter *In Eum* giveth some comfort, that so great a *Person*, should so greatly *love* us, as, for our sakes, to endure all those so many injuries, even to the *piercing* of his very *heart*.

Secondly, *Respicient* (that is) *Re-aspicient*: Not, once or twise, but *often-times* to *look* upon it: that is (as the *Prophet* saith here) *iteratis vicibus*, to *looke againe and againe*: or (as the *Apostle* saith) *Recogitare*, to *thinke* upon it, *over and over againe*, as it were to *dwell* in it for a time. In a sort, with the frequentnesse of this our *beholding* it, to supply the weaknesse and want of our former *attention*. Surely, the more steadily and more often we shall fixe our eye upon it, the more we shall be enured: and being enured, the more desire to doe it. For, at every *looking*, some new *sight* will offer it selfe, which will offer unto us occasion, either of godly *sorrow*, true *repentance*, sound *comfort*, or some other reflexion, issuing from the beames of this heavenly mirror. Which point, because it is the chiefe point, the *Prophet* here calleth us to; even, how to *looke upon* CHRIST often, and to be the better for our looking. It shall be verie agreeable to the Text, and to the HOLY GHOST's chief entent, if we prove how, and in how diverse sorts, we may with profit behold and *looke upon Him*, whom thus we have *pierced*.

First then, *looking upon Him*, we may bring forth for the first effect, that which immediatly followeth this Text it selfe, in this Text, *Et plangent Eum: Respice & plange*. First, *looke and lament*, or *mourne*: which is indeed the most kindly and naturall effect of such a spectacle. *Looke upon Him that is pierced*; and with *looking upon Him*, be *pierced* thy selfe: *Respice & transfigere*. A good effect of our first *looke*, if we could bring it forth. At least wise, if we cannot *Respice & transfigere*, *looke* and be *pierced*; yet, that it might be *Respice & compungere*, that with *looking* on Him, we might be *pricked in our hearts*; and have it enter past the *skinne*, though it go not cleane through: Which difference in this Verse, the *Prophet* seemeth to insinuate, when, first he willeth us to *mourne, as for one's onely sonne*, with whom all is lost. Or, if that cannot be had, to *mourne*, as for a *first begotten sonne*, which is, though not so great, yet a great mourning: even for the *first begotten*, though *other sonnes* be left.

And, in the next Verse, if we cannot reach to *naturall* griefe; yet he wisheth us to mourne with a *Civill*; even with such a lamentation as was made for *Josias*. And *Behold a greater then* JOSIAS *is heere*. comming not (as he) to an honourable death in *battell*; but to a most vile death, the death of a *Malefactor*: And not (as *Josias*) dying without any fault of theirs; but mangled and massacred in this shamefull sort, *for us*; even for us and our *transgressions*. Verily, the dumbe and senselesse creatures had this effect wrought in them (of *mourning*) at the sight of his death; in their kind

2.
With *Iteration*: *Re-aspicient*.
Heb. 12.3.

1. *Respice & transfigere*.

Acts 2.37.

Verse 11.

sorrowing for the murder of the SONNE *of* GOD. And we truly shall be much more senseless then they, if it have in us no worke to the like effect. Especially, considering it was not for them, he suffered all this; nor they no profit by it: but, for us it was; and we by it saved: And yet, they had compassion, and we none. Be this then the first.

<small>2. *Respice & transfige.*</small>

Now, as the first is *Respice & transfigere*, Looke upon him, and be *pierced*: so, the second may be (and that fitly) *Respice & transfige*; Look upon him, and *pierce*: and *pierce* that in thee, that was the cause of CHRIST's *piercing*: (that is) sinne and the lusts thereof. For, as men that are *pierced* indeed with the griefe of an indignity offered, withall are pricked to take *revenge* on him that offers it: such a like affection ought our second *looking* to kindle in us; even to take a wreake, or revenge upon sinne, *quia fecit hoc*, because it hath been the cause of all this. I mean (as the HOLY GHOST termeth it) *a mortifying* or *crucifying*; a thrusting thorow of our wicked passions and concupiscences, in some kind of repaying those manifold villainies, which the SONNE *of* GOD suffered by meanes of them. At leastwise (as before) if it kindle not our *zeale* so farre *against sinne*; yet, that it may slake our *zeale* and affection to *sinne*: that is, *Respice, ne respicias: Respice* CHRISTUM, *ne respicias peccatum*. That we have lesse mind, lesse liking, lesse acquaintance with sinne, for the *Passion*-sake. For that, by this means we do in some sort, spare CHRIST; and (at least) make his wounds no *wider*: Wheras by affecting sinne anew, we do, what in us lieth, to *crucifie Him* afresh, and both increase the *number*, and enlarge the widenesse of his *wounds*.

It is no unreasonable request, That, if we list not *wound* sinne, yet, seeing CHRIST hath wounds enough, and they wide and deep enough, we should forbeare to *pierce* him further, and have (at least) this second fruit of our *looking upon Him*: either to look and to *pierce sinne*; or to *looke* and *spare to pierce* him any more.

<small>3. *Respice & dilige.*</small>

Now, as it was *sinne* that gave him these *wounds*: so, it was love to us that made him receive them, being otherwise hable enough to have avoided them all. So that, He was *pierced* with *love*, no lesse then with *griefe*: and it was that *wound* of *love*, made him so constantly to endure all the other. Which *love* we may read in the *palmes* of *His* hands (as the *Fathers* expresse it, out of *Esa.* 49.16.) For, in the *Palmes of his hands, He hath graven us*, that he might not forget us. And the print of the *neiles* in them, are as *Capitall letters* to record his *love* toward us. For, CHRIST *pierced* on the Crosse is *liber charitatis*, the very *booke of love* laid open before us. And againe, this love of His we may read in the cleft of *His heart, Quia Clavus penetrans factus est nobis Clavis reserans* (saith *Bernard*) *ut pateant nobis viscera per vulnera*. The *point* of the *Speare* serves us instead of a *key*, letting us, through his *wounds*, see his verie *bowells*, the *bowells of tender love* and most kind compassion, that would for us endure to be so entreated. That, if the *Jewes* (that stood by) said truely of him, at Lazarus's grave, *Ecce quomodo dilexit Eum!* when He shed a few *teares* out of his eyes; much more truly may we say of him, *Ecce quomodo dilexit nos!* seeing him shedd, both *Water* and *Blood*; and that in great *plentie*; and that, out of his *heart*.

Joh. 11.36.

Which *sight* ought to *pierce* us with *love* too, no lesse then before it did with *sorrow*. With one, or with both: for, both have power to *pierce*; but specially *Love*: Which except it had entred first and *pierced* him, no *naile* or *speare* could ever have entered. Then let this be the third, *Respice & dilige*: Look, and be *pierced* with *love* of him, that so *loved* thee, that he gave himselfe in this sort to be *pierced* for thee.

And forasmuch as it is Christ his owne selfe, that, resembling his passion on the *Crosse* to the *Brazen Serpent lift up in the wildernesse*, maketh a correspondence between their *beholding* and our *beleeving* (for, so it is *Joh*.3.14.) we cannot avoid, but must needs make that an effect too: Even *Respice & crede*. And, well may we *beleeve* and trust him, whom looking a little before, we have seene so constantly *loving* us. For, the sight of that *love* maketh credible unto us, whatsoever in the whole scripture, is affirmed to us of Christ, or promised in his name: So that, beleeve it, and beleeve all. Neither is there any time, wherein with such cheerefulnesse or fulnesse of faith we crie unto him, My Lord *and* My God, as when our eye is fixed upon the *print of the neiles*, and *on the hole in the side* of him that was *pierced* for us. So that, this fourth duty Christ himselfe layeth upon us, and willeth us from his own mouth, *Respice & Crede*.

4. *Respice & crede.*

Joh. 20.28.

And, beleeving this of him, what is there, the eye of our *hope* shall not look for from him? What would not he do for us, that for us would suffer all this? It is S. Paul's argument, *If* God *gave his sonne for us, how shall he denie us anything with Him?* That is, *Respice & Spera*. Looke upon him, and his heart opened, and from that *gate of hope* promise thy selfe, and looke for all manner of things that good are. Which our expectation is reduced to these two: [1]The *deliverance from the evill* of our present miserie: [2]and the *restoring to the good* of our primitive felicitie. By the death of this undefiled *Lambe*, as by the yeerely Passeover, looke for, and hope for a passage out of *Egypt*: which spiritually is our redemption from the servitude of the power of darknesse. And, as by the death of the *Sacrifice*, we looke to be freed from whatsoever evill: So, by the death of the *High Priest*, looke we for and *hope*

5. *Respice & spera.*

Rom. 8.32.

9 naile] F₂; netle F₁   10 dilige:] F₂; dilige. F₁

for restitution to all that is good; even, to our forfeited estate in the land of *Promise*, which is *Heaven* it selfe, where is all joy and happinesse for evermore. *Respice & Spera*, Looke, and *Looke for*: by the *Lambe* that is *pierced*, to be freed from all miserie; by the *High Priest* that is *pierced*, fruition of all felicity.

6. *Respice & Recipe*.

Now, inasmuch as His *heart* is *pierced*, and his *side opened*; the *opening* of the one, and the *piercing* of the other, is, to the end, somewhat may *flow forth*. To which end (saith Saint *Augustine*) *Vigilanti verbo usus est Apostolus*, the *Apostle* was well advised, when he used the word *opening*; for, there issued out *water* and *blood* which make the sixt effect, *Respice & Recipe*. Marke it *running out*, and suffer it not to *runne waste*, but *receive* it. Of the former (the *water*) the *Prophet* speaketh in the first words of the next Chapter, that out of his *pierced* side ^aGOD *opened a fountaine of water to the house of Israel for sinne and for uncleannesse*: Of the *fulnesse whereof we all have received*, in the *Sacrament* of our *Baptisme*. Of the later (the *blood*) which the *Prophet* (in the ^bIX. *Chapter* before) calleth the *blood of the New Testament*, we may receive this day: for, it will runn in the high and holy *Mysteries* of the *Body* and *Blood* of CHRIST. There, may we be partakers of the *flesh* of the ^c*Morning-Hart*, as upon this day killed. There may we be partakers of the ^d*Cup of salvation*, the *precious blood* ^e*which was shedd for the remission of our sinnes*. Our part it shall be, not to accompt the ^f*blood of the Testament an unholy thing*, and to suffer it to runne in vaine for all us; but with all due regard to receive it so running: for, even therefore was it shedd. And so to the former, to add this sixt, *Respice & Recipe*.

^aZach. 13.1.
^bZach. 9.11.
^cPsal. 116.13.
^d1. Pet. 1.19.
^eMatt. 26.28.
^fHeb. 10.29.

7. *Respice & Retribue*.

And shall we alway *receive grace*, even *streames* of *grace* issuing from Him that is *pierced*, and shall there not from us issue something backe againe, that he may look for and receive from us, that from him have and do daily receive so many good things? No doubt there shall; if *love* which *pierced* Him, have pierced us aright. And that is (no longer to hold you with these effects) *Respice & Retribue*. For, it will even behove us no lesse then the *Psalmist*, to enter into the consideration of *Quid retribuam*: Especially, since we, by this day, both *see* and *receive* that, which he and many *others desired to see*, and receive, and could not. Or, if we have nothing to render, yet (our selves) to returne with the *Samaritan*, and *falling downe at his feete*, with a *loud voice*, to *glorifie His goodnesse*, who finding us in the estate, that other *Samaritane* found the *forlorne* and *wounded man*, healed us, by being *wounded* himselfe, and by his owne death restored us to life. For all which

Psal. 116.12.

33 receive, and] F_2; receive and F_1

his kindnesse, if nothing will come from us, not so much as a kind and thankfull acknowledgement, we are certainly worthy, He should restrein the fountaine of his benefits, (which hitherto hath flowen most plenteously) and neither let us *see*, nor *feele* him any more.

But, I hope for better things: that, *love*, such and so *great love* will *pierce* us, and cause both other fruits, and especially thoughts of *thankfulnesse* to issue from us. Thus many; and many more, if the time would serve: But, thus much severall uses may we have of thus many severall respects, or reflexed *lookings upon* HIM *whom we have pierced*.

Thirdly, *facient se respicere*. For, the HOLY GHOST did easily foresee, we would not readily be brought to the *sight*, or to use our *eyes* to so good an end. Indeed, to *flesh and blood* it is but a dull and *heavy spectacle*: And, neither willingly they begin to look upon it; and having begun, are never well, till they have done, and looke off of it againe. Therfore is the *Verbe* (by the *Prophet*) put into this *Conjugation* of purpose: which to turne in strict propriety is *Respicere se facient*, rather then *Respicient*: They shall procure or *cause*, or even *enjoine* or *enforce themselves to looke upon it*; or (as one would say) *looke*, that they *looke* upon it.

3. With *enforcement of themselves. Respicere se facient.*

For some new and strange *spectacle* (though vaine and idle, and which shall not profit us how strange soever) we cause our selves sometimes to take a journey, and besides our paines, are at expenses too, to *behold* them: we will not only look upon, but even *cause our selves to looke upon* vanities; and in them, we have the right use of *facient se respicere*. And why should we not take some paines, and even *enjoine our selves* to *looke upon* this? being neither farre off, nor chargeable to come to; and since the *looking on* it may so many waies, so mainly profit us? Verily it falleth out oft, that of CHRIST's: *violenti rapiunt illud*. Nature is not enclined; and where it is not enclined, force must be offered; which we call in Schooles, *Actum elicitum*. Which very act by us undertaken, for GOD, and (as here) at His word, is unto him a *Sacrifice* right acceptable. Therfore, *facias*, or *fac facias*; do it *willingly*, or do it *by force*: Do it, I say; for, done it must be. Set it before you and looke on it: or, if you list remove it, and set it full before you, though it be not with your ease, *Respice Looke backe upon it* with some *paine*: for, one way or other, looke upon it we must.

Matt. 11.12.

The necessity whereof (that we may the better apprehend it) it will not be amisse, we know, that these words are in two sundry places, two sundrie waies applied: ¹Once, by S. *John* in the *Gospell*; ²and the second time againe, by CHRIST himselfe in the *Revelation*. By S. *John* to CHRIST, at his

Joh. 19.37.

14 off of] off F_2 35 The necessity] F_2; no para. F_1, F_3

first comming, suffering (as our Saviour) upon the *Crosse*. By CHRIST to himselfe, at his second comming, sitting (as our Judge) upon His *throne*, in the end of the world. *Behold He commeth in the Cloudes, and everie eye shall see Him, yea even they that pierced Him. Et plangent se super Eum omnes Gentes terræ*. The meaning whereof is, *Looke upon Him*, here, if you will: *Enjoine your selves* if you thinke good: Either there, or some where els; either now or then, *looke upon Him* you shall. And, they which put this spectacle farre from them heere, and cannot endure to *look upon Him whom they have pierced, & plangere Eum*, and be grieved for Him, while it is time: a place and time shall be, when they shall be enforced to *looke upon Him*, whether they will or no, *Et plangent se super Eum*, and be grieved for themselves, that they had no grace to do it sooner. Better, compose themselves to a little *mourning* heere, with some benefit to be made by their *beholding*; then to be drawne to it there, when it is too late, and when all their *looking* and *grieving* will not availe awhit. For, there *Respicientes respiciet, & despicientes despiciet*: His look shall be amiable to them that have *respected* His *piercing* heer; and dreadfull on the other side, to them that have neglected it. And, as they that have enured themselves to this *looking on* (heer) shall in that day, *Looke up, and lift up their heads with joy, the day of their Redemption being at hand*. So, they that cannot bring themselves, to *look upon* Him heere, after they once have *looked upon* him there, shall not dare to do it the second time; but crie to the mountaines, *Fall upon us, and to the Hills, Hide us from the face of Him that sitts upon the throne*. Therefore, *Respicient* is no evill counsell. No, though it be *facient se respicere*.

In a word; if thus *causing* our selves to fixe our eyes on Him, we ask, how long we shall continue so doing, and when we may give over? Let this be the answer, *Donec totus fixus in corde, qui totus fixus in cruce*. Or, if that be too much or too hard, yet *saltem* at the least, *Respice in Illum, donec Ille te respexerit*. Looke upon him, till He looke upon you againe. For so he will. He did, upon PETER; and with his look, *melted* him into *teares*. He that once and twise before *denied Him*, and never wept, because CHRIST looked not on Him; then denied, and CHRIST looked on him, and he *went out and wept bitterly*. And, if to *Peter* thus he did, and vouchsafed him so gracious a regard, when *Peter* not once looked toward HIM; how much more shall he not denie us like favour, if, by *looking on Him* first, we provoke him in a sort to a second *looking on us* againe, with the *Prophet*, saying, *Proposui Dominum coram me*, I have set thee, O LORD, before me: and againe, *Respice in me, &c*. *O looke thou upon me, and be mercifull unto me, as thou usest to doe to those that love thy Name*. That love *thy name*, which is JESUS a SAVIOUR; and which love that *sight*, wherein (most properly) thy Name appeareth, and wherein thou chiefly shewest thy selfe to be JESUS a *Saviour*.

And (to conclude) if we aske, how we shall know, when CHRIST doth thus *respect* us? Then truely, when fixing both the eyes of our meditation *upon Him that was pierced* (as it were) one eye, upon the griefe; the other, upon the love wherewith he was *pierced*, we find by both, or one of these, some motion of *grace* arise in our *hearts*: the consideration of his *griefe, piercing* our hearts with *sorrow*; the consideration of his *love, piercing* our hearts with mutuall *love* againe. The one is the motion of *compunction*, which they felt, who when they heard such things *were pricked in their hearts*. The other, the motion of *comfort*, which they felt, who when CHRIST spake unto them of the *necessitie* of his *piercing*, said; *Did we not feele our hearts warme within us?* That, from the *shame* and *paine* he suffered for us: This, from the *comforts* and *benefits*, He thereby procured for us. Acts 2.37. Luc. 24.32.

These have been felt at this *Looking on*; and these will be felt. It may be, at the first, unperfectly; but after, with deeper impression: and that, of some, with such as *Nemo scit, None knoweth, but he that hath felt them*. Which that we may endevour to feel, and endevouring may feele, and so grow into delight of this *looking, GOD, &c.*

VIII

A Sermon on Isaiah 6.6–7 Preached at St. Giles Cripplegate, 1 October 1598

Isaiah 6.6.

Sed advolavit ad me unus ex istis Seraphim *habens in manu sua prunam; quam forcibus sumpserat ab altari. Admovitque ori meo dicens, &c.*

Octob. 1. 1598.

IN the Liturgy of the ancient Church, these words are found applyed to the blessed Sacrament of Christs body and blood; for it is recorded by *Basill,* That at the celebration thereof, after the Sacrament was ministred to the people, the Priest stood up and said as the Seraphin doth here, *Behold this hath touched your lips, your iniquity shall bee taken away, and your sinne purged.* The whole fruit of Religion is, *The taking away of sinne, Isaiah* the twenty seventh Chapter and the ninth verse, and the speciall wayes to take it away, is the Religious use of this Sacrament; which as Christ saith is nothing else, *but a seale and signe of his blood that was shed for many for the remission of sinnes, Matthew* the twenty sixt Chapter and the twenty eight verse; for the Angell tells the prophet, that his sinnes are not only taken away, but that it is done sacramentally, by the touching of a Cole, even as Christ assureth us, that we obtain remission of sinnes by the receiving of the Cup: Now as in the Sacrament, we consider the Element and the word; so we are to divide this Scripture. For first, in that the Seraphin touched his mouth with a burning Cole taken from the Altar, therein we have the element, and the word of comfort which the Prophet received, was, that the Angell said to him, *Behold this Cole hath touched thy lips, and now thine iniquity is taken away, and thy sinnes purged*: And there is such an Analogie and proportion between the Seraphim and the Priests, between the Altar and the Lords Table, between the burning Cole and the Bread and Wine, offered and received in the Lords Supper. As we cannot but justifie the wisdome of the ancient Church, in applying this Scripture to the holy Eucharist: For as, *St. John* sheweth, this vision shewed to the Prophet *Isaiah,* is to be understood of our Saviour Christ, *John* the twelfth and the fourty first verse; for said the Evangelist, *These things said Esay, when he saw*

1–3 A Sermon ... 1598] *ed.*

his glory, and spake of him; and therefore by this burning Cole taken from the Altar, is meant *Christ Jesus*, who *by the Sacrifice of his death which hee offered up to God, his Father, hath taken away our iniquities, and purged our sinnes*, as it is in the six chapter to the *Hebrewes*, and therefore for the confirmation of our Faith wee are here taught, That our sinnes are no lesse taken away by the element of bread and wine, in the Sacrament, then the Prophets sinne was by being touched with a Cole.

    The occasion of this touching is set downe in the former verses of this Chapter, which doe stand upon a *vision* and a *confession*; The *vision* shewed to the Prophet was, *That hee saw the Lord sitting upon an high Throne, as a Judge ready to give Sentence, before whom the very Angells were forced to cover their faces*. The *confession* that hee made was, *Woe is mee for I am uncleane, I am a man of polluted lips, mine eyes have seene the King and Lord of Hosts*: From whence wee learne, that howsoever by the consideration of his former life, and the sinnes that have scaped from him, a man may bee brought to some remorse of Conscience, yet then especially hee is humbled when hee seeth the vision of Gods glory, and therefore nothing is more forcible to bring us to repentance, than to consider that at the last generall day, *Wee shall see* Christ Jesus *the sonne of God come in glory, and sit downe in his Throne of glory, and give Sentence of condemnation upon the wicked*. The Prophet who otherwise was no grievous sinner, but only guilty of omission, for that he had beene silent, and did not glorifie God with his tongue as he should have done, notwithstanding in the sight of Gods glory is touched with remorse & cryeth out, *Woe is me*; Whereby again wee learne that wee sinne not only when wee speake of these things which wee should not, but when wee are silent, when we should apply our tongues to Gods glory; so that though the excellency of our upright and honest conversation bee never so great in the world, yet the Majesty of God is such as shall shew, That even those duties that we have omitted, shall be sufficient to confound us before his glorious presence, unlesse it please him to be mercifull to us; therefore when wee appeare before his judgement-seate, it shall bee in vain for us to alleage what wee have done, forasmuch as the least duty that wee have left undone is enough to condemn us. It shall bee our duty therefore, *notwithstanding all our righteousnesse, to judge our selves worthy to bee destroyed for our iniquities and sinnes of omission, Ezechiel* the thirty sixt chapter and the one and thirtieth verse, and to say with this Prophet *Woe is mee, for I am a man of polluted lips*: We must acknowledge that nothing belongs to us but Woe, and that God may in justice confound us for the least duty we have omitted. Upon this confession made by the Prophet there came an Angell flying from God, which by touching his lips with a hot Coale assured him that his sinne was taken away; wherefore, as by the former wee learne that wee should repent us of our sinnes when wee consider the great Majesty of God, so by this wee are taught what to hope for, that is, that if wee bee penitent God will not bee wanting unto us, but will send a Seraphin unto us, with a word of comfort, to assure us *that all our iniquities are purged.* The outward element appointed by God to confirme his faith, was *the flying of a Seraphin unto him to touch a mouth with a Cole*; the word of invisible grace signifyed by the element was, *that by that touching his sinne was taken away.* In the outward action wee are first to consider the element it selfe, that was, *the burning Cole on the Altar*; next the application performed by a Seraphin, who *tooke the Cole from the Altar, and touched the Prophets lips.* First therefore considering that none can take away sinne but God only, wee must needs confesse that there was in this Cole a divine force and virtue issuing from Christ, who is the only reconciliation for our sins, without which it had not beene possible that it could have taken away sinne. But what is here said of this Cole, is to bee understood of Christ, of whom *Esay* speaketh in this place, *When hee saw the glory of Christ, John* 12.41. for hee is the Cole by which our sinnes are taken away; There are two natures in a Cole, that is, the Cole it selfe, which is a dead thing, and the burning nature and heate that it hath; which setteth out first Christs humane nature, which is dead in it selfe; And then his divine nature, containing the burning force of that is represented in this burning Cole: So the element of bread and wine is a dead thing in it selfe, but through the grace of Gods spirit infused into it hath a power to heate our Soules: for the elements in the Supper have an earthly and a heavenly part. Secondly, that Christ is to bee understood by this burning Cole wee may safely gather, because *his love to his Church is presented with fire, Cantic.* the eighth chapter and the sixth verse. It is said of Christs love, the Coles thereof are fiery Coles, and a vehement flame, such as cannot be quenched with any water, nor the floods drown it, even so all the calamities and miseries that Christ suffered and endured for our sakes, which were poured upon him as water, could not quench the love that he bare us. Thirdly, *quia non solum ardet ipse, sed alios accendit,* so saith *John* the Baptist of him, *There cometh one after me that shall Baptize with the holy-Ghost and with fire,* as it is in the third chapter of *Luke* the sixteenth verse, therefore the graces of the holy-Ghost are also represented by fire, *Acts* 3. the union whereof hath a double representation. First, it is signified by water in Baptisme; for sinne that is derived unto us from another, being as a spot may be washed away with water, and therefore the Prophet saith, *there is a fountaine opened to the house of David, and to the inhabitants of Jerusalem, for sinne and uncleannesse, Zach.* the thirteenth chapter and the first verse, therefore *Ananias* said to *Saul, bee Baptized and wash away thy sinnes, Acts* the twenty second Chapter

[marginalia: Two parts. First, Elementall. Secondly, Invisible grace. First, The Element.]

and the sixteenth verse, that is meant of originall sinne and the corruption of our nature, by which wee are guilty of the wrath of God; but because through the whol course of our life sinne, by custome groweth more to be strong, and to stick fast in our nature, so as no water can take it away; therefore the Grace of God is set out by fire, as having a power and force to burn up sinne; for by custome sinne is bred and setled in our nature, and is *tanquam furni*, drosse that must be tryed and purged by fire, so the holy Ghost speaketh of actuall sinnes, the first of *Isaiah*, and the twenty fift verse, and the sixt chapter of *Jeremiah* and the thirtieth verse, *Ezech.* the twenty second chapter and the eighteenth verse; *The house of Israel is to mee as drosse*, that is by custome of sinne; and in regard of this kinde of sinne there needs not only *water* to wash away the corruption of our nature and the qualitie thereof, but *fire* to purge the actuall sins that proceed from the same.

The sinnes of Commission came by reason of the force of concupiscence, and from the lusts that boyle out of our corrupt nature, and the grace that takes them away is the grace of water in Baptisme; but the sinnes of omission proceede of the coldnesse and negligence of our nature to doe good, such as was in the Church of *Laodicea*, *Rev.* the third chapter and the fifteenth verse, and therefore such sinnes must bee taken away with the *fiery Grace of God*. Secondly, for the quality of the Cole; it is not only a *burning Cole*, but *taken from the Altar*; to teach us that our zeale must bee sanctified and come from the spirit of God. The fires that are appointed by earthly Judges to terrifie malefactors from offending, may draw a skinne over the spirituall wounds of their Soules, so as (for feare) they will eschue and forbeare to sinne, but it is the fire of the Altar, and the inward Graces of Gods spirit that taketh away the corruption and healeth the wound; therefore as in the Law God tooke order *there should ever bee fire on the Altar*, *Leviticus* the sixt chapter and the ninth verse, so for the sinner that is contrite and sory for his sinne, there is alwaies fire in the Church to burne up the Sacrifice of his contrition and repentance, even that fire of Christs Sacrifice. The love which hee shewed unto us in dying for our sinnes is set out unto us most lively in the Sacrament of his Body and Blood, unto which wee must come often, that from the one wee may fetch the *purging of our sinnes*, as the Apostle speaks, and from the other qualifying power *si in luce*, *John* the first chapter & the seventh verse; wherefore as by the mercy of God we have a fountain of water alwaies flowing, to take away originall sinne, so there is in the Church fire alwaies burning to cleanse our actuall transgressions; for if the Cole taken from the Altar, had a power to take away the Prophets sinne, much more the body and blood of Christ, which is offered in the Sacrament; *If the hem of Christs garment can heale*, the ninth chapter of *Matthew* and the twentith verse, much more the touching of Christ himselfe shall procure health to our soules; here we have not somthing that hath touched the Sacrifice, but the Sacrifice it self to take away our sins.

<small>Secondly, the Application.</small>

The application of this Cole is by a Seraphin, for it is an office more fit for Angells than men, to concurre with God for taking away sinne; but for that it pleaseth God to use the service of men in this behalfe, they are in Scripture called *Angells, Job* the thirty fifth chapter and the twenty third verse. *Malachi* the second and the seventh verse, *The Priests lips preserve knowledge, for hee is the Angell of the Lord of Hosts*, and the Pastors of the seven Churches in *Asia* are called *Angells, Apoc.* the first chapter and the first verse; for the same office that is here executed by an Angell is committed to the sonnes of men, to whom, as the Apostle speaks, *Hee hath committed the ministery of reconciliation, 2 Cor.* the fift chapter and the eighteenth verse, to whom hee hath given this power, *that whose sinnes soever they remit on earth shall bee remitted in heaven*, the twentith chapter of Saint *John* and the twenty fift verse. So when *Nathan*, who was but a man, had said to *David, etiam Jehova transtulit peccatum tuum*, the second booke of *Samuel* the twelfth chapter and the thirteenth verse; it was as availeable as if an Angell had spoken to him; And when *Peter* tells the Jewes *that if they amend their lives and turn, their sinnes shall be done away*, their sinne was taken away no lesse than the Prophets was when the Angell touched his lips, *Acts* the third chapter and the ninteenth verse; for not hee that holds the Cole, but it is the Cole it selfe that takes away sinne; and so long as the thing is the same wherewith wee are touched, it skills not who doth hold it; but wee have not only the Cole that touched the Altar, but the Altar it selfe, even the Sacrifice of Christs death represented in the Supper, by partaking whereof our sins are taken away.

<small>Secondly, the Word, or invisible grace.</small>

The word of comfort, whereby the inward Grace is preached unto us is, that the Angell said to the Prophet; *Loe this hath touched thy lips, and thine iniquity shall be taken away, and thy sinnes purged*: concerning which wee finde that the Leper was cured of his Leprosie, not only by the word, but by the touching of Christ; but the Centurion said only *but speake the word and thy servant shall bee whole, Mat.* the eight chapter and the eighth verse; so hee can doe what he will with his only word. It pleased God to take away the Prophets sinnes by touching his lips. And albeit he can take away our sins, without touching of bread or wine, if he will; yet in the councell of his will, he commendeth unto us the sacramentall partaking of his body and blood. It is his will, that our sins shall be taken away by the outward act of the sacrament: The reason is, not only in regard of our selves, which consist of body and soul, and therefore have need both of bodily and Ghostly meanes, to assure us of our Salvation; but in regard of Christ himself, who is the burning Cole. For ever since God ordained, that Christ should take our nature, and *aptare sibi corpus*, in the tenth chapter to the *Hebrewes*, and the fifth verse; that so he might worke our Reconciliation. As Christ became himself a man, having a bodily substance; so his actions were bodily. As in the Hypostasis of the Sun, there is both the Humane and Divine nature; so the Sacrament is of an Heavenly and Earthly nature. As he hath taken our body to himself, so he honoureth bodily things, that by them we should have our sinnes taken away from us. By one bodily sacrament he taketh away the affection unto sin, that is naturally planted in us. By another bodily Sacrament he taketh away the habituall sins, and the actuall transgression, which proceed from the corruption of our nature. And here we have matter offered us of faith; that as he used the touching of a cole, to assure the Prophet that his sins were taken away; so in the Sacrament he doth so elevate a piece of bread, and a little wine, and make them of such power; that they are able to take away our sinnes: And this maketh for Gods glory, not only to beleeve that God can work our Salvation, without any outward means, by the inward Grace of his Spirit; but also, that he can so elevate the meanest of his creatures; not only the hemme of a garment, but even a strawe, (if hee see it good) shall be powerfull enough, to save us from our sinnes. As Christ himself is spirituall and bodily; so he taketh away our sinnes, by means not only spiritual but bodily; as in the Sacrament. For if there be a cleansing power in the Word, as Christ speaketh in the fifteenth chapter of *John*, and the third verse: If in prayer, as *Peter* sheweth to *Simon Magus*, *Pray to God, that (if it be possible) the thought of thy heart may be forgiven thee*, in the eighth chapter of the *Acts of the Apostles*, and the twenty second verse: If in shewing mercy, and giving almes, sinnes shall be forgiven, as *Salomon* saith in the sixteenth chapter of the *Proverbs*, and the sixth verse, *Per misericordiam purgantur peccata*; much more in the Sacrament, wherein both the word and prayer and the works of mercy doe concurre, to the cleansing of sinners from their sinnes: Whereas the Seraphim did not take the coale in his mouth, but with tongs; and applied it not to the Prophets eare, but to his tongue. We learn, that it is not the hearing of a sermon that can cleanse us from sinne; but we must taste of the bodily element, appointed to represent the invisible grace of God. It is true, that meditation privately had, *will kindle a fire in the hearts of many*, in the thirty ninth *Psalm*, and the third verse: And the word, *as it is a fire, Jeremie* the twenty third chapter, and the twenty ninth verse, will also *kindle a man, and heat him inwardly*: But because in the Sacrament all those doe meete together; therefore nothing is so availeable to take away sinne, as the touching of bread and wine, with our lips.

The effect.   The effect of this touching followeth; wherein we are to consider, First, the efficacy of this action. Secondly, the certainty; that as sure as this coale hath touched thy lips; so surely are thy sinnes taken away. Thirdly, the speede, that so soon as the coale touched, presently sinne was taken away and purged. The efficacie standeth, of the removing, or taking away of sinne, and of the purging away of sinne. The taking away, and purging of sinnes, have two uses: Some have their sinnes taken away, but not purged; for something remaineth behinde: Some have *Adams* figge leaves to hide sinne that it shall not appear for a time; but have not *Hezekiah his plaister to heal it*, in the thirty eighth chapter of *Isaiah* and the one and twentieth verse. But by the touching of this Coal, that is, of the body and blood of Christ, we are assured that our sinnes are not only covered, but quite taken away as with a plaister; as the Lord speaks, *I have put away thy transgressions like a cloud, and thy sins as a mist, Isaiah* the fourty fourth and the twenty second verse, whereby the Lord sheweth that our sinnes are scattered, and come to nothing, when it pleaseth him to take them away. The other sense gathered from the word *purging*, is, that God doth not forgive our sinnes, as an earthly Judge forgiveth a malefactor, so that he goeth away with his pardon, without any farther favour shewed him; but that he likewise becometh favorable unto us, and willing to doe us all the good he can: If malefactors can obtain their pardon at the hands of temporall Judges, it is all they can looke for; but they never come to any preferment: But God doth not only give us *veniam* but *gratiam*; as he doth pardon our sinnes, so also he becomes loving and kinde to us: Christ doth not only take us away from God, that he should not proceed to punish us for our sinnes, but offers us up to God, as an acceptable sacrafice, as *Peter* witnesseth, *Christ once suffered for sinnes, the just for the unjust, that he might offer us up to God*, in the first of *Peter* the third chapter and the eighteenth verse; for as the wiseman saith, *Take the drosse from the silver, and there shall proceed a vessel for the refiner, Proverbs* the twenty fift and the fourth verse: So after sinne is taken away from us, our nature is most acceptable to God, because there remaineth nothing but his own nature. Secondly, for the certainty; As thou hast a perfect sense of the touching of this coal, so certainly are thy sinnes taken away; which assurance we are likewise to gather to our selves, in this sacrament; that as surely as we corporally doe taste the bread and wine, so sure it is, that we spiritually feed on the body and blood of Christ, which is communicated unto us by these elements, as the Apostle sheweth, in the first to the *Corinthians*, the tenth chapter, and the fifteenth verse, *that the bread broken is the communion of the body of Christ, that the cup blessed is the communion of his blood*; that by partaking of this spirituall food we may be fed to eternall life. Thirdly, this act was performed with speed, the Seraphin came flying with wings, and being come, he hath a present effectuall power to take away his sinne; for a little before he that cried out, that he was *in woefull case*, verse the fift, *Væ mihi*; by and by being touched and revived with comfort of forgiveness, saith, *Ecce ego, mitte me*, in the eighth verse: whereby we learn, that the touching with the coal thus taken from the Altar, and the participating of the body and blood of Christ, hath a power not only to purge, and heale the sore of our nature; but that it giveth a willingness to serve God more cheerfully and carefully than we did before, it maketh us *ferventes spiritu*, fervent in spirit *Rom.* the twelfth and the eleventh verse; so that we care for nothing nor count our lives precious, *that we may finish our course with joy*, *Acts* the twentieth and the twenty fourth verse.

The summe of all is, that seeing it is a fearfull thing to appear in the presence of Gods Majesty, and knowing that one day we must all appear before his tribunall seat and throne of glory, we do confesse with the Prophet, that albeit we have lived never so upright a life, yet if we have beene silent, when we should have spoken to his glory, if we have omitted never so little a duty, which we ought to have performed, for all that, our case is miserable, untill it please God by the burning coale of his Altar, and, by the sacrifice of Christs body, offered up for us upon the crosse, to take away our sinnes: And that if we truly humble our selves before God, and acknowledge our sinnes, then our sinnes shall be purged by the death of Christ, and by partaking of the sacrament of his bodie and blood; the rather, because in the sacrament we doe touch the sacrifice it self, wheras the Prophets sinne was taken away with that which did but touch the sacrifice.

Then, after the receiving of this sacrament, we must take a view of our selves, whether we can say, *Nonne cor nostrum ardebat in nobis?* Did not our heart burn within us? *Luke* the twenty fourth chapter and the thirty second verse, because in this sacrament we finde a fire of Christs love towards us; And whether we finde in our selves that willingnesse to serve God aright, which was in the Prophet, in the eighth verse, *Behold, send me; Ecce, mitte me*. As in regard of our misery we made the confession of sinfull men; so having experience of Gods mercie in taking away our sinnes; we must make the confession of Angels, crying, *Holy, holy, holy, Lord God of Hosts*.

Lastly, We must not only shew forth the heat of our love to our needy and poor Brethren, by doing the works of mercy; but even to our enemies, as both *Salomon* and the Apostle teach, *If thine enemie hunger, feed him; if he thirst give him drink; for so thou shalt heap coals of fire upon his head*; *Proverbs* the twenty fift chapter and the twenty first verse, and *Romans* the twelfth chapter and the ninteenth verse; For so as thou art a burning coale in thy selfe; so thou shalt kindle in him the coals of devotion to God, and of love to thy self.

IX

A Sermon Preached before the King's Majestie, at White-Hall, on the V. of November. A.D. MDCVI.

PSAL. CXVIII. VER. XXIII. XXIV.

A DOMINO factum est istud, & est mirabile in oculis nostris.
Hæc est Dies quam fecit Dominus; exultemus & lætemur in ea.

This is the Lord's *doing, and it is mervailous in our eyes.*
This is the Day which the Lord *hath made; let us rejoyce and be glad in it.*

To entitle this time to this Text, or to shew it pertinent to the present occasion, will aske no long processe. This Day of ours, This *fift of November*, a day of GOD's *making*; that which was done upon it, was the *Lord's doing*. CHRIST's own application (which is the best) may well be applied here: *This day, is this Scripture fulfilled in our eares.* For, if ever there were a *Deed* done, or a *Day* made by *God*, in our dayes; this *Day*, and the *Deed* of this *Day* was it: If ever He gave cause of *mervailing* (as, in the first;) of *rejoycing* (as in the *second verse*) to any Land; to us this day, He gave both: If ever *saved, prospered, blessed* any; *this day*, He *saved, prospered,* and (as we say) *fairely blessed* us.

The *day* (we all know) was meant to be the day of all our *deaths*; and we, and many were appointed, as *sheepe* to the *slaughter*; nay, worse then so. There was a thing *doing* on it, if it had been done, we all had been undone. And, the very same day (we all know) the day, wherein that appointment was disappointed by *God*, and we all saved, that we might *not die but live, and declare the praise of the Lord*: the *Lord*, of whose *doing*, that *mervailous Deed* was; of whose *making*, this *joyfull Day* is, that we celebrate.

This mercifull and gratious *Lord* (saith *David*, *Psal.* 111.4) *hath so done His mervailous Works, that they ought to be had, and kept in remembrance.* Of *keeping in remembrance*, many waies there be: Among the rest, this is one, of *making*

Luk. 4.21.

Ver. 17.

Psal. 111.4.

27 *in marg.* Psal. 111.4] *LACT*; Psal. 111.5 F_1, F_2, F_3 111.4] *LACT*; 111.5 F_1, F_2, F_3

Dayes; sett, solemne Daies, to preserve memorable Acts, that they be not eaten out, by them, but ever revived, with the returne of the Yeare, and kept still fresh in continuall memorie. *God* himselfe taught us this way. In remembrance of the great *Deliverie* from the *destroying Angell*, He himselfe ordained the day of the *Passe-over* yearly to be kept. The *Church*, by Him taught, tooke the same way. In remembrance of the disappointing of *Haman's bloudie lotts*, they likewise appointed the daies of *Purim*, yearely to be kept. The like memorable mercie did He vouchsafe us: The *Destroyer* passed over our dwellings, this day: It is our *Passe-over*. *Haman*, and his Fellowes had set the *dice* on us, and we by this time had beene all in pieces: it is our *Purim* day.

Exod. 12.3.&c.
Est. 9.26.

We have therefore well done and upon good warrant, to tread in the same stepps, and by law to provide, that this Day should not die, nor the memoriall thereof perish, from ourselves, or from our seed; but be consecrated to perpetuall memorie, by a yearly acknowledgement to be made of it, throughout all generations. In accomplishment of which order, we are all now heere in the presence of *God*, on this day, that He first, by His Act of *doing* hath *made*; and we secondly, by our act of *decreeing*, have *made* before *Him*, his holy *Angells*, and men, to confesse this His goodnesse, and our selves eternally bound to Him for it. And, being to confesse it, with what words of Scripture can we better or fitter do it, then those we have read out of this *Psalme*? Sure, I could thinke of none fitter, but even thus to say, *A Domino factum, &c.*

The treatie whereof may well be comprised in three points. 1. The *Deed* or *doing*: 2. The *Day*, and 3. The *Dutie*. The *Deed*, in these: *This is the Lord's &c.* The *Day*, in these: *This is the day &c.* The *Dutie*, in the rest: *Let us &c.* The other two reduced to the *Day*, which is the center of both. The *Doing* is the cause; The *Dutie* is the consequent: from the *Day* groweth the *Dutie*.

The Division
I.
II.
III.

To proceed orderly, we are to beginne with the *Day*. For, though (in place) it stand after the *Deed*; Yet, to us, it is first: our knowledge is *à posteriori*. The effect ever first, where it is the ground of the rest. Of the *Day* then first.

1. That such *Daies* there be, and how they come to be such. 2. Then of the *Doing*, that maketh them: wherein [1]that this of *David's* was; and [2]that ours is no lesse, rather more. 3. Then of the *Dutie*, how to doe it; by *rejoycing*, and *being glad*, for so, *gaudium erit plenum*, these make it full: How to take order, that we may long and often doe it, by saying our *Hosanna*, and *Benedictus*; for, *gaudium nostrum nemo tollet à nobis*, those will make, that *our joy no man shall take from us*.

Joh. 16.12.

---

35 these] these two F₂

I. Of the *Day*: Such *daies* there be.	**T**HIS is the Day: *This?* Why, are not all daies *made* by Him? Is there any *daies* not made by Him? Why then say we *This is the day, the Lord hath made?* Divide the days into *naturall* and *civill*; the *naturall*, some are *cleere* and some are *cloudie*; the *civill*, some are *luckie daies*, and some *dismall*. Be they faire or foule, gladd or sadd; (as the Poet calleth him) the Great *Diespiter*, the *Father of daies* hath made them both. How say we then of some one *day*, above his fellow, *This is the Day, &c*?

   No difference at all, in the *dayes*, or in the *moneths* themselves: by nature, they are all one. No more in *November*, then another *moneth*: nor in the *fifth*, then in the *fifteenth*. All is, in GOD's *making*. For as, in the Creation, we see, all are the *workes*; and yet, a plaine difference beetweene them for all that, in the manner of making: Some made with יהי *Sit, Lett there be light, a firmament, drie land*; Some, with *Faciamus*, with more adoe, greater *forecast*, and framing; as *man*, that *master-peece* of His *works*, of whom therefore, in a different sense, it may be said: *This is the Creature, which* GOD *hath made* (suppose, *after a more excellent manner*.) In the very same manner, it is, with *daies*; All are His *making*, all æquall, in that; but, that letteth not, but He may bestow a speciall *Faciamus* upon some one day more then other; and so that day, by speciall prerogative, said *To be indeed a Day, that* GOD *hath made*.

Gen. 1.14. 26.

   Now, for GOD's *making*, it fareth with *daies* as it doth with *yeares*. Some *yeare* (saith the *Psalme*) GOD *crowneth with His goodnesse*, maketh it more seasonable, healthfull, fruitfull, then other. And so for *dayes*; GOD leaveth a more sensible impression of His favour, upon some one, more then many besides, by *doing* upon it some *mervailous worke*. And, such a day on which GOD vouchsafeth some speciall *factum est*, some great and publique Benefit; notable for the time present, memorable for the time to come; in that case, of that *Day* (as if GOD had said *Faciamus diem hunc*, shewed some workemanship, done some speciall cost on it) it may with an *accent*, with an *emphasis* be said, *This verily is a Day which* GOD *hath made*, in comparison of which, the rest are as if they were not; or at least were not of *His making*.

Psal. 65.11.

   As for *blacke* and *dismall dayes*, dayes of sorrow and sadd accidents; they are and may be counted (saith *Job*) for no *dayes*: *Nights* rather, as having the *shadow of death* upon them; or, if *dayes*, such as his were, which *Sathan* had *marrd*, then which GOD had *made*. And for common and ordinarie *daies*, wherein as there is no *harme*, so not any notable *good*, we rather say, they are *gone forth* from GOD, in the course of nature (as it were) with a *fiat*, then *made* by *Him*; specially, with a *faciamus*. So, *evill dayes* no *daies*, or *daies marrd*: and *common daies*, *daies*; but no *made daies*: Only those *made*, that *crowned* with some extraordinarie great *Favour*, and thereby gett a dignitie, and exaltation above the rest; exempted out of the ordinarie course of the

Job 3.3,6.

Calendar with an *Hic est*. Such, in the *Law*, was the *Day* in the *Passe-over*, made by God, the head of the yeare. Such, in the *Gospell*, of Christ's *Resurrection*, made by God, *Dies Dominicus*; and to it, do all the Fathers applie this verse. And we had this day our *Passe-over*, and we had a *Resurrection* or παραβολή, as *Isaac* had. But, I forbeare to go further in the generall. By this that hath beene said, we may see, there be daies of which it may be safely said, *This is the day &c* and in what sense, it may be said. Such there be then; that this of ours, one of the them; that, if it be, we may so hold it, and doe the duties that pertaine to it.

David's day heere, was one certainely, *dictante Spiritu*; and they, that are like it, to be holden for such: so that, if ours be as this was, it is certainely *dies à Deo factus*. Now then (to take our rule from the former verse) *Factum Domini facit diem Domini*. It is God's *deed*, that maketh it God's *day*: and, the greater the *Deed*, the more God's *day*. There must be first, *Factum est*, some *doing*: and secondly, it must be *à Domino*, He the *doer*: and thirdly, that *somewhat* must be somewhat *mervailous*: and fourthly, not, in it selfe, so; but, *in our eyes*. These foure goe to it; these foure make any day, a *day of God's making*. Let us see then these foure: First, in *David's* heere, and then in our owne; and if we finde them all, boldly pronounce, *This is the Day, &c.*

First, the *factum est*, in *David's*; what was *done*, sett downe at large in the forepart of the *Psalme*. It was a *deliverance*: all the *Psalme* runneth on nothing els. Every *deliverance* is from a *danger*; and, by the *danger*, we take measure of the *deliverance*. The greater that, the greater the *Deliverie* from it: and the greater the *Deliverie*, the greater the *Day*, and the more likely to be of God's owne *manufacture*. His *danger* first: what should have been done. He was in a great distresse. Three severall times, with great passion, he repeats it, that *his Enemies* [1]*came about him*; [2]*compassed him round*; [3]*compassed and kept him in on every side*: were, no swarme of *bees* so thicke: That they gave a terrible lift or *thrust* at him, to overthrow him; and verie neere it they were. And at last, as if he were newly crept out of his grave, out of the very jawes of death and despaire, he breakes forth and saith, *I was very neere my death*; neere it I was, but *non moriar, Die I will not now*, for this time, *but live* a little longer *to declare the workes of the* Lord. This, was his *danger*: and a shrewd one (it seemeth) it was. From this *danger*, he was *delivered*. This, the *factum est*.

But, *man* might doe all this; and so it be *man's day*, for any thing is said yet. Though it were *great*, it maketh it not God's, unlesse God, God (I say) and not *man*, but God himselfe were the Doer of it: and, if He the *Doer*, He

Exod. 12.2.

Heb. 11.19.

II.
David's day was such.

In it there was
[1]A *factum est,*
A *deliverance.*

From *danger.*
Verse 10.
11.
12.
Verse 13.

Verse 17.

2.
A Domino:
By God, not by *man.*

Verse 8. 9.	denominates the *Day*. This then was not *any mans*, not any *Prince's* doing, but GOD's alone; His *might*, His *mercie*, that brought it to passe: Not any *arme of flesh*, but GOD's *might*; not of any *merit* of His, but of His owne *meere*
Verse 15. 16.	*mercie*. This was *done* by His might: Thrise he tells us of it; *It was the right hand of the Lord, that brought this mightie thing to passe*. This was done by His *mercie*; His *ever-enduring mercie*: foure times he tells us, it was that, did
Verse 1.2.3.4.	it. With that he beginnes, and makes it the key of the *song*. Then, as we have *factum est*, so we have *A Domino*: The *Deed* and the *Doer* both.
3. Et mirabile, and Mervaillous it was. *Zach. 4.10.	GOD's *doings* are many, and not all of one size. The Prophet *Zacharie* speaketh of a *day* of *small things*; and, even in those small, must we learne to see GOD, or we shall never see Him in greater. Yet, so dimme is our sight, that unlesse they be great, commonly we see Him not: nay, unlesse it be great *Usque ad miraculum*, so great, that *mervailous* withall, we count it not worth a *day*, nor worthy GOD: unlesse it be such. But, if it be such, then it is
Psal. 72.18.	GOD's, *Qui facit mirabilia solus*, *Who only workes great mervailes*: then, man is shutt out; and then, GOD's must the *Day* be. *A Domino factum, & mirabile*.
4. In oculis nostris, even in our eyes.	And yet this is not enough. The truth is, all that GOD doth, all His *workes* are *wonderfull*: *Magna, sed ideo parva quia usitata*. Great, wonders, all: but, not *wonderfull*; seeme *small* to us, because they be *usuall*: His *miracles* are no more *mervailous*, then His *ordinarie workes*, but that, we see the one daily, and the other, not. Therefore he addeth [*in our eyes*] for a full period: His *doings*, all *mervailous* in themselves; but, not mervailous, *in our eyes*, unlesse they be rare, and the like not seene before: But then, they be; and then we say, *Digitus Dei est*; It is the *finger of* GOD; nay, the *right hand of God*, that
Exod. 8.19.	brought this mighty thing to passe. Then we give the *day* for *God's*, without more adoe. Now then, we have all that goeth to it: [1] A *Deliverance* wrought; [2] wrought, by *God*; [3] a *wonderfull deliverance*; [4] and that, even *in our eyes*. These make *David's day*, a *day* of *God's making*.
Our Day was such. These foure in *ours*. Factum est: [1]A *deliverance* from a *danger*, a great danger	Will *these* be *found in ours*, and then ours shalbe so too? They will, all of them certenly; and that, in an higher degree, in a greater measure; match *David's day*, and overmatch it in all. I. We were *delivered*, and from a *danger*, that is cleere. How great? (for, that makes the odds.) Boldly I dare say, from a *greater* then *David's*. Thus I shew it, and go no further then the Psalme it selfe.
	1. *David* called upon GOD in his danger; he knew of it, therefore. We did not: we imagined no such thing; but that, all had been safe, and we might

9 size] F_2; sise F_1

have gone to the *Parliament,* as secure as ever. The *danger* never dreamt of, that is the *danger.*

2. His was, by *compassing* and *hemming in*; that is *above ground,* and may be discried from a watch-tower. Ours was by *undermining,* digging deep under ground; that none could discerne.

3. One cannot be *besett,* but he may have hope to breake through, at some part. But heer, from this, no way, no means no possibilitie of escaping. The *danger* not to be discried, not to be escaped, that is the danger.

4. His were a *swarme of bees* (He calleth them so:) they, *buzze* and make a *noise* when they come. Ours, a brood of *vipers, mordentes in silentio; still,* not so much as a *hisse,* till the deadly *blow* had been given.   Ver. 12.

5. His was but of *himselfe* alone; so he saith, *I was in trouble, They came about me, kept me in, thrust sore at me*: But one person, *David's* alone. Ours, of a farre greater extent; *David,* and his three Estates with him. Now, though *David* himselfe were valued by them at *ten thousand* of themselves (and not over-valued neither; for he is worth more; and all Kings like him, no lesse worth:) yet he and they too, must needs be more, then He alone. Not onely *King David* had gone, but *Queen Esther* too: and not onely they, but *Salomon* the young *Prince,* and *Nathan* his *Brother.* Nor these were not all. The Scriptures recount, *David* had *Jehosaphat* for his *Chancellor, Adoram* his *Treasurer, Seraja* his *Secretarie, Sadoc* and *Abiathar* and twenty more, the chiefe of the *Priests, Admo* his *Judge, Joab* his *Generall*; all had gone: His *forty eight Worthies* or *Nobles,* all they too. The Principall of all the *Tribes* in the kingdome: All they too; and many more then these; no man knoweth how many. It is out of question, it had exceeded this of *David's* heer.   Ver. 11. 13.   2. Sam. 18.3.   2. Sam. 20.24.   2. Sam.23.

6. One more. His *danger* (he confesseth) was from *man*: He goeth no further, *I will not feare what* man *doeth unto me.* This of ours was not: meerly mans, I denie it; it was the *Devill* himselfe. The instruments (not as his, a *swarme of Bees,* but) a swarme of *Locusts, out of the infernall pitt.* Not *men*; No not *Heathen men*: Their *Stories*; nay, their *Tragœdies* can show none neer it. Their *Poëts* could never feigne any so *prodigiously impious.* Not *men*; No, not *savage wild men*: the *Hunnes,* the *Heruli* the *Turcilingi,* noted for *inhumanitie,* never so inhumane: Even among those barbarous people, this fact would be accounted *barbarous.* How then? *Beasts*: There were at *Ephesus, beasts in the shape of men*; and θηριτης brutishnesse is the worst, *Philosophie* could imagine of our *nature.* This is more then *brutish*; What *Tiger,* though never so inraged, would have made the like havock? Then, if the like, neither in the nature of *men,* nor *beasts* so be found (it is so unnaturall;) we must not looke to paterne it upon earth, we must to *hell*; thence it was certenly, even from the *Devill.* He was a *murderer from the*   Ver. 6.   Apoc. 9.3.   1. Cor. 15.32.   Joh. 8.44.

beginning, and wilbe so to the ending. In every sinne of bloud, he hath a *claw*; but, all his *clawes*, in such an one as this: wherein so much bloud, as would have made it *raine bloud*; so many baskets of *heads*, so many peeces of rent bodies cast up and downe, and scattered all over the face of the earth.

Joel 2.30. Never such a day; all *Joël's* signes of a *fearefull day, bloud*, and *fire* and the
Mar. 9.29. *vapour of smoake*. As he is a *murtherer*; so we see (in *Marke*) by his *renting* and *tearing* the poore *possessed child* he is *cruell*; and in this, all his cruelties
Exod. 1.16. should have mett together. *Pharoa's* and *Herod's* killing *innocent* and *har-*
Mat. 2.16. *melesse children*; yet, they spared the *Mother: Esau's* crueltie, smiting *mother, children* and all: *Nebuzaradan's* not sparing the *King*, nor his Lords:
Psal. 137.7. *Haman's* not sparing *Hester*, nor her *Ladies: Edom's* crueltie not sparing the *Sanctuarie* nor the walls, *downe* with them *to the ground*: His owne
Job 1.18. smiting the *foure corners* and bringing down the house upon the heads of
19. *Job's children*. Put to all the *cruelties*, in *Jeremie's Lamentations*, the not
Jer. 31.15. *honouring the faces of Nobles, Priests, Judges*; the making so many *widowes* and *orphans*; the voice in *Rama* of *Rachel* comfortlesse. Crueltie, more cruell to them, it spared and left behind, then to those it took away. It yrketh me to stand repeating these: That ever age, or land, but that our age, and this land should foster or breed such monsters!

That you may know it for that perfectly, consider but the wickednesse of it, as it were in full opposition to GOD, and you must needs say, it could not
Gen. 18.23. be His doing: GOD *forbid* (saith *Abraham*) *thou shouldest destroy the righteous*
25. *with the wicked. Kill not dam and young ones both* (saith *Moses* in the *Law*.)
Exod. 22.6. *You shall not touch mine Anointed* (saith GOD in the *Psalmes*). *You shall not*
Psal. 105.15. *pull up the good corne, rather let the tares stand* (saith CHRIST in the *Gospell*.)
Mat. 13.29.
Rom. 3.8. *You shall not do evill, that good may come of it* (saith *Paul* in his *Epistles*.) But,
Dan. 9.27. heer is *Satan* flat contrarie, in despite of *Law, Prophetts, Psalme, Epistle* and *Gospell*: *Hoc est Christum cum Paulo conculcare*, to throw downe *Abraham*, and *Moses*, and *David*, and *Paul*, and CHRIST, and GOD and all, and trample upon them all.

Mat. 24.15. One more yet: that this *abomination of desolation* (so calleth *Daniel*; so calleth our *Saviour*, the uttermost extremitie of all that bad is: so may we this truly:) that this *abomination of desolation* tooke up his *standing*, in the *holy place*.

1. An *abomination*: so it is; abhorred of all flesh, hated and detested of all, that but heare it named: yea they themselves say, they should have abhorred it, if it had taken effect. It is an *abomination*.

2. Every *abomination* doth not forthwith make *desolate*. This had. If ever a *desolate kingdome* upon earth, such had this been, after that terrible *blow*. Neither *root* nor *branch left*, all swept away: *Strangers* called in; *murtherers* exalted; the very *dissolution* and *desolation* of all ensued.

3. But this, that this so *abominable and desolatorie* a plott, stood in the *holy place*, this is the pitch of all. For, there it stood, and thence it came abroad. Undertaken with an *holy oath*; bound with the *holy Sacrament* (that must needs be in a *holy place*;) warranted for a *holy act*, tending to the advancement of a *holy Religion*, and by *holy persons* called by the most *holy Name*, the *name* of JESUS. That these *holy religious persons*, even the *chiefe* of all *religious persons* (the *Jesuites*) gave not onely *absolution*, but *resolution*, that all this was well done; that it was by them *justified* as lawfull, *sanctified* as meritorious, and should have been *glorified* (but it wants *glorifying*, because the event fayled, that is the griefe; if it had not *glorified*) long yer this, and *canonized*, as a very good and holy act, and we had had orations out of the *Conclave* in commendation of it. (Now I think, we shall heare no more of it.) These good *Fathers* they were *David's bees* heer, came hither, onely to bring us *honie, right honie* they; not to *sting* any bodie: or (as in the XXII. verse) they (as *builders*) came into the land, onely for *edification*; not to *pull down*, or to destroy any thing. We see their practise, they begunne with *rejecting* this *Stone*, as one that *favoured Heretiques* at least, and therefore excommunicate, and therefore deposed, and therefore exposed, to any that could handle a *spade* well, to make a *mine* to blow him up; *Him*, and all his *Estates* with him to attend him: (The *corner Stone* being gone, the *walls* must needs follow.) But then, this *shrining* it (such an *abomination*) setting it in the *holy place*, so ougly and odious; making such a treason as this a *religious, missall, sacramentall treason*; hallowing it with *orison, oath,* and *Eucharist*; this passeth all the rest. I say no more, but as our *Saviour* concludeth, when you see such an *abomination* so *standing, qui legit intelligat*; nay *qui videt.* GOD send them, that (not *reade* of it, but) *see* it, and had like to have smelt of it, to learne that, they should, by it: and so I leave it.

Verse 22.

Mat. 24.15.

Tell me now, if this were not *His doing*, and if it should not have beene a Day of His *making*, the *Devill's* owne making?

This should have beene done; this, the *danger*: what was done? This, the *factum fuisset*; what the *factum est*? All these were undone, and *blowen over*; all the undermining disappointed; all this murder, and crueltie, and desolation defeated. The *mine* is discovered, *the snare is broken and we are delivered*. All these, the *King, Queen, Prince, Nobles, Bishops, Judges* both Houses *alive*, all: not a *haire of any of their heads perished*; not so much as the smell *of fire on any their garments. Give thankes ô Israël, unto the Lord thy God in the congregation, from the bottome of the heart*; heere is little Benjamin, thy Ruler, the Princes of Juda &c that they are heere and we see them heere, and that the *Stone* these *Builders* refused, is still the *Head-stone of the corner*.

Dan. 3.27.
Psal. 68.26.
27.
28.
&c.

26 send] sent F_2

That, should have been done; this, was done: and we all, that are heere this day, are witnesses of it; Witnesses above all exception of this *factum est*.

[margin: ²*A Domino*.]

But by whom, whose *doing*? Truely, not mans doing this; it was the Lord's. *A Dæmone factum est illud*, or *fictum est illud*. It was the *Devill's doing*, or *devising* (the *plott*:) *A Domino factum est hoc*, This was *God's doing* (the deliverance.) The *blow* was the *Devill's*: the *ward* was *God's*. Not *man*, but the *Devill*, devised it: Not *man*, but *God* defeated it. He, that *satt in heaven* all this while, and from thence looked down and saw all this doing of the *Devill* and his *limmes*, in that mercie of His, which is *over all his workes*; to save the effusion of so much bloud, to preserve the soules of so many innocents, to keepe this Land from so foule a confusion, to shew still some token, some *sensible token upon us for good, that they which hate us may see it, and be ashamed*; but especially, that that, was so lately united, might not so soon be dissolved; He took the matter into his own hand. And, if ever *God* shewed, that He had *a hooke in the Leviathan's nose*; that the *Devill* can goe no further then his *chaine*: if ever, that there is in *Him* more power to *helpe*, then in *Satan* to *hurt*; in this, He did it. And, as the *Devill's clawes* to be seene in the former; so *God's right hand*, in this mightie thing (He brought to passe) and all the *fingers* of it.

[margin: Psal. 86.17.]

1. To shew it was *He*. He held his peace and kept silence, satt still, and let it goe on, till it came neere, even to the verie period, to the day of the *lott*; so neere, that we may truly say (with *King David*) *as the Lord liveth, Uno tantum gradu, nos morsque dividimur*, there was but a *stepp* betweene death and us. We were upon the point of going to the *hill*, all was prepared, the *traine*, the *match*, the *fire*, *wood* and all, and we readie to be the *sacrifice*, and even then and there, *In monte providebat Dominus*, God provided for our safetie, even in that very place, where we should have been the *burnt offering*; from heaven, *stayed the blow*. It was *the Lord's doing*.

[margin: 1. Sam. 20.3.]
[margin: Gen. 22.7.]
[margin: Verse 8.]

2. When treacherie *hath his course like water*, and creepes along like a *snaile* (it is the *fiftie eight Psalme*) then, to make it *like the untimely birth of a woman*, never to see the sunne (not, as in this, *arserunt sicut ignis in spinis*, was but *a blaze, as in a bush of thornes*: (nay, if it come so farre, it had gone wrong with us:) but, as in that, *priusquam intelligerent spinæ*, or ever the *thornes* gate *heate*, or the *powder*, fire;) then, saith he there, *Dicit homo, Utique est Deus*, Men shall say, verily there is a *God*, and this was His *doing*.

[margin: Psal. 58.8.]
[margin: Verse 9.]
[margin: Verse 11.]

3. And not onely, that it was bewrayed, but that He made them the bewrayers of it themselves; and even according to the place (*Eccl.* 10.) made *things with feathers* to disclose it: When (as in *Psalme* 64.) *their owne tongues* (or, which is all one, *their owne penns*) *make them to fall*: all that consider it, shall be amazed; and then all men shall say, *This hath God done; for they*

[margin: Eccles. 10.20.]
[margin: Psal. 64.8.]

shall perceive it plaine, it is His worke. They shall be charged in *confession*, they shall *sweare*, they shall take the *Sacrament* not to doe it; and yet, contrarie to all this, it shall come out by themselves. Was not this *God's doing*?

4. Yet further, to shew it was so: This which was written, was so written, as diverse of profound wisedome, knew not what to make of it. But then commeth *God* againe (*God* most certenly) and (as in the *Proverbs* 16.10.) puts קשם, a very *divination*, a very *oracle, in the King's lipps*, and his mouth missed not the matter; made him, as *Joseph*, the revealer of Secretts, to read the riddle: giving him wisedome to make both explication, what they would doe; and application, where it was they would doe it. This was GOD certainely. This, *Pharao* would say, none could, unlesse he were *filled with the Spirit of the holy* GOD. It was *A Domino factum*. Pro. 16.10.

Gen. 41.38.

5. Lastly, as that, when it was come forth they were not reclaimed; not then, when they saw, the hand of GOD was gone out against them, and that it was even GOD, *they strave withall*: no, but even then, from hidden *treacherie*, fell to open *rebellion*, and even perished in it (if *God* shewed not a *miracle* of His *mercie* on them) perished there, and perished eternally: as this I say did (that it was *factum à Dæmone*, who never left them, till he had brought them thither:) So, that (before they came thither) GOD cast their owne *powder* in their faces, *powdered* them, and disfigured them with it; and that their quarters stand now in peeces, as they meant, ours should: It is the case of the CIX *Psalme, And hereby shall they know, that it is Thy hand, and that Thou Lord hast done it*, How? in that, they are thus *clothed with their owne shame*, and even *covered with their owne confusion*; that they *fall*, as fast as they *rise*; are still *confounded*, and still *thy servants rejoyce*. These five (as prints) shew, it was *God's hand*. It was the *Lord*, that made the *Day*; it was the *Day*, that the *Lord* made. *Be thou exalted Lord in thine owne strength*. It was thy *right hand*, that brought this mightie thing to passe. Psal. 109.27.

29.

Psal. 21.13.

This will not serve the turne. His *doing* makes it not the *Day*; His *doing* a *miracle*, that makes it: and, that it is too. I take no thought, to prove this point: by the *Law*, the *Prophets*, the *Gospell*. To put them to it; *Moses*: *Enquire now of the daies that are past, that were before us, since the day that God created man upon earth, and aske from one end of heaven to the other, if there came to passe such a thing as this, whither any such like thing have been heard*; and, if we cannot suit it, or sett such another by it, we must needs yield it, for one. By the *Prophets*: *Goe to the Isles and behold, send to Kedar and take diligent heed, and see, if you can possibly* finde the like: if not, confesse it for *mervailous. Come hither* (saith *David*) and *behold, how mervailous God is!* and what is that? that such, as are *rebellious*, are not able to

[3]*Et est mirabile*.

Deut. 4.32.

Jer. 2.10.

exalt themselves: We need not goe so farre, we have it heere to see; We may say to him, *Come hither*. By the *Gospell*: for, so doe they (there) acknoweldge our *Saviour's* for miracles: *Sure we have seene strange things to day*: We never saw it on this fashion: The *like was never seene in Israël*: therefore *mervailous* certainely. It is now no *miracle*, no *strange thing*, to have a *King* delivered: every other yeare, we see it, and therefore wonder not at it. But, to see *King*, *Queene*, their *seed*, all their *Estates* delivered, that is *mirabile*, that is a *new thing created on earth*. I conclude: as, that was the *Devill's doing*, and was *monstrous in our eyes*; so, this is *God's doing*, and it is *mervailous in our eyes*. And againe, upon all these marks, that, as this was a *day*, the *Devill would* have *marred*; so, this is a *day*, that the *Lord made*.

Mervailous then it is: yet, hath it not (as we say) his *full Christendome*, unlesse it be so *in our eyes*. For the time, it was; and that (of the *Psalme*) fitts us well, *When God* (saith He) *turned away the captivitie* (say we, *the destruction*) *of his people, then were we like to them that dreame*. No man, but stood in a maze, as if he knew not well, whither he saw it *waking*, or *dreamt* of it, it was so strange.

And lett me goe further. Not, *in ours* onely; for (sure I am) that which followeth there, is true (*Then said they, inter Gentes*) of other *nations*; The *Lord hath done great things for them*: and we are to blame, if we answer them not, with the *Eccho* there following, *Yea indeed, the Lord hath done great things for us; for which we have cause to rejoyce*. If strangers thinke it strange, and say, and write, *A seculo inauditum*, The like was never heard before: if it were *mervailous in their eyes*, it were very *mervailous*, it should not be so, *in our eyes* too.

I add, they that were the *Actors* of it, *in their eyes*, it is so; and that of the *Apostle* may fitly be applied to them. *Behold ye Despisers and wonder, and vanish for* GOD *hath wrought a Worke in your dayes, a Worke which you your selves that were the doers, shall scarse beleeve, when it shalbe told*: that even astonished themselves, to see it go forward so long, and so suddainly cast downe. Nay I go further, to make it a *miracle* consummate. I doubt not, but it was strange newes, even in *Hell* it selfe, insomuch as even that place had never hatched the like monster before. You see the welcome they in *Hell* gave him of *Assur* (*Esay* XIIII) *What art thou come, that makest the earth to tremble, and dost shake whole kingdomes*? And yet it is well knowne, all his *shaking* was but in a *metaphore*: He never made it *shake actually*, as these would have done: and therefore, this of greater admiration, and (I doubt not, but) more *wonderfull* in *their eyes*: And *ours* are very dimme, if in all other it be, and be not so in *ours*.

Marginal references:
Luk. 5.26.
Mar. 2.12.
Matt. 9.33.
Jer. 31.22.
⁴*In oculis nostris*, in *our eyes*. Psal. 126.1.
In the *eyes* of others. Psal. 126.2.
Verse 3.
Of the very *Actors*. Acts 13.41.
Esa. 14.16.

25 Actors] *F*₂; Actor's *F*₁   33 gave him] *F*₂; gave, him *F*₁

III. The *Duety*.

Then, if such *dayes* there be, if this of ours be one of them, if the fore-part of the verse do, then must the latter also belong to us: If this, the *day*, the LORD *hath made*; then, this, the *day*, wherein we to *rejoyce*: When *He* makes, we to *make*; and our *rejoycing* in it, is our *making* of it.

To *rejoyce*, no hard request, nor heavie yoak, let it not be grievous to us. We love to do it, we seek all meanes to do it in all cases els: then to assay to do it heer. This (sure) the *Prophet* would not require, nor make it the Office of the *day*; but that upon such dayes, GOD himself calls us to *joy*.

And even as, when GOD calleth us to mourning, by *black dayes*, of famine or warr, or the like; then to fall to *feasting* or revelling, is that that highly displeaseth GOD: so, when GOD, by *good dayes*, calleth us to *joy*; then to droop, and not to accommodate our selves to seasons of His sending, is that which pleases Him never a whitt.

What? (saith *Nehemias*, upon such a blessed day as this?) *Droop you to day? Nolite*, at no hand do it, *Dies enim festus est*, it is a *festivall day*: What then? why it is essentiall, it is of the very nature of every *Feast* (saith GOD in His law) *omnino gaudere*, by any meanes, in any wise, therein to rejoyce. And *Nehemia's* promise is to incourage us, that if the *strength of the Lord* be our *joy*, the very joy of the *Lord* shalbe our *strength*.

Nehem. 8.9. 10.

Num. 10.10. Deut. 16.11.

To conclude: Sure I am, that if the *plott* had prevailed, it would have been an high Feast in *Gath*, and a day of *Jubilee* in *Ascalon;* the daughters of the uncircumcised would have made it a *day of triumph*. Let us not be behind them then, but shew as much *joy*, for our *saving*, as they would certenly have done, for our *perishing*.

2. Sam. 1.20.

Exultemus & lætemur. GOD loveth, our *joy* should be full; it is not full, except we have both these, the *bodie* (as it were) and the *soule* of *joy*: the *joy outward* of the *body*, and *gladnesse inward* of the *soule*. (So much do the two words signifie, in all the three tongues.) Both He will have: for, if one be wanting, it is but *semiplenum*, halfe full.

Exultemus and *Lætemur* both

And he beginneth with *Exultemus*, the outward: Not, to our selves within, which we call *gaudere in sinu*, *Joy of the bosome*; but such, so exuberant, as the streames of it may overflow, and the beames of it shine and shew forth, in an *outward* sensible *exultation*. It is a *day*: so would he have us *rejoyce*, that, as by *day light*, it might be seen in our face, habit, and gesture: *Seene*, and *heard* both: therefore he saith (at the XV. Verse) *the voice of joy is in the dwellings of the righteous*. And *in the dwelling* it doth well: But yet, that would not serve his turne; but, *open me* (saith he at the XIX. Verse) the *gates of righteousnesse*, that is, the *Church-doore* (his *house* would not hold him) *thither will I go in*, and *there*, in the *congregation*, in *the great congregation, give thankes to the Lord*: And that so *great a congregation*, that it

Exultemus: the outward joy.

Ver. 15.

Ver. 19.

may *constituere diem solennem in condensis usque ad Cornua altaris*, that they may stand so thick in the *Church*, as fill it from the entrie of the doore, to the very edge of the *Altar*. This same *joy*, that is neither seen nor heard, there is some *levin* of *malignitie* in it; he cannot skill of it. He will have it *seen* in the *countenance*, *heard* in the *voice*; not onely *preaching*, but *singing* forth His *praise*. And that, not with *voices* alone, but with *instruments*, and not *instruments* of the *Queer* alone, but instruments of the *steeple* too, *bells* and all, that so it may be *Hosanna in altissimis*, in the very *highest key* we have. This for *exultemus*.

<small>*Lætemur*, the inward joy.</small>

But, many a close *Hypocrite* may do all this, and many a counterfeit *Shemei* and *Sheba* did all this, to *David*; gott them a *fleering forced countenance*, taken on *joy*: And therefore the other; that *God* will have this joy, not be the joy of the countenance alone, a cleere face, and a clowdie overcast heart; he will have the *gladnesse* of the *heart* too, of the inner man: *Cor meum & caro mea*; the *heart*, as well as the *flesh*, to be joyfull. The *joy* of the *soule*, is the *soule* of *joy*: not a *bodie* without a *soule*, which is but a *carcasse*. Strange *children may* (and will) *dissemble with me* (saith the Psalme XVIII.XLIV.) dissemble a gladnesse, for feare of being noted; and yet within, in *heart*, you wott what. But, *God* calleth for his *de fontibus Israël*, which we reade, *from the ground of the heart*. That is (indeed) the true fountaine of joy, that our *lipps may be faine, when we sing unto Him, and so may our soule, which He hath delivered*. Nay, He delivered both: and therefore, both the *bodie* to rejoyce, and the *soule* to be *glad*. This doth *Lætemur* add, to *exultemus*.

<small>Psal. 16.9.</small>

<small>Psal. 18.44.</small>

<small>Psal. 68.26.</small>

<small>Psal. 71.23.</small>

<small>How to *order* our *joy*.</small>

If then we be agreed, that we will do both, I come to the last, how to *order our joy*, that it may please Him, for whom it is undertaken. It is not every *joy*, that He liketh. Merrie they were, and joyfull (they thought) that kept their King's day (Hos.VII.) by taking in *boule* after *boule* till they were sick again. So they, that *Malachi* speaks of, there came nothing of their *feasts*, but *dung* (beare with it, it is the *Holy Ghost* his own terme) that is, all in the *belly*, belly-cheere. So they, that sate *down to eate and drink, and rose up to play*, and there was all; that is the *Calve's feast*: a *Calfe* can do as much, But *with none of these was God pleased*: and as good no *joy*, as not to the purpose; as not to please *Him*.

<small>Hos. 7.5.</small>
<small>Mal. 2.3.</small>
<small>Exod. 32.6.</small>
<small>1. Cor. 10.5.</small>

That it may be to the purpose, that *God* may take pleasure in it, it must beginne at *Hosanna*, at *Aperite mihi portas Justitiæ*, at the *Temple-doore*; there it must go in, it must *blesse*, and be *blessed* in the *house of the Lord. I will first make joyfull in my house of prayer* (it is God by Esay:) the streame of our *joy*, must come from the spring-head of *Religion*.

<small>Ver. 19.</small>
<small>Esa. 56.7.</small>

---

20 *in marg*. Psal. 71.23] *LACT*; Psal. 71.21 F_1, F_2, F_3
34 *in marg*. Ver. 19] *LACT*; Ver. 9 F_1, F_2, F_3

Well then, to the *Church* we are come: so farr onward. When we are there, what is to be done? Somwhat we must say, we must not stand mute. There to stand still, that, the *Prophet* cannot skill of. That then, we may (there) say something, he heer frames, he heer endites us a versicle, which after grew into such request, as no *Feast* ever without it, without an *Hosanna*: it grew so familiar, as the very *children* were perfect in it. The summe and substance whereof (briefly) is no more, but (which we all desire) that *God* would still *save*, still *prosper*, still *blesse* him, that in His name, is come unto us (that is) *King David* himselfe, whom all in the House and all of the House of the *Lord* blesse in His name. Ver. 25.

Mat. 21.9.

And to very good purpose doth he this: for, *joy* hath no fault, but that it is too short, it will not last, it will be taken from us too soon. It is ever a *barr*, in all *joy, tolletur à vobis*; subject to the *worme*, that *Jona's gourd* was. It standeth us therefore in hand; to begin with *Hosanna*, so to *joy*, as that we may long joy, to pray for the continuance, that it be not taken from us: ever remembring, the true temper of *joy*, is (*exultate in tremore*) not without the mixture of some *feare*. For, this day, we see what it is, a *joyfull day*: *we know not* (saith *Salomon*) *what the next day will be*: and if not what the *next day*, what the *next yeare* much lesse. What will come, we know not; what our sins call for to come, that we know; even that *God* should call to judgement, if not by *fire*, by somwhat els. If it be but for this, it concernes us neerly, to say our *Hosanna*, that the next yeare be as this. It is our wisdome therefore, to make the meanes, for the continuance of it, that *God would still stablish the good worke, He this day wrought in us*; still blesse us, with the continuance of the same *blessings*. Psal. 2.11.

Pro. 27.1.

And this that we may doe, not faintly but cheerefully with the *lifting* up of our *soules*; therefore, as farre as art of spirit can do it, he hath quickned his *Hosanna*, that he may putt *spirit* and *life* in us, to follow him in it, with all fervor of affection: foure times, twise with *Anna*, and twise with *Na*; either of them before, and after; but eight words, and foure of them *interjections*: all to make it passionate; and that so, as (in the originall) nothing can be devised more forcible; and so, as it is hard in any other tongue, to expresse it; which made the *Evangelist* lett it alone, and retaine the *Hebrew* word still. But, this, as neere as I can, it soundeth: *Now good Lord save us yet still, now good Lord prosper us yet still*. Be to us, as last yeare, so, this, and all the yeares to come, JESUS *a Saviour, yesterday and to day and the same for ever*. Verse 25.

And three things doth he thus earnestly pray for, and teacheth us to doe the like. [1]*To save,* [2]*prosper,* [3]*and blesse.*

1. To *save*: that should be first with us; it is commonly last: We have least sense of our *soules*. To *save* us, with the *true saving health*; (it is a word

whereof our *Saviour* JESUS hath his name) it importeth the salvation of the *soule*; properly to that it belongeth, and hath joyned to it *Hosanna* in the *Gospell* (*Hosanna in excelsis*) to shew, it is an high and heavenly salvation.

    2. Then, to *prosper*. If He but grant us the former alone, to have our *soules* saved, though without prosperitie, though with the dayes of adversitie, it is *sors Sanctorum*, the lott of many a *Saint* of His, of farre more worth then we: Even so, we are bound, to thanke him, if, even so, we may be but *saved*. But, if he add also *prosperitie* of the outward, to the *saving* of the inward man, that not so much *as a leafe of us shall wither, but looke what we doe shall prosper*; and that, whatsoever men of evill counsells do, shall not prosper against us; if He not only vouchsafe us *Hosanna in excelsis*, but *Hosanna de profundis* too, from *deep cellars, deep vaults*, those that digg deep to undermine our prosperitie; If He add the *shaddow of his wings*, to shelter us from perills, to the *light of his countenance*, to *save* us from our *sinnes*, then have we great cause to rejoyce yet more: and, both with *exultemus* from without, and *lætemur* from within, to magnifie His *mercie*, and to say with the *Prophet, Praysed be the Lord, that* (not onely *taketh care* for the *safetie*, but) *taketh pleasure in the prosperitie of His servants*.

    3. Lastly, because both these, the one and the other; our future *salvation*, by the continuance of His *Religion* and *truth* among us, and our present *prosperitie* (like two walls) meet upon *the Head stone of the corner*; depend both, first, *upon the Name of the Lord*, and next upon him, that *in His name*, and with *His name*, is *come* unto us (that is) the *King*: (So, do both the *Evangelists, Saint Luke* and *Saint John* supplie; and, where we read, *Blessed be he*, there they read, *Blessed be the King that commeth*:) so that neither of them sure, unlesse *He* be safe; that *He* would blesse him, and make him blest, that, in His blessed Name, is come amongst us. The building will be as *mount Sion*, so the corner stone be *fast*; so the two walls, that meet, never fall asunder. If otherwise: but, I will not so much as put the case; but, as we pray, so trust, it *shall never be removed but stand fast for ever*.

    This then we all wish, that are now in the *House of the Lord*; and *we that are of the House of the Lord* do now and ever, in the Temple and out of it, morning and evening, night and day, wish and pray both, that He would continue forth His goodnesse, and blesse with length of dayes, with strength of health, with increase of all honour, and happinesse, with terror in the eyes of his enemies, with grace in the eyes of his Subjects, with whatsoever *David*, or *Salomon* or any *King*, that ever was happie, was *blessed* with; Him, that in the *Name of the Lord* is come to us, and hath now these foure yeares stayed with us, that he may be blessed, in that Name, wherein

Matt. 21.9.

Psal. 1.3.

Luk. 19.38.
Joh. 12.13,15.

Psal. 125.1.

he is come, and by the *Lord*, in whose Name he is come, many and many yeares yet to come.

And, when we have put this *incense* in our phialls, and bound *this sacrifice with cords, to the altar* fast, we blesse you and dismisse you, to eat your *bread* with *joy*, and to drinke your *wine* with a *cheerfulle heart*: for, GOD accepteth your worke; your *joy* shall please Him: this *Hosanna* shall sanctifie all the *joy*, shall follow it.

To end then. This *Day*, which the *Lord* hath thus *made* so *mervailously*; so *mervailously* and *mercifully*; let us rejoyce in the *Maker*, for the making of it, by His doing on it that deed, that is so *mervailous in our eyes*, in all *eyes*; returning to the beginning of the *Psalme*, and saying with the *Prophet*: *O give thankes to the Lord for he is gracious &c. Lett Israël, lett the house of Aaron, yea lett all that feare the Lord, confesse that His mercie endureth for ever.*   Verse 1.2.3.4.

Who onely doth great wonders. Who remembred us when we were in danger, And hath delivered us from our enemies, with a mighty hand and stretched out arme. And, as for them, hath turned their devise upon their owne head. And hath made this day, to us, a day of joy and gladnesse. To this GOD of GODS, the LORD of heaven, glorious in holinesse, fearefull in power, doing wonders, be, &c.   Psal. 136.4.
23.
24.
12.

X

A Sermon Preached before the Kings Majestie at Whitehall, on Christmas Day. ANNO 1609

GALAT. 4. vers. 4, 5.

When the fulnesse of time was come, God sent his Sonne, made of a woman, made under the Law.
That, He might redeeme, them that were under the Law, that wee might receive the Adoption of sonnes.

IF, *when the fulnesse of time commeth*, God *sent his Sonne*: then, When *God sent his Sonne, is the fulnesse of time come*. And as this day, *God sent his Sonne*. This day therfore, (so oft as by the revolution of the yeere it commeth about) is to us a yeerely representation of *the fulnesse of time*. So it is: and a speciall honour it is to the *Feast*, that so it is. And we our selves seeme so to esteeme of it. For we allow for every *month* a *day*, (Looke how many *months* so many *dayes*) to this *Feast*; as if it were, and we so thought it to be, the *full* recapitulation of the whole yere.

This honour it hath, from *Christ*, who is the *substance* of this, and all other *Solemnities*. Peculiarly, *à Christi missâ*, from *Christs sending*. (For, they that read the ancient writers of the *Latin* Church, *Tertullian*, and *Cyprian*, know that *Missa*, and *Missio*, and *Remissa, and Remissio*, with them are taken for one. So that *Christi missa* is the *sending of Christ*.) And when then hath this Text place so fit, as Now? Or what time so seasonable to entreat of it, as This? Of *the sending of his Sonne*; as, *when God sent his Sonne*: Of *the fulnesse of time*; as, on the yeerely returne and memoriall of it.

To entreat of it then. The Heads are two. 1. Of *the fulnesse of time*. 2. And of that, wherewith it is *filled*. 1. *Times fulnesse*, in these, *whence the fulnesse of time came*. 2. *Times filling* in the rest, God sent his Sonne, made of a woman, made under the Law, &c.

11 IF,] IF Q_1 21 *Cyprian*,] *Cyprian* Q_1 22 *Remissa*,] *Remissa* Q_1
27 two.] two: Q_1

In the former, (*Quando venit plenitudo temporis,*) there be foure points. 1.
1. *Plenitudo temporis*, That, *time* hath a *fulnesse*; or, that there is a *fulnesse of time*. 2. *Venit plenitudo*. That, that *fulnesse commeth*, by steps and degrees, not all at once. 3. *Quando venit*. That, it hath a *Quando*, (That is,) There is a time, when *time* thus *commeth* to this *fulnesse*. 4. And, when that *When* is? And that is, *When God sent his Sonne*. And so passe wee over to the other part, in the same Verse, *Misit Deus*; *God sent his Sonne*.

For the other part, (touching *the filling of time*.) There be *Texts*, the right 2. way to consider them, is to take them in pieces. And this is of that kinde. And if wee take it in sunder, we shall see, as it is of *fulnesse*, so a kinde of *fulnesse* there is in it: every word, more *full* then other: every word, a step in it, whereby it riseth still higher, till by *seven* severall degrees it commeth to the top, and so the *measure is full*. 1. *God sent*, the first. 2. *Sent his Sonne*, the second. 3. *His Sonne made*, the third. 4. And that *twice* made, *made of a woman*, the fourth. 5. *Made under the Law*, the fift, every one *fuller* then other, still.

And all this, for some *persons*, and some *purpose*. The persons, *Ut nos,* 3. *that we*. The purpose, *reciperemus, that we might receive*. Nay, (if you marke it) there be two *Ut's, ut ille, ut nos*, that *He might*, and, that *wee might*. He might *redeeme*: and *we* might *receive*, that is, *He* pay for it, and, *wee* reape the benefit. 6. A double benefit, of *Redemption* first from the state of persons cast and condemned, *under the Law*, which is the *sixt*. 7. And then, of translation into the state *of adopted children* of God, which is the *seventh*; & the very *filling* up of the measure.

All which, we may reduce to a double *fulnesse*. *Gods*, as much as *Hee* can send. *Ours*, as much as *we* can desire. *Gods*, in the five first. 1. *God sent*. 2. *Sent his Sonne*. 3. *His Sonne made*. 4. *Made of a Woman*. 5. *Made under the Law*. And *Ours* in the two latter, 6. *We are redeemed*, the sixt. 7. *We receive adoption*, the seventh.

In that of *Gods*, every point is *full*; The thing sent, *full*. The *sending*, and the *maner* of sending, *full*. The *making*, and the two *maners* of making, *Of a woman*, and, *under the Law*, both *full*. And *our fulnesse* in the two latter, the *effects* of these two *Actes*, or *makings of a woman under the Lawe*, *Redemption*, and *Adoption*, which make up all. That, when we were *strangers* from the *Adoption*; and not that onely, but lay *under the Law*, as men whom sentence had passed on: From this latter, wee are *redeemed*, (Hee *under the Law*, that we *from under the Law,*) that, (being so *redeemed*) we might further *receive the adoption of children*, (and as Hee *the Sonne of man*: So we might be made *the sonnes of God*.) Which two are as much as we can wish. And this is *Our fulnesse*.

14 *woman*,] woman Q_1 19 *He* pay] *Hee*, pay Q_1
36 *Law*,) that] *ed.*; *Law*) That Q_1, Q_2; *Law*,) That F_1

4. And to these, I will crave leave to adde another *fulnesse* of *Ours*, rising out of these, and to make a *motion*, for it. That, as it is the time, when *wee* from God, *receive* the *fulnesse* of his *bounty*: so it might be the time also, when *He* from us, may likewise *receive* the *fulnesse* of our *duetie*. The time, of *His Bounty-fulnesse*, and the time, of *our Thanke-fulnesse*: That it may be *Plenitudo temporis, quâ ad illum, quâ ad nos*; downeward, and upward; from *Him* to *us*, and from *us to Him* againe: and so bee both wayes, *The fulnesse of time*.

Quando venit plenitudo temporis.

1. Plenitudo temporis.

FIRST, there is a *fulnesse* in Time. The terme, *Fulnesse*, carieth our conceit to *measure* straight, from whence it is borrowed: which, is then said to bee *full*, when it hath as much, as it can hold. Now, God *hath made all things in measure*: and if all things, then *Time*. Yea, *Time* it selfe is by the Apostle called, *Mensura temporis*, The measure of time. As then, all other *measures* have theirs; so the *measure* of *Time* also hath *his fulnesse*, when it receiveth so much, as the capacitie will conteine no more. So, *Time* is a *measure*: it hath a *capacitie*: that hath a *fulnesse*. That, there is such a thing, as, *the fulnesse of time*.

Sap. 11.17.
Eph. 4.13.

2. Venit plenitudo.

But, nothing is *full* at first: no more is *Time* by and by. *Venit plenitudo*, it commeth, not at once, or straightwayes, but by steps and paces, neerer and neerer: *Fills*, first a quarter, and then halfe, till at last it come to the brim. And *degrees* there be, by which it commeth. *Ecce palmares posuisti dies meos*, Psal. 39.6. From which word *palmares*, it is an observation of one of the Fathers, a man may reade his *time* in his owne *hand*: there is a likenesse betweene a mans *hand*, and his *time*. As in the *hand*, visibly there is an ascent, the fingers rise still, till they come to the top of the middle finger; and when they be come thither, downe againe by like descent, till they come to the little, which is the lowest of all: So is it in our *time*; It riseth still *by degrees*, till we come to the *full* pitch of our Age, and then declineth againe, till we grow to the lower end of our *dayes*. But, howsoever it may be (as it oft falles out) the descent is sudden, wee goe downe headlong without degrees, goe away in a moment; yet, ever this holdeth, to our *fulnesse* we come not, but *by degrees*.

Alcuin.

3. Quando venit.
Joh. 7.6.

Now thirdly, this *comming* hath a *Quando venit*, a *time*, when it *commeth* thither. As a time there is a great while, when wee may say, *Nondum venit hora*, the time is not yet come, while the *measure* is yet but in *filling*: So at

---

19 thing, as,] thing as Q_1 22 Fills] F_1; Fill's Q_1, Q_2 25–26 his *time*... visibly there is] his *time*. In his owne *hand*, visibly there is Q_1, F_1

the last, a time too, that we may say, *Venit hora*, the time is now *come*, when the *measure* is *full*: That is, A *time* there is, when *time commeth to the full*: As in the *day*, when the *Sunne* commeth to the *Meridian Line*: in the *moneth*, when it commeth to the point of *opposition* with the *Moone*: in the *Yeare*, when to the *Solstice*: In *man*, when he commeth to his *full* yeres: for that is the *fulnesse of time* the Apostle alledgeth, in the three verses before.

Joh. 12.23.

And, when is that *When*, that *time* thus *commeth* to his *fulnesse*? *Quando misit Deus*, when God sends it: for, *Time* receives his *filling* from God. Of it selfe, *time* is but an *emptie measure*, hath nothing in it: *Many* dayes and monethes runne over our heads, *Dies inanes*, sayth the *Psalmist*. *Menses vacui*, sayth *Job*: *Emptie dayes*, Psal. 78.33. *Void monethes*, without anything to fill them, Job 7.3.

4. Quando

That which *filleth time*, is some memorable thing of *Gods* powring into it, or (as it is in the Text) of *his sending*, to *fill* it withall. *Misit Deus* is it: and so commeth *Time* to be more or lesse *full*; thereafter as that is, which *God sends* to *fill* it.

Now, many memorable *missions* did *God* make, before this heere; whereby in some measure, hee *filled* up certaine times of the yeere under Moses, and the *Prophets*: all which, may well be termed, *The implements of Time*.

But, for all them, the *measure* was not yet *full*: *filled* perhaps to a certaine *degree*, but not *full* to the *brimme*: *full* it was not (seeing it might be stil *fuller*) till *God sent* That, then which, a more *full* could not be *sent*.

And, That *He* sent, when *He* sent his *Sonne*, a *fuller* then whom, *He* could not *send*, nor *Time* could not *receive*. Therefore, with the *sending Him*, when that was, *Time* was at the top, that was the *Quando venit*, then it was *plenitudo temporis*, indeed.

And, well might that *Time*, be called *the fulnesse of Time*. For, when *He* was sent into the world, in whom *the fulnes of the Godhead dwelt bodily*. In whom *the Spirit was not by measure*. In whom was *the fulnesse of grace and trueth*. Of *whose fulnesse we all receive*, when *He* was sent, that was thus *full*, then was *Time* at the *full*.

1.

And well also might it be called, *the fulnesse of Time*, in another regard. For, till then all was but in *promise*, in *shadowes*, and *figures*, and *prophecies* onely, which *fill* not, God knowes. But when the *performance* of those *promises*, the *body* of those *shadowes*, the *substance* of those *figures*, the *fulfilling* or *filling full* of all those *Prophecies* came, then *came the fulnesse of Time*, truely so called. Till then, it *came* not: then, it *came*.

2.

17 *missions*] F_1; *mission's* Q_1, Q_2 make,] make Q_1 28 *bodily*.] bodily: Q_1 29 *meas-ure*.] measure: Q_1 32 called,] called Q_1 *in marg.* 2.] F_1; *om.* Q_1, Q_2 33 For,] For Q_1
37 then,] then Q_1

3. And well might it bee called the *fulnesse* of *time*, in a *third* respect. For, then the Heire, (that is *the world*) was come to his *full age*: and so, that the fittest *time*, for *Him* to bee *sent*. For to that, compareth the Apostle their estate then; that, the former times under *Moses* and the *Prophets* were as the Nonage of the world; *sub Pædagogo*, in the 3. *Chapter, ver.* 24., ὑπὸ στοιχεῖα, at their *A.B.C.* or rudiments, (as in the very last words before these.) Their estate then, as of *Children* in their minority, *litle differing from servants*. For, all this while, *nondum venit*, the *fulnes* of *time* was not yet *come*. But a *time* there was, as for *man*; so for *mankind* to come to his *full* yeeres: That *time*, came with *Christs comming*, and *Christs comming* with it, and never till then, was the *fulnesse of time*; but then, it was.

And let this bee enough, for this point; more there is not in the *Text*. But if any shall further aske, why *then*, at that age of the world, the world was at his *full age*, just then, and neither sooner nor later? I know, many heads have bene full of devices, to satisfie mens curiositie in that point. But, I hold it safest, to rest with the Apostle (in the second verse) on Gods ὑποθεσμία. Let that content us. Then was the time, for that was *Tempus præfinitum à Patre*, the time appointed of the Father. For, even among men, (though the *Father* being dead) the Lawe setteth a time, for the *Sonne* to come to his heritage: yet the *Father* living, no time can be prefixed, but onely when it liketh Him to appoint; and the *Father* here, liveth; and therefore let his προφεσμία stay us. *The times and seasons, He hath put in his owne power, it is not for us to know them.* This is for us to know, that, with his appointment, we must come to a full point. So doth the *Apostle*: and so let us, and not busie our selves much with it. *Time* is but the *measure* or caske, that wherewith it is *filled*, doth more concerne us. To that therefore let us come.

Acts 1.7.

2. God sent.

1. The *degrees* are *seven* (as I said.) To take them, as they rise. *Misit Deus, God sent*. That standeth first; and, at it, let our first stay be. That, will fall out, to make the *first* degree. For, even this, that *God sent* at all, *Ipsum mittere Dei*, this very *sending* it selfe, is a degree. It is so; and so we would reckon of it, if we knew the *Sender*, and who *He* is; the *Majestie* of his presence how great it is, and how glorious, how farre surpassing all we can see on earth.

For *Him*, for such an one as *Hee*, to condescend, but to *send*; is sure a degree. For, ynough it had beene, and more then ynough, for *Him*, to be *sent to*; and not to *send*, *Himselfe*. To have sit still, and bene content, that we might *send* to *Him*, and have our message and petition admitted; and not, *He send* to us. That had beene as much as we could looke for, and well, if wee might have

---

1 in marg. 3.] F_1; 2. Q_1, Q_2 2 then the] then, the Q_1 7 these.)] F_1; these) Q_1, Q_2 9 as for] as, for Q_1 11 then, it] then it Q_1 21 here, liveth] here liveth Q_1 24 *Apostle*:] *Apostle*, Q_1 36 admitted;] admitted, Q_1

A SERMON PREACHED ON CHRISTMAS DAY 1609

bene vouchsafed but that. But it was *He*, that *sent*, not *we* to *Him* first, nay, not *we* to *Him* at all, but, *He* to *us*.

He to us? And what were *we*, that *He to us? Us*, (as elsewhere he termeth us) *meere Aliens from Him*, and *His Houshold*; Not that onely, but *Us*, in case of men, whom the Law had passed upon. (So is our estate described in the end of the Text:) for *Him*, to *send to Us*, so great as *Hee*, to *such* as *we*; to thinke *us, tanti*, so much worth, as to make any *mission*, or motion, or to disease any about *us*; This, may well be the *first*. Be it then so; that to *us*; or *for us*, or *concerning us*, God would trouble *Himselfe*, to make any *sending*. A *fulnesse*, there is in this. *Full Hee* was; *a fulnesse* there was in *Him*, (even the *fulnesse of compassion* in His bowels over our estate,) else such a *Sender*, would never once have *sent*. Ephes. 2.12.

God sent; Sent, and *sent his Sonne*. That, (I make no question,) will beare a *second*. *Others* He might have *sent*; and *whosoever* it had bene Hee had *sent*, it might well have served our turnes. If, sent by the hand of any his *Servants*, any *Patriarch, Prophet*, any *ordinary messenger*, it had beene ynough. So hitherto had bene his *Sending*. So, and no otherwise, ever till now. His Sonne. 2.

Then, if to *send* by *any* may seeme sufficient; to *send His Sonne*, must needs seeme *full*. For, ever the more excellent the *Person sent*, the more honourable the *sending*: the *greater He*; the *fuller it*. Now, *greater* there is not, then *His sonne*, His *first*, His *onely begotten Sonne*, *in whom the fulnes of the Godhead dwelt*; In sending *Him*, He sent the greatest, the best, the *fullest* thing He had. Colos. 2.9.

To heape the *measure* up yet more, with the *cause* of his *sending*, in the word ἐξαπέστειλε; It was *voluntarie*. Hee sent him not for *need*: but for meere love to us, and nothing else. There was no *absolute necessitie*, that He should have sent *Him*. Hee might have done what Hee intended by the meanes and ministerie of some besides. God could have enabled a *Creature*; a *Creature* enabled by God, *and the power of his might*, could soone have *troad downe Sathan under our feete*. But, if it had bene any *other* He had sent; his love and regard to us, had not shewed so *full*. It had bin *ostendit Deus charitatem*, but not, *Ecce quantam charitatem ostendit Deus*. Whomsoever He had sent besides, his love had not bene *full*, at least not *so full*, as it should have beene, if He had sent *his Sonne*. That therefore it might be *full*, and so appeare to us for *full; Misit Deus filium suum*. Enough it was, in compassion of our estate, to have releeved us, by *any*: Men that are in need to be releeved, care not, *who* they be that doe it. Enough then for *compassion*: but 1. John. 3.1.

---

1 *He*, that] *he* that *Q₁*   19 sufficient;] sufficient, *Q₁*   21 *He*; the] *He*, the *Q₁*
31 sent;] sent, *Q₁*   36 *full; Misit*] *full, Misit Q₁*

not enough, to manifest *the fulnesse* of his love, unlesse to releeve us, *He sent his owne Sonne.*

Made. 3.   This is *full*, one would thinke: Yet, the *Manner* of his *sending* him, is *fuller* still. *Misit Filium; Filium factum.* Sent his Sonne; His Sonne *made.* Sent Him, and sent Him *made.* This is a *third.* For, if He would have sent Him, He should not have sent Him, *made*: but as He was, *neither made, nor created*, but like himselfe, in his owne estate, as was meete for the *Sonne of God*, to bee sent. To *make Him* any thing, is to *marre Him*, be it what it will be. To *send Him made*, is to *send Him marred*, and no better. Therefore, I make not doubt, *Christs sending* is one degree, *His making* is another: So *to sende*, as withall *to make*, are two distinct measures, of this *filling.* As He is, Hee is a *Maker*, a *Creator*: If God *make Him* any thing, Hee must be a thing *made*, a *Creature*; and that, is a great disparagement. So that, howsoever the *Time* is the *fuller*, for this; He is the *emptier*: πλήρωμα χρόνον κένωμα Χριστοῦ, The fulnesse of Time, is his emptinesse; The exalting of that, his

Phil. 2.7.   abasing. And, this very *Exinanivit seipsum*, emptying Himselfe, for our sake, is a pressing downe the *measure*: and so, even by that, still the *measure* is more *full.*

Yea, the very *maner* of this *making*, hath his encrease too, addeth to it still. In the word γενόμενον which is not every *making*, but *making it his nature*. To have *made* Him a bodie, and taken it upon him for a time, till He had performed his Embassage, and then laid it off againe, that, had bene much: But so to be *made*, as once *made* and *ever made*: so to take it, as never lay it off more, but, continue so still, γένεσθαι, it to *become his very nature*; so to *be made*, is to *be made* indeed, so to *to be made* is to *make* the *union full.* And to *make* the *union with us full*, He was content, not to be *sent* alone, but to be *made*, and that γένεσθαι, to be *made so*, as never *unmade* more. Our *manhood* becomming his *nature*, no lesse then the *Godhead* it selfe: This is *Filium factum* indeed.

Made, and twise *made*, (for so it is in the verse) *factum ex*, and *factum sub*, *made of*, and *made under*. *Of a woman; under, the Law.* So, two *makings* there bee, either of them of it selfe, a *filling* to the *measure*, but, both of them, maketh it perfectly full.

Made of a woman. 4.   *Made*, first *of a woman*: that, I take cleerly to be *one.* For, if *Hee*, if the *Sonne of God* must be *made a Creature*; it were meet, He should *be made*, the best *creature* of all. And if *made* of any thing, (if any one thing, better then another) of that: *made* some glorious Spirit, Some of the orders of the

John 1.14.   Angels. Nay, *made*, but *made* no Spirit, *Verbum caro factum est*, The word

---

3–4 *fuller still*] *fuller still Q₁*   4 *Misit Filium*] *Misi Flium Q₁*   6 made, nor] made nor *Q₁*
24 off more] *LACT*; of more *Q₁, Q₂, F₁*   31 made of,] made of *Q₁*   So, two] So two *Q₁*

became flesh: *made*, but *made* no Angel: *Nusquam Angelos*: He in no wise tooke the *Angels* nature upon Him. Heb. 2.16.

But *made man*, First I will aske with *David, Domine, quid est homo?* Lord, what is man? And then, tell you his answere: *Homo quasi res nihili.* Man is like a thing of nought. And this he was *made*, this he became, *made man, made of a woman; did not abhorre the Virgines wombe,* (as wee sing daily, to the high praise of the *fulnesse of his humilitie*, to which his Love brought Him for our sakes.) For, *whatsoever* else He had bene *made*, it would have done us no good. In this then, was the *fulnesse* of his Love, as before of his *Fathers*, that He would bee *made*, and was *made*, not *what* was *fittest* for *Him*, but *what* was *best*, for *us*: not, *what* was most for his *glory*, but *what* was most, for our *benefit* and behoofe. Psal. 144.3.

Made of a woman. For *man* He might have bin *made*, and yet have had a body framed for Him *in heaven*, and not *made of a woman*. But when he saith, *Factum ex muliere*, it is evident, He passed not *through Her as water through a Conduite Pipe*, (as, fondly dreameth the Anabaptist.) *Made of, Factum ex: Ex, dicit materiam.* Made of Her; She ministred the matter, *Flesh of her flesh. Semen mulieris.* The seed, and *Semen intimum substantiæ*, that is the principal and very inward chiefe part of the *substance*. Made of that, made of her very *substance*. Gen. 3.15.

And so have we here now in one, both twaine his *Natures*. *God sent his Sonne*, There his *Divine: made of a woman*, Here his *humane Nature*, That, from *the bosome of his Father*, before all worlds: this, *from the wombe of his mother*, in the world. So that, as from *eternitie*, *God* his *Father* might say, that verse of the Psalme. *Filius meus es tu, hodie genui te*: Thou art my Sonne, this day have I begotten thee. So, in *the fulnesse of time*, might the *Virgin his mother*, no lesse truely say, *Filius meus es tu, hodie peperi te*: Thou art my Sonne, this day have I brought thee into the world. Psal. 2.7.

And heere now, at this word, *made of a woman*, He beginneth to concerne *us* somewhat. There groweth an alliance betweene *us*: For *we also* are *made of a woman*. And our hope is, as, He will not be confounded, to bee counted *inter natos mulierum*: No more will He bee, (saith the *Apostle*) to say *in medio fratrum*; to acknowledge us, his *Brethren*. And so by this *Time* He groweth, somewhat *neere us*. Heb. 2.1. Rom. 8.29.

This now, is *full* for the union with our nature, *to be made of a woman*. But so to be *made of a woman*, without He be also *made under the Law*, is not neere enough yet. For, if he be out of the compasse of the *Law*, that the *Law* cannot take hold of Him, *factum ex muliere* will doe us small pleasure. And He was so borne, *so made of a woman*: As, the veritie, of His conception, is in Made under the Law. 5.

39 As, the] As the Q_1

this *factum ex muliere*: So, the puritie, is in this, that it is but *ex muliere*, and no more; Of the *virgin* alone, by the power of the *Holy Ghost*, without mixture of fleshly generation. By vertue whereof, no originall soile was in Him; *Just* borne He was, and *Justo non est lex posita*, No law for the Just, no law could touch him. And so wee, never the better, for *factum ex muliere*.

1. Tim. 1.9.

For, if one be in debt and danger of the *Law*, to have a *Brother*, of the same blood, *made of the same woman*, both (as we say) *lying in one belly*; will little availe him, except He will also, come under the Law, that is, become his Surety, and undertake for him. And such was our estate. As Debters we were, by vertue of *Chirographum contra nos*, The hand writing that was against us. Which was our *Bond*, and we had forfeited it. And so, *factus ex muliere*, to us, without *factus sub lege*, would have bin to smal purpose.

Col. 2.14.

No remedy therefore, Hee must bee new *made*, *made* againe once more. And so Hee was, cast in a new mould, & at his second *making, made under the Law*, under which if He had not *beene made*, we had beene marred: even quite undone for ever, if this had not beene done for us too. Therfore, He became bound for us also, entred Bond anew, tooke on Him, not only our *nature*, but our *Debt; our Nature*, and *Condition* both. *Nature*, as men: *Condition*, as sinful men; expressed in the words following; [*Them, that were under the lawe*] for that was our *Condition*. There had indeed beene no capacitie in him, to doe this, if the former had not gone before, *factum ex muliere*; if He had not bene, as we, *made of woman*; but the former was for this; *Made of a woman* He was, that He might be *made under the law*: Being *ex muliere*, He might then become *sub lege*, which before He could not, but then he might and did: And so, this still is the *fuller*.

And when did He this? when was *He made under the lawe*? Even then, when he was *circumcised*. For this doth S. *Paul testifie*, in the *third* of the *next Chapter; Behold, I Paul testifie unto you, whosoever is circumcised, factus est debitor universæ legis*. He becomes a debter to the whole lawe. At His *Circumcision* then, He entred *Bond* anewe with us, and in signe that so He did, He shed then a few drops of his blood, wherby He signed the *Bonde* (as it were) and gave those few drops then, *tanquam arrham universi sanguinis effundendi*; as a pledge or earnest, that *when the fulnesse of time came*, He would be readie to shed all the rest; as He did. For, I would not have you mistake, though we speake of this, *sub lege*, being under the law, in the termes of a *Debt* sometimes: yet, the truth is, this *debt* of ours was no *money debt*, we were not *sub lege pecuniaria*, but *Capitali*: and the *debt* of a *Capitall*

Gal. 5.3.

---

8 also, come] also come Q_1 19 *Them, that*] *Them that* Q_1 21 capacitie] captivitie Q_1
22 *woman*; but] *woman*, but Q_1 28 *Chapter;*] *Chapter,* Q_1 33 *effundendi*;] *effundendi* Q_1,
34 rest;] rest, Q_1

law, is death: and under that, under *Death* He went, and that the worst *death* law had to inflict, even the *Death of the Crosse*, the most bitter, reprochful, cursed death of the *Crosse*. So that upon the matter, *factus sub lege*, and *factus in Cruce*, come both to one; one amounts to as much, as the other. Well, this He did undertake for us, at His *Circumcision*: and therefore then, and not till then, He had his name given him, the name of *Jesus a Saviour*. For then, tooke He on him the *Obligation* to save us. And looke, what then at his *Circumcision* He undertooke, at his *Passion* he paid, even to the full, and having paid it, *delevit Chirographum*, cancelled the sentence of the lawe, that till then, was of record, and stoode in full force against us. Luk. 2.21.

 Col. 2.14.

Howbeit all this, was but one part of the lawe, But He was *made sub lege universâ*, under the whole law, and that, not by his *death* onely, but by his *life* too. The one halfe of the law, (that is, the *Directive* part) He was *made under* that, and satisfied it, by the Innocencie of his life, without breaking so much, as one jot or tittle of the lawe: and so, answered that part (as it might be, the *Principall*.) The other halfe of the lawe, which is the *Penaltie*, He was under that part also, & satisfied it, by suffering a wrongfull death, no way deserved, or due by him, and so answered that (as it might be the forfeiture.) So, He was *made under both, under the whole law*. Satisfying the *Principall*, there was no reason, He should be lyable to the *forfeiture*, and *penaltie*: yet, *under that* He was also. And all, that the whole law might be satisfied fully, by His being under both parts, and so, no part of it light upon us.

These two then, 1. *Made of a woman*. 2. *Made under the lawe*, ye see, are *two* severall makings, and both very requisite. Therefore, Either hath a severall *Feast*, they divide this *Solemnitie* betweene them. *Sixe dayes* a peece, to Either; as the severall moities of this *fulnesse of time*. This day, *Verbum caro factum*, The Word made flesh: That day, *Him that knew no Sinne, He made Sinne*; (that is) made him undertake to be handled as a *Sinner*, to be *under the law*, and to endure what the lawe could lay upon Him. And so now, the thing sent is *full*: and *fully sent*, because, *made*: and *fully made*, because, *made once* and *twise* over: fully made *ours*, because fully united to us: *Made of a woman* as wel as we. *Made under the Lawe* as deepe as we, Both *ex muliere*, and *sub lege*. So of our nature (*of a woman*,) that of our condition also (*of a woman*,) that of our condition also (*under the lawe*:) So, fully united to us in nature, and condition both. Joh. 1.14.

 2. Cor. 5.21.

3. And so we are come, to the *full measure* of His *sending*. And, that we are come to the full, ye shall plainely see, by the *overflowing*, by that which Verse 5.

---

15 tittle] title Q₁   21 under that] vener that Q₁   all, that] all, His Q₁   22 by His] by that Q₁   29 Sinne, He] Sinne; He Q₁   Sinne; (that] Sinne, (that Q₁   32 because, made] because made Q₁   twise] twice Q₁

we receive from this *fulnesse*, which is the latter part of the verse, and is our *fulnesse*, even the *fulnesse*, of all that we can desire. For, if we come now to aske, For whom, is al this adoe? This *Sending*, This *making*, over and over againe? It is *for us*. So is the conclusion, *ut nos*, that *wee* might from this *fulnesse*, receive the *full* of our wish. For in these two behinde, *Redemption*, and *Adoption*; to be *redeemed*, and to be *adopted*, are the *full* of all, we can wish our selves.

The transcendent Division, of *Good* and *Evill*, is it, that comprehendeth all. And heere it is. Our desire can extend it selfe no further, then to be rid of all *evill*, and to attaine all, that *good* is. By these two, (being *redeemed*, and being *adopted*) we are made partakers of them both. *To be redeemed from under the law*, is to be quit of all *evill*. *To receive the Adoption of children*, is to be stated in all that is *Good*. For, all *Evill* is in being *under the law*, from whence we are *redeemed*; and, all *Good*, in being invested, in the heavenly Inheritance, whereunto we are *adopted*. Thus stood the case with us: *Aliens we were from God His Covenant*, & his kingdome: More then that, *Prisoners* we were, fast layed up *under the Lawe*. From this latter we are *freed*: of the former, we are *Seised*: And what would we more?

Onely, this you shall observe, that in the *Idiom* of the *Scriptures*, it is usuall; two points being set downe, when they are resumed againe, to beginne with the latter, and so ende with the former. So is it here, At the first, *made of a woman, made under the Law*. At the resuming, Hee beginnes with the latter, *made under the Lawe, That He might redeeme them, that were under the Lawe*. And then comes to the former, *made of a woman*, made the Sonne of man, *That we by adoption might be made the Sonnes of God*. But this we are to marke, it is He that is at all the *cost* and *paine*: and we, that have the *benefit* by it. At the *redeeming* it is, *ut ille*: At the *receiving* it is, *ut nos*.

Briefly of either: And first, of our *Redeeming*. *Redeeming* (as the word giveth it) is a second buying, or buying backe of a thing, before *aliened* or *sold*. Ever, a former *sale* is presupposed before it. And such a thing there had gone before. A kinde of *alienation*, had formerly beene, whereby we had made away our selves, (for a *sale* I cannot call it, it was for such a trifle) our nature *aliened* in *Adam*, for the *forbidden fruit*; a matter of no moment. Our *Persons* likewise, daily wee our selves *alien* them, for some *trifling pleasure*, or *profit*, matters not much more worth. And, when we have thus passed our selves away, by this *Selling our selves under sinne*, the Law seizeth on us, and under it wee are συγκεκλεισμένοι *Cap.* 3.23. even *lockt up*, as it were in a Dungeon, *tyed fast with the cordes of our sinnes, Prov.* 5.22: the sentence

---

3 adoe?] adoe Q_1 9 further, then] further then Q_1 17 were, fast] were fast Q_1
22 first, *made*] first *made* Q_1

passed on us, and wee waiting but for execution. What evill is there not, in this estate, and on every soule that is in it? Well then, the first *ut*, the first ende is, *To get us ridde*, from under this estate.

He did it: not by way of *intreaty*, step in and beg our pardon: That would not serve; *Sold* wee were, and *bought* wee must be. A *price* must bee laide downe for us: To get us from *under the Lawe*, it was not a matter of *Intercession*, to sue for it, and have it. No, He must *purchase* it, and *pay* for it. It was a matter of *Redemption*.

And, in *Redemption* or a *Purchase*, wee looke to the *Price*. For, if it bee at any easie rate, it is so much the better. But with an high *price*, He *Purchased* us; it cost Him *deare* to bring it about. *Non auro, nec argento.* Neither of them would serve, at an higher rate it was, even *pretioso sanguine.* His precious blood, was the *price*, we stood him in. Which He payed, when *He gave his life a ransome for many*. 1. Pet. 1.18,19.
Mat. 20.28.

It stood thus, between *Him* and *us*, in this point of *Redemption*. Heere are certaine *malefactors, under the Lawe*, to suffer, to be executed. What say you to them? Why, I will become *under the Lawe*, suffer that they should, take upon me their execution, upon *condition*, they may be quit: In effect so much, at his *Passion* He said, *Si ergo me quæritis Jo.* 18.6. *If you lay hold on me*, if I must discharge all, *Sinite hos abire*, Let these goe their way, Let the price I pay be their *Redemption*; and so it was. And, so wee come, to be *redeemed from under the Lawe*.

And this is to be marked, that *Them that were under the Lawe*, and, *We that are to receive*, are but one, *one and* the *same persons* both: But being so *redeemed*, then we are our selves. Till then, the *Apostle* speaks of us, in the *third person, Them, that were under the Lawe*, as of some strangers, as of men of another world, none of our owne: But now being *redeemed*, the stile changeth. Hee speaketh of us, in the *first* person *ut nos*, that we: for till now we were not our owne, we were not our selves, but now we are: till this, it was the *old yeere* still with us, but with the *new yeere*, commeth our new estate.

Being thus *redeemed*, we are got from *under the Lawe*: and that is much. Till a party come to bee once *under it*, and feele the weight of it, hee shall never understand this aright; but then he shall. And if any have beene *under it*, he knowes what it is, and how great a *benefit* to bee got thence. But is this all? No, He leaves us not heere; but to make the *measure* compleat, yea, even to *flowe over*, He gives us not over, when he had rid us out of this wretched estate, till He have brought us to an estate, as good, as He himselfe is in. After our *Redemption*, we stood, but as *Prisoners enlarged*; that was all: But, That we might receive the Adoption of children 7.

32 *redeemed*] redeemed Q_1

still we were as *strangers*, no part, nor portion in God, or his kingdome: nor, no reason, we should hope for any. He now goeth one step further, which is the highest and furthest step of all. For further then it, He cannot goe.

That we might receive the Adoption, (that is) from the estate of *Prisoners condemned*, be translated into the estate of *Children Adopted*. Of *Adopted*: for, of *naturall*, wee could not: That is His *peculiar* alone, and He therein onely above us, but else, fully to the joynt fruition, of al that He hath, which is fully as much, as we could desire. And this is our *Fieri* out of His *Factum ex muliere*. We made the *Sonnes of God*, as Hee the *Sonne of man*; We made partakers of his *Divine*, as He of our *humane nature*. To purchase our pardon, to free us from death, and the lawes sentence, this seemed a small thing to Him: yea this is *Lex hominis*. Mans goodnesse goeth no farther; & gracious is the *Prince*, that doth but so much. For who ever heard of a *condemned* man, *Adopted* afterward; or that thought it not enough and enough, if Hee did but scape, with his life? So farre then to exalt his bountie, to that *fulnesse*; as *pardon*, and *Adopt* both, *Non est lex hominis hæc*. No such measure among men, *Zelus Domini Exercituum*, *The zeale of the Lord of Hosts*, was to performe this: *The fulnesse of the Godhead, dwelt in Him*, that brought this to passe.

For (to speake of *adopting*:) We see it dayly; No father *adopts*, unlesse He be *orbe*, have no childe; or if He have one, for some deepe dislike, have cast him off. But God had a *Sonne*, *The brightnes of his Glorie*; *The true character of his Substance*: and no displeasure there was; No, *In quo complacitum est*, In whom He was absolutely well pleased: yet, would He by *adoption*, for all that, *bring many Sonnes to Glory*. Is not this *full* on his part?

We see againe, no *Heire* will endure to heare of *Adoption*, nay, nor divide his Inheritance, no not with his *naturall Brethren*. Then, that the *Heire* of all things, should admit *joynt Heires* to the Kingdome hee was borne to; and that admit them, not out of such, as were *neere* him, but from such as were *strangers*, yea such as had beene *condemned* men *under the Lawe*, Is not this *full*, on his part? To purchase us, and to purchase for us, both at once? And not to *doe* this for us alone, but to *assure* it to us: For, as his *Father*, in this verse, sends Him: So, in the next verse, *He* sends *the Spirit of his Sonne*, to give us *seisin* of this our *Adoption*: whereby we now call him, the Jewes *Abba*, the Gentiles *Pater*, as *Children* all, and He *our Father*, which, is the priviledge of the *Adoption*, we heere receive.

marginalia:
2. Pet. 1.4.
2. Sam. 7.19.
Es. 9.7.
Heb. 1.3.
Mat. 17.5.
Heb. 2.10.
Heb. 1.2.
Rom. 8.17.

20 adopts] Q_1; adopt's Q_2 22 off] *LACT*; of Q_1, Q_2, F_1 25 Glory.] Glory, Q_1
27 *in marg* Heb. 1.2] *ed*.; Heb. 1.3 Q_1, Q_2, F_1, *LACT*

And now, are we come to the *fulnes* indeede. For this *Adoption*, is the *fulnes* of our option, We cannot extende; we, our *wish*: or He, his *love and goodnes* any further. For, what can we aske, or He give more, seing in giving this, He giveth all He is worth? By this time, it is *full Sea*. All the Banckes are *filled*. It is now, as *Ezekiels waters*, that hee sawe *flowe, from under the threshold of the Temple*: that tooke him to the *ancles* first, then to the *knees*, after to the *loynes*, at last, so *high risen*, there was no more passage. Ezek. 47.3,4,5.

1. From the *fulnes* of his *Compassion*, he *sent* to release us: 2. from the *fulnese* of His *love*, He *sent his Sonne*: 3. In the *fulnes of Humilitie*, He *sent him made*: 4. *Made of a Woman*, to make a *full union* with our *nature*. 5. *Made under the Lawe*, to make the *union* yet more perfectly *full* with our *sinfull condition*: 6. That we might obteine a full deliverance, from all *Evill*, by being *redeemed*: 7. and a full estate, of all the *joy* and *Glory* of his heavenly inheritance, by being *adopted*. So, there is *fulnes*, of all handes. And so much, for the *fulnes of the Benefit*, we receive.

Now, for the *fulnes of the duetie*, we are to perform this day. For, *in the fulnes of time*, all things are to be *full*. *Plenitudo temporis, tempus plenitudinis*. And, seing God hath suffered us to live, to see the yeare run about, to this *plenitudo temporis*: if it be so, on *Gods* part; meete also, it be so on *Our's*: and that *we*, be not *emptie*, in this *fulnes of time*. It is not fit, if *He* be at the *brincke*, that *we* be at the *bottom*. But, as *we* be willing, to receive of his: So *we* be like willing, to yeeld Him of *ours* againe; of *our duety* (I meane:) that it, to him, in a measure, & proportion be like *full*; as his *Bountie*, hath beene *full* above measure, toward us. That so *from us*, and on *our parts*, it may be *plenitudo temporis*, or *tempus plenitudinis*, the *fulnes of time*, or *time of fulnes*, choose you whether.

1. And, a *time of fulnes* it wilbe, (I knowe) in a sense: of *fulnes of Bread*, of *fulnes of braverie*, of *fulnes of sport*, and *pastime*: and this it may be. And it hath beene ever, a *joyfull time* in apparance, for it should be so: *with the joy* (sayth Esay a verse or two before, *Puer natus est nobis*, unto us a Childe is borne) *that men rejoyce with, in harvest*. Not to goe from our *Text* here, with the joy of men that are come out of *prison*, have scaped the *Lawe*, with the *joy* of men, that have got the reversion, of a *goodly heritage*. Only, that we forget not the principal, that this *outward joy*, eate not up, evacuate not our *spirituall joy*, proper to the *Feast*: that we have in mind, in the middest of our mirth, the cause of it, *Christs sending*, and the benefits that come thereby. And, it shall be a good signe unto us, if we can thus rejoyce, if Esa. 9.3.

---

19 *Our's*] Ours Q_1 21–22 to receive...willing,] *om*. Q_1, F_1 29 apparance] appearance F_1

this our joy can be *full*, if we can make a *spirituall* blessing, the object of our mirth. *Beatus populus, qui scit jubilationem*. Blessed is the people, that can rejoyce on this manner.

Psal. 89.15.

2. And, after *our joy-fulnesse*, or *fulnes of joy*, *our fulnes of thankes*, or *thank-fulnes*, is to ensue: for, with that *fulnesse*, we are to celebrate it likewise. Our *minds* first, and then our *mouthes*, to be *filled* with blessing, and praise, and thankes to Him that hath made our times, not to fall into those *emptie* ages of the world; but to fall within this *fulnes of time*, which *so many Kings & Prophets desired to have lived in*, but fell short of; And lived then, when the times were *full* of shaddowes, and promises, & nothing else. How instantly they longed, to have held such a *Feast*, to have kept a *Christmasse*, it is evident, by Davids *Inclina cælos*; by Esaies *Utinam disrumpas Cælos, Bow the Heavens, and Breake the Heavens*: How much (I say) they longed for it: and therefore, that we make not light account of it.

Luk. 10.24.

Psal. 144.5.
Es. 64.1.

To render our *thankes* then, and to remember to doe it *fully*, To forget none: To *Him* that *was sent*, & to *Him*, that *Sent*; *Sent his Sonne*, in this; the *Spirit of his Sonne*, in the next verse. To beginne with *Osculamini filium*, it is the first duetie enjoyned us this day, to *kisse the Babe* new borne, that when his *Father* would *send Him*, sayd, *Ecce venio*, so readily: and when he would *make Him*, was content with *Corpus aptasti mihi*, to have a body made him, meete for him to suffer in: who willingly yeelded to be our *Shilo*; to this ἀπέστειλε heere; yea to be not onely *Christ*, but an *Apostle* for us, Heb. 3.1. even *the Apostle of our profession*.

Psal. 2.12.

Psal. 40.7.

Gen. 49.10.

And not to *Him* that *was sent* and *made* alone: but, to the *Father* that *sent Him*, and to the *Holy Ghost* that *made Him*, (as by whom He was conceived.) To the *Father*, for his *mission*; The *Sonne*, for his *Redemption*; the *Holy Ghost*, for his *Adoption*; For by him it is wrought. He that *made Him the Sonne of man*, doth likewise *regenerate us*, to the state of the *Sonnes of God*. And this for our *thankefulnesse*.

3 And, to these two, (to make the measure *full*) to joyne, the *fulnesse of duetie*, even whatsoever *duetifull* minded persons, may yeeld to a *bountifull minded*, and a *bountifull handed* Benefactor. And with this to begin, to consecrate this first day of this *fulnesse of time*: even with our *service* to Him at the *full*; which, is then at the *full*, when no *part* is missing: when all our *dueties*, of *preaching*, and *praying*, of *Hymnes*, of *offering*, of *Sacrament*, and all, meet together. No *fulnes* there is of our *Liturgie*, or publike solemne service, without the *Sacrament*. Some *part*; yea, the chief *part* is wanting, if that be wanting. But our *thanks* are surely not *full*, without the Holy *Eucharist*, which is by interpretation, *Thankesgiving* it selfe. *Fully* we cannot say, *Quid retribuam Domino?* but we must answere, *Calicem salutaris*

Psal. 116.12,13.

8 world; but] world, but Q_1 12 cælos;] cælos, Q_1

accipiam, we *will take the cup of salvation*, & with it in our hands *give thanks* to *Him*; render Him our true *Eucharist*, or real *Thanksgiving* indeed. In which *cup* is the *blood*, not only of our *redemption* of the *Covenant*, that freeth us from the *Law*, and maketh the *Destroyer passeover us*: but of our *Adoption* of the *new Testament* also, which intitles us, and conveyes unto us (*Testament-wise*, or by way of *Legacie*) the estate we have in the joy and blisse of his heavenly kingdome, whereto we are *adopted*. We are then made partakers of Him, and with Him of both these His benefits. We there are made *to drinke of the Spirit*, by which *we are sealed, to the day of our redemption, and adoption* both. So that, our freeing from *under the lawe*, our investiture into our new *adopted* state, are not fully consummate without it.   Mat. 26.28.

   1. Cor. 12.13.
   Ephe. 4.30.

And what? Shall this be all? No, when this is done, there is allowance of 12. *dayes* more, for this *fulnesse of time*: that, we *shrinke* not up our *duety* then into *this day* alone, but in the *rest* also remember, to redeeme some *part* of the day, to *adopt* some *howre* at the least, to bethinke our selves of the *duetie*, the *time* calleth to us for: that so, we have not *Jobs dies vacuos*, no daye quite *emptie* in this *fulnesse of time*. Hereof assuring our selves, that what we doe in this *fulnesse of time*, will have *full* acceptance at His hands. It is the *time of his birth*, which is ever a *time* as *accepted*, so of *accepting*, wherein, what is done, will be *acceptably* taken to the *full: fully* accepted, and fully rewarded by Him, of *whose fulnesse we all receive*: with this condition, *of grace for grace*, ever one grace for an other.   2. Cor. 6.2.

   Joh. 1.16.

And so, growing *from grace to grace*, finally from this *fulnes*, we shal come to be partakers of another yet behinde, to which we aspire. For all this, is but the *fulnesse of time*: but that, the *fulnesse of eternitie*, when time shall be runne out, and his glasse emptie, *Et tempus non erit amplius*; which is, at His next *sending*. For yet once more shall God *send* him, and He come againe. At which comming, we shall then indeed receive the *fulnesse* of our redemption, not from the *Law* (that we have alreadie) but from *Corruption*, to which our bodies are yet subject; and receive the *full fruition* of the *Inheritance*, wherto we are heere but *adopted*. And then it will be perfect, compleat, absolute *fulnesse* indeed, when we shall all *be filled* with the *fulnesse of him that filleth all in all*. For, so shall all be when nothing shall be wanting in any: for *God shall be all, in all*. Not as heere He is, something, and but something in every one; but then *omnia in omnibus*. And then the *measure* shall be *so full*, as it cannot *enter* into us, we cannot hold it: we must *enter* into it; *Intra in gaudium Domini tui*.   Apo. 10.6.

   Ephe. 1.23.
   1. Cor. 15.28.

   Mat. 25.21.

To this we aspire, and to this in the *fulnesse* appointed of every one of our times, *Almightie God* bring us, by *Him*, and for *His sake*, that in this *fulnesse of time*, was *sent* to worke it for us, in his person: and worke it in us, by the operation of his *blessed Spirit*. To whom, &c.

20 *acceptably*] acceptebly Q_1

XI

A Sermon Preached before His Majestie, on Sunday the fifth of August last, at Holdenbie, ANNO DOM. 1610

1. CHRO.16.22
Nolite tangere Christos meos.
Touch not mine Anointed.

I. 2. 3.   HEre is a Speech: but wee know not *Whose*, nor *to Whom*, nor yet (well) *concerning Whom*; onely concerning certaine Persons, whom the Speaker (whosoever he is) calleth *His Anoynted*. It behooveth us, to know these three, who they be.

The person, *whose* the speech is, *Persona loquens*, Hee that saith *Meos, Him* we finde at the 14. verse. *Ipse est Dominus Deus noster, He is the Lord our God*: God it is, that speaketh here, *He* that challengeth them for *His*, by calling them, *Mine*.

The persons, *to whom*: in the verse before, *Non reliquit hominem*: *He leaveth not a man*. So, it is, *to all* in generall: but specially *to some*, more quicke of *touch* then the rest, whose fingers are never well, till some way or other, they bee *touching*, whom God would not have *touched*.

The persons, *concerning whom*, (whom, Hee stileth, *His Anointed*) will fall out to prove, the Princes of the earth. Wee must not say it, but prove it, (say it now, prove it anon.)

Now, as if some body were about to offer them some wrong; here commeth a voyce from heaven, staying their handes, and saying, *See you touch them not. Quos Deus unxit, homo ne tangat*. Whom God hath Anointed, Let no man presume to touch.

Of which, it may wel be said, as the Psalmist saith to us, every day, *Hodie si vocem*: To day, if ye will heare this voice, harden not your hearts, and ye may: For, as this day (now ten yeeres,) from the same Person, and the same place, a like voice there came, concerning *His Anointed*, in whose presence

28 this voice] his voice Z, F₁

we stand. That GOD would not have *His Anointed touched*, this Text is a witnesse, and this day is a witnesse: The Text, *dixit*, The day, *factum est*.

Touching the same point, when time was, in this place you heard, *Ne perdas*: you shall heare it againe now, but, from an *higher person*, under a straiter charge, and with *a larger compasse*.

^{Referred unto the Text next before, 1. Sam. 26.19}

The *person higher*; for, that was *David*: *Sed ecce maior Davide hîc*: but behold, a greater then *David* is here. This, is no voice on earth (neither of Prophet nor Apostle) we now heare: *Audivi vocem de cælo*, Wee heare a voice from heaven: And thence, neither of Saint, nor Angell, but of God himselfe. To shewe his care of them (*His Anointed*) hee would have none give the charge about them, but himselfe; himselfe in person, *Non alienæ vocis organo, sed oraculo suæ*: from none other, but from his owne mouth.

1.

The *charge straiter*: for, there it was, *Destroy not*, the worst that could be: Here it is, *Touch not*, the least that may be; and so, even that way, amended much.

2.

The *compasse larger*: That, was to *Abishai*, but one man; and it was, concerning *Saul*, one King onely; and therefore it was in the singular, *Ne perdas*: This is, *Nolite*, and *Christos*: the number altered, of a larger extent farre, even to *All men*, concerning *All his Anointed*. *Nolite*, in the plurall, that is, None of you: *Christos* in the plurall, that is, None of them. *Them, not touched*, not *Any of them; You, not touch*, not *Any of you. Non reliquit hominem*: He leaveth not a man, but forbiddeth *All*. Now, out of this plurall, you may deduce any singular; Out of *Christos*, any King: Out of *Nolite*, any partie: Out of *Tangere*, any hurt: and so, not *any man*, to doe *any hurt* to *any his Anointed*.

3.

A Commandement it is, and I may safely say, *Primum, & magnum mandatum*, The first and great Commandement, touching the safeguard of Princes.

^{This Text, the first and great Commaundement concerning this point.}

The *first*: For, (as the verses before shew) it was the first given, in this kinde, and that before all other, in the Patriarchs time, long before *Moses*, under the Law of Nature.

The *greatest*, not onely because it is of the *greatest* in heaven, and concerning the *greatest* in earth: but for that it is the originall maine precept, touching Princes and their safetie, or (as the phrase is) the fundamentall law, upon the which all the rest are grounded, unto the which all the rest reduced, and from the which all the rest derived. Davids *Destroy not*, is but an abstract of this *Touch not*. Aske him what Text he had for his *Ne perdas*: hither he must come, this must be it, and none other. This *Nolite tangere* is the maine wing of protection; *Ne perdas*, or any other particular, is but a feather of it.

The Division. To see the parts of it. A Precept it is, and negative, and the negative precept is of the nature of a *fence*, and the *fence* leadeth us to the thing fenced. First of all then, we take it in sunder, and make two parts of it: and set *Christos meos* in the midst, whose the fence is; and then, *Nolite tangere*, as it were a circle or *fence* round about them.

Christos meos hath in it, two things: not onely *the parties*, whom they should not: but *the reason* why they should not *touch them*. Not *touch*? Whome *not touch*? *His Anointed*. And why *not touch*? Even because, *His Anointed*.

In *Christos meos* taken together, are the parties *non tangendæ*: Againe, in *Christos meos* taken in sunder and weighed apart, are two reasons couched, *de non tangendo*.

Why *not touched*? first, they bee *His*: And secondly, *what of His*? *His Anointed*. These two, be two severall: *His anointed*, is more then *His*: for all that be *His*, be not *Anointed*.

His alone, were enough; that they bee *His*, they pertaine to *him*, and so, *he* to see them safe.

But then besides, they be the very choise and chiefe of *his*, *His anointed*, and so, a more speciall care of them, then the rest.

And then (from the nature of the word) not onely *his anointed, Uncti eius*: but *Christi eius, His Christs*, which is the highest degree of *his anointed*: for higher then that, ye cannot goe.

And last, what that is, that maketh them thus, *his anointed*: to knowe whether they may be stripped of it, or no.

Then come wee to the Circle or *Fence*, and that we may divide too: for, *Nolite tangere*, is a double *fence*, from the *acte* and from the *will*. *Touch not*, (so we read) where the *touch*, the *acte*, is forbidden. *Nolite tangere*, (so reade the Fathers) where the *will* to *touch* is forbidden likewise. *Nolite*, that is, Have ye not the *will* nor so much as an inclination to doe it. So, both the *acte* and *will* of *touching* is restrained: the *acte*, in *tangere*; the *will*, in *Nolite*.

In the former, wee are to take the extent of *Tangere*, and *Christos*: 1. To what matters *Tangere* will reach: 2. In howe many points to *Christos*: And in the latter, to what persons in *Nolite*.

And so, see we the summe of the Text, which is sufficient enough to keepe Kings from *touching*, if it selfe might be kept untouched: but as the times are, the Text it selfe is touched, there needes a second *Nolite tangere* for it. To that end then, to see the Text safe and well kept, the three persons

---

3 sunder] sun-| der [last syllable as catchword only] Z   3–4 and make...whose] *meos*, whose Z; in the midst: *meos*, whose F_1 16 *His*] I. *His* F_1 18 But] 2. But F_1 20 And] 3. And F_1 25 *in marg.* II F_1 26 *fence*, from] *fence*, ¹from F_1 *acte* and] *act*, ²*and* F_1 29 *will* nor] *will*, not F_1

in it, all to joyne together: *Kings,* touching whom; and *Subjects,* to whom; and *GOD* himselfe, by whom it is given in charge. And if the two former doe their parts, God will not faile in his.

Let me adde one thing more. That this Text, besides that it is a *Commandement,* it is also a *Thankesgiving*; But both have but one errand, the *Kings safetie.*

A *Commandement* it is *from God*: the very stile, the moode *Nolite,* giveth it for no lesse.

And a *Thankesgiving* it is *to God;* for it is a verse of a Psalme, of a *Halleluja* Psalme, of the first *Halleluja* Psalme: (There bee twentie of them in all, this is the first of them all.)

A *Commandement* it is; for it is proclaimed with sound of Trumpet, and that by *Banaiah* and his companie. And a *Thankesgiving* it is; for it is sung with solemne musicke by *Asaph,* and the *Queere,* at the sixe and seven verses before. It is both, and both wayes we to have use of it.

First, as of a *Commandement* from God, to teach us this duetie towards Gods *Anointed*. I trust, wee will performe better dueties to them then this: but whatsoever we doe besides, what good wee doe them, *Ne noceat,* not to touch them, to doe them no hurt.

1.

And, never so much neede of this doctrine, as now, when by a late heavie accident, wee see, wretches there are, dare attempt it: And other, (and they the more wretches of the twaine) that did dare to avow it: Did (I say) for, now they would seeme to disavow it; but so poorely, and faintly, as all they say, may holde, and yet an other like acte, be done to morrow.

And then secondly, as a *Thankesgiving* to God, who hath set the print of this commandement, upon this day; in cutting short this day, two wicked Impes, that went about to breake it, by *touching,* and more then *touching,* the Lords *Anointed.*

2.

And, never were we so much bound to doe it, as this yeere: For that, this yeere, upon this fresh occasion, truely wee may say, He that dealt thus with us, *Non taliter fecit omni Nationi,* Hee hath not so dealt with all Nations, nor hath every King found him so gracious. Others, have not in theirs; I speake it with compassion: wee have in ours; I speake it to our comfort, and to the praise of GOD. Both these wayes.

Psal. 147.20.

---

14 six and seven] sixth and seventh F_1 16 *in marg.* 1.] om. Z, F_1 22 Did (I say) for,] Did dare (I say;) for, Z, F_1 25 *in marg.* 2.] om. Z, F_1

Christos meos.

Christos meos, who they be.

An honourable Title to beginne with: and begin with it we must: the very Grammar Rules leade us to it. *Anoynted,* is but an Adjective, wee are to seeke the Substantive for it. But besides, wee are to finde *who* they be, whom we are *not to touch,* lest we *touch* them unawares: And as well, that we may know the right, and doe them their right; as, that we may discerne them from the wrong: for wrong there be, that call themselves *Christos Domini,* whom the holy Ghost never christened by that name.

Marke 13.21.

As, of Christ himselfe, many come and say, *Ecce, hîc est Christus, ecce illic:* Here is Christ, and there is Christ, and deceive many: So, of these *Christes* here likewise; See, heere is *Christus Domini,* and there hee is, and no such matter. Our first point then is to know, *who* they be.

Patriarchs, Christi Domini.

These in the Text here, were the *Patriarchs,* it cannot bee denied. They be set downe by their names, *Abraham, Isaac, Jacob,* touching whom, *primâ intentione,* this charge is given, that they be *not touched.*

And let not this seeme strange: For in the first world, the *Patriarchs* were principall persons, and (as I may safely say) Princes in their generations; and for such, holden and reputed by those, with whom they lived. I may safely say it: for of *Abraham* it is in expresse termes said by the *Hethites,*

Genes. 23.6.

Audi Domine, Princeps Dei es inter nos, Thou art a Prince of God, that is, a mighty prince, *here among us:* As indeede a Prince hee shewed himselfe,

Genes. 26.16.

when he gave battell and overthrow to foure Kings at once. Of *Isaac* no lesse may be sayd, who grewe so mightie, as the king of *Palestine* was glad to intreat him to remoove further off, and not dwell so neere him: and then, to

Verse 28.

goe after him in person, and sue to him, there might be a league of amitie

Genes. 48.22.

betwene them. And the like of *Jacob,* who by his sword and bow, conquered from the *Amorite* (the mightiest of all the nations in *Canaan*) that Countrey which by Will he gave to *Joseph* for his possession. It was neere to *Sichar,* wel knowen; you have mention of it, Joh.4.5.

Great men they were certainly, greater then most conceive: but be their greatnesse what it will, this is sure, they were all the Rulers the people of God then had, and besides them, Rulers had they none, And that is it we seeke; *Pater* was in them, and ἀρχή too, *fatherhood,* and *government:* and

In Psal. 104.

these two made them *Patriarches, & unctos ante unctionem* (saith S. *Augustine*) *Anointed,* before there was any materiall *Anointing* at all.

In them then this terme began, and in them it held so long, as they had the government in them: But *Patriarches* were not alwayes to governe Gods

Princes, Christi Domini

people, but *Kings,* in ages following, were to succeed in their places. And so

20–1 God...prince,] (that is, a *mighty Prince*) F_1 29 Joh.] *John* Z, F_1 34 *in marg.* In Psal. 104] In Psal. 140 Z, F_1

A SERMON PREACHED THE FIFTH OF AUGUST 1610

did succeed them; succeede them in the word *Pater*, and in the word ἀρχή both, both in the right of their *fatherhood*, and the rule of their *government*, as *Fathers* of their Countreys, and *Governors* of their Common-wealths. Where the *Patriarchall* rule expired, the *Regall* was to take place, being both one in effect: For, *Abraham* the *Patriarch*, is termed a *Prince*, Genesis 23.6. and to make even, *David* the Prince is termed a *Patriarch; Let me speake boldly unto you of the Patriarch David*, saith *S. Peter*, Acts 2.29. So that two things wee gaine here: 1. That *ius Regium* commeth out of *ius Patrium*, The *Kings* right from the *Fathers*, and both holde by one Commandement. Then 2. that this Text bindeth, as a Lawe of Nature, being given for such, to the old world, long before the Law came in any Tables.

Now, that as in other things, so in this terme of *Christi Domini*, *Kings* doe succeed the *Patriarchs*, we have first, our warrant from the *holy Ghost*, applying this terme here, after, to ^a*Saul*, to ^b*David*, to ^c*Salomon*, to ^d*Ezekias*, to ^e*Josias*, to ^f*Cyrus*, Kings all. Secondly, from the *Councels*. The third general Councel of *Ephesus*, The great Councell of *Toledo* the fourth. The great Westerne Councell of *Francford*. Thirdly, from the consent of *Fathers*. To dispatch them at once, so saith the Councel of *Francford*, *B. Hieronymus & cæteri S. Scripturæ tractatores, &c. S. Hierom* and the rest of the writers on Scripture, all, understand it not of others, but of *Kings*. Yea, lastly from their owne Writers, *Cajetan*, and *Genebrard*, who themselves so apply it, upon this very place.

^a1 Sam. 12.3,4.
^b2 Sam. 19.21.
^c2. Chron. 6.42.
^dAbac. 3.13.
^eLam. 4.20.
^fEsai. 45.1.
Append. ad Tom 4. pag. 1097 *can* 74. *Pag.* 649. *Editio Venet.*

Nay, *Kings* they will graunt, (they can neither will, nor choose;) But then they would hemme in others likewise, to entercommon in the Title, as the *Pope*, as the *Cardinals*, and as any else, save them that be indeed. But that, they must doe then without booke: For, in this Booke warrant have they none. For this terme [*Christi Domini*] here, originally ascribed to the *Patriarches*, is ever afterward, without variation, continually appropriate to *Kings*, and to *Kings* onely, all the Bible through. The question is, whether we will speake, as the *holy Ghost* doeth, or no? If wee will, then upon a just survey taken of all the places, where the worde *Christus Domini* is to bee found in Scripture, three and thirtie they be in number. Of which, one only is in the New, and that is of our *Saviour* himselfe: The rest, all in the Old. Foure times by GOD, *Mine Anoynted*; Sixe times to GOD, *Thine anoynted*: Ten times of GOD, *His Anointed*: Twelve times in termes terminant, GODS *Anoynted*. Of which, twise it is sayd of the *Patriarchs*; Here, and in the 105. Psalme (which two places are indeed but one.) All the rest are said either of *Christ*, or of *Kings*, all: and never applied to any other, but to them only. And here wee joyne issue: If to any other the *Scripture* apply *Christos*

Princes onely in Scripture have the title of *Christi Domini.*

Luc. 2.26.

Verse 15.

24 entercommon] enter-common Z; enter common F₁

Domini, we yeeld: If to none but them, we cary it. For, what reason have wee, if the *Scripture* appropriate it to them, and none but them; to take it from them, and give it to others, to whom the *holy Ghost* never gave it?

<small>Though other persons anointed, yet none called the Lords anointed.</small>

Yet have I no meaning to denie, but that others, not onely *persons*, but (if they will) even *things* too, were *anoynted* under the Law. *Persons*, as *Priests* and *Prophets*: *Things*, as the *Tabernacle*, and the *vessels* of it, even to the very *fireforkes*, *ashpans* and *snuffers*. But though they were so, yet none of the *things*, nay nor any of the *persons*, have ever the name given them, of *Christus Domini*. No *Prophet*, of all the fellowship of the *Prophets*, no *Priest*, no not the *high Priest* himselfe, ever so called. It may bee, *Annointed*, but not the *Lords Annointed*: it may be *uncti*, but not *Christi*: or, in a corner of one Chapter of the *Maccab.* [*Christi*] once, but not with his full Christendome, not *Christi Domini*. Still they fall short: and *Christus Domini* followes the *King*, and him onely.

Yea, this ye shall observe in their owne olde Translator: that the same word in Hebrewe and Greeke, when hee speaketh of the *Priest*, hee ever turneth it *unctus*; when of the *King*, *Christus* ever: as if of purpose hee meant by this word, to make a partition betweene them. Any will thinke there was surely meant them some speciall prerogative more then the rest: that from the rest it is given them, and ever to them, and to none of the rest.

<small>Heb.1.4,5.</small>

Wee may well conclude this point then with the Apostle: *They are made so much the more excellent then the rest, by how much they have obtained a more excellent name then the rest. For unto which of all the rest at any time said hee, Thou art mine Anointed?* Enough, to settle this terme upon *Kings*. The Holy Ghost attributes it to them, and none but them. Wee to understand it of them, and none but them. It is, and so let it be, their owne due stile, their proper denomination. *Touch not mine Anointed*. Who be they? If wee goe by the booke, *Princes*: why then, *Touch not Princes*.

<small>*Meos*, the claime whose they be.</small>

Christos meos, who they be, wee see. But in these words (we said) there are not only the *parties*, whom they should not: but the *reason* why they should not *touch* them. And not one *reason*, but two at the least. Now then, let us take the words in sunder, and weigh either by it selfe, seeing either word is a *reason de non tangendo*. First, *whose* they be: *His*, *Meos*. Then *what of His*: *His anointed*. And *His anointed*, is *Christi eius*: Which (it may bee) will amount to two *reasons* more. *Meos* is his *claime*: *Christos* his *character*, or speciall marke.

Meos, his *claime*: which word is not slightly to be passed by. It is to the purpose. To *claime*, is to *touch*. He that saith, *Meos*, he that *claimes* them,

---

<small>3 it?] it. F_1 15 their ... Translator] their owne, in the olde Translator Q_1 that] that, Q_1</small>

toucheth them: *toucheth* their free-hold (as we say.) He that sayth, *Touch them not*, sayth, *Claime them not*. Some question there is growen *whose* they be. Two *claimes* there are put in, and laide to them, besides. *Meos*, saith the *Pope*: and *Meos*, say some for the people: but neither say true: *God*, hee saith *Christos meos*, and *Hee* onely hath the right so to say.

Meos, saith the *Pope*. For hee, or some by his Commission, used to annoint the *Emperours*, and because he was master of the *Ceremonie*, he would be master of the *substance* too: and *his* they were. The *Pope*, he was *Gods*, and they were *his anointed*, and of him had their *dependence*, and he to depose them and to *dispose* of them, and to doe with his owne what hee list. And this *claime*, is not yet given over. For hee that shall marke the *Popes* faintnesse, when some *Kings* are sought to be *touched*, Nay, are *touched* indeed; out of *his Meos*, will easily thinke he is well enough content they bee *touched*, though they be GODS *Anointed*, if they be not *His* too: *Touch not his*: Not *His*: as for *others*, it skilleth not, *touch* them, who will.

But this *claime* by the *Ceremony*, is cleane marred, by this Text: for when these words here were spoken, there was no such *Ceremonie* instituted, it was *Non ens*, no such thing then *in rerum naturâ*. That came not up, till *Moses*: Now these here in the Text, were in their graves long before *Moses* was borne; No *Meos* then; no *claime* by the *Ceremonie*.

And after it came up, no *Priest* went out of *Jury* to *Persia* to cary the *Ceremonie* to *Cyrus*: yet, of him, saith *Esay*, *Hæc dicit Dominus, Cyro Christo meo*, Thus saith the Lord, to *Cyrus mine Anointed*, and yet never came there any *oyle* upon his head. So that even after it was taken up, yet the *Ceremonie*, and the *claime* by it, would not holde. The trueth is, the *Ceremony* doth not any thing; onely declareth what is done. The *partie* was before, as much as he is after it; onely by it is declared to be, that hee was before, and that which he should have beene still, though hee had never so beene declared. The trueth may and doeth subsist, as with the *Ceremonie*, so without it. It may be reteined, as with some it is, and with us it is; and it may be spared, as it is with others: Spared, or reteined, all is one, no *claime* groweth that way.

But last of all, where it was used, as by *Samuel* to *Saul*, by *Sadoc* to *Salomon*: yet they *claimed* nothing in the *parties*, they anoynted, but called them still *Gods*, and never their *owne Anoynted*. They knew no *claime* lay by it: Nay, if it had beene a *Sacrament*, as it was but a *Ceremonie*; he that ministreth the *Sacrament*, hath no interest in the *partie* by it, but *God* alone; and then much lesse hee that performeth but a *Ceremonie*, is to plead any *Meos*. So that every way, this *claime* vanisheth, of *Christi Pontificis*.

_{Lay no title to them.}

_{I. *Meos*, the Popes claime.}

_{2. Esai 45.1.}

_{3.}

---

1 free-hold] free hold Q_1, Z, F_1 10 *dispose* F_1; dispose Q_1, Q_2, Z

2.
Meos the peoples claime.

Now then, a second *claime*, an other *Meos*, hath of late begun to be buzzed of, as if they were *Christi populi*, and helde of them. And whatsoever matter is, the Cardinall himselfe waxeth very earnest for it; (I thinke, because he seeth the *Popes* arme groweth short, and loath hee is, but that there should bee still some handes to *touch them*;) Hee will not so much, as give *God* leave to appoint *Saul* or *David* of himselfe, but hee taketh upon him to *suspend* them both, untill the *people* with their suffrage come in, and ratifie *Gods* doing.

But this *claime* likewise falleth to the ground, even by this Verse: then must wee goe mend our Text here. For if so: *God* was properly to have said, *Nolite tangere Christos vestros, Touch not your Anoynted*; for to the *people* he speaketh. And seeing it is to them hee speaketh; of all others *Meos* cannot be theirs, unlesse we wil glosse it thus, *Meos (id est) non meos*; *Mine* (that is) *none of mine*, but *your owne*. And then sure hee should have done them some wrong, to have forbid them *to touch* that, which was *their owne*. The *Pope* saith, He can make *Christum Dominum, Christ the Lord himselfe*: if he could so doe indeed, it were not altogether unlike, he might make *Christum Domini*. But *God* helpe, if the *people* fall to make *Gods*, or to make *Christs*, if they shal take *Gods* verse from him, and say, *Nos diximus, Dii estis*, We have said, ye are *Gods*: yea, and *Christs* too, and change it, *Thou shouldest have no power unlesse it were, Data desuper, Given from above*, saith He, They, unlesse it were *data desubter*, unlesse it *were given you hence from beneath*: then, must we goe change all our Texts that sound that way. Enough to let you see, they both *claime* that is none of *theirs*, but *Gods*.

Psal. 82.6.
John 19.11.

3.
Meos Gods claime.
Chap. 4.14.
Verse 22.
Verse 29.
Verse 14.

To give in evidence now, for *Gods* right; That his *Meos* is the onely true *claime*, that *His* onely they be. Three times over, it is told us by *Daniel* in one Chapter, that the *Kingdomes* bee *Gods*, and that *Hee giveth them, to whom Hee will*, as having the sole *propertie* of them. And it is said there, that this is, *Sententia vigilum, & Sermo Sanctorum*. And, if it be *Sententia vigilum*, they are scarce well awake, that thinke otherwise; And if it bee *Sermo Sanctorum*, they talke prophanely, that speake otherwise. And this verely was the divinitie of the *Primitive Church* concerning *Kings*, which, of all, had least cause to favour them. *Cuius iussu nascuntur homines, eius iussu contituuntur Principes; By whose appointment they bee borne men*; (and that is, neither by *peoples*, nor by *Popes*) by his appointment, and no other, are they made Princes, saith old *Irenæus*. *Inde illis potestas, unde spiritus; Thence have they their power, whence they have their breath*, saith *Tertullian*. And that is from neither, (I am sure) but from *God* alone.

Lib. 5.
Apolog. pag. 675.

12 And...speaketh;] *om. Z, F₁*   12 of] Of *Z, F₁*   18 or to make] or make *F₁* 19 *diximus*,] *diximus Q₁*   29 this is,] *F₁*; This is *Q₁, Q₂, Z*   34 *Principes*] *Q₁, Z, F₁*; *Princeps Q₂*

His they be: for, *His* their *Crowne, Diadema Regis in manu Dei*, Esai 62. _{Verse 3.}
And, as if he saw a hand come from heaven with a *Crowne* in it, so speaketh
hee in the 21. Psal. *Tu posuisti, Thou hast set a crowne of pure gold upon his* _{Verse 4.}
head. *His*, their *scepter*, or rod: *Virga Dei in manibus eius*, Gods rodde in his
hand, Exod. 17. of *Moses*. *His* their *throne*, *Sedebat Salomon in throno Dei*, _{Verse 9.}
Salomon sate upon Gods throne, 1.Chron. 29. Nay, long before, in the Lawe _{Verse 23.}
of Nature, sayth Job, *Reges in solio collocat in perpetuum*: He takes them by _{Job. 36.7.}
the hand, and placeth them in the Throne, and that *in perpetuum*, there to
sit, in themselves, and their succession for ever. *His*, their *Anointing*: *Oleo* _{Psal. 89.21.}
sancto meo, with *mine* holy oyle: The *anointing His*, therefore the *Anointed*.
And if all these, their *Crowne*, their *Scepter*, their *Throne*, their *Annointing*
His; then *His* they bee, *Christi Domini*. And of *Christi Domini*, wee shall
shewe twelve faire evidences, in expresse termes, *Gods Anointed*. And ten
more, we shall bring forth, with an *Eius*, a plaine reference to *Him*, *His*
anointed. *Christi Pontificis*, *Samuels* or *Sadocs anointed*: *Christi populi*, *Judas*
or *Israels anointed*, *non legitur*, we shall not finde. *His* they be then.

Now inferre. *His*, therefore hand off, what have you to doe with that is
none of yours? what to claime or to *touch*, that is *His*? *Nolite tangere meos*.
This onely, and no more but this, in very equitie were enough, *Touch not*
mine. This for *Meos*: Now to *Unctos*.

His then: but, not as All are, by a generall tenure; but *His*, as *his Anointed*, _{Anointed.}
by a more speciall and particular kinde of interest. *His Anointed*, is more _{Uncti.}
then *His*, for all *His* are not *annointed*: for if all were *anointed*, there should
bee none left to *touch* them: wee might strike out this verse, the charge were
in vaine, there were none to receive it. If all be *Uncti*, where should be
Tangentes? Wee must then, needs leave a difference betweene *Christiani* and
Christi. For, holding, all that are Christians, all Gods people *Anointed* and
holy alike; it will follow, why should *Moses* then, or any take upon him to be _{Num. 16.3.}
their Superiour? And so we fall into the olde contradiction of *Core*: which is
all one with the new paritie, and confusion of the *Anabaptists*, or those that _{Jude 11.}
pricke fast towards them.

But the very Ceremonie it selfe serveth to shewe, somewhat is added to
them, by which they bee *His*, after a more peculiar maner then the rest, to
whome that is not added. Oyle it selfe designeth Sovereigntie: powre
together water, wine, vineger, what liquor you will, oyle will bee uppermost: And that is added by their *anointing*. Besides then, this generall
claime *Mine*, here is his speciall signature, *Anointed*, whereby they are
severed from the rest. His hand hath *touched* them with his *anointing*, that

---

6 *in marg.* Verse 23] *LACT*; Verse 21 Q_1, Q_2, Z, F_1 11 their *Crowne*] *ed.*; their *Crowne* F_1;
Their *Crowne* Q_1, Q_2, Z 29 And] F_1; and Q_1, Q_2, Z

188   A SERMON PREACHED THE FIFTH OF AUGUST 1610

no other hand might *touch* them. Things *anointed*, of our selves wee forbeare to touch; but specially, if the *anointing* have the nature of a marke, that we wrong it not: And this hath so, these are so marked, that wee might forbeare them. And yet more specially, if wee have a Caveat, not to doe it, as here we have. *Nolite tangere unctos,* Touch not them that I have anointed.

<small>Anointed, yet not *Uncti*, but *Christi*, which is more.</small>

This were all, if it were but, *Anointed*: but, there is yet a further matter then all this: For it is not *Unctos*, but *Christos meos*: Wee reade it, *Mine Anointed*, In the Hebrew, Greeke and Latine, it is more full. In Hebrew, *my Messiah's*; in Greeke and Latine, *Christos meos*, that is, *my Christes*, which is farre more forcible. Somewhat, we may be sure was in it, that all the old writers uniformely forbore to turne it *Unctos*, which is enough for *Anointed*, and all have agreed to turne it *Christos*, that is, *Christes*, which is a great deale more. It seemes, they meant not to take a grain from this charge, but to give it his full weight. And it cannot but weigh much with all that shall weigh this one point well, that Princes are taken into the societie of *Gods* Name, in the Psalme before, and here now, into the societie of *Christs* name, in this: and so made *Synonymi*, both with *God*, and with *Christ*, specially since *God* himselfe it is, that *so stileth* them: for he flatters not (wee are sure.) *God* himselfe is a *King, King* of all the earth, and *Christ* is his *Heire of all*, as appeareth by his many *Crownes on His head, Apoca.* 19.12. Those whom *God* and *Christ* vouchsafe to take into the charge of any their kingdomes, them, they vouchsafe their owne names, of *God* and of *Christ*. They two, the first Kings, to these other the after-Kings ruling under them, and in their names.

<small>Psal. 47.8.</small>

<small>Anointed not with every ointment, but with holy, and so, *Sacri*. *Psal. 89.21.</small>

A third graduall reason then there riseth here. All *anointed* are not *Christi*: for all *anointing* is not *Chrisme*. *Chrisme* is not every common, but an *holy annointing,* a sacred signature. **Oleo sancto meo,* with mine *Holy oyle* have I *Anointed* them. *Meo,* to make them *his*: *Sancto,* to make them *sacred*. Hee might have taken this oyle out of the Apothecaries shop, or the merchants ware-house: He did not, but from the Sanctuarie it selfe, to shew their calling is sacred, sacred as any, even the best of them all. From whence the Priests have theirs, thence, and from no other place the King hath his; from the Sanctuary both. The *anointing,* is one & the same. All, to shew that *sacred* is the *office,* whereunto they designed, *sacred* the *power* wherewith they indued, *sacred* the *persons* whereto it applied. And for such were they held all the Primitive Church through. Their *writ, Sacri apices*; Their *word, Divalis iussio*: Their *presence, Sacra vestigia*: (the usual stile of

---

<small>14 charge,] charge Q_1 20 Heire of all,] F_1; heire of all Q_1, Q_2, Z 21 Crownes...head] F_1; Crownes...head Q_1, Q_2, Z 24 after-Kings F_1; after Kings Q_1, Q_2, Z 28 to make] Q_1, Z, F_1; to to make Q_2</small>

the *Councels*, when they spake of them.) And when they ceased to knowe themselves for *his*, (that here saith *Meos*) and to hold of *him*, then lost they their holines. He that tooke from them the one, tooke to himselfe the other. Now then, will yee inferre? Holy they be, their *Anointing* halowed: therfore *Nolite tangere sacros*, Touch not mine *holy ones*. No more *touch Moses* then the holy *Mount* which neither man nor beast might touch upon paine of death: No more touch *David*, then the holy *Arke*. It is not good touching of *holy* things. In the 13. chap. before, *Uzza* so found it.

Exod. 19.12.
Heb. 12.10.

Verse 10.

And yet still me thinks we fall short: for it is not *Sanctos* neither, it is more then *Sanctos*, it is *Christos*: In which word, there is more then in *Commune Sanctorum. Omnes Sancti non sunt Christi; at Reges Christi*. We cannot say of all Saints they be Christs, Of *Kings* we may; Verely, every degree of holinesse, will not make a Synonymie with *Christ*. Hee was *Anointed*, saith the Psalme, *Oleo exultationis supra socios*, with an *holy oile*, or *chrisme above his felowes*. To hold this name then of *Christos Domini*, it is not every ordinary holinesse will serve, but a speciall, and extraordinary degree of it above the rest, which they are to participate, and so doe, from *Christ* whose name they beare, eminent above others, that cary not that name; as if they did in some kinde of measure partake *Chrisma Christi*, even such *chrisme* as wherewith *Christ* is *Anointed*. And, the inference of this point, and the meaning of this stile of *Dii* and *Christi* is, as if hee would have us, with a kinde of analogie, as carefull in a maner to forbeare *touching* them, as we would be to touch GOD, or the Sonne of GOD *Christ* himselfe. It is not then *Meos*, nor *unctos meos*, nor *Sanctos meos* onely; but it is *Christos meos*, Mine, and that *Anoynted, Anoynted* with *holy Oyle*: So *Anoynted*, and with Oile *so holy*, as it raiseth them to the honour of the denomination of the *Holie of Holies*, Christ himselfe. These 4. degrees, and from them these foure severall reasons, are in *Christos meos*.

Annointed not with every holy oyle, but with a speciall above the rest, and so *Christi*.

Psal. 45.8.

One thing more of *Christos meos*: For I should doe you wrong certeinly, if I should slip by it, and not tell you what this *Anointing* is, and leave a point loose, that needeth most of all to bee touched. Upon misconceiving of this point, some have fallen into a fancie, *His Anointed* may forfeit their tenure, and so cease to be *His*, and their *anointing* drie up, or be wiped off, and so kings be *unchristed*, and cease to be *Christi Domini*, and then, who that will, may *touch* them.

What this *Anointing* is.

They that have beene scribling about Kings matters of late, and *touching* them with their pennes, have beene foully mistaken in this point. Because,

6 Mount] Mount, Q_1 11 Reges] Reges, Q_1 20 chrisme as] as chrisme Q_1, Z,
27 Holie of Holies] Z, F_1; Holy of holies Q_1: holy of Holies Q_2 4.] foure Q_1 34 unchristed, and] un-christed, F_1

annointing in Scripture doeth otherwhile betoken, some Spirituall grace; they pitch upon that, upon that taking of the word, and then, *anointing* it must needs be some grace, some *gratia gratum faciens*, making them religious and good Catholiques, or some *gratia gratis data*, making them able or apt for to governe. So that, if he will not heare a Masse, no Catholicke, no *Anointed*. If after hee is *anointed*, hee grow defective, (to speake their owne language) proove a Tyrant, fall to favour Heretickes, his *anointing* may be wiped off, or scraped off; and then, you may write a booke *De iustâ abdicatione*, make a holy league, *touch* him, or blow him up as ye list. This hath cost Christendome deare: It is a dangerouos sore, a *Noli me tangere*; take heed of it, *touch* it not.

_{It is no spirituall grace.}
_{Lam. 4.20.}
_{Esai. 45.1.}
_{2. Sam. 19.21.}
_{1. Sam. 26.9.}

Before I tell you what it is, I may safely tell you, that this it is not. It is not religion, nor vertue, nor any Spirituall grace, this Royall *anointing*. *Christus Domini* is said not onely of *Josias*, a King truely religious, by Jeremie; but of *Cyrus* a meere Heathen, by Esai; not onely of *David* a good King, but of *Saul* a tyrant, even then when he was at the worst. Religion then is not it, for then *Cyrus* had not beene; nor Vertue is not it, (especially the vertue of clemencie) for then *Saul* had not beene Gods *Anointed*. If it were Religion, if that made Kings; then had there beene of olde no Kings, but those of *Juda:* and now, no Kings but those that be Christen. But by *Cyrus* case we see, one may be *Christus Domini*, and yet no Christian.

Among Christen, if the orthodox truth were it; *Constantius, Valens, Valentinian* the yonger, *Anastasius, Justinian, Heraclius*, I know not how many, had beene no Emperors; yet all so acknowledged, by the Christians of their times.

Then, if Religion make them not, Heresie will not unmake them. What speake I of Heresie? Harder is the case of Apostasie, yea hardest of all: yet, when *Julian* from a Christian, fell away to be a flat Pagan, his *anointing* helde, no Christian ever sought, no Bishop ever taught to *touch* him. And it was not *quia deerant vires*, that their hand was too short; it is well knowen, farre the greater part of his Armie were Christians, and could have done it, as appeared instantly upon his death, by their acclamations to *Jovian* his Successor, *Christiani sumus*.

_{Gen. 49.5,6,7. and 35.22. and 38.16. and 49.14.}

Will yee see it in the Patriarchs? These in the Psalme heere, were holy and good men. But, twelve Patriarchs there were presently after, of whom, *Simeon* and *Levi*, were two very Tyrants; *Reuben*, scarce honest; nor *Juda* no better then he should; *Issachar* by his blessing, should seeme none of the wisest, (as it might be *Roboam*:) yet were they numbred with the twelve, and were Patriarches still, no lesse then the other.

2 pitch] F_1; picke Q_1, Q_2, Z 17 not it] not is Z 19 if that] if, that, Q_1

And after the Patriarches, *Saul* the first king (that there might bee no mistaking) with his *anointing*, there came no grace to him. The Spirit of God came indeed upon him, but hee was *anointed*, and gone from *Samuel* first: And the same Spirit as it came, so it went, and left him afterward: and Gods *Anointed* he was before it came, and Gods *Anointed* hee remained after it was gone againe, and that no lesse then before, and is so termed by *David* ten times at the least.

Unxit in Regem, Royall unction gives no grace, but a just title onely, *in Regem*, to be king: that is all, and no more. It is the administration to governe, not the gift to governe well: the right of ruling, not the ruling right. It includes nothing but a due title, it excludes nothing but usurpation. Who is *Anointed*? On whome the right rests. Who is *inunctus*? He that hath it not. Suppose *Nimrod*, who cared for no *anointing*, thrust himselfe in, and by violence usurped the Throne, came in rather like one steeped in vinegar, then *anointed* with oyle, rather as a Ranger over a Forrest, then a Father over a familie. He was no *anointed*, nor any that so commeth in. But on the other side, *David*, or he that first beginneth a royall race, is as the head; on him is that right of ruling first shed; from him it runs downe to the next; and so still, even to the lowest borders of his lawfull issue. Remember *Job, Reges in solio collocat in perpetuum*. It is for ever. Gods claime never forfeits: His character never to bee wiped out, or scraped out, nor Kings loose their right, no more then Patriarches did their fatherhood.

Not, but that it were to be wished, both *Anoyntings* might goe together, and that there might goe, as there doeth, a fragrant odor from the precious oyntment which is shed upo[n] them, at their Crowning: so a like sent from their Vertues, and they no lesse vencrable for their qualities, then for their callings; and happy the people, *qui currunt in odore unguentorum Principis sui*, that can trace their Prince by such a savour; This we are to wish for, and pray for dayly, and use all good meanes it may bee. But, if it be not, ever hold this, Allegiance is not due to him, because hee is vertuous, religious or wise, but, because he is *Christus Domini*. Let this be still in your minde; GOD saith not, *Touch him not*, Hee is a good Catholique, or, indued with this vertue, or that: *Touch him not*, Hee deserveth well, or at least doeth no harme. No, these would faile he saw, or be said to faile, though they failed not; Wee should never then have done, never have bene quiet. But, this he saith, *He is mine Anointed*. Marke that well, GOD giveth no other reason here, nor *David* after, in as evill a Prince as might bee. That is the true reason then, and wee to rest in it, and let other fansies goe.

margin:
1. Sam. 10.9,10.
1. Sam. 16.14.

It is *Jus regnandi*.

Gen. 10.9.

Job 36.7.

Cant. 1.4.

19 next;] next? Z   26 Vertues,] Vertues: Q₁

192　A SERMON PREACHED THE FIFTH OF AUGUST 1610

<small>*Tangere*, the Acte forbidden.</small>

　　Now, by whose appointment they be set, by his Commaundement they be fenced; Fenced from *touching*, and that is the lightest, and least; consequently from whatsoever is greater or worse. What talke you of *Non occides*, or *Ne perdas*? I tell you, *Ne tangas, Touch them not*.

　　Yet, are we not so sillily to understand it, as if one might not *touch* them at all, not for their good: For how can they be *Anointed*, but they must bee *touched*? No, the Verse before telleth us, it is for their hurt, this *touch* is forbidden. *Non permisit nocere*. He suffered no man to doe them hurt, to that end saying, *Touch them not*. Yea, the very word it selfe, without any glosse, giveth as much, which is נגע properly *plaga*, and that is, *tactus noxius*, a hurtfull *touch*, that leaveth a marke behinde it, *Qui tangit & angit*, as the Verse is. For, it is good yee understand, this phrase is taken from the Devil: & good reason: for whosesoever the fingers be, his the *touch* is, when

<small>Job. 1.11. and 2.5.</small>

GODS *Anoynted* are *touched*. He calleth it but *touching Job*, but *touching*, when he did him all the mischiefe he could devise. And his nature, and the nature of hurtfull things, is well set out by it. Few things are so good, *ut in transitu prosint*, as they onely *touch*, and doe good: Evill is far more operative, if it but *touch* and away, if it but blow, or breathe upon any, it is found to doe mischiefe ynough.

<small>The extent of *Tangere*, how many wayes touch.</small>

　　To speake then of this *touching*, and the extent of it. Where the Scripture distinguisheth not, neither doe we: but let the word have his full latitude. *Nolite tangere* is generall, no kind is limited: then, not to *touch* any maner of way.

<small>I.</small>

　　There is none so simple, as to imagine there is no *touch*, but that with the fingers end, *immediate*. The *mediate*, with a *knife* or with a *Pistoll*, that is a *touch*: if wee *touch* that whereby they are *touched*, it is all one.

　　Againe, be the *touch* so as we feele it, or be it by meanes unsensible, as of *poison*, or *sorcerie*, it is a *touch* still, and these no lesse guiltie: no lesse? nay a great deale more, as the more dangerous of the twaine. One shall be *touched*

<small>Deut. 27.24.</small>

and know not *how, when*, or by *whom*. *Cursed be he, that smiteth his neighbour secretly*, saith the Law. His *neighbour?* much more his *Prince*, between which two there is as great a distance, as between *Non occides*, and *Non tanges*. In a word, as it is the lightest, so it is the largest terme hee could choose. For *non est actio nisi per contactum*, saith the Philosopher. Nothing can be done, but a *touch* there is, some *touch*, superficiall, or vertual, immediate or mediate, *cominus* or *eminus*, open or privie, and all come under *tangere*. For it is not *Nolite sic tangere*, touch not this way or that: but, *Nolite tangere*, touch not any way at all, let nothing be done at all, to doe them hurt.

<small>13　whosesoever] whose soever Z; whose-soever F_1　　15　devise.] devise? Z　　30　*in marg.* Deut. 27.24] Deut. 27.34 Z, F_1　　36–37　not *Nolite*] no *Nolite* Z, F_1</small>

A SERMON PREACHED THE FIFTH OF AUGUST 1610

And is there no *touch*, but that of the *violent hand*? The *virulent tongue*, doeth not that *touch* too? and the *pestilent pen* as ill as both? *Venite, percutiamus eum linguâ*, say they in *Jeremie, Come, let us smite him with the tongue*. If *smite* him, then *touch* him (I am sure.) There is (saith Salomon) that *speaketh* (and is there not also that writeth?) *words, like the pricking of a sword. Et qui, quos Deus ungit, eos pungit*, commeth not he, within the compasse of this charge? Yes, they be Sathans weapons both *tongues* and *pennes*, have their points and the edges: their points, and pricke like a sword; their edges, and cut like a razor; both *touch*, and with the worst *touch* that is, *tactus dolore cordis*: therefore the worst, because of the best part. These, it is Gods meaning to restraine. You may see it by the verse before: *Non dimisit hominem calumniari*, saying, *Nolite tangere*. So that even *calumnia*, is a *touch*. You may see it exemplarily, in the Patriarchs: One of Gods *Nolite tangere's* was to Laban touching Jacob, and this it was: *Vide ne quid loquare durius*: See you give him no ill language, no foule wordes, for they *touch* too: *Touch* him not so. As well to Shimeis *tongue*, as to Jacobs *hand*, is this *Nolite tangere* spoken.

Is this all? What say you to the *touch* with the foote? the foot of pride upon the necks or Crownes of Emperours (though no cricke or bodily paine ensued?) Wil not *Nolite tangere*, reach to *Nolite calcare*? Yes certainely; This *Nolite tangere*, was a stronger Text against it, then *Super aspidem & Basiliscum*, was a Text for it.

Yea, I goe further: by an undecent and over familiar *touch*, voyd of the reverence, that is due to them, *læditur pietas*, duety taketh hurt, and wrong is offered to his *Anointed*. *Mary Magdalen* was not about to have done our Saviour any harme, when after his resurrection shee offered to *touch* him; onely because she did it as to one mortall (where the case was altered now) and not with the high reverence pertayning to his glorified estate, shee heard, and heard justly, *Noli me tangere*. The *touch* which any way impeacheth the high honour of their *Anointing, Nolite tangere*, takes hold of that too.

Touch them not, Not them. And when we say, *Not them*, meane wee their persons onely, and not their States? Are not they *touched*, when those are wronged? They that *touch* their *Crowne* and *dignitie*, their *Regalia*, shall wee say they *touch* them not? Yes, no lesse, nay rather more. For, then the *Anointed* are properly *touched*, when their *Anointing* is, and that is their *State* and *Crowne*, as deare every way, and as precious to them, as their life. Indeed *touch* one, and *touch* both. If their *State* hold not holy, no more will their *persons*. It hath ever bene found, if their *Crowne* once goe, their life

2.
Prov. 12.18.

Gen. 31.24.

3.

4.

1.
The extent of *Christos*, how many ways they *touched*.

3-4 Jeremie...tongue] F_1; rom. Q_1, Q_2, Z   14 to Laban touching Jacob] touching *Laban* to *Jacob* F_1 33 dignitie,] dignity. Z tarrieth not long after. And even in this point also, it may safely be said, that the loose and licencious *touching* their *State*, with Mary Magdalens *touch*, without the regard due to it, as if it were a light matter, that might be lifted with every finger, falleth within the reach of this *Nolite*; I list not dilate it, it would be looked to. These light and loose *touchings*, are but the beginnings of greater evils.

2. Againe, *Not them*. Sathans motion was twofold: One, that he might *touch* that was Jobs: The other, that *touch* himselfe: and in either of these, hee reckoned that hee should *touch* him home. They are *touched*, when that is *touched* that is theirs. It was so here directly: Pharaoh, one of them, to whom originally, nay the very first of all, to whom this *Nolite* was spoken, *touched* not Abraham himselfe; it was Sara was wronged: In Sara, was Abraham *touched*. So God esteemed it, and gave his first *Nolite tangere* in that point. So, even unto Her wrong, doeth this *touch* extend, takes in Her too, as being the one halfe, yea, one and the same person with the Lords *Anointed*.

3. *Not them*. One more yet: For two kinds of *Anointed* I finde in Scripture: Saul, and David: the one *in esse*, the other in *fore*: one *in being*, the other *to be*. If David had beene *touched*, (Saul yet living) though but *Anointed* to succeede, I make no doubt, this Commandement had bene broken: For we are bound by it, to preserve the *anointing*, not onely upon the head, but even in the streames, running downe from it: that with the King himselfe, the whole race Royall is folded up in this word, every one of them in their order, that not one of them is to be *touched* neither.

Nolite: The *will* forbidden.

This barre then, is set to the *touch* every way, and to the *touch* of them, and every of theirs, every way. But, there is a further matter yet: For, (if wee marke it well) it is not, *Ne tangite*, but *Nolite tangere*: *Nolite*, (that is) have not so much as the *will*, once to goe about it. So that, not onely *tactus*, the *touch* is forbidden, but *voluntas tangendi*, the very *will* to doe it: For that *will* is *tactus animæ*, the soules *touch*, the soule can *touch* no way but that. And Gods meaning is absolute: neither bodie nor soule should *touch*, neither the body by *deede*, nor the soule by *will*.

And *Nolite* standeth first, beginneth the Text: for indeed with that, is the right beginning: The Devill *toucheth* the *will*, before the *hand* ever *touch* Gods *Anointed*: He doeth *mittere in cor*, put a *will* in the *heart*, before any doe *mittere manum*, put foorth their *hand* to doe it. Therefore, even *velle tangere* was to be made a crime, and that a capitall crime. And so it is: for, in

Verse 21.

the attainder of the two Eunuches, Esth. 2. there was no more in the Inditement, but *voluerunt*, they *would* have done it, they *would* have *touched*

7 One] ¹One F_I 8 The] ²The F_I 17–18 *in being ... to be*] F_I; rom. Q_I, Q_2, Z

Ahasuerus: that being proved was enough, they died, and died justly for the *will*, though no *touch* followed. Pitie it should be otherwise. Hee *toucheth* not alwayes, that hath a *will* to *touch*; hath a will to *touch* the throat, *toucheth* but a tooth: what though? To breake *Nolite*, *voluit* is enough; and *voluit*, hee would have *touched*, at another place.

They that laide the Powder ready, and lighted the match, it was but *voluerunt*, (as God would) it *touched* not any: but righteous and just was their execution, to teach them, or others by them, *Ne tangite*, is not it: *Nolite tangere* is the charge: and, if you breake *Nolite* onely, it is enough, though *Tangere* and it never hap to meet.

Of which *Nolite*, I hold it very pertinent to touch the *extent* also, as I did even now of *tangere*, the *touch* it selfe, and of the *persons*, to whom it may reach; that we may see, it is true in the verse before, *Non reliquit hominem*, he leaves not out a man, hee exempts not any from it. I wil not once speake of *subjects*, no question of them: over whom they are *Anointed*, them it toucheth neerest, and bindeth them fast. But this I say, that even *forreiners*, borne out of their Allegiance, are within it. The *Amalekite* was a stranger, none of *Sauls* lieges, borne out of his dominions; yet died for saying hee had *touched Saul*, & that sheweth that even *Aliens* here, *sortiuntur forum ratione delicti*, are that they are intended, within this *Nolite*.

Yea, even such *Aliens* as are in open hostilitie, even at that time, they are in Campe and in Armes against a King, they are bar'd by this *Nolite*, and are to spare him. So saith *David* in his mourning song for *Sauls* death: He blames there the Philistims, as if they had done more then they might, in so *touching Saul*, considering hee was a King, with holy oyle *anointed*, as if they ought, even in that respect, to have spared him. So that this *Nolite* is a Law of *Nations*, making their *persons* so sacred, as even in the battell they are to bee forborne, and their lives saved.

Yea, if we looke to the wordes next before, it is given even to Kings, this *Touch not*. The parties were *Pharao* King of Egypt, and the two *Abimelechs* kings of Gerar, and even they in particular charged: Not *to touch* (for *Pharao* did *touch*) not to *will to touch*, for *Abimelech* went no further. Kings not *to touch* them, none but God *to touch* them: As if it were another law of nations, not one King *to touch* another, but, by vertue of this *Nolite*, each to spare, and to save the others life.

And the difference in religion maketh here no let: for, these being Egyptians and Philistims to whom it was given; there can bee no greater difference then betweene them and the Patriarchs in the worship of God: for all that, not *to touch* them though. Which is *ad erubescentiam nostram*, to our

The extent of *Nolite* to whom it reacheth.

1.

2.

2. Sam. 1.10, 13.

3.

2. Sam. 1.21.

4.

5.

1. Cor. 6.5.

---

11 Nolite] Nolice Z   17 in marg. 2. Sam. 1.10, 13] *LACT*; 2. Sam. 1.9, 13 Q_1, Q_2, Z, F_1
39 in marg 1. Cor. 6.5] 1 Cor. 6.4 Z, F_1

shame, that heathen men, and Idolaters were kept from it by this charge, and now (I will not say) Christians, but holy religious men, Friers, and Priests, yea, and martyrs forsooth, will not be held in by it, but they will be *touching*.

And last of all, this restraint of *will* and *deed*, it is not in the singular, *Noli*, to this or that private man; it is in the plurall, *Nolite*, and so reacheth to whole multitudes. *Nolite*, will serve even people and Countreys, to restraine them also. I wonder at it, It is Gods maner, to give his precepts in the singular. Witnesse the whole Law, and all the ten Commandements in it. How happeneth it, the number here is changed? Somewhat there is in that. He saw multitudes might assay it as well as single men, and take libertie to themselves, thinking to be priviledged by their number. To make sure, he putteth it in a number that encloseth them too. For, be they many, or be they few, *Nolite* will take them in all. So, neither *Subject*, nor *Alien*, nor *Enemy*, nor *King*, nor *People*; nor one *religion*, nor other; nor one, nor many, *Non reliquit hominem*, None left, none exempt, not *any* to *touch* them, not *any*, to *will* to *touch* them. For with *Nolite* God toucheth the heart, and so many as God toucheth their hearts, will have *idem velle, & nolle*, make *His will*, their *will*, & wil obey it. This is the summe of the Charge; Here is the Double Fence, I spoke of. *Touch not*, By which he raiseth, as it were, an high wall about them, that none may reach over to them. And then, with *Nolite*, diggeth deepe even *in profundum cordis*, the very depth of the heart, & casteth a trench there, and so they be double fenced. Or you may (if you will) call them the Cherubims two wings spread over *His Anointed*, to protect them. *Touch not*, one wing; *Nolite*, the other, reaching as the Cherubims wings did, from one wall to the other, covering them from all, that none may come any way to doe them hurt. And by this we see the full of this Text; Wee se it, but we are to feele it also; and see whether the Text be whole, whether it be well kept, and have taken no hurt.

_{How this text is observed.} The Charge is short, ye see; a *Hemistichion*, but half a verse; *Touch not mine Anointed*: foure words only, and but six syllables: One would thinke, it might well be caried away, and well be kept: But, as short as it is, we see it is not though; For, the very *Text* is *touched* and broken. And, I speake not of inferiour *touchings*, that every tongue is walking, and every penne busie, to *touch* them and their rights, which they are to have, and their dueties which they are to doe; And if they doe not, then I know not what, nor themselves neither. This is too much, but I would it were but this.

Hands have beene busie of late, and that in another more dangerous manner. Two fearefull examples wee have in two great Kings: one, no very

---

21–22 heart, & casteth] heart, casteth Q_1, Z; heart; casteth F_1

long time since; the other, very lately made away: not so farre from us, but that they may, and (I trust) doe *touch* us. What shall I say? I would this were the worst.

Yea, I would this were the worst: for, this hath happened in former times too. This Psalme, he that indited it and set it, (*David*) he living, *Ishbosheth* his neighbour king was slaine upon his bed. The like hath happened then, broken it hath beene, in former ages. But then, upon revenge, or ambition, or hope of reward, or some other sinister respect; never, upon conscience, and religion, till now. *Nolite tangere*, was still good Divinitie, till now. The *Text* it selfe never *touched*, never taken by the throat before, and the contradictorie of it given in charge, [*Touched they may be, Touch them notwithstanding*:] Never bookes written, to make men willing, to Gods *Nolite* before. *Baanah*, hee upon hope of reward, slew *Ishbosheth*: *Bigthan*, upon revenge, would have done the like to his liege Lord. *Zimri*, upon ambition, slew his master. But, Religion came never forth with the knife in her hand till now: a Kings life was never a Sacrifice to expiate sinne, before.

And wil ye but consider the great oddes betwixt those *Touchers*, and these of late? They, ever, ere they went about it, cast how to escape; and when they had done it, fled and hid themselves, as guiltie to themselves of evill they had done: These, stirre not an inch, as if they had done that, they might well stand to. Those formerly, grew ever contrite, at their ende detesting the Acte, and crying God mercy: These now, rejoyce in it, as if by it, they had done God a piece of good service. Then yet, it was ever a crime, and a grievous crime, and they that did it, were generally upon the first report, ever condemned by all men, none to defend them: Now, it is, *multis laudantibus* (you know the Booke) it findeth many to justifie, nay to praise it, *& immortalitate dignum iudicantibus*, and thinke them worthy immortalitie, for their worthy Act. Yea, write they not further? *Præclarè cum rebus humanis ageretur, si multi;* It were a merry world, if there would many so exercise their fingers, to keep them in ure. And to Kings themselves, (Gods *Anointed*) dare they not to say? This is *salutaris cogitatio*, an wholesome meditation for them next their heart to thinke, *se eâ conditione vivere,* they live in that case and condition, *ut non solùm iure*, that they may not onely be slaine lawfully, *sed cum laude, & gloriâ perimi possunt*; but to the praise and glory of them that shall do it. How now! What is become of our Text? of *Nolite tangere* with these? Are wee not fallen into strange times, that men dare thus print, and publish, yea even *prædicare peccatum suum*, preach and proclaime their sinnes, even these sinfull, and shamefull positions, to the eyes and eares of the whole world? whereby, Gods *Anoynted* are

The Text it selfe touched, and a Nolite given to it.

1.

2.

3.

1. *Mariana pag. 45.*

2. *Pag. 60.*

3. *Pag. 61.*

33 and] or F_1

198   A SERMON PREACHED THE FIFTH OF AUGUST 1610

endangered, mens soules are poisoned, Christian Religion is blasphemed, as a murtherer of her owne Kings, God in his Charge is openly contradicted, and men made beleeve, they shal go to heaven, for breaking Gods Commandements.

O, But now wee have all great cause to rejoyce. The booke is condemned, if wee may beleeve it. Whether condemned or no, that wee knowe not: this is too sure, eleven yeeres agoe, set out it was, and that authorized, and so went eight whole yeeres, by their owne confession, and even the whole eleven, for ought that we know. How went it foorth so allowed at the first? How went it so long uncontrolled? without an *Index expurgatorius* at least.

The Censure upon Mariana idle.

But, now lately wee have newes, that some few yeeres since, it was censured in a privie Provinciall Councill. But, that was as strange a Censure, as ever was heard of, a Censure *sub silentio*, kept close, and none knewe of it but themselves: fast or loose; Censure, or no Censure, as they pleased. If any such censure were, why made they it not as publicke as their Approbation? The Approbation the world seeth: Their Censure we but heare of, and peradventure it is but a tale, neither. Why came it never to light, till the deed was done, and it was too late? Why heard we not *Jacobs* voyce, till we had felt *Esaus* hands? But, this is all they have to say for themselves: after so great a losse, this we must be faine to take for paiment.

But, I aske, is it condemned? Indeed no; but the matter so faintly caried, as all they say, standing for good, he that wil give the like attempt againe, may. For, what say they? An *Usurper* may be *deposed*; so they all agree. And is it not in the power of *Rome*, to make an *Usurper*, when it will? If he have no right, he is an *usurper*: if he be lawfully *deposed*, his right is gone. If he but favour Heretiques, nay, though he favour them not, the Pope may *depose* him, *Non hoc tempore, sed cùm iudicabit expedire*: and that done, he hath no right, then is hee an *usurper*, and ye may *touch* him, or doe with him what ye will.

What say they then further? *A private man may not doe it, by his owne authoritie.* Not by his owne, but may hee by some other? Belike, some other then there is, whereby he may. Authoritie then there is, and it may bee given, and when it is given him, he may doe it. And so we are, where we were before. And this is their condemning: indeed the condemnation of the world, if they love darknesse so well, as to be deluded by it.

First they will doe it: will doe it? have done it, *touched, touched* in the highest degree, against *Tangere*. It may bee against their wils; nay, *voluntarie*, have

---

5 O, But] Q_1 [*catchwords*]; But Q_1, Q_2, Z, F_1 10 uncontrolled?] uncontrolled; F_1
11 least.] least? F_1

done it *wittingly*, and *willingly*, against *Nolite*. But, it may be repent themselves: Nor that; For, they give a charge, against this Charge, willing men, and making men willing, to doe flat against it, to *touch*, even the *Text*, and breake it, and spare not: by holding, They may bee *touched* for all it.

What is then to bee done of us? The more busie they, to suggest the devils motion, *Mitte manum, & tange*; The more earnest wee, to call on GODS Charge here, *Nolite tangere Christos eius*. The more resolute they, to be *touching*; The more carefull wee, to looke to their fingers. The more they endevour to breake downe this double Fence; the more wee to labour to strengthen it. How will that bee? Our selves not to *touch* them? I will not speake of that, for shame. I trust, GOD hath so *touched* all our hearts, as we detest the least thought that way. Never was any, truely partaker of the inward *Anoynting* of a Christian man, but hee was ever fast and firme to the royall *Anoynting*. That, we will doe: and that is not all; (I trust) wee will doe more then so, even provide a *Nolite tangere* for the Text too, keepe that from *touching*, and that will keepe GODS *Anoynted* untouched: Keepe one, and keepe both.

The Text it selfe to be preserved and kept untouched.

Three persons there bee in the Text. 1. *Gods Anointed* themselves, touching whom it is given. 2. *We all, Non reliquit hominem*, not leaving a man of us out, to whom it is given. and 3. Hee that saith, *Meos*, God that giveth it. The two first, to doe their parts toward it, wee to looke to ours; and God will come in at his turne, and not faile with his part, we may be sure.

By the three persons in the Text.

Let me begin with *Christos Domini*, whom it toucheth: that they would bee *touched* with it, and not lay themselves open to this *touch*, nor carelessly goe where they may be within the reach, or fall into such fingers, as tickle to be *touching* them: Not to put it upon, *What shall be shall be. Non est bonæ, & solidæ fidei, sic omnia ad voluntatem Dei referre, & ita adulari, ad unumquemque dicendo, Nihil fieri sine iussione eius, ut non intelligamus aliquid esse in nobis ipsis.* It is *Tertullian*: and most true it is, That it is neither good, nor sound divinitie, in these cases, to put all upon the will of God, and every one to flatter himselfe or others, saying, Nothing can be done without God will, but to conceive aright, that withall there is somewhat belongs to our part. Therefore subordinately to serve Gods providence, with our owne circumspect foresight and care, knowing, that his providence doeth not always worke by miracle. This day it did: every day it will not doe so. That Hee *gives his Angels charge over them that tempt him not*, that doe not *mittere se deorsum*, cast themselves wilfully into danger. That *Baltazars* dayes were numbred, when he forgat his duetie, not before. That hee hath indeed

1. Gods Anointed.

Psal. 91.11.
Matt. 4.6.
Dan. 5.26.
Psal. 20.6.

18 Text] *Z*, *F*₁; Text, *Q*₁, *Q*₂   20 and 3.] 3. And *F*₁   36 gives...him not *F*₁; gives...him not *Q*₁, *Q*₂, *Z*

Acts 27.30–32. promised to save his *Anointed*: but he promised *Saint Paul* also *his life, and all theirs with him in the ship*, and that by an Angel: for all that, *Paul* would not let the *Mariners go away with the boat*, but *cut the rope*, and said, *If these tarie not in the ship, we cannot bee saved*, for all the Angels promise. Let his *Anointed* say & do the like: keepe your mariners about you in the name of God, keep your selves with that state and guard, that is meete for the Maiestie of Princes: and thinke God saith to you, *Christi mei, nolite tangi*, Be you willing to keepe your selves from being *touched*, and I for my part, will not be behind.

This way onely is now left them. Another way there was, that Gods
Exod. 19.12. *Anointed* might not be *touched*; To set lists about them, as about the holy Mount, that is, Lawes, whereby, (that desperate wretches might not *touch*
Gen. 26.11. God *Anointed*) Gods *Anointed* might *touch* them first. I finde, *Abimelech* made a law to strengthen this Law of God, made a list about this very *Nolite*, a law upon paine of *Morte morietur*. And this was wont to keepe them from approaching. But, if that which should give strength to the law, and make it a law to the conscience, Divinitie, if that be corrupted, if it be a matter of the *will*, as appeareth by *Nolite*, and the *will* bee made wilfull, (an horrible sinne, being now become an heroicall and holy acte:) these listes wil not holde them, the lawe commeth too late. For, if men growe wilfull, it is well knowen, *Vitæ alienæ Dominus est, quisquis contemptor est suæ*. And who would not be *Contemptor suæ*, if he may be sure to bee *Comprehensor æternæ*? Then doe but once perswade them, that for their *touching* they shall streight goe to heaven, and no *Anointed* shall ever stand before them, *Nolite* is gone then: take order for *Tangere* howe we can.

2.
The Subject.
Our part then, is, (and to us it is spoken, & to us properly doth *Nolite* belong) Every man in his place to doe his best. They that are his *Priests*, by bowing their knees dayly, and lifting up their hands to God: They that in the place of Counsaile, by all the wayes of wisedome: They that in the Seate of Justice, by just and due execution: All, by all the meanes they can, *hanc talem terris avertere pestem*, to devise and procure (if it may bee) *ne velint*, that evill disposed hands *would not*: but howsoever, *ne possint*, that they may not be able, if they would, *to touch, His Anointed*. It must be in part, by carying a continuall eye, and keeping a continuall watch over them; or a shorter way, by remooving them farre enough off, that are in any likelihood to doe it; and those be such, as holde, Gods *Anointed* be *tangibiles*, and may be; nay in some case, be *tangendi*, and ought to be *touched*.

1 Saint] F_1; S. Q_1, Q_2, Z 1 in marg. Acts 27. 30–32] *ed.*; Acts 27.30, 31 *all other edns.*
1–2 *his life...the ship*] F_1; his life...the ship Q_1, Q_2, Z 3 *Mariners...boat*] F_1;
mariners...boat Q_1, Q_2, Z *cut the rope*] F_1; cut the rope Q_1, Q_2, Z 27 belong)] F_1;
belong.) Q_1, Q_2, Z 32 *possint*] Z, F_1; *possuit* Q_1, Q_2

A SERMON PREACHED THE FIFTH OF AUGUST 1610   201

God himselfe in *Cores* case and *Dathans* (who went about to *touch Moses* and *Aaron*, not in their persons, but estates only) sheweth us the best way: Hee gave order, that a generall *Nolite tangere* went out against them and theirs, that no man should come neere them, but all shun them and their company, as having them in a generall detestation. Gods course would be followed; that seeing their consciences are seared, and they feare not Gods voice here from heaven, they might feele the full measure of his vengeance upon earth, and might assure themselves, upon the least discoverie, of but a *will* to *touch*, but a *will* to doe that execrable Acte, to incurre an universall detestation, to have all rise against them, to have all the hatred of earth powred upon them and theirs, to bee the outcasts of the Commonwealth, and the *Maranathas* of the Church; yea, they and their names for ever to be an abhorring to all flesh. Nothing in this kind is too much: this way, if no way els, to keep them from it: which is lesse then they should suffer; but all that we can doe.

Num. 16.21, 24.

The best is, if we faile not in our duety; though neither wee, nor the *Anointed*, can take perfect order against them; the *Anointer* can, can and will, as this day hee did. And the rather he will doe it, in the time to come, if we turne to him, to thanke him for that is past. To him then let us turne, that he may take the matter into his own hand. If his *Nolite tangere* will not prevaile, his *Nolo tangi*, will: and if hee say, *Nolo tangi*, have they never so bent a *will*, doe what they can, they shall not (for their lives) bee able to doe them hurt.

3. God himselfe will joyne with them.

Two points there bee in this Charge, both expressed in the verse next before. *Non permisit*, He suffered none to attempt it; *sed corripuit*, but them that did, hee put them to rebuke. Put to rebuke, wee turne *Corripuit*; it is properly to take up short, and that is, by a *touch*, or rather by a *twitch*. And so hee hath ever done, and so he will ever doe: *Tangentes tangentur*, or rather *Tangentes corripientur*, if they *touch*, they shall be *twitched*, be taken short, and cut short for it, (all the sort of them.) Have beene (I am sure.)

I beginne with *Corripuit*: for that never faileth: for sure God will not suffer *His anointed*; nor Christ, *His Synonymos*, those of his name, to bee *touched* for nought: if not his *name* it selfe to be *taken*, neither those that beare it, to bee *touched* in vaine. And there is nothing more kindly, then for them that will be *touching*, to bee *touched* themselves, and to be *touched* home, in the same kinde, themselves thought to have *touched* others. You

By *Corripuit*.

---

12 they and their] Z, F_1; their Q_1, Q_2 16–17 wee...*Anointer* can,] wee can take perfect order against them; *nor the Anointer*; the *Anointer* can Q_1 22 (for...lives)] for...lives Q_1 30 them.)] F_1; them) Q_1, Q_2, Z 32 anointed;] anointed, Q_1 Christ,] Christ Q_1

may see it in the first, in *Pharaoh*, the very first that *touched* the Patriarch *Abraham*. It is said, God *touched* him for it, (and it is the very same word which God useth here in willing not to *touch*) God *touched* him, and *touched* him *tactibus maximis*, with many a grievous *touch*: wee read, *plagued* him with many plagues. And indeed he *toucheth* them so, that he plagueth them that have beene busie in this kinde. Grievous are the *touches* they are *touched* with here on earth; of Pincers red hote, and boiling Lead: but, who knoweth the *touches* of the place, whither (being unrepentant) they must needes goe? which, besides that they are *maximi*, (in another manner of degree then these here) are *æterni* withall, and not ended in an houre or two, as these are. *Tactibus maximis tangentur*, they shall bee *touched* indeed throughly, as the first was.

[Gen. 12.17.]

And looke, as he began in the Patriarchs, so hath he ever held on in *His Anointed*, the kings that ensued. The first that ever touched his kings, *Baana* and *Rechab*, were *touched* for it: and cut shorter, both by the hands, wherewith they *touched*, and the feet, wherewith they went about it. Aske the rest, if it were good *touching*. *Shimei touched* but with the *tongue*; his necke was *touched* with the sword. *Bigthan* and *Tharez* said nothing, did nothing, but onely with their *will*: their necks were *touched* with the halter, *tactibus maximis*, the greatest *touch* or twitch that is here. And so (to make short) were al the rest, even to those two that were this day put to a foule rebuke, and cut short in their going about it. Besides the Cherubims wings then, to protect kings, here you have, in *Corripuit*, the blade of a sword shaken, to keepe the way to them.

[2. Sam. 4.12.]
[1. Reg. 2.46.]
[Ester 2.23.]

But what comfort is it, if *Corripuit* come to the malefactor, if he be cut short, and if the King miscarie withall? *Baana* and *Rechab*, they that killed *Ishbosheth*, were cut short, shorter by the heads; but *Ishbosheth*, he died for it. I confesse, there is small comfort in *Corripuit*, unlesse *Non permisit nocere*, goe withall; in shortening them, without saving *His Anointed*. And that is our comfort, the comfort of this day, which wee meet to give thanks for, that both these went together, *Non permisit nocere*, and *Corripuit* both.

[By *Non permisit*.]

You know, at the beginning I told you, besides that it is a *Commandement*, it is also a *Thanksgiving*. It is so, in that it is a verse of a Psalme, a Psalme of *Halleluja*, the first Psalme of *Halleluja*, of all the twentie.

[The thankesgiving.]

Now in that he hath placed this duetie, and set it in a psalme; his will is, men should come to it with pleasure, cheerefully, and as it were singing.

[1. Psal. 119.54.]

---

9 which, besides] which besides, Q_1 9–10 (in...here)] in...here, Q_1 20–21 And so...the rest,] And so to make short, of all the rest, Q_1 33-34 a Psalme of *Hallelujah*,] om. F_1

When we speake of it, we doe it speculatively; when we sing it, that would be with affection.

In that it is in the first *Halleluja* of all, it sheweth (as I thinke) that Gods *Anointed* are the *persons*, which (saith the Apostle) *Ante omnia*, before all, wee are to pray for; which (saith the Prophet here) before all, we are to praise God for, for them, and their keeping out of evill hands. Their safetie we are to put in our first *Halleluja*.

2.

1. Tim. 2.2.

This *Halleluja* is a Psalme purposely for the bringing home of the Arke. And that sheweth, his Arke, and *His Anointed* are allied, and that no sooner is the Arke well come home, but this *Commandement* goeth foorth streight from it, first of all, before all other: That all may know, what account they were to make of this duetie, how high regard to have *His Anointed* in, in that the Arkes welfare and theirs, are so inseparably knit together. And indeede, experience hath taught it; The wel setling of the Arke, dependeth much upon the safetie of the Prince.

3.

1 Chro. 16.1.

Now this Psalme, as it was sung with all the musicke could be invented, of winde, of hand, and of voice, to shew, the preservation of Kings is a benefit extraordinarie, that requireth so solemne a Thanksgiving:

4.

1 Chro. 16.5, 42.

So besides, it is ordered every day after, to be sung *iugiter coram Arcâ* (that is) to be the ordinarie Antheme of their dayly service; to shew, it is a duetie perpetuall, that needes so dayly a remembrance, to wit, the care of their preservation.

5.

1 Chro. 16.37.

For last of all, that all the praise and thankes here in the psalme, are for this *Nolite*, that all the psalme was set to come to this verse, it is plaine. There bee 29. verses more in the psalme it selfe, (it is the 105. Psalme.) But assoone as ever they once come to this verse, all the rest, all the verses following, are cut off; they goe no further in the psalme, then till they come to it; and then breake off all those behind, and streight goe to another Psalme, (for this is all of the 105. and the next verse is the first of the 96. psal.) So that this verse, plainly was the end and upshot of all the Psalme besides.

6.

---

4 *in marg.* 1. Tim. 2.2.] *ed.*; 1 Tim. 2.1. *all edns.*   9 *in marg.* 1 Chro. 16.1] *LACT*; Verse 1 Q_1, Q_2, Z, F_1 14 setling] setting Z 17 *in marg.* 1 Chro. 16.5, 42] *LACT*; Verse 5. 42. Q_1, Q_2, Z, F_1 20 *in marg* I Chro. 16.37] *LACT*; Verse 37 Q_1, Q_2, Z, F_1
21–22 perpetual...preservation.] perpetuall (the care of their safegard) that needes so dayly a remembrance. Q_1 25 29.] 92 Z; ninetie two F_1 105.] hundredth and fift F_1
27 it...breake] it; breake Q_1 28 and streight] and then streight Q_1 anotherPsalme,]another, Q_1
29 105.] hundreth and fift, F_1 96. psal.] ninetie sixt *Psalme* F_1 30 all...besides] all the rest. Q_1

Of this Verse then, of His *Nolite tangere*, and of *His Nolo tangi*, besides of a famous *Non permisit nocere* in this kinde, this Day is a memoriall to us, and to all our posteritie, even to the children yet unborne: In GODS *Anointed*, not *touched* I cannot say, for *touched* he was, and more then *touched*: But, in the *touch*, there is no great matter (we said,) but for the *hurt*; so that in the end, *not hurt*, is as good, as *not touched*. As good, nay better, for a *Halleluja*. For, to be *touched*, as he was, and to take no *hurt*, is a greater delivery farre, then at all not to be *touched*. To goe through the Red sea, and not wet a threed: To have bene in the fornace, and no sent of the fire; that is the miracle. So, to have bene *touched*, and taken by the throat, (that the marke was to be seene, many dayes after;) To be *thrust at* and *throwen downe*, as Hee was, and yet no harme, (*Híc est potentia,*) Here was the power, and here was the mercy of GOD; Here it was certainely, and that so sensible, ye might even *touch it*.

1. And here *Halleluja* first, and wee to praise him, that when *Nolite tangere*, would not serve in word, made *Non permisit nocere* to serve in deed. Came forth, first, with *non permisit nocere*, as with his shield, & so shielded him, that Hee suffered him not to take any hurt at all; *Anointed* the shield, made it slippery, their hands slid off, their *touch* did him no harme. *Non permisit*,

2. was as His shield, that he brought foorth to save Him. But besides it, he brought foorth his sword too, & cut them short: *Corripuit eos*, was his sword, *touched* them with it, and twitched them for *touching his Anointed*, *touched* them with Pharao's *tactus maximi*, that the markes of it will bee seene upon them and theirs, for ever.

3. For either of these severally, a severall *Halleluja*: but especially, for not severing them, but letting them meet and go together, *Eripuit*, and *Corripuit*, both joyntly arme in arme. Not either alone, this, or that. Not, *permisit nocere, sed corripuit*, suffered them to do hurt, but rebuked them: No, but *Non permisit, & corripuit* both, suffered them not to doe any hurt; and rebuked them, and cut them short too besides.

And this happy conjunction of these both, is it, which maketh the speciall encrease of our thankes this yeere, more then the last, or any before. For that, since, and very lately, GOD, that suffered not *Him*, hath suffered some other King, to bee *touched*, as farre as his life. True. Hee that did that execrable acte, *Corripuit eum*, GOD *touched* him, touched him as hee

---

1 and...besides] (and...besides) Q_1 2 kinde,] Q_1, F_1; kinde; Q_2 6 As] *new para*. As Q_1 9 threed] thred Z, F_1 10–11 (that...after;)] that...after; Q_1 16 in word] Z, F_1; in the word Q_1, Q_2 18 suffered...all;] suffered him to take no hurt at all; Q_1 23–24 touched...and] *touched* them, and Q_1 27 that. Not] F_1; that, Not Q_1, Q_2, Z   34 True.] Z, F_1; True: Q_1, Q_2

did the Mountaines, *Tange montes, & fumigabunt*, touched him, till hee smoked againe. What of that? In the meane time a great Prince is fallen. But *permisit nocere*, He suffered the King to take hurt: And as for *non permisit nocere*, GOD did not Him that favour.

Psal. 144.5.

Not Him, but *Ours* He did: And did it, for the maner, not without miracle, if we compare the cases. For, Hee was then sitting in the midst of divers his Nobles, No likelyhood, that any would come neere Him, to offer but *to touch* Him: If he did, there was odds, there would have bene many a *Non permisit*, he should never have bene suffered to doe it. One man, for all that, one, and no more, did it; Divers were neere him; None of them, All of them kept Him not from his harme. But *Ours*, was all alone, shut up, and so left as one forsaken; not many, nay not any, no helpe at all, neere him. And not one alone, and no more, but three there were to *touch* Him: yet even then, even in that case, GOD *non permisit nocere*, suffered not, not any of them, nor all of them, to *touch* Him, so as they did him any *hurt*.

1.

And even in the maner of the *Non permisit*, God shewed himselfe more then marveilous: for, it was not, God onely suffered him not to be hurt; but miraculously he made, that of them that came to breake his *Nolite*, even of them, one, that was set, that was readie armed to have *touched*, and to have hurt him; hee, even that partie, *non permisit*, would not, did not suffer the other to doe Him any *hurt*; *sed corripuit*, but rebuked him, gave the *noli tangere* to the other, spake this very Text, and stayed his hand, that would have done it. This was a *Non permisit* indeed, worth a *Halleluja*, and after it, came there at the least three other *Non permisits* more. But I have presumed too much alreadie: I will not enter into them, but ende.

2.

The more they were, the more are wee bound to magnifie God, and to blesse his holy name, yeerely, yea weekely, yea daily to sing our *Halleluja* of praise, and thankes to him for this dayes *Non permisit*, and for this dayes *Corripuit*, for them both. That, what he speakes in this Text, he made good upon this day: Shewed, He would not have His *Anointed touched*: Shewed, He was displeased with them, that did *touch* him: kept Him without *hurt*, and cut them short: shortned their armes, they could doe Him no *harme*, shortened their lives for attempting to doe it: *scattered them* first, *in the imaginations of their hearts*; and then after, made them perish in that their wicked Enterprise: And hath made this *Nolite*, this Precept, to us, *Præceptum cantabile*, a Precept Psalme-wise, that wee may sing it to him. There is another, in another place, of another dittie and tune, wherein, hee takes up a dolefull complaint, thus: *But thou hast cast off thine Anointed, and art displeased with him. The dayes of his life hast thou shortened, & cast his Crowne downe to the ground.* With them indeede it is, *Præceptum flebile*, but with us, *Cantabile*. Praise we him for it.

Psal. 119.54.

Psal. 89.38, 44, 45.

And withall, pray wee also, that as this day he did not, nor hitherto hee hath not; so hencefoorth *malignus ne tangat eum*, the malignant wicked one may never *touch* Him: never may any have the *will*; or if have the *will*, never have the *power* to doe Him *hurt*: Suffer Him not *to be touched*; or, if suffer Him *to be touched*, suffer not their *touch* to doe him any *harme*, no more then this day it did: Make all *Nolentes*, with his *Nolite*; if not, come with his *Non permisit*, that he may ever be safe: and straight after, with his *Corripuit*, that they may ever be taken short, that offer it. This day hee suffered them not: nor let him ever suffer any. This day he cut those short; so may hee ever doe them all: And ever make this Statute, our Song, all the dayes of our Pilgrimage. This is now the tenth yeere, and so these the *Decennalia* of it: That as this day it is, so it may still be celebrated, from ten yeeres to ten yeeres, many ten yeeres more. Which God grant, &c.

1. John 5.18.

XII

A Sermon Preached before the King's Majestie at Greenwich on the XXIV. of May, A.D. MDCXVIII. being Whit-Sunday.

ACT. CHAP. II

Sed hoc est, quod dictum est &c.

VER. 16. *But this is that, which was spoken by the Prophet* JOEL.
17. *And it shalbe in the last dayes (saith* GOD*) I will powre out of my* SPIRIT *upon all flesh, and your sonnes and your daughters shall prophesie, and your young men shall see visions, and your old men shall dreame dreames.*
18. *And, on my servants, and on mine hand-maids, I will powre out my* SPIRIT, *and they shall prophesie.*
19. *And I will shew wonders in heaven above, and tokens in the earth beneath, bloud, and fire, and the vapor of smoke.*
20. *The Sunne shalbe turned into darkenesse, and the Moone into bloud, before that great and notable Day of the* LORD *come.*
21. *And it shalbe, that whosoever shall call on the name of the* LORD, *shalbe saved.*

These words may well serve for a Sermon, this day: they were a part of a *Sermon*, preached as this day. The first *Whitson-Sermon*, that ever was: the first *Whit-Sunday*, that ever was. S. *Peter* preached it. And this was his Text, out of the second Chapter of the *Prophet Joël*. As CHRIST, the last yeare, out of *Esai*: so *Peter*, this, out of *Joël*. Both tooke Texts: both, for the *day*, & for the present occasion.

The occasion of this heer, was a lewd surmise given out by some, touching the gift of *tongues*, this day sent from heaven.

---

8 VER. 16.] F_2; VER.17. F_1 9–17.] F_2; 16. F_1 17 20.] F_2; 28. F_1 21 part] F_2; pat F_1

It shalbe my first note. That looke, how soone GOD from heaven had sent His *fiery tongues* upon His *Apostles*; the *Devill* from hell presently sent for his *fiery tongues*, and put them in the mouthes of his *Apostles*, to disgrace and scoffe at those of GOD's *sending*.

Ye may heare them speake (at the thirteenth verse:) *Well fare this same good new wine; these good fellowes have been at it, and now they can speake nothing but outlandish: some little broken Greek or Latin they had, and now out it comes.*

Thus, that which was indeed *grande Miraculum*, they turned into *grande ludibrium*. Of the great Mysterie of this day, they made a meer mockerie. Those, that were *baptized with the Holy Ghost*, they traduced, as if they had soused themselves in *new wine*. Heer is the *Holy Ghost's* welcome into the world. This use doth the Devill make of some men's wits and tongues, to powre contempt on that, which GOD powreth forth, all that ever they can; even *to worke despite to the Spirit of Grace*.

Mat. 3.11.

Heb. 10.29.

The Summe.

Being to make an apologie for himselfe, and the rest, (and indeed, for the *Holy Ghost*) Saint *Peter* first prayes audience (at the XIV. verse.) Then tells them soberly, they misse the matter quite (at the XV.) It was too early day, to fasten any such suspition, upon any such men as they were (to be gone, before *nine in the morning*.) But, this he stands not on, as not worth the answering.

Heer (at this *Verse*) he tells them, it was no *liquor*, this: specially, no such as they surmised. If it were any, if they would needs have it one, it was the *Prophet Joël's*, and none other. Something *powred on*, nothing *powred in*. Nothing, but the *effusion* of the *Holy Ghost*. This is it, that was spoken by the Prophet *Joël*.

2. Pet. 1.19.

So, *habemus firmiorem sermonem propheticum*: and this, which seemed to happen thus on the sudden, it was long since foretold; and alleadges for it this text of the *Prophet*, that such a thing *there should come to passe*, an *effusion of the Spirit*, and that a strange one. And this they would find it to be; this *Prophesie* (of the *Spirit powred*) this day fulfilled in their eares.

The Division.

Of which Text, the speciall points be two. ¹Of the *Spirit's powring*: ² Of the *end* whereto.

I.

The first, I reduce to these foure. ¹The *Thing*: ²the *Act*: ³the *Partie by whom*: ⁴the *Parties upon whom*. ¹*De Spiritu meo*, is the thing ²*Effundam*, the act: ³*Dicit Dominus*, the partie by whom. ⁴*Super omnem carnem*, the parties upon whom it is powred.

22 this: specially,] this specially F_2

Then, the *end* whereto. And in that, foure more. The last *end* of all, in the last word of all, *salvabitur*. That, is the very end: and a blessed end, if by any meanes we may attaine to it. Then are there three other conducting to this. Two maine ones; and one accessorie, but yet as necessarie as the other. ²Close to it, in the end, there is *calling on the Name of the* LORD: *He, that calleth on the Name of the* LORD, *shalbe saved.* ³And farthest from it, at the beginning, there is *prophetabunt*, to call upon us to that end: *And my servants shall prophesie.* ⁴And, between both these, there is a *Memorandum* of the *Great Day of the* LORD. Which is not from the matter neither, nor more then needs. For then (at that day) we shall stand most in need of *saving*: if we perish then, we perish for ever. And the mention and memorie of that *Day*, will make us not *despise prophecie*, nor forget *invocation*; but be both more attentive in *hearing* of *prophecying*, and more *devout in calling on the Name of the* LORD. So, it may well go for a third conducting meanes, to our salvation.

Now, to bring this to the Day. This (it is said) shalbe *in the last daies*. Which with *Saint Peter* heer; and with *Saint Paul* (*Heb*.1. 1.) yea, and with the *Rabbins* themselves, are the dayes of the *Messiah*. So, of our *Messiah* CHRIST (to us) and of none other. Of whose dayes, this is the very last. For, having done his errand, He was to goe up againe, and to send His *Spirit* downe, to doe His, another while: which is the worke of this *day*. As His first then, the *taking of our flesh*, so His last, the *giving of His Spirit*: the giving it abundantly, which is *effundam* heere.

It remaineth, that we pray to Him, who thus, *of His Spirit powred forth* this day, that He would vouchsafe on the same day to *powre* of it on us heer: that we may so hold this *Feast* (the *memorie* of it) and so heare the words of this *prophesie*, as may be to *His good acceptance*, and our *owne saving* in the great *Day, the Day of the* LORD.

OF the *thing powred* first. *De Spiritu meo*, the *Spirit* of GOD. First of Him, to give Him the honour of His owne *Day*.

The Spirit, is of Himself Author of *life*; and heer is brought in, as Author of *prophesie*. They both are in the *Nicene Creed*: ¹the *Lord and Giver of life*, ²and *who spake by the Prophets*. *Life* and *speech* have but one instrument, the *spirit* or breath, both. Of it, these foure.

1. *Prophesie* can come from no nature but *rationall*: The *Spirit* then, is *natura rationalis*. And determinate it is, distinct plainly heer two wayes. ¹The *Spirit*, from Him, whose the *Spirit* is; Him that sayes, *de Spiritu meo*.

II.

I.
Of the *spirit's* powring.
De Spiritu.

---

12 *prophecie*] *prophecying* F_2 13 *prophecying*] *prophecie* F_2 21 As His] F_2; As his F_1 22 so His] F_2; so his F_1 32 Himself] F_2; himself F_1

²That which is *powred*, from Him, that *powreth* it; *Fusus à Fusore*. Being then *natura rationalis determinata*, He is a *Person* (for, a *person* is so defined.)

    2. Secondly, *effusion* is a plaine *proceeding* of that, which is *powred*: as *spiration* is so too, in the very body of the word *Spirit*. So, a *Person proceeding*.

    3. Thirdly, being a *Person*, and yet being *powred out*, He behoves to be GOD. No *Person*, *Angell* or *Spirit*, can be *powred out*, can be so *participate*. Not at all: but not *upon all flesh*, not dilated so farre. GOD onely can be that. So, the *Person*, the *Proceeding*, the *Deitie* of the *Holy Ghost* (all) in these words. And not a word of all this mine: but thus deduced, by Saint *Ambrose*, and before him, by *Dydimus Alexandrinus* Saint *Heirom's Master*.

    4. But fourthly, you will marke: It is not *my Spirit*, but *of my Spirit*. The whole *Spirit*, *flesh* could not hold: not *all flesh*. And parts it hath none. 1. Understand then, *of my Spirit*, that is, of the *gifts* and *graces* of the *Spirit*. *Beames* of this *light*: streames of this *powring*. Other where, others: heer, the gift of *prophesie and tongues*.

<small>Luk. 4.18.
The text of
last yeare.</small>   2. Which *de Spiritu* is also said, to keep the difference between CHRIST and us. *Upon Him* the *Spirit* was: The *Spirit* of GOD *upon Me*, last yeare. Upon *us*, not the *Spirit:* but, *de Spiritu, of my Spirit* onely, this year.

<small>2.
The *Act*,
Effundam.</small>   The next is the Act, *effundam*: In it, foure more. ¹The qualitie, in that it is compared to a thing liquid, *fulfil*, *powred out*. This seemes not proper. *Powring* is, as it had been *water*; He came in *fire*. It would have been *kindled*, rather then *powred*. True, but Saint *Peter*, in proper termes, makes his answer, referr to their slaunder: and that was, *that it was nothing but new wine*, a *liquor*. Their objection being in a thing *liquid*, his answer behoved to be accordingly. And well it might, so: CHRIST had so expressed it: both <small>Cap. 1.5.</small> lately in His promise, *Ye shalbe baptized with the Holy Ghost within few* <small>Joh. 7.39.</small> *dayes*: And formerly, under the termes of *waters of life* (*Joh*. VII.) where Saint *John's* exposition is, *This He spake of the Spirit*. Not (then) given, but to be given, streight upon CHRIST's *glorifying*, which is now this very day. The *Holy Ghost* then, is not all *fire*.

    And this *qualitie* falls well with the two graces, of ¹ *prophesie*, and ²*invocation*, heer given. ¹*Prophesie*: *Moses* (the great Prophet) likened it, to <small>Deut. 32.2.</small> the *dew falling upon the herbs*, or *the raine powred on the grasse* (*Deut*. XXXII.) And that likening is so usuall, as [פורה *Moreh*] the word in Hebrew for *raine*, is so for a *Preacher*, too; that it poseth the Translators,

---

5 3.] *LACT*; 3, F_1; 3, F_2 9 And] F_2; and F_1 14 Other where] Otherwhere F_2
23 answer, referr] answer referre, F_2

which way to turne it: and even in that very Chapter of *Joël*, whence this text is taken. Ver. 23.

²And, *invocation* is so too; a *powring out* of *prayer*, and of the very *heart* in prayer.

³And, the *third* of the *later Day* may be taken in, too. Then there shalbe a *powring* forth also of all the *phialls* of the *wrath* of GOD.

2. The *qualitie* then first: the *quantitie*, no lesse. For, *powring* is a signe of *plentie*: *Effundam*, not *aspergam* (the first prerogative of this day.) For, the *Spirit* had beene given before this time: but never with such a largesse. *Sprinkled* but, not *poured*. Never till now, in that bounty, that now. This was reserved for *Christ*. For, when there was *copiosa sanguinis effusio* on His part, there was likewise to be, *copiosa Flaminus effusio*, on the *Holy Ghost's*. He, as liberall of his *grace*; as *Christ* of his *blood*. That there might be to us *copiosa redemptio*, betweene them both, it is *effundam copiose* in both. Psal. 130.7.

3. *Effundam* tells us further, the *Spirit* came not of himselfe: not till He was thus *poured* out. It is not *effluet*, but *effundam*. *Sic oportet impleri*, that so, order might be kept, in Him (in the verie *Spirit*) and we by Him taught to keepe it. Not to start out, till *we be sent*; nor to goe on our owne heads, but to stay *till we be called*. Not to *leake* out, or to *runne* over; but, to stay til we be *poured* out, in like sort. Seeing CHRIST would not goe un-sent, *Misit me*, last yeare: Nor the HOLY GHOST run *un-poured*, this yeare: it may well become us to keepe in, till we be *poured* and *sent*, eny yeare. And yet, the *Spirit* is no lesse ready to *runne*, then GOD is to *poure* it. One of these is no barr to the other. *Ecce ego, mitte me. Ecce ego*, Behold I am readie (saith *Esai*;) and yet, *mitte me*, Send me, for all that. *Effluence*, and *Effusion*; *Influence* and *infusion* will stand together well enough. Luk. 22.37.

Esay. 6.8.

4. Lastly, *effundam* is not, as the *running* of a *spout*. To *poure*, is the *voluntarie act* of a *voluntarie Agent*, who hath the vessell in his hand, and may *poure* little, or much; and may choose whither he will poure eny at all, or no. As, *shut the heaven* from raining: So *refreine the Spirit* from *falling* on us.

²And when He *poures*, He strikes not out the head of the vessell, and letts all goe: but moderates his *pouring* and dispenses his *gifts*. *Poures* not all, upon every one; nay, not upon eny one, all: but *upon some in this manner, upon some in that*: Not to each, the same. And to whom the same, not in the same measure, though: but, to some, *five*; to some, *two*; to some, but *one* talent. The Text is plaine for this. There are diverse assignations in it: ¹To diverse parties; *Sonnes, servants, old men*, and *young men*: ²Of diverse gifts; 1 Cor. 12.

Matt. 25.15.

---

1 *in marg.* Ver. 23.] F_1 *placed by printer's error at* p. 210, *l.* 33, *causing unnecessary LACT emendation to* Acts 2.33.   9 largesse. *Sprinkled* but, not] largesse, *Sprinkled*, but not] F_2 14 *in marg.* Psal. 130.7] *LACT*; Psal. 103.7 *all other edns.*   16 not *effluet*] no *effluet* F_2 *impleri*] *ed.* (*Vulg.*); *implere all edns.* that so] F_2; That so F_1 33 *in marg.* 1. Cor. 12] 1 Cor. 12.4–11 *LACT*

prophesies, visions, and *dreames.* ³And them, of diverse degrees: one cleerer then the other; the *vision,* then the *dreame. Singulis prout vult,* at the *Pourer's* discretion, *to each as pleaseth Him best.*

1. Cor. 12.11.

3 The Party powring. *Dicit Dominus.* Psal. 110.1.

The Party Pouring is *Dicit Dominus,* the *Lord that said.* But, *Dixit Dominus, Domino meo, The Lord said to my Lord:* Which of these? The later (*Domino meo*) *My Lord, David's Lord* and ours; *Dominum nostrum,* in our *Creed* (that is) CHRIST. How appeares that? directly at the thirtie three verse after. *He being now exalted by the right hand of* GOD, *and having received the promise of the Holy Ghost from the Father, He hath poured out this, that ye now see and heare.* CHRIST then. And not the *Father?* Yes, *He* too: For, of Him, *Christ* is said to *receive* it. Not onely *Dixit Dominus Domino meo;* but, *dedit Dominus Domino meo.* And so, as in the nineteenth of *Genesis, Pluit Dominus à Domino: From the Lord, the Lord poured it.* And but one *Effundam,* with but one *effusion* both; as, with one *spiration,* He came from both. Both, with one *effusion poure* Him: Both, with one *spiration* breath Him. It is expresly so set downe, *Revelation, Chap.* 22. *The fountaine of the water of life issued from the seat of* GOD *and of the Lamb.* So have you heere the whole *Trinitie:* ¹*Quis,* ²*Quid,* ³*à Quo;* the *Father,* by the *Sonne,* or the *Sonne* from the *Father, pouring out the* HOLY GHOST.

Gen. 19.24.

Revel. 22.1.

2. And may we not also finde the two *natures* of Christ heere? *Effundam* is *fundam ex. I will poure, out:* Out of what? what the cisterne into which it first comes, and out of which it is after derived to us? That, is the *flesh* or *humane nature* of *Christ:* On which it was poured at His *conception,* fully to endow it; For *in Him the fullnesse of the God-head dwelleth bodily* (marke that, *bodily.*) And it was *given to Him without measure,* and *of His fulnesse we all receive.* From this *Cisterne,* this day, yssued the *Spirit,* by so many *quills,* or *pipes* (as it were) as there are severall *divisions, of the graces of the Holy Ghost.* And so now we have both *à Quo,* and *ex Quo.* The *Divinitie,* into His *Humanitie,* pouring the *Spirit,* which from His *flesh,* was *poured* downe, this day, *super omnem carnem,* upon all flesh. Which fitly brings in the next: *Super omnem carnem.*

Col. 2.9.
Joh. 1.16.

4. The parties upon whom. *Super omnem carnem.* 1 Cor. 9.9. Joh. 1.24.

On whom this *pouring is* (which is the last point:) *Super omnem carnem.* In which there are *three points,* as the words are three. ¹*Carnem* first (that is) men. For *doth* GOD *take care for oxen* (saith the *Apostle*) or for eny *flesh,* but ours? No, not for eny *flesh;* but the *flesh* which the *Word* did take. And, for that He doth.

But, we are *Spirit* too, as well as *flesh*: and, in reason, *Spirit* on *Spirit,* were more kindly. There is neerer alliance betweene them.

Yet you shall finde the other part (*flesh*) is still chosen.

3 Him] F₂; him F₁

1. First, to magnifie his *mercie* the more, that part is singled out, that seemeth further removed; nay, that is indeed quite opposite to the *Spirit* of GOD heere poured out. For, what is *flesh*? It is *proclaimed* (XL. of *Esay*) *It is grasse*. And not *gramen*, but *fœnum*, that is *grasse withering* and *fitt for the Scithe*. Is that the worst? I would it were: But *caro peccati*, *sinfull flesh* setts it further of, yet. *Upon sinfull flesh*, He should have *poured* somewhat els, then his *Spirit*.

So, two oppositions. ¹*Flesh* and *Spirit* absolutely in themselves. ²Then, *sinfull flesh*, and the *Holy Spirit*. All which commends his *love* the more, thus to combine things so much opposite. This *first*.

And withall (that, which right now I touched) to shew the introduction to this conjuction of these so farre in opposition either to other, Even *Verbum caro factum* that made this *symbolisme*. By which, *a gate of hope was opened to us* (by his incarnation) *in spem*, of our *inspiration*, which this day came *in rem*. For, his *flesh exalted to the right hand of* GOD remembred us, that were *flesh of his flesh*, and derived downe this fountaine of living water to it, *saliens in vitam æternam*; *Springing*, and raising us with it, whence it came (for, water will ever rise as high as the place from whence it came) that is, up to *heaven*, up to *æternall life*.

2. *Super*, upon it: *Upon it*, is without, on the outside of it. Had not *fundam in*, been better then *fundam super: Into them*, then *upon them*? Not a whit.

Indeed, both waies, I find the *Spirit* given. At CHRIST's *baptisme*, the *Dove came upon Him*. At His resurrection, *insufflavit*, He *breathed it into them*. And so hath He parted his *Sacraments: Baptisme* is *effundam super, upon us*, from without: the *Holy Eucharist*, that is *comedite*; that goeth in. Upon the matter, both come to one. If it be *poured on*, it *sokes in*, *pierces* to the very center of the *soule* (as, in *Baptisme, sinne* is washed thence, by it.) If it be *breathed* in, it is no sooner at the *heart*, but it workes forth, out it comes againe: Out at the nosthrills in *breath*; Out at the *wrest* in the beating of the *pulse*. So, both (in effect) are one.

1. But it is *Super* heere, for these reasons. First, that we may know, the *graces* of the *Spirit*, they are ἔξωθεν, *from without*; *In us*, that is *in our flesh*, they grow not: neither they nor *any good thing*, els. And not onely ἔξωθεν, *from without*; but Saint *James* his ἄνωθεν too, *from above*, from the *Father of lights*. Both these are in *super*: and but for these we might fall into a phansie, they grew within us and sproong from us; which (GOD knoweth) they doe not.

2. Another reason is, for that [*upon*] is the Præposition proper to initiation, into eny *new Office*. So is the manner, by some such outward cæremonie *upon*,

---

1. *Super carnem.*
Esay. 40.6.

Ver. 33.

Joh. 4.14.

2. *Super.*

Luk. 3.22.
Joh. 20.22.

Jam. 1.17.

24 upon Him] F_2; upon him F_1 At His] F_2; At his F_1

to initiate. By *annointing*, or *pouring oyle upon*. By *induing* [*induemini*] putting some *robe* or other ensigne *upon*. By *imposition* or *laying hands, upon*. All *upon*. *Baptisme* (which is the Sacrament of our *initiation*) is therefore so done. So, the *Dove came upon* CHRIST. The *tongues* (heere) *upon* these, to enter them, either, into their new offices.

<small>Verse 3.</small>

3. A third (last but not least) to enure them to this Præposition *super*, which many can but evill brook. No *super*, no *superioritie* they; all *even*, all *æquall*; *fellowes* and *fellowes*. The *right hands of fellowship*, if you will; but not so much, as *imposition of hands, super*. For, if *super*, then *sub* followes: *if upon*, then we *under*; if *above*, then we *beneath*. But, no *sub* with some: *submitt* neither *head*, nor *spirit* to any. Yet, *super Me*, said CHRIST last yeare: and it may become any that became *Him*: it may well become *super carnem*. *Super* then must stand, and be stood upon: *Confusion* will come, if it be not.

<small>Gal. 2.9.</small>

<small>2.
Super *omnem carnem*.</small>

Super carnem, super omnem carnem. Upon flesh, and *upon all flesh*. Not, some one: not *Jewe's-flesh* alone: In regard of whom, this *omnem* is heer specially put in. For, they had in a manner engrossed the *Spirit* before, by a *Non taliter omni*. And yet, *upon them* too; for, *upon their sonnes* and *their daughters* (as it followeth:) but *upon them*, now, no more then *upon any* other. This is a second prerogative of this Day. The first, *effundam*, that is. ¹Before, sparingly sprinkled; now, *plentifully powred*. ²Now againe, *super omnem*: Before, *upon* but *some*; now indifferently, *upon all*.

<small>Psal. 147.20.</small>

For so, when we way *all*, we meane, *none is excluded*, but now may have it. *He hath put no difference between them and us* (saith Saint *Peter*.) *Non est dinstinctio* (saith Saint *Paul*.) The *partition is throwne downe* now. Go but to the letter of the Text, *All flesh*. ¹No *Sexe* barred; upon *sonnes* and upon *daughters*: so either *sexe*. ²No *age*: upon *young* men and upon *old*: The one, *visions*; the other, *dreames*. ³No *condition*: on *servants*, as well as *sonnes*; on *handmaids*, no lesse then *daughters*. ⁴No *Nation*: for (if ye marke) the *Spirit* is *powred* twise: *Upon their sonnes*, in this; And againe, *Upon his servants* in the next verse. *His servants*, whither they be their *sonnes* or not; whose *sonnes* soever they be: though the *sonnes* of them, that are (perhaps) strangers to the first covenant. (And yet, even then, GOD had ever His servants, as well, out of that *Nation*, as in it.)

<small>Acts 15.9.
Rom. 10.12.
Eph. 2.14.</small>

<small>Ver. 18.</small>

Now, in signe that thus [*upon all flesh;*] they heard them speake the tongues of *all flesh*, even of *every Nation under heaven*. That, where before, a *few in Jewrie*; now many, all the world over: No longer now, *Notus in Judæâ DEUS*; *His way should be knowne upon earth, His saving health among all Nations*.

<small>Acts 2.5.
Psal. 76.1.
67.2.</small>

<small>19 that is.] F_2; that is.) F_1</small>

Yet, not *promiscuè* though, without all manner limitation. No: the text limits it. I must againe put you in mind, of the two *powrings* mentioned in it. One, the *super omnem carnem*, in this the XV. verse: The other, the second, *super servos meos*, in the next (the XVIII.) And *super servos meos* is the qualifying, of *super omnem carnem*. *Upon all flesh* (that is) *all such as wilbe my servants*; as will give in their names to that end; *as will call upon me: Quicunque invocaverit*, so concludes *Joël*: As *will beleeve* and *be baptized*, so concludes Saint *Peter*, heer, his *Sermon*. This gives them the capacitie, makes them *vessels* meet to receive this *effusion*. By which, all *Turks, Jewes, Infidels*, are out of the *omnem*: and counterfeit *Christians*, too; that professe to serve him, but, all the world sees whom they serve. And by this, much *flesh* is cutt of from *omnem carnem*. But so with this qualifying, *upon all*. For any other, I know not. And this for the *powring*.

And now, *Utquid effusio hæc?* To what end, all this? For it is not to be imagined, this *powring* was casuall, as the turning over of a tub: nor, that the *Spirit* did run *wast*: then it were, *Utquid perditio hæc?* An *end* it had. And that followes now: *And your Sonnes &c.* The *Spirit* is given to many *ends*; many *middle*, but *one last*; and that last, is in the last word, *salvabitur*. The *End* then of this *powring*, is the *salvation* of *mankind*. *Mankind* was upon the point to perish, and the *Spirit* was *powred*, as a precious *balme* or water, to recover and to save it. So, the *end* of all is (and marke it well) that the *Spirit* may *save* the *flesh*, by the *spiritualizing* it. Not the *flesh* destroy the *Spirit*, by *carnalizing* it. Not the *flesh* weigh downe the *Spirit*, to earth, hither: but the *Spirit* lift up the *flesh* thither to *heaven*, whence it came.

To this last, heer are *three middle conducing ends* more. ¹*Prophesie* first; ²*Invocation*, last: both which are well heer represented; three waies. ¹In the *tongues* (the *symbole* of the HOLY GHOST, this day:) The one, *Prophesie*, being GOD's *tongue* to us: the other, *invocation*, being our *tongue* to GOD. ²In the *Spirit* (Both being acts of the *Spirit*, or *breath*:) *Prophesie breathes* it unto us: *Prayer breathes* it out again. ¹In the *pouring*: Both, *pourings* (after a sort:) that, which *Prophesie* doth infuse, poure in at the eare; *Invocation* doth *refundere*, or *powre* forth back again in prayer, out of the *heart*.

And beside these two, a *third* there is, which is wedged in between them both, as stirring us, first and last, both to heare *Prophesie* more attentively, and to practise *invocation* more devoutly (which I wish may never depart out of our minds) the *memorie* of the *later day*.

Thus they stand, subordinate. That men *may be saved*, they are to *call upon the Name of the* LORD (that, at least.) That they may so *call* to purpose, they are to be called to it, & directed in it, by *& Prophetabunt*. And, that they might performe this, to all *flesh*, they were to speake with the *tongues of*

II.
The *end*, whereto.
Salvabitur.

Meanes to that end.
¹*Prophesie*.
²*Prayer*.

3.
Memorie of the *later day*.

all flesh; which was the gift (heer) of this day (without just cause scoffed at.) But, *tongues* are but as the *caske*, wherein *Prophesie* (as the *liquor*) is conteined. I will set by the empty caske, and deale with *Prophetabunt*, the *liquor* in it onely.

[1]*Prophetabunt.*
Pro. 29.18.
Esai. 12.14.
15.
16.

Prophesie, stands first in the Text, *Without which* (saith *Salomon*) the *people must needs perish*. That saying (of *Esai*) is much used by the *Fathers; Tenebræ & palpatio, donec effunderetur super nos Spiritus de excelso. All is darke: men doe but grope, till the Spirit be powred on us from above*, to give us light, by this gift of *Prophesie*.

This terme is kept by *Joël*, as well, when he speakes of GOD's servants (that is) of us, as when of *them and their Sonnes*: And ever after, in the New Testament, it is reteined still as an usuall terme, by the *Apostle*, to the *Corinthians, Ephesians, Thessalonians*, all his *Epistles* through.

But not in the sense of *foretelling* things to come. For, so can it be verified onely upon *Agabus*, *Saint Philip's daughters*, and upon *Saint John*: which are too few, for so great an effusion, as this. That (indeed) was the chiefe sense of it, in the Old Testament: And well, while CHRIST was yet to come. CHRIST He was the stop of all *Propheticall prædictions*. Then, it had his place, that. But now, and ever since *Christ* is come, it hath in a manner left that sense (at least, in great part) and is not so taken in the New.

Rom. 10.15.

The sense, it is there taken in (to expound this place of *Peter*, by another of *Paul*, citing this very same Text of the *Prophet, Rom.* 10.) is *& Prophetabunt* (heer) by *quomodo Prædicabunt* there, *Prophesying* (that is *Preaching*.) Whereby, after a new manner, we doe *Prophesie* (as it were) the meaning of Aunceient *Prophesies*: not *make* any *new*, but *interpret* the *old*, well; take of the *veile of Moses's face*. Finde CHRIST, finde the *Mysteries* of the *Gospell*, under the types of the *Law*; applie the old *prophesies*, so as it may appeare, the *spirit of prophesie, is the Testimonie of* JESUS: And, he the best *Prophet* now, that can doe this, best.

Exo. 34.33.
2 Cor. 3.13.
Revel. 19.10.

Ver. 31.

This sense, we prove by these in the Text. The *Spirit was powred on them, and they did prophecie*. What did they? How *prophecied Saint Peter?* He *foretold* nothing: All he did, was, he applied this place of the *Prophet*, to this Feast. And a little beneath, the passage of the XVI. *Psalme* to CHRIST's Resurrection. And after that, the place of *another Psalme*, to His *Ascension*.

Psal. 16.10.
Ver. 34.
Psal. 110.1.

And the rest (on whom it was *poured*, too) how *prophesied* they? All (we read) they did, was *loquebantur magnalia Dei*, they *uttered forth the wonderfull things of God*, but *foretold* not any thing, that we finde. So as, to *Prophecie* (now) is to *search out*, and *disclose* the hidden things of the *Oracles of* GOD, and not to tell before hand, what shall after come to passe.

Ver. 11.

22 *in marg.* Rom. 10.15] *ed.*; Rom. 10.13.14. F_1, F_2; Rom. 10. 13. 15. *LACT*

But, what say you to *Visions* and *Dreames* heer? Little: they pertain not to us. The Text saith it not. You remember the two *powrings*: ¹One *upon their sonnes*: ²The other *upon His servants*. This latter, is it by which we come in. We are not of *their sonnes*; we claime not by that, GOD make us *His servants*; for, by that word, we hold.

Now, in this later *powring, on His servants* (which onely concernes us) *visions and dreames* are left out quite. If any pretend them now, we say with *Jeremie* (Cap.XXIII. Ver.XXVIII.) *Let a dreame go for a dreame*, and *let my word* (saith the LORD) *be spoken as my word: Quid paleæ ad triticum*, What mingle you *chaffe* and *wheat*? We are to lay no point of *religion* upon them, now: *Prophesie, preaching* is it, we to hold our selves unto now. As for *visions* and *dreames, transeant*; let them go.

But then, for *prophesie* in this sense of opening or *interpreting* Scriptures; is the *Spirit powred upon all flesh*, so? Is this of *Joël*, a proclamation for libertie of *preaching*; that all, *yong* and *old, men-servants* and *maid-servants*, may fall to it? Nay: the *shee-sexe*, Saint *Paul* tooke order for that betimes; cutt them of, with his *Nolo mulieres*. But, what for the rest? may they? For, to this sense hath this Scripture been wrested by the *Enthusiasts* of former Ages; and still is, by the *Anabaptists* now. And by mistaking of it, way given to a foule error, as if all were let loose, all might claime, and take upon them (forsooth) to *prophecie*. 1. Cor. 14.34.

Nothing els this, but a malitious devise of the Devill, to powre contempt upon this gift. For (indeed) bring it to this once, and what was this *day* falsly surmised, will then be justly affirmed, *musto pleni* (or *cerebro vacui*, whither you will; but *musto pleni*) drunken Prophets then, indeed: howbeit not with *wine* (as *Esai* saith) but with another as heady a humor, and that doth intoxicate the braine as much as any must, or *new wine*: Even of *selfe-conceited ignorance*, whereof the world growes too full. But it was no part of *Joël's* meaning, nor Saint *Peter's* neither, to give way to this phrensie. Esa. 51.21.

No? Is it not plaine? the *Spirit is powred upon all flesh*. True, but not *upon all*, to *prophesie*, though. The text warrants no such thing. In the one place it is: *And your sonnes shall:* In the other, *and my servants shall:* But, neither is it, *all their sonnes*: nor *all his servants shall*. Neither (indeed) can it be. There must be some *sonnes*, and some *servants*, to *prophesie* to: to whom these *Prophets* may be sent: to whom this *prophesie* may come. All *flesh* may not be cutt out into *tongues*; some left for *eares:* some *auditors*, needs. Els a *Cyclopian Church* will grow upon us, where all were *speakers*, no *body* heard another. Ἀκούει οὐδεὶς οὐδὲν οὐδένος.

25 *in marg.* Esa. 51.21] *LACT*; Esa. 1.21 *all other edns.*

How then, shall the *Spirit be powred upon all flesh?* well enough. The *Spirit of prophesie*, is not all GOD's *Spirit*; He hath more beside. If the *spirit* or *grace* of *prophesie* upon some: the *Spirit of grace and prayer* (in *Zacharie*) upon the rest. So, between them both, the *Spirit* wilbe *upon all flesh*, and the proposition hold true: *Prophetabunt* must not make us forgett *invocaverit*. All the *Spirit* goes not away in *prophecying*; some left for that too; and there, is the *quicunque (Quicunque invocaverit)* and no where els.

<small>1. Cor. 14.31.</small>

But, if Saint *Peter* will not serve, Saint *Paul* shall: He is plaine, *Ye may all prophesie one by one:* What, the *shippers* of *Holland* and all? I trow not. But (*all*) there, is plaine. *All*, that is, *all that be Prophets*. And, I wish, with all my heart (as did *Moses*) that all GOD's *people were Prophetts*: but, till they be so, I wish they may not *prophecie*; no more would *Moses* neither. Now, in the same Epistle, Saint *Paul* holds it for a great absurditie, to hold, *all are Prophetts*. With a kind of indignation, he asks it, *What, are all Prophets?* No more, then all *Apostles*; as much t'one as t'other. Then, if all be not *Prophetts*; all may not *prophecie* (sure.) For, with the *Apostle* in the same place, the *operation* (that is, the *act of prophecying*) the *administration* (that is, the *office or calling*) and the *grace* (that is, the *enhabling gift*) these three, are ever to go together. No act in the Church lawfully done, without them all. Then the Apostle's [*you all may*] is, *all you may, that have the gift*.

<small>Num. 11.29.</small>

<small>1. Cor. 12.29.</small>

And not, you that have it neither (the *gift*) unlesse you have the *calling* too: For, as GOD *sent gifts*, so He *gave men* also, *some Apostles, some Prophetts*. *Men* for *gifts*; as well, as *gifts* for *men*. *Misit*, in CHRIST, as well as *unxit* (last yeare.) And, in *his servants, vocavit*, as well as *Talenta dedit*. Not to be parted, these.

<small>1. Cor. 12.28.</small>

<small>Mat. 25.14.</small>

I conclude then. *Et prophetabunt*: but such as *have been at the doore of the Tabernacle*, as have been the *sonnes of Prophetts; men set apart* for that end. And yet even they also, so, as they take not themselves at libertie, to *prophesie* whatsoever takes them in the tongue; the *dreames of their owne heads*, or the *visions of their owne hearts*; but remember their *super*, and know, there be *Spirits* also, to *whom their spirits be subject*. So much for the *seventeenth* and *eighteenth Verses*.

<small>1. Cor. 14.32.</small>

<small>2. The Meane betweene both, The later Day.</small>

But now how come we thus suddeinly, *to the signes of the later day, and to the day it self?* For they follow close (you see.) It is somewhat strange, that from *Et Prophetabunt*, he is streight at *Doomes-day*, without more adoe.

The reasons which I finde, the *Fathers* render of it, are these. First, the close joyning of them, is to meete with another dreame that hath troubled the Church, much. And that is, that it may be, there wilbe another *powring*

<small>33 now how] how now F_2</small>

yet, after this, and more *Prophets* rise still. Every otherwhile, some such upstart *spirits* there are, would faigne make us to so beleeve. Heer is a discharge for them.

No (saith *Joël*) looke for no more such daies as this, after this: Therefore to this *day*, he joynes immediately; from this *day*, he goes presently to the *later day* (as if he said, you have all you shall have.) When this *powring* hath run so farr as it will, then commeth the end; when this is done, the world is done: No new *spirit*, no new *effusion*; this, is the last. From CHRIST's departure, till His returne againe; from this day of *Pentecost* (a great Day and a notable) till the *last great and notable Day of all*, between these two dayes, no more such Day. Therefore, in the beginning of the Text, he called them the *last dayes*, because no dayes to come after them. No *pouring* to be looked for, from this first *day*, of those *last*. No other but this, till *dies novissimus novissimorum* the very last day of all; till He *powre* downe *fire* to consume all *flesh*, that, by the *fire* this day kindled by these *fiery tongues*, shall not be brought to know *Him*, and call *upon His Name*.

A second is, Being to speake by and by of *salvabitur*, that we should be *saved*, He would let us see, what it is we should be *saved* from. That helpeth much, to make us esteeme of our *saving*. *Saved* then from what? From *blood*, and *fire*, and the *smolder of smoke*; that is, from the heavy signes heer: and from that (which is after these, and beyond all these farr) the *Great* and *terrible Day of the* LORD. This sight of *undè*, from whence, will make us apprize our *saving* at a higher rate, & thinke it worth our care, then, in that day to be *saved*.

And last, it is set heer, *per modum stimuli*, to quicken us, *Ut scientes terrorem hunc*, saith *Saint Paul*, that entring into a sad and sober consideration of it, and the terror of it, we might stirr up our selves by it, to prepare for it. And set it is betweene both, to dispose us the better to both. To that which is past (*& prophetabunt*) to awake our attention to that: and to that which followes (*invocaverit*) to kindle our devotion in that; and so by both, to *make sure our salvation*.

2. Cor. 5.11.

The *day of the Lord*, the *Prophet* calls it (*dies Domini*;) as it were opposing it, to *dies servi* to our dayes heer. As if he said, These are your *dayes*, and you use them (indeed) as if they were *your owne*. You *powre* out your selves into all *riott*; and know no other *powring* out but that: you see not any great use of *prophecying*; thinke, it might well enough be spared: you speake your pleasures of it, and say, *musto pleni*, or to like effect, when you list. These are *your dayes*. But, know this, when yours are done, GOD hath His *day* too, and His *day* will come at last; and it will come *terribly* when it comes.

When that *day* comes, how then? *Quid fiet in novissimo*, the *Prophet's* ordinarie question; *What will ye doe at the last*, How will you be *saved*, in Die illo, in that Day?

Jer. 5.31.

We speake sometime of *great dayes* heer: alas, small in respect of this. There is matter of *feare* sometime in these of ours: Nothing, to the terror of this. *Great* it is, and *notable*, as much for the *feare*, as for any thing els in it. This, a *terrible* one indeed, *& quis potest sustinere*, Who can abide it? saith *Joel* in this very *chapter*. Looke to it then. On whom He *powreth* not His *Spirit* heer, on them He will *powre* somewhat else there, even the *Phials of His wrath*: possibly before, some; but then all, certeinly.

And that you may not onely heare of this day, but see somewhat to put you in minde of it, *Ecce Signa*: Terrible signes shall come upon *earth*, *Sword and fire*: from the *sword, pouring out of bloud*; from *fire*, a choking vapor of *smoke*, or (as the *Hebrew* is) a *Pillar of smoke*: which then doth *palmizare* goeth up streight like a pillar or a palme-tree, when the *fire* encreaseth more and more: for when it abateth, it boweth the head and decaieth; which this shall never doe.

Nay further, *wonders in heaven*. For these *tongues* of heaven thus despised, *heaven* shall shew it selfe displeased, too; the *lights* of *heaven* (as it were) for a time put out, for contempt of the *heavenly light*, this day kindled. The *Sun darke*, as if he hid his face: the *moone red as bloud*, as if she blushed, at our great want of regard, in this, a point so neerly concerning us.

For (indeed) these *Eclipses*, though they have their causes in nature, as the *rainbow* also hath: Yet what hinders, but as the *rainbow*, so they may be *signes* too, and have their meaning in Scripture, assigned; and even this meaning heer. This I see, that all *flesh* are smitten with the kinde of horrour and heavinesse, when they happen to fall out: as if they portended somewhat, as if, that they portended, were not good: for *dies atri*, they have been and are reckoned, all the world over.

Mat. 24.8. But these *are but the beginnings of evills*, scarse the *dawning* of that day: But, when the *Day*, it selfe commeth, *the Great Day*, then it will *powre downe*, and who (saith *Joël*) may abide it? A faire *Item* for them, that despise *Prophecies*; and so doing, make voyd the Counsell of God, against their owne soules.

I have much marvailed, why on this Sunday (*Whit-Sunday* as we call it) the *day* of the *White Sunn*, the *Prophet* should present the *Black Sunn* thus, unto us. But the *Prophet* did nothing, but as inspired by the Holy Ghost: which makes me thinke, he thought the *fire* of that day, would make the *fire* of this burne the cleerer: and, that *powring* downe make this *powring* passe the readier: that he thought that day, a good meditation for this, and for such I commend it to you, and so leave it: And come to *Invocaverit*, the onely meanes left us now, to escape it.

3.
Quicunque invocaverit.

I dare not end with *Prophetabunt*, or with this; I dare not omit, but joyne *invocaverit* to them. For what? From *Prophetabunt*, come we to *Salvabitur* streight, without any *medium* betweene? No, we must take *Invocaverit* in our way; no passing to *salvation*, but by and through it. For what? is the *powring of the Spirit*, to end in *preaching*; and *preaching* to end in it self (as it doth with us; a *circle of preaching* & in effect nothing els) but *poure in prophesying enough*, and then all is safe? No: there is another yet, as needfull, nay more needfull to be called on (as the current of our Age runns) and that is *Calling on the name of the Lord*.

This, it grieveth me to see, how *light* it is sett; nay, to see, how busy the devill hath beene, to *powre contempt* on it, to bring it in disgrace with disgracefull termes: to make nothing of *Divine Service*, as if it might be well spared, and *invocaverit* (heer) be stricken out.

But marke this Text well, and this *Invocation*, we make so sleight account of, stickes close, is locked fast to *Salvabitur*: closer and faster, then we are aware of.

Two errors there be, and I wish them reformed: One, as if *Prophesying* were all we had to doe; we might dispense with *Invocation*, let it goe, leave it to the *Queer*. That is an error: *Prophesying* is not all; *Invocaverit* is to come in too: we to joyne them, and joyntly to observe them, to make a conscience of both: It is the *Oratorie of Prayer powred out* of our *hearts*, shall *save us*; no lesse then the *Oratorie of preaching powred in* at our *eares*. 1.

The other is, of them that doe not wholy reject it; yet so depress it, as if 2. in comparison of *Prophesying*, it were little worth. Yet (we see) by the frame of this Text, it is the higher end: the calling on us by *prophecie*, is but, that we should *call on the Name of the Lord*. All *prophesying*, all *preaching*, is but to this end. And indeed *Prophecie* is but *gratia gratis data*: and (ever) *gratis data* is for *gratum faciens*; a part and a speciall part whereof is *invocation*. There is then, as a conscience to be made of both; so a like conscience to be made of both; not to set up the one, and magnifie it, and to turne our backe on the other, and vilifie it. For, howsoever we give good words of *invocation*; yet what our conceit is, our deeds show.

I love not to dash one religious duty against another; or (as it were) to send challenges between them. But, as much as the Text saith, so much may I say: And that is, that it hath three *speciall prerogatives*, by this verse of the *Prophet*.

1. First, it is *effundam* (ours) properly; and *effundam Spiritum meum*, the *powring out* of *our Spirit* (to answer that of God's *Spirit* in the Text.) *Prophetabunt* is not ours, none of our act, but the act of another. The streame of our times tends all to this, To make Religion nothing, but an *auricular profession*, a matter of ease, a meer sedentarie thing: and our selves,

26 speciall] F_2; specall F_1

meerly *passive* in it; sitt still, and heare a *Sermon*, and *two Anthems*, and be *saved*: as if, by the act of the *Queer*, or of the *Preacher*, we should so be (for, these be their acts) and we do nothing our selves, but *sit* and *suffer*: without so much as anything done by us, any *effundam* on our parts at all; not so much as this, of *calling on the Name of the* LORD.

2. The second: This hath the *quicunque*. We would faine have it, *quicunque prophetiam audiverit*, he that heares so many *Sermons* a *weeke*, cannot choose but be *saved*: But it will not be. No: Heer stand we *preaching*, and *hearing Sermons*; and neither they that heare *prophecying*, nay nor they that *prophesie* themselves, can make a *quicunque* of either. Witnesse, *Domine, in nomine tuo prophetavimus*, and LORD *thou hast preached in our streets*, and yet it would do them no good: *Nescio vos*, was their answer for all that.

<small>Mat. 7.22.
Luke 13.26.</small>

And yet how faine would some be a *prophecying?* It would not save them, though they were: and is it not a preposterous desire? we love to meddle with that, pertaines not to us, and will do us no good: that, which is our *duty*, and would do us good, that care we not for.

Tongues were given for *prophesie*. True: but, no *quicunque* there, for all that: but to whom none are given to *prophesie*, to them yet are there given to *invocate*. And there comes it in, the *quicunque* lies there: *de Spiritu meo super omnem carnem*, heer it comes in; at *invocation*, not at the other. Let it suffice; It is not *quicunque prophetaverit* heer, *Quicunque invocaverit* it is. The *Prophet* saith it, the *Apostles* say it both, πᾶς ὃς ἂν. Peter, heer; Paul, *Rom*.X.XIII.

Last, this is sure; *invocaverit* is ἐχόμενον σωτηρίας, it stands neerest, it joines closest to *salvabitur*: Both one breath, one sentence: the words touch, there is nothing between them. *Salvabitur* is not joined hard to *prophetabunt*; it is removed farther of. To *Invocaverit* it is; a degree neerer at least. Nay, the very next of all.

The Text shewes this (in a sort) but the thing it self more: for when all comes to all, when we are even at the last cast, *salvabitur* or no *salvabitur*, then, as if there were some speciall vertue in *invocaverit*, we are called upon, to use a few words or signes to this end, and so sent out of the world with *invocaverit* in our mouthes. Dying, we call upon men for it; living, we suffer them to neglect it. It was not for nothing, it stands so close, it even touches *salvation*: It is (we see) the very immediate act next before it.

And yet I would not leave you in any error concerning it: To end this point; shall *invocaverit* serve then? needs there nothing but it? no *faith*, no *life*: Saint *Paul* answers this home: He is direct (X.*Rom*.) *How can they call upon Him, unlesse they beleeve:* So, *invocation* presupposeth *faith*. And as peremptorie he is, II. *Tim*. II. *Let every one that calleth on* (Nay, that but nameth) *the name of the* LORD, *depart from iniquitie:* so, it presupposeth *life*

<small>Rom. 10.14.

2. Tim. 2.19.</small>

too. For, if *we incline to wickednesse in our hearts*, GOD *will not heare us.* No *invocation* (that) not *truly so called*; a *provocation* rather. But putt these two, *faith* and *recedit ab iniquitate* to it, and so, who so *calleth upon Him*, I will put him in good Sureties, one *Prophet*, and two *Apostles*, both to assure him, he *shalbe saved.*

Psal. 66.18.

4.
Salvabitur.

And that is it, we all desire, to be *saved. Saved*, indefinitely. Applie it to any dangers, not in the *Day of the* LORD onely, but even in this *our Day*: For, some *terrible dayes* we have even heer. I will tell you of one; The signes heer sett downe, bring it to my mind: A day we were *saved* from (the *Day* of the *Pouder-treason*) which may seem in a sort heere to be described, *blood and fire*, and *the vapor of smoke*: a *terrible day* sure, but nothing to the *Day of the* LORD.

From that we were *saved*: but we all stand in danger, we all need *saving* from this. When this *Day* comes, another manner of *fire*, another manner of *smoke*. That *fire* never burnt; that *smoke* never rose: but, this fire shall *burne and never be quenched*; this *smoke* shall not vanish *but ascend for ever*. I say no more, but, in that, in this, in all, *Qui invocaverit, salvus erit: Invocation* rightly used is the way to be safe.

Rev. 19.3.

This then I commend to you. And of all *invocations*, that which *King David* doth commend most, and betake himselfe to, as the most effectuall and surest of all: and that is, *Accipiam calicem salutaris, et nomen* DOMINI *invocabo*: To *call on his Name with the Cup of Salvation taken in our hands*. No *invocation*, to that. That, I may be bold to add (which is all that can be added) *Quicunque calicem salutaris accipiens, nomen* DOMINI *invocaverit, salvus erit*. Another *effundam* yet, this.

Psal. 116.13.

Why, what vertue, is there in the taking it, to helpe *invocation*? A double. For whither we respect our sinnes; they have a *voice, a cry, an ascending cry*, in Scripture assigned them. They *invocate* too, they call for somwhat; Even for some *fearefull judgement* to be powred downe on us: and I doubt, our owne *voices* are not strong enough, to be heard above *theirs*.

1.

But *bloud*, that also hath a *voice*: specially *innocent blood*, the *bloud of Abel*, that *cries loud* in GOD's eares: but nothing so loud as the *bloud* whereof this *cup of blessing* is the *communion*; the voice of it, wilbe heard above all: the cry of it, will drowne any cry els. And, as it cries higher: so it differs in this, that it cryes in a farre other key; for far *better things then that of Abel*: not for *revenge*, but for *remission* of *sinnes*; for that, wherof it is it self the *price* and *purchase*, for our salvation in that great and terrible *Day of the* LORD, when nothing els will *save* us, and when it will most import us; when if we had the whole world to give, we would give it for these foure syllables, *salvabitur, shalbe saved*.

Heb. 12.24.

31 But *bloud, that*] F_2; But, *bloud that* F_1

2.   But it was not so much for sin, *David* took this *cup*; as to yeeld God *thanks* for all His benefits. In that case also, there is speciall use of it: and both fit us. As the former, of *drowning* of our *sinn's* crye; so this also. For, to this end, are we heer now mett, to render publikely and in solemne manner, our *thanksgiving*, for His great favour this day vouchsafed us, in *powring out His Spirit*; and with it, *His saving health upon all flesh, all that call upon Him*: then, to take place, when we shall have speciall use of it, in the *Great Day*, the *Day of the* Lord. And very agreeable it is, *per hunc sanguinem, pro hoc Spiritu*, for the *powring out of this his Spirit*, to render Him thanks with the *bloud, that was powred out* to procure it [and this is our last *effundam*, and a reall *effundam* too:] For this *effusion*, of both, the one, and the other, and for the hope of our *salvation*, the worke both of the one, and of the other.

To the finall atteinment whereof, by *His holy word of prophesie*, by *calling on His Name*, by this *Sacrament* of *His bloud powred out*, and of *His Spirit powred* out with it, He bring us. &c.

XIII

A Sermon Preached at White-hall, on Easter day the 16. of April. 1620

John Chap. X

Maria autem stabat juxta monumentum, &c.

Ver. 11. *But Marie, stood by the Sepulchre, weeping, and as she wept, she stouped, and looked into the Sepulchre,*
12. *And saw two angels, in white, sitting, the one at the head, the other at the feete, where the body of Jesus had lyen.*
13. *And they said to her, Woman, why weepest thou? She said to them, They have taken away my Lord, and I know not where they have laid Him.*
14. *When she had thus said, she turned herselfe about, and saw Jesus standing, and knew not that it was Jesus.*
15. *Jesus saith to her, Woman, why weepest thou? whom seekest thou? She (supposing He had beene the gardiner) said to him, Sir, if thou have borne Him hence, tell mee where thou hast laid Him, and I will take Him thence.*
16. *Jesus saith to her, Marie: She turned herselfe, and said to Him, Rabboni; that is to say, Master.*
17. *Jesus saith to her, Touch me not, for I am not yet ascended to my Father: But, goe to my brethren, and say to them, I ascend to my Father and to your Father, and to my God and your God.*

THIS LAST VERSE WAS NOT TOUCHED.

IT is Easter day abroad: And it is so in the text. We keepe *Salomons* rule, *Verbum diei in die suo*: For, all this (I have read) is nothing else, but a report of Christs rising, and of His appearing this Easter day morning, His very first appearing of all. S. *Marke* is expresse for it, that *Christ* was no 1. Reg 8.59.

Mar. 16.9.

---

1 Preached at White-hall] Preached before the King's Majestie, at White-hall F_1 5 Maria...&c.] *om.* F_1 25 Easter day] F_1; Eastr day *Q*; *Easter Day MS*

sooner risen this day, but, *He appeared first of all to Mary Magdalene*: which first appearing of His, is here by S. *John* extended, and set downe at large. The summe of it is, 1. The seeking *Christ* dead; 2. The finding *Him* alive.

The Maner of it is, That *Mary Magdalene* staying still by the Sepulchre, first she saw a vision of Angels: and after, she saw *Christ* himselfe. Saw *Him*, and was herselfe made an Angel by *Him*, a good Angel, to cary the Evangel, the first good and joyfull tidings of *His* rising againe from the dead. And this was a great honour (all considered) to serve in an Angels place. To doe that at *His* Resurrection (*His* second birth) that, at *His* first birth an Angel did. An Angel first published that, *Mary Magdalen* brought first notice of this. As hee, to the Shepherds; so shee, to the Apostles, the Pastours of *Christs* flock; by them to be spred abroad to the ends of the world.

To looke a little into it.

1. *Mary* is the name of a woman:
2. *Mary Magdalen*, of a sinful woman.

1. That, to a woman first, it agreeth well, to make even with *Eve*; that, as by a woman came the first newes of death; So, by a woman also might come the first notice of the Resurrection from the dead. And the place fits well: for, in a garden, they came, both.

2. That, to a sinfull woman first; that also agrees well. To her first that most needed it: most needed it, and so first sought it. And it agrees well, *He* be first found of her, that first sought *Him*: Even in that respect she was to be respected.

In which two, there is opened unto us *a gate of hope*, two great leaves (as it were) one that no infirmity of sex (for a woman we see:) the other, that no enormitie of sin, (for a sinfull woman, one that had the blemish, that shee went under the common name of *peccatrix*, as notorious and famous in that kinde:) That, neither of these, shall debarre any to have their part in *Christ*, and in *His* Resurrection; any, that shall sccke *Him* in such sort, as shee did. For, either of these *non obstante*, nay notwithstanding both these, she had the happinesse; To see *His* Angels (and that was no small favour:) To see *Christ* himselfe: And that, first of all, before all others, to see and salute *Him*: And, to receive a commission from *Him* of *Vade & dic*, to goe and tell, (that is, as it were) to be an Apostle, and that to the Apostles themselves, to bring them the first good newes of *Christs* rising againe.

---

7 *His* rising againe] His rising, *MS*   20 well...that] well, too. To her first, ^{as one} that *MS*   25 (as it were) one that] (as it were.) One: that   see:) the] F_1; see: (the Q; see): The *MS*   32 To...himselfe:] to See & *to salute Christ Himself. MS*   32–33 others... And,] others: and, to receive *MS*   33–34 *Him of Vade & dic*, to goe and tell,] *Him to go and tell* ^*MS*; to be an]   34 to...an] to be made an *MS*   35 bring] bear *MS*

There are three Parties that take up the whole Text: and if I should divide it, I would make those three Parties the three parts; ¹*Mary Magdalene*, ²the *Angels*, ³and *Christ* our Saviour.

Mary Magdalen begins her part in the first verse, but she goes along through them all.   I.

Then the *Angels* part in the two verses next. ¹Their *appearing*, ²and their *speech* to her: *Appearing*, in the twelfth; *Speech*, in the thirteenth.   II.

And last, *Christs* part in all the rest. ¹His *appearing*, ²and *Speech*, likewise. *Appearing*, first, *unknowen*, in the fourteenth, and *His speech* then, in the fifteenth.   III.

After, *His appearing*, and *speech* againe, being *knowen*, in the sixteenth and seventeenth. ¹Forbidding her, *Mane & tange*, to *stay*, and to *touch*, ²and bidding her, *Vade & dic*, to get her quickly to *His* brethren, and tell them, *His* resurrection was past, for (*ascendo*) Hee was taking thought for *His* ascension, and preparing for that. Thus lieth the order, and the parts.

The use will be, that we, in our seeking, cary our selves as she did: and so may we have the happinesse, that she had, to finde *Christe*, as *Hee* is now to be found in the vertue of *His Resurrection*.

VER. 11.

But Mary, stood by the sepulchre, weeping, and as shee wept, shee stouped, and looked into the sepulchre.

Of the favours vouchsafed this same *fœlix peccatrix*, (as the Fathers terme her) this day, ¹To *see* but *Christs* Angels, ²To *see Christ* at all, ³To *see Him* first of all, ⁴But, more then all these, to be employed by *Him* in so heavenly an errand; reason wee can render none that helped her to these, but that, which in a place *Christ* himselfe renders, *Quia dilexit multùm*, Because shee loved much.   Luke 7.47.

She loved much: we cannot say, Shee beleeved much. For, by her *sustulerunt* thrise repeated, at the second, thirteenth, fifteenth verses, it seemes, shee beleeved no more, then just as much as the High Priests would have had the world beleeve, that *He was taken away by night*.   Matt. 28.13.

---

4 begins ... the] beginns the *MS*   6 *Angels* part in] *Angells*, in *MS*   8 And ... in] Last, *Christs*, in *MS*   9 *unknowen* ... fourteenth] unknowen 14ᵗʰ *MS*; 9–10 then, in the fifteenth.] then. 15. *MS*   11 After, *His appearing*] no new para. *MS*   11–12 *knowen* ... seventeenth.] knowen 16. & 17. *MS*   17 may we have] may have *MS*   18 found] found. *MS*   in the vertue of *His Resurrection*] *MS* added in author's hand   19–22 [*rule*] VER. 11. ... *the sepulchre*.] *MS om*.   24 ¹To *see* but *Christs* Angels,] *MS om*.;   24–5 ²To ... then all] ¹To *see Christ*, at all, ²To *see Him* first of all, ³But, more then both *MS*

Defectus fidei non est negandus, affectus amoris non est vituperandus: It is *Origen*, we cannot commend her faith; her love, we cannot but commend; And so doe: Commend it in her, commend it to you. Much it was, and much good proofe gave she of it. Before, to *Him* living: now, to *Him* dead. To *Him* dead, there are divers: [1]She was last at *His* Crosse, & first at *His* grave: [2]Stayed longest there, was soonest heere: [3]Could not rest, till shee were up to seeke *Him*: [4]Sought *Him*, while it was yet darke, before shee had light to seeke *Him* by.

But, to take her as wee finde her in the Text, and to looke no whither else. There are, in the Text, no lesse then ten, all arguments of her great love, all, as it were, a commentarie upon *dilexit multùm*. And even in this first verse, there are five of them.

1. The first, in these words; *stabat juxta monumentum*, that she stood by the grave. A place, where faint love loves not to stand. Bring *Him* to the grave, and lay *Him* in the grave, and there leave him: but come no more at it, nor stand not long by it. Stand by *Him*, while *He* is alive, So did many, stand, and goe, and sit by *Him*. But, *stans juxta monumentum*, Stand by *Him* dead, *Marie Magdalen*, she did it, and she onely did it, and none but she. *Amor stans juxta monumentum*.

2. The next is in these, *Maria autem stabat. But Marie stood.* In the *autem*, the *but* (that, helpes us to another.) *But Mary stood* (that is asmuch to say, as) others did not, *But*, she did. *Peter* and *John* were there but even now. Thither they came, but not finding *Him*, away they went. They went: *But Marie* went not, she *stood still*. Their *going away* commends her *staying behinde*. To the grave *she came* before them, From the grave *she went* to tell them, To the grave *she returnes* with them, At the grave *she stayes* behind them. *Fortior eam figebat affectus*, saith *Augustine*, a stronger affection fixed her, so fixed her, that she had not the power to remove thence. Goe, who would, she would not, but *stay, still*. *To stay* while others doe so, while company stayes, that is the worlds love: But *Peter* is gone, and *John* too: all are gone, and we left alone; then to *stay*, is love, and constant love. *Amor manens, aliis recedentibus*, Love, that when others shrinke and give over, holds out still.

ver. 8.

3. The third in these, *she stood, and she wept*; And, not a teare or two: but *she wept* a good (as we say;) That the Angels, That *Christ* himselfe pitie her, and both of them, the first thing they doe, they aske her, *Why wept she so?* Both of them begin with that question. And, in this, is love. For, if, when *Christ*

1–2 *vituperandus*: It is *Origen*, we] *vituperandus*. We *MS*, *F*₁ 5 divers: [1]She] diverse before:. *MS* 7 were up to seeke *Him*:] were so. *MS* 13 *in marg*. 1.] *MS*, *F*₁ 20 *in marg*. 2.] *F*₁ om. 21–2 But Mary...others] But Marie, that is as much to say, others *MS* 23–24 But Marie...stood still.] but Marie stood still. *MS* 34 a good] agood *MS* 35–36 Both of them begin] Both beginn *MS* *stood at Lazarus graves side and wept*, the Jewes said, *See how he loved him*: may not we say the very same, when *Mary stood at Christs grave and wept, See, how she loved him?* Whose presence she wished for, *His* misse she wept for; whom she dearely loved, while she had *Him*, she bitterly bewailed, when she lost *Him*. *Amor amarè flens*, Love running downe the cheekes.

The fourth in these, *And as she wept, shee stouped, and looked in*, ever and anon. That is, she did so *weepe*, as, she did *seeke* withall. *Weeping* without *seeking*, is but to small purpose. But, her *weeping* hindered not her *seeking*; Her sorrow dulled not her diligence. And, diligence is a character of love, comes from the same root, *dilectio & diligentia* from *diligo*, both. *Amor diligentiam diligens*.

To *seeke*, is one thing: not to give over *seeking*, is another. For, I aske, why should she now looke in? *Peter* and *John* had looked there before, nay had beene in the grave, (they.) It makes no matter: Shee wil not trust *Peters* eyes, nor *Johns*, neither. But, she her selfe had before this, looked in, (too.) No force, she will not trust her selfe, she will suspect her owne eyes, she will rather thinke she *looked* not well before, then leave off her *looking*. It is not enough for love, to *looke* in once. Thus we use, this is our manner when we seeke a thing seriously, where we have sought already, there to seeke againe, thinking wee did it not well, but, if we now looke againe, better, we shall surely find it, then. *Amor quærens ubi quæsivit*. Love, that never thinkes, it hath looked enough. These five.

And, by these five, we may take measure of our love, and of the true *multum* of it. *Ut prosit nobis ejus stare, ejus plorare, & quærere* (saith Origen) that her *standing*, her *weeping*, and *seeking*, wee may take some good by them.

I doubt, ours will fall short. *Stay* by *Him* alive, that we can, *juxta mensam*: but *juxta monumentum*, who takes up his standing there? And our love, it is dry eyed, it cannot *weepe*, it is stiffe-joynted, it cannot stoupe to *seeke*. If it doe, and wee hit not on *Him* at first, away wee goe, with *Peter* and *John*; wee stay it not out with *Mary Magdalen*. A signe, our love is little, and light, and our *seeking* sutable, and so, it is without successe. We find not *Christ*, no mervaile: but *seeke Him* as shee *sought Him*, and we shall speed, as she sped.

Ver. 12.

And saw two Angels, in white, sitting, the one at the head, the other at the feet, where the body of Jesus had lien.

1–2 him: may] Him? May *MS*   3 him?] Him. *MS*   10–11 Amor...diligens.] Amor solicitè quærens seu dilectio diligens. *MS*   17 leave off] leave *MS*   18 this is] so is *MS*   33 Ver. 12.] *in marg. MS*   34–35 And saw...had lien.] *MS om.*

For what came of this? Thus *staying* by it, and thus *looking in*, againe and againe, though she saw not *Christ* at first, shee *sees his Angels*. For so it pleased *Christ* to come by degrees: *His Angels*, before *Him*. And, it is no vulgar honour, this, to *see* but *an Angel*, what would one of us give to see but the like sight?

We are now at the *Angels* part. Their *appearing*, in this verse. There are foure points in it. ¹Their *place*, ²Their *habit*, ³Their *site*, ⁴and their *order*. ¹*Place*, in the grave, ²*Habit*, in white; ³*site*, they were sitting; ⁴and their *order in sitting*, one at the head, the other at the feet.

I.

Rev. 14.13.
Psal. 116.15.

The Place, *In the grave* shee saw them: and *Angels* in a *grave*, is a strange sight, a sight never seene before, not till *Christs* body had beene there, never, till this day; this the first newes of *Angels* in that place. For, a *grave*, is no place for *Angels* (one would thinke) for wormes, rather: Blessed *Angels*, not but in a blessed place. But, since *Christ* lay there, that place is blessed. There was a voice heard from heaven, *Blessed be the dead, Precious the death, Glorious the memorie* now, *of them that die in the Lord*. And, even this, that the *Angels*

2.

disdained not now to come thither, and to sit there, is an *auspicium* of a great change to ensue in the state of that place. *Quid gloriosius Angelo? quid vilius vermiculo?* saith *Augustine. Qui fuit vermiculorum locus, est & Angelorum*. That which was the place for wormes, is become a place for Angels.

Rev. 7.9.

Their *Habit, In white*. So were there divers of them, divers times, this day, seene, *in white*, all, in that colour. It seemes to be their *Easter day* colour; for at this Feast, they all doe their service in it. Their *Easter day* colour, for it is the colour of the *Resurrection*. The state whereof when *Christ* would represent upon the Mount, *His raiment was all white, no Fuller in earth could come neere it*. And, our colour it shall be, when rising againe, wee *shall walke in white robes, and follow the Lambe withersoever he goeth*.

Eccles. 9.8.

Heaven mourned on *Good-Friday*; the Eclipse made all then in blacke. *Easter day*, it rejoyceth, *Heaven and Angels all in white. Salomon* tells us, it is the colour of joy. And, that is the state of joy, and this the day of the first joyfull tidings of it, with joy ever celebrated, even *in albis*, eight dayes together, by them that found *Christ*.

3.

In white, and *sitting*: As the colour, of joy: so, the situation, of rest. So wee say, *Sit downe*, and *rest*. And so, is the grave made by this mornings

---

6 at the *Angels* part.] at the 12ᵗʰ, the *Angells* part. *MS* *appearing*,] appearing first, *MS*   11 beene there, never,] been there. Never, *MS*   16 And, even this,] And this, *MS*   17 is an] it is an *MS*   18–19 *Quid...vermiculo?*] added in marg. *MS* *Qui fuit...Angelorum*] /~~Locus~~ qui fuit/ ~~Ante~~ vermiculorum, /~~locus, jam est et~~ /~~modo~~ *Angelorum*. *MS*   19–20 That...Angels.] *MS* om.   23–24 Their...Resurrection.] in marg. in author's hand replacing ~~It is the colour of Resurrection~~. *MS*   25–26 Fuller in earth] fuller on the earth *MS*; fuller in the earth F_1

worke, a place of *rest*. *Rest*, not from our labours onely, so doe the beasts rest when they die: But, as it is in the 16. Psalme (a Psalme of the *resurrection*) a *rest in hope*; hope, of rising againe, the members in the vertue of their head, who this day is risen. So, to enter into the rest, which yet *remaineth for the people of God*, even the Sabbath eternall.

Psal. 16.9.
Heb. 4.9.

Sitting, and in this order *sitting, at the head, one; at the feet, another, where His body had lyen*.

4.

1 Which order may well referre to *Christ* himselfe, whose body was the true *Arke* indeed, *In which it pleased the Godhead to dwell bodily*; and is therefore heere betweene two *Angels*, as was the *Arke* (the type of it) betweene the two *Cherubims*.

Col. 2.9.
Exod. 25.19.

2 May also referre to *Mary Magdalen*. She had *annointed his head*, she had *annointed his feete*: at these two places, *sit the two Angels*, as it were to acknowledge so much for her sake.

Mat. 26.7.
Joh. 12.3.

3 In mysterie they referre it thus. Because *caput Christi Deus*, the Godhead is the head of Christ, and *His feet* (which the Serpent did bruise) *His manhood*; that either of these hath his Angell. That, to *Christ man*, no lesse then to *Christ God*, the Angels doe now their service. *In principio erat verbum*, His Godhead, there an Angell: *Verbum caro factum, His manhood*; there, another. And *let all the Angels of God worship Him* in both. Even in *His* manhood, at *His* cradle (the head of it) a queere of Angels; At *His* grave (the feete of it) Angels likewise.

1 Cor. 11.3.
Gen. 3.15

Heb. 1.6.
Luk. 2.13.

4 And lastly, for our comfort (thus.) That, henceforth even such shall all our graves be, if we be so happy as to *have our parts in the first resurrection*, which is of the soule from sinne. We shal go to our graves *in white* (in the comfort, and colour of *hope*) lye betweene *two Angels*, there: they guard our bodies, dead, and present them alive againe at the resurrection.

Rev. 20.6.

1 Yet before we leave them, to learne somewhat of the Angels: specially, of the *Angell that sate at the feete*. That, betweene them there was no striving for places. He that sate *at the feet*, as well content with his place, as he that *at the head*. We, to be so, by their example. For, with us, both the Angels would have beene *at the head*, never a one *at the feete*: with us, none would be at the *feet* by his good will, *Head-angels* all.

2 Againe, from them both. That, inasmuch, as the *head* ever stands for the beginning, and the *feete* for the end; that we be carefull, that our beginnings onely bee not glorious (O an Angel at the head in any wise)

---

1 *Rest . . . from*] Not, of rest from *MS*   7. beasts rest] beasts *MS om.*   13 *in marg.* Joh. 12.3] *MS, LACT*; Joh. 11.3 *Q, F₁ feete:*] feet, *MS*   15–16 *Deus,theGodhead*]*Deus.* 1. Cor.11.3.the*GodheadMS*   15*inmarg.*1Cor.11.3]*MSom.*   19 *factum, His*]*factumestHisMS* 23 4] *MS, F₁ om.*   (thus.) That,] thus: that *MS*; all] *F₁ om.*   25–26 *white* (in . . . *hope*)] *white, in . . . hope, MS*   28 Angels: specially] *angells* specially *MS* 33 *Head-angels*] Head angells *MS*

232   A SERMON PREACHED ON EASTER DAY 1620

but that wee looke to the *feete*, there be another there, too. *Ne turpiter atrum Desinat*, that it end not in a blacke Angel, that began in a white. And this for the *Angels appearing*.

VER. 13.

And they said to her, Woman, why weepest thou? She said to them, They have taken away my Lord, and I know not where they have laid Him.

Their question.   Now to their *speech*. It was not a dumb shew, this, a bare apparition, and so vanished away. It was *visio & vox*, a vocall vision. Heere is a dialogue, too. The *Angels speake to her*.

And they aske her, *Quid ploras?* Why she wept? what cause shee had to weepe. They meane, she had none (as indeed no more she had.) All was in
Gregorie.   error, *piæ lachrymæ, sed cæcæ*, teares of griefe, but false griefe, imagining that to be, that was not, *Him* to be dead that was alive. She *weepes*, because shee found the grave emptie, which God forbid she should have found full, for then *Christ* must have beene dead still, and so, no Resurrection.

And this case of *Marie Magdalen* is our case oftentimes. In the error of our conceit, to weepe where we have no cause; to joy, where we have as little. Where we should, where wee have cause to joy, we weepe: and, where to weepe, we joy. Our *ploras* hath never a *quid*. False joyes, and false sorrowes, false hopes, and false feares this life of ours is full of, God helpe us.

Now because she erred, they aske her the cause, that she alledging it, they may take it away, and shew it to bee no cause. As the *elench, à non causâ pro causâ* makes foule rule among us, beguiles us, all our life long.

Her answer.   Will ye heare her answere to, *Why weepe you?* Why? *sustulerunt*, that was the cause, *Her Lord* was gone, *was taken away*.

1.   And a good cause it had beene if it had beene true. Any have cause to grieve, that have lost, lost a good Lord, so good and gracious a Lord, as *He* had beene to her.

2.   But that is not all: a worse matter, a greater griefe then that. When one dieth, we reckon him *taken away*; that is one kind of *taking away*. But his dead body is left; so, all is not taken from us; That, was not her case. For, in

---

4 VER. 13.] *in marg. MS*   5–6 *And... laid Him.] MS om.*   7 Now... speech.] *no new para.* (And now (to the 13th vers.) to their Speech.) *MS*   9–10 The *Angels...* wept?] The angells speak to her; & *ask her quid ploras Why she wept? MS*   13 She *weepes*] *new para. MS*   23 the *elench*] that *elench MS*   30–32 When... her case] For w When one... note her case *added in marg. MS*   32 us; That] us, that *MS*

saying (*her Lord*) she meanes not, *Her Lord* alive, that is not it; she meanes
not, they had slaine *Him*, they had *taken away* his life (she had wept her fill
for that, already.) But, *her Lord*, that is, his dead body. For, though *His* life
was gone, yet *His* body was left. And, that was all, she now had left of *Him*
(that, shee cals *Her Lord*) and, that, they *had taken away* from her, too.
A poore one it was, yet some comfort it was to her, to have even that left
her, to visite, to annoint, to doe other offices of love, even to that. *Etiam viso*   *Ambros.*
cadavere recalescit amor, at the sight, even of that, will love revive, it will
fetch life of love againe. But now, heere is her case; that, is gone, and all,
and nothing, but an empty grave, now left to stand by. That S. *Augustine*
saith well, *sublatus de monumento*, grieved her more, then *occisus in ligno*, for,
then something yet was left; now, nothing at all. Right *sustulerunt*, taken
away quite and cleane.

And thirdly, her *nescio ubi*. For though *He* be *taken away*, it is some   3.
comfort yet, if we know where to fetch *Him* againe. But here, *He* is gone,
without all hope of recovery, or getting againe. For *they* (but shee knew not
who) *had caried Him* (she knew not whither) *laide Him* (shee knew not where)
there to do to *Him* (she knew not what.) So that now she knew not, whither
to go, to find any comfort. It was *nescio ubi*, with her, right. Put all these
together, *His life taken away, His body taken away, & caried no man knowes
whither*; and, doe they aske, *why she wept*? or, can any blame her for it?

The trueth is, none had *taken away Her Lord*, for all this: for, all this   *Her errour.*
while *Her Lord* was well, was, as shee would have had *Him*, alive and safe.
He went away of himselfe, none caried him thence. What of that? *Non*   *Augustine.*
credens suscitatum, credidit sublatum, for want of beliefe *He was risen*, shee
beleeved, *He was caried away*. Shee erred in so beleeving, there was errour
in her love, but there was love in her errour too.

And, give me leave to lay out three more arguments of her love, out of   Yet, her
this verse (to make up eight, towards the making up of her *multùm*.)   love.

1. The very title shee gives *Him* of *Dominum meum*, is one, *My Lord*, that
she gives *Him* that terme. For, it shewes her love and respect was no whit
abated, by the scandall of His death. It was a most opprobrious, ignomini-
ous, shamefull death Hee suffered, such, as in the eyes of the world, any
would have been ashamed to own *Him*, (or say of *Him*, *Meum*:) But, any

---

1–2 Aug: Not ~~occisus in ligno, onely But sublatus de monumento~~] *in marg.* MS   4 And, that
was all,] And that, was all, *MS*   she now had] she / ^{now}/had ~~now~~ *MS*   5 (that ... *Lord*)]
(/^{that she calls}/~~of~~ her Lord) *MS*   10–13 That S. *Augustine* ... cleane.] *added in marg.*
MS   14–15 For though ... But here] *added in marg.* MS   17 (she ... whither)]
she ... whither *MS*   20–21 His life ... whither] *added in marg.* MS   24 *in marg.*
Augustine] F_1, LACT *om.*   28 to lay out] to lay you forth MS   30 meum ... that]
meum. My Lord, is one: that *MS*   34 (or ... *Meum:*)] (or said *meum*): MS

would have beene afraid to honour Him with that title, to style Him, *Dominum meum*. Shee was neither. *Meum*, for hers, *Dominum meum*, for her *Lord*, shee acknowledgeth Him, is neither ashamed, nor afraid to continue that title still. *Amor scandalo non scandalizatus.*

2. Another (which I take to be farre beyond this.) That, shee having looked into the grave a little before, and seene never an *Angel* there; and of a sudden looking in now, and seeing *two*, (a sight, able to have amazed any; any, but her) It mooves not her at all. The suddennesse, the strangeness, the gloriousnesse of the sight, yea even of *Angels*, moove her not at all. Shee seemes to have no sense of it, and so to be in a kinde of extasie all the while. *Domine, propter te est extra se*, saith *Bernard. Amor extasin patiens.*

3. And thirdly, as that strange sight affected her not a whit: so neither did their comfortable speech worke with her at all. Comfortable, I call it, for they that aske the cause, why, (*why weepe you?*) shew, they would remoove it, if it lay in them. Neither of these did, or could moove her, or make her once leave her weeping: she wept on, still (*Christ* will aske her, *quid ploras?* by and by againe.) If shee finde an *Angel*, if she finde not *her Lord*, it will not serve. She had rather finde her dead body, then them in all their glory. No man in earth, no *Angel* in heaven can comfort her, none but *He* that is *taken away, Christ*, and none but *Christ*; and, till she find *Him* againe, her soule refuseth all maner comfort: yea, even from heaven, even from the *Angels* themselves: These three. *Amor super amissum renuens consolari.*

Thus shee, in her love, for her supposed losse, or *taking away*. And what shal become of us, in ours then? That lose *Him* [1]not once, but oft, [2]And not in suppose, as she did, but in very deed, [3]And that, by sinne (the worst losse of all,)[4]And that, not by any others *taking away*, but by our owne acte, & wilfull default; and are not grieved, nay not moved a whit, break none of our wonted sports for it, as if we reckoned *Him*, as good lost as found. Yea, when *Christ*, and the *holy Ghost*, and the favour of God, and all is gone, how soon, how easily are we comforted againe for all this? that, none shall need to say, *quid ploras?* to us, rather, *quid non ploras?* aske us, why we weepe not, having so good cause to doe it, as wee then have? This for the *Angels* part.

---

2 *Dominum meum.*] *MS; Dominum. Q, F₁, LACT* 3 shee acknowledgeth] she doth acknowledge *MS* 5 this.)] *MS*; this) *Q, F₁* 7 sudden] sodein *MS* 7–8 (a sight ...her)] a sight hable to have amazed eny, Eny but her *MS* 8–9 The suddennesse...not at all.] *not in MS* 10 and so] *not in MS* 15 cause...shew] cause shew *MS* 22 refuseth] refuses *MS* even from heaven,] *MS om.* 25 [1]not once, but] *MS om.* 26–27 [2]And...[3]And...[4]And] *not numbered in MS* 29 for it] *MS om*

Ver. 14.

When she had thus said, she turned her selfe about, and saw Jesus standing, and knew not that it was Jesus.

Alwayes the Angels (wee see) touched the right string, and shee tells them the wrong cause, but yet the right, if it had beene right.

Now, to this answere of hers, they would have replied, and taken away her errour touching her *Lords taking away*; that, if she knew all, shee would have left her *seeking*, and *sit* her downe by them: and left her *weeping*, and beene *in white*, as well as they.

But, here is a *supersedeas* to them: The *Lord* himselfe comes in place. (Now come wee from the *seeking Him* dead, to the finding *Him* alive.) For, when *Hee* saw, no *Angels*, no *sight*, no *speech* of theirs would serve, none but her *Lord* could give her any comfort; *Her Lord* comes. *Christus adest.*

Adest Christus, nec ab eis unquam abest, à quibus quæritur, saith *Augustine.* *Christ* is found, found by her; And this case of hers, shall be the case of all that seriously seeke *Him*. This woman heere, for one, shee sought *Him* (we see.) They that went to *Emmaus* to day, they but talked of *Him* sadly, and they both found *Him*. Why, *He is found of them that seeke Him not.* Esa 65.1. but, of them that *seeke Him*, never but found. *For, thou Lord never failest them that seeke Thee.* Psal. 9.10. *God is not unrighteous, to forget the worke and labour of their love that seeke Him.* Heb. 6.10.

So, finde *Him* they shall, but happly not all so fully at first, no more then shee did. For, first (to try her yet a little further) *He* comes unknowen, stands by her, and she little thought it had beene *Hee*.

A case that likewise falls out full oft. *Doubtlesse He is not farre from every one of us,* saith the Apostle to the *Athenians*. But *He is neerer us many times then we thinke; even hard by us, and we not aware of it,* saith *Job*. And, *O si cognovisses & tu,* O if wee did know (and it standeth us in hand to pray that we may know) when He is so; for, that is *the time of our visitation.*

Acts 17.27.
Job. 9.11.
Luke 19.42.

Luk. 19.44.

Saint *John* saith here, *the Angels were sitting*: Saint *Luke* saith, *they stood.* Luk. 24.4. They are thus reconciled. That, *Christ* comming in presence, the *Angels* which before *were sitting, stood up*. Their *standing up*, made *Marie*

---

1 VER. 14.] *in marg. MS* (to the 14ᵗʰ verse) *from MS*   2–3 When she had...was Jesus.] *MS om.*   11 wee from] we by her; And] found & *MS*   14 Adest Christus.] Christus adest. *MS*   15 found, found *MS om.*   16–17 Him (we see.) They] Him They *MS*;   17 to day] *MS om.*   18 Esa 65.1.] *in marg. MS*   20–21 worke and labour] works and labors *MS*   22 happly] *MS*; happily Q, F₁, *LACT*   not all so] not so *MS*   23 For, first (to...further)] For first, to...further, *MS*;   24 stands] stood *MS*   26 *in marg.* Job. 9.11] *MS om.*   27 saith Job] saith Job. 9.11. *MS*   28–29 know (and...know)] know, and...know, *MS*   31 Luk. 24.4.] c.24. v.4. *MS*

Magdalen turne her to see who it was they rose to. And so, *Christ* she saw, but, knew *Him* not.

Not onely not knew *Him*, but misknew *Him*, tooke *Him for the Gardiner*. Teares, wil dim the sight, and it was yet scarse day, and shee, seeing one, and not knowing what any one should make in the ground so early, but he that dressed it, she might well mistake. But it was more then so: *Her eyes were not holden* onely, *that shee did not know Him*, but over and beside, *He did appear* ἑτέρᾳ μορφῇ in some such shape as might resemble the *Gardiner*, whom shee tooke *Him* for.

Proper enough it was, it fitted well the time and place (this person.) The time, It was the Spring: The place, It was a garden (that place is most in request at that time) for that place and time, a *Gardiner* doth well.

Of which her so taking *Him*, Saint *Gregorie* saith well, *Profectò errando non erravit*. She did not mistake in taking *Him* for a *Gardiner*: though she might seeme to erre, in some sense, yet in some other she was in the right. For, in a sense, and a good sense, CHRIST may well be said to be a *Gardiner*, and indeed is one. For, our rule, is, *Christ*, as *He* appeares, so *He* is, ever: No false semblant in *Him*.

1 A *Gardiner He* is then. The first, the fairest garden that ever was (Paradise) *He* was the *Gardiner*, it was of *His* planting. So, a *Gardiner*.

2 And ever since it is *He* that (as God) makes all our gardens greene, sends us yearely the Spring, and all the hearbs and flowers we then gather; and neither *Paul* with his planting, nor *Apollo* with his watering, could doe any good without him. So a *Gardiner* in that sense.

3 But not in that alone; But *He* it is that gardens our soules too, and makes them, as the Prophet saith, *Like a well watered garden*, weedes out of them whatsoever is noysome or unsavoury, sowes and plants them with true rootes and seedes of righteousnesse, waters them with the dew of *His* grace, and makes them bring forth fruit to eternall life.

But it is none of all these, but besides all these, nay over and above all these, this day (if ever) most properly *He* was a *Gardiner*. Was one, and so after a more peculiar manner, might take this likenesse on *Him*. *Christ* rising was indeed a *Gardiner*, and that a strange one, who made such an hearbe grow out of the ground this day, as the like was never seene before, a dead body, to shoote foorth alive out of the grave.

I aske, was *He* so this day alone? No, but this profession of *His*, this day begun, *He* will follow to the end. For, *He* it is, that by vertue of this mornings act, shall garden our bodies, too: turne all our graves into garden plots: Yea, shall one day turne land and Sea and all into a great garden, and so husband them, as they shal in due time bring forth live bodies, even all our bodies alive againe.

Long before did *Esai* see this and sing of it, in his song *Esa.* 26.19. resembling the Resurrection to a Spring garden. *Awake and sing* (saith he) *ye that dwell for a time are as it were sowen in the dust, for His dew shall be as the dew of hearbs, and the earth shall shoot forth her dead.* So then: He appeared no other, then *He* was: A *Gardiner He* was, not in shew alone, but *opere & veritate*, and so came in *His owne likenesse*. This for Christs appearing. Now to *His speech* (but, as *unknowen* still.)

Vers. 15.

Jesus saith to her, Woman, why weepest thou? whom seekest thou? She (supposing he had beene the Gardiner) said to Him, Sir, if thou have borne Him hence, tell me where thou hast laid Him, and I will take Him thence.

Still *she wept*: So *Hee* begins with *quid ploras?* askes the same question the Angels had before; onely quickens it a little with *Quem quæris, Whom seeke you?* So, *quem quæris, quærit à te quem quæris*, whom she sought, He asks her whom she sought? *Si quæris, cur non cognoscis? si cognoscis, cur quæris?* saith *Augustine.* If she *seeke* Him, why knowes she Him not? If shee know Him, why seekes she Him still? A common thing with us (this also.) To seeke a thing, and when we have found it, not to know, wee have so; but even *Christum à Christo quærere*, to aske *Christ* for *Christ*. Which however it fall in other matters, in this seeking of *Christ*, it is safe. Even when we seeke *Christ*, to pray to *Christ*, to helpe us to finde *Christ*; we shall doe it full evill without Him.

This *quid ploras*, it comes now twise. The Angels asked it, wee stood not on it, then. Now, seeing *Christ* askes it againe, the second time, wee will thinke there is something in it, and stay a little at it. The rather, for that it is the very opening of His mouth, the very first words that ever came from

<small>Christs question unknown.

Augustine.</small>

<small>1 I aske...alone?] *MS om.* No, but] And *MS* 26.19] *in marg. MS*; in his song *Esa.* 26.19] *MS om.* *MS om.* 12 and so] *MS om.* *MS* 14 Ver. 15. *in marg. ms* 14–17 vers ....*him thence.*] *ms om.* *om. wept*] *weeps f*₁ 20 *you*] *ye ms* 21–22 *quæris?* saith] *quæris* saith *ms* this also. *ms* 24 thing, and] thing and; *ms* know, wee] know we *ms*
4 plots: Yea,] plotts yea *MS* 9 dwell for a time] *MS om.* as it were] speech, but...still. 13 speech...still.)] 18 *marg. ref.*] *ms* 23 us (this also.)] us, 32 words] word *ms*
7 Esa.</small>

Him, that He spake first of all, after His rising againe from death. There is sure some more then ordinary matter in this *quid ploras*, if it be, but even for that.

Thus say the Fathers; [1]*That Marie Magdalen standing by the grave side*, and there *weeping*, is thus brought in, to represent unto us, the state of all mankind before this day, the day of *Christs* rising againe, *weeping over the dead, as doe the heathen that have no hope*: comes *Christ* with His *quid ploras*, *Why doe you weepe?* As much to say, as *ne plores*, Weepe not; why should you weepe? There is no cause of *weeping* now. Henceforth none shall need to *stand by the grave to weepe* there any more. A question very proper for *Easter-day*, for the day of the *Resurrection*. For, if there be a rising again, *quid ploras*, is right, *why* should shee, *why* should any *weepe*, then?

So that this *quid ploras* of *Christs*, wipes away teares from all eyes, and as we sing in the 30 *Psalme* (whose title is, the *Psalme of the Resurrection*) *puts off our sackcloth*, that is, our mourning weeds, *girds us with gladnesse*, puts us all *in white* with the *Angels*.

Ploras then: leave that for *Good-friday*, for His Passion: *Weepe* then, and spare not. But, *quid ploras*, for *Easter-day*, is in kinde, (the Feast of the *Resurrection*) why should there be any *weeping* upon it? Is not *Christ* risen? Shall not He raise us with Him? Is He not a *Gardiner*, to make our bodies sowen, to grow againe? *Ploras*, leave that to the *heathen, that are without all hope*; but to the Christian man, *quid ploras?* Why should hee weepe? he *hath hope*: the Head is already risen, the members shall in their due time follow Him.

I observe, that foure times this day, at foure severall appearings, [1]at the first (at this heere) He askes her, *quid ploras? Why she wept?* [2]Of them that went to *Emaus, quid tristes estis? Why are ye sad?* [3]Within a verse following this Text (the 19.) Hee said to the Eleven, *Pax vobis, Peace be to them*: [4]And to the women that met Him on the way, χαίρετε that is, *Rejoyce, bee glad*. So, no *weeping*, no *being sad*, now; nothing this day, but *peace* and *joy*: they doe properly belong to this feast.

And, this I note the more willingly, now, this yeere; because the last *Easter* we could not so well have noted it. Some *wept* then; all were *sad*, little *joy* there was, and there was a *quid*, a good cause for it. But blessed be God that hath now sent us a more kindly *Easter*, of this, by taking away the cause of our sorrow then, that we may preach of *Quid ploras*, & be far from it. So much for *quid ploras, Christs* question. Now to her answer.

---

2 even] *added in author's hand MS*   5 there *weeping*] *weeping* there *MS*   6 againe, *weeping*] again. Weeping *MS*   7 hope: comes] hope. Comes *MS*   8 Weepe not;] Weepe not. *MS*;   8–9 why...weepe?] *MS om.*   14 30 Psalme] 30. Psal. v. 11 *MS*   15 *MS* 7 girds] and girds *MS*   25 first...heere)] first, at this heer, *MS*   35 then,] then. *MS* that we...it.] *MS om.*

A SERMON PREACHED ON EASTER DAY 1620

She is still where she was; at *sustulerunt* before, at *sustulisti*, now: *si tu sustulisti*: we shall never get that word from her.

But, to *Christ* shee seems somewhat more harsh, then to the *Angels*. To them she complaines of others, *They have taken*. *Christ* she seems to charge, at least to suspect of the fact, as if He looked like one that had beene a breaker up of graves, a carrier away of corses out of their place of rest. Her (*if*) implies as much. But pardon love: as it feares where it needs not, so it suspects oft where it hath no cause. He, or any that comes in her way, hath done, *hath taken Him away*, when love is at a losse. But *Bernard* speakes to *Christ* for her; *Domine, amor quem habebat in Te, & dolor quem habebat de Te, excuset eam apud Te, si fortè erravit circa Te*: That the love she bare to Him, the sorrow shee had for Him, may excuse her with Him, if she were in any error concerning Him, in her saying, *Si tu sustulisti*.

And yet, see how God shall direct the tongue. In thus charging Him, *Prophetat & nescit*, She sayes truer then shee was aware. For indeed, if any tooke *Him away*, it was He did it. So, she was not much amisse. Her *si tu*, was true, though not in her sense. For, *quod de ipso factum est, ipse fecit*. All that was done to Him, He did it Himselfe. *His taking away, virtus fuit, non facinus*, was by His owne power, not by the act of any other: *Et gloria, non injuria*, No other mans injurie it was, but His owne glorie, that shee found Him not there. This was true, but this was no part of her meaning. Origen.

Chrysologus.

I cannot here passe over two more Characters of her love, that so you may have the full ten I promised.

One, in *si tu sustulisti eum*, in her *eum*, in her [*Him*.] *Him*? which *Him*? Her affection seems so to transport her, as shee sayes no man knowes what. To one, a meere stranger to her, and shee to him, shee talks of one thrise under the terme of *Him*, *If thou hast taken Him, tel me where thou hast laid Him, and I will fetch Him; Him, Him, & Him*, & never names Him, or tels who He is. This is *Solæcismus amoris*, an irregular speech, but loves owne Dialect. Him is enough with love, who knowes not who that is? It supposes every body, all the world bound to take notice of Him whom we looke for, onely by saying, Him, though wee never tell his name, nor say a word more. *Amor, quem ipse cogitat, neminem putans ignorare*. 1.

The other is in her *ego tollam*; If hee would tell her where hee had laide Him, she would go fetch Him (that she would.) Alas poore woman, shee was not able to lift Him. There are more then one, or two either, allowed to 2.

---

2 get . . . her.] gett <s>out of that</s> the word from her *MS* 4–5 charge . . . fact,] charge (at least to suspect) *MS* 7 love:] love, *MS* 8 her way] *MS*; our way *Q*, *F*₁, *LACT* 11 That the] The *MS* 13 in her saying] / ⁱⁿ ˢᵃʸⁱⁿᵍ \ *MS* 24 One, in] *no new para. MS* 26–27 thrise . . . terme] / ᵗʰʳⁱˢᵉ ᵇʸ ᵗʰᵉ ᵗᵉʳᵐᵉ \ *MS* 27–8 Him, If . . . & Him] *added in marg. MS* 30 is?] is. *MS* 35 fetch] fett *MS*

240 A SERMON PREACHED ON EASTER DAY 1620

Joh. 19.39. the carrying of a corps. As for *His*, it had more then *an hundred pound weight of myrrhe and other odours* upon it, beside the poise of a dead body. She could not doe it. Well, yet she would doe it, though. *O mulier, non mulier* (saith *Origen*) for *ego tollam* seemes rather the speech of a Porter, or of some lustie strong fellow at least, then of a silly weake woman. But love makes women more then women, at least it makes them have νοῦν ὑπὲρ ἰσχὺν, the courage above the strength, farre. Never measures her owne forces, no burden too heavie, no assay too hard for love, *& nihil erubescit nisi nomen difficultatis*; And is not ashamed of any thing, but that any thing should be too hard or too heavie for it. *Affectus sine mensurâ virium propriarum.* Both these argue *dilexit multùm.* And so now you have the full number of ten.

Ver. 16.

Jesus saith to her, Mary: She turned her selfe, & said to Him, Rabboni; that is to say, Master.

Christs second speech.

Now *magnes amoris amor.* Nothing so allures, so drawes love to it, as doth love it selfe. In *Christ* specially, and in such in whom the same minde is. For, when *her Lord saw*, there was no taking away *His taking away* from her, all was in vaine, neither men nor *Angels*, nor *Himselfe* (so long as *Hee* kept *Himselfe gardiner*) could get any thing of her, but *her Lord* was gone, *He was taken away*; and that for the want of *Jesus*, nothing but *Jesus* could yeeld her any comfort; *Hee* is no longer able to containe, but even discloses *Himselfe*; And discloses *Himselfe* by *His* voice.

For, it should seeme, before, with His shape, Hee had changed that also. But now, Hee speaks to her in His knowen voice, in the wonted accent of it, does but name her name, *Mary*, no more, and that was enough. That was

Augustine. as much to say, *Recognosce à quo recognosceris*, she would at least take notice of Him, that shewed He was no stranger by calling her by her name. For, whom we call by their names, we take particular notice of. So God sayes to

Exod. 33.17. *Moses, Te autem cognovi de nomine, Thou hast found grace in my sight, and I know thee by thy name.* As God, *Moses*; So Christ, *Mary Magdalen*.

And this indeede is the right way to know *Christ*; to be knowen of *Him* first. Gal. 4.9. the Apostle saith, *Now wee have knowen God* (and then correcteth himselfe) *or rather have beene knowen of God.* For, till *Hee* know us, wee shall never know *Him* aright.

1 As for *His*] as for it /ᴴⁱˢ\ *added in author's hand MS* *in marg.* Joh. 19.39] Joh. 9.39 F₁ 4 a Porter] some porter *MS* 5 silly] seely *MS* 8 for love,] *MS om.* 9 And] *MS om.* 11 now] *added in author's hand MS* 12 Ver. 16.] *in marg. MS* 13–14 *Jesus saith...Master.*] *MS om.* 17 His] of *His MS* 26 *in marg.* Augustine] 'Gregorie' Augustine *in author's hand MS* 32 Gal. 4.9] Gal. c. 4. v. 9 *MS*

And now, loe, *Christ* is found, found alive that was sought dead. A cloude may be so thick, we shal not see the Sunne through it. The Sunne must scatter that cloud, and then wee may. Here is an example of it. It is strange, a thicke cloude of heavinesse had so covered her, as, see *Him* shee could not, through it; this one word, these two syllables [*Mary*] from *His* mouth, scatters it, all. No sooner had *His* voice sounded in her eares, but it drives away all the mist, dries up her teares, lightens her eyes, that shee knew *Him* straight, and answeres *Him* with her wonted salutation, *Rabboni*. If it had lien in her power to have raised *Him* from the dead, shee would not have failed, but done it (I dare say.) Now it is done to her hands. Her answer.

And with this, all is turned out and in. A new world, now. Away with *sustulerunt*; *His taking away*, is taken away quite. For, if *His taking away* were her sorrow; *Contrariorum contraria consequentia. Si de sublato ploravit, de suscitato exultavit*, we may be sure; If sad for *His* death, for *His taking away*; then glad for his rising, for His restoring againe. Surely, if she would have bene glad but to have found but His dead body; now she findes it, and Him, alive, what was her joy, how great, may wee thinke? So that, by this she saw *Quid ploras* was not asked her for nought, that it was no impertinent question, as it fell out. Well now, He that was thought lost, is found againe, and found, not, as He was sought for, not a dead body, but a living soule, nay, *a quickening Spirit*, then. And that might *Marie Magdalen* well say. Hee shewed it, for He quickened her and her Spirits, that were as good as dead. You thought you should have come to *Christs* Resurrection to day, and so you doe. But, not to His alone, but even to *Marie Magdalens* resurrection, too. For, in very deed, a kind of resurrection it was, was wrought in her, revived, as it were, and raised from a dead & drowping, to a lively and cheerfull estate. The *Gardiner* had done his part, made her all greene, on the soddaine. Augustine.

1. Cor. 15.45.

And all this, by a word of His mouth. Such power is there in every word of His, so easily are they called, whom *Christ* will but speake to.

But, by this we see, when He would be made knowen to her after his rising, Hee did choose to be made knowen by the eare rather then by the eye. By hearing rather then by appearing. Opens her eares first, and her eyes after. *Her eyes were holden*, till her eares were opened; comes *aures autem aperuisti mihi*, and that opens them. Luc. 24.16.
Psal. 40.6.

With the Philosophers, *hearing* is the sense of wisedome. With us, in divinitie, it is the sense of faith. So most meet. *Christ* is the *Word*; hearing

---

1 And now] *no new para. MS* A cloude] *new para. MS* 8 in marg. Her answere] *MS om.* 8 If it] *new para. MS* 11 And with] *no new para. MS* 12 sustulerunt;] *sustulerunt, now: MS* For, if] *new para.* Now, if *MS* were] was *MS* 13 in marg. Augustine] Ambrose. Aug. *MS* 14 we may be sure] *added in MS* 17 alive,] alive: *MS* by this] now *MS* 20 in marg. 1. Cor. 15.45] 2. Cor. 14.45 *F₁* 21 Spirit, then] Spirit *MS* 22 You thought] *new para. MS* 25 and raised] as raised *MS* 29 His, so] His. So *MS* 34 that opens them.] there it began. *MS*

242   A SERMON PREACHED ON EASTER DAY 1620

then (that sense) is *Christs* sense; *voce quàm visu*, more proper to the *Word*. *Psal. 48.8.* So, *sicut audivimus* goes before, and then, *sic vidimus* comes after. In matters of faith the eare goes first, ever, and is more use, and to bee trusted before the eye. For, in many cases faith holdeth, where sight faileth.

Psal. 95.7. This then is a good way to come to the knowledge of *Christ*, by *Hodie si vocem*, to *heare His voice*. Howbeit, it is not the onely way. There is another way to take notice of Him by besides, and we to take notice of it. On this very day we have them both.

For, twise this day came *Christ*, unknowen first, and then knowen, after. To *Marie Magdalen*, here: and to them at *Emmaus*. *Luc. c. 24.* To *Marie Magdalen*, unknowen, in the *shape* of a *Gardiner*. To those that went to *Emaus*, unknowen, in the likenesse of a *Travailer* by the way side. Came to be knowen to her by His voice, by the word of His mouth. Not so to them. *Luk. 24.32., 35.* For, many words He spake to them, and they felt them *warme at their hearts*, but, knew Him not for all that. But, *He was knowen to them in the breaking of the bread*. Her eyes opened by speaking a word: their eyes opened by the breaking of bread. There is the one way and the other way, and so now you have both. And now you have them, I pray you make use of them. (I see I shall not be able to goe further then this verse.)

It were a folly to fall to comparisons, *Committere inter se*, to set them at oddes togither, these two waies: as the fond fashion now adaies is, whether is better, Prayer or Preaching: The *Word*, or the *Sacraments*. What needs this? Seeing we have both, both are ready for us; the one now, the other by and by. Wee may end this question, soone. And this is the best and surest way to end it, to esteeme of them both, to thanke Him for both, to make use of both, having now done with one, to make triall of the other. It may be (who knowes) if the one will not worke, the other may. And if by the one or by the other, by either, or by both, it be wrought, what harme have we? In case it bee not; yet have we offered to God our service in both, and committed the successe of both to Him. He will see they shall have successe, and in His good time (as shalbe expedient for us) vouchsafe every one of us as Hee did *Marie Magdalen* in the Text, to *know Him and* *Philip. 3.10.* *the vertue of His Resurrection*; and make us partakers of both, by both the meanes before remembred, by His blessed Word, by His holy mysteries; the meanes to raise our soules heere, the pledges of the raising up of our bodies hereafter. Of both which *He* makes us partakers, who is the Author of both, JESUS CHRIST *the Righteous, &c.*

4 For, in] In *MS*   7 by besides,] by, *MS*   7–8 On this ... them both.] They wear on this very day both. *MS*   10 *Luc. c. 24.*] *MS om.*   16 by speaking a word:] with speaking, by His word. *MS*   19 (I see ... this verse.)] *MS om.*   21 whether] whither *MS*   25 them] *MS om.*   30–31 they shall have successe,] it / ^{shall have successe} \, *in author's hand MS*   33–4 by ... remembred] by the meanes of both *MS*   36 hereafter] also *MS*

APPENDIX 1

St. Paul's Cathedral MS 38F22.01, fos. 51ʳ–67ʳ

[51] A sermon preached at the spittle by M[aster] Andrewes the wednesday in Easter weeke. *April. 10. 1588*

1 Timothy 6. 17. Charge them that are rich in this world, that they be not high minded, and that they trust not in vncertaine riches but in the living God, which giveth vs abundantly all things we enioy
  18. That they doe good, and be rich in good workes, and ready to distribute, and communicate.
  19. Laying vp in store for themselves a good foundation against the time to come, that they may obteyne eternall life.

10   The commendation of the word of God (right honorable, right worshipfull, and beloved in o[ur] Savio[ur] Iesus Christ) is that every word of it (although not every word, in every place, by hymselfe alone) is one thing though not alike, for every parcell of scripture hath his owne force, and a full^fitt^scripture hath a full ^his fuller^force in the auditory fitt for yt

15   This scripture which I have read, is playne whose it is and to whome it belongeth, and as a godly father sayth of *Psal.41. Blessed is he that iudgeth rightly of the poore*, that it is *scriptura pauperum*, the poore mans scripture; so this scripture may be rightly called, (though in a divers sence) *scriptura divitum*; the rich mans scripture. And if this be the rich mans scripture, then

20   it is very fit for this place/, for that this auditory (as I thinke) is an auditory of rich men/, for no where is ther such vse of merchandize as heer wher the princes are marchants, and their cheapemen are the nobles of the earth, *Isay.23.9*. Nowher are the like sommes lent vnto princes *Ezechiel.27.33*. Nowhere doe they sucke the abundance of the sea, & the treasures hid in

25   the sand in like measure. *Deut.33.19*. Therfore when as I gave all diligence to speake not onely true things, but also seasonable, both for this tyme & place; I was directed to this scripture, of which I must say, as St Augustine said in the like case, *Deus tam faciat commodum quam est accommodum* [51v] I will pray God to make it as profitable in you, as it is fitt for you.

30   This scripture hath his name given it, even in the very first word, *Charge* (saith he) *the rich &c* it is a charge, as also to whome it is directed; namely to

the rich of this world. It consisteth of four members, whereof 2 are negative; for the removing of 2 abuses; the first, *that they be not high minded*, The second, that *they trust not in their riches/*, the reason is added, (which is a maxime and^a^ground in ther law of nature;) that we must trust to no vncerteyne thing,) of the *vncertainty of riches*. The other two are affirmative; concerning the true vse of riches,/first *charge them that they trust in God;* the reason, *because he giveth them all things aboundantly/*, The second that they doe good; that is the substance, the quantity, *that they be rich in good workes*; the quality, *that they be mercifull to distribute & communicate vnto others*: and all these are one charge, the occasion of them all doth follow, because by this meanes *they shall lay vp in store for themselues a good foundation against the time to come*, the end *that they may obteine eternall life*.

And to begin, *Charge the rich men of the world &c.* My beloved, heer is a charge a *præcipe*, a p[re]cept, or a write directed vnto *Timothy*, & to those that are of his commission, that he should call before him the rich men of *Ephesus*, & so they the other rich men of the earth, and give them a charge. Charges are vsually given at the assises, & in courts, and at the bench, and from thence the word is drawen as it appeareth in *Acts. 5.28. Did not we charge you straitly* said the counsell & the chiefe priest,/wherby it apeareth that in such an assembly as this is, the lord of heaven doth keep a court, whervnto all that are in the world, and so they [that] least of all seeme, w[hich] are the rich of the world doe owe sute & service/, & as princes & kings have their lawes, their commissioners, theyr ministers, their courts, & court dayes, for the [52] mayntenaunce of their peace; so the lord of lords hath his lawes & statutes *Rom. 7.* his p[re]cepts & commissions .*Mat. 28 ite prædicate* goe preach the gospell his lawyers & counsellors, whom Augustine calleth *diem*^*diuini*^*iuris consultos* his courts *in occulto conscientiæ*, in the hid & secret part of the heart and conscience *Psal. 7.* for the p[re]servation of his peace that none of his may be offended or offend in the 165 of *psal. 119.* or if otherwise, that they that give the offence may be seared with an hote iron, agaynst the fearfull day of the lord. All men must learn therfore, so to p[re]pare themselves to these meetings, as to appeare before the lord in the lords court, wher we must receive a charge, which we must thinke how to excute when the court is broken vp/who is he that standeth not w[ith] feare & reverence, before an earthly barre to receive a charge/heer you must come to hear a charge of the lord of hostes: Truly this charge is worthy as great attention as the charge of any prince/, weigh w[ith] yo[ur]selves, whether it have so much force or no. St Augustine saith, *absit ut non sit, sed utinam vel sit*, it is meet that it should have better attention, I would wish it had so much, I would we could say w[ith] a true face that we are willing to doe as much for god as for an earthly man, but whether you can or no, yet as o[ur] Savio[ur] Christ said of Iohn Baptist, *this is that Eliah which was to come if you will receive it*, so say I of this p[re]cept, this is [that] charge if you will receive it, & I will adde further, this is that p[re]cept w[hich] concerneth the plentifull vse of all yo[ur] goods and riches, in the second verse of my text, and if this be not inough, I will adde further this is that p[re]cept which concerneth yo[ur] everlasting life in the last verse of my text for in the well hearing or evill hearing of this charge consisteth your eternall welbeyng.

Secondly let vs consider whom this charge doth concerne *Charge (saith he)* [52v] *the rich^of this world.^*shall I tell yo^u, he speaketh to the rich: you know yo[ur] owne names: yo^u know best who these rich men are; you are the rich men he speaketh vnto. It is the manner and the fault of the world, that men will especially exercise their gifts on those that have no need of them. It is an old similitude of the cobwebb, that they take fast hold of the litle flyes, but the great & mightie ones breake through,/ as their are many cobwebbe lawes, so the same corruption that was the cause therof would also make cobwebbe divinitie, for they would not have this charg given to great & rich men. though they are in great daunger, & in many snares, wherby it commeth to passe (I know not how, that they are exempted from this court, & are not called, either for that they thinke themselves wise inough, & so that they need not this admonition, or that it belongeth to those that are more noble then themselves, or at least that they should receive it of those, that are more honorable then themselves wherby it falleth out that we of the ministery, doe often forget the warning given vs *Psal.49.16. not to feare when a man is made rich or when the glory of his house encreaseth*, the reason is yeelded in 17 verse, *for that when they dye they shall take nothing away with them, neither shall theyr glory descend after them*. It may be resting vpon the wrong conceiving of the 18 verse *if we speake well of them they will do well vnto vs*: ffor the rich men can be content to thinke well of the ministers, as long as they speake well of them, but if they enter once to ransacke their consciences, then p[re]sently they say *odi Micheam filiu[m] Iimlæ* I hate Micheas the sonne of Iimlah: and who would willing live in the disgrace of a mighty man? nay who would beare the wrath of a magistrate, or the heavy looke of a man in authoritie? And heerby it commeth to passe, that though we will not be like the eunuch, & p[er]swade the p[ro]phet to speake good vnto the kinge, [53] yet we will learne w[ith] Balaam neither to blesse nor to curse. But I will not learne for you the vpholsters science, for this teacheth many of vs the vpholsters craft which *Ezechiel. 13.* speaketh of to stuffe quishions & pillowes well & lay them vnder the elbowes, so that we will not be of the p[ro]phet Isayahs occupation; that is we will not take a trumpet, & sound it aloud, & disease the people, & tell them of their syns, for feare of getting Esaus portion, or loosinge Balaams promotion. In a word this maketh that Ionah was never more vnwilling to deliver his charge at Niniveh, then Tymothy was to deliver it at Ephesus, & therfore the Apostle giveth hym another charge even before this charge *verse. 13.* of this cap. wher he hath a new write directed vnto hym, charging hym in the syght of God who quickneth all thinges, & before Iesus Christ who vnder Pontius Pilate witnessed a good confession, that he should keepe this commaundement w[ith]out spott, & vnreproveable vnto the apearing of Iesus Christ, which in due tyme he shall shewe &c. This charge is delivered in very peremptory & very rigorous termes, so as beyng will [*sic*] considered it will make vs all to tremble. *I charge thee* (saith he) *in the sight of God that quickneth all things, and before Iesus Christ,* laying before his eies his death & passion, & charging hym as he would aunswere it at the dreadfull day of iudgm[ent] that he keepe this Commandm[ent] &c. and because he knew that favo[ur] & hono[ur] would p[re]vaile w[ith] vs, & that we feared earthly lords & princes, he telleth vs of the king of kyngs & lord of lords, & because he knew we feare the pompe & glittering shewes of the world, he telleth vs of one that dwelleth in the light, w[hich] none can atteine vnto, whom nevere man saw, neither can see, & because he knew we feared the power of this world, w[hich] endureth but for a tyme & is mortall, he telleth vs of one whose power is for ever, who onely hath immortality. Weigh this I beseech you, *nunquid scripsimus nos?* [53v] If we write it not, & that o[ur] pens dealt not in it, o[ur] pens cannot blot it out, vnlesse we o[ur]selves wilbe blotted out of the booke of life, in the last of the Revelation. It is not o[ur] charge *cogit nos Paulus iste* this Paule is a very importunate fellow, he forceth vs to give it, for if it were not for that this fearfull charge were laid vpon vs, &^if^we were ~~never~~ not threatned o[ur]selves we would never execute it, neither would we ever have any thing doe w[ith] [*sic*] the rich of this world, we would never deale in a thing so full of daungers, often very chargeable & ever vnsavery. I for my p[arte] would say with Augustine *in ista otiosa securitate nemo me vinceret,* in this discreet idlenes, no man should goe beyond me. But this charge standing in force *cogit nos Paulus iste,* this *præcipio tibi* compelleth vs *præcipere divitibus* to charge the rich. Therfore we charge not before we are charged o[ur]selves. we terrefy you not but that we fyrst feare o[ur]selves, & I would god we did both feare together. This may serve to stand betweene vs & yo[ur] displeasure, & seying the commission is penned, & that rich men are in it *nominatim, except the leaven of affection* shew it selfe marvelously in vs we cannot but charge you, because otherwise the lords wrath could lye heavy vpon vs.

Charge the rich &c. This is the first poynt of the charge that they be not high mynded. This charge is given fyrst against that, w[hich] though a man have all other vertues, yet beyng w[ith] them it spoileth them all w[hich] is pride. And secondly agaynst that which is the root, prop & stay of this bittere branch, namely, trust in o[ur] riches. Ever synce o[ur] first father by infection tooke this *morbum Sathanium*, this divelish disease, o[ur] nature hath bene so light, that every little thing puffeth vs vp, & setteth vs alofte, yea the chiefe of the children of men are altogether higher then vanitie [54] *Psal. 62.9.* Many times when the gifts are low the mind is high. The bramble *Iudges 8.* had his mind higher then the highest *Cedar in Lebanon*: when we see in o[ur]selves any small thing more then is in o[ur] bretheren, p[re]sently we fall into Simons case *Acts. 8.* we seme to be τὶ μεγα some great thing. But if we grow to perfect growth in any thing then p[re]sently it is Hamans case *Ester 3.* who but he? who was he that the kyng could hono[ur] more then hym? nay who was ther that the king would hono[ur] but him? poore Mordecai might have no hono[ur]. This is that we learne of the Devill: *Discite a me Diabolo quia superbus sum*, but of Christ we must learne another lesson *Discite a me Christo quia mitis sum*, because I am meeke & gentle *Mat. 11.* will soone learne the Devils lesson, w[hich] is pride, but we will not learne Christs lesson which is humility, we will not learne of Christ but of the devill, we are his schollers: and having once learned this lesson of hym, we are ready to corrupt o[ur]selves, & whatsoever w gifts we have, either in wisdome, manhood, law, divinitie, learning, or eloquence, every one of them serveth for a stirrope to mount vs aloft, in o[ur] owne conceits, & riches doth overrule them all, for whereas every one of the former, is of force as it were is w[ith]in his owne circuit, onely riches p[re]vaileth beyond all circuite & compasse, let vs examine them all, wisdome ruleth in counsell, manhood in the field, law in the iudgment-seat, divinity in the pulpit, learning in the schooles, & eloquence in p[er]swasion, onely riches raigne w[ith]out limitation, it ruleth all the former, it ruleth w[ith] all of them, & it overruleth all of them, his circuite is the whole world, for when he saith, charge the rich, he p[re]sently addeth of this world, because it standeth altogether at the devotion of riches, & it willeth onely w[hat] riches will as the wise man saith *Ecclesiastes. 10. 19. Pecuniæ obediunt omnia*, all things answere mony: riches mustereth all the former gifts & all of them [54v] obey it. Let vs goe lightly over them all; wisdome ruleth in the court & in counsell, so doe riches. In the court of the great^king^Artaxerxes *Ezra 4. 13. 22.* riches p[re]vailed against counsell, & hyndered the course of building the temple, & I doubt mony can doe much in every court. Manhood ruleth in the warre, so doe riches, experience teacheth vs [that] w[ith]out it ther can be no warre: and what els ledd (though some say expelled) the Switzers out of ffraunce, w[ith]out striking one blow, but in shew only. Phillip of Macedon was wont to win a field, when he listed with his mony, as now Phillip of Spayne doth. Law governeth in the seate of iustice, so doe riches, & oftentimes it turneth iudgm[ent] into gall, & the frute of righteousnes into wormewood. *Amos. 6.12.* by the much sharpnes of sentence p[ro]nounced, & oftener it turneth it into vineger, through long standing & long delaying of sentence. Divinitye ruleth in the church & pulpit, so doe riches, for w[ith] a set of sylver peeces saith Augustine the high priests brought *concionatorem mundi* the p[re]acher of the world Iesus Christ, to answere at the barre. Learning ruleth in the schooles, but now mony setteth vs all to schoole, it maketh vs all infants, it will have *cathedram*, we must sit in *subsellijs*, learning is now but the vsher, riches sitteth in the chayre, & highest seat. Eloquence ruleth in p[er]swasion, & so doe riches. When Tertullus *Acts. 24.* had made a long oration against Paule, ffelix looked that another orator should have spoken, namely that something should have bene given hym, & if that orator had spoken, Tertullus oration had bene cleane dasht: loe this will I give, *tantum dabo*, is a very short but a pithy refutation, *tantum dabo* did more then all the rest could do *tantum valent quatuor syllabae* foure syllables are of so great force & riches raigne every wher. But some thinke that it is not the power & force of riches that beare the great sway, but that it is some sorcery or [55] witchcraft [that] lurketh vnder them, for indeed the sorcerer Symon Magus *Acts. 8.* vsed this p[er]swasion to Peter. It is a world to enter into discourse what the rich may doe in the world: sith riches may doe so much it is no marvell though riches be so much set by, *cum magna faciant quid mirum si magnifiant*, & if they be so much set by, it maketh the rich man also to be so much set by, & so they beyng so much esteemed, it maketh the rich men so much to esteeme of themselves, & so they are proud & high minded.

St Augustine saith that all frute nourisheth a worme, as the peare hath his worme, the nutt hath his worme, the beane hath his worme, so also riches have theyr worme, & the worme of riches is pride. Heer I might take occasion to iustefy the wisdome of god in giving this charge, but I beseech you lete me not be put vnto it. The prophet David warneth vs *psal. 62. 10.* that if riches *encrese we should not set our harts theron*, & the wise man *Prov. 30. 8.* prayeth the lord saying *give me not riches least I be proud*, And the Apostle Paul saith heer *charge the rich men of this world that they be not high minded*. Hono[ur] god & ease me so much, there was high & iust cause why the lord should give commandem[ent] that this charge should be put in execution. If any say ther is iust cause & yet goeth on saying what, then? that will not serve you are you able to accuse any? My beloved it is not the manner of the court, it is o[ur] p[ar]te only to deliver the charge & to exhort you that if none be proud, that none would be proude, & if any be proud that they would be lesse proud, & if any be humble that they would be humble still, & if any be not humble that they would be, we are to charge you to enquire & be p[re]sent, & it is yo[ur] p[ar]te [that] shall receive the charge to examine if any be high-minded, & to accuse them, & if any be accused it is their parts to acquite & defend themselves, & to prove their innocencie if they [55v] be innocent, if not to sue to the lord speedely for p[ar]don, for feare least his heavy displeasure light vpon them.

When a Iudge giveth charge concerning treason, he wisheth I dare say w[ith] all his hart that his charge might be in vayne, rather then that he should fynd any who offend. A Phisition when he hath tempered his potio[n] dsyreth that it might be throwen in the chanell so [that] the patient may recover by some other meanes, & so it is my desyre that ther may not one man be found guiltie amonst all these hearers. I wish that this charge might be given in vayne, for those charges are best w[hich] are in vayne, and those sermons are best which are p[re]ached in vayne, I meane in vayne when ther is no need of them, but not if theyr be cause why this charge should be given such things should be spoken against & it be not corrected, so if ther be cause why this charge should be given I am sory. And if it came to be but [that] among so great riches, ther must be some pride, then hear the charge & search yo[ur]selves while ther is hope of grace, that you be not tried when ther is no hope of mercie, but only feare of damnation w[hich] [that] you may doe, I will enforme you how to trie yo[ur]selves, referring you to the records & braunches of the statutes of the lords high courte of parliament in heaven, laying them out vnto you. The points are .3. first whosever he is whose mind is so high, that he looketh on his bretheren as a man out of the top of a lead he is high minded, for as St Augustine sayth *excipe pompatica hæc, et volatica,* they are the same that you are; they have not *vestem communem* the same coate w[ith] you, but they have *cutem communem* the same skinne, and w[ith]in a fewe daies when as you die, if a man come w[ith] a Gomer & measure, all that you cary w[ith] you, they shall cary awaye as much w[ith] them as you, and w[ith]in a short time, a man shall not be able to [56] discerne betweene their shoulder blade & yo[urs], nor betwixt ther skull & yo[urs] ther skinne bone & sinnewes are all one w[ith] yours.

Therfore if any be a child of Anak *Nu[m]bers. 13. 34.* a looke downe, such a one as in whose sight his bretheren seeme like grasshoppers, or whether it appeare in drawing vp his eylids *Prov. 30. 13.* or in a proud looke *Psal. 101. 5.* such a one as David a man after god[es] owne heart could not beare his looke, & therfore god will abide it: or if ther be any that vse a proud dialect of speech as was that of Saules. 1. Sam. 20. 27. *vbi est filius iste Ishai* wher is this son of Ishai, or if he come to the Pharisees *non sum sicut iste Publicanus*, or if ther be any that be like the pikes that must have a long walke in their ponde[s], & none must come in ther way, they will suffer none to be in it but themselves, who thinke all the litle fishes to be made for them, & to serve them, no, no say of the poore, we care not w[hat] become of them so we may welter & wallow still in o[ur] wealth *Ezech. 11.3.* & (let vs build o[ur] houses & encrease o[ur] good[es]) who walke like roaring lyons, & can abide none to be w[ith] them *Zephan. 3.3.* & delight to be much feared, & will never be reconciled if they once take an offence, & will not suffer any iniury, but like Lamech *Gen. 4.* for one drop of bloud will have a mans life, or they will die for it, or will doe iniurye to whome they list, for why? we will have it so like *Hophni. 1. Sam. 2.15.* or except it be so we cannot governe like Iezebell. & therefore we will draw them before the iudgm[ent] seat[es] *Iames. 2.6.* & we will weary them out w[ith] law, as ther be many among vs who for trifles and matters of no valew will bring their bretheren before the iudgment seat, & set them before the throne, I say if ther be any such he is high minded.

Secondly he that climbeth so high that the boughes will beare hym no longer, he & his mind are both to high: if ther be any that beareth [56v] hymselfe beyond his abilitie & calling, wherof p[ro]ceed treasons *2. Timoth. 3.4.* & are become now despereate for that they have alreadie swolne more then their skin can hold, who lash on more of the leather then they are able to beare & so they are become προπετεις & their enterprises are προδοται, who when as they have lost all in one calling they would seeke to plant it agayne in another. Agayne consider whether they passe their calling, whether it be in excesse of diet as Nabal would be making a feast like a kyng whenas he was neither king nor magistrate but playne M[aster] Nabal, or whether it be in excesse of apparell, wherin the pride of England as the pride of Ephraim testifieth against her in her face *Hosh. 5.5.* or whether it be in lifting the gate to high, that is in excesse of building *Prov. 17.19.* or whether it be in keeping to great a trayne w[hich] was Esaus fault who must have in his trayne 400 *Gen. 32.6.* when as the fourth p[ar]te of them would have served his father Iaacob, or whether it be in making to high alliaunce as *2. Kings.14.9.* The thistle in Lebanon would needs mary the Cedars daughter, wherin they shall exceed their condition, or if ther be any who having skill in the law, (w[hich] is an excellent thing) or if there be any who be wise & expert in matters of pollicie, if they thinke p[re]sently they are so wise as no man is like them, & so thinke that by their wisdome they are able to master all cases, & to overrule all divinitie, & to teach the Bishops to governe, so stretching themselves above their lynes, as the Apostle saith *2. Cor. 20.14.* & so make the people to rise against the priests as the prophet *Hoshea 4.4.* complayneth, & will set themselves over all those that are set overe them in the lord. *1.Thess. 5.12.* w[hich] the Apostell rep[ro]veth very sharply *Rom. 12.* If I say ther be any such, he is high mynded.

[57] Thirdly if any man exalt his mind, any of both these wayes, the lord hath appoynted his prophets to prune them *Hoshea. 6.5.* & his word to pull downe all that shalbe exalted against it it [sic]. *2.Cor.20.4.* If ther be any man that setteth hymselfe w[ith] this shott, & is so high minded as [that] he will not beare the words of exhortation, nor cannot hear the charge, this man is very high minded. Nabal in *1.Sam. 25.17.* was so surrely in his riches, [that] he could not abide to be spoken vnto of his faults: & Abner. *2. Sam. 3.7.8.* for a word of his adulterous life, with one of Sauls minions, layd the plott, that cost his M[aster] Ishbosheth his kingdome. Ahab because *Miceah* the prophet would not tell him plausible things as the false prophets did, although he told hym true things professed enmitie towards hym, & wheras the false prophets were fed at his owne table, he tooke order for Miceahs dyet, that he should be fed w[ith] bread & water. If then ther be any that will not be trimmed & pruned by the word of god, who when he heareth the words of the curse blesseth himselfe in his hart, & promiseth peace vnto himselfe when he feeleth no shew of alteration in him, but walketh still according to the stubbornes of his owne heart *Deut. 29.19.* or if ther be any [that] in hearing the word of god, beyng but flesh & bloud will take vpon him to iudge of it, & say this is well spoken & this is spoken foolishly, so giving hymselfe to vaine babling & to counselling w[ith] flesh & bloud *Gal. 1.16.* this is the Pharisees case & let them know they scoffe at god & not at man: or if ther be any to whom the word of god is a reproch, & they be not delighted w[ith] it *Ierem. 6.20.* or if ther be any to whom the ephod seemeth contemptible as it did vnto Micol, these are high minded & they lift themselves vp not agaynst man but agaynst god, not agaynst the earth but agaynst the heaven, & if any man be so high minded he knoweth his case: Therfore love & reverence the word of god, it is [the] roote that doth beare you, the maiestie wherof keepeth all subiects in obedience: [57v] for if it were not for that the lord had saide *ego dixi dij estis*, a charge out of this o[ur] charge, the people would fall a maddering by & by, & the madnes of the world would not beare the maiestie of goverment [sic], but they would runne headlong & overthrow all chayres of estate, and all authoritie, for the rep[re]ssing of w[hich] synne, & punishing of it in Iacke straw you beare a worthy memoriall in yo[ur] scuchion of this citie. Therfore you must make much & esteeme of the word of God if you will continue long, you must hear this charge, for when you shall passe away it shall stand still, & if you will hear it, it will make you also to continue for ever.

This is the first point of the charge, concerning the w[hich] let every man doe his endevo[ur], to pull downe this pride, for the lord cannot abide it neither in the king *Deut. 17.20.* nor in the Angels in the epistle of Iude. 6. verse, much lesse in mortall men. This pride will never be pluckt vp so long as the root of it remayneth: the root of it is a vayne confidence in riches, not as some say a subordinary confidence in them, as in secondary meanes, but an inordinate confidence in them as *[blank]* to god, wherby we transfer the homage which is due to god, vnto a plate of sylver, or to a wedge of gold, & ther by vnto the devill, for *Dij gentium dæmonia sunt the gods of the heathen are divels* & the p[ro]phet David saith, that ther idols are sylver & gold, & we by an inversion may well say sylver & gold are the Idols of the rich of this world.

We may examine o[ur]selves heerof namely whether we make them o[ur] god[es] or no? by 2 wayes. the first is taken out of *Prov. 22.* we must search whether the lord be o[ur] strength & confidence or no, w[hich] we shall know if we consider what it is, which in all the neede we have we cleave fastest vnto, & what it is that in these cases cleaveth fastest vnto vs. ffor every thinge when as it is assaulted, moveth that first & trusteth that most wherin his [58] principall strength consisteth, whether it be his tuskes or his hornes or his taile. The poore man in his need trusteth in god & in his owne innocency that is his strength, & the horne of his salvation. *Psal. 18.* The mightie mans trust is in his might, of whom the p[ro]phet *Amos. 6.13.* sayth *that they reioyce in a thing of nought, and say have we not gotten vs hornes by our owne strength*. The rich mans confidence in his riches, so much saith he will discharge it, this much mony will dispatch such a case, so much will stop such a mans mouth, neither is god in all their cogitations. what will you then say vnto me, do you accuse any of this synne? No I accuse none p[ar]ticulerly, *Aures omniu[m] pulso et mentes* I speake in the eares of you all, & I speake to the conscience of you all.

The second meanes to know whether we make o[ur] riches o[ur] confidence, or no? is this, we must consider that as they be the first things that commeth to o[ur] mind, in o[ur] troubles, so whether it be the last meanes that we put in execution & the last that we flie vnto, as riches are vnto the rich man a strong citie. *Prov. 18.11.* & a sure castle to w[hich] after they are beaten from the walles, they fly for succo[ur]. And they when as they are forsaken of god, of all good men, & of the goodnes of ther owne cause & of the truth of ther matter, & that none of these will stand by them, yet the pride of their owne harts will not suffer them to let their cause fall, & then they flie vnto their riches, knowing that they will stand by them, & so wheras by reason of their vniust cause, they cannot say vnto the lord thou art my trust, then they runne vnto their money & make gold their hope, & say vnto the wedge of gold thou art my god & my confidence *Iob. 31.14.* thou shalt deliver me, & as thou hast redeemed me once, so I shalbe againe in the like danger redeemed of thee, therby putting his trust in the multitude of his riches *Psal. 52.7.* The p[ro]phet Micah pronounced a woe vnto them that

imagine iniquitie & worke wickednes because [58v] their hand[es] are mightie *cap.* *2.1.* But if any man can say, though I be rich yet w[ith] all my riches I have not done any thing against the truth but for the truth. *2. Cor. 13.8.* or if he can say though I be riche yet to doe evill I am poore,
5 although I be wise yet w[ith] all my wisdome I am foolish to doe evill, I dare discharge that man the court. Thinke this privately w[ith] yo[ur]selves, & I dare warrant you, if good [*sic*] be god & if ther be any truth in him, that, you shall obteyne peace & prosperitie by it, vse yo[ur] selves to this examination & you shall find great comfort in it at the last.
10 *Charge the rich men of this world that they be not high minded*, & why not high minded? the reason is added because riches are vncerteyne, & how vncerteyne, *Salomon* teacheth vs *They will vanish away (saith he) they have the wings of an eagle Prov. 23.5.* This is the vncertaintie of riches, now we have them, now we see them, let vs but turne o[ur]selves & looke for them
15 & they are gone. If we could pinion the wings of riches, or as St. Paule saith if we could nayle them downe, then were ther some cause why we might trust in them, but they are very vncerteyne, the harvest of the land is vncerteyne, but the harvest of^the water as^Isayah calleth it is much more vncerteyne. I know it is a reason why the m[ar]chants gaine should be the
20 greatest gayne, for that he putteth all that he hath on venture, & hazardeth his good[es] his body his life & all that he hath, for by sea men often loose their good[es], nay their bodies, & I doubt (& for a doubt I feare it is to true,) sometime they loose their soules also.
Agayne if riches be not vncerteine how then commeth it to passe that the
25 rich men themselves are so vncerteine, & be so soone vndone, & that he that was even a litle before of the greatest credite, now ther bills will not be taken, & the rich men themselves when as they deale one w[ith] another, doe [59] acknowledge this to be true in that they seeke such assurances & writings, yea more strong then any assurance? ffor why should they seeke
30 such assurances? but that they doe acknowledg heerby the vncerteyntie of riches. I know they p[re]tend mortalitie, for that men are mortall, but they meane indeed the mortality of riches. wherfore they are vncertayne Paule telleth vs they are vncerteyne, he calleth them men, but he by & by addeth the rich of this world, concerning which addition, divers writers both old &
35 new are of the opinion (as of the new M[aster] Calvin, St Augustine of the old) that this is an addition w[ith] a diminution, & as it were a barre in the armes wherby the vncertantye of riches are shewed, for that they are of this world, & as they are of this world, so must they savo[ur] of the same, & as the world is fickle, so must they likewise be fickle. *Charge them that they*
40 *trust not &c* He nameth not riches barely, but the vncertayntie of riches. This kind of speech is often vsed in the scriptures. *2. Iohn. 3.17.* the holy

ghost calleth them the world[es] good. *Mat. 13.22.* o[ur] Savio[ur] Christ calleth it the deceitfulnes of riches. David *Psal. 49.16.* Calleth it the glory of a mans house it is not the glory of man but the glory of his house, & *Salomon Prov. 3.16.* calleth them god[es] blessings: but he telleth vs w[ith]all, they are but the blessings of his left hand, for the blessings of his right hand are length of dayes & immortality, & this the holy ghost setteth downe to the end, [that] we should not ioy if we have a few minerals subiect vnto vs, but that in all humilitie & weldoyng towards o[ur] bretheren we should write o[ur] names certeyne in the booke of life.

Riches then are vncerteyne, & therfore vncerteyne because they are of this world, & yo^u must leave them to the world, they are none of yours. *Si vestra sint* (saith Gregory) *tollite ea vobiscum, ac no[n] vestra sunt, hic acquirunt[ur]* [59v] *hic dimittuntur, imò hic amittuntur.* If they be yo[urs] take them w[ith] you when you goe, but they are none of yo[urs], heer they are gotten, heer they are left nay heer they are lost. This is therfore the certeyntie of riches that they are vncerteyne, we must leave them when we die, or loose them while we live, they have *finem tuu[m]*, or *finem suum*, thy end on their owne end, yo^u must either leave them or they will leave you. Iob taried still butt his wealth left him, Dives went but his riches staid behind hym, Abraham & divers others staied & they staid w[ith] them. Paule in *2. Cor. 11.26.* whenas he would glory he gloryeth in his frailty in that he had bene in dangers & perils of waters, of robbers, of his owne nation, among the Gentiles, in the citie, in the wildernes, in the sea, and amongst false bretheren. Riches are in greater dangers then all these for to compare them, the Apostle was in p[er]ils of waters, they are in perill both of fyre and water, he was in danger of fyre robbers, they are in danger of robbers by land, & rovers by ~~saye~~ sea, he was in perill of his owne nation, they are in danger of o[ur] owne nation, & of others also, he was in danger in the citie, they are in danger in the citie, not only of yo[ur] familiar friends, servaunts & factors, but of straungers also, he was in perill of the wild beasts in the wildernes, they are in daunger both of the wild beast the Sycophant, & of the tame beast the flatterer, he was in daunger of the sea, they are in daunger both of shipwracke by sea & overthrow by land, he was in daunger of false bretheren, & so are they also in perill of false bretheren, namely of the wilfull bankrupt, & the deceitfull lawyer who are to deale the one of them w[ith] yo[ur] good[es], the other w[ith] yo[ur] deed[es] writings & evidences. *Musculus* writeth that when in a sermon he bad his hearers earnestly to beware of mothes, that [60] they laughed at hym & sayd theyr maydes would looke well inough vnto that, but he told them that his meaning was not so to be vnderstood as that he ment it of the mothes, that corrupted ther garm[ents], but (sayd he) what say you to those *vrbanæ*

tineæ those citie mothes those bankrupts, that eate vp & consume yo[ur] wealth, & what say you to those *forenses tineæ* those westminster hall moths (I trust I may speake it w[ith] the favo[ur] of the godlye lawyers ther) who devo[ur] & consume yo[ur] deed[es] & evidences. It is almost incredible to
5 consyder how great wealth these two mothes doe consume. Let it be that riches be certeyne, yet we shall have no certeynty of them, except we o[ur]selves also were certeyne, for ther can be no certeyntie of any two things to continue together, vnles both of them were certeyne, we take vpon vs to make leases of o[ur] land[es] & riches for 60 years when as we
10 o[ur]selves cannot have leases of them for 3 houres: when we have built o[ur] howses neu[er] so high, & filled o[ur] treasuries never so full, if god say vnto vs *hac nocte* this night shall they take thy soule from thee, we must then yeeld them backe to hym from whom we received them: The having of them is vncertayne. St Iames. 1.11. compareth them to the grasse w[hich]
15 withereth & whose flower fadeth. Ther is vncerteyntie in the getting of riches, & ther is vncerteyntie of the tarying of riches w[ith] vs, & of o[ur] tarying w[ith] them. But what if they were certeyne in their owne nature, what were we the better, vnles we were also certeyne to keep them, but this vncertainty in the keeping of them is double: the fyrst I know not neither
20 can you vnderstand it because of the mercifull governm[ent] of o[ur] prince, for some princ[es] when they fynd any one more subtle headed then the rest, whom they thinke fitt to serve their tourne, hym they favo[ur] & give countenance vnto, & place hym in authoritie abroad in the land, vsing them as instrum[ents] to looke into rich mens dealings, & to fynd
25 some faults therin, that so vpon the leasat occasion ther [60v] goods must be seased into the kings hand to encrease his treasury, & so at length also, when as these men themselves have gathered together great store of wealth, they will find some peeping hole into there estate also & empty them, vsing them as sponges when they swing about to gather water vntill they be full,
30 & then they wring them drye: but I say god be praised by reason of the gratious & peaceable goverm[ent] of o[ur] prince, neither can I vnderstand this my selfe, neither can I make you to vnderstand it.

The second vncertayntie is by reason of the vnquietnes of the estate, Iob compareth riches vnto cobwebs, all that w[hich] a man shall weave all his
35 life longe, in one halfe houre a barbarous souldyer shall come w[ith] his broome & sweepe it cleane away. Now we looke for great daungers & perilous tymes. And good cause why, for he that knoweth his m[asters] will & doth it not is worthy to be beaten w[ith] many stripes. We all for the most p[ar]te know o[ur] m[asters] will, but few practise it & therfore it must
40 needs be that we must be beaten w[ith] many troubles & therfore in this respect o[ur] riches remayne vncertayne to be kept.

The third vncertentie of riches is in respect of the conveyance of them, for when as we are not to keepe them o[ur] selves, yet if we were certeyne to whome we should leave them, ther were then some shew of certeyntie in them: doe not we say dayly that make enheritances, but god makes heyres, many a sonne rosteth not the venison their fathers gate in hunting, & the fathers dep[ar]te leaving their chests to theyr sonnes, who spend their wealth faster then the snow melteth against the sunne. flatter not yo[ur]-selves, deceive not yo[ur]selves, say not this is the way of the world that some should get & some should loose no my beloved it is not the course of nature, it is the iudgm[ent] of god, for by the course of nature, this [61] place might have enriched the realme w[ith] many worshipfull & honorable families, but fewe of them remayne now, though we see that by the course of nature, some of them have continued 500 yeares. say not therfore that this is the way of the world, but it is the way of the iudgm[ent] of the lord against some for the evill getting ther good[es], agaynst othersome for the evill keeping them, & if you will not hearken to the lords charge yo[u] shall also tast the same in iudgm[ent] although not in this life yet in the life to come.

The last vncertayntie of riches is in respect of the ten[ure] & possession, ther are troubles in the getting of them, troubles in the keeping of them, & troubles in the bestowing of them, yet they bring this certeyntie w[ith] them in theyr vncerteynty that we must leave them behind vs. Iob sayth naked came I into the world, & we must cary away nothing w[ith] vs: but we must cary away w[ith] vs all o[ur] syns, yo[ur]s teno[urs] yo[ur] possessions yo[ur] fruitions & enioying of them & yo[ur] conveyances are all vncerteine. This is a large point & I shold never get out of it except I breake it of: ther is one behind w[hich] is worst of all, these things are vncerteine but this is certeine, yo[ur] pride will not forsake you it will goe w[ith] you, the synnes that you commit will follow you & cleave fast vnto you, when yo[ur] riches shall leave you, & this certeyntie of synne breed[es] the vncerteyntie of yo[ur] soules, as Iob saith 27.8. *what avayleth it the hypocrite when he hath heaped up riches if god take away his soule*: then is he as the staffe of reede *Isay. 38.6.* wherupon if a man leaue it will goe through the hand, I have knowen some that have wished that they had never seene the riches w[hich] they now see, if at the houre of death they might not see those synnes w[hich] they doe see: this poynt would be well stood vpon, for heervpon is it that Chrisostome saith if all the creatures in the world [61v] had teares they would poure them all fourth for this cause my beloved it is the gratious hand of god that the wealth of the world should so totter & reele, because we should not set o[ur] stay & rest vpon it, but one the lord of heaven, for if now that it is so brickle & so vncerteine fond men set their delight so much one it: what would they do if the lord had made it certeyne? then what poore mens right? what widowes copy? or what orphanes legacy should be free from invasion?

Charge them that be rich men in this world that they be not high minded neither trust in the vncerteinty of riches, but that they trust in God. The 3d poynt of the charge is this that they should trust in god. The apostle battereth not downe the castle, but that he erecteth them another to trust in. So the wise man Salomon *Prov. 18.10.11.* when he throweth downe the castle of the rich man, he opposeth & setteth vp against it the castle of the iust, w[hich] is the name of the lord, *qui vult securus sperare, speret in eo qui non potest perire*, who never deceived neither himselfe nor those that trusted in hym, in whom is no vncerteyntie, no not so much as any variablenes or shadow of change. *Iames. 1.11.* he faileth none that trust in hym, that look vpon hym, that fancy nothing but hym.

Charge them that they trust in the living God. The reason why he would have them trust in god is for that he is a living god, he is no dead Idoll, he is not like the canker & moth eaten gods, who are dead, & neither give life to themselves, nor to you, nay it cannot p[re]serve life, nor take away the least disease from you, neither the ache from yo[ur] teeth, nor the palsie from yo[ur] hand[es], nor the gowte from yo[ur] feet, neither can it adde one heares breadth to yo[ur] stature, nor one minute to the howre of yo[ur] life this canker eaten god (as o[ur] Savio[ur] Christ saith) must be kept vnder [62] locke & key from the thiefe, it is a shame to trust in this moth eaten god, w[hich] if you stay but a day or two you shall see inough of it hang out in yo[ur] streets: oh trust not in them, let it never be sayd that the livinge trust in the dead, as the p[ro]phet Aggai exhorteth, but trust in the living God, who giveth you life & is able to quicken you, so p[re]serve, & deliver you & for this mortall life to give you an immortall life, *qui vivit et dat vitam* who is not only a living god but he is also a giving God, he geteth vs not onely life & yeares, & dayes, but he also giveth vs hornes w[ith] w[hich] we may both defend o[ur] life, & run agaynst those that would take it from vs, he giveth vs all things, for the earth is the lords & all that therin is, all the earth is his temple, silver & gold are the lords, he giveth them vnto ~~you~~ thee, he might have given them to the brother of lowe estate, & he might make thee stand at his gate, as he standeth now at thine.

He geveth vs riches, we gett them not by o[ur] wisdome or pollicie, for you see many men wiser then yo[ur] selves who want them many men of vnderstanding have them not, neither all those that labo[ur] for them: but they are the gift of god, & except the lord blesse yo[ur] labors it is in vayne for you to rise earely or to lie downe late & to eate the bread of sorrow *Psal. 127.* why are you then so proud of them? The lord giveth them the lord will take them away: he giveth vs all things aswell corporall as spirituall aswell temporall as eternall he giveth vs althings even *a pane nostro quotidiano* from o[ur] dayly bread *vsque ad regnu[m] cæloru[m]* to the kingdom of heaven, in the end of the same prayer he giveth vs all things even vnto hymselfe, himselfe & all.

Then if all that we have be meere donative, & that we hold all [that] we have by franke almoigne at the will of the will of the lord [sic] only [62v] consydering ther is no other tenure nor no othere custome in o[ur] lord[es] court, If I say it be so why boast you then of any of any thing, *quid non accepisti*, name any one thing that you have not received & boast of that: If this be true that you have nothing but that you have received, why boast you so of yo[ur] riches? But conclude w[ith] Ciprian who hath a worthy sentence often cited by St Augustine *De nullo gloriandu[m] est quia nullu[m] est nostru[m]*, adde vnto it *Nulli fidendu[m] est quia nullum est nostru[m]*. we must glory of nothing for that we have nothing or o[ur] owne, neither must we trust any thing, for that we have nothing of o[ur]selves, let vs trust in god that giveth all things to every one to enioy, for it is the great goodnes of god that not only giveth vs all things to have them, but it is the same goodnes of god that giveth vs to enioy them, for to have & possesse any thing w[ith]out making vse & benefit of it is an vntimely byrth, but blessed be god that hath not onely given vs all things plenteously to possess but that hath also given vs health p[ro]speryty & peace to enioy them, so that every one may eate his portion w[ith] ioye, he hath not dealt w[ith] vs as he hath dealt w[ith] the poore, he hath not given vs things for vse onely & necessity, but for fruition & pleasure, he giveth the Israelits not only manna for food but also quailes for lust *Psal. 78.* he giveth Salomon not only horse & lynnen for necessity, but apes, ivory & peacocks for pleasure *2. Chron. 9. 12.* he hath given the poore *indumenta* clothing for need, but he hath given you *ornamenta* coverings for comelynes he hath given them alimenta norishm[ents] for their food, but he hath given you *delectamenta* delicates for pleasure. Trust therfore in him as he reioiceth in yo^u, & hath given you such abundance of good things so plenteously, so as plenteously may Israell now say hath the lord powred his blessings vpon vs, you could not alwayes say so, but now you may say blessed be god [63] that blesseth vs w[ith] such blessings, yea blessed be the people w[hich] are so blessed, & blessed is the people whose god is the lord. This would move the harts of all p[ro]fessors, & stirre them vp to be thankfull vnto the lord who giveth all things, ther is no goodnes to the lord[es], he geueth all things w[ith]out exprobration, w[ith]out except, beyond compentency, plenteously, this is a violent argum[ent], if this will not p[er]swade you to be thankfull, you shall not need Moses nor o[ur] Savio[ur] Christ to teach you,

for the devill hymselfe will teach you, for he saith *Iob. 1. 9.10.11.* vnto the
lord, doth Iob feare thee for nought, thou hast made a hedge about him &c
if Iob be so affected then learne you also my beloved to feare god, & to be
thankfull vnto hym because he hath so blessed you, it must needs be a great
fault in any man, that the devill findeth fault w[ith], but especially it must
be a great fault in rich men, & he must need[es] be very vnthankfull when
the devill reproveth, if the lord will not condemne you for it the devill will.

Charge the rich of this world that they doe good and be rich in good workes &c
Ther enioying must be ioyned w[ith] well doyng: this last point was very
plausible concerning the plenty of those things w[hich] we receive of the
lord: but heerof the Apostle inferreth this consequent vpon that Antecedent, if [the] lord hath bestowed so many good things vpon you, & hath
given you all things plenteously to enioy, then you ought also to doe good
by giveing to others: if god have given you all things then how much the
more you give to those that want, so much the more like are you vnto hym,
& if the lord give vnto you to the end that you should distribute &
p[ar]ticipate vnto others why then should you goe about to make the
bushell great & the pecke small as the prophet Amos saith, & so bring the
plenty of heaven into the pe=[63v]nurie of the earth. The Apostle telleth
you heer that you must be ready to distribute, you must be riche &
plenteous in all good works, that you may have plenty for ever *Prov.
11.25.* and this doth the Apostle inferre very well of a very godly zeale to
the godly, that if the lord have given you πρόσκαιρον ἀπόλαυσιν not for a
fewe dayes or weeks but for all yo[ur] dayes, then you must bestowe one
yo[ur] bretheren, that yo[ur] enioying may be ioyned, w[ith] well doyng,
that you yo[ur] selves may doe well & p[ro]sper, & so the lord bring
weldoyng vpon England.

The Apostle could not have devised to have placed it more excellently
then heer because o[ur] to much enioying spoileth o[ur] weldoing, o[ur] to
much lavishnes eateth & destroyeth o[ur] riches so that we cannot exercise
iustice, distributative & commutative w[hich] S[t] Basill com[ar]eth to the 7
leane kyne that ate vp & devoured the seven fat kine, & to the 7 leane eares
w[hich] consumed the 7 fatt eares, so p[ro]digalitie destroyeth all good
doyng as he saith φιλοτιμία *est ὡς ἀκολασίας* ambition is as the whetstone
of p[ro]digalitie, w[hich] whetteth it to so sharpe, that it maketh it shave so
cleane & cut so deepe, that it leaveth vs but a little wealth to practise o[ur]
weldoyng, therfore ther must be lesse pride amongst vs before ther be more
weldoing for pride breedeth p[ro]digalitie.

Heer the apostle teacheth vs [that] ther be two vses of o[ur] wealth, the
first concerning the fruition of it, the second concerning the true vse of it.
we must not only enioy o[ur] wealth, but we must doe good also, we must

not doe the one alone, but we must doe both together as the wise man techeth vs *Prov. 5.15.* that ther must be 2 vses of the water in the cisterne, fyrst that thou mayst drinke of it thyselfe, they must be thyne & thyne only, but yet the founteines must flow foorth into the **[64]** streets: So the lord hath poured water into o[ur] cisterne, not only that we should enioy it but that others also should take good by it: & a wiser then Salomon, o[ur] Svio[ur] Iesus Christ *Iohn. 13.* hath 2 vses of his bagge, the first to furnish them w[ith] things necessary: secondly to give to the poore: this was the vse of o[ur] Savio[ur] Christs purse, & if yo[urs] be like his it must be the vse of yo[urs] also. A great many know no more vse of their wealth then the brute beasts & vnreasonable creatures, who reioyce alwaies to have p[ro]vender in the manger & to have their furniture fayre & new about them. Many know no more vse of their wealth then *Dives* did *Luke. 16.12.* to fare deliciously every daye, & to pamper their bodies, & if he have any regard of his pewfellow the soule, it is w[ith] the other rich epicure in the Gospell who said to his soule, my soule take thy rest & be mery for thou hast store laid vp for thee for many yeares, who looked for no other ioy in the life to come, but we must looke for treasures in heaven, & therefore we are to know another vse of o[ur] riches namely to doe good & to be rich in good works. let vs thus thinke on god. This wealth that I see heer he hath given me to enioy & to doe good w[ith]all, the fyrst vse of my riches I have had long inough, now what have I done in the second. These rich men enioy litle ioy that fayle in the second vse: The two rich men in the gospell had abundance, they enioyed much and so doe I, but the other ioy they had not, why? they did no good. Abraham enioyed his riches & had another ioy w[ith]all & received lazarus into his bosome because he received hym into his bosome heer vpon earth: so also did Iob, & so did zacheus Therfore o lord give me thy grace to enioy that ioy heer, that I may enioy the other ioy in heaven w[ith] Abraham, & that my life may be like theirs, w[ith] whom I wish my soule to be.

[64v] Thirdly we are to see what it is to doe good. If you aske me what it is to doe good, it is not as the world saith not to doe hurt (for men thinke now adayes, that he is an honest man who doth no harme to his neighbors) but it is *facere aliquid boni* to doe some good thing. The saying of St Augustine is most excellent in this sence, *quod non vultis facere illud bonu[m] non est*, that w[hich] you will not doe that is not good, so [that] to doe good is to doe some good thing, & not to doe no harme. It were a happy thing if this saying of Augustine might be affirmed of vs all. But the Papists speake it to the common obloquy of the whole realm that you will not doe that w[hich] is good, they say that in the p[ro]testants religion hath an attractive vertue in it, for they draw riches vnto them & hold them very fast but they have the gout in their feet, the palsey in their fingers, & the [*blank*] in theyr bowels, when they should give any thing either to the reliefe of the poore, or to the redemption of captives, they say we are become as horseleaches, of whom Solomon speaketh who crie still give give, bring in bring in, but there is no geving out: have you no regard vnto this? be diligent to doe good, give to them that want, I call for it to discharge my owne soule, I call for it, & I take God to witnes I call for it: to you therfor to you that have wherw[ith] you may doe good I call for it, tell me not of yo[ur] faith *Iames. 2.18.* nor of thy religion, of w[hich] you heard very notablie yesterday. if thou doest no good thou hast no faith, thou hast no religion, doe good or you will never be able to aunswere it in the iudgment day, whenas you shall not be asked of the height & depth of yo[ur] mony, neither of the multitude of yo[ur] riches, but captives you have redeemed, what fatherles children you have holpen, what widowes you have visited, then what will you answere? You have heard what it is to doe good, namely to visite the [65] fatherles & the widowes & to redeeme captives. I beseech you therfore to doe that is good. I speake not as though I thought the Papists assertion to be true, but I forbid them in any popish citie in christendome to shew such a company of fatherles children brought vp so as these are w[hich] are heer before yo[ur] eyes, w[hich] are but a handfull of the whole heape, or els to read of the like in all the world, I flatter not, be it spoken to the glory of the eternall god, *non nobis domine, non nobis sed nomini tuo gloriam tribue*, not vnto vs lord, not vnto vs, but to thy name geve the glory *Psal. 115.* I will prove it that learning in the foundation & amplifying of colledges, & the mayntenance of the poore, in giving perpetuities to almes howses is more encreased w[ith]in these 40 yeares last past when o[ur] gospell did begin to flourish (& not then first start vp as they say) then in any 40 yeares vnder popery. I speake p[ar]tly of myne owne knowledge, & p[ar]tly by good information, & so comparing 30 yeares w[ith] 30 yeares or 40 yeares w[ith] 40 yeares, so many time for time in the time of light, shall match so many in the time of darknes But yet this I must say, that we have had a greater peace & a more quiet tyme then ever they had, & therfore we should πλεονάζεσθαι 2. *Pet. 1.8.* we should abound in good workes & exceed them. This is more then they reckon of, yet looke not to them but to yo[ur]selves & come one so farre that yo[u] may snaffle them in this theme, [that] they may not once open their mouthes in this matter, thus it should be & thus o[ur] gospell requireth, doe good to others, be beneficiall to those that communicate w[ith] you in spirituall things, but so also as that you be beneficiall to yo[ur] bretheren in Christ Iesus, for this end it may be the lord hath given you yo[ur] wealth. Ester came to the kingdome & Nehemiah to his great authoritie for this end, namely that they should be covering ~~the~~ Cherubes to the church of god, & stretch their wings over it *Ezech. 28.* & if you be covering Cherubims to the church of god, & to the people in this world you shall **[65v]** syng w[ith] the Cherubims in the world to come: Heer have these two daies bene made very iust complaint of symony & selling of spirituall livings wherof the Papists accuse vs not seying it in themselves, for the Pope as he hath dispenced w[ith] the subiects othes to their princes^against the 3d commandm[ent], stirring [the] subiects to rebellion^against ~~the~~ their princes whom they depose from governm[ent] (as in the bull of *Pius Quintus, dicimus Reginam Elizabetham cecidisse ab omni iure regnandi* we affirme that the Queene Elizabeth hath no right to governe) against the fift commandment as he hath dispenced w[ith] murther & poisoning of princ[es], as of the late prince of *Orange* against the 6. commandm[ent] (as w[ith] the death of the late prince of *Orange*,) & as he hath dispensed w[ith] fornication & the synne of vncleannes (in the mayntenance of their stewes) against the 7 commandement, so hath he of late also sent over his dispensations & licenses to all popish patrones in this land to sell their benefices for as much as they can, even if it might be w[ith] the sound of a drumme, so as they send over some small portion to the relief of Papists beyond the seas, & to the maintenance of their seminaries. But to leave them you must doe good & be plenteous in good works, In succoring the necessitie of the Saints you must have yo[ur] bosomes open heer to receive *Lazarus* into yo[ur] bosomes, it were a goodly sight to see Lazarus in a rich mans bosome, & ther shall be never a rich man w[ith] Lazarus in his bosome in heaven, vnles he have had a lazarus in his bosome heer on earth, who hath not relieved the comfortles estate of the poore, the weake estate of orphanes, the miserable estate of widowes, the distressed estate of strangers, the discouraged estate of poore schollers, all those must be succored, but ther are other w[hich] must not be succored, w[hich] are those idle vagabond beggers, w[hich] lie in the streets. I hope ther wilbe honorable regard taken of this matter The strangers that are succored by vs have this care of the poore, that they **[66]** relieve them so as none of them goe about, shall they have this care of the poore that they relieve them, & shall we that are their succorors be lesse carefull of o[ur] poore then they: let vs p[ro]vide for this matter, & so shall we doe great good to them in redeeming their bodyes from divers dangerous & noisome diseases, to their soules in redeeming them from idlenes & other syns w[hich] abound among them, to the common welth in redeeming to it many rotten members w[hich] may heerafter doe good in it, & then you shall have the blessing of god vpon you, even that blessing that ther shall not be a beggar in the street. You have the substance have also the quality be rich in good works, & not in good word[es], not in the goodnes of the tongue, but in the goodnes of the hand, be rich in good doyng. you must not be like the tree that Plinie speaketh of, that beareth leaves as broad as any target, but his frute is not as big as a beane. You must not talke targets & do beanes, you must not talke in set speech, & quainted termes wherin much of o[ur] religion consisteth now a dayes, but you must doe good, but now men had rather build them barnes to put in πάντα τὰ ἀγαθα all ther good[es], then to be rich in good works & releving the poore. what? may not then a man be rich? yes, saith the apostle some may be rich, but they must not have all in their barnes, the apostle would not have them not to be rich, but he would have them to be rich in the world to come. If thou be be [*sic*] *dives in arca* rich^in^the chest, see whether thou be *dives in conscientia* rich in they conscience: thou art so rich in the queenes bookes, so thou be also so rich in god[es] booke, thou art so much worth *in terra morientiu[m]* in the land of the dying, see that thou be so much worth *in terra vivantiu[m]* in the land of the living. Paule p[er]swadeth thee that thou be rich in doyng good, **[66v]** for to doe good sparingly *2. Cor. 8.* that belongeth to the brother of base estate. It is not yo[ur] worke. in the law at the building of the tabernacle, the poore gave hear & badgers skins toward[es] it, the rich gave silke purple gold & sylver, & o[ur] Savio[ur] Christ in the gospell requireth that they to whom much is geven, should give much, & as you are seased in the queenes bookes so are you bound to p[er]forme accordingly: & as you are seased in god[es] books so are ye bound to p[er]forme. you must abound in good workes you must περισσεῦσαι *Gal. 6*.

And you must ποστιζεδς^προίστασθαι^that is goe before yo[ur] bretheren *Titus. 3.8.* as you are knights, Aldermen, m[asters], wardens of the livery of yo[ur] companyes & so are in abilitie before others, so must you also in good works be before others. Yo[ur] sonnes gayne & prophet is so much, it commeth in so fast as great bookes of accounts will scarcely hold it, but a litle scrole not to bigge as my hand will hold yo[ur] liberalities, you will spend at a banket you know not what, what you will give to the redeeming of captives all the world seeth what. Yo[ur] enioying shall cost you pounds, but for well doing pence will suffice. ther is no coherence in this.

Heer I might charge & exhort you in the name of god the father & the lord Iesus Christ, who shall apeare in flames of fire & w[ith] his mightie angels, to render vengence to them that obey not the gospell I might pray you in the name of the father who hath loved you, & called you to his holy calling that you receive not this charge of me but of the lord hymselfe, Looke not vpon me I beseech you, for I most willingly acknowledg my selfe vnmeet to give this charge, & more fit to receive it my selfe, beyng a man compassed w[ith] the same infirmities that you are, although I might commaund you, yet according to humanity I bessech you **[67]** looke not one me but on the lord Iesus Christ, who gave me in charge to speake: deceive not yo[ur]selves, surely ther is a heaven, ther is a hell, ther will be a iudgm[ent], ther will be day wherin we shalbe demaunded of that we have received of the lord. & you of that you have received from vs. thinke not that when this charge is ended it will vanish away & so regard it not. But the daye will come when it shalbe requyred at yo[ur] hand[es]: w[hich] day wilbe fearfull to those who in regard of ther riches thinke basely of ther bretheren.

 Therfore when tyme & ability serveth thinke of this day you never stood in such need as you doe now, thinke of it that though it tary in comming yet when it commeth it wilbe a heavy day, & therfore lay vp for yo[ur]selves a sure foundation, against that day by doying good & beyng rich in good works & relieving the poore, succoring of the fatherles & redeeming of the captivs: This is not a casting away of riches but a treasuring vp of them, it is not a doyng of good to others alone but also to yo[ur]selves. And for this sandy foundation w[hich] endureth but for a tyme, it is the laying vp of a steady foundation on w[hich] you may lift vp yo[ur] stately buildings, w[hich] beyng founded they will stand sure. And this is indeed to be high minded: oh be so high minded, Paule had this ending in this exhortation & this shall be my end, & I beseech god it may be all o[ur] ends.

APPENDIX 2

Table of Correspondence
Sermon at St Mary's Hospital, 1588

XCVI Sermons (this edn., pp. 59–118) page & line nos.	St Paul's MS 38F22.01 (*APPENDIX 1*) page & line nos.
40.1–11	243.1–9
40.12–41.7	243.10–29
41.12–27	243.30–244.12
41.28–42.18	244.13–36
42.18–32	244.36–245.8
42.33–43.32	245.9–246.3
42.33–44.7	246.3–24
44.8–12	246.21–3
44.13–34	246.24–38
44.35–39	246.40–247.3
44.39–45.2	*om.*
45.3–32	247.3–34
45.33–4	*om.*
45.35–46.23	247.34–248.22
46.24–34	248.22–29
46.34–47.2	*om.*
47.2–11	248.29–37
47.12–20	248.37–249.6
47.21–48.35	249.7–250.14
48.35–39	*om.*
49.1–37	250.15–41
49.37–50.8	*om.*
50.9–52.4	251.1–252.8
52.5–53.12	252.9–253.9
53.13–54.3	253.10–32
54.4–55.4	253.32–254.20
55.5–7	*om.*
55.8–38	254.21–255.5
56.1–4	*om.*
56.5–57.2	255.5–32
57.3–58.9	255.33–256.26

58.10–17	om.
58.18–59.10	256.26–257.3
59.11–12	om
59.12–14	257.4–5
59.14–18	om.
59.19–32	257.5–14
59.33–61.8	257.15–258.17
61.9–41	258.17–259.7
62.1–63.2	259.8–38
63.3–65.16	259.39–260.34
65.16–66.4	om.
66.5–68.2	260.34–261.37
68.3–69.14	262.40–263.32
69.14–71.11	om.
71.12–73.7	261.37–262.40
73.8–79.33	om.
79.34–80.20	363.33–264.8
80.20–39	264.9–20
81.1–7	om.

EXPLANATORY NOTES

ABBREVIATIONS USED IN MARGINALIA

Biblical

Abac.	Habbakuk
Act.(s.)	Acts
Ag.	Haggai
Am.	Amos
Apoc.	Apocalypse (Revelation)
Cant.	Canticles (Song of Songs, or of Solomon)
1, 2 Chro.	1, 2 Chronicles
Colos.	Colossians
1, 2 Cor.	1, 2 Corinthians
Dan.	Daniel
Deut.	Deuteronomy
Eccles.	Ecclesiastes
Ecclus., Eccus.	Ecclesiasticus
Eph., Ephes.	Ephesians
Es., Esa, Esai., Esay.	Esay (Isaiah)
Est.	Esther
Exod.	Exodus
Ezek., Eze.	Ezekiel
Gal.	Galatians
Gen., Genes.	Genesis
Hab.	Habbakuk
Hag.	Haggai
Heb.	Hebrews
Hos.	Hosea
Isai.	Isaiah
Jac., Ja., Jam.	James
Jer.	Jeremiah
1, 2, 3 Jo.	1, 2, 3 John
Joh., Johan.	John
1, 2 Kin., King.	1, 2 Kings
Lam.	Lamentations
Lev., Levit.	Leviticus
Luc., Luk.	Luke
1, 2 Mac.	1, 2 Maccabees
Mal.	Malachi
Mar.	Mark
Mat., Matt., Matth.	Matthew
Mic.	Micah
Nehem., Nehe.	Nehemiah

Num., Numb.	Numbers
1, 2 Par.	1, 2 Paralipomenon (Vulg.; = 1, 2 Chron.)
1, 2, 3 Pet.	1, 2, 3 Peter
Phil., Philip.	Philippians
Prov., Pro.	Proverbs
Psal., Ps., Pss.	Psalm(s)
1, 2 Reg.	1, 2 Kings
Rev.	Revelation
Rom.	Romans
1, 2 Sam.	1, 2 Samuel
Sap.	Sapientia (Wisdom)
1, 2 Thess., Thes.	1, 2 Thessalonians
1, 2 Tim.	1, 2 Timothy
Tit.	Titus
Zach.	Zacharia
Zeph.	Zephaniah

Other

Ver.	Verse
Cap.	Caput (chapter)
Ep., Epist.	Epistle
Hom.	Homily
Lib., l.	Liber (book)
Obj.	Objection
Resp.	Response
Serm.	Sermon

ABBREVIATIONS USED IN COMMENTARY

Place of publication is London unless otherwise stated.

Andrewes's Works

AS	ΑΠΟΣΠΑΣΜΑΤΙΑ SACRA: or A Collection of Posthumous and Orphan Lectures... Never before extant, ed. anon., pref. by Thomas Pierce (1657)
LACT	Works of Andrewes, in The Library of Anglo-Catholic Theology, ed. J. P. Wilson and J. Bliss (Oxford, 1841–54), as follows: vols. i–v, XCVI Sermons (1841–3) vol. vi, Pattern of Catechistical Doctrine and Other Minor Works (ed., anonymously, by Charles Eden (ODNB), 1846) vol. vii, Tortura Torti (1851) vol. viii, Responsio ad Apologiam Cardinalis Bellarmini (1851) vol. ix, Opuscula Quædam Posthuma [Latin works only] (1852) vol. x, Preces Privatæ (1853) vol. xi, Two Answers to Cardinal Perron, and other Miscellaneous Works [includes English works from OP] (1854)

OP	*Reverendi in Christo Patris, Lanceloti, Episcopi Wintoniensis, Opuscula Quædam Posthuma*, ed. William Laud and John Buckeridge (1629)
Preces	*The Preces Privatæ of Lancelot Andrewes*, ed. and trans. F. E. Brightman (1903; repr. Gloucester, Mass., 1983)
XCVI	*XCVI. Sermons by... Lancelot Andrewes*, ed. William Laud and John Buckeridge (1629)

All citations of Andrewes's catechetical lectures, unless otherwise stated, are to *The Pattern of Catechistical Doctrine* (1650).

Patristic, Theological, and Liturgical Texts

ACW	*Ancient Christian Writers*, ed. J. Quasten et al. (Westminster, Md., and London, 1946–67; Westminster, Md., 1970–)
ANCL	*Ante-Nicene Christian Library* (25 vols., Edinburgh, 1864–97)
BCP	*The Boke of Common Praier* (1559)
FC	*Fathers of the Church* (Washington, DC, 1947–)
FEWRH	*The Folger Library Edition of the Works of Richard Hooker*, W. Speed Hill, gen. ed. (7 vols., Cambridge, Mass., 1977–89)
LF	*Library of the Fathers of the Holy Catholic Church* (43 vols., Oxford, 1838–74)
PG	*Patrologia Græcæ*, ed. J. P. Migne (162 vols., Paris, 1857–66)
PL	*Patrologia Latina Database* (Chadwick-Healey, 1995) = *Patrologia Latina*, ed. J. P. Migne (221 vols., Paris, 1844–64)
Summa	Thomas Aquinas, *Summa Theologica*, ed. and trans. Thomas Giltz et al., 61 vols. (1964–81)
[Luther,] *Werke*	*Luthers Werke im WWW* (ProQuest Information and Learning Co.); = Luther, *Wiemarer Ausgabe* (100 vols., Weimar, 1883)
[Luther,] *Works*	*Luther's Works*, ed. J. Pelikan and H. T. Lehmann (54 vols., St Louis, 1955–76)

Libraries

BL	British Library
Bodl.	Bodleian Library, Oxford
CUL	Cambridge University Library
PCCL	Pembroke College Cambridge Library

Other Reference Works

Foster	Joseph Foster (ed.), *Alumni Oxoniensis... 1500–1714*, 4 vols. (Oxford, 1891–2).
McK	R. B. McKerrow, *Printers' and Publishers' Devices in England and Scotland, 1485–1640* (1949)
ODNB	*The Oxford Dictionary of National Biography* (Oxford, 2004–5)
OED	*Oxford English Dictionary*
STC	Pollard and Redgrave, *A Short-Title Catalogue of Books Printed in England, Scotland, and Ireland... 1475–1640*, 2nd edn., 3 vols. (1976–91)

Tilley	Maurice Palmer Tilley, *A Dictionary of the Proverbs in England in the Sixteenth and Seventeenth Centuries* (1950)
Venn	John Venn and J. A. Venn, *Alumni Cantabrigiensis... to 1751*, 4 vols. (Cambridge, 1922–7).
Wing	Donald V. Wing, *A Short-Title Catalogue... of English Books... 1641–1700*, 3 vols. (1945–51)

Biblical

AV	Authorized ('King James') Version (1611)*
Bishops'	*The. Holie. Bible.* (1568)*
Douai-Rheims	*The Holie Bible... out of the authentical Latin* (Douai, 1609–10)*
cap.	Lat., 'caput' (chapter)
Geneva	*The Bible... according to the Ebrew and Greeke* (1587)*
juxt. Hebr.	Vulg., Psalms, from Hebrew
juxt. LXX	Vulg., Psalms, from Septuagint
LXX	Septuagint
NT	New Testament
OT	Old Testament
Trem.	*Biblia Sacra sive libri canonici... facti ab I[mmanuel] Tremellio & F[rancisco] Junio* (1581)
v., vv.	verse, verses
Vulg.	*Biblia Sacra Iuxta Vulgatem Versionem*, ed. B. Fischer et al. (Stuttgart, 1969)

* From *The Bible in English Database* (Chadwick-Healey, 1996)

OTHER WORKS FREQUENTLY CITED

In addition to standard patristic and biblical texts, the following primary and secondary sources are used frequently throughout the commentary, cited in short form.

Cardwell, Edward, *Documentary Annals of the Reformed Church of England*, new edn., 2 vols. (Oxford, 1844).
Calvin, John, *Institutes of the Christian Religion by John Calvin*, trans. Henry Beveridge, 2 vols. (1879; repr. 1957).
Chamberlain, John, *The Letters of John Chamberlain*, ed. N. E. McClure, 2 vols. (Philadelphia, 1939).
Collinson, Patrick, *The Elizabethan Puritan Movement* (1967; repr. Oxford, 1990).
Donne, John, *The Sermons of John Donne*, ed. George Potter and Evelyn Simpson, 10 vols. (Berkeley, 1953–62).
—— *Complete English Poems*, ed. C. A. Patrides, new edn., rev. Robin Hamilton (1994).
Ferrell, Lori Anne, *Government by Polemic: James I, the King's Preachers, and the Rhetorics of Conformity* (Stanford, Calif., 1998).
Fincham, Kenneth (ed.), *The Early Stuart Church, 1603–1642* (Basingstoke, 1988).
Fulke, William, *Works*, ed. C. H. Hartshorne and R. Gibbings, 2 vols. (Parker Society, vols. 17, 18; Cambridge, 1843, 1848).
Isaacson, Henry, *The Life and Death of... Lancelot Andrewes*, printed with Thomas Fuller, *Abel Redivivus* (1651).
Lake, Peter, 'The Laudian Style: Order, Uniformity and the Pursuit of the Beauty of Holiness in the 1630s', in Fincham (ed.), *Early Stuart Church*, 161–86.
—— 'Lancelot Andrewes, John Buckeridge, and Avant-Garde Conformity at the Court of James I', in Peck (ed.), *Mental World*, 113–33.
Lossky, Nicholas, *Lancelot Andrewes the Preacher (1555–1626)*, trans. Andrew Louth (Oxford, 1991).
MacCulloch, Diarmaid, *Tudor Church Militant: Edward VI and the Protestant Reformation* (1999).
McCullough, Peter, 'Making Dead Men Speak: Laudianism, Print, and the Works of Lancelot Andrewes, 1626–1642', *Historical Journal*, 41 (1998), 401–24.
—— *Sermons at Court: Politics and Religion in Elizabethan and Jacobean Preaching* (Cambridge, 1998).
Milton, John, *Complete Shorter Poems*, ed. John Carey (1968).
—— *Paradise Lost*, ed. John Carey (1967).
Neale, J. E., *Elizabeth I and her Parliaments*, 2 vols. (1953).
Peck, Linda Levy, *The Mental World of the Jacobean Court* (Cambridge, 1991).
Shakespeare, William, *The Complete Works*, ed. Stanley Wells and Gary Taylor (Oxford, 1986).
Story, G. M., *Lancelot Andrewes: Sermons* (Oxford, 1967).
Tyacke, Nicholas, 'Lancelot Andrewes and the Myth of Anglicanism', in Peter Lake and Michael Questier (eds.), *Conformity and Orthodoxy in the English Church c.1560–1660* (2000), 5–33.
Voak, Nigel, *Richard Hooker and Reformed Theology* (Oxford, 2003).
Welsby, Paul A., *Lancelot Andrewes* (1958).

TWO MOST EXCELLENT PRAIERS...

Text. THE WONDERFULL | Combate (for Gods glorie | and Mans saluation) be-|tweene CHRIST and | Satan. | *Opened in seuen most excelent, lear-| ned and zealous Sermons, vpon the | Temptations of* CHRIST, *in | the wildernes, &c.* | Seene and allowed. | [type orn.] | LONDON | Printed by Iohn Charlwood | for *Richard Smith:* and are to | be sold at his Shop, at the | West doore of Paules. | 1592.; (hereafter *W*), sig. A1^r–A6^r. These sermons, printed with the prayers presented here, were published anonymously and presumably without Andrewes's consent. Charlwood entered his copy 'under th'andes of [the] Bishop of London' on 3 August 1592. The publisher, probably anxious about his right to publish, protested to 'the Christian Reader' that 'as the Author to me is not certainly knowen, so am I driven to let them passe without name: desiring you to suspend your judgements' (sig. :4^r). However, Andrewes's authorship has never been in doubt; the anonymous dedicatory epistle to Lord Keeper Sir John Puckering teased that 'the Tree from whence this heavenlie fruite was gathered, may well be discerned both by the beautie and taste', and praised the author as 'a sweete sounding Cimball, or rather a singuler instrument in Gods Church' (sig. :3^v). The sermons, without the prayers, were again printed without authority, but attributed to Andrewes, in 1627 as *Seven Sermons*.

Having come to the printer in 1592 from 'a Gentleman (a friend of mine)', the texts in *W* cannot be taken as strictly authorial, and are most likely reconstructions by hearers. The prayers (as well as the sermons) indisputably bear Andrewes's diction and structure. The former are cognate with three other exemplars of 'prayers before sermon' in English attributed to Andrewes: *The Private Devotions... of Lancelot Andrewes* (1647, pp. 152–61, and 161–6), and Trinity College Cambridge MS B.14.49, pp. 105–10. In addition, two complete prayers before sermon are incorporated into the Latin sermons *Concio ad Clerum pro Gradu Doctoris* and *Concio... in discessu Palatini* (*OP*, 1–3, 74–5). The prayers edited here also survive in a seventeenth-century MS copy in Bodl. MS Rawl. C. 412, fos. 49^r, 68^r–72^r, headed 'Bp. *Andrews's* prayer before sermon in Q: *Elizabeth*'s reign'. These four prayer texts have been published in parallel columns with commentary by P. J. Klemp as 'Lancelot Andrewes's "Prayer before Sermon": a Parallel-text Edition' (*Bodleian Library Record*, 11.5 (Nov. 1984), 300–19; hereafter *K*). Klemp's work is compromised by ignorance of both *W* and the Latin exemplars. Collation proves that the Bodl. MS is simply a mid-seventeenth century transcript from *W*, with several small but obvious errors of omission by the copyist, and therefore of less authority for an edition.

Headnote. Prayers before sermon, also called 'bidding prayers', were an official form prescribed by royal injunctions and canons, not the *BCP*. They derive directly from the pre-Reformation forms for 'bidding of the bedes', vernacular prayers for the laity led by the priest during mass. Successive revisions under Henry VIII, Edward VI, and Elizabeth gradually realigned the prayers with the sermon, rather than the eucharist, and enjoined intercessions (in order) for the church, state, clergy, nobility, and commons, and praise for the Christian departed. 'The forme of biddinge the prayers to be used generally in this uniforme sorte' was promulgated in Elizabeth's *Injunctions* of 1559 (sigs. D4^v–5^r; also Cardwell, *Documentary Annals*, i. 235–6). The Elizabethan text is:

> Ye shall pray for Christes holy catholike church, that is, for the whole congregation of christen people, dyspersed throughoute the whole worlde, and specially for the church of Englande and Irelande. And herein I require you most specially

to pray for the Quenes moste excellent majestie our soveraigne lady Elizabeth Quene of Englande, Fraunce and Irelande, defendour of the faith, and supreme governour of this realme, aswell in causes ecclesyasticall as temporall.

you shal also pray for the ministers of gods holy word and Sacramentes, aswel Archbyshops and bishoppes, as other pastures [*sic, 'pastors'*] and curates.

you shall also pray for the Quenes moste honorable counsayle, and for all the nobylitie of this realme, that al and everye of these in their callynge, maye serve truly and painfully, to the glory of god and edifiyng of his people, remembringe thaccompte that they must make.

Also you shall praye for the whole commons of this realme, that they may live in true faith and feare of god, in humble obedyence and brotherly charytie one to tother.

Finally, let us prayse god for all those whych are departed out of this life in the faith of christ and pray unto god, that we have grace so to direct our lyves after their good example, that after this lyfe, we with them may be made partakers of the gloriouse resurrection, in the lyfe everlastinge.

This text was reproduced almost verbatim as Canon LV in 1604, with the added instruction, 'always concluding with the Lords prayer' (*Constitutions and Canons Ecclesiastical* (1604), sig. K3ᵛ). This institutionalized what was already conventional, as seen here (p. 4, l. 6).

Although known as 'prayers before sermon', in practice preachers often incorporated them into the beginning of the sermon itself, either after the declamation of the text, the *exordium*, or the *divisio*. As Peter Heylyn explained—using Andrewes to illustrate the third of these options—Canon LV's 'before' the sermon meant 'before the substance of it (the preface & division being only a *manuduction* thereunto, & no part thereof) as Bishop *Andrews* allwaies used it, or else between the text, and Sermon, as others no lesse eminent' (*Ecclesia Vindicata* (1657), 343). Heylyn also cited five sermons from *XCVI. Sermons* that bear fragmentary textual evidence ('footsteps') of Andrewes's practice of placing a prayer like that presented here after the *divisio* in his sermons. He then adds the more complete witness of the Latin sermons from *OP* (*above*) as conclusive evidence (p. 331). This would suggest that the omission of the prayer was a routine part of either Andrewes's preparation of fair copies of his sermons after delivery. Reinstituting the same significantly alters the form of Andrewes's sermons as readers have come to know them in print.

The statutory form of the prayer was a template which dictated the order and subject matter of petitions that were in practice adapted, with varying degrees of freedom, by individual preachers for their own use in the pulpit. Hence, 'prayers before sermon' are examples of humanist *imitatio* that digest an original exemplar to create a wholly new work inspired by it. Using *amplificatio*, both of *exempla* and diction, Andrewes's prayer turns the prescribed form into a composition that reflects his own characteristic pastoral, liturgical, and theological concerns. Most striking is the addition of a short preliminary act of penitence, modelled on the *BCP* general confessions (p. 1, ll. 3–24). All four surviving prayers in *K* include such a preface, though that presented here is the most fully developed. It focuses on confessing sins associated with sermon hearing. This reminds the auditory that proper preaching is a corporate act that demands as much from the listener as it does from the preacher. Moreover, this is an early illustration of Andrewes's lifelong concern to inscribe the sermon into corporate liturgical worship. The second part of the prayer commences the five-part progression through the statutory subjects for intercession: the church (p. 1, l. 27–p. 2, l. 36), sovereign (p. 3, l. 13–p. 4, l. 3), nobility (p. 4, ll. 4–8), clergy (p. 4, ll. 9–12), magistrates and commons (p. 2, l. 37–p. 3, l. 10). Notably absent from this and all texts in *K* is thanksgiving for the witness of the faithful departed. The prayer concludes instead with an ascription of praise to Christ as mediator and advocate, and recitation of the Lord's Prayer. Striking throughout, and unique to Andrewes, is his emphasis on a reciprocal economy of prayer wherein as the congregation prays for other parts of the church, those other parts simultaneously pray for it. Analogously, Andrewes returns often to the hope that the congregation should pray for others as it would wish to be prayed for by them. This logic finds apt expression in several chiasmic constructions whereby form perfectly mirrors sense (e.g. p. 2, ll. 10–14). Andrewes thus articulates a Cranmerian vision of worship as fundamentally corporate—*common* prayer. His brief allusion to 'the unchristian and unhappy contentions of these days of ours' (p. 2, ll. 5–6) suggests a liberal distaste for the multiple schisms in Christendom, while his conflation of church and state (p. 2, ll. 26–7) appeals again to Cranmer's ideal of an inclusive, visible, national church. The pointed allusion to the 1588 defeat of the Armada (p. 2, ll. 29–30) fixes an anterior date for composition, and the inclusion of prayers for the Mayor and Aldermen make clear that this prayer was used not in Cambridge, but in London as vicar of St Giles's Cripplegate or prebend of St Paul's.

Further Reading. For the evolution of the Bidding Prayer, see F. E. Brightman, *The English Rite* (1915), ii. 1020–45; a briefer summary is Francis Procter and W. G. Frere, *A New History of the Book of Common Prayer* (1961), 254–6; other early modern examples of the form are reprinted in H. O. Coxe, *Forms of Bidding Prayer* (1840); seventeenth-century practice, with sustained treatment of Andrewes, is found in Peter Heylyn's tract, written in the 1630s, 'In prescribing a Set Form of Prayer to be used by Preachers before their Sermons', printed as part III of *Ecclesia Vindicata* (1657).

p. 1, 3. *Exercises*: catechetical lectures or sermons.

3–5. *That...our selves*: cf. Morning Prayer, invitation to confession (*BCP*), 'And although we ought at all times humbly to acknowledge our sinnes before God, yet ought we must chiefly so to doe, when we assemble and meet together, to render thanks for the great benefits that wee have received at his hands, to set foorth his most worthy praise, to heare his most holy word, and to aske those things which be requisite & necessary'.

5. *mercie seat*: lit., the covering of the Ark of the Covenant (Exod. 25: 17); by extension, the seat or throne of God in Heaven (Heb. 9: 5).

9–10. *by reason...offences*: cf. Morning Prayer, invitation to confession (*BCP*), 'the Scripture moveth us...to acknowledge and confesse our manifold sins and wickednesse'.

11. *divers*: diverse; many different.

20–3. *That so...comfort*: cf. Holy Communion, third collect 'to be said after the offertory when there is no Communion' (*BCP*), 'grant...that the wordes, which wee have heard this day with our outward eares, may through thy grace be so grafted inwardly in our hearts, that they may bring foorth in us the fruit of good living'; also Andrewes, 'Before Preaching', 'therefore of our very Lord and Master I cease not to ask that, whether by the utterances of his Scriptures or by the converse of brethren or by the inward and sweeter teaching of his inspiration, He will vouchsafe to learn me what things I can in such sort put forth' (*Preces*, 257); according to David Stokes (1591?–1669), Andrewes's pupil at Westminster School, Andrewes always read this passage (from Fulgentius) to himself 'upon his *Preaching daies*', and it was 'written with his own hand (in his Hebrew Bible...)' (*Verus Christianus* (1668), 3, 4).

20. *inward*: inwardly; within us; cf. prev. n.

28. *parts*: functions (in the sixteenth century used in the plural when referring to a number of persons).

p. 2, 1. *Militant Church*: members of the church on earth (vs. the 'Church Triumphant' in heaven); cf. Holy Communion (*BCP*), 'let us pray for the whole state of Christs Church militant here on earth'.

3–4. *the former age*: of Roman Catholicism in England.

4–5. *contentions... ours*: both between Protestants and Roman Catholics, and between Protestants themselves.

7. *this Church*: Church of England.

8–9. *poore afflicted members*: those in need; cf. Holy Communion (*BCP*), 'comfort & succour all them which... be in trouble, sorrow, neede, sicknesse, or any other adversitie'.

10. *crosse*: 'adversity', but with added Christian sense of 'bearing one's cross' (cf. Matt. 16: 24).

13. *to become suters for us*: become suitors, petitioners to God; to pray for us.

18–22. *And forasmuch... affliction*: perennial concern of Andrewes's that those, whether individuals or churches, blessed with peace and prosperity are in greater need of prayer and moral vigilance than the afflicted because of the pitfalls of wealth and complacency; cf. 'Sacrilege a Snare', and 'A Sermon Preached at St Marie's Hospital' (this edn.).

30. *mervailous deliverance*: from the Spanish Armada, July 1588.

34. *open our eies*: cf. Ps. 119: 18.

34. *encline our harts*: cf. Ps. 119: 36.

39. *Defendresse of the faith*: originally, papal title (*Fidei Defensor*) conferred upon Henry VII and Henry VIII; applied after the Reformation with reference to the royal supremacy.

p. 3, 5. *degrees*: lit., steps in an ascent, here with the queen at the top; by extension, social classes, rank.

8–9. *many arguments... of late*: evidence (e.g. the failure of assassination plots against Elizabeth, and of the Armada) of England's status as favoured by God.

14–15. *Councell... councels*: punning on the proper noun 'Privy Council' (the private council of the queen), the concrete noun 'council' (an advisory body), and the abstract noun 'counsel' (advice).

16. *right reverend Fathers*: the bishops.

17–18. *inferior Ministers*: clergy below the rank of bishop or dean (priests and deacons).

21–2. *Governors... Citie*: the Lord Mayor and Aldermen of the City of London.

27–8. *that glorious calling*: both the duty to keep one's social station and one's Christian vocation; cf. Rom. 10: 13, Geneva gloss: 'true calling upon the Name of God is the testimonie of true faith, & true faith, of true vocation or calling, and calling, of true election'.

33. *deaw of his blessing*: cf. Prov. 19: 12.

41. *alone*: only, sole.

p. 6. *Our Father, &c.*: the congregational recitation of the Lord's Prayer (Matt. 6: 9–13).

THE PATTERN OF CATECHISTICAL DOCTRINE

Text. THE | PATTERN | OF | CATECHISTICAL DOCTRINE | AT LARGE: | OR | A Learned and Pious Exposition | of the Ten COMMANDMENTS, | With An INTRODUCTION, Containing the Use | and Benefit of Catechizing; the generall Grounds of Religion; and the truth of Christian Religion in particular ... By the Right Reverend Father in God | *LANCELOT ANDREWS*, late Bishop of | WINCHESTER | ... LONDON, | Imprinted by *Roger Norton*, and are to be sold by *George Badger*, | ... *Anno Dom.* 1650. Printed notes taken from Andrewes's Cambridge catechetical lectures appeared as early as 1630. Two editions in at least six settings appeared in the period 1630–41 as *The Patterne of Catechisticall Doctrine*, but, presumably to avoid contravening Laud's royal patent for publishing the bishop's works, these unauthorized texts were published without attribution to Andrewes. These are from notes taken by hearers in outline form. *LACT* mistook them for an 'original work of Andrewes', and edited one of the three 1641 texts in full (vol. vi). With the collapse of Laudian print controls in 1641–2 there appeared the first text of the lectures (with other sermons) openly attributed to Andrewes, *The Morall Law Expounded* (Wing 3140; hereafter *M*). This was an open bid by the editor, John Jackson, and the puritan bookseller Michael Sparke, to appropriate Andrewes's legacy for the cause of Parliament.

The 1650 *Pattern* (hereafter, *P*) is a riposte to the earlier editions, which its anonymous editor dismissed (ostensibly on textual grounds) as 'a heap of broken rubbish'. *P* was printed 'in vindication of the Author' by presenting 'the Authors own Copy, revised and compared with diverse other manuscripts, which though it were not perfected by himself, nor intended for publick use, yet being the onely Copy he had, as is acknowledged under his hand in the beginning of the Book, and containing many Marginal Notes, and alterations throughout the whole made by himself in his latter years'. This autograph manuscript (now lost) was allegedly passed, *c.*1641, 'to one of those, to whom the perusal of his papers were committed'—presumably Laud or one of his chaplains (the other royal patentee, Buckeridge, had died in 1631). The work of editing the manuscript was then intrusted 'to an able, industrious and worthy Gentleman, who ... had some relation with the Author whilst he lived'. That editor, however—daunted by the 'variety of all kinde of Learning, both Divine and Humane' in the lectures that required documentation—in turn handed the project over to another of 'more leizure and abilities then himself' who brought the project to completion with publication in 1650 (*P*, sig. **3ʳ–4ʳ). The identity of this succession of editors is not known. However, one of them was very likely to have been Henry Isaacson (1581–1664), Andrewes's quondam secretary, first biographer, and most devoted lay acolyte, who published a small stream of Andrewesiana throughout the Commonwealth and Interregnum.

The Laudian editors of *P* were anxious to neuter any traces of what the puritan editors of *M* had gloated over—evidence that Andrewes had, in the 1580s, espoused more mainstream Calvinist doctrines and churchmanship. *P* therefore interpolates, as a corrective, passages from Andrewes's later works (mostly from *XCVI. Sermons*) that defend Laudian principles, as well as short editorial essays that 'clarify' any points where Andrewes might have been seen to depart from hallmarks of Laudian churchmanship, such as episcopal and patristic authority, and ceremonial worship. The care with which *P* distinguishes these from the main text convinces this ed. that the latter itself is not contaminated with ideas from Andrewes's later thinking unless they might be those added later by Andrewes himself in the manuscript from which *P* was set. Ed.

has corroborated this by comparing the texts edited here from *P* with the cognate passages in *M*, and those from the 1641 text edited by *LACT*: *A Patterne of Catechisticall Doctrine . . . With Additions* (London, R.B. for William Garrett, 1641; Wing A3146; hereafter *G*.). In the text presented here, ed. has omitted the interpolations of editorial commentary and extracts from Andrewes's later works supplied in *P*. Their place in the text, however, is noted in square brackets; elisions by ed. of other matter are marked by '***', and their contents documented in the annotations.

To summarize this ed.'s view of the characteristics and merits of the three textual traditions of Andrewes's catechistical lectures: (1) *P*, as a text set from the author's manuscript, holds the primary claim to authority; it must be used carefully to distinguish between authorial text and editorial interpolation; it shows weaknesses in scholarship when handling biblical languages and patristic sources, but its documentation of scriptural allusion and citation is superior; (2) *G*, the last witness in a series of related editions from as early as 1630 (all associated with the bookseller William Garrett), prints in outline form notes taken by hearers with minimal editorial intervention or expansion; the *LACT* edition of this text supplies some helpful documentation of sources, but the *G* texts are by far the most skeletal of the three textual traditions; (3) *M*, from an undescribed copy text (but presumably a set of notes by a hearer) expands the outline form of *G* and its predecessors and presents the lectures as continuous expository prose; as a reading text, it is therefore often clearer than the note forms of *P* and *G*, and is used in the notes here to supply glosses on some very truncated passages in *P*; *M* also preserves far more Greek and Hebrew than *P*, and its citation of patristic sources is more thorough.

The typesetting of *P* is frequently wanting. Ed. has silently standardized its minor typographical inconsistencies (spacing after enumerations and abbreviations, possessive *'s*), and ignored the random italicization of the first letters of capitalized proper nouns, e.g. 'Prophet').

Headnote. *P* is a lengthy work, and only small representative selections from it are presented here. *In toto*, it is a complete set of 110 lectures on the Ten Commandments, divided first into twenty introductory lectures on the principles of religion, catechizing, and biblical law, followed by between four and seventeen lectures on each of the individual Commandments. (This numerical analysis assumes that *P*'s 'chapters' correspond to lectures.) Andrewes was appointed catechist of Pembroke Hall, Cambridge, of which he was Fellow, in 1578. According to Isaacson, the lectures on the Commandments were delivered in that office 'every Saturday, and Sunday at three of clocke afternoone' in Pembroke chapel (*Life and Death*, sig. *2^r). They must therefore have stretched over at least two if not three academic years, which is consistent with the pattern of the dated lectures on Genesis delivered at St Giles's Cripplegate and St Paul's in the 1590s and printed in *AS*. A printed marginal note in the preface to *P* dates the lectures '*Anno* 1585' (sig. *[1]^r). This is the only known dating of the lectures, and is perhaps corroborated by the publication dates of sources used by Andrewes in the portions edited here. Andradius's *Defensio Tridentinae* appeared in 1580, making it impossible for these lectures to have been Andrewes's first as catechist. The principal work refuted, Stapleton's *Principiorum* (see below), had appeared in 1578, and portions of it were attacked in print by Andrewes's college Master, William Fulke, in 1579. However, Andrewes's surviving annotated copy (PCCL 3.16.4), is the edition of 1582.

Like many Oxford and Cambridge college catechisms (vs. those for school and parish children), Andrewes's are formal academic lectures. However, texts in the *G* tradition (those derived most directly from hearers of the original spoken lectures) do contain remnants of 'question and answer' structures which do not remain in *M* or *P*.

Further Reading. For the print history and ideological appropriation of the catechetical lectures, see McCullough, 'Making Dead Men Speak'; for the significance of the lectures in the development of Andrewes's churchmanship, see Tyacke, 'Lancelot Andrewes'; the definitive study of catechisms in early modern England, with reference to Andrewes *passim*, is Ian Green, *The Christian's ABC: Catechisms and Catechizing in England c.1530–1740* (1996).

p. 5, 5–6 *INTRODUCTION CHAP. XIII*: Andrewes's exposition of the Ten Commandments began first with a series of twenty general introductory lectures covering pedagogical points about catechizing, proofs of religion in general, and of Christianity in particular (against the competing arguments of atheism, paganism, Judaism, and Islam), as well as principal points of contention between Roman Catholics and Protestants, and on the nature of the Mosaic law. The first selection presented here, Chapter XIII, treats the methods of interpreting scripture practised by '*the two chief parties that lay claim to Christian Religion, Papists and Protestants*' (p. 52). Andrewes's rules for biblical interpretation are classically Protestant, and reflect the frenzy of engagement with Catholic apologies for the Council of Trent and the Rheims New Testament, in particular Thomas Stapleton's *Principiorum Fidei Doctrinalium* (Paris, 1579), and Dieguus Payva Dandrada ('Andradius'), *Defensio Tridentinae Fidei Catholicae* (Cologne, 1580). On several points he echoes the anti-Catholic polemic of Fulke. But most striking is the degree of similarity between Andrewes's lectures, and the later work of his Cambridge contemporary, William Whitaker. Whitaker was chief guardian of Calvinist orthodoxy in the university, Fellow of Trinity, Regius Professor of Divinity (1580), and Master of St John's (1586). In 1588 he published at Cambridge his *Disputatio de Sacra Scriptura*, a large-scale treatment of precisely Andrewes's subject here, in response to both Stapleton and Robert Bellarmine's later *Disputationes* (Ingolstadt, 1587). The response to Bellarmine by Whitaker, and the absence of the same in Andrewes, confirms that Andrewes's work predates Whitaker's. Although the terms of the dispute were to some extent supplied by their common adversary (Stapleton), and both men were articulating typically Protestant views from within a close circle of Cambridge theologians, the similarities documented below suggest that Andrewes's lectures were, if not a direct source, then at least a contribution to the intellectual context on which Whitaker drew. Andrewes is distinguished from Whitaker, however, on two significant points. First, he does not insist, as Whitaker, on the primacy of scripture itself for interpreting scripture ('the supreme decision and authority in the interpretation of the scripture should not be ascribed to the church, but to the scripture itself', Whitaker, *Disputation* (see below), 447; cf. also pp. 488–95). Second, unlike Whitaker, he carefully highlights the grounds on which Protestants and Roman Catholics do agree, whereas Whitaker is uniformly antagonistic to Rome. Whitaker is cited here from William Fitzgerald's translation for the Parker Society, *A Disputation on Holy Scripture, against the Papists* (Cambridge, 1849).

In this chapter in *P* there are six interpolated passages of later commentary and passages from Andrewes's later work; their positions in the text presented here are noted in square brackets, and their contents summarized in the notes. They uniformly qualify the original text's Protestant de-emphasis of the authority of the church and patristic scholarship, often coming closer in spirit to the Roman Catholic arguments

Andrewes was in fact attacking. They are as indicative of Interregnum Anglican longing for hierarchical church authority as they are of Andrewes's own later thought.

7. *And... true way*: in the immediately preceding lectures, Andrewes had argued the certainty of Christianity's claims to religious truth ('the true way') over Judaism and Islam.

17. *[Addition 1]*: to illustrate '*what the sense of this reverend Authour was in his latter years, concerning points that are manifest, and matters controverted*', paraphrase of an excerpt on the need for the church to focus on general points of doctrinal agreement, rather than minor disputed points, from Andrewes's sermon before King James, Christmas 1607 (*XCVI*, 18–19).

19. *the Fathers*: early Christian writers; usually applied by Protestants to those of before *c*.500; some, especially Roman Catholics, extended this to include major medieval theologians.

19. *Councels*: assemblies of ecclesiastics convened to settle points of doctrine and relations with the civil state; in the early church, 'general' or 'ecumenical' councils could claim to be universal, but following the Great Schism between Eastern and Western churches (from 1054), assertions of papal supremacy vexed claims to conciliar authority, a problem made even more acute by the Reformation.

19. *the Church*: local and national churches often interpreted scripture variously in matters of ceremony and discipline.

23–24. *build... Rock*: cf. Matt. 7: 24–5.

p. 6, 1. *wrest*: wrench, forcefully pull away or out of shape.

2. *Hilary... auferre*: Lat., 'to bring sense to the scripture, not to carry it away'; summary of a recurring argument in Hilary of Poitiers, *De Trinitate* (cf. *PL*, 10.51B–52B), that heresies are born not from the scriptures themselves, but from the interpreter taking the wrong sense from them; Whitaker quotes Hilary to the same effect (*Disputation*, 461, 492).

6. *naturall man*: person acting only with the capacities of human nature, unaided by divine grace.

7–8. *Augustine... reddit*: Lat, 'not the vivacity of believing, but the simplicity of belief brings salvation'; cf. Augustine, *Contra Epistolam Manichaei*, iv. 5: 'quippe turbam non intelligendi vivacitas, sed credendi simplicitas tutissimam facit' (*PL*, 42.175); ('indeed [it is] not the liveliness of understanding, but the simplicity of believing that makes most secure').

10–11. *Eunuch... Philip*: Acts 8: 27–39.

14. *[Addition 2]*: paraphrase of Hugo Grotius on 1 Cor. 12, acknowledging that the gift of interpretation can extraordinarily fall upon the unlearned, but that '*the ordinary power and gift of interpretation alwayes was and is in the Church, and the Bishops*'; an argument much closer to those by Stapleton and Andradius here refuted by Andrewes (p. 6, ll. 15–23).

18. *Stapleton... them*: response to Stapleton, *Principiorum*, x. vii (pp. 374–7), on the gifts of the Holy Spirit, which include interpretation (1 Cor. 12: 11); Stapleton insists on the diversity of the recipients of gifts, as well as of the gifts themselves, to argue that all people do not receive the gift of interpretation, against the Protestant use of the text to justify the universal Christian right (i.e. of laity as well as clergy) to interpret the scriptures; the qualification made by Stapleton over which Andrewes gloats here is the chapter's awkward explanation (p. 377B) of how Origen was given the gift of scriptural interpretation before becoming a priest; cf. also Whitaker, *Disputation*, 410–14.

21. *Amos...Jeremie*: Amos 1: 1, Jer. 1: 1; cf. Whitaker (*Disputation*, 478), 'Isaiah, who was educated in the royal court, hath a much purer and more elegant diction than Amos, who had lived amongst the shepherds, yet this shepherd speaks in such a manner as to be intelligible'.

22–23. *Andradius...howsoever*: Andradius, *Defensio*, Bk. II ('*De Sacrae Scripturae*'), strictly defends the Council of Trent's limitation of interpretative authority over disputed points of scripture to bishops in council and the papacy (Session 4, canon 1). For his round dismissal of private interpretation and a summary of his defence of episcopal-papal authority, see *Defensio*, 417–23, 435–7.

25. *Apices...jus*: legal commonplace; *G* (p. 104) is slightly fuller, 'It is well said in Law, that *Apices juris nont sunt jus*; each small quiddity of the Law is not the Law'; cf. Edward Leigh, *A Philologicall Commentary* (1658), 'the Law of *England* respects the effects and substance of the matter, and not the very niceity of form and circumstance... *apices juris non sunt jura*' (p. 144).

27. *Aquinas...rules*: the four points which follow summarize Aquinas, *Summa Theologica*, I. Q1. A10 ('Whether in Holy Scripture a word may have several senses'), a proof text also expounded by Whitaker (*Disputation*, 408–9).

38. *a trope*: metaphor.

p. 7, 4. *sectaries*: members of a religious sect; schismatics.

11–22. *We...must be judged*: *G* does not contain a corresponding paragraph; *M* (p. 67) does.

14–16. *Augustine...good life*: cf. Augustine, *De Doctrina Christiana* II. ix. 14 (*PL*, 34.42): 'Deinde illa quae in eis aperte posita sunt, vel praecepta vivendi, vel regulae credendi, solertius diligentiusque investiganda sunt: quae tanto quisque plura invenit, quanto est intelligentiae'; ('therefore, in those things which are clearly set open, either precepts for living, or rules of believing, can be diligently and skillfully searched for'); also quoted by Whitaker (*Disputation*, 394) to prove the same point.

17–18. *Chrysostome...manners*: Chrysostom, *Homilies...on...Thessalonians* (*LF*, xiv. 14), 'all things are clear and open that are in the Scriptures; all things that are necessary are plain'; Whitaker rejects an interpretation of the same by Bellarmine, 'that he [Chrysostom] is speaking only of the historical books; which is false: for he says of *all things necessary to salvation*... "they are all manifest, clear, and easy"' (*Disputation*, 396–7).

19–21. *Melchior Canus...wrangle*: Melchior Cano, *De Locis Theologicis Libri Duodecim* (Salamanca, 1563), 'Quanquam, fateor, nonnulla sunt scripturae loca, quae in alium atque alium sensum trahi ne à contentiosis quidem possunt. Quis enim illud torqueat, quod Paulus ad Corinthios scripsit, alii per spiritum dari sermonem sapientiae, aliis sermonem scientiae, alii interpretationem sermonem?' (pp. 101–2); ('Although, it must be admitted, that there are not no places at all in scripture in which one can draw out all the senses without being contentious. Who indeed would twist what Paul wrote to the Corinthians [to say that] the spirit gave everyone the language of wisdom, everyone the language of knowledge, everyone the language of interpretation?'); Andrewes is of course ignoring the fact that Cano uses the exemplum ironically to argue against the Protestant belief in the universal interpretability of scripture.

21–22. *Ireneus...judged*: cf. Irenaeus, *Five Books...against Heresies*, Book II, ch. 28.2–3 (*LF*, lxii. 174–6).

23–24. *means...reduced to six*: Whitaker (*Disputation*, 466–73) expounds a list of 'those means [of interpretation] which are proposed by our divines' that corresponds almost exactly to Andrewes's here. It differs only in having two means additional to Andrewes's: interpreting scripture according to the 'analogy of faith', and the recourse of the unlearned to teachers (pp. 472–3).

26–27. *first place, Prayer*: cf. Whitaker (*Disputation*, 468), 'this [prayer] should be always the first means, and the foundation of the rest'.

27–29. *Augustine... contemplation*: from *Scala Paradisi*, attr. in the period to Augustine, but now attr. to St Bernard of Clairvaux or Prior Giugi V (*PL*, 40.998), 'Beatae igitur vitae dulcedinem lectio inquirit, meditatio invenit, oratio postulat, contemplatio degustat'; ('so then the sweetness of the blessed life seek by reading, find by meditation, ask by prayer, and taste by contemplation'); also quoted by Whitaker, attr. Augustine (*Disputation*, 467).

30. *conference*: comparison; refutation of Stapleton, *Principiorum*, XI. x (p. 421), titled '*Collatio locorum in qua gloriatur tantopere hodie Protestantes, fallax est interpretandi Medium*' ('The collation of places in which the Protestants today glory in all their works, is false as a means of interpretation').

30–32. *Saint Augustine... number*: *G* (p. 106) cites in its text '*August.2. de Doctrina Christiana, cap.* 8'; cf. *De Doctrina Christiana*, II. vi. 8 (*PL*, 34.39), 'Nihil enim fere de illis obscuritatibus eruitur, quod non planissime dictum alibi reperiatur' ('there is therefore almost nothing in [the Scriptures] that is found to be obscure, which is not found very clearly said in another place'); paraphrased, without attribution, in Whitaker (*Disputation*, 471), 'one place must be compared and collated with another; the obscurer places with the plainer or less obscure'.

33. *counsel... Ghost*: the scriptures (dictated by the 'counsel' of the Holy Spirit).

34. *Inspectu fontium*: Lat., 'look to the source'; *G* (p. 106) cites 'Aug. *de Doctrina Christiana, cap.* 11.4'; cf. *De Doctrina Christiana*, II. xi (*PL*, 34.42), 'Ut ignorantia signorum tollatur, necessaria est linguarum cognitio, ac praesertim graecae et hebraeae' ('For removing ignorance of signs [words], it is necessary to know languages, chiefly Greek and Hebrew'); cf. Whitaker (*Disputation*, 468), 'we ought to know the original languages.... consult the Hebrew text in the old Testament, the Greek in the new: we should approach the very fountain-heads of the scriptures, and not stay beside the derived streams of versions'; refutation of Stapleton, *Principiorum*, XI. xii (pp. 432–7), titled, '*Quòd inspectio fontium, textus scilicet Hebraici vel Graeci, incertum est*' ('That the looking to the original, that is the Hebrew and Greek text, is uncertain').

38. *Dialect, Idiom or Stile*: cf. Whitaker (*Disputation*, 470), ' in dealing with the words we should consider which are proper, and which figurative and modified'; refutation of Stapleton, *Principiorum*, XI. ix (pp. 420–1), titled '*Observatio phrasis seu styli S. Scripturae Medium interpretandi incertum*' ('The observation of phrases according to the styles of the holy scripture is an uncertain means of interpretation').

39. *as the Apostle speaks*: cf. *M* (p. 68), 'as *Heb*.5.v. last... *Have our senses exercised*, that we may know the Holy Ghost when he speaketh'.

p. 7, 39–p. 8, 1. *crucifying... concupiscence*: Gal. 5: 24, Col. 3: 5; examples of metaphor in Scripture, part of the Holy Ghost's rhetorical 'Stile'; cf. *M* (p. 68), 'For the Holy Ghost useth divers idioms, that are not to be found in other writers; as the crucifying of mans flesh, the mortifying of his concupiscence, &c. Therefore we must be perfect in these'.

5–6. *Oculus... intent*: cf. *G* (p. 106), '*Oculus ad scopum*, the Eye intent to the scope'; and Whitaker (*Disputation*, 470), 'we ought to consider the scope'.

9–10. *Hilary...spoken*: cf. Hilary of Poitiers, *De Trinitate*, iv. 14 (*PL*, 10.107C), 'Intelligentia enim dictorum ex causis est assumenda dicendi', ('certainly the meaning of things said is known from the reasons for saying them'); probably Andrewes's own wordplay changed 'dictorum' to '*Doctorum*', which reading exists also in *G* (pp. 106–7); *M* (p. 68) corrects to Hilary's original: '*E causis dictorum sumenda est intelligentia dictorum*. From the causes of things that are spoken, the understanding of them is to be taken'.

13. *Antecedents...Circumstance*: cf. Whitaker (*Disputation*, 470), '[consider the] end, matter, circumstances...the antecedents and consequents of each passage'; refutation of Stapleton, *Principiorum*, XI. ix (pp. 418–19), '*consideratio antecedentium & consequentium...sit...incerta*' ('the consideration of antecedents and consequents is uncertain').

15–18. *Ireneus...Scripture*: cf. p. 7, ll. 21–2 and n.

18–23. *Stapleton...sufficient at all*: refutation of Stapleton, *Principiorum*, XI. xi (p. 418D); cf. Whitaker (*Disputation*, 474), 'What? Do our opponents find fault with these means? Not altogether; but yet neither do they entirely receive them. Stapleton...admits that they are highly conducive, but says that they are not firm, certain, or of uniform avail'.

25. *they*: Roman Catholics.

38. *without them*: outside of, beyond, our rules; in error.

p. 9, 1. *[Addition 3]*: lengthy essay (pp. 55–6) by the editor marginally glossed 'of peoples submitting to the judgement of the Church', which, although denying the infallibility of the church, insists that '*in matters doubtful the safest way is to submit to the judgement of the Church*'; Andrewes himself is not invoked; authorities cited are Suarez, Cajetan, Aquinas, William Bedel, and William Chillingworth.

3–6. *fathers...not expound alike*: cf. Whitaker (*Disputation*, 455), 'we...demand of them, when we are to know that the fathers agree? For certainly in most places they are at variance; so that their authority will be but small'.

7. *[Addition 4]*: brief editorial completion (indeed, qualification) of Andrewes's own sentence: '*yet, where they all agree...their exposition ought to be received, for therein they deliver the sence of the whole Catholick Church derived from the Apostles...otherwise Christ might have no Church.*'

8–13. 2. *In their expositions...carelessely*: a corresponding paragraph is absent from *G* (p. 108), but present in *M* (p. 69).

8. *the literal sense*: this paragraph adopts a typically Protestant attitude to interpreting multiple senses in scripture—privileging the literal sense and cautioning against excessively symbolic interpretations, but not dismissing the latter entirely; cf. Whitaker, 'we affirm that there is but one true...sense of scripture, arising from the words rightly understood, which we call the literal: and we contend that allegories, tropologies, and anagoges are not various senses, but various collections from one sense, or various applications and accommodations of that one meaning' (*Disputation*, 404); cf. next nn.

9. *in their Homilies*: homilies of the Apostolic Fathers, most likely Origen, famous for often extravagant allegorical interpretations; cf. Whitaker, 'others, however, enumerate other kinds of mystical senses, as the tropological, the allegorical, and anagogic; of which we read a great deal in Origen and the rest' (*Disputation*, 403).

10. *tropological*: lit., pertaining to the second of the four traditional senses in allegorical interpretation, that which pertains to human behaviour; but here used less technically as a synonym for 'figurative', or the generally allegorical (cf. *OED sa* 1, 2); cf. p. 6, ll. 30–32.

12–13. *S. August... carelessely*: M (p. 69) has the fuller, 'So saith *Augustine* against *Julian*. That in controversies, that fell not in their time, the Fathers *loquebantur obscurè, controversiâ nondum motâ; in caeteris loquebantur securè, controversiâ nodum notâ*; spake obscurely, the controversie not yet moved; in the rest they spake securely, the controversie not yet knowne'; diction close to this appears in neither Augustine's *Contra Julianum*, nor his *Contra Secundam Juliani Responsionem, Imperfectum* (*PL*, 44, 45). The spirit, if not the letter, of this argument informs especially the first two books of the former wherein Augustine addresses the lack of consensus about Original Sin among earlier fathers; cf. *Against Julian*, I. vi. 22, 'there are other matters on which at times even the most learned and excellent defenders of the Catholic rule do not agree, without the breaking the bond of faith, and one speaks better and more truly about one thing and another about another' (*FC*, xxxv. 26).

14–16. *Basile... time*: Basil, *Epist. IX*, criticizes Dionysius for compromising his orthodox arguments with unnecessarily shrill rhetoric (*PG*, 32.90–1). The terms ἀγωνιστικῶς ('agonistikos', antagonistically) and δογματικῶς ('dogmatikos', dogmatically), are Andrewes's.

19–22. *Cardinal Cajetan... Andrad.*: Andradius discusses and endorses Cajetan's example at length (*Defensio*, 443–9); Whitaker (*Disputation*, 466) deploys the same evidence.

26–32. *controversy... Augustine... man speaketh*: Jerome and Augustine's epistolary quarrel was a *cause célèbre*, and perhaps the most infamous example of a public dispute between eminent fathers; for a brief summary and bibliography, see A. D. Fitzgerald (ed.), *Augustine through the Ages* (1999), 461. Augustine does not use the commonplace 'non quis, sed quid', though it does aptly summarize his argument (*Epist.* 82) in response to Jerome's appeal to patristic evidence; cf. *Saint Augustine: Letters 1–82* (*FC*, xii. 410–12). See also Whitaker (*Disputation*, 455), 'Chrysostom and Jerome excuse the dissimulation of Peter related by Paul; on the other hand Augustine and Ambrose think it sinful'.

32–35. *Jerome... indulged*: probably a commentary on the Psalms once attr. to Jerome, but called into question by Erasmus and others; cf. Fulke, 'A Rejoinder to J. Martial's Reply' (1580), in *Works*, ii. 207 8.

37–39. *Petrus... his person*: cf. Stapleton, *Principiorum*, VI. i (p. 206F), who cites Jerome on Matt. 16: 18 as authority for Peter's person (not his faith) as the rock upon which Christ would build the church ('quia totius Ecclesiae Petra futurus esset, & super eum tota aedificanda Ecclesia'); probably the scripture most contested between Roman Catholics and Protestants; for a rehearsal of the arguments and contested patristic evidence, see Fulke, *A Defense* (1583), in *Works*, i, 225–31.

p. 10, 1–7. *Saint Aug.... Decalogue*: Rome and the Lutheran churches followed Augustine's enumeration of the Commandments; the Eastern, and later, the Reformed churches in England and Switzerland did not.

10–11. *Action... and Canon*: Andrewes disputes both the process of argument by which councils debate matters ('Action'), and the canons (legislative acts of a church council) which result from that process. Cf. *M* (p. 70), 'For Councels; they are divided into Action and Canon: for the Action, it is either intollerable or shameless; or they must confesse infinite writings; so that they confesse, the action may erre. For the Canon, there is not one place among a thousand that hath the indefinite sentence of the Fathers.'

15–22. *Councils of Constance... Florence*: a succession of Councils (Constance, 1414–18; Basle, 1431–49; Ferrara and Florence being, along with Rome, the successive transferred sites for that of Basle from 1438) wrestled successively with the two Great Schisms—Constance with that of the rival 'anti-popes' at Avignon, Rome, and Pisa (1378–1417), and Basle with the longer-standing split between Eastern and Western Christendom. Constance enacted the decree *Haec Sancta*, asserting the primacy of general councils over the papacy, and settling the schism by electing Martin V (1415); his successor, Eugenius IV attempted by papal decree ('*bull*'; 1431) to dissolve the next Council at Basle, but was ignored and forced to issue a second bull (1433) contradicting his former, which allowed a reaffirmation by the Council of *Haec Sancta*. At Florence in 1439, a short-lived union with the Greek church was accomplished, but in response to a splinter-council and rival pope persisting at Basle, Eugenius was able to reassert by papal bull the supremacy of popes over councils. Andrewes has here chosen easy targets to illustrate contradictions between conciliar and papal decrees. *G* (pp. 109–10) makes the point much more briefly: 'The Canon. And thereof we see some plaine opposite, one to another; as in the two generall allowed Councils, the one of *Constance*, the other of *Basil*; whereof the one setteth down that the Councils could erre; and so also the Pope, and that the Council was above the Pope; the other affirmeth the quite contrary'.

24. *[Addition 5]*: editorial caveat acknowledging the possible error of councils, but concluding, '*yet for the peace of the Church their decrees tye us to external obedience, that is, not to oppose them, if there be no fundamental errour*'.

26. *East and West*: the breach between the Eastern church and the Roman Catholic church is traditionally dated from 1054, the year that Pope Leo IX of Rome and Oecumenical Patriarch Cerularius of Constantinople anathematized and excommunicated one another. The Union of Florence (1439) was revoked by Constantinople in 1484.

29. *Arrians*: followers of Arius (d. 336), who held the chief Christian heresy of denying the divinity of Christ; repudiated at the Council of Nicaea (325), but flourished, especially in the East, until the Council of Constantinople (381); *G* (p. 110) levels the charge of Arianism specifically against Eastern bishops ('And if we should follow their Bishops, many of them have been *Arians*, so that here is both ambiguity and perill').

30–32. *Basile...thrice*: *G* (p. 110) cites '*Basil cap. 27. de Spi. sancto*'; cf. *De Spiritu Sancto*, xxvii. 66, 'And whence comes the custom of baptizing thrice?' (*LF*, viii. 42; *PG*, 32.55).

33. *[Addition 6]*: acknowledgement that the church is not infallible, '*but that the Church is the ordinary interpreter of Scripture to her children, and that they ought to submit to her*'; then quoting Andrewes on the value of patristic consensus for settling disputed points of scriptural interpretation, from a sermon on the second commandment preached at St Giles's, Cripplegate, 1592 (*XCVI*, pt. 2, pp. 27–8).

36–38. *Damasus...Liberius*: cf. Jerome, *Chronicon* (*PL*, 27.697, 684, respectively); the same catalogue is rehearsed by Fulke, *A Discoverie* (1580), in *Works*, ii. 349–50.

p. 11, 3–7. *Honorius...Monothelites*: Honorius I (Pope, 625–38), posthumously anathematized by the Council of Constantinople (681) for a letter (c.634) used in the formulation of Monotheletism, the heresy which ascribed only a divine will (vs. both a divine and a human will) to the incarnate Christ; Honorius' ill-fated letter has been a centrepiece of arguments against papal infallibility ever since.

9. *writings of Beda...corrupt*: probably ironic; the works of the Anglo-Saxon Bede, 'The Venerable', were universally admired for their clarity and orthodoxy, but became a lightning rod for Roman Catholic–Protestant debate with Thomas Stapleton's trans-

lation of Bede's *History of the English Church*, prefaced with Stapleton's table of forty-five 'Differences between the primitive faith of England... and the late pretended faith of the Protestants'; see Fulke, 'An Overthrow' (1580), in *Works*, ii. 5–27.

11. *Lords supper to infants*: a current point of dispute between Fulke and his antagonists; cf. Fulke, *A Sermon Preached... within the Tower* (1581), 'For S. Paule forbiddeth any man or woman, to presume to the Lordes Table without examination and judging of themselves, which thinges because infantes cannot performe, it can be none other, but a meere prophanation of the Lordes Supper, to minister it unto young infants, even as it was of them which ministred it unto dead bodies upon the same erronious persuasion of the necessitie thereof unto eternall life' (sig. H2^r).

17–19. *Stapleton... authority*: points argued *in extenso* by Stapleton, *In Principiorum*, x. xi and xiiii (esp. pp. 385A–B, 393A–B), aptly summarized by the respective index entries, '*Episcoporum praecedentium interpretatio authoritatis molem obtinet*' ('the precedent of bishops possesses the greatest weight of authority in interpretation') and '*Episcopus in causa fidei potius consulendus quam doctor Theologus, etsi doctissimus*' ('in matters of faith the opinion of a bishop is stronger than a doctor of divinity even though he [may be] more learned').

19–21. *Andradius... rules*: cf. p. 6, ll. 22–23 and n.

24. *First Commandement*: Exod. 20: 2–3 ('I am the Lorde thy God... thou shalt have none other Gods before me').

25. *CHAP. XI*: Andrewes's first twelve lectures on this commandment treat the nature of God as lawgiver, and seven 'virtues' that should be consequent to acknowledging God as 'Lord': knowledge, faith, and fear of God, humility, hope, prayer, and love of God. The extract presented here is the bulk of his treatment of the sixth of these, prayer ('invocation'); passages not included are marked '***' in the text, and summarized in the notes. There are no interpolations of editorial matter or excerpts from Andrewes's later work in this chapter in *P*. The high view of prayer expressed here, especially the primacy of liturgical prayer, anticipates much of Andrewes's later commendation of prayer as an antidote to excessive sermon-hearing; cf. 'A Sermon Preached... Whit-Sunday', this edn., pp. 207–24.

32. *prayer is divided*: The scheme Andrewes elaborates here by way of diagram and exposition is ancient. The earliest such division is found in Origien's third-century *De Oratione* ('Of Prayer'), which Andrewes knew well. It was a template for his elaborate *Preces Privatæ*, composed *c*. 1590 and privately used and revised by him throughout his life (see *Preces*, 11–15). He also expounded these same structural principles of prayer in a series of later Elizabethan sermons or lectures, probably delivered at St Paul's or St Giles's Cripplegate *c*.1589–1601, and printed (without authority) in 1611 as *Scala Cœli, Nineteene Sermons Concerning Prayer* (also *LACT*, v. 301–476).

33. *Deprecation*: *OED* (sn 2) cites 1596 as the first usage of the term meaning 'prayer for the averting or removal (of evil, disaster, etc.)'.

33. δέησις: Gr., 'dĕēsis'; petition, supplication.

36 *Precation*: praying (for which *OED* cites this ex.); fr. Lat., 'precari' ('to pray').

38. προσευχή: Gr., 'prŏsĕuchē'; prayer.

39. ἔντευξις: Gr., 'ĕntĕuxis'; intercession, prayer.

p. 12, 1. εὐχαριστία: Gr., 'eucharistia'; 'thanksgiving'.

5. *rationem boni*: Lat., reason, object of good.

16. *mitiga iram tuam*: Lat., lit., 'soothe your wrath'; cf. Vulg. Ps. 84: 4 (juxt. LXX), '*mitigasti omnem iram tuam*' ('thou hast mitigated al thy wrath', Douai-Rheims).

18. *Saints*: in the general Protestant sense; believers.

20–21. *sins of omission... himself*: cf. 'we have left undone those things which we ought to have done, and we have done those things which we ought not to have done' (*BCP*, confession at Morning and Evening Prayer); and 'sins... committed by thought, word, and deed' (*BCP*, confession in Order for Holy Communion).

27. *maxime deprecandum*: Lat., 'greatly to be prayed for'.

38. *hoc solum... Domine*: cf. Vulg. (2 Par. 20: 12), 'hoc solum habemus residui ut oculos nostros dirigamus ad te' ('this onlie we have least, that we direct our eies to thee', Douai-Rheims).

p. 13, 1–2. *Nomen Domini... fortissima*: cf. Vulg. (Prov. 18: 10), 'turris fortissima nomen Domini' ('a most strong towre, the name of our Lord', Douai-Rheims).

10. προσευχή: see n. above.

16. *keep at a stand*: arrested state of movement or thought; here, to rest complacently on saving grace.

22–24. *Chrysostome... prayed*: not identified.

26. *Quicquid... petimus*: cf. Vulg. (1 John 5: 14), 'quia quodcumque petierimus secundum voluntatem eius audit nos' ('whatsoever we shal aske according to his will, he heareth us', Douai-Rheims).

29. *unum necessarium*: Lat., 'one necessity'.

30. *unum... Jehovah*: Lat., 'one thing I have petitioned for from Jehovah'.

31. κατ' ἐξοχήν: Gr., 'kat[a] ĕxŏchēn' ('principally', 'most specially').

35–37. *Saviour... deny us*: Luke 11: 13.

39. *competency*: sufficiency.

p. 14, 1–2. *S. Augustine... non amplius*: cf. Augustine, *Ep. CXXX*, vi. 12, 'ergo sufficientiam non indecenter vult, quisquis vult, nec amplius vult' (*PL*, 33.498); ('therefore one does not desire sufficiency indecently, when one wants that and not more').

4–5. *as Christ... thy will*: Matt. 19: 35–6.

11. *mentioned before... omnia*: earlier in the lecture, Andrewes had briefly touched on the problem of whether everyone ('*omnis*') received everything ('*omnia*') asked for in prayer: 'there can be no more said then that every one that asketh shall have, and whatsoever you aske you shall have' (*P*, 144).

15–17. *S. Augustine... non petes?*: cf. Augustine, *Sermones de Scripturis LXI*, v. 6, 'quanto magis dabit bonus, qui nos hortatur ut petamus; cui displicet, si non petamus? Sed cum aliquando tardius dat, commendat dona, non negat' (*PL*, 38.411); ('how much more the good one [God] gives us, who urges us to pray, who is displeased if we do not pray? But sometimes when he gives slowly, he is making the gifts more valuable, not denying [them]').

29–35. *Job... Swyne... Paul... their good*: summary of Augustine, *Enarr. in Psalm. LXXXV*, 9 (*PL* 37.1088).

33. *S. Isidore*: marg. cites Isidore's *Sententiae* (often known in the period as *De Summo Bono*), iii. 1; that chapter contains no sentences on prayer *per se*, but no. 4 is similar in spirit, 'justo temporalia flagella ad aeterna proficiunt gaudia; ideoque et justus in poenis gaudere debet, et impius in prosperitatibus timere' (*PL*, 83.653B); ('the temporal sufferings of the just man gain him everlasting joy; in the same way, the just man pays a penalty to rejoice, while the wicked man [pays a debt] in his prosperity to fear').

35–41. *S. Aug.... great things*: cf. Augustine, *Sermones de Scripturis LXI*, v. 6, 'Diu desiderata, dulcius obtinentur: cito autem data, vilescunt.... Servat tibi Deus, quod non vult cito dare; ut et tu discas magna magne desiderare' (*PL*, 38.411); ('the longer the desiring, the sweeter the obtaining: something quickly given is less regarded.... God retains from you that which he does not want to give you quickly, so that you learn to desire more greatly great things').

p. 15, 4–7. *A fourth... for thee*: cf. Chrysostom, *Hom. on Matthew XXV*, 4, 'for even [Paul], when in much danger and affliction, often besought God that the temptations might depart from him: nevertheless God regarded not his request, but his profit, and to signify this He said, "My grace is sufficient for thee, for my strength is made perfect in weakness." So that before He hath told him the reason, He benefits him against his will, and without his knowing it' (*LF*, x. 175).

5–6. *quod novit utilius*: Lat., 'what he finds more useful'.

9–10. *Chrysostome... aguish prayers*: not identified in Chrysostom; perhaps an error for Basil, 'childish prayers', *Epist. CXCIX*, xxviii. 3.

10–12. *S. Aug.... use ill*: Augustine, *In Joannem Evang. Tract. LXXIII*, 1, 'Male ergo usurus eo quod vult accipere, Deo potius miserante non accipit' (*PL*, 35.1824); 'that which one would like to receive for a bad purpose, God preferably in his mercy will not let him receive'.

14–18. *S. Aug.... then himself*: cf. Prosper of Aquitaine, *Sententiae Delibatae ex Augustino CCXII*, 'fideliter supplicans Deo pro necessitatibus hujus vitae, et misericorditer auditur, et misericorditer non auditur. Quid enim infirmo sit utile, magis novit medicus quam aegrotus' (*PL*, 45.1876–7); ('faithfully asking for the necessities of this life, God both mercifully hears and mercifully does not hear. That which is meet for the sick man is better known by the doctor than the patient').

23–26. *S. Aug.... pray for thee*: attr. Augustine, *Sermo XXII* ('De Consolatione Fratrum'), 'nam, ut ait venerabilis pater Ambrosius, Si pro te tantum rogaveris Deum, tantum tuum meritum possides: sed si pro omnibus rogaveris, omnes pro te rogabunt' (*PL*, 40. 1272); ('for as the venerable father Ambrose says, if you will pray God entirely for yourself, you will have all your reward: but if you will pray for everyone, all shall pray for you'); the original is Ambrose, *De Cain et Abel*, ix. 39, 'si pro te roges tantum, solus, ut diximus, pro te rogabis. Si autem pro omnibus roges, omnes pro te rogabunt' (*PL*, 14.336B); ('if you pray entirely for yourself, let us say that you shall pray for yourself alone. If, however, you pray for everyone, everyone shall pray for you').

27–31. *S. Gregory... for others*: cf. Gregory the Great, *Moralia* x. 20, 'sed quia quisquis pro aliis intercedere nititur, sibi potius ex ipsa charitate suffragatur, recte subjungitur' (*PL*, 76.760D); ('but whoever strives to intercede for others, rather supports himself out of that same goodness, rightly joined to it').

31–37. *S. Chrysostome... then necessity*: summarizes the concluding argument of Chrysostom, *Hom. LX on Matthew* (*LF*, x. 374–5).

40. *prayer in our Liturgie*: *M* (p. 219) has, 'in the ancient Liturgy of the Church, there is first a prayer for them that are without the Church... then for those that be in the Church'. Ed. has not identified a prayer with such a structure in the Great Liturgy of the Eastern church, but similar intercessions for non-Christians are a hallmark of the Western liturgy for Good Friday. The 'orationes solemnes' from the Sarum Rite include petitions 'pro hereticis et scismaticis', 'pro perfidis judeis', and 'pro paganis... idolis suis' (*Sarum Missal*, ed. J. Wickham Legg (1916), 111–12). These were in turn abbreviated by Cranmer in the third solemn collect for Good Friday (*BCP*): 'mercyfull God... have mercy upon all Jewes, Turkes, Infidels, and heretikes, and take from them all ignoraunce, hardnes of heart, and contempt of thy word'. In delivery, Andrewes may

have called attention to both the original and the Cranmerian survival, hence the variant texts's citation of an 'ancient Liturgy' (Sarum and its predecessors) and 'our Liturgie' (*BCP*).

p. 16, 8–16. *Gregory... pray for you*: summary of Gregory the Great, *Hom. in Evang. xxvii*, 8 (*PL*, 76.1209A–D).

27. *Quid retribuam Domino*: Vulg., Ps. 115: 12 (juxt. LXX).

40–41. *the Heathen... bounty*: G (p. 182) reads, 'The Heathen could say, *Gratus animus est mea benignitatis*; A thankfull mind is all which kind and good heart aimeth at'; cf. Cicero, *Oratio Pro Cnaeo Plancio*, xxxiii, 'etenim, iudices tum nihil est, quod malim quam me et gratum esse et videri. Haec est enim una virtus non solum maxima, sed etiam mater virtutum omnium reliquarum'; ('For indeed, gentlemen, while I would fain have some tincture of all virtues, there is no quality I would sooner have, and be thought to have, than gratitude. For gratitude not merely stands alone at the head of all the virtues, but is even mother of all the rest').

p. 17, 3–4. *The Hebrews... Scripture*: *P* uses only the Latin and English translations of these terms in the enumeration that follows (p. 17, ll.5–40, p. 18, ll.1–2); the four Hebrew words are kept in *M* (pp. 220–1).

7. ἀνωθέν: Gr., 'anōthĕn'; 'from above' (James 1: 17).

9–13. *Augustine... own acquiring*. Andrewes has here recast Augustine's observation from 'knowing' and 'not knowing', to 'having' and 'not having'; cf. *Sermones de Temp. CCLXV*, viii. 9, 'Qui se dicit scire quod nescit, temerarius est: qui se negat scire quod scit, ingratus est' (*PL*, 38.1223); ('he who says that he knows what he does not know, is rash: he who says he does not know what he does know, is ungrateful').

18–21. *Bernard... grace*: cf. Bernard, *In Feria IV Hebd. Sac.*, 11, 'quod videlicet tantae charitati ingratus fuerim, quod spiritui gratiae contumeliam fecerim, quod sanguinem testamenti pollutum duxerim, quod conculcaverim Filium Dei' (*PL*, 183.296A–B); ('because clearly I had been ungrateful to the greatest love, had reproached the spirt of grace, had polluted the blood of the testament, and had trampled upon the Son of God').

21. *disease of the Israelites*: complaints ('murmuring') against God and Moses by the Israelites in the forty years between the exodus from Egypt and entering the promised land of Canaan; cf. Exod. 16: 2–3, 17: 3, Numb. 14: 2–3, Deut. 8: 14–17.

22–24. *Augustine... against him*: Augustine, *In Joann. Evang. Tract. XXVI*, 11, 'nam de nulla re magis Dominum offendisse ille populus dictus est, quam contra Deum murmurando' (*PL*, 35. 1612); ('in no one thing did that people more offend the Lord, it is said, than in murmuring against God').

34–36. *Chrysostom... of them*: Chrysostom, *Hom. on Matthew XXV*, 4, 'For the best preservative of any benefit is the remembrance of the benefit, and a continual thanksgiving' (*LF*, x. 174).

p. 18, 1–2. *his last Psalm... duty*: the 'last Psalm' is 150; but Andrewes alludes to 148 ('beastes and all cattell: creeping things, and flying foule. Kings of the earth, and all people: Princes, and all Judges of the earth... Let them praise the Name of the Lord', vv. 10–13); cf. *G* (p. 225), 'and if there were no men, wee should call upon the creatures to praise God, *Psa.* 148'.

14–18. *Chrysostom... any other*: not identified.

26. *the end*: purpose.

30. *best member*: noblest part of the body.

37–38. *Saint Chrysostoms... neglect it*: not identified.

p. **19**, 3. *predicare*: Lat., 'praedicare'; lit., to warn or instruct; to preach.

6. *Doxology... honour &c.*: gen., any ascription of glory to the Trinity; the form conventional after sermons—'To whom with the Father, the Son, and the Holy Ghost be all honour and glory, now and forever, Amen'—is a form of the 'Lesser Doxology', or *Gloria Patri*, itself based loosely on biblical ascriptions of glory to the Godhead (cf. Rom. 16: 27, Rev. 5: 13).

9. εὐχαριστία: the Gr., 'eucharistia', lit., 'thanksgiving', is here applied to the sacrament of Holy Communion; although commonly so applied since early Christian times, it is not a strictly biblical use, except in the fact that Christ 'gave thanks' at the institution of the Lord's Supper (cf. Matt. 26: 27), or, more generally, that the service itself is (as for Andrewes here) the highest act of thanksgiving for Christ's sacrifice. The conjunction of both prayer and sacrament in εὐχαριστία are typical of Andrewes, and similar to the statement of Chrysostom in a homily quoted elsewhere in the lecture: 'for this cause even the awful mysteries... which are celebrated at every communion, are called a sacrifice of thanksgiving, because they are the commemoration of many benefits, and they signify the very sum of God's care for us, and by all means they work upon us to be thankful' (*Hom. XXV(.4) on Matthew*; *LF*, x. 174). Use of the word was hotly contested by Roman Catholics and Protestants, the former being keen to accuse the latter of emptying the sacrament of sacrificial real presence in favour of a merely commemorative thanksgiving (see Fulke, *A Defence*, in *Works*, i. 502–6); throughout his career, 'eucharist' was Andrewes's preferred term for the sacrament.

11–12. *it ends... on high &c.*: the 'Gloria in Excelsis', or 'Greater Doxology', an ancient hymn of Gr. origin, dating from the fourth century, inspired by the angels' hymn to the shepherds at the Nativity (Luke 2: 14); in *BCP* (1552) Cranmer moved the 'Gloria' from its traditional place at the opening of the eucharist, to the end of his order for Holy Communion as a climactic declaration of praise and thanksgiving.

14. *church exercises*: church services; liturgies.

29. *quid retribuam*: see p. 16, l. 27 and n.

34–35. *Deus vult... beneficiorum*: Lat., 'God wishes our gratitude to be for making us able to receive greater benefits'.

36–38. *Ten lepers... saved him*: Luke 17: 11–19.

38. *gratis*: free; unrewarded.

p. **20**, 1–7. *Bernard saith... formerly*: cf. Bernard of Clairvaux, *In Capite Jejunii. Serm. I*, 4, 'siquidem etiam fluminis aqua, si stare coeperit, et ipsa putrescet, et inundatione facta superveniens, repelletur. Sic plane, sic gratiarum cessat decursus, ubi recursus non fuerit: nec modo nihil augetur ingrato, sed et quod acceperat vertitur ei in perniciem' (*PL*, 183.170A); ('just like a stream of water, if it begins to stand still, and putrifies, and the flood rises up, it is driven back. Just as clearly, if thanks cease to come down, there will be nowhere for them to return: neither can an ungrateful man augment anything, but instead turns everything he receives into ruin').

7–17. *The same Father... was in them*: summary of Bernard of Clairvaux, *Sermo de Div. XXVII*, 4–5 (*PL*, 183.613C–615A).

17–19. *Prosper... thanksgiving*: attr. more specifically in *M* (p. 223) to '*Prosper* in his second booke *de vocatione gentium*', but ed. does not find a similar passage in Prosper of Aquitaine, *De Vocatione Omnium Gentium*, ii (*PL*, 51).

21-25. *the leper ... some think*: cf. Chrysostom, *Hom. on Matthew XXV*, 3, 'now some say, that for this intent He bade him tell no man, that they might practise no craft about the discerning of his cure; a very foolish suspicion on their part.... He bids him "tell no man," teaching us to avoid boasting and vainglory. And yet He well knew that the other would not obey, but would proclaim his benefactor' (*LF*, x. 173).

26. ***: there follows here (*P*, 151-2) exposition of five 'rules to direct us that our invocation may be rightly grounded', viz., urgency, constancy, humility, reasonableness, persistence.

27-28. *Now because ... helps to it*: since prayer is a means in itself it cannot (logically) also have means, but only aids ('helps') to it; cf. *M* (p. 226), 'prayer it selfe is a meanes, and the meanes of all means: therefore it hath means, i.[e.] helpes; none to beginne it, but to helpe it'.

32. *want*: lack.

37-38. *canticum ... beneficium novum*: Lat., 'a new song for a new benefit'; cf. Vulg. Ps. 97: 1, 'Cantate Domino canticum novum quia mirabilia fecit' ('Sing to the Lord a new song, for he has done marvellous things').

p. 21, 7-13. *Fathers call ... so alms*: common patristic images and arguments; '*Jejunium orationis robur*' in fact seems closest to Bernard of Clairvaux, *In Quadrag. Serm. IV*, 2, 'Jejunium orationem roborat, oratio sanctificat jejunium' (*PL*, 183.177A; 'fasting strengthens prayer, prayer sanctifies fasting'); various combinations of fasting, almsgiving, and prayer as 'wings' to God occur frequently in Augustine; cf. *Sermo de Temp. CCV*, 3, 'Hae sunt duae alae orationis, quibus volat ad Deum' (*PL*, 38.1040); ('these things [righteousness and almsgiving] are the two wings of prayer, with which it flies to God'); and *Enarr. in Psalm. XLII*, 8, 'vis orationem tuam volare ad Deum? Fac illi duas alas, jejunium et eleemosynam' (*PL* 36.482); ('do you want your prayer to fly to God? Use these two wings, fasting and almsgiving'); also found in Chrysostom, cf. *Hom. de Precatione* (*PG*, 64.463B).

10. *Dan.4.24 [in marg.]*: reference to a point not preserved in *P*, but present in *M* (p. 227), '*almes*, whereof *Daniel* was a Preacher, *cap*. 4 *v*. 24. to *Nabuchadonoser*', i.e. Daniel's exhortation to Nebuchadnezzar that he 'breake off [his] sinnes by righteousnes, and [his] iniquities by mercy toward the poore'; Andrewes here sides with the Rhemists who insisted on 'redeem thy sins with alms' as the translation of the Vulg. 'Redime eleemosynis peccata tua'; Fulke (*Defence*, in *Works*, i. 447) condemned this as fostering 'popish penance and satisfaction'.

15-18. *Si oratio ... of others*: cf. Chrysostom, *On the Incomprehensible Nature of God*, Hom. III, 34, 'When you call upon the Lord by yourself, he does not listen to you in the same way as when you invoke him along with your brothers. Here in church you have something more. Here you have the oneness of mind, the unison of voices, the common bond of love, the prayers of the priests'; and Hom. III, 36, 'if the prayer of a single person is so powerful, much more so is the power which is offered along with many other people' (*FC*, lxxii. 110-11).

19. *oratio fidei ... oratio sensus*: Lat., 'prayer of faith as well as prayer of feeling'; 'prayer of hope' (p. 30, l. 22) is an error; cf. *M* (p. 227), 'yet I may have the prayer of faith'.

24. ***: The chapter concludes (*P*, 153-4) with a catalogue of 'signes ... that our prayers are rightly qualified, and like to prevail' (earnestness, confidence of forgiveness of sins, patience, true thankfulness).

26. *Second Commandement*: 'Thou shalt not make to thyself any graven image.... Thou shalt not bow down to them, nor worship them...' (Exod. 20: 4-5).

NOTES TO PP. 21–22

27. *CHAP. VII... affirmative part*: Andrewes's first three lectures on the second commandment (*P*, 192–204) expounded its 'negative' injunction against the worshipping of images; the subsequent seven lectures (*P*, 204–30) treated the 'affirmative' rules implied in it for how to worship properly; cf. p. 32, ll. 34–7. Chapter VII (*P*, 214–21), presented here in its entirety, prompted no interpolations by the editors of *P*. It contains the scripturalist foundation for all of Andrewes's later calls for bodily reverence in worship, and is his earliest expression of the arguments that would underwrite the 1630s Laudian campaign for ritual conformity.

30. *first Commandment... internal*: in the fourth lecture on the first commandment, Andrewes explained that it held precedence over the second commandment 'because spiritual worship required in the first, is before outward worship, prescribed in the second' (*P*, 99).

33–34. *Tishtacaveh... Tagnabod*: transliterations of Heb. verbs 'bow down' and 'serve'; from Exod. 20: 4–5; by modern standards, more accurately, *tishtahweh*, and *ta'abedem*.

p. 21, 39–p. 22, 2. *the fathers... darknesse*: cf. Orsisius, *Doctrina de Institutione Monachorum*, xxxv, 'non sumus filii noctis, neque tenebrarum. Si ergo sumus filii lucis, debemus scire quae lucis sunt, et facere fructus luminis in omni opere bono: quod enim manifestatur, lux est' (*PL*, 103.467A–B); ('we are not the sons of night, nor of darkness. If therefore we are the sons of light, we must show that we know what light is, and to make the fruit of the light in everything through good work: that which is manifest, that is the light').

6. *close*: hidden.

10–11. *conjunctions copulative*: cf. John Milton, *Accedence Commenc't Grammar* (1669), 'a Conjunction is a part of Speech, that joyneth Words and Sentences together. Of conjunctions some be Copulative, as *et* and, *quoque* also, *nec* neither. Some be Disjunctive, as *aut* or. Some be Causal, as *nom* for, *quia* because, and many such like' (p. 39).

13. [καὶ]: Gr., 'and'.

20–21. *a distinction... other places*: Andrewes here departs markedly from mainstream English Calvinism which was anxious to avoid the perceived Catholic extreme of declaring churches as spaces more holy or sanctified than any other of human creation. These remarks anticipate Hooker's similar defence of the 'beauty of holiness' by nearly twenty years (*Lawes*, v. 16, 25; *FEWRH*, ii. 60–1, 113–17), and are the foundation of Andrewes's more well-known Jacobean views as well as the subsequent Laudian campaign for the beautification of churches as distinctly holy places (see Tyacke, 'Lancelot Andrewes'; and Lake, 'Laudian Style').

27. *the preacher*: Solomon (cf. Eccles. 1: 1).

28. *observa pedem utrunque*: cf. Vulg. (Eccles. 4: 17), 'custodi pedem tuum ingrediens domum Dei' ('Take heede to kepe thy foote, when thou entrest into the house of God', Douai-Rheims).

29. *inferior members*: lesser parts of the body (i.e. feet).

34. *Honor signi*: Lat., lit. 'honour of [by] the sign'; symbolic worship or reverence.

35–36. *Exinanivit... no reputation*: cf. Vulg. (Phil. 2: 7), 'sed semet ipsum exinanivit formam servi accipiens'; and Geneva, 'but he made himself of no reputation & tooke on him the forme of a servant'; in 'A Sermon... on Christmas Day. Anno 1609' (this edn., p. 168, l. 16), as here and elsewhere, Andrewes (like Douai-Rheims) prefers the etymological specificity of 'emptied himself' ('*exinanivit*').

36. *Humiliavit se*: cf. Vulg. (Phil. 2: 8), 'humiliavit semet ipsum factus oboediens usque ad mortem' ('he humbled himselfe, and became obedient unto the death'); part of Andrewes's text for Easter, 1614 (*XCVI*, 469–80), which elaborates Christ's humiliation as precedent and cause for genuflection at the name of Jesus (Phil. 2: 10).

40. *spoliavit me honore*: cf. Vulg. (Job 19: 9), 'spoliavit me gloria mea et abstulit coronam de capite meo' ('hee hath spoyled mee of mine honour, and taken the crowne away from mine head').

p. 23, 2. *Nudatio capitis*: Lat., lit. 'nakedness of the head'.

2–6. *a cap... a servant*: cf. Jean Bodin, *The Six Bookes of the Common-weale*, trans. R. Knolles (1606), 'the wearing of a cap was in auntient time the marke of them that were but lately made free, to cover their heads that were shaven when they were slaves' (p. 121); and Plutarch, *The Philosophie [Moralia]*, trans. P. Holland (1603), 'afterwards when he entred *Rome* in triumph for this victorie; the said *Terentius* followed hard after his [Scipio's] triumphant chariot, wearing a cap of libertie on his head, like an affranchised slave, and avowing that he held his freedome by him' (p. 450).

16. *knees... to Baal*: the quotation of 1 Kings 19: 18. in Rom. 11: 4 was a controverted point of translation. Gregory Martin objected to the Bishops' Bible's 'which have not bowed the knee to [ye image of] Baal' for its interpolation of 'image', without textual warrant, as an opportunistic Protestant critique of reverence or worship of images (Fulke, *Defence*, in *Works*, i. 202). Andrewes prefers the Rheims reading to validate proper adoration of God, not images of him.

20. *Honor facti*: 'worship in [by] deed'.

22–23. *Honor exhibitus facto*: 'worship shown in doing'.

28–29. *Christ... you not*: Vulg. (Matt. 25: 12).

41. *mature*: Lat., 'early', 'speedily'.

p. 24, 9. *Tribe of Levi*: cf. 'Sacrilege a Snare' (this edn., p. 87, ll. 3–10 and n.).

14–15. *antipsalm... our Church*: Ps. 95, the 'Venite Exultemus Domino', first canticle (hence 'ante', 'before', or 'first' psalm) at Morning Prayer (*BCP*); here a characteristically literal reading of v. 5 ('O come, let us worship and fall down, and kneel before the Lord our Maker').

26–27. *exhibiting... going out*: suggests genuflection upon entering and departing from church; cf. the instructions for the same by both clergy and laity *passim* in Andrewes's 'Notes on the Book of Common Prayer' (*LACT*, xi. 144–58).

39. *depositionem magnificientiæ*: Lat., lit., 'the putting off of magnificence' (dignity).

p. 25, 8–21. *True... lawfull authority*: careful acknowledgement of scriptural precedents for standing at public prayer, but severely limited by insistence upon observance of the prayer book rubrics which require kneeling.

22–31. *In private... rise up*: although making concessions to liberty of posture in private prayer, Andrewes's preference for kneeling is clear. *M* (p. 275) is more emphatic against sitting: 'Sitting at prayer time is not warranted by the word.' Contrast John Merbecke, *A Booke of Notes* (1581), 'some foolishly imagine that praier is made either better or worse, by the jesture of our bodyes.... it skilleth not after what sorte our bodyes be placed, so that the minde being present with God, bring her purpose to passe' (pp. 582–3).

p. 26, 22–24. *Sacraments... unto eternal life*: in Cranmer's first *BCP* (1549), the priest distributed the elements using the words from the Sarum mass, in English: 'The body [blood] of our Lorde Jesus Christe which was geven for thee, preserve thy bodye and soule unto everlasting lyfe.' The books of 1552 and 1559 added to this the memorialist 'Drink this in remembrance that Christ died for thee, and feed on him in thy heart by faith, with thanksgiving.' Significantly Andrewes only marshals the more sacrificial diction as an argument for bodily reverence in receiving communion.

27–28. *sitting...unlawful*: terse rejection of puritan complaints against kneeling to receive communion; *BCP* enjoined reception kneeling, but many preferred the Edwardine practice of receiving communion seated, to avoid any hint of adoring the elements of a sacrificial mass and to imitate the Last Supper (see MacCulloch, *Tudor Church Militant*, 159–60); cf. John Whitgift, *An Answere to...An Admonition to the Parliament* (1572), 'the meetest gesture for praying and thanks gyving is kneeling: but those that receive the Eucharist, pray and give thanks, *Ergo* the metest gesture for them is kneeling' (p. 100); and Hooker, *Lawes*, v. 68. 3 (*FEWRH*, ii. 346), 'our kneeling at communions is the gesture of pietie. If wee did there present our selves but to make some show or dumbe resemblance of a spirituall feast, it may bee that sitting were the fitter ceremonie, but comming as receivers of inestimable grace at the hands of God, what doth better beseeme our bodies at that hower then to bee sensible witnesses of minds unfainedly humbled?' (*FEWRH*, ii. 346).

p. 27, 3. *opposite*: 'hostile, antagonistic, adverse' (*OED sa* 4.a).

4. *Wise man*: Solomon.

8. *stiffe necked*: obstinate, haughty; cf. Acts 7: 51.

9. *knees...Elephant*: popular sixteenth-century belief that elephants could not bend their knees; not in *M* or *G*; cf. Andrewes, Easter 1614, 'and verily, He will not have us worship Him like *Elephants*, as if we had no joynts in our *Knees*' (*XCVI*, 475–6, where the point is fulsomely elaborated); the metaphor became part of Laudian idiom; cf. Antony Farindon asking, 'Whether it be indeed Religion that maketh their knees as the knees of the Elephant, and putteth them in the same posture at Church which they use in a Theatre, and maketh them more bold with their God then with their fellow-Dust and ashes' (*LXXX Sermons* (1672), 757).

12–16. *S. Chrysostome...comest not*: not identified.

29–30. *some come...sermon begin*: early example of Andrewes's lifelong complaint against the common practice of attending sermon instead of service; cf. 'A Sermon Preached...on Easter Day' (this edn.), pp. 242 and nn.; 'A Sermon Preached... Whit-Sunday' (this edn.), pp. 220–23 and nn; also Andrewes, Gunpowder Anniversary 1617, 'devotion is the proper, and most kindly worke of *holinesse*....now, in what honour, this part of *holinesse* is; what accompt we make of this *service*, do but tell the number of them that be heere at it, and ye shall neede no other certificate' (*XCVI*, 992).

34. *compact...it self*: quoting first Geneva ('compact together in it selfe'), then *BCP* ('at unitie in itselfe').

38–39. *In Discordia...separation*: cf. Augustine, *Enarr. in Psal. CXXVII*, 3 (*PL*, 37.1679).

p. 28, 9–10. *separation...language*: Gen. 11: 1–9.

12–13. *Chrysostome...hailstones*: not identified.

14–16. *Augustine...Revelation*: not identified; cf. Rev. 1: 15, 19: 6.

17. ἐν παντὶ φόβῳ: Gr., 'en panti phŏbŏ', 'in all fear' (1 Pet. 2: 18).

21–24. *Apostles...fled*: Matt. 26: 40–56.

25. *Jacob...night*: confusion of Jacob's fear of Esau with his fear of Laban (the error exists also in *M* and *G*); upon stealing away from the latter with his daughters, Jacob

confessed 'thus I was in the day, the drought consumed mee, and the frost by night, and my sleep departed from mine eyes' (Gen. 31: 40).

28–31. *Chrysostome... mid-day*: cf. Chrysostom, *Homilies on the Acts*, xliii, which commends the zeal and vigilance of those who listened to Paul, in contrast to the diffidence of modern congregations, but does not use precisely this epigrammatic summary (*NPNCF*, xi. 263–4).

32. *natural man*: see p. 6, l. 36 and n.

33. *the two former*: eating and drinking.

40. *Vigilate... dormiunt*: cf. Vulg. (1 Thess. 5: 6–7), 'igitur non dormiamus sicut ceteri sed vigilemus et sobrii simus qui enim dormiunt nocte dormiunt et qui ebrii sunt'; ('Therefore let us not sleepe as do other, but let us watch and be sober. For they that sleepe, sleepe in the night, and they that be drunken, are drunken in the night.')

p. 29, 3. *crosse*: contrarious, oppositional.

3. *sleep at Church*: the occasion of the following anecdote, recorded by John Aubrey, might have animated Andrewes's point here: 'There was then at Cambridge a good fatt Alderman, that was wont to sleep at Church... [the] good man was exceedingly troubled at it, and went to Andrewes his chamber to be satisfied in point of Conscience. Mr. Andrewes told him that was an ill habit of body not of mind .... Andrewes then told him, he would have him make a good heartie meale as he was wont to doe, and presently take out his full sleep; he followed his advice, came to St Maries church, where the Preacher was prepared with a sermon to damme all who slept at Sermon, a certaine signe of Reprobation. The good Alderman having taken his full nap before lookes on the Preacher all sermon time, and spoyled his designe.... Andrewes was most extremely spoken against and preached a[gainst] for offering to assoile, or excuse a sleeper in Sermon time' (*Brief Lives*, ed. K. Bennett, Oxford, forthcoming).

4–5. *Actio... unlawful*: a commonplace; cf. George Chapman, *A Widdowes Tears* (1612), 'This tale... suited | with action clothed with such likely circumstance' (IV. i); and William Ames, *The Marrow of Sacred Divinity* (1642), 'for a singular action is always clothed with its circumstances, upon which the goodnesse or evillnesse of it doth not a little depend' (p. 238).

7–8. *Non dormiet... dormitabit*: Vulg. (Isa. 5: 27).

12. *In prima... peccati*: cf. Seneca, *Epist. XCVII*, 14, 'prima illa et maxima peccantium est poena peccasse' (the first and worst penalty for sin is to have committed sin').

14–15. *Cains murder... blood*: Gen. 4. 10.

15. *Sodoms heat... &c.*: Gen. 19: 5, 24.

24. *ardens cor*: Lat., lit., 'a burning heart'; an ardent heart.

25–27. *a Father... compatible*: cf. Bernard of Clairvaux, *Serm. de Div. XVI*, 2, 'sicut autem corporis natura est sanitas, ita cordis natura est puritas: quia turbato oculo non videbitur Deus; et cor humanum ad hoc factum est ut suum videat Creatorem' (*PL*, 183.580B); ('but just as the natural state of the body is health, so the natural state of the heart is purity: because clouded eyes do not see God; and the human heart is that which is made to see the Creator').

33. *in domo lætitiæ*: Lat., 'in a house of mirth'; cf. Eccles. 7.4.

p. 30, 3–4. *fools... not present*: cf. Andrewes on sermon hearing, Gunpowder Anniversary 1617, 'we come to it, if we will: we go our waies, when we will: stay no longer, then we will: and listen to it, while we will: and sleep out, or turne us and talke out, or sit still, and let our mindes rove (the rest) whither they will' (*XCVI*, 992).

5. *risus*: Lat., 'ridicule'.

16–17. *Heathen...simulato*: Cicero, *Pro Sext. Rosc. Orat.*, xiii. 37, 'vultu saepe laeditur pietas' ('filial duty is often violated by a look').

30. *Qui...me audit*: Vulg. (Luke 10: 16).

31. σίγα λαός: Gr., 'siga laŏs', 'people, be silent'.

35. *constantia...divino*: Lat., 'constancy in divine worship'; cf. *M* (p. 280), 'And the Fathers say, that that place is taken out of *Esay* 32.17. *Cultum justitiae silentium* [lit., "the worship of righteousness is silence"]'.

38. *discedere a lege*: Lat., 'to depart from the reading'; cf. *M* (p. 280), 'used in *Psalm*. 119.118. they had a relation to the departing out of the Congregation, when the Law was a reading'; cf. Ps. 119: 118, 'thou hast troden downe all them that depart from thy statutes'.

40. *lex Talionis*: Lat., 'the law of retaliation' (*OED* cites 1597 as the earliest English use); cf. Lev. 24: 20 ('Breach for breach, eye for eye, tooth for tooth: as he hath caused a blemish in a man, so shall it be done to him againe)'.

p. 31, 1. *Quare...Domine*: Vulg. (Ps. 21: 2).

2. *Quare...serve*: parody of Vulg. (Ps. 21: 2).

4. *Discedite a me*: Vulg. (Matt. 25: 41).

7. λαος ἄφεσο: Gr., 'laŏs aphĕso', 'let the people depart'.

9. *Council of Carthage*: 4th Council of Carthage (398); canon 24, 'sacerdote verbum faciente in ecclesia, qui egressus de auditorio fuerit, excommunicet' ('while the priest is ministering the word in the church, he who leaves the auditorium shall be excommunicate'); *Conciliorum Omnium Volumina Quinque* (Venice, 1585; i. 759; Andrewes's copy is PCCL 4.11.17–21).

17. *in quam...prospicere*: Vulg. (1 Pet. 1: 12).

22. *Ut...facies*: Lat., 'you shal do as you hear'; cf. Vulg. (Deut. 27: 10), 'audies vocem eius et facies mandata atque justitias quas ego praecipio tibi' ('thou shalt heare his voice, and doe the commandementes and justices, which I command thee', Douai-Rheims).

23–24. *ultra speciem*: Lat., 'beyond a pretence'.

24. *ut...audieris*: Lat., 'as you hear you shall be heard'.

32–38. *Augustine...looke for?* Not identified. An equivalent passage does not appear in *G*, but cf. *M* (p. 281), '*Mal.* 1.14. a way to examine us. God maketh there a very abject, and as *Augustine* saith, an unlawfull comparison; to compare himselfe to a great King on earth: and *vers*.8. he reasoneth, If you should offer such a gift to your Prince, would he accept thy person?' Thus, after acknowledging that Augustine found the comparison demeaning to God, Andrewes uses the texts from Mal. to argue by analogy that one would not behave in the presence of an earthly king the way many behave in the presence of God himself. Andrewes returned in greater detail—but without the Augustinian caveat—to these images from Mal. in Gunpowder Anniversary 1617, 'In *Malachie's* time, things were growen much to this passe...to think any service... would serve GOD well enough. When they were come to this, GOD is faine to take state upon Him, and to tell them plainely, He would have them know, He is a King, and a Great King....He knoweth no reason, why any King or creature on earth, should be used with more respect, or served with more reverence, then He' (*XCVI*, 991). For the 1617 context, see Tyacke, 'Lancelot Andrewes', 30–1. A less well-known early example of these sentiments is in Andrewes's lecture at St Giles, 23 Sept. 1599 (on Gen. 4: 16), 'the point that wee are to gather hence for our instruction, is, That we conceive of the

Church, and place of Gods presence, as we doe of the place of the Princes presence; for we reverence such places though the Prince be absent; though we have no visible apparition of his presence' (*AS*, 458).

p. 32, 13. *Misericordiam... Sacrificium*: cf. Vulg. (Matt 9: 13, quoting Hos. 6: 6), 'misericordiam volo et non sacrificium' ('I wil mercie, & not sacrifice', Douai-Rheims).

16. 2. *The second signe*: the enumeration of parts in all texts is flawed, each in a different way. Here '2.' follows from '1.' (p. 31, l. 31); the 'second signe' follows from the 'good signe' described in p. 31, ll. 31–40. These 'signs' are points for self-scrutiny whereby the believer can judge whether his or her worship is proper. A 'third' follows, l. 19.

23. *the sixth rule*: evidence that at some stage or in some state the lecture was divided into 'rules'; *M* also has remnants of such a scheme, but collation does not provide a logical pattern for its reconstruction.

24–27. *Hierome... Gods service*: not in *G*; *M* adds, '*Hierome* on *Numb*. 36.13. no man may be a curtaine in the Lords house, unlesse he hath a hooke and a tache'; this itself contains an error for Exod. 36: 13 ('After, he made fiftie taches [*marg*: Or, hookes] of golde, and coupled the curtaines one to another with the taches'); ed. cannot identify such a gloss by Jerome or the other authors in *PL*.

p. 33, 1. *Fourth Commandement*: Exod. 20: 8–10, 'Remember the Sabbath day, to keepe it holy [...]'.

2. *CHAP. II*: *P* divides Andrewes's lectures on the fourth commandment into twelve chapters (pp. 259–308). The first five (pp. 259–85) concern the required 'rest' on the sabbath; the remainder treat the ways to 'sanctify' the sabbath (worship, works of mercy, well-trained clergy, proper places of worship). The chapter presented here (*P*, 262–7)—Andrewes's major statement on the theology (vs. the practice) of Sunday as the Christian day of worship and rest—has been more contested than any other work by Andrewes since at least the 1630s. A succession of controversialists, and later of scholars, have read the lectures less in the context in which they were written, than in the polemical terms of mid-seventeenth-century debates over 'sabbatarianism'—the strict observance of Sundays associated especially from the mid-1590s with puritans and nonconformists. Andrewes's high view of Sunday's sanctity—especially the belief in its divine institution, the moral obligation of Christians to observe it, and the right of the civil magistrate to enforce it—does in fact parallel later godly views of the sabbath.

But, if the date 1585 is accepted for this lecture, it is very nearly coincident with what scholars accept as the *locus classicus* of sabbatarian theology in England—the incipient presbyterian fraternity of the Dedham Classis, which formally debated the sabbath question in the spring of 1584. As J. H. Primus has shown, there was no single 'puritan' position on this point, a fact revealed by the division of opinion between two debating clergy at Dedham, Richard Crick and Henry Sandes ('The Dedham sabbath debate: more light on English sabbatarianism', *Sixteenth Century Journal*, 17 (1986), 87–102). As Primus's generous quotations from the manuscript records of the debate show, Sandes's principal beliefs correspond with those of Andrewes here: that sabbath observance was not merely an Old Testament ceremony since it had been refounded by Christ and the apostles on the day of the Resurrection (Sunday); that it could not be changed or abrogated by the church; and that although any number of secondary symbolic meanings could be soundly applied to understanding the Christian Sunday, its original and always fundamental *raison d'être* was the worship of God.

What has not been properly appreciated, however, is that Andrewes's motives for such positions could differ from those of emergent 'puritans'. Sandes's affirmation that the sabbath 'was not a church conclusion but came from heaven' (quoted in Primus, p. 93) should be seen as a godly hedge raised against dictation of church practice by ecclesiastical (episcopal) authority. But for Andrewes, the same argument flows from a characteristic inclination to hedge ecclesiastical authority with *jure divino* theology. Similarly, the worship which is for Sandes the 'principal end' of the sabbath is defined as godly preaching, whereas for Andrewes it is a worship not defined only by sermons, but also the reverent celebration of the sacraments, set forms of prayer, and good works. Furthermore, Andrewes, much more than the Dedham group, had in his sights the extremely radical teachings of separatists like Henry Barrow, who argued for the complete abolition of the sabbath as a mere Jewish ceremony that had been abrogated by the Gospel. Hence Andrewes has as a polemic target an adversary quite different from seventeenth-century sabbatarians keen to make more rigid the English church's pre-existing commitment to Sunday observance.

Charles I's reissue (1633) of James I's 'Book of Sports' (1618), which allowed moderate recreations on Sunday afternoons, reignited sabbatarian controversy. Antagonists of Archbishop Laud, such as Henry Burton, viewed this (with some justification) as an attack on English traditions of sabbath observance enshrined in the official homily 'Of the Place and Time of Prayer' (*Book of Homilies*, 1568). And they were quick to seize upon Andrewes's catechistical lectures as the ultimate weapon for use against the party that openly idolized Andrewes as their most revered authority. As Burton witheringly put it in his *Brief Answer to a late Treatise of the Sabbath Day* (Amsterdam, 1635?), 'I might here also adde what is sayd in that Booke, which is intituled, *A Patterne of catecheticall Doctrine*, and printed at London 1630. which though it have not Dr. Andrewes name prefixt unto it; yet it is well knowne, it was his worke, (even *ex ungue Leonem*) being his Catecheticall exercise in Cambridge, as I have been credibly informed, and whereof I have the Manuscript by mee, which I keep as an Antiquity. I know the booke will not very well relish with our adversaries palate' (p. 15). Burton refers here to both a print copy (the earliest exemplar of the *G* group of texts), and, tantalizingly, to a manuscript. Presumably the latter was one of the many sets of notes taken by hearers said to have circulated widely among the devout. However, Burton's citation of readings found in his MS but not in his printed text, confirm that his MS was related to that used to set *M*, or *P*, or, possibly, that Burton's MS was in fact the copy text of *M* itself (see p. 34 l. 39– p.35 l. 2, 37–8; p. 37, l. 28 and nn.). Burton scores a palpable hit against the Laudian apologists with his use of Andrewes, and accurately points up how far Laudians like Francis White were willing to stray from the consensus represented by Andrewes and Hooker in order to defend the right of ecclesiastical authority to govern public worship. But Andrewes's reasons for insisting on the moral duty of observing the sabbath were not the same as Burton's. Although, as Kenneth Parker has shown, Andrewes as a Jacobean bishop remained a stern disciplinarian against sabbath-breakers, he was also a consultant to James I for the 'Book of Sports' (*The English Sabbath* (Cambridge, 1988), 99–100, 134–7), and defended Sunday pastimes as long as they did not conflict with his benchmark for proper observance, reverent worship at appointed times and places.

Given the susceptibility of Andrewes's lectures to use by their critics, Laudian propagandists were anxious to distance this part of Andrewes's legacy not only from themselves, but from Andrewes himself. The most obvious example of this was Laud and Buckeridge's omission of any of the catechetical texts from their authorized editions of Andrewes (1629). Commonwealth Laudians went even further. Peter Heylyn asserted in 1656 that Andrewes had gone so far as to order his chaplains 'not to own any thing for his, that was said to have been taken by notes from his mouth'. More dubiously (given the evidence of *P*), he went on to claim that 'in discourse with those about him he would never own it, nor liked to have it mentioned to him, so he abolished (as it seemeth) his own original copy' (*Extraneus Vapulans*, 127). One year later, the editor(s) of *P* continued this exercise in damage control by adding extensive passages from Andrewes's later work to their presentation of this lecture (see nn. to '*Addition 7*' and '*Addition 8*', below). These attempt to distance Andrewes from what in his own lifetime had been a hallmark of his orthodox conformity, but by the 1650s could be appropriated as a defence of puritan reform.

4. *Sanctification*: cf. Andrewes, St Paul's lecture, 'the honor which is given this day is holinesse, which is expressed by sanctifying or hallowing' (*AS*, 130); in the first lecture on the fourth commandment (*P*, 261), Andrewes defined 'sanctification' as, 'when God appointeth any thing to an holy use, he is said to sanctifie it, and when man applieth it to the use to which God hath so appointed it, he is said also to sanctifie it'.

11. *res finitae*: Lat., lit., 'things of finitude'.

27. *servile work*: '[after L. *opus servile* (Vulg.), a literal rendering of Heb.] . . . : in religious use applied *spec*. to laborious or mechanical work forbidden to be done on the Sabbath' (*OED sa* A.1.c).

34. *Rest . . . subordinate end*: Andrewes avoids extreme prescriptiveness here by not enumerating exactly what to do and what not to do on Sundays, emphasizing instead the general need for the moral profitability of sabbath rest. Cf., from the St Paul's lecture, 'touching the rest from things inhibited, it is somewhat dangerous to speak of it because our nature is given to such extremes', and, 'least while men avoid prophanesse, they fall into that precisenesse of the Jews, as to think it death and deadly sinne to doe any thing at all on the Sabbath day' (*AS*, 138, 139), and below, p. 38, ll. 17–21. Elsewhere (*P*, 282–5) Andrewes upholds sabbath strictures against harvest, trade, travel, and building, but these are carefully qualified by caveats against any literalism that might privilege the legalistic means over the spiritual ends of sanctification.

p. 34, 1. *[Addition 7]*: this is a lengthy insertion (*P*, 263–5) designed to frustrate any desired alignment of Andrewes with strict sabbatarianism. The two-part thesis is judicious: first, that '*the scope of this reverend Author, is not here to prove, that the command of the sabbath is wholly Moral, and in no part ceremonial, but to prove against the Anabaptists, Familists, and other sectaries, who denie all distinction of dayes under the Gospel*'; and second, that '*his opinion seems to be, that the Lords day which we observe, instead of the sabbath, is* jure divino . . . *yet, that the Jewish sabbath . . . is abolisht by the death of Christ*' (p. 263). The editor supports the first argument with a short excerpt from Andrewes, Easter 1618, where he argues that Sunday was instituted by Christ himself in the act of his resurrection (*XCVI*, 529). The second is supported by a lengthy extract from Andrewes's *Speech delivered in the Starr-chamber against . . . M. Traske* (*OP*, part 2, pp. 63–75; also *LACT*, xi. 83–94). In 1618–19 Traske had been prosecuted in Star Chamber, of which Andrewes was a member, for preaching the Christian observance of the Jewish sabbath and dietary laws. The portion of Andrewes's speech defending Traske's censure quoted here summarizes the evidence for the Christian Sunday from scripture, the fathers, and the ancient church councils

(*OP*, 72–5). Significantly, Burton (*Answer*, 13–15) quotes exactly these passages to support the opposite claim.

7. *Genesis 2.3*: 'And God blessed the seventh day, and sanctified it: because that in it he had rested from all his worke, which God created and made'; also the text for a lecture by Andrewes on 27 April 1591, at St Paul's (*AS*, 128–41).

9. *many think...ceremony*: '*the Anabaptists, Familists, and other sectaries, who denie all distinction of dayes under the Gospel*' (see prev. n.); i.e. those radical sects who believed that the freedom of the Gospel included a freedom from any ceremonial religious observance, including Sunday; in fact a tiny minority of opinion in England, only tentatively represented in the works of Henry Barrow (see Parker, *English Sabbath*, 101).

12. *Saviours rule...Polygamie*: Matt. 19: 8; *G* (p. 264) reads 'Do as Christ did in the cause of divorce'; *M* (p. 329) also has '*Polygamie*'; since Christ goes on to discuss remarriage after divorce (v. 9), the two could be considered synonymous; contrast Milton's different use of the same evidence in favour of divorce, 'but they were to look back to the first institution, nay rather why was not that individual institution [prohibition of divorce] brought out of Paradise, as was that of the Sabbath, and repeated in the body of the Law, that men might have understood it to be a command?' (*Doctrine and Discipline of Divorce* (1643), 30).

13. *call it to*: recall it to; judge it by.

16–18. *A thing...annexed*: a law cannot be dismissed as merely ceremonial if part of ('annexed to') the performing of it is an action that may be ceremonial.

20. *type out*: 'prefigure or foreshadow as a type; to represent in prophetic similitude' (*OED sv* 1.a; citing 1598 as the first usage).

21–23. *Paradise...mans innocency*: ceremonies or symbols which prefigure a later fulfilment of their imperfect representations of truth were logically impossible in prelapsarian Eden; ceremonies and symbols are a necessary product of the Fall. Hence, the day of rest, declared before the Fall, is a revealed moral truth in itself, and thus not a mere symbol or ceremony (cf. ll. 1–7). The Dedham Classis minister Sandes also argued that if sabbath worship was necessary for Adam, it was even more necessary for fallen man. And, like Andrewes, he finds 'ceremonial appendices', or worthy symbolic readings of the meaning of the sabbath, but distinguishes them from the reasons for it. The 'principal end' of the sabbath was not the provision of a type or sign that would find its fulfilment in Christ, but, 'the end why it was commanded is that his word might be heard and his spirit more effectually to work in them' (quoted in Primus, p. 98).

24. *[Addition 8]*: an unusual disagreement by the editor(s) of *P* with Andrewes: '*This is to be understood of such Ceremonies as had reference to Christ as a redeemer...for otherwise ceremonies which have a moral signification...might stand with mans estate in Paradise, for what was the tree of life but a ceremony* [i.e. symbol]'.

28. *Saviour...nor ceremony*: repeated in similar terms in Andrewes's St Paul's lecture (*AS*, 136).

35. *avocations*: 'that which has the effect of calling away or withdrawing one from an occupation. *Hence*, A minor or less important occupation' (*OED sn* 3; citing 1642 as the first usage).

p. 34, 39.–p. 35, 2. *Deuteronomie...accessory*: Deut. 5: 15; cf. Burton, *Answer* (p. 15), quoting his texts of Andrewes's lectures, '*and if they say it prefigured the rest that wee shall have from our sinnes in Christ. Answ. Wee grant it (as comming in afterwards Deuter.*

5. 15. as it is in my Manuscript) and therefore the day is changed, but yet no Ceremony prooved'; *G* (pp. 264–5) reads verbatim as Burton quotes here (i.e. without the citation of Deut. 5: 15); Burton's MS, therefore, derived from a source related either to *P* or *M* (which also includes the citation, p. 329); crucially, however, both *P* and *M* make clear that thanksgiving for the deliverance from Egypt was only a secondary ('accessory') reason for keeping the sabbath, which Andrewes then uses (see next n.) as precedent for the evolution and addition by peoples and churches to the reasons for sabbath observance—precisely the kind of temporal ('ceremonial') flexibility of observance which Burton wishes to deny; see also ll. 2–8.

2–3. *adde... benefits received*: cf. Andrewes's remarkable peroration on Easter 1611 (24 Mar.), which compounds the celebration of Easter itself, Sunday generally, the feast of the Annunciation, the king's Accession Day, and the collective national 'resurrections' from the Gowrie and Gunpowder plots (*XCVI*, 443–6).

3–5. *Exodus... their labour*: Exod. 20: 10.

6–8. *these ends... accessory end*: cf. p. 34, l. 39–p.35, l. 2 and n.

10. *preventing... grace*: Augustinian distinction between the two primary forms of God's free grace; 'prevenient' ('preventing') grace, that which comes before any act of human will, anterior to and responsible for conversion and justification (cf. 2 Tim. 1: 9); and 'subsequent' grace ('following grace'), that which, after conversion and in the process of justification, involves the cooperation of the human will; cf. Augustine, *De Grat. et Lib. Arb.*, 2, 5.

25. *Adam never kept it*: position expounded in David Primerose, *A Treatise of the Sabbath* (1636); cf., 'it is not probable, that God from the beginning sanctified the seventh day to ordaine it to *Adam* for a day of rest, because *Adam* in the estate of innocency should not have had any use of such a day. For he was without sin, which might have hindred him to serve God continually, and therefore needed not a signe, which by the similitude of a bodily rest and cessation, might teach him to cease and rest from sin' (p. 86).

27–28. *sanctifie... in practise*: cf. Primerose, *Treatise*, on Gen. 2: 3, 'so it shall be a narration made in this place occasionally, according to the ordinary custome... of *Moses*, when in the historicall relation of things that were come to passe long before, they find occasion to speak of things happened since, specially of those that were come to passe in their time when they wrote, to interlace, upon that occasion, a short rehearsall of them, with the narration of things more ancient, and to speake of both in such a manner, as if they had happened in the same time' (p. 79).

29. *materia prima*: Aristotle, *Physics* I the primal physical matter of the universe.

34. *rem ante usum*: Lat., 'the thing before the use'.

39. *Again... confusion*: when quoting his printed text's citation of Deut. 4: 13,14 (cf. *G*, 265; this edn. p. 35, l. 36), Burton (*Answer*, 16) adds a marginal note, 'So there should be confusion. Manuscr.', which again suggests that Burton's MS of the lectures is closely related to *P* and *M* (the latter reads, 'Againe, beside the *Confusion* and breach of *Order*', p. 330).

p. 35, 41–p. 36, 3. *Fathers... another kinde*: cf. Peter Comestor, *Historia Scholastica*, xi, 'nunquid est Saul inter prophetas...? Quasi dicat: cum non sit de genere prophetarum' (*PL*, 198. 1304D); ('is Saul among the prophets...? Which is like saying, he is not of the sort of the prophets').

11–13. *Thirdly... God's image*: conventional beliefs; cf. Hooker, *Lawes*, I. i, xii (although the 'law' Andrewes discusses here corresponds more exactly to Hooker's 'law of reason'; see Voak, *Richard Hooker*, 113–14).

17–18. *Christ delivering... Lord, &c.*: Matt. 22: 36–40.

24. *Parisius and Politianus*: not identified; possibly Guillaume Perault *alias* Peraldus, and Prosper Poliziano (*fl.* 1480), Florentine humanist; the Council of Trent maintained that the third (here, second; see next n.) commandment pertained to ceremonial, not moral law.

25. *second Commandment*: against worshipping graven images.

26–27. *three... five*: i.e. the third, second, fourth, and fifth commandments.

31–32. *typical ceremonies*: cf. p. 34, ll. 16–18 and nn.

36–37. *Jerusalem was destroyed*: by Titus, 70 CE.

p. 37, 18. ἡμέρα κυριακῇ: Gr., 'hēmĕra kuriakē'; 'the Lord's day' (cf. Rev. 1: 10).

28. *as long... Church militant*: Burton (*Answer*, 16), concludes his quotation from his printed text of Andrewes with the triumphant coda, 'and my Manuscript addeth, *And yet a Sabbath*, Act. 1. 12. So that this lasteth as long, as the Church militant. So there.' *M* does not include a reference to Acts 1: 12 ('they returned... a Sabbath dayes journey'), but does use the key term '*Sabbath*' instead of 'Lords day' (l. 27): 'the *Sabbath* lasteth as long as the *Church militant*'. This is the best evidence that Burton's MS was closer to the copy text for *M*, if not the very same.

36. *other great work*: Pentecost (Whitsunday); the sending of the Holy Spirit fifty days after the Resurrection (Acts 2); the association of Sunday with the Holy Spirit, and the three persons of the Trinity, dates from the writings of Isidore of Seville (6–7th century), and was strongly marked in late medieval Western Catholicism, but disappeared with the *BCP*; the Trinitarian encomium to Sunday which follows here is thus perhaps another example of Andrewes's liturgical nostalgia.

p. 38, 6–7. *Fourth... CHAP.IX*: in the previous lectures, Andrewes had treated the reasons for the commandment; he here (*P*, 298–9) turns to the first 'means' or manner of keeping it, proper places of public worship. The final two chapters on the commandment (*P*, 301–9) treat the clergy, schools, tithes, and securing proper observance by others.

13. ***: brief precis of the later section on properly trained clergy.

16–17. *joyned... one Nature*: cf. Hooker, *Lawes*, v. 12. 5., 'These two commandementes therefore are in the law conjoygned, *Ye shall keep my Sabboths, and reverence my sanctuarie*' (*FEWRH*, ii. 52).

17–20. *those men... prophane it*: early specimen of anti-puritan satire, and a palpable hit at the hypocrisy of those who demanded strict sabbath observance, yet neglected the buildings in which that observance took place; Andrewes (not unlike Ben Jonson decades later) had a reputation for exposing such godly pretensions in 1580s Cambridge; cf. Aubrey, 'the Puritan faction did begin to increase in those dayes, and especially at Emanuel College.... [t]hey preached up very strict keeping and observing the Lords day: made upon the matter damnation to breake it, and 'that' twas lesse sin to kill a man than—yet these Hypocrites did bowle in a private green at their colledge every sunday after Sermon: and one of the Colledge, (a bowing friend to Mr L. Andrewes,) to satisfie him, one time lent him the key of a private back dore to the Bowling green on a Sunday evening, which he opening discovered the zealous Preachers with their Gownes off at earnest at play. but they were strangely surprized, to see the entery of one that was not of their Brotherhood' (*Brief Lives*, ed. Bennett).

20–21. *pari... ambulare*: Lat., lit., 'walk along together'; 'go together'.

21–24. *no more... transient*: remarkable assertion not only of the sacrality of physical churches, but prioritization of the same over worship itself, which surpasses the later views of Hooker and even 1630s Laudians; cf. Hooker, *Lawes*, v. 12. 6, 'when therefore we sanctifie or hallowe Churches, that which we doe is onlie to testifie that we make them places of publique resort, that wee invest God him selfe with them, that we sever them from common uses' (*FEWRH*, ii. 53); for Laudian views, see Lake, 'Laudian Style', esp. pp. 164–5.

32–34. *Apostle reproves... God?* cf. Hooker, *Lawes*, v. 12. 5, 'Out of those thapostles wordes, *have ye not howses to eate and drinke*, albeit temples such as now were not then erected for the exercise of Christian religion, it hath bene neverthelesse not absurdlie conceived that he teacheth what difference should be made betwene house and house; that what is fit for the dwellinge place of God and what for mans habitation he showeth' (*FEWRH*, ii. 52).

32. **Have ye not*: the editor of *P* signals here his own marginal note, '*That by ἐκκλεσια, *Church, is there meant, not the persons, but the place, is the opinion of most of the Fathers*', citing Augustine, Basil, Jerome, Chrysostom, Theophilus (of Antioch), Theodoret, and Oecumenius (of Tricca), 'cum aliis' ('among others'). For debate over 'ekklesia' (Lat., 'ecclesia', 'church') as the physical or hierarchical church, vs. the congregation(s) of believers themselves, see Fulke, *Defence*, in *Works*, i. 227–9.

p. 39, 1–2. *Chrysostome... celebrated*: Chrysostom, *Homilies on the Epistles... to the Corinthians*, xxvii. 5 (*LF*, xii. 160–1); cf. David Lindsay, *The Reasons... Touching the Reverend Receiving of the Holy Communion* (1619), '*Chrysostome* saith, that *Paul* in 1. *Cor.* 11. calleth that a Supper, which should rather haue beene called, a Dinner, or a breake-fast, if hee had respected the time: but hee calleth it so, *Ut remitteret illos iam inde, ad illam vesperam qua Dominus tremenda mysteria tradidit,* That hee might send them back to that evening, wherein our Lord delivered these fearefull mysteries' (p. 103).

2–3. *like an oyster board*: as Tyacke has shown ('Lancelot Andrewes', 15), Andrewes here redeploys—in a daring ideological reversal—Marian Catholic satires against Edwardian communion tables ('boards'). The simile probably condemns tables not only for being what Catholics (and Andrewes) considered an inappropriately common piece of furniture for the sacrament, but also the godly Protestant custom of receiving communion seated around that table. According to Foxe, the Marian dean of Westminster Weston and Bishop White of Lincoln taunted Latimer and Ridley at their trials (1555) for having 'set an oyster table instead of an altar' (*Actes and Monuments*, (1583), x. 1458, 1466; xi. 1370, 1765, 1931); another Marian martyr, John Hooper, complained in his *Apologie* (printed posthumously, 1562), that Marian Catholics had 'banished the holye supper of the Lorde, and call the table wher the communion was used, an oyster borde, and the breade appointed to that use, oyster bread' (sig. Cii^r). The oyster table insult was again traded in the Laudian altar disputes, but these authors cite only Foxe, and seem unaware of (or strategically ignore) Andrewes's use of the image; cf. Peter Heylyn, *A Coale from the Altar* (1636), 21–2; Heylyn, *Antidotum Lincolniense* (1637), 68; John Williams, *Holy Table, Name and Thing* (1637), 20–1, 192; William Prynne, *A Quench-Coale* (1637), 54.

6. ευσχημοσυνη: Gr., 'euschēmosunē'; 'decency', 'decorum'.

7–8. *inter graviora legis*: Lat., 'among the most important of laws'.

12. *[Addition 9]*: lengthy (*P*, 299–300) transcript of passages from later Andrewes, Hooker, and mid-seventeenth-century apologists '*concerning the adorning of the house of God*'; the former are Andrewes's explicit criticisms of the neglect of church buildings from court sermons for Ash Wednesday 1593 and Easter 1615 (*XCVI*, 294–5, 483,

485); from Hooker, a tally of main arguments from *Lawes*, v. 11–17 (*FEWRH*, ii. 47–65); and finally pamphlets by the Laudians Richard Steward (*An Answer... to Dr Samuel Turner, concerning... alienating the lands of the Church*, 1647) and John Warner (*Church-Lands not to be sold*, 1647); and the Jesuit Francisco Suarez's 'De Sacrilegio', from *Operis de Religione* (1624).

the Person: of the priest or minister.

A SERMON PREACHED AT SAINT MARIES HOSPITAL

Text.   *XCVI. Sermons*, Part II, *Certaine Sermons Preached At sundry times, upon severall occasions* (1629, F_1 editor's copy), pp. [1]–[26]; collated with F_2 (Bodl. Antiq.c.E.1632.2), and F_3 (editor's copy).

Headnote.   This is a sermon of great importance in Andrewes's œuvre on three counts. It is his earliest datable sermon to survive in complete form, presumably set, like the others in *XCVI. Sermons*, from an authorially prepared fair copy. Second, it is the only printed sermon text by him for which there also survives a transcript of the sermon as it was actually preached. The latter is in Saint Paul's Cathedral manuscript 38F22.01 (hereafter *SPMS*), fos. 51^r–67^r, and is transcribed in Appendix 1 (hereafter *A1*). Appendix 2 presents a line-by-line table of correspondence between the *XCVI. Sermons* and *SPMS* texts. Careful students of this sermon should study the significant changes Andrewes evidently made between the text as prepared (*XCVI*) and as actually preached (*A1*). The complete contents of *SPMS*, and the differences between the two versions of the sermon, are more fully described in the headnote to *A1*. Finally, this is the only extant sermon preached by Andrewes at one of London's two great outdoor pulpits. There is no record of him preaching at the greatest of these, Paul's Cross, hence the added significance of this sermon from the other, St Mary's Hospital. Both pulpits demanded sermons that were free-standing orations, preached outside of any liturgical context. This accounts for the 'Spital Sermon' also being Andrewes's longest—the *XCVI* text is twice the length of the great court sermons; and even the shorter *A1* is half as long again as the court pieces, and would have required approximately two hours to deliver. Stylistically, the sermon is therefore unlike his others: more copious and digressive than the clipped, condensed pieces preached at court, the preacher here elaborating more *exempla*, using less asyndetic syntax, and indulging in more contemporary social and political commentary.

St Mary's Hospital lay in the open suburbs north of the City between Bishopsgate, Shoreditch, and Spitalfields, on the site of the modern-day Liverpool Street Station. On the eve of the Reformation this priory hospital housed some 180 invalids, but was surrendered to Henry VIII at the Dissolution and converted into dwellings. But there survived in the former churchyard the covered stone pulpit 'like to that in *Paules Church yard*' where part of the City's most famous sermon series continued to be preached. On Good Friday was appointed a sermon at Paul's Cross on the Passion of Christ, followed by sermons on the Resurrection at the Spital on the mornings of the Monday, Tuesday, and Wednesday after Easter. On the following Sunday, the auditors returned to Paul's Cross to hear another preacher 'make rehearsall [review] of those foure former Sermons... and that done, he was to make a sermon of his owne studie, which in all were five sermons in one'. The preachers at Paul's Cross were appointed by the bishop of London, but those at the Spital by London's Court of Aldermen, who, with the Lord Mayor, attended in full ceremonial regalia, along with the orphan children of Christ's Hospital in their blue coats. The Aldermen formed London's mercantile and political elite: freemen elected from among the members of the leading livery companies to represent each of the City's twenty-six wards. At the Spital, they were seated opposite the pulpit in the lower part of a 'faire builded house in two stories', the upper gallery being occupied by 'the ladies and Aldermens wives' who could stand 'at a fair window, or sit at their pleasure' (John Stow, *A Survey of London*, ed. Charles Kingsford, 2 vols. (1908; rev. edn. 1971), i, 167–8).

In February 1588 the City's Recorder was ordered by the Aldermen to write to 'Master Doctor Bisse, Master Doctor Powell, and Master Andrewes of Cambridge' to 'intreate them from this Cyttye to take paynes to preach at St Marye Spyttle on the Mundaye Tewesday and Wednesdaye in the Easter weeke' (Corporation of London Record Office, Rep. 21 p. 527). These sermons, along with the Good Friday sermon at St Paul's, by 'M[aster] Bright', all survive in unique copies in *SPMS* (see Headnote to *A1*). These compose the only complete surviving set of London Spital sermons. Andrewes alludes to the two sermons which had immediately preceded his, and twice commends the amount of money collected for charity after the sermons on the two preceding days, and in years past (pp. 97, 98, 111). Finally, a marginal note in Bisse's sermon (*SPMS*, fo. 29^v), identifies 'M. D: Holland'—Dr Thomas Holland (d. 1609), recently returned from the Low Countries as chaplain to the Earl of Leicester, and appointed Regius Professor of Divinity at Oxford in 1589—as the divine who preached the climax of the series, the 'Rehearsal Sermon', on Low Sunday. No text of this survives.

The City Easter sermons in this year were delivered at the height of two great social crises: mobilization for defence against the Spanish Armada, and the height of the presbyterian *classis* movement, both of which inflect the sermons of all three preachers. Their compliments and appeals to City generosity are carefully calibrated to acknowledge the pain of the huge tax burdens imposed upon the City only weeks before by the Privy Council for mobilizing ships, soldiers, and horse. They also offer sharp rebukes of puritan anti-clericalism, ceremonial nonconformity, simony, and the patronage of the same by wealthy citizens and lawyers, which reflect many of Andrewes's concerns in his Cambridge catechetical lectures (1585), and anticipate his larger-scale attacks on the same at Cambridge in the 1590s (see 'Sacrilege a Snare', this edn.). Moreover, the issues that would erupt only months later in the Marprelate Controversy were clearly in all these preachers' sights.

Although ostensibly sponsored to expound the great mysteries of Easter, by Elizabethan times the Spital sermons had become primarily associated with the charitable collections taken at them. These were usually designated for the ransom of captive merchants and mariners and the support of the City's hospitals. Although dozens of later Spital sermons survive, there are only three extant (excluding those in *SPMS*) which pre-date Andrewes's: Thomas Drant's for Easter Tuesday 1570 (part two of *Two Sermons*, 1570) and 1572 (*A Fruitfull and Necessary Sermon*, 1572), both reprinted in *Three Godly and Learned Sermons* (1584); and one (undated) by Edwin Sandys (*Sermons* (1585), 225–59). All three are sermons on almsgiving which praise and encourage City initiatives for poor relief and satirize conspicuous consumption by the rich. Drant's 1570 effort also includes a sustained attack on Roman Catholic biblical and patristic scholarship, his for 1572 an attack on the doctrine of Purgatory, and Sandys's refutes the Catholic doctrine of the efficacy of works. In 1588, Bright, Bisse, Powell, and Andrewes similarly combine exhortation to almsgiving, warnings to the rich, and rejoinders to Roman Catholicism, in what had become a conventional Spital formula. What Andrewes does with the components of this formula, however, is innovative rather than conventional.

As Peter Mack observes, Andrewes is 'gentler with the wealthy', and, 'rather than accusing the rich, he would prefer to befriend them and to find uses for their wealth' (*Elizabethan Rhetoric* (2002), 286). Part of this sympathy must be rooted in the wealth of Andrewes's own family derived from London trade: his father was a prosperous mariner and Warden of Trinity House, the guild which governed the Port of London. The preacher's three surviving younger brothers would rise to prominence in other City guilds. Although cast in biblical metaphor, Andrewes's evocation of London merchants' dependence on the sea, and his extensive use of the technical legal and financial language governing trade, rings true from personal experience. Andrewes speaks here respectfully, though firmly, as a son of the City. Notably absent is the jealous zeal of Drant's estates satire. Andrewes furthers a sense of cooperation, rather than confrontation, between himself and his auditory by exploiting the full theatrical potential of the Spital setting: he sustains throughout the sermon the punning conceit of standing before the 'court' of Aldermen as a judge trying a legal case, even alluding deftly to the gathered orphans of Christ's Hospital as both witnesses and evidence (p. 65), and constantly calling the listeners to self-examination, rather than brow-beating them. And his use of the technical language of bills of exchange (pp. 74–75) as a metaphor for laying up in heaven the 'credit' of good works is a masterstroke of choosing a vocabulary familiar to his audience as cover for an avant-garde theological position.

The place and auditory of the Spital also account for some of the sermon's literary distinctiveness. No sermon by Andrewes is larded with more colloquial, mercantile, and proverbial language than this, reflecting his stated decision that 'I will not answer, as in the *Schooles*; I feare, I should not be understood; I will go grossely to worke' (p. 95). This conscious attempt to use popular diction probably also accounts for the remarkable number—unsurpassed in any other sermon in this edition—of usages that either pre- or post-date those cited in *OED*, or that are entirely unique to Andrewes. Unique usages are 'in-bearing' (p. 78, l. 36), 'lashed on' (p. 49, l. 8), 'countermeanes' (p. 51, l. 36), 'under-meanes' (p. 57, l. 37), 'forgrowen' (p. 70, l. 31), and 'discommon' (p. 70, l. 35); significant pre-datings of *OED* citations are 'altitudes' (p. 45, l. 6), 'transcendent' (p. 45, l. 34), 'Estate' (p. 49, l. 16), 'abate' (p. 50, l. 10), 'ventureth' (p. 53, l. 27), 'attractive' (p. 66, l. 13), and 'instillation' (p. 60, l. 30); *'consumed'* (p. 74, l. 13), and 'overcast' (p. 69, l. 37) significantly post-date *OED* citations. (Of these, however, only two—'lashed on' and 'attractive'—appear in *A1*; see Headnote to *A1*.) Such linguistic inventiveness puts Andrewes on a par with Shakespeare, and accounts for his appeal at this time to the likes of Thomas Nashe and John Lyly (see Introduction).

But more significantly, Andrewes here grasps in a new way the Protestant nettle of how to account for works of charity within a reformed soteriology. Drant's and Sandys's Spital sermons exemplify the conventional Protestant approaches: either to commend works simply as the duty of the elect and evidence of their faith (Drant, *passim*), or to reject explicitly the Roman Catholic belief that 'our owne woorkes before wee have faith are preparations to grace' (Sandys, *Sermons*, 236). Bisse, too, on Easter Monday 1588, made the same points *in extenso* (*SPMS*, fos. 26ᵛ–28ᵛ). But Powell, preaching the day before Andrewes on James 1: 26–7 ('*purer religion... is this, to visite the fatherless and widowes*'), took a startlingly avant garde, indeed anti-Calvinist, position by demurring, 'lett us never stand to dispute with the papists concerninge meritts and good workes, let me have care to serve God and to doe good... and then if the lord shall give me salvation what is that to me, whether he give it me for desart or of his free mercye these are but triffles [trifles], & are not to be stood one [on]' (*SPMS*, fo. 50^r). Andrewes pointedly praised this effort in his own sermon (p. 66), and, in a similar spirit, Andrewes's governing aim was the pastoral one of guiding his auditory to salvation, and asserts a role for charitable works within that process. Andrewes's choice of text is itself suggestive, since it, as well as Powell's text from James to which he also appeals, were themselves favourite Catholic proof-texts for refuting justification *sola fide*, and urging the efficacy and merit of works. Andrewes justifies his choice from 1 Tim. on the grounds that it is an apt '*Scripture* for *rich men*' (p. 40), but he then cleverly plays to the proverbial self-interest of the rich by arguing that if they crave a rich reward, they should lay up '*for themselves*' in the store-house of heaven '*good workes*'. Andrewes, like Powell on James 1: 26–7, makes little attempt to qualify the simple logic of his chosen text that doing good works is a way to '*lay hold of æternall life*'. Doing so steers clear of Calvinist notions of election, and inserts works into the economy of salvation. The effort is not entirely consistent, as he does briefly reject the efficacy of works while refuting the Rheims gloss on his text. But he then goes on to argue in language borrowed, but not acknowledged, from the same Rheims translation, that works are a secondary 'foundation' with faith for justification (pp. 77–8). In itself, the notion of any foundation other than faith, however 'secondary', is a significant step away from mainstream English Protestant orthodoxy.

Sources. Andrewes's entering the lists of Protestant and Roman Catholic debate over works of charity draws on a body of print too vast and diffuse to document here. Debate over justification *sola fide* was a particular feature of the early Reformation, reappearing early in Elizabeth's reign in the wake of John Jewel's *Challenge Sermon* (1560), and *Apology for the Church of England* (1564), with another renascence in tracts prompted by the arrest, interrogation, and trial of Edmund Campion (1581–2). For these, see Peter Milward, *Religious Controversies of the Elizabethan Age* (1977). Out of this tradition, Andrewes retails a long list of Catholic allegations of Protestant neglect of works (p. 66). Exact sources have proved elusive; in fact, it is easier to find Protestant complaints about such allegations than the allegations themselves (cf. Archer, 'Charity', 225–6 (see below)). Andrewes also engages very subtly with the Catholic English translation of the New Testament (Rheims, 1582). His Pembroke head, William Fulke, whom Andrewes would succeed in the following year, had been the leading antagonist of the translation, but Andrewes shows here (though tacitly) an avant-garde willingness to accept some of its diction, and even theology. Andrewes's usual display of patristic learning is also on show here, proof that London worthies were not averse to scholarship. But there are inflections of that scholarship that suggest Andrewes took into account the City's more reformed sensibilities: the Protestant favourites Augustine and Chrysostom are the most frequently cited, with a rare acknowledgement of Calvin's existence, and a unique citation in his works of the impeccably reformed Wolfgang Musculus of Augsburg (d. 1563), praised by Drant at the Spital in 1570 for 'yeld[ing] better sucke and sense from the scripture, then all the Jesuites: nay, then all the writers of all the papasie' (*Two Sermons*, sig. Dii^r). This sermon's treatment of the rich and poor is closely related by theme and exempla to Andrewes's 1596 court Lent sermon on Luke 16: 25 (*XCVI*, 309–19). The discovery of *SPMS* reveals how carefully Andrewes engaged with the two previous Spital sermons preached by Bisse and Powell (see Headnote to *A1*); the major points of contact between them and Andrewes, both tacit and acknowledged, are documented in the notes here.

Further Reading. This sermon is given close analysis by Peter Mack as an exemplar of 'rhetoric and dialectic in Elizabethan religious discourse' in *Elizabethan Rhetoric* (2002), 265–86 *passim*. For an excellent overview of the social and religious politics of wealth and poverty in early modern London, see Ian Archer, 'Material Londoners?' in Lena Cowen Orlin, *Material London, ca. 1600* (2000), 174–92; for trends in charitable giving, and charity appeal sermons, see Archer, 'The Charity of Early Modern Londoners', *Trans. of the Royal Historical Society*, 6th series, 12 (2002), 223–44; and Susan Brigden, *London and the Reformation* (1989), 470–83. For levies on London during the Armada crisis, see Archer, 'London Military Levies, 1509–1603' (http://senior.keble.ox.ac.uk/fellows/iarcher/levies/htm#1588). For the presbyterian *classis* movement, see Collinson, *Elizabethan Puritan Movement*, 6.3.

p. 40, 5. *I. Tim. . . . XIX*: the text quoted is closest to Geneva, but with some significant variants: *'uncertenty of riches'* for 'uncertaine riches', *'plenteously'* for 'abundantly', and *'lay hold of æternall life'* for 'obtain eternal life', all of which are closer renderings of the New Testament Greek, the first and third of which are cited or adopted (respectively) by AV; the text quoted in *A1* (p. 243, ll. 3–9) is Geneva, without these variants; two other surviving Spital sermons on this text are Joseph Hall, *The Righteous Mammon* (1618), and John White, *Two Sermons . . . the latter at the Spittle* (1613).

6. *high-minded*: arrogant.

14. *Place and Auditorie*: the physical 'Place' of preaching, and those listening to the sermon; 'congregation' is a later term for the latter; 'Auditorie' more accurately reflects the early modern distinction between hearing sermons and participating in a liturgy.

19. *peculiar*: particular, specific.

20. *reached*: given to.

21. *streightway*: straightaway; immediately.

p. 40, 25–p.41, 1 *this place . . . as heer*: encomium, in biblical language, to the mercantile wealth represented in the auditory by the Lord Mayor and Court of Aldermen (see Headnote); whether from importing manufactured luxury goods from abroad, or exporting raw domestic goods like wool, City fortunes were fundamentally maritime (a *'Harvest of the water'*); City merchants were key sources of often huge loans to *'Noblemen'*, and indeed to the queen herself (*'Princes of the earth'*).

5–6 *Faxit Deus . . . accommoda*: *A1* (p. 243) cites 'St Augustine', but unidentified in *PL*.

7–23. *1. This . . . the publique*: Mack offers a lapidary gloss on this *divisio* as an exemplar of the importance of logical analysis to Andrewes's sermon structure: 'Initially Andrewes divides into type of text, persons addressed and content . . . as a letter might be analysed in a commentary on Cicero. Then content is subdivided into negative and positive commands. The two negative . . . are followed by a reason, derived from a maxim. . . . Each positive command is provided with its own reason, the second being further subdivided, in accordance with Aristotle's *Categories*, into substance, quantity and quality. . . . On top of this intensely dialectical reading of the organisation of the text, Andrewes will lay a grammatical analysis and a rhetorical amplification of the words employed' (*Elizabethan Rhetoric*, 273). To this should be added, of course, that the work of the division is not simply to show logical structure, but to show how that structure derives from the scriptural text itself.

8. *his name*: its name.
11. *branches*: parts or divisions of an oration or sermon.
15. *Ground*: fundamental principle.
15–16. *Law of Nature*: cf. Hooker, 'Law rationall therefore, which men commonly use to call the law of nature, meaning thereby the Law which humaine nature knoweth it selfe in reason universally bound unto... comprehendeth all those thinges which men by the light of their naturall understanding evidently know... to be... good or evill for them to doe' (*Laws*, I. 8. 9; *FEWRH*, i. 90)
    23. *communicate*: 'to give, bestow (a material thing)' (*OED, sv* 3.a).
    28. *Praecipe divitibus*: Vulg. (1 Tim. 6: 17); 'charge them that are rich'.
    30. *convent*: 'to summon, to cite; to summon on a charge of' (*OED sv* 3.c).
    31. *rich men of Ephesus*: Paul's letter is addressed to Timothy and the church at Ephesus; cf. also Acts 19: 35.
    33. *Charges... Bench*: in the county trials of civil and criminal justice in England ('*Assizes*'), charges against a defendant were read from the judge's '*Bench*'. The name is from OF '*assise*', 'act of sitting down, sitting, seat' (*OED*). Andrewes's phrase 'use to be' refers to practice presently in use (not the past tense 'used to be').

p. 41, 33–p. 42, 32. *Charges... let him heare*: Mack compares Andrewes's opening summary of his text to 'the manner of the fullest grammatical commentary on a classical text', and his application of it here to his audience like a schoolmaster 'drilling his class on a sentence from Cato' (*Elizabethan Rhetoric*, 266).
    34. παράγγελλε... *Consistorie*: Gr., 'para[n]gĕllĕ', by command or charge. Here the judge (metonymically '*Bench*') in the court ('*Consistorie*') is the High Priest charging Peter and the apostles after their miraculous delivery from prison (Acts 5: 17–28).

p. 42, 1. *suit and service*: in the feudal legal sense, 'attendance at court and personal service due from a tenant to his lord' (*OED 'suit'* I.2.a).
    2. *Court-daies*: 'a day on which a court (legal, administrative, etc.) is held' (*OED*).
    5–6. *Augustine... Consultos*: Augustine, *Serm. LII*, iv. 9: 'Paulum recito, idoneum juris divini consultum' (*PL*, 38.358); ('I appeal to St Paul, a skilled counsel in divine law').
    7–8. *peace... take away*: cf. from 'The Second Collect at Evening Prayer' (*BCP*), 'Give unto thy servants that peace which the world cannot give'.
    10–13. *This... discharge*: summary of the preceding legal conceit of preachers (lawyers) prosecuting God's (the judge's) cases in their auditory's consciences (court); the repetition of '*Court*' also puns on the corporate presence of the Court of Aldermen at the sermon; as London's governing body, it was its responsibility to enforce ('discharge') judgments after its meetings were adjourned ('broken up'), vocabulary applied here to the expected enactment of the preacher's precepts by them upon their departure from his sermon.
    16. *Barre*: the barrier before a judge where prisoners are tried.
    21–22. *Absit... vel sic*: Augustine, *Serm. CLIX*, vi. 7: 'Absit ut sic, sed et utinam vel sic' (*PL*, 38.871); ('Not in the same way, but would that it were in the same way').
    25. *Statute-Books*: books containing Acts of Parliament.
    38. *to preferre*: 'to promote (*to* a position or office of dignity)' (*OED, sv* I.1.a).

p. 43, 1–5. *Lawes... Cobwebb-Divinitie*: Tilley L116.
    9. *whither*: whether.
    11. *meane*: of low estate.

12. *Counsaile*: the Queen's Privy Council.

24–29. *Balack's counsaile... Esau's portion*: Num. 24: 11; 1 Kings 21; Gen. 25: 30–4.

26–27. *stuffe cushions... elbowes*: Tilley P329; to curry favour by saying what people want to hear; to pull punches; *A1* (p. 245) cites Ezek. 13 (17–18); also used by Bisse on Easter Monday, 'so fareth it nowadayes when our great masters have got them soft pillowes under ther heads & soft cushions under ther elbowes they sleep, & even then is sathan busye to sowe tares' (*SPMS*, fos. 29^{r-v}).

28. *disease*: to discomfort, annoy.

29. *wote*: know.

30–32. *Jonah... Ephesus*: Jonah 1: 2–3; 1 Tim. 1: 3–4.

33. *Apostle*: Paul.

35. *Verse 13... &c*: *A1* (p. 246) suggests that this verse was read or paraphrased here.

36. *hable*: able.

37. *Streightly*: strictly.

p. 44, 7. *feareth*: inspires with fear; frightens (*OED sv* I.1).

8. *place*: a triple pun on the office of the preacher, the august occasion and setting of the Spital sermon itself, and the text in scripture he here expounds.

9–10. *Nunquid... Augustine*: Lat., lit., 'Can we blot out anything that we have received? If we blotted anything out, we fear being blotted out'; cf. Augustine, *Serm.* XL, iii. 5: 'Numquid ego delere illud possum? Si delevero, timeo deleri' (*PL*, 38.246); ('Can I blot anything out? If I blotted anything out, I fear being blotted out').

10. *We*: preachers.

18. *Processe... us*: legal charge, mandate.

19–20. *Augustine... vinceret*: cf. Augustine, *Serm. CCCXXXIX*, iii. 4: 'nam ad istam securitatem otiosissimam nemo me vinceret' (*PL*, 38.1481); ('for in this most leisurely freedom from responsibility, no one could outdo me').

23–24. *Cogit... iste*: Lat., 'We consider this Paul'.

28–29. *the great Day*: Judgement Day.

31. *nominatim*: Lat., 'named', 'specified'.

32. *levin*: leaven; lit., 'yeast'; fig., any agent that causes change; cf. Matt. 13: 33; 1 Cor. 5. 8.

40. ἀδηλότης: Gr., adēlotĕs; 'uncertainty' (1 Tim. 6: 17).

p. 45, 3. *first Fathers*: first parents (Adam and Eve); *A1* (p. 247) reads 'first father' (Adam).

4–5. *Pride... fire*: cf. Augustine, *Serm.* LXI, ix. 10: 'Nam qui nolunt divites fieri, vel qui non curant, vel non ardent cupiditatibus, non avaritiae facibus accenduntur, sed divites sunt, audiant Apostolum. Hodie lectum est, Praecipe divitibus hujus mundi. Praecipe. Quid? Praecipe ante omnia, non superbe sapere. Nihil enim est quod sic generent divitiae, quomodo superbiam' (*PL*, 38.412); ('For those who do not wish to become rich, nor care to be, or who do not burn with greed, or who are not kindled by the torch of avarice, but are rich, they should listen to the Apostle. Today it was read, "Charge the rich of this world. Charge them." What? Charge them before all else, "not to be high-minded". There is nothing that riches are so likely to breed as pride.')

6. *altitudes*: lit., 'height in the air', but also fig. here, 'lofty mood, ways, airs, phrases' (*OED sn* 8); this example of the latter sense significantly pre-dates the earliest such usage cited in *OED* (1616); not in *A1*.

11. *then is*: than is.

12. τις μέγας: Gr., tis mĕgas ('a certain high and mighty [man]').

17. *Discite à me*: Vulg. (Matt. 11: 29); 'learne of me'.

22. *circuite*: circuit; gen., a 'sphere of action', but also in the sermon's metaphorical legal vocabulary, 'the visitation of the judges for holding assizes' in a particular geographical jurisdiction (*OED sn* 2.b, 4.a).

23. *Manhood... Field*: prowess on the battlefield.

24. *Schooles*: 'the faculties composing a university; universities in general' (*OED sn* II.7.b).

30. *the Wiseman*: Solomon.

31. *answer*: answer to, obey.

33. *bound*: limit, confine.

34. *transcendent*: 'that which transcends, surpasses, or excels something else, or things generally' (*OED, sn* B.3); this sense of the adjective absolute significantly predates the first use cited in *OED* (1613); not in *A1*.

39. *wan*: won.

39. *Deventer*: prosperous Dutch port lost to the Spanish by mercenary English governors appointed in 1586 by the Earl of Leicester; not in *A1*.

40. *Switzers... France*: Elizabeth and her Council had invested money and hope in the German Protestant campaign of Baron von Dohna against the Spanish client Duke of Guise in eastern France in Nov.–Dec. 1587. But Dohna's ill-disciplined and unpaid Swiss mercenaries easily accepted the terms of surrender offered by the Catholic Henry III. See Garrett Mattingly, *The Defeat of the Spanish Armada* (1959), 149–55. *A1* (pp. 247–8) adds the further exempla of mercenary strategies by Philip of Macedon and Philip of Spain.

41. *strooken*: stricken; struck.

p. 46, 1. *wormewood*: lit., a proverbially bitter plant; here fig., 'an emblem or type of what is bitter and grievous to the soul' (*OED sn* 2).

3. *yer*: ere; 'before anything else is done' (*OED, sadv* A.4.b).

4–6. *sett of silver... Barre*: Christ was betrayed by Judas to trial ('the Barre') for thirty '*silver peeces*' (Matt. 26: 15). The epithet for Christ, '*Concionatorum mundi*' ('Preacher of the world'), is Augustine's (*Serm. CLXIV*, ii. 4.; *PL*, 38.896).

6. *Disciple... Master*: parody of Matt. 10: 24; here, the '*Master*' is money.

7. *setteth... to schoole*: 'to subject to teaching; often, to presume to correct (one's superior)' (*OED* 'school', *n* I.1.c).

9. *Usher*: assistant to a schoolmaster.

9. *Master*: schoolmaster or head of a college.

9. *Chaire*: university professorship; *A1* (p. 248) reads, 'it [money] will have *cathedram*, we must sit in *subselliis*', that is, money will have the chair ('*cathedram*') or throne reserved in university divinity schools for the vice-chancellor or other president at an academic disputation, while academics ('we') sit in the lowest stalls or benches ('in *subseliis*'); perhaps an ironic allusion to the dispute over allegedly Genevan practice whereby in parish churches the minister sat in a lower place than the richest members of the congregation; cf. Richard Bancroft, *A Survay of the Pretended Holy Discipline* (1593), 'admit but of their elderships into every parish, & then you have them, who will prove it out of the word of God, that there ought to be such a separation of their Aldermen, (every one of them, though he be but a Cobler) from the rest of the Idiots' (p. 326); equally parodied, though, is the notion that Genevan magistrates would relegate a sovereign to a place lower than the preacher, thus offending the English

principle of royal supremacy over the church, '*Sedeat itaque inferiori subsellio: let him therfore sit in a lower seat, then the preacher of the word of God, and the Prophet: that he may both see and acknowledge himselfe to be subject to the threats of the word....* I am perswaded it would greatlie trouble the subjects of *England*, to see such a Metamorphosis in her Majesties Chappell' (pp. 327–8).

14–15. *Tertullus... Tantum dabo*: in Andrewes's summary of the orator Tertullus's accusations against Paul before Felix (Acts 24: 1–26), he stresses v. 26 ('[Felix] hoped also that money shoulde have bene given him of Paul, that he might loose him: wherefore hee sent for him the oftner, and communed with him'). The 'greater Orator' is the money (a bribe) that could have 'dasht' Tertullus's accusations and won Paul his freedom. But Andrewes's repeated epithet for bribery—'*Tantum dabo*' (Lat., 'I give you something', lit., 'so much', i.e. a bribe) alludes not to Acts, but to yet another great 'Orator', Cicero. Seneca the Elder's *Controversiae*, I. vii. 1, which considers the execution of Cicero, includes the ironic taunt, '"Vt uno ictu pereat, tantum dabo"; pro Cicerone sic liceat pacisci' ('"I will give such-and-such an amount for his death at a single blow": may one bargain thus for Cicero?'). This, in turn, is a parody of Cicero's account (*Verrine Orations*, II. v. 118) of an executioner's sneer to a grieving mother, 'Ut uno ictu securis adferam mortem filio tuo, quid dabis?' ('Well now, what offers [will you give me] for making an end of your son with one blow of my axe?')

16–17. *Tantùm... syllabæ*: see 'A Sermon Preached ... vi March, A.D. MDXCIIII' (this edn.), p. 110, ll. 28–29 and n.

22. *estates*: social degrees, ranks.

25. *sett by*: valued; trusted in.

25–29. *Et divites... by themselves*: not identified.

31. *As riseth... blood*: Tilley G298.

31–34. *Augustine... Pride*: Augustine, *Serm. LXI*, ix. 10 (*LACT*): 'Et alius est vermis mali, alius pyri, alius fabae, alius tritici. Vermis divitiarum superbia' (*PL*, 38.412–13); ('And there is a worm for every apple, every pear, every bean, every grain of wheat. The worm of riches is pride').

p. 46, 39–p. 47, 1. *runne David... javeline*: 1 Sam. 19: 33.

4. *the Prophet*: David.

6. *the other Prophet*: Solomon.

6–7. *Give me... proud*: cf. Prov. 30: 8–9.

13. *our Court*: the Court of Aldermen.

13. *us*: preachers.

17. *endite*: indite; 'to enjoin as a law, precept, or maxim' (*OED*, sv 2); probably also with the sense of the related word 'indict', 'to bring a charge against; to accuse ... esp. by legal process' (*OED sv* I.1).

19. *approve*: prove; demonstrate.

24. *tempered*: mixed.

26. *kennell*: gutter; cf. *A1* (p. 249), 'throwen in the channel'.

29. *Sessions*: Quarter Sessions, the quarterly sittings of the Justices of the Peace for criminal and civil proceedings; the Assizes (see p. 41, l. 33 and n.).

31–2. *I joy... will joy*: Phil. 1: 18.

34. *our Office*: preaching.

36. *fearefull... judgement*: Heb. 10: 27.

p. 48, 2. *Records... Ghost*: scripture (the author of which was 'the *Holy Ghost*').

5. *Leades*: roof.

6. *Excipe...volatica*: Lat., lit., 'these pomposities and transient things that are welcomed'; cf. Augustine, *Serm. LXXI*, 6: 'Adhuc vana, adhuc inutilia, adhuc pompatica et volatica, ita Christo sancto magnificato, adhuc ista requiruntur?' (*PL*, 38.469); 'Still vanities, still useless things, still pomposities and transient things—with the blessed Christ thus already magnified—still such things are sought after?'

7–8. *vestem... cutem communem*: cf. Augustine, *Serm. LXI*, ii. 2: 'divitiae... homines extolluntur, magis amantes vestem fulgentem, quam cogitantes communem cutem' (*PL*, 38.410); ('riches puff men up, [who are] more in love with splendid clothes than thinking about their common skin'; i.e. the skin they have in common with the poor).

9. *Joyner*: woodworker; here, coffin-maker.

10–12. *carrie away... one of you*: cf. Augustine, *Serm. LXI*, viii. 9: 'Certe quando aliquo casu vetera sepulcra franguntur, ossa divitis agnoscantur. Ergo dives audi Apostolum: Nihil intulimus in hunc mundum. Agnosce, verum est. Sed nec auferre aliquid possumus' (*PL*, 38.412); ('Indeed, when you break open an ancient tomb, you cannot tell the bones of a rich man. Therefore, rich man, listen to the Apostle: "We brought nothing into this world." You know that this is the truth. But neither can we take anything [out of this world]'); both allude to 1 Tim. 6: 7.

12. *incedere... insericati*: 'to go arrogantly among others'; cf. Augustine, *Serm. LXI*, vii. 8: 'Inflatus obsericatus ista loquitur de pannoso' (*PL*, 38.412); ('The puffed-up man richly clothed [lit., covered] talks like this about the man in rags').

18–19. *David... owne heart*: 1 Sam. 13: 14.

20. *Dialect*: manner of speaking; here, condescendingly.

22. *Pharisee's... sicut*: Vulg. (Luke 18: 11); 'I am not like [other men are]'.

23. *Pikes*: large freshwater fish, proverbially rapacious (Tilley F311); cf. Falstaff's boast, 'If the young dace be a bait for the old pike, I see no reason in the law of nature but I may snap at him' (Shakespeare, *2 Henry IV*, III. ii. 320–2).

28. *implacable as Lamech*: Gen. 4: 23 (*LACT*).

36. *in-bearing*: other usages of this as a noun not identified; but clearly related to 'bearing', 'the carrying of oneself (with reference to the manner); carriage, deportment; behaviour, demeanour' (*OED svbl. n.* I.2.a), with the adverbial 'in-' adding a sense of intrusiveness or being 'overbearing'; cf. also the sense of 'to bear' as 'to exalt or lift up oneself upon, to plume oneself, presume' (*OED sv¹* II.19); also the Scottish use of 'inbearing' as an adjective (the only *OED* citation of the word, with only nineteenth-century examples, but closest to Andrewes here) as 'intrusive, officious, meddlesome'; not in *A1*.

37. *over-crow*: 'to crow or exult over; to triumph over; to overpower' (*OED*, *sv*).

p. 49, 4–13. *The late treasons... the old*: Roman Catholic plots against Queen Elizabeth, which culminated in the Babington Plot, and the subsequent trial and execution of Mary Queen of Scots (1586–7); ambition and pride were the vices traditionally associated with treason and rebellion, but Andrewes may here allude specifically to the fourteen Babington conspirators, who were well known for gallantry and flamboyance; moralized propaganda after their executions (September 1586), stressed their lust for wordly goods and dissatisfaction with their stations, as in the description of Henry Dun, who 'lived (reasonably) wealthely: but it seemeth, the humour of the man, was not contented with a reasonable vocation', as was revealed in his boast to a friend that he would 'see me within one quarter of a year to walke up & down with twenty men after me' (George Whetstone, *The Censure of a Loyal Subject* (1587), sig. E4^r).

7–8. *swolne...skinne*: swollen with ambition; cf. Shakespeare, 'Caesar's ambition, | Which swell'd so much that it did almost stretch | The sides o'th' world' (*Cymbeline*, III. i. 50).

8. *lashed on*: 'to lavish, squander' (*OED* sv¹ I.4); 'lash' in this sense is usually with 'out' (*OED* cites no examples with 'on'); Andrewes uses the phrase again at p. 63, l. 30, and in Lent 1596 ('our too much lashing on, to doe good to our selves'; *XCVI*, 317); cf. Thomas Manton, *One Hundred and Ninety Sermons* (1681), 'bastard goods of a base and transitory nature, as pleasure, profit; we may easily *over-lash* and exceed in these things. But *on* holiness which is more high and noble, and is truly good, and of greater vicinity and nearness to our chiefest good, than those other things are, we cannot exceed' (p. 303; italics added); *A1*, however (p. 250, 'who lash on more of the leather then they are able to beare'), uses the phrase in the sense of 'to lace (a garment)' or 'to truss (clothes)' (*OED* sv² 1, 2).

10. προπετεῖς: Gr., 'prŏpĕtēis', 'reckless' (2 Tim. 3: 4).

11. προδόται: Gr., 'prŏdótai', 'traitorous' (2 Tim. 3: 4).

14. *passing*: surpassing; over-reaching.

15. *condition*: social rank; class.

16. *Estate*: state (*OED*, sn 10), which pre-dates the first citation of the usage in *OED* (1605); *A1* (p. 251) uses the more conventional 'chayres of estate' (cf. *OED* sn 4.d).

21–25. *excesse...Cedar's daughter*: conventional litany of moralists' complaints against the evidences of Tudor class mobility; 'sumptuary laws' attempted to restrain luxury expenditure on clothing, domestic building, and retinues that were seen to threaten class distinctions (cf. ll. 4–13 and n.); 'alliance' by marriage between different social classes for social and financial advancement was ostensibly disapproved of, but not uncommon.

24. *perking*: 'to exalt oneself or thrust oneself forward ambitiously or presumptuously; to behave impudently or insolently; to play the upstart' (*OED*, sv¹ I.1.c).

p. 49, 34–p. 50, 6. *Divinitie...our dayes*: primarily alluding to the presbyterian *classis* movement's agitation for the abolition of episcopacy and reform of the clergy; but also a typical conformist-clerical complaint against civil lawyers' frequent alignment with religious nonconformists against ecclesiastical (canon) law, such as their power to withdraw cases from ecclesiastical to common law courts by writs of prohibition, and their denunciation of the ex officio oath used to incriminate nonconformist ministers; see Collinson, *Puritan Movement*, 266–7, 421–2.

36. *professed with us*: members of our profession (ministers; preachers).

p. 50, 1. *stretching...your line*: cf. 1 Cor. 10: 14.

4. *cup-shotten*: drunken.

5. *breaking compass*: going outside one's bounds, sphere of knowledge.

5. *outreaching*: punning on two principal senses, 'to overreach; to deceive, cheat; to outwit', and 'to reach too far; to go beyond bounds' (*OED* sv¹, 2, 3).

6. *rents...Nett*: puritan, and (more radically) presbyterian agitation for further reform of the Church.

6–7. *Only...contention*: Prov. 13: 10 (*LACT*).

10. *abate*: 'to put down, put an end to, do away with' (*OED* sv¹ I.2, citing 1585 as the last usage); the word-play that follows is indebted to the literal etymological sense from the Lat. *battere*, 'to beat down, demolish, destroy'; not in *A1*.

11. *his Prophetts*: literally, the OT Prophets, but by extension, any preacher.

14. *without the shot of it*: beyond the range of it (scripture and preaching).

14. *suffer*: bear.
16. *bide*: both 'to remain in expectation, to wait'; and 'to endure, suffer, bear, undergo' (= 'abide'); (*OED sv* I.1, II.9).
17. *durst*: darest.
22. *choler*: anger, rage.
29. *high-minded...generations*: parody of Ecclus. 44: 7.
32. *Tush*: 'an exclamation of impatient contempt or disparagement' (*OED*).
33. *prate*: 'babble; speak at length without a point' (*OED*).

p. 51, 2. ἐκμυκτηρίζειν: Gr., ěkmuktērizěin, 'mock, ridicule' (Acts 16: 14).
3. *sack*: sweet wine.
7–8. *account...Micholl's case*: 2 Sam. 6: 14–23 (*LACT*).
14. *Ego...estis*: Vulg. (Ps. 82: 6); 'I have said that ye are gods'.
14. *parcell commission*: a compound noun coinage ('parcel-commission'); part-commission, partial commission; cf. A_1 (p. 257), 'a charge out of this o[ur] charge'.
16. *runne headlong...estate*: A_1 (p. 251), reads 'would fall a maddering by & by', the verb probably a scribal error for 'madding' (to go mad), unless a recondite pun on 'maddering', to dye with madderwort, producing (royal?) purple or scarlet.
18–19. *Jack Straw...scotcheon*. Straw led armed rebels (his 'meiny', 'many') in the 1381 London Peasants' Revolt. The legend retailed here—that the heraldry ('*scotcheon*') on the Lord Mayor's seal commemorated Mayor William Walworth's killing of another leader in the rebellion, Wat Tyler—was refuted by Stow (*Survey*, ed. Kingsford, ii. 219–21).
22–24. *flower...for ever*: cf. also 1 Pet. 1: 24.
28–29. *Patimini...extirpantem*: Lat., 'suffer the pruning hook that trims, so that you do not have to suffer the axe that completely uproots'.
36. *countermeanes*: an original coinage; 'counter' ('against', 'opposed to') + 'means' ('agency', 'course of action'); not in A_1.
37. *under-meanes*: another original coinage (see prev. n.); riches should be a subordinate ('*under-*') means to serve God; part of a very tight double antithesis between the improper use of riches as inordinate '*countermeans*', vs. their proper use as subordinate '*under-meanes*'; not in A_1.

p. 52, 16–17. *Horne...salvation*: Ps. 18: 2 (*LACT*); cf. also Luke 1: 69.
19. *push*: 'to thrust or butt with the horns: chiefly biblical' (*OED, sv* I.3).
19. *consumed*: 'to consummate, accomplish, complete' (*OED sv^2*); *OED* cites no example of this sense after 1541; probably also with punning overtones of 'to spend (goods or money)...to waste, squander' (*OED sv^1* 2); not in A_1.
22. *Neither...thoughts*: Ps. 10: 4 (*LACT*).
23. *affaires*: business affairs.
24–25. *Aures...convenio*: Lat., 'I beat against the ears of all; I am congenial to the conscience of only a single one'; cf. Augustine, *Sermo LXXXII*, ix. 12: 'Aures omnium pulso: sed conscientias quorumdam convenio' (*PL*, 38.512); ('I beat against the ears of all, but am congenial to the conscience of only a few').
28. *lightly*: briefly.

p. 53, 3. *arreigned*: 'called to account'; or, more formally, 'to indict before a tribunal' (*OED sv^2* 1, 2).
4. *dic...Augustine*: Lat., 'speak, speak, but speak it inwardly to yourself'; Augustine, *Sermo LXVII*, v. 8, 'Sed dic: dic, et intus dic' (*PL*, 38.437).
22. *pinion*: clip.

24–25. *harvest... trades*: merchant trade by sea is more hazardous (financially and materially) than by other routes and means.

27. *ventureth*: 'to take the risk of sending... where loss or detriment is possible' (*OED sv* I.3); pre-dates the earliest such usage cited in *OED* (1599): 'Others like merchants venture trade abroad' (Shakespeare, *Henry V*, I. ii. 192); but cf. Drant's 1572 Spital exhortation to give alms: 'you must venture it, therefore now venture it. Venture, for after many dayes ye shall receave it agayn' (*A Fruitfull... Sermon*, sig. C1^v); not in *A1*.

27. *traffique*: 'the transportation of merchandise for the purpose of trade' (*OED* 'traffic' *n* 1.a).

28. *hazard*: to risk; gamble.

28. *venture*: 'the chance or risk of incurring harm or loss' (*OED sn* I.2.a).

29. *venturer*: 'one who undertakes or shares in a commercial or trading venture, esp. by sending goods or ships beyond seas; a merchant-venturer' (*OED sn* 2).

33. *bills*: bills of exchange; written promises to pay later for goods already received (cf. *OED sn*^{3} 9.a); see p. 74, ll. 24–27 and n.

34. *Assurances... Exchange*: premiums paid (with a bill of exchange; see prev. n.) against the possible loss of goods; cf. modern 'insurance' (*OED* 'assurance' *n* II.5).

35. *securitie*: 'a document held by a creditor as guarantee of his right to payment' (*OED sn* II.10).

37. *conveyances*: transfers of property between parties, or the documents of such transfers (cf. *OED sn* I.7).

p. 54, 7. *Calvin... Augustine*: cf. Calvin on 1 Tim. 6: 17, 'he first speaks slightingly of riches, for the phrase *in this world* is intended to lower them in our esteem' (*Calvin's Commentaries*, trans. T Smail, vol. vi (1964), 282); and Augustine, *Sermo XXXVI*, ii. 3 (*LACT*), '*Praecipe*, ergo, inquit, *divitibus hujus mundi. Non adderet, hujus mundi*, nisi quia sunt et divites non hujus mundi?' (*PL*, 38.215); ('"Charge", therefore, he says, "the rich of this world." Would he not add "of this world" unless there were some who were rich and not of this world?').

8. *barre... armes*: horizontal '*barre*' in a heraldic coat of '*armes*' popularly understood as a mark of illegitimacy (*OED* 'bar' *n*^{1} I.6).

9. *enthwite*: entwite; to reproach (*OED*).

10. *entrance*: an introduction.

14. *Holy Ghost's fashion*: expressing the conventional belief that the Holy Spirit is the author, by inspiration, of scripture.

15. *magnifically*: 'in eulogistic terms' (*OED*).

20. *plate... furniture*: the most prominent categories of domestic luxury goods: ornamental and table silver, tapestries, fine wood furniture.

22. *Saint Chrysostome's note*: 'He did not say, note, "when their glory is increased," but *the glory of their house*. All these things that I enumerated, after all... are the glory of the house, not of the person living in the house' (Chrysostom, *Commentary on the Psalms*, ed. and trans. R. C. Hill (1998), i. 343–4).

22–23. *Salomon... left hand*: Prov. 3: 16 (*LACT*).

24. *to learne*: to teach (*OED sv* II.4.a).

25. *stay*: 'to support, sustain, strengthen, comfort' (*OED sv*^{2} 1.b).

25–29. CHRIST... *booke of life*: Luke 10: 17–20 (*LACT*).

32–37. *Denique... leave them*: perhaps a confusion of sources; although Andrewes proceeds to quote Gregory the Great (see next n.), this seems to paraphrase Augustine,

Sermo LXI, viii. 9: 'sed forte quia nihil attulisti, et hic multa invenisti, aliquid hinc tecum ablaturus es?' (*PL*, 38.412); ('But certainly if you brought nothing with you [into this world], and you have found much [in the world], [you think that] you can take some of it with you?').

35–36. *Hic... dimittuntur*: cf. Gregory the Great, *Epistola XXIX*: 'Cum igitur finis nostri dies advenerit, ubi nobis erit omne quod modo cum tanta cura quaeritur et cum sollicitudine congregatur? Non ergo honor, non divitiae quaerendae sunt, quae dimittuntur' (*PL*, 77.885A); ('Now then, when our last days shall come, where will be all those things that we have sought after with such great care and with solicitude hoarded up? Neither honour nor riches are to be sought after, but left behind'); cf. *A1*, p. 254, ll.11–13.

38. *disjunctive*: from logic, 'a statement or condition of affairs involving a choice between two or more statements or courses; an alternative' (*OED*, *sn* B.1.b).

p. 55, 2. *Luk.12. (in marg.)*: Luke 12: 15–21; *LACT* emends this citation to Luke 16: 22 (the rich man and Lazarus), but the earlier parable (the rich man with many barns) is clearly more apt and intended here.

16. *Rovers by Sea*: pirates.

18. *removed as*: as removed as.

18. *Moore... Dunkerker*: the geographical and national range of pirates and privateers which preyed on English merchant vessels (Moroccan in the Mediterranean, Spanish in the Atlantic, and French in the English Channel); not in *A1*.

20. *factours*: mercantile agents, commission merchants (cf. *OED sn* I.3).

21. *Publican*: tax-gatherer; here, customs agent.

28–32. *Musculus... Creditors?*: Musculus treats this passage in *In Evangelistam Matthæum Comentarii* (Basle, 1578), 160–1, but does not retail this anecdote there.

31. *seely*: silly; 'weak, feeble, frail; insignificant, trifling' (*OED sa* A.2.a).

32. *Tineæ urbanæ*: 'city moths'; perhaps an adaptation of the marginal gloss 'Tineæ aulicæ' ('court moths') in Musculus, *In Evangelistam Matthæum*, 161.

33. *vent*: market (*OED sn^3* 2).

33. *merchandizes*: merchandise.

34. *Tineæ forenses*: Lat., 'legal moths' (cf. l. 32 and n.); lawyers.

34. *Westminster-Hall*: seat of the common law courts.

36. *evidences*: 'document by means of which a fact is established; esp. title-deeds; in the fifteenth to sixteenth centuries often in collective sense = "documents"' (*OED sn* III.8); cf. Powell, Easter Tuesday, 'they that have great enheritaunces and possessions will read ther evidences and writinges over and over agayne that they may be perfect in them' (*SPMS*, fo. 43^v).

36. *estates*: 'an account of the state or condition of anything; a "statement" of particulars' (*OED sn* 8).

p. 56, 3. *fretted*: frayed.

13. *Fee simple*: absolute possession without limitation on type of heirs (*OED*).

15. *Hâc nocte*: Vulg. (Luke 12: 20); 'this night'.

18–20. *life... vanished away*: James 4: 14.

25–38. *Prince... live under*: tactful—and tactical—comparison of Elizabeth's dealings with the City with that of her royal predecessors; probably recalls the extortion of wealth from the City by Henry III, Edward II, and Richard II, who '[took] hold of small matters, and coyned good summes of money out of them' (Stowe, *Survey*, ed. Kingsford, ii. 214;

cf. also Raphael Holinshed, *Chronicles*, 6 vols. (1807–8), ii. 818–19, 580–1); the overt praise for Elizabeth's 'gracious government' is no doubt intended to ease the pain of huge levies on the City for arming against the Armada (see Headnote); *A1* (p. 255) expands the anecdote, but without reference to chronicles or any specifically English context; cf. Bisse, Easter Monday, 'although that now you are very much charged for munition, for souldiers, for mayntenaunce of a the navye for the defence of the realme, which you have most bountifully yeilded vnto even almost beyond your power, so as it might seeme vntimely to remember other things vnto you now yet shall not be amisse to repeat them vnto you now that when you shall be better able you shall goe foreward in them' (*SPMS*, fo. 26ᵛ).

32. *roule*: roll.

p. 57, 6. *garboile*: tumult; rebellion or riot (*OED*).

10–11. *How many ... uncertaintie*: religious unrest and war in France, and more immediately, the Low Countries; not in *A1*.

13–14. *knoweth ... stripes*: Luke 12: 47 (*LACT*).

20. *descend*: passed on by inheritance.

24. *heritages*: cf. *A1* (p. 256), 'enheritances'; estates passed on by inheritance (*OED sn* 1); Drant made the same point at the Spital in 1572: 'Heyres appare[n]t I saye are not always heyres at your death' (*A Fruitfull ... Sermon*, sig. C1ᵛ).

25–26. *many sonnes ... hunting*: cf. Tilley C321.

26. *accompt*: account.

32. *way of the world*: Job 22: 15 (Bishops): 'Hast thou marked the way of the world, wherin wicked men have walked?'

p. 58, 6. *wrastle out*: wrestle; struggle with.

40. *sad*: serious; grave.

p. 58, 41–p. 59, 2. *Chrysostom ... we be*: not identified.

9. *copie*: copyhold; a lease (*OED sn* 5.a).

23. *Worldling's*: 'one who is devoted to the interests and pleasures of the world' (*OED*).

26. *Nam ... perire*: Lat., 'let him who hopes to be secure, hope in Him who cannot perish'; cf. Augustine, *In Psalmum LXXXIV*, 8: 'qui vult securus gaudere, in illo gaudeat, qui non potest perire' (*PL*, 37.1073); ('let him who wishes to rejoice in safety, rejoice in Him who cannot perish').

p. 60, 3–4. *moath-eaten ... thiefe*: Matt. 6: 19–20.

5. *living ... the dead*: cf. 2 Cor. 1: 9.

5. *Trust ... living GOD*: cf. 1 Tim. 4: 10, 6: 17.

6. *is life himselfe*: cf. John 5: 26.

7. *quicken himselfe ... you*: cf. Rom. 8: 11.

8. *spirit and visitation*: cf. Luke 1: 68, 78.

12. *that liveth ... giveth*: *A1* (p. 257) quotes the tag in Latin ('*qui vivit et dat vitam*').

13. *hornes*: biblical emblem of power, defence, or resistance (cf. 2 Sam. 22: 3); the slightly expanded image in *A1* (p. 257) is explicitly one of horns as both a weapon of defence and of offensive attack.

17. *Ag.2.9. [in marg.]*: AV Haggai 2: 8; the reference is to the verse numbering in the Geneva and Bishops' Bibles.

18–19. *thou broughtest ... naked*: Job 1: 21.

21. *ask*: beg.

25–27. *bread... in vaine*: parodic conflation of John 3: 27 and Ps. 127: 3.

27. *recognisance*: legal bond or obligation.

28. *Dominus dedit*: Vulg. (Job 1: 21), 'the Lord giveth'.

29. *Dominus abstulit*: Vulg. (Job 1: 21), 'the Lord taketh away'.

32–33. *Si... gloriaris?* Vulg. (1 Cor. 4: 7), 'if thou hast received it, why rejoycest thou?'

37. *panem quotidianum*: Vulg. (Matt. 6: 11; *LACT*), 'daily bread'.

37–38. *Regnum cælorum*: Vulg. (Matt. 6: 13; *LACT*), 'kingdom of heaven'.

39. *giveth us himselfe*: cf. Eph. 5: 2; Tit. 2: 14.

40. *Donatives*: 'a donation, gift, present; *esp*. one given formally or officially, as a largess or bounty' (*OED sn* B.1).

41. *franck almoigne*: lit. 'free alms'; tenure by free gift of charity, or of God (*OED*).

p. 61, 1. *quid... accepisti?* Vulg. (1 Cor. 4: 7), 'what hast thou, that thou hast not received?'

3–5. *Cyprian's... nostrum*: Augustine, *Retractionum*, ii. 1: 'Quod volens etiam martyr Cyprianus ostendere, hoc totum ipso titulo definivit, dicens: *In nullo gloriandum, quando nostrum nihil est*' (*PL*, 32.630); ('Which the martyr Cyprian wishing to make clear, he glosses this whole verse [1 Cor. 4.7], saying, "glory in nothing, when nothing is ours".') cf. Cyprian, *Testimonia adversus Judaeos*, III. iv (*PL*, 4.734).

14. *untimely birth*: miscarriage; abortive birth.

21–22. *Manna... lust*: Psal. 78: 29 (marg. cit.), 'so they did eate and were well filled: for he gaue them their desire', summary of God's provision of food in the Wilderness (Ps. 78: 25–9; cf. Exod. 8); Andrewes anticipates the noun 'lust' from verse 30 ('they were not turned from their lust').

22–23. *Ophir... Peacockes*: 1 Kings 10: 11, 22 (*LACT*).

24. *indumenta*: Lat., 'clothing'; cf. Vulg. (Job 24: 7), 'nudos dimittunt homines indumenta tollentes quibus non est operimentum in frigore'; ('[the wicked] cause the naked to lodge without garment, and without covering in the colde').

25. *ornamenta*: Lat., lit. 'ornaments'; here, 'rich clothing'.

26. *alimenta*: Lat., 'food'; cf. Vulg. (1 Tim. 6: 8), 'habentes autem *alimenta* et quibus tegamur his contenti sumus' ('therefore when wee have foode and raiment, let us therewith be content').

26. *delectamenta*: Lat., 'delicacies'.

31–p.62, 10. *Israël... in us*: A_I (p. 259) condenses these paragraphs, and omits the specifically nationalistic application to England.

31 *the Prophet*: David.

p. 62, 11–p. 63, 2. *The arguement... heavenly condition*: A_I (pp. 259–60) rearranges and condenses these arguments and exempla.

11. *arguement is forcible*: cf. A_I (p. 258, l. 40), 'this is a violent argum[ent]'.

30. *exprobation*: upbraiding, reproach.

p. 62, 34–p.63, 2. *as men... condition*: cf. Acts 14: 15–17.

8–9. *consequent... antecedent*: from logic; the 'consequence', or logical conclusion that follows from ('will inferr upon') a prior proposition ('antecedent').

12. *liker*: more like.

16–17. *Epha... Hin*: Hebrew dry and liquid measures, respectively; here the falsifying of them by false merchants; A_I (p. 259, l. 18) uses the Anglicisms 'bushell' and 'pecke' and specifies the quotation from Amos (8: 5).

25. πρόσκαιρον ἀπόλαυσιν: Gr., 'prŏskaipŏn apŏlausin'; 'temporary enjoyment' (Heb. 11: 25).

27–28. *So enjoy...too*: *A1* (p. 259, l. 27) concludes the passage with a specific application to 'England'.

29. *cleane*: completely.

29–32. *Our too...selves*: *A1* (p. 259, ll. 29–31) reads, 'o[ur] to much lavishness...-destroyeth o[ur] riches so that we cannot exercise iustice, distributative & commutative'; this language does not appear in the *XCVI* text, and perhaps alludes to points made by Powell the day before, 'I shold also have spoken of Iustice aswell commutative in number weight and measure, as also distributive in proportion ether Arithmeticall or Geometricall, these things are now gone out of the church' (*SPMS*, fo. 48ʳ).

33–36. *Basil...of it*: not identified; redeployed, without attribution to Basil, in 'Sacrilege a Snare' (this edn., p. 90, ll. 10–16).

34. ἐφ᾽ ἃ μὴ δεῖ: Gr., 'ĕph a mē dei' 'these things are not necessary'.

35. ἐφ᾽ ἃ δεῖ: Gr., 'ĕph a dei'; 'these things are necessary'.

36–37. Ἀκόνη...*whetstone*: Basil, *Hom. XXI*, "ἀλλὰ τὴν δαπάνην μετατιθέντες ἐπὶ τοῖς χείροσί, καὶ τὸ φιλότιμον ἀκόνην πονηρίας" (*PG*, 31.169C); ('but because we have traded extravagance for worse, and because we make pride the whetstone of baseness for those who pursue it'); the Gr. φιλότιμον can mean both 'pride' and (self-aggrandizing) 'munificence'; Andrewes's ἀσωτίας ('prodigality') perhaps recalls the latter sense of φιλότιμον, or is a simple mistake for the original πονηρίας ('baseness'); *A1* complicates the crux further (p. 259, l. 34) with its bilingual reading, "φιλοτιμία est ὡς ἀκολαστίας" ('pride is like intemperateness'). Andrewes repeats the exemplum, with only slightly different diction, in Lent 1596 (*XCVI*, 317): 'The saying of *Saint Basil* is highly commended, that ἀκόνη τῆς ἀσωτίας ἡ φιλοτιμία, *Pride is prodigalitie's whetstone*. And so it is (sure;) and setts such an edge upon it in our expenses, that it cutts so deepe into our *receipt*, and shares so much for *purple* and *linnen*, as it leaves but a little for *Lazaru*'s [*sic*] portion.'

p. 64, 12–13. *for us*: because of us.

17. *compt of*: take account of; account for.

21. *suiters*: suitors; supplicants.

32. *pew-fellow*: 'a fellow-worshipper...a companion, an associate' (*OED*).

36. *consequently*: 'with proper sequence or connexion (of thought, reasoning, etc.); consistently' (*OED*, sadv 3).

p. 65, 4–5. *Abraham...Lazarus*: Luke 16: 19–31.

7. *Job...Zachæus*: Job 29: 12–13; Luke 19: 8–9 (*LACT*).

13–16. *Yet...be partaker*: cf. Powell, Easter Tuesday, 'now adays he is accounted a righteous and just man that hurteth no man, that doth no man wronge but giveth every man his due. Is he mercifull? doth he visitt the widowes and fatherles? doth he kepe himself unspotted of the world, then is he indeed religious, otherwise he is not' (*SPMS*, fo. 48ʳ).

16–p. 66, 4 *But, it...want neither*: not in *A1*.

17. *the Schooles*: the university Divinity Schools, where theological points were debated in formal academic disputations; cf. 'Sacrilege a Snare' (this edn., Headnote).

18. *grossely*: in plain terms.

18. *These...your eyes*: the poor attending the sermon; probably the orphan wards of Christ's Hospital, one of the City's charitable institutions (see Headnote); cf. Bisse,

Easter Monday, 'If I wold sett examples^of good works^before your eyes, I might speake of this notable monument, the hospitall, wher so many poore children which otherwise were like to perish are mayntayned and most aboundantly provided for' (*SPMS*, fo. 25ʳ); and Powell, Easter Tuesday, 'to visite the fatherles we have a notable example here before our eyes, and ther are more of these workes done here in this cittye then almost in all the land agayne' (*SPMS*, fo. 48ʳ).

20–21. *sundry... now sitt*: previous generations of Lord Mayors and Aldermen.

26. *enjoy*: to give pleasure to (*OED sv* 2.a).

27. *to lighten*: 'to remove a burden from, relieve (the heart or mind); to cheer, comfort' (*OED sv¹* I.2).

28. *forecast*: 'forethought, prudence' (*OED sn* 1.a).

30. *depositum*: Vulg. (1 Tim. 6: 20), 'O Timothee depositum custodi' ('O Timotheus, keepe *that which is committed unto thee*';); Rheims leaves the word untranslated ('keepe the *depositum*').

32. *deposita*: pl. of '*depositum*' (see prev. n.).

33. *feoffees of trust*: trustees (of the '*depositum*'; see prev. nn.).

34. *gainsaying*: speaking against (*OED sv* 3).

34–35. *unpreaching Prelates... onely*: bishops ('*Prelates*') and priests ('*Pastors*') who do not preach regularly (or at all), and thus 'feed themselves' (in the literal sense) out of their incomes, but offer no spiritual food to their congregations; cf. Bisse, Easter Monday, 'It is not enoughe therfore to sowe seede and to teach doctrine only... it cannot be done by an howers preachinge. This is no puritanisme, as some of o[ur] cleargy epicures ~~affirme~~ call it, but this is Christianisme to be defended... hereof ariseth it that we have so many seminary preists amonge vs... for that now men thinck it enough to have ther Quarter sermons' (*SPMS*, fos. 29ᵛ–30ʳ); unlike Bisse, however, Andrewes only retails this concern as a way to criticize the perceived hypocrisy of the rich who hold this view; calls for the abolition of the higher clergy and the better fostering of a preaching clergy were central to radical proposals for religious reform in the parliament of 1586–7, and would soon be a *leitmotif* in the Marprelate pamphlets; continued presbyterian agitation flourished underground in London, often supported financially by wealthy London merchants; cf. Collinson, *Puritan Movement*, 85–6, and Neale, *Parliaments*, ii. 218.

36–37. *If... sincere*: challenge to City magnates to criticize themselves as harshly for not giving to the poor as they criticize ministers for not preaching.

36. *begoon*: begun.

p. 66, 3. *bread of æternall life*: cf. John 6: 35.

5–9. *Augustine... doe good*: not identified; perhaps a reworking of Augustine, *Sermo LXXXV*, iii. 4: 'Audi quid: Divites sint in operibus bonis. Quid est hoc? Expone, Apostole. Multi enim quod nolunt facere, nolunt intelligere' (*PL*, 38.522); ('Listen to which: "let them be rich in good works". What is that? Explain it, Apostle. Many do not want to do what they do not want to understand.'); *A1* (p. 260, l. 35–6) quotes differently (adding a second '*non*' in the second clause), perhaps with an improvement on the sense that simply not doing something bad is not the same as doing something good; cf. p. 65, ll. 13–16 and n.

6. *backward*: reluctant.

10–13. *Papists... doe good*: Catholic polemic routinely accused Protestants of ignoring good works; debate on this issue was a prominent part of the pamphlet war sparked by the missions of Edmund Campion and Robert Parsons in the 1580s (see next nn.); cf.

Bisse, Easter Monday, 'I speake this to stoppe the mouthes of those who affirme that we have no good workes in the church of England.... [t]he papists object further unto us that though these good deeds be now done yet if it wer not for our doctrine more wold be done then ther is' (*SPMS*, fo. 27ʳ).

13–14. *One...from you*: see Headnote.

13–14. *Religion...from you*: 'Religion has strengthened your magnetic force so much that nothing can be pulled from you', punning on the precious metals and money to which the rich are 'magnetically' attracted; cf. *A1* (p. 260, l. 41), 'an attractive vertue'; '*attractive*' in the figurative sense of 'drawing as by magnetic influence' pre-dates the earliest usage cited by *OED* (sv A.4.b; from *Hamlet*, III. ii. 117); the only other such usage cited is Andrewes, *Patterne of Catechistical Doctrine* (1642, p. 109): 'Love is the lode-stone attractive of love'; cf. also Good Friday 1605, 'if our *hearts*...be *iron*, they cannot choose but feele the *magneticall force* of this *load-stone*'; and 'A Sermon Preached...Easter Day...1620' (this edn., p. 240, ll. 15–16 and n.)

16. *chiragra*: gout in the hand.

17–19. *Another...nothing els*: cf. Thomas Harding, *An Answere to Maister Juelles Chalenge* (1565), that Protestants 'be geve[n] over to the lustes of their fleshe, which have no delite ne feeling of God, which like Turkes and Epicures seeki[n]g onely for the com[m]odities and pleasures of this world, have no regard of the lyfe to come' (p. 236).

18. *Salomon's horseleches*: Prov. 30: 15 (*LACT*); used by Andrewes himself against hypocritical Protestant greed in 'Sacrilege a Snare' (this edn., p. 90, l. 9–7).

19–20. *All...faith onely*: cf. Thomas Harding, *The Apologie of Fridericus Staphylus*: 'good workes by the deniall of fre wil being wiped away, faith must do the dede. Luther therefore and all his felow heretikes teach the sufficiency of only faith to salvation' (p. 161ᵛ); *A1* omits specific reference to salvation *sola fide*; cf. Bisse, Easter Monday, 'on that poynt of justification by faith alone which we teach, here they crye out aloud, here ther bookes are full, they say we have no exhortation to virtue, but that we sett open a gate to all liberty, because we teach justification by faith only charging us that we give license and encoragem[ent] to all sinne, teachinge that men may doe what they will so they beleve only' (*SPMS*, fo. 27ʳ).

22–23. *They say...Charges*: cf. Stanislaus Hosius, trans. Thomas Harding, *Of the Expresse Worde of God* (1567): 'Thou seest...of what sort is the preaching of those... Gospellers.... Those men commaund naught ells, but that eche man stedfastly beleeve, and rest well assured that he standeth yn the state of grace...how so ever his workes be' (pp. 9ʳ⁻ᵛ).

26–27. *Domine...clamavi*: Lat., 'Lord, you know what I have said, you know what I have spoken about, you know what I have cried out about'; not in *A1*; cf. Augustine, *Serm. de Script. CXXXVII*, xii. 15, 'Domine, scis quia dixi, scis quia non tacui, scis quo animo dixi, scis quia flevi tibi' (*PL*, 38.762); ('Lord you know what I have said, you know what I have not been silent about, you know what I have lamented to you about').

35. *Saint James saith*: James 2: 14–17 (*LACT*).

36–37. *Pure religion...widowes*: James 1: 27; the text of Powell's sermon preached the previous day.

37. *as...yesterday*: strong endorsement of Powell's avant-garde sermon; see Headnote, and cf. Powell's peroration, 'Care not you my beloved for the great knowledge of the world but study and labour to goe one in good workes and to doe good vnto all to visite the fatherles and widowes and to kepe your selves vnspotted of the world, and here I end. &c.' (*SPMS*, fo. 50ᵛ).

p. 67, 3. *great Day*: Judgement Day.

5. *feeding... succouring*: cf. Matt. 25: 31–46.

12. *Rhemes*: Rheims (or Reims); French cathedral city, home from 1578 to 1593 of the English Roman Catholic college or seminary which produced the Rheims New Testament in 1582; *A1* (p. 261, l. 18) omits the specific references to Rheims and Rome.

12. *Christen*: Christian.

12–14. *a shew... Moonday*: not the charitable collections taken at the Spital sermons on Easter Monday and Tuesday (cf. Headnote; also p. 76, ll. 22–24; and *A1*, p. 261, ll. 19–21), but the orphans of Christ's Hospital present; the Christ's children were the 'handfull of the whole heape' provided for in the City's other hospitals; Bisse, on Easter Monday, read out, in the middle of his sermon, the traditional roll-call of the numbers housed in all of them, 'Therfore first accordinge to the customc of the place I will rehearse vnto you the number of them that be partakers of this your liberalitye. At this present you have in the both hospitalls &c.' (*SPMS*, fo. 26^v).

15–16. *Chariotts... horsemen*: epithet used in 2 Kings 2: 12, and 13: 14 to describe Elijah and Elisha, respectively; cf. Geneva gloss to the latter verse: 'Thus they used to call the Prophets and servants of God by whom God blessed his people... meaning that by their prayers they did more prosper their countrey, then by force of armes'; it seems that Andrewes applies the epithet here to the citizens of London who benefited from the 'heape' of charity collected at the Spital sermons, although there might be tacit praise for the preachers (latter-day Elijahs and Elishas) who inspired that charity by their sermons; not in *A1*.

22. *Schooles... Colledges*: the foundation of grammar schools was a particular feature of the Edwardian reformation; colleges in the universities had also benefited directly from the redistribution of monastic wealth; for Andrewes's bitter complaint against the misuse of the latter, see 'Sacrilege a Snare' (this edn.).

24. *these forty yeares*: the years since the Reformation, dated here from the accession of Edward VI (1547).

25. *not... starting up*. Protestants were sensitive to Roman Catholic accusations that they had heretically started a new church, rather than carefully reformed the ancient one.

33–34. *thirtie yeares... trouble*: Elizabeth (acc. 1558) had reigned over a stable Protestant church for thirty years, perhaps here contrasted to the thirty years of troubled religious change between Luther's *Theses* (1517) and Edward's accession (1547); cf. Bisse, Easter Monday, 'm[asters] have not you sowen the good seede of the word of God these 30 yeares/ have not you taught and delivered good and wholesome doctrine/ whence then commeth it that the church is overgrowne with so many evills' (*SPMS*, fo. 20^r).

38. φιμοῦν: Gr., 'phimŏun'; 'muzzle', 'silence' (1 Pet. 2: 15).

38. *snaffle*: to bridle, restrain; a 'snaffle' is a bridle-bit for horses (*OED* sv^1; sn^1).

p. 68, 8–9. *tree... bean*: the *ficus*, or fig; cf. Anglicus Bartholomaeus, trans. Stephen Bateman, *Batman upon Bartholome* (1582) (fos. 291^b–292^a, 'Plin[y]. saith... the leaves thereof are full broad, and shaped somewhat lyke to a shield, and beareth many apples, but they be small, & passe unneth ['underneath', 'less than'] the bignesse of a Beane'.

9. *targett*: target; 'a light round shield or buckler' (*OED* sn^1 1).

9. *then*: than.

12. *queint*: quaint; 'clever, smart; full of fancies or conceits; affected' (*OED sa* A.6).

12. *sett phrases*: 'a short, pithy, or telling expression; sometimes, a meaningless, trite, or high-sounding form of words' (*OED* 'phrase' *n* 3); here also formulaic, as if from a textbook ('*sett*'); cf. Shakespeare, *Othello* (Q_1, 1622), 'Rude am I in my speech, | And little blest with the set phrase of peace' (where most editors prefer F_1's 'soft phrase'; I iii. 82–3).

16. πάντα ἀγαθὰ: Gr., 'panta agatha'; 'all the goods' (Luke 12: 18; *LACT*).

19. ἐν τῷ νῦν αἰῶνι: Gr., 'ĕn tōi nun aiōni'; 'in the present age' (1 Tim. 6: 17).

22. *Queene's bookes*: tax assessment books.

23–24. *land ... living*: common biblical epithet for heaven or the state of election; cf. Ps. 142: 5, Is. 53: 8.

29. *mary then*: indeed; a mild oath of affirmation (from 'by St Mary').

31. φειδομένως: Gr., 'phĕidŏmĕnōs'; 'abstemiously', 'stingily' (2 Cor. 9: 6; *LACT*).

39. *sessed*: assessed, taxed.

p. 69, 2. *sessement*: assessment, rate of taxation.

2. *Col.1.10. [in marg.]*: *LACT* omits, presumably on the grounds of the more exact quotation here of 2 Cor. 9: 8. (see next n.); although Andrewes does not quote Col. 1: 10, its sense is pertinent.

3. περισσεῦσαι: Gr., 'pĕrissĕusai'; 'to superabound in' (2 Cor. 9: 8).

4. προΐστασθαι: Gr., 'prŏïstasthai'; 'take precedence', 'practice' (Tit. 3: 8; *LACT*).

6. *Lords ... Livery*: hierarchical list of dignitaries attending the sermon, descending from the Lord Mayor to the wealthier freemen of the livery companies.

7. *Wards*: administrative divisions of the City of London, whose representatives composed the Court of Aldermen.

7. *Companies*: London livery companies.

9. *tell*: count.

10. *compt-bookes*: account books.

11–12. *lash out*: 'to lavish, squander' (*OED*, 'lash' v^1 I.4).

12. *Captive's redemption*: charitable collections taken at the Spital Sermons were routinely designated for the ransom of English captives abroad, usually merchant-mariners and seamen; cf. Bisse, Easter Monday, 'I might also perswade you to the redeeminge of those captives from the bondage of the turke who art bone of your bone and fleash of your fleash and therfore you ought to be touched with ther miseryes as with your owne, not knowinge what may fall vpon any of you' (*SPMS*, fo. 27ʳ); and Powell, Easter Tuesday, 'If ther be any religion left in England then where is the redeeminge of captives' (*SPMS*, fo. 48ʳ).

13. *cast*: 'to reckon, calculate, estimate' (*OED sv* VI.38.a).

19. Ἐξ ἀνάγκης: Gr., 'Ĕx anagkēs'; lit., 'out of, or by, constraint' (2 Cor. 9: 7; *LACT*).

20. ἐκ λύπης: Gr., 'ĕk lupēs'; lit., 'out of grief'; begrudgingly (2 Cor. 9: 7; *LACT*).

27. *Rogo's*: Lat., lit., 'I ask's'; questions, instructions.

28–29. *dauncing ... threshold*: Zeph. 1: 9; cf. Geneva gloss: 'He meaneth the servants of the rulers which invade other mens houses, and rejoyce and leape for joy when they can get any praye [i.e. 'prey'] to please their master withall'.

29. *failing ... eyes*: cf. Job 31: 16.

30. *instillation ... dropp*: 'the action of instilling; introduction (of a liquid) drop by drop' (*OED sn* 1, citing 1608 as first usage); not in A_1.

33. *had as leef*: would rather, would prefer to.

34. *seed-time*: the season of sowing seed; proverbially in contrast to harvest (cf. Gen. 8: 22).

35. *Hilaris... satio*: Lat., 'cheerful giving [is a] fair sowing'; cf. Tilley H72, G128.

37. *overcast*: 'clouded over, dull, gloomy'; *OED* cites 1625 as the earliest usage of the literal sense, and no examples of the transferative sense used here (*OED sppl a* 2); not in *A1*.

38. *gladnesse... countenance*: cf. Deut. 28: 47; Acts 2: 46; Prov. 15: 13.

p. 70, 2. *giving... receiving*: cf. Acts 20: 35.

3. *communicate*: to give, bestow (a material thing)' (*OED sv* 3.a).

4. *this word*: '*communicate*' (see prev. n).

6. εὐπροσόδους: Gr., 'ĕuprŏsŏdous', 'well-disposed towards'.

8. *Devill's... lending*: usury; condemned by Andrewes in similar terms in his B.Th. degree thesis argued at Cambridge in 1585: 'ut ille ætate nostrâ, non minus eleganti dixit *Chymiam Satanæ*' ('De Usuris', *OP*, 136); ('and in our age, it is not less elegantly called "the Devil's alchemy" '); orthodox opinion (both Classical and Judaeo-Christian) condemned profit from interest as the unnatural 'breeding' of an inanimate object (gold), here figured as an alchemical trick practised by the devil.

13. *analogie of faith*: exegetical principle based on Augustine, *De Doctrina*, i. 15, and common phrase in Protestant assertions of scripture as the best interpreter of scripture, based on Rom. 12: 6 ('let us prophecie according to the portion of faith'); cf. the Rheims commentary on Rom. 6: 17: 'they must never... take of man or Angel, any new doctrine or Analogie of faith, as the Protestants call it'; and William Fulke, *A Rejoynder to Bristows Replie* (1581), 'exposition of the scriptures or prophesying must be according to the analogie of faith. Rom. 12. But faith is builded upon the worde of God, and not upon the custome of men: therefore exposition of the scriptures, must be according to the word of God, and not after the usage of men' (p. 384); cf. 'Pattern of Catechistical Doctrine' (this edn., p. 6, ll. 1–3 and nn).

14–16. *Heirome... use*: cf. St Jerome (attr.), *Commentarii Epistolas Pauli*, 1 Tim. 6: 'communicare vero, multum dare' (*PL*, 30.888b); ('"to communicate" really means "to give to many"').

17. *pitch*: 'the highest (or extreme) point, top, summit, apex' (*OED sn*^{2} IV.15).

20. *Societies and Foundations*: charitable institutions like colleges, schools, and hospitals.

27–28. *eat up... many*: cf., from the anon. 'Discourse of Corporations', quoted in David Harris Sacks, 'The Greed of Judas: Avarice, Monopoly, and the Moral Economy in England', *Journal of Medieval and Renaissance Studies*, 28.2 (1998), 'all Monapolies have bin condemned by all politique men and in all well governed Comonweales, as a cause of dearth and scarcitie... contrarie to the nature and kinde of all Societies' (p. 263); Sacks's article is a brilliant study of the Christian Aristotelianism that informs Andrewes's condemnation of monopoly here.

29. *singulare commodo*: Lat., 'individual advantage, use'.

30. *civil livings*: the godly, including their merchant patrons, were quick to criticize the higher clergy for hoarding or 'appropriating' ecclesiastical livings; here Andrewes turns the tables by applying the metaphor to greedy merchants who 'appropriate' secular livelihoods ('civil livings').

31. *forgrowen*: 'overgrown, misshapen' (*OED sv* 1); archaic even in Elizabethan English; *OED* cites Andrewes for the last example of its use (1601); not in *A1*.

35. *discommon*: 'disfranchise' (*OED sv* 1.a, citing this usage as an example); not in *A1*.

36. *first privation*: foremost, or worst deprivation; perhaps the 'first' deprivation of Adam and Eve from society with God at their expulsion from Eden.

p. 71, 3-4. *they... mightily*: trustees of charitable foundations who embezzle endowment profits intended for the poor.

5-6. *Shall... things?* Jer. 5: 9, 29.

8. *suffer... exhortation*: Heb. 13: 22 (*LACT*).

11. *the charge... vaine*: conclusion of polite deference to the auditory ('the charge I make against you may be unnecessary').

14. *Saints*: distinctly Protestant understanding of 'saints' generally as members of the church, not specific historical individuals canonized by it.

23. *Church militant*: members of the church living on earth.

23-24. *Church triumphant*: members of the church in heaven.

27-28. *heard... these dayes*: Bisse, Easter Monday, enveighed against simony at length (*SPMS*, fos. 30^v-30^r), cf., 'for now ther is open Simony and buyinge sellinge of spirituall livings in the church of England, And surely it is a thinge to be observed, & I have observed it all the dayes of my life, that these buyers of spirituall livings had never any care of the church of God, nor were ever ledd with a zeale to teach the church' (fo. 30^v); and Powell, Easter Tuesday, 'I my selfe have knowne a doctor of divinity both learned and abell to teach, and godly to have stoode with an unlearned minister such as was not worthy to feede swine, yet he hath bene preferred and the other putt by, because he went not to the same markett the other did, he gave not as largely as the other' (*SPMS*, fos. 47^v-48^r).

29. *Arke*: the Ark of the Covenant (Exod. 25: 18-21); here a metaphor for the church.

33-34. *Pope doth... their Prince*: Pope Pius V's 1570 bull *Regnans in excelsis* excommunicated and deposed Queen Elizabeth, thus releasing English Catholics from bonds of loyalty to her; with the imminent invasion of the Spanish Armada (which was acting on the authority of the bull, and, if successful, would have called on English Catholics to rebel), the 18-year-old bull was dangerously pertinent; A_1 (p. 262) is even more expansive and explicit, quoting *Regnans in excelsis*, and citing the assassination of the Protestant William of Orange (1584).

34-38. *fift Commandement... eighth*: Andrewes accuses the papacy of breaking four of the Ten Commandments: the fifth, honouring father and mother (here, the monarch); the sixth, against murder (from *c*.1580 Catholic apologists defended as meritorious the assassination of heretical rulers); the seventh, against adultery (papal refusal to dissolve the marriage of Henry VIII and Katherine of Aragon, which Henry and the reformers argued was '*incestuous*'); and the eighth, against stealing (here '*Simonie*', the sale of clerical livings).

35. *daggs*: daggers.

37. *stewes*: brothels.

p. 72, 1-5. *Licence... Seminaries*: allegation that the Pope instructed recusant Roman Catholics who held the presentation of clerical livings ('*Patrons of his marke*') to sell them ('*Simonie*') and use the profits to support English Roman Catholic priests trained abroad for service in England ('*Seminaries*'); ed. finds no documentation for this alleged scheme; Andrewes may be playing to the gallery with his own anti-Catholic scaremongering; A_1 (p. 262) also retails the accusation, but without the alledged evidence of confessions from interrogated Catholic priests; Powell, Easter Tuesday, only ventures that the Church of England is open to Roman Catholic charges of simony, 'of the simony and sacriledge in o[ur] church this is that the Papists crye out agaynst and for which they promise themselves most certayne victory agaynst vs' (*SPMS*, fo. 47ᵛ).

3. *by... the drumme*: vendors heralded sales by beating drums, hence '*by the drum:* by public announcement, publicly' (*OED sn¹* I.1.c); often applied metaphorically to the simoniacal sale of clerical livings; cf. Sir Edmund Hellowes, trans., *Familiar Epistles* (1574), no. 375, 'Unto him yt offered most silver... the priesthoode was given, as when a garment is sold by the drumbe' (cit. *OED*); and Francis Godwin, *A Catalog of Bishops* (1601), 'he which was woont to sell all other ecclesiastical promotions as it were by the drum, bestowed this Archbishopricke freely' (p. 32).

6–11. *Seeing... better service*: having accused recusant patrons of the sacrilegious use of church property and livings, Andrewes here infers that rich Protestant lay patrons are guilty of the same sin; not in *A1*; but cf. 'Sacrilege a Snare' (this edn.).

16–17. *Lazarus... bosome*: Luke 16: 22–4.

23. *Strangers*: foreigners.

23. *discontented*: 'deprived or devoid of contentment' (*OED sppl.a.* 1).

29. *honourable... redresse*: City scheme to take 200 orphans off the streets and set them to work sewing woollen goods in Bridewell Hospital, to be funded by income from Christ's Hospital, Dec. 1587–Feb. 1588 (CLRO Rep. Bk. 21, fo. 507ᵛ; Journal of Common Council 22 fo. 158ᵛ; Guildhall Lib., MS 12806/2, fos. 393, 394); not in *A1* (cf. p. 262); cf. Bisse, Easter Monday, 'I require of you that you wold continew and goe one in the enterprise you have begonne in bridwell for the trayninge vp of these 200 children in divers trades' (*SPMS*, fo. 26ᵛ); Powell, Easter Tuesday, was more specific, 'add to these good workes and goe forward in them, concerninge the mayntenaunce of these 200 children in the mystery of clotheworkinge, in the bridewell it wilbe very profitable vnto the commo[n]wealth, and it wilbe a sweet smellinge sacryfice in the nostrills of the lord, even a sacrifice of mercy, this is the seminary and as it were the proppe and staye of kingedomes' (*SPMS*, fo. 48ᵛ).

32. *exiled... Strangers*: autonomous congregations of exiled French and Dutch Protestants sheltered by the City and diocese of London; also judged by modern historians as 'paragons of charitable endeavor' for their support of their own indigent members (Archer, 'Charity', 241).

36. *good cheape*: a 'quasi-adj.': 'that is a good bargain, that can be purchased on advantageous terms; low-priced, cheap' (*OED* 'cheap' *n* II.8).

37. *quitt*: satisfy, pay.

41. *naughtinesse*: 'wickedness, viciousness, depravity' (*OED sn* 1.a).

p. 73, 15. *Da... retinere*: Alanus de Insulis, *De Arte Praedicatoria*, cap. VI ('De Avaritia'): 'Vis esse mercator optimus, foenerator egregius et prudens mercenarius? Da quae non potes retinere' (*PL*, 210.124c); ('Is it the nature of a great merchant to be an admirable usurer and a prudent mercenary? Give that which you cannot retain').˙

17. *De... Christus*: Lat., '"I ask for [that which is] mine", says Christ'; cf. Matt. 20: 15.

19–20. *quod... accepimus*: Vulg. (1 Chron. 29: 14), 'and of thine owne hand we have given thee'.

26. *lay up... selves*: Matt. 6: 20.

26. *leese*: probably 'lease' (rent-out), but perhaps with a pun on 'leese' = 'to lose'.

28–35. *Augustine... lose it*: *LACT* suggests St Augustine, *Serm. LXXXV* and *Serm. LXI*, both used by Andrewes earlier in this sermon. The allusion here is in fact to *Serm.*

XXXIX, iii. 5: '*Facile tribuant, communicent* [1 Tim. 6: 18]: veluti aqua frigida perfunditur, rigescit, stringit sinum, et dicit, Non perdo labores meos. Infelix, perdere non vis labores tuos? Ecce morieris, et qui nihil huc attulisti, nihil hinc potes auferre: cum nihil abstuleris, nonne perdidisti omnes labores tuos?' (*PL*, 38.242–3); ([to say to a rich man,] '"give freely and distribute": is as if you poured cold water [over him]; he goes stiff, he recoils, and says, "I will not lose my labors." Unhappy man, do you fear to lose your labours? Behold, you will die, and as you brought nothing here with you, so you can take nothing out with you: and as you will take nothing out with you, will you not have lost all your labours?').

37–38. *Judas...bagg*: John 12: 3–8.

38. *Utquid perditio?* Vulg. (Mark 14: 4), 'To what ende is this waste?'

p. 74, 1.ἀγαθοεργεῖν: Gr., 'agathŏĕrgĕin', 'to do good' (1 Tim. 6: 18).

3. *dimittere*: Lat., 'to give up, abandon'.

3. *præmittere*: Lat., 'send before, send on ahead'.

15. *strange land*: foreign country; cf. Ps. 137: 4.

18. *Utquid respicimus?* Lat., 'how [by what means] may we look?'

19. *entertainment*: welcome, hospitality.

21. *ought*: anything.

24–27. *By exchange...receive it heer*: in Elizabethan trade, 'the exchange contract was a covenant whereby a person, usually a merchant-banker, advanced a sum of money in exchange for an instrument which was payable in another place, at a future date, and in a different kind of currency. Such an instrument was called a bill of "exchange".' The purpose of bills of exchange was 'to avoid the shipping of specie and the danger of loss during the trip'. Andrewes's epithet '*Cambium caeleste*' ('heavenly exchange') parodies the technical legal term for bill of exchange ('cambium per litteras') and the subcategories of the same ('cambium reale', 'cambium siccum', 'cambium fictum'). (Raymond de Roover, *Gresham on Foreign Exchange* (1949), 94–9.)

32. *put case*: suppose.

33. *baggs*: moneybags.

33. *currant*: current, currency that is legal tender.

34. *base*: debased, counterfeit (*OED sa* II.15).

35. *Quare non facis?* Lat., 'Why do you not do [it]?'.

36. *Adires trapezitas*: Lat., 'Go to the money-changers' (cf. Matt. 25: 27; *LACT*).

37–38. *Pauperes sunt campsores*: Lat., 'the poor are the bankers [treasurers]'; cf. Edward Phillips, *The New World of English Words* (1658), '*Cambio* (Spanish) a Burse, or Exchange, whence comes *Cambsor*, a Banker, or Money-changer' (sig. F3^r).

38. *Da...thesaurum*: Lat., 'Give to the poor and you shall receive treasure'; cf. Vulg. (Matt. 19: 21), 'da pauperibus et habebis thesaurum in caelo'.

39–41. *Where...* CHRIST's *bill*: dense allusion to the NT promise that Christ's satisfaction of the debt of human sin is superabundant, going beyond even the amount required for literal satisfaction of that debt; the mercantile vocabulary hints at Christ's parables of the unjust steward (Luke 16: 1–13), and the just king who punishes a servant unwilling to forgive debts (Matt. 18: 23–35).

39. *Quod...uni*: Lat., 'Why, there is a great one'.

39–40. *Ego resolvam...mercedem*: Lat., 'I shall cancel it; not demand interest, but give interest'.

p. 75, 2. *earst*: erst; 'in the first place' (*OED, sa* A.2).

3. *Utopia*: in the lit. sense, 'no place'; 'a fiction' (*OED*); possibly with anti-Catholic overtones, as John Foxe, *Actes and Monuments* (1583, viii. 1017), 'I do not...thinke, that...there is any such fourth place of Purgatory at all (unles it be in M. Mores Utopia[;] Utopia that is to say, *Nusquam*, no place)'.

7–13. *When...commandeth it*: Andrewes's emphasis on the spiritual benefit of almsgiving and good works for the doer is a daring reorientation of conventional Protestant denunciations of the efficacy of works; even Powell, who offered a striking dismissal of quarrelling with Roman Catholics over the efficacy of works (quoted in Headnote), praised works as an outward obligation of religion that would be rewarded by God in this life ('lett vs goe one in good workes, and then the lord will p[ro]sper and bless vs in this life', *SPMS*, fo. 50^r), not as a part of the nature of religion itself that brought reward in heaven.

14–16. *Widow...Sarepta*: 1 Kings 17: 1–16 (*LACT*), a *locus classicus* for exhortations to almsgiving, amplified, for example, in the official Elizabethan homily 'Of Alms-Deeds'; cf. Mack, *Elizabethan Rhetoric*, 282–3.

19. *prove*: 'to make trial of, put to the test' (*OED sv* 1.a).

23–25. *bosomes...Lazarus*: cf. Luke 16: 20–5.

29. *husbandman casts*: farmer sows; cf. Matt. 13: 3–12.

32. *compt*: account.

37. *for altogether*: 'for all time to come' (*OED, sadv.* B.3); cf. 'for good'.

p. 76, 1. *fulnesse of time*: cf. Gal. 4: 4.

1–3. *harvest...retribution*: Matt. 13: 37–40 (*LACT*).

15–16. *thousand...a day*: 2 Pet. 3: 8 (*LACT*).

18–19. *Sed...aliud*: Lat., 'but for some other thing I know not of'.

22. *Date and Dabitur*: Lat., '"Give" and "it shall be given"'; cf. Vulg. Luke 6: 38 (*LACT*).

23–24. *our carefull...encrease*: allusion to the pattern of charitable collections taken at past Spital sermons; viz.: 'our careful command to give (*our...Date*) at the sermons in 1586 (*last yeare save one*) was repaid in the present (*in presenti*) by a great receipt (*Dabitur* = 'ye shall receive') in 1587 (*last yeare's encrease*)'; see Headnote.

26. *Habetis hic*: Lat., 'you shall have it here'.

27. *Habete illic*: Lat., 'have it there'.

31. *opera eorum*: Lat., 'their works'.

34–35. *Jona's gourd*: Jonah 4: 6–7 (*LACT*).

36. *ground-worke*: foundation; cf. Heb. 3: 14, Rheims gloss: 'faith is the groundworke of our creation in Christ, which if we hold not fast, al the building is lost'; the term is not used in the Protestant translations or glosses.

37. ἐν τῇ φυλακῇ: Gr., 'ĕn tē phulakē', 'in the prison'.

37. ἐν τῇ βασιλικῇ: Gr., 'ĕn tē basilikē', 'in the palace'.

p. 77, 2–3. *perillous note...foundation*: criticism of the marginal note on this verse in the Rheims translation, 'Almes deedes and good workes laide for a foundation and ground to attaine everlasting life. So say the doctors upon this place'.

5. *fundamentum*: Lat., 'a foundation'.

8–9. *Apostles...foundations*: cf. also Rev. 21: 14 (*LACT*).

11. *Eph.3.18. [in marg.]*: Eph. 3: 17 in all English translations except Geneva; cf. next n.

8–12. *lowest...foundations too*: calling the apostles a secondary foundation to Christ (with its implicit endorsement of the apostolic succession of bishops by divine right) as an analogy for justifying works as a secondary foundation to faith is an avant-garde combination of both *jure divino* episcopacy and anti-Calvinist doctrines of justification (see next n.).

11–12. *Charitie... workes of charitie*: Andrewes here massages Eph. 3: 18 (or 17; cf. prev. n.), which in Geneva and Bishops' reads 'that ye, being rooted and grounded in love'. Only Rheims reads 'rooted and founded in charitie'. The wordplay on 'foundations' ('founded') and the latinate 'charitie' instead of 'love' links Andrewes's argument to the Rheims text. Moreover, Geneva glosses 'love' as God's love 'which is the roote of our election'. But Rheims insists that 'not faith only must be in us, but charitie which acco[m]plisheth al vertues'. In spite of his rejection of Rheims' 'perillous note' on his main text, like the Rheims translators, Andrewes does reject 'love' defined as predestinate election, preferring instead works of 'charitie' as a joint foundation with faith for 'al vertues' (Andrewes's 'the *graces* within us'; l. 9). His diction here edges close to Reginald Pole's in *A Treatie of Justification* (Louvain, 1569), which lauds faith as a 'foundation' upon which works erect the 'building' of justification: 'for as in a building there must be a foundation to bear up the house... and yet it is to no purpose to laie a foundation if a man builde nothing upon it... even so is there in our Justification, as it were a foundation... and a perfect building' (p. 60ʳ). Andrewes does, however, shift the same metaphor again in a Protestant direction (ll. 32 ff.). For a similar formula expressed later in his career, see 'A Sermon... Preached With-Sunday' (this edn., p. 222, ll. 36 ff.).

15–18. *drift... stabilitie*: another very cautious intervention on justification by faith alone; although the letter of the classic Protestant case is firmly put ('not... *justifying*'), the ensuing reiteration of Paul's qualification that works carry a '*stabilitie*' not to be confused with the '*uncertaintie*' of riches still departs in spirit from mainstream *sola fideism*.

18–19. *Magnificat at Matins*: in the *BCP*, the Magnificat is appointed for Evening Prayer, not Morning Prayer ('*Matins*'); hence, wrong, out of place.

24. *faster*: firmer.

25. πάντα... οὐδεμία: Gr., 'panta ĕkčina bĕhaia, mĕtabolē ŏudĕmia' ('all of these things are steadfast; there is no change'). Chrysostom, *Hom. XXIV on Matt.* (7: 4–7), treats this idea, but not in these words, which are perhaps Andrewes's own brief paraphrase. Cf. also Chrysostom, *Hom. IX on 2 Tim.* (4: 8): 'None can stand upon water, but upon a rock all find a secure footing. Worldly things are as water, as a torrent, that passes away... spiritual things are as a rock' (*LF*, xii. 256).

29–31. *Chrysostome... groundworke*: cf. Chrysostom, *Hom. XVIII on 1 Tim.* (6: 17): 'If thou seekest riches, seek those that are stable and enduring, and which are the fruit of good works' (*LF*, xii. 160).

36. *plott*: plot of ground (for building).

p. 78, 5. *raise upon*: build upon.

5. *O... pretio!* Lat., 'O how meet a reward!'

10. *to you-ward*: toward you; for you.

11–12. *not... your salvation*: another statement of the reformed position that by their nature ('*naturá*') works are a foundation of one's assurance of salvation, but not a foundation of salvation itself ('to *God-ward*'); cf. Church of England, 'Articles of Religion' (1571), no. 12: 'good workes... folowe after justification... and do spring out necessaryly of a true and lively faith'.

27. *prospect*: view.

28. *staple ware*: goods that were the monopoly of The Staple, a royally licensed group of wool merchants, hence valuable (cf. *OED* 'staple' n^2 4); or, more generally, the principal product of any place or group of merchants.

31–32. *readings... true life*: a tacit compliment to the Rheims translation of this clause—'that they may apprehend the true life'—which, unlike all Protestant English translations ('readings') since Tyndale, follows Vulg. ('aprehendant veram vitam').

32. *in this*: in this life.

33–36. *Augustine... die*: cf. Augustine, *Sermo LXXX*, 2: 'omnis enim vita ista nostra, infirmitas' (*PL*, 38.494–5); ('this whole life of ours is a disease').

36. *He lives... die*: although attributed to Augustine ('*he saith*'), not positively identified; cf. Augustine, *Sermo XXXIX*, 5; also Gen. 2: 17; Ps. 89: 48.

40. *ill favoured*: 'offensive (to some other sense than sight, or to the mind)' (*OED sa*, b); here, bad-tasting.

p. 79, 1. *scarifying*: surgical incisions or scratches made to heal a sore or wound (cf. *OED svbln.* b).

1. *searing*: scorching or cauterizing a wound.

6. *eeke*: eke; 'increase, add to, lengthen' (*OED sv* 1).

14–15. *yeares... never faile?* Heb. 1: 12.

16. *haply*: perhaps; by chance.

16. *abridges*: shortens; reduces.

21. *leese*: lose.

24. *pecunia... perditionem*: Lat. (not Vulg.), 'Thy monie perish with thee' (Acts 8: 20).

26. *tentations*: temptations.

27. *noisome*: harmful, noxious.

29–30. *Quibus... curabo?* Lat., 'With what words shall I cure you?'

33. *the Court*: lit., the Court of Aldermen assembled for the sermon; but punning on the congregation as a judicial 'court' assembled to hear the preacher's 'judgment' handed down in his sermon (cf. pp. 41–42 and nn.).

35–36. *I might... Jesus*: 1 Tim. 6: 13 (*LACT*).

37–39. *who shall... CHRIST*: 2 Thess. 1: 7–8 (*LACT*).

p. 80, 1–2. *humanum... men*: Vulg. (Rom. 6: 19); cf. *A1* (p. 263), 'according to humanity'.

3–6. *beseech... unto Him*: composite of four salutations by Paul: Rom. 12: 1, 1 Cor. 1: 3, 2 Thess. 2: 16, 2 Thess. 2: 1.

9. *countenance*: 'bearing, demeanour, comportment' (*OED sn* I.1).

9. *autoritie*: authority.

10. *unmeet*: 'unsuitable' (*OED sa* 4).

11. *fellowship*: appointment, or office; here, ordination.

12. *dispensing... Charges*: administering the sacraments, and preaching; the two duties of a minister in the Church of England.

20. *O... your life*: Wisd. 1: 12 (*LACT*).

24. *basely*: 'at small value or esteem; meanly' (*OED sadv* 5).

25. *vaine riches*: cf. Matt. 6: 19, Geneva gloss, 'those mens labours are shewed to be vaine, which passe not for the assured treasure of everlasting life, but spend their lives in scraping together fraile and vaine riches'.

25. *vaine confidence*: a common epithet unique to the commentaries in the Geneva Bible; cf. glosses to Ps. 146: 3, Mic. 5: 10.

26. *belly... backe*: indulging in excessive food for the '*belly*' and fine clothes for the '*backe*'; cf. Solomon's sarcastic dismissal of the wicked rich, Eccles. 9: 7–8, and the Geneva gloss on v. 8, 'Rejoyce, be merie, and spare for no cost. Thus spake the wicked belly gods.'

27. *sparing good*: cf. 2 Cor. 9: 7: 'so let him give, not grudgingly, or of necessitie: for God loveth a cheerefull giver'; Geneva glosses 'grudgingly' as 'with a sparing and nigardly heart'.

30. *in novissimo*: Vulg. (John 12: 48, Job 19: 5), 'at the last', i.e. Last Judgement.

32. *devill's charge*: Satan's claim on damned souls at the Last Judgement; the image relies more on late medieval iconography than scripture, but cf. Rev. 12: 9–10 for Satan as 'the accuser'.

p. 81, 2. *Saint Paule's end*: the end of the sermon's text (1 Tim. 6: 19).

3. *immortal... wise*: 1 Tim. 1: 17.

SACRILEGE A SNARE

Text.   Sacrilege a Snare. | A | SERMON | PREACHED, | *AD CLERUM,* | In the *University* of *Cambridg*, by the | *R. REVEREND FATHER IN G*OD | *Lancelot Andrews:* | Late L. BISHOP of *WINCHESTER.* | When he proceeded Doctor in *Divinity:* | Translated for the benefit of the Publike. | [...] | *LONDON,* | Printed *by T. B.* for *Andrew Hebb*, at the *Bell* in | *St. PAUL'S* CHURCH-YARD. 1646. (Wing A3151; hereafter, *Q*). The copy text used is Bodl. Sermons 1 (16), collated with BL Thomason E.364 (reproduced on *EEBO*; collation revealed no variants). This sermon first appeared in its original Latin in *OP* (1629), the volume of Andrewes's Latin works edited under royal warrant by William Laud and John Buckeridge. It is there titled only '*Concio ad clerum pro gradu doctoris, &c.*'(without separate title-page). The Latin text is hereafter *O*. The anonymous but faithful English translation presented here omits only Andrewes's prayer before the sermon (*O*, 1–3), and one sentence specific to the sermon's original context (this edn., at p. 84, l. 40; see n.). *Q* also translates Andrewes's frequent quotations from Greek and Hebrew, but leaves intact most of those in Latin. *Q*'s title is the translator's, taken from the scriptural text. The printer Thomas Badger inherited the controlling rights to the texts in the Laudian editions of Andrewes from his father, Richard Badger (publisher of *XCVI* and, jointly with Andrew Hebb, *OP*) in 1641. A manuscript annotation on the BL copy dates the sermon's publication 'Decemb: 1st'. The translator or compositor of *Q* favoured several unconventional spellings that are foreign to Andrewes's own authorial English, and could cause unnecessary distraction to the modern reader; these have been silently amended by the editor: 'ei' for 'ie' (e.g. 'preist', 'veiw'), 'Cedar' (Kedar), 'mantenance' (maintenance), 'Levits' (Levites), 'chang' (change), and 'tith' (tithe). Also silently amended is one incorrect possessive ('will's' to 'wills') and two non-sequential superscript numbers. Also corrected are four typographical errors in biblical citations. *Q* is edited here for the first time. *O* is included in *LACT*, x. 7–28; an outline in quotations from *O* by John Warner, bishop of Rochester (1581–1666) is in Bodl. MS Engl.th.b.4, fos. 237[r]–238[v].

Headnote.   This sermon had a complex political and literary significance both during and after its author's life. *O* was originally preached *ad clerum* ('to the clergy') in the university church of St Mary in Cambridge as part of the requirements for proceeding to the degree of Doctor of Divinity. The candidate also had to have completed five years in residence after proceeding BD, participate in the Divinity Acts (see Sources, below), and preach within a year thereafter at Paul's Cross (*Documents Relating to the University... of Cambridge* (1852), i. 460). Andrewes proceeded BD in 1585 and DD in 1590 (Camb. Univ. Archives MS Degr. 3, fo. 7^v). The date of Commencement in that year, and thus the latest possible date for the sermon, was 7 July. As part of a university exercise, this sermon is a piece of donnish display that surpasses even the erudition of his court sermons. The Latin is not only florid, but larded with quotations from Classical history and literature, as well as patristics and scripture. (Although some of the former are obscured in the English translation, they are documented in the notes.) The tone is in keeping with the Divinity and Commencement Acts' festive combination of *gravitas* and entertaining ostentation.

In content the sermon is a remarkably ambidextrous attack on the Henrician reformation's legacy of alienating church property to the crown and laity, including the system of exchange and leasing of church lands and the impropriation of tithes reintroduced by Elizabeth in 1559. Andrewes's sweeping condemnation of any misuse of church property that deprives the clergy of its rightful maintenance allows him to articulate both 'puritan' concerns (e.g., the evils of non-residence and poor preaching standards among the clergy) as well as a sacerdotalism that dares to criticize the martyred fathers of the early Reformation, the queen, and prominent courtiers. On one hand, the sermon is deeply engaged in Archbishop John Whitgift's final campaign against the presbyterian movement in the wake of the Marprelate Controversy and puritan agitation in Parliament (1588–9). (Andrewes was appointed Whitgift's chaplain at this time, and was intimate with his protégé, Richard Bancroft.) Fundamental to presbyterian proposals for the abolition of the hierarchical clerisy was the replacement of the system of parochial tithes (wherein the clergy received and administered their own incomes) with a system of flat-fee stipends collected and distributed to ministers by the state or by lay elders. To the establishment, this was an offensive subjugation of the clergy to the laity, or, in Andrewes's terms here, a 'devouring' by the laity of the 'sacred' things belonging to the church. Andrewes's sensitivity to extreme nonconformity was probably further heightened by his harsh interrogation of the imprisoned Isaac Barrow in March 1590. On the other hand, the queen herself is also indicted for a system of patronage paid for by another kind of sacrilegious 'devouring'—the alienation of church property for crown profit and distribution to favourites. Andrewes differs from other episcopal apologists, notably Bancroft, in his strident demand that the church's financial independence be defended from both the crown and court as well as presbyterians; it should be noted, however, that the very public venues for Bancroft's surviving works on the subject (e.g. Paul's Cross) did not afford him the luxury of bold theorizing allowed to Andrewes here in the rarified context of the University Commencement acts (which Andrewes acknowledges in the one sentence in *O* omitted in *Q*; see n. to p. 84, l. 40).

There are three more immediate backgrounds to the sermon: Whitgift's defeat of proposals in 1585 for the 'farming', or investment, of tithes for further crown profit; the Privy Councillor Sir Francis Knollys's ongoing support at court of puritan and presbyterian reforms; and the crisis over presbyterian cells active in Cambridge at the time of the sermon. One of the presbyterian ringleaders in the university, John Alvey, included as part of his campaign of pro-puritan civil disobedience in the winter of 1589–90 the non-placeting of motions in the University Senate, including that for Andrewes's proceeding DD. The lack of an exact date for this sermon makes it impossible to judge whether it made Andrewes Alvey's target, or whether Andrewes in it responds to Alvey's insult. But the episode, and the sermon, make very clear Andrewes's status as the leading anti-puritan in Cambridge at least five years before the predestinarian debates that mark his coming-out as a doctrinal anti-Calvinist.

The sermon's second lease of life was in print. As the first text presented in *O* (1629), it advertised William Laud's controversial policy of unstitching Tudor erastianism by wresting from the laity as much control of ecclesiastical affairs (including property and livings) as possible. But proof of the sermon's breadth of appeal is then seen in its redeployment by presbyterian interests in December 1646 in the English version presented here. The presbyterians—once Andrewes's *bêtes noires*, but in the realignment of ecclesiastical politics after the Civil War, the new conservatives—were engaged in a protracted debate with Independents in parliament over the new church polity. Although episcopacy and the *BCP* had been abolished, Independents reviled the presbyterian retention of the old parochial system of tithes and livings. *Q*—a sermon by one of the old church's most august defenders of clerisy, translated 'for the benefit of the Publicke', and with the imprimatur of the presbyterian censor John Downame—was overtly recycled as a defence of its original opponents. As such, it is emblematic of the Independent charge articulated by John Milton (at precisely the time of *Q*'s publication) that 'New *Presbyter* is but old *Priest* writ large' (Sonnet XIII).

Sources. The sermon is most intimately linked with Andrewes's Divinity Act thesis, 'Tithes ought not to be abrogated', argued, like the sermon, as part of the requirements for his proceeding DD at Cambridge in Trinity Term 1590. Andrewes's liberal quotations from the thesis in the sermon suggest that the sermon was preached after the thesis was argued. Like the sermon, the thesis was first published in Latin in *O* as *De Decimis, Theologica Determinatio*, and then in English early in 1647 as *Of the Right of Tithes: A Divinity Determination* (hereafter *RT*; clearly a companion piece to *Q*). The thesis argues in thirteen points for the unambiguous validity of tithes *de jure divino*. This was a position unheard of since the reign of Mary. Andrewes acknowledged how avant-garde his argument was by noting that 'I am to treat of a hard point, nor is there any by whose candle I shall light mine', and then asking the judges to grant 'pardon, as is meet, to me the first that make experiment' (*RT*, 5). Significantly, Andrewes demurred from *RT*'s divine right argument in *Q* (p. 88, ll. 7–10). Andrewes's quotations from *RT*, which cluster in the sermon's defence of tithes in its first part, are documented here.

Quotations from non-Christian poets and historians abound in this sermon, unlike their very occasional and muted appearance in his City and court sermons, and include Homer, Virgil, Cicero, Juvenal, Seneca, Josephus, Herodotus, Florus, and Justinus. Although certainly a part of the *ad clerum* genre's academic display, they are also no doubt intended to antagonize puritans who objected in principle to the use of secular learning in sermons. The source for Andrewes's controlling gloss on his text—that Solomon was prompted to utter this proverb by court embezzlement of Temple funds—has eluded the editor. Andrewes seems to attribute this to rabbinical '*Interpreters*' (pp. 82, 83). Neither the most widely used rabbinical commentaries on the Proverbs—Solomon Ben Isaac, Abraham ben Ezra, and Levi ben Ghershom, *In Proverbia Salomonis commentarii Trium Rabbinorum* (Milan, 1520); *Mishle Shelomoh ben David, Proverbia Salomonis* (Munster, 1524)—nor the major Protestant and Roman Catholic commentaries—Cajetan (Tomaso de Vio), *Parabolae Salomonis* (Paris, 1545); Ralph Baynes, *In Proverbia Salomonis...Commentarium* (Paris, 1555); Ludwig Lavater, *In Librum Proverbiorum* (Zürich, 1562); Jean Mercier, *Commentarii in Salomonis*

Proverbia (Geneva, 1573); Johannes Arboreus, *Commentarii... in Proverbia Salomonis* (Paris, 1549); Phillip Melancthon, 'Explicatio Proverbiorum', in *Operum... Pars Secunda* (Wittenberg, 1562)—assert this historical gloss.

Q shares arguments and language with a wide range of both presbyterian and anti-presbyterian polemic. In particular, the imagery of devouring holy things was familiar from presbyterian accusations of episcopal avarice. Whole paragraphs of precisely this language from Walter Travers's 1573 *Ecclesiae Disciplinae* were reinjected into the vernacular debate when quoted for rebuttal by Bancroft in 1589 (*A Sermon Preached at Paules Crosse*, 27–8). Andrewes, however, not only refutes presbyterian arguments, but does so with the brilliantly ironic appropriation of the presbyterians' own vocabulary. Andrewes also seems to have been familiar with the arguments and language of Whitgift's 1585 position against the farming of tithes, printed in John Strype, *The Life and Acts of... John Whitgift* (1718), Appendix, pp. 100–2. For Sir Francis Knollys's petitions and letters against the hierarchical clergy (in response to Bancroft's 1589 sermon) see Strype, *Whitgift*, 292–3, 311–13, 349–50.

Further Reading. For tithes and impropriations, see Christopher Hill, *The Economic Problems of the Church from Whitgift to the Long Parliament* (1956), ch. 5. For Elizabethan erastianism, see MacCulloch, *Tudor Church Militant*, ch. 4. The standard studies of the Elizabethan episcopate's fortunes are Felicity Heal, *Of Prelates and Princes: A Study of the Economic and Social Position of the Tudor Episcopate* (1980), and *Hospitality in Early Modern England* (1990), ch. 7. For Andrewes and Cambridge puritanism, see H. C. Porter, *Reformation and Reaction in Tudor Cambridge* (1958), 159–94; Strype, *Whitgift*, 320; and Tyacke, 'Lancelot Andrewes'. For Laud's implementation of Andrewes's views on lay involvement in church finances, see Kevin Sharpe, *The Personal Rule of Charles I* (1992), 308–17, 392–402. For the debates in the Long Parliament between advocates of presbyterian and Independent church polity, J. T. Cliffe, *Puritans in Conflict* (1988), 101–34.

p. 82, 1–3. *A Sermon... Cambridg*: from title-page of *Q* (see Text above).

4–5. *PROV.... HOLY*: AV (which, by the date of translation, 1646, was the standard English version); like *O*, this follows the translation derived from the Septuagint, 'Laqueus est homini devorare Sacra'; Vulg. reads 'ruina est hominis devorare sanctos' ('It is destruction to a man to devour holy things').

8. *tenor*: continuous course of meaning in something written or spoken (*OED*); cf. Gen. 43: 7, Exod. 34: 27 (AV); and 'A Sermon Preached... the V. of March A.D. MDXCIIII' (this edn., p. 113, l. 20).

16. *Grater*: one who grates, harasses. *O*—'Nec inter δημοβόρους Βασιλέας erat Salomoni'—quotes Homer, *Iliad*, II. i. 228–31 (Achilles' condemnation of Atreides), 'Far better to your mind | is it, all along the widespread host of the Achaians | to take away the gifts of any man who speaks up against you. | *King who feed on your people* (δημοβόρους Βασιλέας)' (trans. R. Lattimore). δημοβόρους (dēmoborous) = lit., 'devourer of the common stock' (*Iliad*, ed. Walter Leaf, 2nd edn., 1900).

17. *on the Clergy*: *O* keeps a stricter parodic parallelism with the immediately preceding Homeric quotation (see previous note) with the coinage κληροβόρους (klēroborous, 'devourer of the clergy').

17. *Alienating*: transferring ecclesiastical property to secular ownership.

18–19. *Vow-breakers... points at*: the full text of Prov. 20: 25 (AV) is, 'It is a snare to the man who devoureth that which is holy: and after vowes, to make inquirie.'

20. *stomach*: in the literal sense, but also transferatively, 'appetite'; O reads '*Œsophagus*' ('gullet').

23. *Interpreters*: perhaps the '*Rabbies*' (p. 121, l. 16), or rabbinical commentators (see Sources).

p. 82, 25–p. 83, 2. *answer... Court Vanities*: this historical scenario seems, for Andrewes, an unusually specific commentary on actual events and individuals. Grandees and gentry of all religious persuasions were beneficiaries of ecclesiastical revenues granted by the queen. In March 1588, the Earl of Leicester had petitioned for a scandalously huge income from the vacant sees of Durham, Ely, Oxford, and Bristol. But he had died eight months before Andrewes's sermon, and the '*Counsellor*' who most busily 'laboured to perswade' the queen for the radical restructuring of the church along presbyterian lines was Sir Francis Knollys, Treasurer of the Queen's Chamber (here, the '*Threasury*' for '*Court* Vanities'?). He circulated a position paper at court against the superiority of bishops dated 31 March 1590, and his efforts were too zealous for his royal kinswoman, who temporarily denied him access to Court for his pains in May 1590 (Strype, *Whitgift*, 349–52). The timing of this episode fits exactly with the Divinity Acts season in Cambridge during which the sermon was preached, and may have emboldened Andrewes. For Knollys, see also *ODNB*; Neale, *Parliaments*, ii. 225–9; Peter Lake, *Anglicans and Puritans?* (1988), 146, 222–3; and Collinson, *Elizabethan Puritan Movement*, 497–8 n.

25–26. *Wise... Prince*: Solomon.

27. *His Father*: King David.

p. 83, 3. *diduce*: deduce; to derive, go back over ('Paulò rem repetam altius', O).

8–10. *men... under the Crosse*: criticism of the Church of England for not endowing its clergy and places of worship with greater dignity in the 'Peace' that followed the early Tudor reformations and persecutions. The image of 'groaning under the Cross' (cf. Gal. 6: 12, 14) was a leitmotif for Protestant suffering under Mary promulgated largely through Foxe's publication of the letters of the Marian martyr John Philpott. Of many examples, cf. his valediction to Lady Vane: 'Farewell on earth, whome in heaven, I am sure, I shall not forget. Farewell under the crosse most joyfully' (Foxe, *Actes and Monuments* (1583), xi. 1837). In *RT*, Andrewes uses similar language to argue that tithes were due during persecution as well as peace: 'But what say you of that *other*, under the *Cross*? Of that, which was so full of *glorious Martyrs*? Although it be an unjust demand, that the *Church* should be in no better condition when *flourishing*, then when *afflicted*... [t]he same did the *Church* ever think concerning *Tithes*, when *she suffered persecution*, and when she was *free* from *it*' (p. 16).

13. *Carved works*: O (p. 4) reads 'tabulata *Cedrina*', lit., 'planks of cedar'; however, 'tabula' can also mean a painted panel or picture; three-dimensional images in churches were particularly repellant to strict Protestants; cf. Thomas Lever, *A Treatise of the Right Way* (1575), asking whether, 'carved and painted images, be any other things, than the open and abhominable spoile & robbery of... the holie Churche'.

18. *evill eye*: 'look of ill-will'; cf. Matt. 7: 22 (*OED* 'evil' 6.a).

24. *accession*: 'addition, augmentation, increase' (*OED sn* 6.a).

24–26. *which hapned... President*: another caustic comment on the Dissolution under Henry VIII. In 1536 Henry's chief minister Thomas Cromwell created a new department, the Court of Augmentations, to handle the Crown's collection of seized monastic wealth and the proceeds from the new system of tithes. The irony is pointed: Solomon appointed a court officer, *'Jehiel'*, to collect for the edification of the Temple; Henry did so to despoil it.

27–30. *David... Jeroboam*: Andrewes continues his satire against Tudor impropriations and neglect of churches in the veiled speech of Old Testament story: David (Henry VIII) left to his heir, Solomon (Edward VI), great wealth in the *'Threasury'* for construction of a new Temple (the Church of England; cf. 1 Chron. 28, 29). Andrewes further imagines the insidious advice of counsellors and courtiers (*'Court-Ratts'*; see next note) keen to pocket the funds from the Temple project. This has no scriptural basis, and requires Andrewes to imagine a plot by schemers perhaps (*'haply'*) like Jeroboam, a traitorous servant to Solomon (1 Kings 11: 26–40). If Elizabeth might be understood as included in the Solomonic image, this could continue the satire aimed at Sir Francis Knollys (p. 82, l. 25–p. 83, l. 2 and nn.).

30. *Court-Ratts*: proverbial epithet in both English and Latin (*'Palatii Sorices'*, O), variously attributed in the Renaissance. Cf. Thomas Nash, *Quaternio or A Fourefold Way to a Happie Life* (1633), 201: 'Adulatores sunt sorices & tineae palatii, qui nocte die & abque; arrodunt, corrodunt, & devorant' ('flatterers are the rats and moths of palaces, who day and night are gnawing, corroding, and devouring'), quoting German humanist Ulrich von Hutten's 1519 *Aula Dialogus*, 18. Lodowick Lloyd, *The Tragicoemedie of Serpents* (1607) asserts that '*Constantine* the Emperour cals *Sorices Palatii*, the rats of the Court' (p. 81). One commentator on Prov. 20: 25 also compares the man who snatches holy things to a mouse: 'muscipula est viro celeriter quippiam proprium sanctificare' (Ralph Baynes, *In Proverbia Salomonis*, 88).

31–32. *House... no sieling*: another Old Testament text (Hag. 1: 4, 'Is it time for you, O yee, to dwell in your sieled houses, and this house lie waste?') with a contemporary application. The dereliction of church buildings, particularly the collapse of chancels, was a focal point for expressing nostalgic regret over the excesses of the Reformation. Shakespeare's 'bare ruined choirs' (Sonnet 72) is only the most famous.

32–33. *CHRISTS head... waste*: early example of Andrewes's fondness for using St Mary Magdalen's anointing of Christ's feet, and Judas's objection to it (Mark 14: 4–6), as an analogue for puritan resentment at adorning Christ's 'body', the church; see his sermon on the text before Elizabeth in Lent, 1592 (*XCVI*, 273–84), which condemns conspicuous consumption by the laity at the expense of poor relief and endowment of churches and clergy.

35–38. *inquisition... True-hearted King*: continues the satire against counsellors who attempt by subterfuge to turn sovereigns' duties to God and church to private gain, by alluding to Joab's slander and murder of Abner (2 Sam. 3), who had transferred his loyalty from Saul to David ('the True-hearted *King*'); there is an implicit warning to Elizabeth to follow David's example.

p. 83, 39–p. 84, 1. *occasion... conjecture*: Andrewes here concludes his satiric use of the Old Testament with a speculative answer to his opening question, 'Whence then, or what had He [Solomon] to do with *Sacrilegious persons...* whom this Verse points at?' (p. 82, ll. 18–19); he claims support in rabbinical commentaries ('the *Rabbies*') on Proverbs, and the whole passage has deftly yoked 'sacrilege' to evil counsel of the monarch (see Sources).

1–4. *these Counsellers... Kingdome*: conventional use of panegyric praise as a warning or implied criticism: Elizabeth (one of the 'like godly *Princes*') will not listen to 'such Petitions', or she risks 'the *Ruin*' of her 'Kingdome'. Andrewes probably alludes to a bill to limit pluralism and non-residence debated in the parliament of 1589, or to

Knollys's petitions against the superiority of bishops. The former was promoted by Knollys and timidly defended by Lord Burghley, both members of the Privy Council ('These Counsellers'), but quashed by Whitgift and the queen (Neale, *Parliaments*, ii. 225-9).

7. *whether*: whither, where.

8. *Sacred Patrimony*: inheritance intended for ecclesiastical use; but also more generally an inheritance from God; cf. the Mosaic laws for the patrimony of the Levitical priesthood (Deut. 18: 1-9).

9. *stupifying or deading*: numbing or deadening; literal translation of 'obstupefaciendos' (*O*), 'stupefying, rendering senseless'.

11-12. *Laying... HOLY Things*: generally, any misappropriation or misuse of church property, but here specifically the use of church property for private gain by laymen (hence, a likely pun on '*laying hands*').

12. *improvements*: increases in clergy stipends.

13. *impairings*: deteriorations, weakenings; thus, literally, the decay or active spoliation of church buildings, but by application, the general weakening of the church's financial and social status. Andrewes no doubt has in mind also impropriations, the lay control of clerical livings, a legacy of the Dissolution, when livings formerly in the gift of monastic houses were bought by or granted to lay patrons who not only had the right of appointing incumbents, but also to the receipt of the parish tithe. To critics like Andrewes (and later more forcefully William Laud) this system amounted to a subjugation of the clergy to the laity. Finally, the Crown itself was guilty of impropriations on a grand scale through its control of appointments of higher clergy (deans and bishops). Elizabeth was notorious for leaving sees vacant for years while absorbing their revenues, and for offering bishoprics only on condition that the new incumbent alienate large amounts of episcopal property to the crown in exchange (see Heal, *Prelates and Princes*, ch. 9). Andrewes himself refused offers, *c.*1590, of both Ely and Salisbury that came with such conditions with the retort, 'I will not be made a *Bishop*, because I will not *alienate Bishop's lands*' (Buckeridge, *Funeral Sermon*, app. to *XCVI*, 19).

14-15. *there... Future tense*: also *RT* (p. 4).

15 16. *what for... Gold*: *O* ('præ Sacrâ auri fame nihil est *Sacrum*') quotes Virgil, *Aeneid*, iii. 57 (*LACT*); the arborified Polydorus laments his murder for gold by Lycurgus: 'To what crime do you not drive the hearts of men, *accursed hunger for gold* ("*auri sacra fame*")?' (ll. 56-7).

17. *restitution... SACRILEGE*: 'restitution' is used here not in the common sense of 'paying back to a rightful owner', but of 'restoring a thing or institution to its original form' (*OED sn* 5.a). As the ensuing paragraph confirms, Andrewes thus here lodges one of the most explicit critiques of the Henrician and Edwardian reformation before the 1620s: that the reformation of the church was to many but a 'pretence for *SACRILEGE*'. His criticism may reach to Elizabeth herself, who, though a subtle enemy to Edwardian evangelicalism, may be seen here as perpetuating earlier Tudor erastianism (cf. MacCulloch, *Tudor Church Militant*, ch. 4).

18-19. *those Worthies*: the leaders of the English Reformation; Archbishop Thomas Cranmer must at least be primarily intended, but Andrewes and his audience probably understood the larger pantheon of Marian martyrs and reformers eulogized in Foxe's *Actes and Monuments*; to Andrewes, they purchased doctrinal reformation at the expense of decent maintenance for the church ('*Churches Patrimony*'). Cf. Heal's documentation that the sees held by reformers Cranmer, Ridley, Goodrich, and Holgate were spared alienations while they did not object to the process in other dioceses (Heal, *Prelates and Princes*, 135–6). Andrewes's negative comments on the early reformers are in striking contrast to other establishment apologists who appealed fulsomely to their memory as a reproach to disloyal presbyterians (cf. especially Bancroft, *A Sermon Preached at Paules Crosse*, 57–61).

22–23. *almost...to You*: recasting of Gen. 14: 17–24; after rescuing Lot and other citizens of Sodom from captivity, Abram was blessed by the priest-king Melchizedek, and then 'the King of Sodom saide to Abram, Give me the persons [*marg*: soules], and take the goodes to thy selfe' (v. 21), i.e. 'give me the hostages with their freedom, and take in reward their belongings'; Abram refused, according to the Geneva gloss, because 'he would not that his liberalitie should be hurtfull unto others'. Andrewes thus suggests that the fathers of the English Reformation, like the king of Sodom, came close ('*almost said*') to stripping their 'people' (the new church) of their rightful worldly possessions for the sake of securing the spiritual freedom of their '*Soules*'. Abram is therefore the greater '*Worthy*' (prev. n.), or patriarch, because he refused any material gain at his peoples' expense. Andrewes here skirts the fierce debate between William Fulke and Gregory Martin over the sacerdotal-eucharistic interpretation of Gen. 14: 17–18 (cf. Fulke, *Defence*, in *Works*, i. 147–9).

23–25. *But...both deceived*: true prophets and patriarchs, John 'the *Baptist*' (Matt. 11: 8) and '*ABRAHAM*', did not seek or sell God's patrimony in 'Kings Courts'.

26–31. *Which Errour...speake of*: highly asyndetic syntax, exaggerated by the translator's close rendering of the original Latin; detailed notes follow, but a general paraphrase is: 'This error, though it is a small one (especially if compared with their great deeds), we may yet justly fear [that] if it is not resisted soon, [it is one that] will lie heavily on later generations. In this last point, intelligent men who heed Prov. 14.4 predict [that] barbarism, or something worse, [will be the result].'

26–27. *a small...by them*: this careful compensating compliment to the 'acts' performed by the worthies of the English Reformation (prev. nn.) shows just how daring his earlier criticism was. The translator's accurate 'great and famous acts' ('magna illa illorum κατορθώματα', O) has an unmistakable, and appropriate, Foxeian ring.

28. *seasonably*: fittingly, at the right time, with the implied sense here of 'urgently'.

29–30. *Pro. 14.4...cleane*: 'By the oxe is ment labour, and by the crib the barne: meaning, without labour there is no profite' (Geneva gloss); thus, 'in a succeeding age if there are no clergy to labour, the church will be empty'.

30. *presage*: predict, foretell.

30. *Barbarisme*: both the more specific 'rudeness or unpolished condition of language' and the more general 'opposite of civilization' (*OED sn* 1, 2); since Andrewes goes on to express fears of the collapse of the universities, as well as the ruin of holy places, both senses are likely in play; the later sense of 'barbarous cruelty' (*OED sn* 3) is not present here. Cf. Whitgift against farming of tithes: 'It would utterlye decay the Studie of *Divinitie*, by discouraging the Studentes thereof, both present and to come, and so at length bring in *Barbarisme*' (Strype, *Whitgift*, App., p. 100).

30–31. *somewhat...speake of*: atheism. Like his contemporaries, Andrewes held that atheism was a worse moral and social state than even non-Christian ('barbarous') religious cultures, which at least intuited by natural reason the existence of God or gods. Cf. his use of the 'Nations...discovered within these hundred years...in the

Americane part of the World... the Natives whereof, though in a manner they seemed barbarous... yet were they not without a kinde of Religion' as a refutation of atheism in *The Pattern of Catechisticall Doctrine* (1650), 23.

31–32. *falsly... without cause*: 'I may be wrong; in fact I hope God proves me so; but I am sure that I do not speak rashly or without cause'.

34. *come to ruin*: *Q* here obscures in *O* ('ruere *Res Sacras* & retro sublapsas referri volumus') a quotation from Virgil, *Aeneid*, iii. 57 (*LACT*); Aeneas laments the sack of Troy and the ravishing of the sacred Pallium as 'ex illo fluere ac retro sublapsa referri spes Danaum' ('from that time the hopes of the Danaans ebbed and, stealing backwards, receded').

36. *aneil*: anoint.

36. *bitter juice*: the (moral of) the scriptural text.

40. *And indeed...*: *Q* here omits the first sentence from the paragraph in *O*: 'Nec ego ista pro vulgi concione dicerem: sed soli jam sumus; & vel hîc hodiè, vel nusquam dicenda sunt.' ('I did not use to say these things publicly in a sermon; but we are alone; and they are to be said here today, or on no other occasion.') The translator of *Q* presumably judged this as unnecessary for the public context of print in 1646.

p. 85, 2. *lukewarme*: cf. Rev. 3: 16.

3. *put up*: 'submit to, endure, suffer quietly' (*OED* 'put', 56.p.(a)).

18. *Light... allowing Oyle*: criticism of Protestant enthusiasm for promulgating the 'light of the Gospel' (2 Cor. 4: 4.) without providing maintenance for academic study ('*Oyle*') by students before ordination; cf. *RT*'s wish that the present age 'have taken care not onely of *increasing the light*, but also of *allowing oil*. Which because not done, this evil spreds daily more and more, and the *devourers* of *Church-Revenues* whisper up and down in corners... that the *Church* may be impleaded and sued for the remainder of *Tithes*' (pp. 4–5).

38. *Augustus... tax*: Luke 2: 1.

p. 85, 40–p. 86, 2. *Under... Aaron*: Andrewes here draws on rabbinical and humanist numismatics describing the purported iconography of two forms of the Hebrew shekel, or silver coin. These traditions, which project iconography from much later periods onto Mosaic times ('Under the *Law*'), are collected in Caspar Waser, *De Antiquis Numis Hebraeorum... Libri III* (Zürich, 1605) (*LACT*). Allegedly, the 'sacred' shekel, kept with the Ark of the Covenant, was stamped with the miraculous rod of Aaron (Exod. 16: 32–4; 17: 1–10) as an emblem of the dignity of the Aaronic (Levitical) priesthood. A later shekel for public circulation was stamped in Hebrew with the monarchical inscription 'King David and King Solomon his son' (Waser, *De Antiquis Numis*, 59^v–73^r).

3–7. *One... both*: Moses the civic leader and Aaron the priest epitomized Andrewes's ideal of good government by autonomous but mutually supporting civic and ecclesiastical authorities. His fullest treatment of the Mosaic-Aaronic ideal is the sermon preached before the queen in Lent, 1591 on Psalm 77: 20 ('Thou diddest leade thy People like Sheepe, by the hand of Moses and Aaron' (*XCVI*, 273–84).

8. *Doves... sacred Tribute*: Mary and Joseph's offering of doves at the presentation of Christ in the Temple (Luke 2: 23–4) satisfied the required offering to the priest ('*sacred Tribute*'); Christ's endorsement of paying tribute to Caesar (Matt. 22: 21) satisfied that to 'the *Prince*'.

14. *heavenly Hierusalem*: Heb. 12: 22 (*LACT*).

14. *Encomium*: also *O*; 'expression of praise; panegyric' (*OED*).

p. 87, 3. *Priests & Levites*: ubiquitous OT epithet for the collective Temple priesthood; the Levites were a distinct order claiming descent from Levi (cf. p. 85, 40–p.86, 2 and n.) who had special charge over Temple furniture, singing, and the teaching of the law; their duties are detailed in 1 and 2 Chron.; cf. 'Pattern of Catechistical Doctrine' (this edn.), p. 24, l. 9.

3–10. *Priests & Levites... Temple*: cf. *RT*: 'The *Levites* had right to *Tithes*: But *the Ministry* of the Gospel, as it is more excellent in *nature*, and more eminent in *dignity*, so, is more profitable in its *use*, then was theirs. Our people receive *more* and *greater* benefits from *us*; therefore they ought to pay *more*, *Reason* presently insinuates' (p. 23).

24. *Of Indiction*: by command; required by authority.

26. *second member*: the second part of the sermon's biblical text, which Andrewes does not address (cf. p. 85, ll. 28–30 and n.).

26. *prosecute*: pursue.

38. *showre of Manna*: cf. Exod. 16: 35.

p. 87, 41–p. 88, 3. *Abraham... then written*: Abram, in reponse to Melchizedek's blessing (see p. 84, ll. 22–23 and n., and next n.) was the first to offer the tithe, an offering of 10 per cent of one's goods or income for sacred use. This anticipated the requirement of tithing as part of the codified Jewish law 'not then written' (cf. Lev. 27: 30–3).

7–9. *Indeed... by Positive*: even defenders of tithes, like Hooker, argued that although the OT example was a 'sensible' (i.e. 'tangible', 'not insignificant') one, as a law it had been abrogated by the NT. This stopped short of claiming that the tithe was owed by moral ('*Natural*') law, and maintained instead that it was to be imposed by the exercise of consent and reason in legislation or royal decree ('*Positive*' law). *RT* argues that Abraham paid tithes to Melchizedek 'by no *politike* constitution... no, nor by any *ceremonial law*', but 'by the *law* of *nature*' (p. 24); as a type of Christ, Melchizedek's example proved that 'the *right* of *Tithes* remaineth under *Christ*' (p. 7). Contrast Hooker, *Lawes*, v. 79.7–17 (*FEWRH*, ii. 453–63); cf. Lake, *Anglicans and Puritans?*, 223–4; and next n.

12. *23. of St. Matth.*: Christ's condemnation of the Pharisees' petty tithing of 'mint, and annise, and cummine', while ignoring 'weightier matters of the Law'; in *RT*, Andrewes uses patristic glosses on the verse to argue that Christ abrogated only insubstantial ceremonial observance of the Law, 'But, concerning this of Tithe, his words are express, *Ye ought not to leave them undone*' (pp. 10–11).

13–15. *I came... Church*: Andrewes's falling back to 'received opinion' hints that were he to 'dispute', not 'preach', he would argue that tithes were a moral requirement imposed by God, not merely a ceremonial or statutory requirement '*of the Church*'. *RT* in fact prosecutes *in extenso* the *jure divino* argument for tithes as required, not abrogated, by the New Covenant (see Sources). This is a good example of Andrewes's characteristic avoidance of outright engagement in controversy from the pulpit on grounds that it is pastorally unedifying (whereas it is appropriate in academic disputation; see n. to p. 84, l. 40). It is also possible that Andrewes's caution here is an act of self-censorship if the *jure divino* views previously expressed in *RT* had been condemned in debate; alternatively, the purported irenicism may simply save Andrewes the work of arguing many cases which he can instead state and proceed.

16. *II. Nehe: 10.33 [in marg]*: confusion of Vulg. and Geneva names for these books; Geneva = Ezra, Nehemiah; Vulg. = 1 & 2 Ezra.

16. *Shekel*: standard unit of weight (*c.*4 oz.) in the OT; in NT times it came to refer to a silver coin of *c.*5 oz.

18. ὁρισμοὺς: Gr., 'hōrismous'; 'decrees'.

18. διαταγὰς: Gr., 'diatagas'; 'arrangements'.

25-29. *Augustine... the Tithe*: also quoted in *RT* (p. 23), from a sermon now doubtfully attributed to St Augustine, *Sermo CCLXXVII*, '*De reddendis decimis*' (*LACT*; *PL*, 39.2267). The text of the sermon accepted by modern scholarship lacks the last clause quoted by Andrewes ('Sed servo tibi novem, da mihi Decimam'; 'but I grant Nine to thee, give me the Tithe'). However, it appears in the passage as quoted by the early medieval theologians Walafridus Strabo (*De Rebus Ecclesiasticus*, cap. xxvii); and Burchardus Wormaciensis (*Libri decretorum*, cap. cxxxiii), both in print in the sixteenth century.

32. *strait*: restrictive.

32-34. *By this... Dove*: also *RT*, p. 24.

34. *Crow... Dove*: Juvenal, *Satire*, ii. 63 (*LACT*): 'Dat veniam corvis, vexat censura columbas'; ('Our censor's rule condemns the doves while acquitting the ravens').

37. *Councils of the Church*: Andrewes devotes the tenth argument of *RT* to conciliar declarations of the right of tithes (pp. 17-18).

39-40. *Lawyer... to him*: Justinian, Roman emperor (527-65), was famous for the 'Code of Justinian' (529) which formed part of the *Corpus Juris Civilis*, the classic formulation of Roman law which included a definitive statement of the relationship between imperial and ecclesiastical authority. This stresses interdependence of the two estates without the subjugation of either, like that Andrewes exemplifies in the government of Israel by Moses and Aaron and sees threatened by erastianism in the Church of England. Andrewes here claims that even the 'absolute', or definitive, Justinian was anticipated in this principle by the law God gave to Moses. Hence '*the Lawyer himselfe*' can refer to God, the ultimate author, or to Moses, the recipient of that law who then declared it to Israel.

40. *She*: the Church.

p. 89, 2. *custome*: custom, precedent.

5. *Covenants of salt*: Jewish covenants ceremonially sealed with salt, held to be everlasting (cf. Num. 18: 19).

7. *antiquated*. 'obsolete' (*OED ppl. a.* 2).

7-8. *antiquated... unprofitablenesse*: cf. *RT*: 'So that no Law is to be antiquated or disanulled, which is not either *weak* or *unprofitable*. The Law concerning Tithes is a Law *going before*, an ancient Law: Let any man shew me either the *weakness* or *unprofitableness* thereof, I will joyn hands and grant the cause' (p. 13).

7. ἀσθενές or ἀνωφελές: Gr., 'asthĕnēs or anōphĕlēs'; 'weakness or uselessness' (Heb. 7: 18; *LACT*).

8-14. *For I ... point*: also, with minor differences in syntax, *RT*, 14.

12-13. *Improper Proprietaries*: elaborate multivocal pun on 'impropriations' (see p. 84, 13 and n.), achieved by word-play on the Lat. root *proprius*, the literal etymological sense of which is 'one's own, special, peculiar', carried into English as 'a property or quality of a thing itself, something inherent' (*OED*). The Lat. derivative 'proprietarius' ('proprietary') is one to whom something so belongs. Thus in the negative '*improper*' there inheres a critique of false ownership much stronger than the general English sense of 'incorrect'. This emphasizes the impropriety of the seizure of church property or tithes (impropriations) by laymen, the '*Improper Proprietaries*'.

15. *Tithe... a stipend*: cf. also *RT*: 'those *stipendiary proportions* are not to be *sought after*, or rather (for that is too little a great deal) are utterly to be *rejected*' (p. 12).

Andrewes's primary target here is presbyterian proposals to divert funds from the abolition of bishops, cathedrals, and collegiate churches and the parochial system of tithes into a national system of flat-fee stipends to parish clergy. He also, however, has in mind any aggregation of livings in the hands of the laity, as with the extant problem (in his view) of ministers appointed and paid by lay-rectors in England. For the latter, see Collinson, *Elizabethan Puritan Movement*, 339–41.

17–18. *Church of Scotland... Leafe*: Andrewes is more explicit about his source in *RT*: '*Scotland* also hath exempted it self from *Tithes*. There is in print a complaint of *John Knox*, exhibited in the *name* of the *Ministers* to the *Parliament at Edinburgh, Anno Domini* 1565, *December* 25. When I read the eight leaf of it, it pities me for them: I say... beware' (p. 14; he concludes here as in *Q*). The allusion is to Knox, 'The Superintendents Ministers and commissioners... to all faithfull', an open letter appended to *A Sermon Preached by John Knox* (1566). Page eight ('*the eighth Leafe*') decries the redirection of tithes from the ministers and poor to lay interests. For the General Assembly's petition to Queen Mary and her Council against crown control of clerical livings, see *Acts and Proceedings of the General Assemblies of the Kirk of Scotland... Part First* (Edinburgh, 1839), 70–2 (*LACT*). Andrewes's positive appeal to Scottish presbyterians is a savvy appropriation of an erstwhile enemy for his own ends, and must certainly have appealed to the 1646 promulgators of the sermon who looked to Scotland for their model of presbytery in England. Contrast Bancroft's much less sophisticated use of Knox and the Scottish kirk as straw men in *A Sermon Preached at Paul's Cross*, 55–6, 72–7.

19–20. *the Boys... beware*: proverb which Erasmus cites as 'common currency' (*Adagia*, LB II 496E; see also Tilley M612); such moral sentences formed the first material for reading and memorizing by 'the Boys' in grammar schools; the verb used in *O* ('cantillant'; '*sing*', *Q*) can mean 'recite' or 'repeat', hence Andrewes probably envisions a schoolroom recitation, not a literal song.

23. *Twelve Tables*: seminal summaries of Roman law (451–450 BCE), used as foundations for subsequent codes, often printed in medieval and later collections of canon law; cf. Thomas Wilson on abuse of church livings, 'Thus God is robbed, learnyng decaied, England dishonored, and honestie not regarded. Thold Romaines not yet knowyng Christ, and yet beyng led by a reverent feare towardes God, made this lawe. *Sacrum sacroue commendatum qui clepserit, rapseritue, parricida est* He that shall closely steale, or forcibly take awaie that thyng, whiche is holy, or geven to the holy place: is a murderer of his countrey' (*The Arte of Rhetorique* (1553), 20).

29 νοσφίξεσθαι: Gr., 'nŏsphizēsthai'; 'embezzle'.

37. *Seneca's Mastiffe*: Seneca, *Epist.*, lxxii. 8 (*LACT*).

p. 90, 1. *up with*: 'to commend, praise' (*OED* 'up' adv. 32.e).

1. *grounds*: lands.

5–6. *bone... afore*. cf. Seneca, *Epist.* lxxii. 8: 'Did you ever see a dog snapping with wide-open jaws at bits of bread or meat which his master tosses to him? Whatever he catches, he straightway swallows whole, and alwayes opens his jaws in the hope of something more'.

7. *dropsie*: hydropsy, in which the patient suffers insatiable thirst.

8–9. *a kin... Give*: retailed by Andrewes as example of Roman Catholic accusations of hypocritical Protestant greed in 'A Sermon Preached at Saint Maries Hospital' (this edn., p. 66, l. 18).

11. *starvlings*: starved or emaciated animals or people.

14. *blowing upon*: cf. Isa. 40: 24.

25–26. *capacity ... they say*: in a specific legal sense, 'no legal qualification of right'; 'they' being lawyers.

27. *Numb. 18 [in marg.]*: Num. 18: 26 (*LACT*).

28. *St. Matth. 22. [in marg.]*: Matt. 22. 37–8 (*LACT*).

35–36. *We ... appertain to God*: ordained ministers; priests; cf. Heb. 5: 1 (*LACT*).

39. *Levit. 5. [in marg.]*: Lev. 5: 15.

p. 91, 7. *Pharaoh ... Table*: Gen. 40: 22.

9–10. *pay ... build Houses*: private bankrolling of mercenary soldiers to resist Spain in the Low Countries and Ireland, and the construction of extravagant country houses for the conspicuous display of wealth and entertainment of the queen; both were particularly sensitive enterprises in the 1580s and 1590s, and often paid for by wealth impropriated from the church; cf. Andrewes's 1593 complaint before Elizabeth that domestic 'endlesse *building*' was '*rubbish*' (*XCVI*, 293); Andrewes may also have in mind the burdens of taxation and mustering imposed upon the clergy in the recent Armada campaigns (contrast his apology for crown levies against City merchants for the same in 'A Sermon Preached at St Maries Hospital', this edn., pp. 56–57 and n.).

11. *wicked Athalia*: 2 Chron. 24: 7 (*LACT*).

12. *wicked Achan*: Josh. 21: 19–26.

13–15. *Joas ... slippery Peace*: Joash (2 Chron. 24: 4–22).

16–18. *Jeroboam ... Tithes*: 1 Kings 12: 25–33; 2 Chron. 13: 6–12.

18–19. *Tobias ... Convenience*: Tobiah (Neh. 13: 4–11).

19–21. *Baltazar ... Sacrilegious*: Belshazzar (Dan. 5: 1–4).

21. *EPIMANES ... All*: Antiochus Epiphanes (*O* also has Ἐπιμανὺς) twice sacked Jerusalem (169–8 BCE), slaughtering and enslaving thousands, stripping the Temple treasures, and desecrating Jewish rites and ceremonies (1 Macc. 1); cf. also Josephus, *Jewish Antiquities*, XII. v. 3–4 (*LACT*).

21–23. *Judas ... crime*: John 12: 4–8.

24. *Sacrilegious Couple*: Ananias and Saphira (Acts 5: 1–10).

32–35. *Drones ... Holy uses*: condemnation of donnish indulgence; Cambridge (and Oxford) colleges had as the principal aim of their endowments ('our Fathers goods') the training of clergy, and much collegiate income after the Reformation came from appropriated ecclesiastical livings; in this satire, the fellows are cast as non-working male bees ('*Drones*') who feast on the fruit of their benefactors' labours; Andrewes accuses them of avoiding the hard work of parish ministry, which required resignation from the college fellowship, or hiring a poorly paid curate, in order to idle ('tarry') instead at college. The passage is important evidence of the Whitgiftian establishment's vulnerability to puritan accusations of the evils of clerical non-residence.

33. *playes, and vanities*: the universities were one of the most important venues for amateur drama (usually part of Christmastide revels) in the early modern period. See F. S. Boas, *University Drama in the Tudor Age* (1914), and cf. n. to p. 93, ll. 21–22.

36. *spend ... riotous Living*: like the Prodigal Son, who 'wasted his substance with riotous living' (Luke 15: 13).

37–38. *former Devouring ... our selves*: at the Dissolution ('that former *Devouring*'), Oxford and Cambridge colleges were major recipients or purchasers of appropriated livings formerly held by monastic foundations.

p. 91, 39–p. 92, 3. *And indeed ... manners*: Andrewes argues that irresponsible stewardship of livings by colleges sets a dangerous example for lay patrons of clerical livings. His vision of pastoral dystopia strikingly anticipates John Milton's indictment of the Laudian clergy in *Lycidas* (1637): 'Of other care they little reckoning make, | Than how to scramble at the shearers' feast, | And shove away the worthy bidden guest; | Blind mouths! that scarce themselves know how to hold | A sheep-hook, or have learned aught else the least | That to the faithful herdman's art belongs!' Like Milton, Andrewes may be guided here by the irony that a pastor ('a person who feeds') is the last person who should desire to be fed himself. Milton criticizes precisely the kind of clericalism that Andrewes inspired in followers like Laud; yet both Andrewes and Milton address the same problem of inadequate clerical provision in the parishes.

6. *those Locusts*: greedy lay patrons, here cast as one of the seven plagues of Egypt (Exod. 10: 12–20).

8. *waits*: serves.

11. *Caiphas... Priest*: John 8: 14.

35. *Field... of bloud*: Acts 1: 18–19.

35–36. *gifts... of Heaven*: one of the freer translations in the sermon—the original of which is '*Anathemata Templi* ne tollant, anathemate enim *Divino* implicari'—which obscures Andrewes's word-play on the root sense of *anathema* as something 'set apart'; the holy things in the Temple can thus be in a positive sense '*Anathemata Templi*', while those who dare to touch them can be anathematized or cursed ('*anathemate*') by God.

38. *Fowling*: hunting birds with traps or snares.

p. 93, 6–20. *goes about... devoure*: 1 Pet. 5: 8 (*LACT*).

20. *Prophane stories*: non-biblical histories.

21–22. *Cambyses... to himselfe*: cf. Heroditus, *Histories*, iii. 27–30 (*LACT*). Cambyses of Persia's killing of the Egyptian calf-god Apis, the torture of its priests, and desecration of the temple at Memphis was cited as the first instance of the insanity brought on as a direct result of his crimes. '*Jupiter Hammon*' was the supreme deity in North African mythology. The lurid history of Cambyses was the subject of one of the earliest English history plays (also strongly indebted to the morality play tradition), *The Life of Cambises King of Percia* (1569), which does not dramatize this episode. Its author, Thomas Preston, was at the time of Andrewes's sermon master of Trinity Hall and vice-chancellor of Cambridge, and therefore probably present.

22–23. *Brennus... and his*: Brennus, chieftain of the Asiatic Gauls, sacked Delphus and desecrated its rites and temple, prompting the destruction of him and his army by a divine earthquake and tempest (M. Junianus Justinus, *Justini ex Trogi Pompeii historiis externis libri XXXXIIII*, xxIIII. viii; *LACT*).

23–25. *Crassus... Holy things with*: M. Licinius Crassus, proconsul of Syria (54 BCE), stripped the Temple at Jerusalem of its gold, and was later killed after capture by the Parthians (Josephus, *Antiquities*, XIV. vii. 3; Plutarch, *Crassus*, XXXI–XXXIII). The account by L. Annaeus Florus, *Epitome of Roman History*, includes the further elaboration that 'molten gold was poured into his gaping mouth, so that the dead and bloodless flesh of one whose heart had burned with lust for gold was itself burnt with gold' (I. xlvi. 11, trans. E. S. Forster) (*LACT*).

25–26. *Sacred stories*: biblical histories.

32. *close*: forecourt.

36–39. *Judas... snare*: John 12: 6; Matt. 26: 14–16, 27: 5.

p. 94, 5. *things... Holy use*: Andrewes composed the first post-Reformation English liturgies for the consecration of church buildings and furniture; see 'The Forme... in Consecrating the Newe Church Plate' (*LACT*, xi. 158–63) and 'Bishop Andrewes' Form of Consecration of a Church and Churchyard' (*LACT*, vi. 306–33).

11. *Satan... his heart*: Luke 22: 3–6; cf. also Acts 5: 3 (*LACT*).

26. *in the very act*: John 8: 4 (*LACT*).

36. *as a storme*: cf. Nah. 1: 3.

38. *an Axe*: cf. also Matt. 3: 10 (*LACT*).

38–39. *Moth consuming*: Matt. 6: 19–20.

p. 95, 1. *Apoplexie*: a sudden death, caused by haemorrhage on the brain.

1. *Hectik*: a prolonged, wasting fever.

2–3. *Pump... Billowes*: Andrewes's antithesis contrasts how a ship can be sunk from water entering from both below and above deck: a '*Pump*' removed water that had seeped into the hold of a ship below; '*billows*', sea swells or waves caused by high winds, overwhelm the vessel from above.

3. *Thunderbolt of St. Peter*: Acts 5: 1–5.

20. *valley of Achor*: Josh. 7.

25. *rents*: rips or tears; with a possible pun on financial church 'rents'.

28. *inexplicable*: in the literal sense, 'that cannot be unfolded, untwisted, or disentangled' (*OED*), as from a snare.

36–40. *S. Augustin's... increased*: attr. Augustine, *Hom*. XLVIII, 3 (*PL*, 39.1912; *LACT*).

p. 95, 40–p. 96, 1. *One devourer... Lawyers*: attr. Augustine, *Serm*. CCLXXVII, 2. (*PL*, 39.2267; *LACT*).

16. *draught*: a long single drink or gulp.

17. *this great Assembly*: members of the university attending the sermon.

32. *long*: for long.

33. *Say... of men?* 1 Cor. 9: 8 (*LACT*).

34–35. *Honour... Arts*: cf. Cicero's defence of honour and support paid to the liberal arts in *Tusculan Disputations* I. ii (*LACT*).

38–39. *Crib... Provender*: cf. *RT*: 'Every Laborer is worthy of his hire. Whether he cut his own Vine, or feed his own Flock: and, *the Ox must not be muzzled that treadeth out the Corn*' (p. 21). This (without acknowledgement) quotes Knox, 'Worthy is the laborer of his wages. And againe you shall not mussell the mouth of the Oxe that treadeth forth the corne' ('The Superintendents', fo. 8ᵛ).

40. *A wiser... Solomon*: Christ.

p. 97, 2–3. *his College... Fryers*: anti-Catholic jibe; some Roman Catholic apologists for the mendicant orders (those which, like the Franciscans and Dominicans, foreswore ownership of common property and relied instead on solicited alms) claimed as a precedent the example of Christ and his twelve disciples.

9. *Bishop... Hospitality*: Andrewes, like Whitgift, blamed puritan anti-prelatical sentiment for the abandonment of the custom of a bishop offering hospitality—alms, feasting, and lodging—in his diocese. Appeals for a revival of episcopal and clerical hospitality were also standard justifications for their appeals for greater subsidy to the clergy. See Heal, *Hospitality*, ch. 7.

13. *holdfasts*: misers.

17–19. *Old Canon... wanting*: the '*Consecration*' of bishops. In the Sarum Rite ('the *Old Canon*'), after the laying on of hands, the new bishop was anointed on the head and hands, his hands were then gloved, and he was given the pastoral staff (crozier) as a sign of pastoral authority (hence, '*Filling of the hand*'). Cranmer's first Ordinal (1550) omitted anointing and gloving; the second (1552) and Elizabethan (1559) omitted also the presentation of the pastoral staff. Instead, the new bishop was presented only with a bible. Andrewes's nostalgic preference for the older rites goes so far as to suggest that without the crozier ('the last'), episcopal unction ('the first') was pointless. This is a stunning rejection of the reformed English understanding that bishops were commissioned as guardians of scripture, in favour of an avant-garde view of bishops as anointed guardians of discipline. For the entrenchment of this dichotomy in the Jacobean episcopate, see Kenneth Fincham, *Prelate as Pastor* (1990). For anointing of kings, see 'A Sermon Preached... the Fifth of August Last' (this edn.), p. 185, ll. 21–32 and nn.

19. *Dathan*: Andrewes's allusion to the story of the rebellion of Korah, Dathan, and Abiram (Num. 16) consolidates the sermon's gradual equation of clerical dignity with episcopal power, introduced by his oblique reference to the bishop's crozier (see prev. n.). Dathan and his followers were swallowed up by the earth (v. 30) for protesting against Moses's and Aaron's civil and religious superiority, citing as the ground of their complaint the belief (strikingly akin to the Reformed dictum of the 'priesthood of the believer' which underwrote presbyterianism) that 'all the Congregation are holy every one of them... wherefore then lift you up your selves above the Congregation of the Lord?' (v. 3). God commanded that the brazen censers of the rebels be recast as adornments for the altar (v. 38).

20. *Assupim... Parbar*: transliterations of Hebrew place names (1 Chron. 26: 15, 18).

31. *1 Kings 12.31 [in marg.]*: cf. also 1 Kings 13: 33 (*LACT*).

34. *bras'd*: i.e. 'brazed', hardened (like brass) with impudence.

34. *sticke not*: do not stop or hesitate.

34–35. *a long Gowne*: the black gown designating academic status as an MA, the disputed minimum for clerical attire (supplemented at divine service with a white surplice).

35. *prate by the houre-glasse*: 'prattle (preach badly) for an hour'; by convention, early modern sermons were to last one hour.

35. *huddle out*: confusedly heap up (in a bad sermon); *Q*'s translation obscures *O*'s quotation from Homer, *Iliad*, II. ii. 213 (*LACT*): "ἄκοσμά τε πολλα τε", from the first description of Thersites, 'who knew within his head *many words, but disorderly*'.

36. *PROPHET*: minister; cf. 'A Sermon Preached... on Whitsunday 1618', this edn., pp. 216–17.

p. 98, 2. *prised at*: apprised at; valued at.

6. *Eldad or Medad*: Num. 11: 24–9.

10–11. *Will... Reward?*: *O* reads 'Ecquid erit *pretii?*' ('What then shall be the reward?'); cf. Cicero's quotation of the epic historian Ennius as an epigram to *De Senectute* (*LACT*), 'O Tite, si quid ego adivero curamue levasso | Quae nunc te coquit et versat in pectore fixa, *Ecquid erit praemi?*' ('O Titus, should some aid of mine dispel | The cares that now within thy bosom dwell | And wring thy heart and torture thee with pain, | *What then would be the measure of my gain?*').

12. *Thirty pieces*: of silver; the price paid Judas to betray Christ (Matt. 26: 15).

13–16. *many... sacred work*: cf. Whitgift against farming of tithes: 'if this Suite should be granted, it would... dryve the Learned... to some other Trade of Lyfe, more gaynfull unto them. For every Waterman on the *Thames*, earneth more by his Labours, then the greater Parte of severall Ministers in *England* should do by their Benefices' (Strype, *Whitgift*, App., p. 102).

19. *taile of Prophets*: Isa. 9: 15.

24. *grounds*: basis; means by which.

27. *to bite... another*: disputes among fellow Protestants aired openly in pulpits.

31. *dilapidations*: literally the decay of ecclesiastical buildings for which incumbents or patrons were responsible; applied here metaphorically to the church as well as literally to church buildings.

p. 99, 5. *Some... Acts. 28.24*: epigram added by the 1646 editor or publisher.

7–9. *Octob.... Downame*: *imprimatur*, or license to print, of Parliamentary censor John Downame (d. 1652), presbyterian minister beneficed in London, formerly an opponent of Laud.

A LECTURE ON GENESIS 2.18 (THE CREATION OF EVE)

Text. *ΑΠΟΣΠΑΣΜΑΤΙΑ SACRA:* | OR | A Collection of posthumous and orphan | LECTURES: | Delivered at St. PAULS and St. GILES his Church, | BY | *The Right Honourable* | AND | *Reverend Father in God* | *LANCELOT ANDREWS*, | [rule] | Never before extant. | [...] | LONDON, | Printed by *R. Hodgkinsonne*, for *H. Moseley, A. Crooke,* | *D. Pakeman, L. Fawne, R. Royston*, and *N. Ekins*. 1657 (pp. 197–204; *AS*). The texts in this posthumous folio claim to be the typeset transcripts of a manuscript volume of notes taken by the anonymous Elizabethan hearer(s?) of lectures preached by Andrewes between 1590 and 1603, and never otherwise printed. The late discovery of a hitherto unknown manuscript proves that at least the Genesis lectures derive from an authorial manuscript (see Introduction, n. 18). That there was little editorial intervention between the manuscript notes and the printed text is suggested by their summary outline form, the preservation of shorthand abbreviations, spelling, and orthography long outdated by 1657, absence of marginal apparatus, and the inclusion of a preface by Thomas Pierce written only after the whole was typeset. The notes vary widely in thoroughness, some being only one- or two-page outlines; others reach full sermon length. As Pierce cautioned, '*every Reader may imagine by the beauty of these* Ruines, *what kinde of* Buildings *he should have seen if he had seen them standing in their integrity*' (sig. 3)(3^v–4)(4^r). Pierce, a strident Laudian, characterized the volume as being the work of commercial publishers '*who commonly* live *and* subsist, *not by being* over-tender *of the* Names *and* Reputations, *but by* publishing *the* Writings *of those especially, whom they think the most* vendible *and famous* Authors' (sig. 4)(1^r). The typesetting is not of the highest standard, and some of the sermons are sloppily placed out of chronological sequence. But Pierce did admit, '*I have something to alledge by way of Apologie for the* Printer, *by whose devotion of* care *and* cost, *these* Fragments *were thus collected*' (sig. 4)(4^r). The consortium of publishers included the leading Stuart propagandist Richard Royston, publisher of *Eikon Basilike* and later bookseller to Charles II, and the royalist Humphrey Moseley, 'remembered as the most prestigious literary publisher of the time' (Lois Potter, *Secret Rites and Secret Writing: Royalist Literature, 1641–1660* (1989), 7–22).

Headnote. This lecture is part of a lengthy series on each verse of Gen. 1: 1–3: 13, delivered at St Paul's Cathedral between 13 October 1590 and 12 February 1591/2 (*AS*, 657–9, 1–35, 660–2, 36–89, 115–312). The series continued with lectures on the remaining verses of Genesis 3 and all of 4 at St Giles's Cripplegate between 18 June 1598 and 17 February 1599 (*AS*, 305–499). Tyacke ('Lancelot Andrewes', 13–14) suggests that the hiatus in the series was a decision by Andrewes to '[desist] in 1592 rather than provoke a controversy' with the lectures' anti-Calvinist content. He further speculates that such views might have been more safely broached in the suburban parish rather than in the more prominent cathedral venue. A more mundane reason for the abrupt halt in 1592 might be that this was the time at which Andrewes suffered the serious illness which Isaacson blamed on his excessive assiduity in preaching: 'witnesse Saint *Giles* Pulpit and that in Saint *Pauls* Church, where he read the Lecture thrice a weeke in the Terme time. And indeed what by his often Preaching at St. *Giles*, and his no lesse often reading in St. *Pauls*, he became so infirme, that his friends despaired of his life' (*Life*, sig. *2^v).

The lecture presented here is a good example of Andrewes's routine dealing, as a pastor and prebendary, with matters of practical moral divinity of the sort with which he is not usually associated because of the predominance of solemn feast day sermons as a royal chaplain in *XCVI. Sermons*. On the subject of the creation of Eve, this is, in effect, a practical homily on marriage. But even on this topic Andrewes appears in an avant-garde light, with views on women that are decidedly more liberal than those of mainstream late Elizabethan theologians which even pointedly attack the open misogyny of popular satires against women (the scurrilous wit of poets like John Donne, active at the Inns of Court at this time, comes immediately to mind).

Sources. Typically, Andrewes relies heavily on a (here unspecified) patristic consensus, the dominant shape of which can be identified as Augustinian, indebted primarily to that father's tract *De Bono Conjugali* ('On the Goodness of Marriage'), and his exegetical *De Genesi ad Litteram Liber* ('On the Literal Interpretation of Genesis'). With Augustine, he departs from the earlier views of Chrysostom on the place of sex and procreation before the Fall. The strikingly positive views on female goodness, and the interpretation of God's careful deliberation in Gen. 2: 18, however, are most directly comparable to Luther's *Lectures on Genesis* (first delivered 1535–6, printed in Latin from 1544 in Wittenberg and Nuremberg; not printed in English until the nineteenth century).

Further Reading. Andrewes pursued in greater detail the relative responsibility of Adam and Eve for the Fall in subsequent lectures delivered between 11 and 27 November 1591 (*AS*, 249–88). For a fine survey of emerging English Protestant views on the place of Eve in the Fall, and the advice literature on godly marriage, see Christine Peters, *Patterns of Piety: Women, Gender and Religion in Late Medieval and Reformation England* (2003), chs. 12 and 13, respectively.

p. 100, 1–3. *A Lecture... 1591*: ed.; individual lectures in *AS* were printed without titles, headed only by the scriptural text of each.

4–5. *Dixerat... commodum ipsi*: not Vulg.; cf. Trem. (Gen. 2: 18), 'Dixerat autem Jehovah Deus, non est bonum hominem esse solum: faciam ei auxilium accomodum ipsi'; ('And the Lord God said, It is not good that the man should be alone: I will make him an helpe meet for him').

8. *certifieth*: assures, guarantees.

15–18. *Ephes. . . . his side*: Cf. Ephes. 5: 22–33. Paul's famous typological analogy between earthly matrimony and the 'great mystery' (*'magnum Sacramentum'*) of the marriage ('espousage') of Christ (the bridegroom) and the church (the bride) does not itself apply the example of Adam and Eve. Following a tradition rooted in Augustine (*In Joann. Tract.* IX), Andrewes imports another Pauline type, that of Christ as a 'second Adam' (1 Cor. 15: 22, 45) to support the typology of Adam gaining his spouse (Eve) 'out of his side', and Christ redeeming his spouse (the Church) through the Passion (one of the wounds of which was a piercing in the side, John 19: 34). Cf. George Abbot, *An Exposition upon . . . Jonah* (1600), 'By the dying of Christ, the Church is made, as Eve was made by Adams sleeping, which is Saint Austens comparison' (p. 164).

18–20. *I told . . . first Chapter*: cf. lecture on Gen. 2: 7, 18 May 1591, 'now touching the 7. verse, at which I said beginneth the repetition of the Historie of Man and his generation . . . we read, *Gen.* 1.26. that Man was created, but not whence, nor how, nor after what sort. . . . [t]herefore that which briefly he touched, omitting some things there, now here he supplyeth, shewing that God first made the Man, and out of his side took the Woman' (*AS*, 149).

20. *Moses*: traditionally, author of Genesis.

21. *Marem . . . eum*: not Vulg.; cf. Trem. (Gen. 1: 27), 'marem & foeminam creasset eos' ('man and woman created He them'); *'eum'* ('him') is an error for *'eos'* ('them').

24–25. *We have . . . hitherto*: lecture on Gen. 2: 7, 18 May 1591 (*AS*, 149–55).

28. *the Fathers say*: standard patristic commentaries on Genesis are those by Origen, Jerome, Augustine, and Chrysostom.

p. 101, 5. *non est . . . faciamus*: unlike the text quoted at the head of the sermon, closer to Vulg. (Gen. 2: 18), 'non est bonum esse hominem solum faciamus ei adjutorium' ('it is not good for man to be alone: let us make him a helpe', Douai-Rheims).

11. *Covenant . . . man*: lectures for 17 and 19 June 1591 expounded Gen. 2: 16, 17 (God's commendation of the fruits of the garden, and his forbidding of the tree of the knowledge of good and evil) as the first ceremonial laws of worship and obedience, which constituted the first covenant of mankind's ecclesiastical duty to God (*AS*, 183–92).

12. *œconomicall*: 'pertaining to a household or its management' (*OED*, 'economical', 1.a); previously, Andrewes had treated Gen. 2: 3 as God's institution of worship (*AS*, 128–41); Gen. 2: 18 contains the divine institution of the family, and by extension, society; Luther, *Lectures*, does the same (*Works*, i. 115).

22. *lege ipsa antiqua*: 'itself [by or of] an ancient law'.

25. *Gods Dixit*: 'God's "he said"'.

25. *tenor*: meaning.

26–27. *dixit Deus . . . before*: 'God said', reiterated upon each new act of Creation (Gen. 1), thus treated repeatedly in the previous lectures.

27. *qui dicendo . . . facit*: Lat., 'he who makes by saying, makes by the word'.

33. *fiat*: Lat., 'let there be'.

34. *faciam*: Lat., 'let me make,' or, 'I shall make'.

36. *fiat lux*: Lat., 'let there be light'.

p. 102, 5–13. *Some . . . crosse Gods will*: informed by a typical Protestant concern to rehabilitate the intrinsic goodness of woman; cf. Luther, *Lectures*, '[Eve] was in no respect inferior to Adam, whether you count the qualities of the body or those of the mind' (*Works*, i. 115); and Thomas Becon, *Worckes* (1564), 'the woman is before God of no les price and dignitie then man is, so that they, which so contemptuously and despitefully either write or speake of the feminine kinde, doo greate dyshonour to God' (sig. CCCCCLXIX^r); Andrewes's implication that Eve's goodness counteracts the natural tendency of man to misogyny is unusual; cf. Milton, *Paradise Lost*, 'nothing lovelier can be found | In woman, than to study household good, | And good works in her husband to promote' (ix. 233–5).

19–27. *Fathers... argument and reason*: Augustine is less definitive on God's deliberative diction in Gen. 2: 18, suggesting either that God said this in Adam's mind directly or through an angel, as well as the possibility that 'the writer [Moses] is referring to the reason-principle which was primordially in the Word of God... the reason-principle to which scripture also referred previously in the words, "And God said, 'Let there be this or that'" ' (*De Gen. ad Litt.*, ix. ii. 3; *ACW*, xli. 72). Andrewes is much closer here to Luther, *Lectures*, discussing the creation of Adam, 'He says, "Let us make." Therefore he includes an obvious deliberation and plan; he did nothing similar in the case of the earlier creatures .... God summons himself to a council and announces some sort of deliberation' (*Works*, i. 56).

31. *bonum est*: Lat., 'it is good'.

32. *ergo faciendum est*: Lat., 'therefore it is to be done'.

32. *malum est*: Lat., 'it is evil'.

33. *ergo non faciam*: Lat., 'therefore I may not'.

35. *He saith... domino*: 'God does not say, "This is not good for me", but rather, "this is not good for the lord" ', i.e. not good for Adam, lord over Eden (Gen. 1: 26).

37. *expedit... abeam*: cf. Vulg. (John 16: 7), 'expedit vobis ut ego vadam', ('it is expedient for you that I goe away').

38. *q.d.*: abbr. Lat., *quasi dictum* ('as if one should say').

p. 103, 1. *commoditie*: private advantage or interest.

3. *ground*: basis, foundation.

3–9. *reversing... wicked men*: potentially an implicit criticism of double predestination; the same logic informs Andrewes's unambiguous insistence that even after his sin and punishment, Cain could have regained a state of grace through repentance, argued in lectures at St Giles's, Aug.–Sept. 1599 (*AS*, 422–68).

13–14. *thoughts words and deeds*: cf. General Confession at Holy Communion of sins 'committed, By thought, word, and deed' (*BCP*).

15. *è contra*: Lat., *ex contra*; 'conversely', 'vice versa'.

19–20. *We read... good*: lecture on Gen. 1: 29–31, delivered 11 Feb. 1591 (*AS*, 105–11).

28–29. *solus sapiens Deus*: Lat., lit., 'the only wise God'; patristic epithet variously applied to the Incarnate Word (Christ), the Holy Spirit, and the Trinity; cf. Didymus Alexandrinus, trans. Jerome, *De Spiritu Sancto*, 21 (*PL*, 23.122A); Augustine, *Contra Max. Episc. Arian. XVI* (*PL*, 42.755); and Peter Lombard, *Collect. in Ep. Pauli*, 66 (*PL*, 191.1534A).

29. *Psalmist... alone*: Ps. 83: 18, 'thou, which art called Jehovah, art alone, even the most High over the earth'.

31. *Angells... an Host*: cf. Luke 2: 13.

35–37. *firmament... and Beasts*: Gen. 1: 16, 7, 12, 22, 24.

40. *væ Soli*: Vulg. (Eccles. 4: 10), 'vae soli quia cum ruerit non habet sublevantem'; ('Woe to him that is alone: because when he falleth, he hath none to lift him up', Douai-Rheims).

p.104, 7. *Husay... 17.7*: Hushai; *AS* incorrectly reads '1 Sam. 17.7'.

11. *Moses...solus*: cf. Vulg. (Lev. 13: 46), 'omni tempore quo leprosus est et inmundus solus habitabit extra castra' ('al the time that he is a lepre & uncleane, he shal dwel alone without the campe', Douai-Rheims).

12. *Ducam...eos*: Lat., lit., 'I shall lead them into solitude [the wilderness?] and I shall teach them'; the exact reference paraphrased here is unclear, but cf. Isa. 56: 7, on God's acceptance of foreign proselytes (Andrewes's 'Schollars'?), 'adducam eos in montem sanctum meum et laetificabo eos in domo orationis meae holocausta eorum et victimae eorum placebunt mihi super altari meo quia domus mea domus orationis vocabitur cunctis populis' (Vulg.); ('Them wil I bring also to mine holy mountaine, and make them joyfull in mine House of prayer: their burnt offerings and their sacrifices shall be accepted upon mine altar: for mine House shall be called an house of prayer for all people'); cf. also Vulg. (Ps. 106: 4, 6–7, juxt. Hebr.), 'erraverunt in solitudine in deserta via .... de adflictione eorum eripuit eos et duxit illos per viam rectam'); ('They wente astraye in the wildernesse in an untroden waye, & founde no cit[i]e to dwell in .... he delyvered them from their distresse. He led them forth by the right waie', Coverdale, Ps. 107); cf. also Hos. 2: 14.

14. *Christ...solitarie places*: cf. Matt. 4: 1, 26: 36–44.

21. *In resolving...concordance*: good example of interpretation of a difficult passage by 'the analogy of faith', or 'conference of places' (cf. 'A Sermon Preached at St Maries Hospital', this edn., p. 70, l. 13 and n.).

23–24. *non est...tangere*: cf. Vulg. (1 Cor. 7: 1), 'bonum est homini mulierem non tangere'); ('It were good for a man not to touche a woman').

27. *bonum morale*: 'a moral good' (not to eat of the forbidden tree).

28. *bonum naturale*: 'a natural (human) good' (conjugality in marriage).

31. *meet*: fitting, proper.

34–36. *Christ saith...marriage*: Mark 12: 25.

p. 104, 40–p. 105, 1. *circumstances...concordant*: warnings to 'distinguish' ('*distingue*') and 'compare' ('*concordant*') '*circumstances, places, times and persons*' of difficult biblical texts, hallmark of Augustine's exegetical method; cf. 'Pattern of Catechistical Doctrine,' this edn., p. 7, ll. 30–32.

9. *in the...Hebrews*: Heb. 2: 10.

10. *Gen. 1*: Gen. 1: 28.

16. *after the fall*: acceptance that sexual relations and the possibility of procreation was part of the perfection of Eden; cf. Augustine, *De Gen. ad Litt.*, IX. iii. 6., 'I do not see what could have prohibited [Adam and Eve] from honorable nuptial union and the bed undefiled even in paradise', rejecting the previously held view (cf. Chrysostom, *Hom. in Gen.* xviii. 4, *De Virginitate* xiv. 5–6) that marriage and procreation was only a product of the Fall (*ACW*, xli. 73); Augustine (*De Gen. ad Litt.*, IX. x. 16–18), however, ruled out any 'pleasure' in Edenic sex (*ACW*, xli. 80–2), while Luther, *Lectures*, allowed that it 'would have taken place without any bashfulness... accompanied by a noble delight, such as there was at that time in eating and drinking' (*Works*, i. 119).

18. *propter fornicationem*: Lat., 'because of [or, for the sake of] fornication'; one of the traditional justifications for marriage; cf. Solempnizacion of Matrimonye (*BCP*), 'it was ordeined for a remedy agaynste sinne and to avoide fornication, that suche persones as

have not the gifte of continencie might mary, and kepe themselves undefiled members of Christes body'.

19–22. *encrease...fewer families*: cf. Augustine, *De Bono Conjugali* ix. 9, arguing for the superiority of celibacy to marriage, 'there is no lack of numerous progeny and an abundance of generation whence holy friendships might be sought out. In this regard it is gathered that in earliest times of the human race...the saints were obliged to make use of this good of marriage.... But now, since the opportunity for spiritual relationship abounds...they who wish to contract marriage only to have children are to be admonished that they practice the greater good of continence' (*FC*, xxvii. 22).

22–23. *Moses...take place*: 'Moses's "good" (the good of spousal conjugality, Gen. 2: 18) must take precedence'.

23. *Pauls (bonum non)*: 'Paul's "[it is] not good"' to touch a woman (1 Cor. 7: 1).

25. *Adhærere...Ps. 37.6.*: mis-citation of Ps. 37: 7 ('Hold thee still in the Lord').

40–41. *Christ...Oxen, &c.*: perhaps an example of the note-taker inaccurately summarizing Andrewes, or (less likely) a quite loose application by him of the parable of the marriage of the king's son (Matt. 22: 1–14): the ill-natured guests are distracted from attending the wedding by 'going their wayes, one to his farme, another to his merchandize' (v. 5), not by themselves 'marrying a wife'. The guest 'plucked away from God' was the hapless 'man who had not a wedding garment' (vv. 11–13).

p. 106, 1. *inter...solitudinem*: Lat., 'between solicitude [anxiety] and solitude'.

7–8. *to condemn...Papists doe*: conventional Protestant criticism of Roman Catholic justifications of monasticism and clerical celibacy, which drew heavily on Pauline asceticism (cf. 1 Cor. 7: 25–40); Roman teaching held that marriage conveyed sacramental grace, but the Reformed rejection of monasticism and clerical celibacy, and its greater emphasis on 'mutual comfort' (*BCP*) as a just cause for marriage, removed the implication in Roman practice that celibacy was a superior state; Andrewes imputes to 'Papists' both a legal condemnation ('condemn', fr. Lat. *condemnare*) and a general scorn ('contemn', fr. Lat. *contemnere*) of matrimony (*OED*).

15–22. *second objection...misery*: probably a rejoinder to Hermetic or cabbalistic philosophy; cf. Andrew Marvell, 'The Garden', 'Such was that happy garden-state, | While man there walked without a mate: | After a place so pure, and sweet, | What other help could yet be meet?' (ll. 57–60); see Nigel Smith (ed.), *The Poems of Andrew Marvell* (2003), 153, 158.

26. *causa...non*: Lat., 'an absolutely necessary case'; Andrewes is unusual here to argue that Adam would have—or at least could have—fallen even had Eve not been created.

35. *Non...viri*: Lat., 'not from [her, but] from of the side of the man'; debate, often playful, on the relative responsibility of Adam and Eve for the Fall was a commonplace; Andrewes's view here is strikingly similar to Amelia Lanyer, *Salve Deus Rex Judeorum* (1611, ed. Susanne Woods, 1993), ll. 761–832; cf. esp. ll. 809–10, 'If any Evill did in her remaine, Beeing made of him, he was the ground of all'; contrast 1 Tim. 2: 14.

39. *advantage*: 'a favouring circumstance...the opposite of *disadvantage*' (*OED* sn 5.a).

p. 106, 41–p. 107, 1. *seed...the Serpent*: Gen. 3: 15.

3–6. *grief...felicity*: Peters (*Patterns of Piety*, 310) suggests that the deep Christocentrism of Protestant interpretations of the Fall enabled an increased prominence of such *felix culpa* readings in early modern England.

9. *Faciam adjutricem*: 'I shall make a helper' (Gen. 2: 18); see p. 101, l. 34 and n.
10. *fiat*: 'let there be'; cf. Vulg. (Gen. 1: 3, 6).
12. *presently*: 'immediately, instantly' (*OED, sadv* 3).

15. *to post up*: accounting metaphor, 'to carry (an item or entry) into the proper account' (*OED, sv* 'post', V.8.b).
28. *headily*: 'precipitately, hastily' (*OED sadv*).
30–31. *Micholl... Saules making*: Michal (1 Sam. 18: 27).

A SERMON PREACHED BEFORE QUEEN ELIZABETH...
VI MARCH, A.D. MDXCIIII.

Text. *XCVI* (1629, F_1, author's copy), 299–308; collated with F_2 (1632, Bodl. Antiq. c.E.1632.2, pp. 299–308); F_3 (1635, editor's copy, pp. 299–308), and *LACT*, ii. 61–77; F_2 provides several corrections of typographical errors accepted here, as well as some suggestive adjustments to punctuation recorded in the apparatus; F_3 continues the process of modernizing Elizabethan spellings begun in F_2.

Headnote. This is the fourth surviving court Lent sermon by Andrewes; he appears in the court Lent rota on weekdays during Lent from 1590, with only the sermons for 1592 and 1595 not surviving (McCullough, *Sermons at Court*, 'Calendar'; *XCVI*, 263–308). The sermon's date (1594), once argued by Tyacke to be 1595, has been confirmed by McCullough and accepted in Tyacke's later work. Scholars have largely fixed on this sermon's breathtaking frontal assault on the defining doctrine of Elizabethan Calvinism, the predestined security ('perseverance') of the elect. Andrewes's uncompromising interpretation of Lot's wife as an exemplum of the 'imperseverant' sinner who can fall from grace (p. 109, l. 4)—and the corollary that salvation is only secure as long as human will voluntarily cooperates with the divine will to preserve it—roundly contradicts early Luther, Calvin, and the English reformed consensus. Not noted before, however, are the many strong similarities (in arguments and exempla) between this sermon and Andrewes's even earlier lecture on perseverance delivered at Cambridge, *c*.1585 (see Sources, below). But this sermon is the earliest statement from the highly public court pulpit of the defining element in later Jacobean and Caroline doctrinal debates over 'Arminianism', and anticipates by a full year the academic explosion over William Barrett's and Peter Baro's anti-Calvinism at Cambridge in 1595. Perhaps the only other non-university Elizabethan text that asks such challenging questions about predestination is Christopher Marlowe's *Dr Faustus* (1588?).

This sermon also continues Andrewes's previous Lent sermons' subtle use of penitential Lenten themes as occasions for exhortation to proper government of church and state. The sermon on Lot's wife, however, is particularly sophisticated in the way it expounds at length the ostensibly private virtue of perseverance, only to apply it dramatically to the queen in its peroration. The overt concluding praise of Elizabeth as 'Queen of vertues' (pp. 121–22) confirms as fact the possibility felt throughout the rest of the sermon that Lot's wife is a counter-type of the monarch who listened to the sermon from the elevated royal closet in the Hampton Court chapel royal. Just as Spenser (*Faerie Queene*, 1. iv) portrays Lucifera as a parody of Elizabeth, Lot's weak, backsliding wife is a parody of the queen whose motto was '*Semper eadem*' ('Always the same'). At several points, Lot's wife's failings are cast in terms suggestive of Elizabeth's successes (cf. pp. 114-15 and nn.). But Andrewes's panegyric is of course also a warning, or at least an exhortation, to Elizabeth to continue in her course of steadfastness, and probably sounds a note of approval for the recent consolidation of Whitgift's and Elizabeth's authority over Protestant nonconformists.

Finally, the sermon is an excellent example of Andrewes's literary craftsmanship. The key word 'memores' ('remember') and its derivatives are woven in and out of the sermon with the ever-expanding referential significance of the subject in a complex fugue. To prepare the sermon's triumphant peroration, Andrewes deftly employs (pp. 119-20) sequences of imperative clauses beginning, 'Remember', in imitation of the Litany, the *BCP*'s penitential liturgy. The thematic imagery of salt also composes an important emblematic and moral image system. Finally, the gendered imagery used to advise and praise the queen is a masterpiece of suggestive restraint. The majority of the sermon is animated by the tension between the negative example of Lot's wife (traditionally an epitome of the faithless and unfaithful woman) and her implied opposite, Elizabeth. But when Andrewes finally openly applies the sermon's central virtue, perseverance, to his queen, he cannily substitutes a male type from the Bible—Zerubbabel—and, briefly but profoundly, from Cicero, the young Roman girl Cloelia, who exemplifies fortitude by having the heart 'of a man' (p. 121 and nn.). Andrewes thus safely distances Elizabeth from any taint of the feminine weakness embodied in Lot's wife, and reprises one of Elizabeth's own most famous self-characterizations—'I know I have the body but of a weak and feeble woman, but I have the heart and stomach of a king' ('To the Troops at Tilbury', 1588; in *Collected Works*, ed. Leah Marcus, et al. (2000), 326).

Sources. Andrewes's usual display of learning—both patristic and classical—is on display here, but the sermon owes no sustained debt to any previous exegesis of his text. Augustine and, in particular, Bernard, are mined here for pithy moral *sententiae* rather than whole arguments or *exempla*. Several common patristic arguments link this sermon to Andrewes's earlier catechetical lecture at Cambridge on the first commandment. There he insisted on perseverance as an element of that commandment's injunction to 'have no other Gods before me'. Andrewes appeals here also to Josephus and Herodotus for brief historical points, but the antiquarian and topographical lore about the destruction of Sodom and Gomorrah on which Andrewes draws was conventional. For the notes below, I have used the full summary of this matter gathered in the works of Heinrich Bünting (Magdeburg, 1598), trans. R.B. and printed in England from 1608 as *Itinerarium Totius Sacrum Scripturae*; I quote from the edn. of 1682.

Further Reading. For dating, see Tyacke, 'Archbishop Laud', in Fincham (ed.), *Early Stuart Church*, 63, McCullough, *Sermons at Court*, 'Calendar', and Tyacke, 'Lancelot Andrewes', 18; Lossky, *Lancelot Andrewes*, epitomizes the political content of Andrewes's early court Lent sermons, and offers a brief but sound reading of this sermon's concluding prayer for the queen (pp. 102-8); for this sermon as Andrewes's 'coming out' as an anti-predestinarian, see Tyacke, 'Lancelot Andrewes', 18-19; for the wider context of late 1590s anti-predestinarian debates in the universities, see Nicholas Tyacke, *Anti-Calvinists: The Rise of English Arminianism c. 1590-1640* (Oxford, 1987), 29-40; Elizabeth's religious conservatism and resistance to change praised by Andrewes here is trenchantly surveyed by MacCulloch, *Tudor Church Militant*, 191-213.

p. 108, 7. *Memores... Lot*: Vulg.

9. *A Part... II. Lesson*: *BCP* calendar appoints Luke 17 as the second lesson to be read at Morning Prayer on 6 March.

10. *no one... so short*: for the number of words, technically a tie with John 11: 35 ('And Jesus wept'), which had to wait until the AV (1611) to become, with the omission of 'And', the shortest verse in the Bible. Cf. Donne, *Sermons*, iv. 324–5.

15. *Memento*: Lat., 'remember' (imperative).

17. *with all*: withal, moreover.

24. *Sodomites laughed*: Gen. 19: 14.

25. *Lot's storie*: Gen. 19: 1–29.

p. 109, 3. *the Sodomites*: Andrewes ignores the conventional association between the men of Sodom and the sin of buggery. In his Cambridge catechistical lecture on the seventh commandment ('Thou shalt not commit adultery'), Andrewes had included in a catalogue of sexual sins (including masturbation and nocturnal emission) the orthodox denunciation of sodomy as a sin against matrimony, procreation, and nature, and the sin for which 'God himself cáme down and sate in judgement against the five Cities, which plot of ground is an unprofitable Seat to this day... called *Lacus Asphaltites*, of the unfruitfulnesse of it, answerable to the sterility of this sin' (*Pattern of Catechistical Doctrine*, 449). In the context of this sermon, however, the Sodomites are remembered not for any particular sin, but as unrepentant sinners in general, who spurn the admonitions of God, his angels, and his servant Lot. This allows a sharper parallel to be drawn between them and Lot's wife, and a focus less on moral theology than on the doctrine of perseverance and election (cf. next n.).

4. *imperseverant*: not cited in *OED*; a simple negation of the doctrinal sense of *perseverant*: having the quality or nature of persevering to eternal salvation; but *cf.* Shakespeare, C*ymbeline*, 'yet this imperseuerant thing loues him in my despite' (F_1), dubiously emended to 'imperceiverant' (Oxford, 4. l. 14).

5. *relapsing righteous persons*: regenerate and justified ('righteous') Christians who, through wilful, unrepented sin, fall back ('relapse') to an unregenerate state of damnation; a remarkable refutation of dominant English Calvinist orthodoxy (see Headnote).

13. *Qui cecidit... resurgat*: Lat., 'he who has fallen, is cast down to rise up'; cf. Jer. 8: 4 ('qui cadet non resurget', Vulg.; 'Shall they fall and not arise?', Geneva).

14. *Qui stat... cadat*: Lat., 1 Cor. 10: 12, 'let him who standeth see that he doth not fall' (Geneva); cf. Vulg. ('qui se existimat stare videat ne cadat').

18–19. *errors of Ur*: Lot followed his uncle Abram (Abraham) on the several nomadic removals commanded by God; the first was from Ur to Haran. The Bible makes no explicit judgement on the moral state ('errors') of Ur (Gen. 11: 31, 12: 1), but this was assumed by Christian commentators—cf. the explanation in Thomas Lanquet and Robert Crowley, *An Epitome of Chronicles* (1559), that Abram left 'because he wold not be defiled with ye wicked supersticions and idolatrie of the Babylonians' (p. 15). Andrewes may also be punning on 'error' as both 'the action or state of erring' (*OED sn* III) and its Latinate sense of 'roaming or wandering' (*OED sn* I.1).

22. *ne putescamus*: Lat., 'that we do not putrefy'.

27. *Mnason*: Acts 21: 16 (*LACT*).

28. *make new Proselytes*: criticism of evangelism—the conversion of new believers ('*proselytes*')—carried out at the expense of confirming the existing faithful and respecting antiquity and conformity; in Andrewes's view, applicable to both Roman Catholic missionaries and zealous Protestant nonconformists.

29. *Venite ad me*: Vulg., Matt. 11: 28 ('come unto me').

29–30. *Manete in me*: Vulg., John 15: 4 ('abide in me').

33–39. *Philosophie... & tu*: catalogue of examples from the traditionally recognized professions (philosophy, law, medicine, theology) of the necessity of maintaining a state of moral good (perseverance) as well as initiating it; cf. following nn.

33. *tueri... quærere*: '"protecting" as no less important than "to seek"'; from the Latin commonplace, 'Non minor est virtus quam querere parta tueri' (Ovid, *Ars Amatoria*, ii. 13), 'protecting what you have is no less a virtue than seeking new things'.

34. *Habendum... Tenendum*: '"having" is just as important as "holding"'; the Latin terms were conventional in patents granting offices and titles; cf. Thomas Pierce, *A Vindication of the Kings Sovereign Rights* (1683), 'this the King gave under the Great Seal... wherein the *Habendum* and the *Tenendum*, is not of the Bishop of *Sarum*... but of *Him* the said *King*' (p. 10); cf. Andrewes, *Pattern of Catechistical Doctrine*, 'in the common conveyances at Law, there is, *Habendum & tenendum* to have and to hold; we have formerly seen *Quid habendum*, what we were to have, now we are to see *Quid tenendum*, what we must hold and keep' (p. 187).

35. *regiment*: 'rule of diet or mode of living' (*OED sn* 5).

35. *recidivation*: relapse (here, medical, but cf. p. 164, l. 2 and n.).

37. *Ne corruat*: Lat., 'that it be not thrown down'; cf. Num. 14: 42 (Vulg.), 'nolite ascendere non enim est Dominus vobiscum ne corruatis coram inimicis vestris' ('Goe not up (for the Lorde is not among you) lest ye be overthrown before your enemies').

37–38. *Nisi credideritis*: cf. Isa. 7: 9 (Vulg.), 'si non credideritis non permanebitis' ('If ye beleeve not, surely ye shall not be established').

38. *Ne perpluat*: Lat., 'that it does not rain through'.

39. *Si permanseris... tu*: Vulg., Rom. 11: 22, 'in te autem bonitatem Dei si permanseris in bonitate alioquin et tu excideris' ('but toward thee, bountifulnesse, if thou continue in his bountifulnesse: or els thou shalt also be cut off'); by applying this verse to the individual believer, Andrewes flatly contradicts the Geneva gloss: 'and wee must marke here, that hee speaketh not of the election of euery private man which remayneth stedfast for ever, but of the election of the whole nation'.

p. 110, 1. *this vertue*: perseverance.

4. ἀψίκορόν τὶ: Gr., 'apsikoron ti'; 'a fickle element'.

6. *The Prophet*: David.

9. *sine sale putescere*: 'without salt, putrefy'.

10. *corned*: preserved with salt.

11. *to draw us on*: to entice us.

17. *called coram*: called before (an authority); cf. Rudolf Gwalter, *An Hundred... Sermons uppon the Actes* (1572), 'how many which through false doctrine... had provoked the wrath of God? yet none of them were called *Coram*' (p. 199).

17–18. *Nemo... deseruerunt*: cf. Vulg., 2 Tim. 4: 16, 'in prima mea defensione nemo mihi adfuit sed omnes me dereliquerunt' ('at my first answering no man assisted me, but all forsooke me').

20. *Etsi... ego*: Lat., 'as it is with others, it is not so with me'; cf. Vulg., Matt. 26: 33, 'et si omnes scandalizati fuerint in te ego numquam scandalizabor' ('though that al men should be offended by thee, yet will I never be offended').

21. *Etsi... ille*: Lat., 'as it is with others, it is not so with him'; cf. prev. n.

24. *amaze*: bewilderment.

28–29. *quantum... Syllabæ*: Lat., 'how mighty are these five syllables'; adaptation of Caesarius of Arles, *Homilia XIX* (*PL*, 67.1082B), on the word 'peccata' ('sins'), 'quantum valent tres syllabae' ('how mighty are three syllables').

34–36. *Saint Augustine... our lives*: Augustine, *En. in Psalmos LXIX*, 9 (*PL*, 36.874), 'Et ipsa in via, jam liberata de Sodomis, retro respexit; ubi respexit, ibi remansit: facta est statua salis, ut condiat te' ('and in that very road of escape from Sodom, she looked back; where she looked back, there she remained: made a pillar of salt to season you'); repeated in *En. in Psalmos LXXV*, 16 and *LXXXIII*, 3 (*PL*, 36.968; 37.1057).

p. 111, 1–2. *us... Remembrancers*: ministers, preachers; Luther similarly prefaces his exposition of the destruction of Sodom with an apologia for ministerial reproof of sin, and (as Andrewes here, pp. 109–10) distinguishes sharply between obstinate and occasional sinners (Lectures on Genesis, Luther, *Works*, ed. Pelikan, iii. 240; also *Werke*, xliii. 46–7).

4. *Recognosce... cognesce*: Lat., 'recalling... learning'.

8. *the Philosopher*: Aristotle (cf. 'A Sermon Preached... the Fifth of August', this edn., p. 192, 34).

9–10. *Nihil... our selves*: cf. Andrewes, *Scala Coeli* (1610), 'when we would settle our selves to pray, *Nihil tam longè abest a nobis, quàm orare vt decet*' ('nothing is so far from us as to pray properly', p. 57ᵛ).

11. παραρρύειν: Gr., 'pararrhuëin', flow out, drift away (Heb. 2: 1).

11. *glasse*: mirror.

13–14. *Memento's*: characteristic treatment of a word as a substantive object in itself; the '*Memento's*' are, first, the key word in Andrewes's biblical text, and, here, the first word in a series of injunctions; but these are treated also as concrete objects serving to remind, warn, or hint of future events, definitions which emerged only in the 1580s (*OED sn* 2.a, b).

14. *Memento... lutum tu*: cf. Vulg., Job 10: 9, 'memento quaeso quod sicut lutum feceris me et in pulverem reduces me' ('remember, I pray thee, that thou hast made me as the clay, and wilt thou bring me into dust againe?').

15. *Memento... ventus*: Vulg., Job 7: 7, 'memento quia ventus est vita mea' ('remember that my life is but a wind').

16. *Memento tenebrosi temporis*: cf. Vulg., Eccles. 11: 8, 'meminisse debet tenebrosi temporis' ('yet hee shall remember the daies of darkenesse').

19–22. *store-house... Memorie of others*: Andrewes's division of human knowledge into written 'Memorie' (history) and lived 'Experience', though largely conventional, bears comparison with the treatment of the same in Book II of Sir Francis Bacon's *Advancement of Learning* (1605); for Andrewes's intimacy with Bacon, see Welsby, *Lancelot Andrewes*, 225–7.

23. *Tantùm hesterni sumus*: cf. Vulg., Job 8: 9, 'hesterni quippe sumus' ('For we are but of yesterday'), and Geneva gloss: 'meaning, that it is not ynough to have the experience of our selves, but to be confirmed by the examples of them that went before us'.

26. *interrogare... pristinam*: cf. Vulg., Job 8: 8, 'interroga enim generationem pristinam' ('inquire therefore, I pray thee, of the former age').

34. *sample*: exemplify; be an example of.

34–35. *if... therafter*: 'if success were to follow the eschewing of it'.

35. *storie*: history, narrative (not, in the modern sense, fiction).

p. 112, 1. *Shew-bread*: loaves of bread ceremonially kept before the Holy of Holies in the Temple as a symbol of the covenant between God and his people (Exod. 25: 23–30).

4–5. *Memento... antiquorum*: Vulg., Deut. 32: 7 ('remember the dayes of olde').

5. *Recordamini... Seculi*: Vulg., Isa. 46: 9 ('remember the former things of old').

5–6. *State... antiquas*: cf. Vulg., Jer. 6: 16, 'state super vias et videte et interrogate de semitis antiquis' ('stande in the waies and beholde, and aske for the olde way').

6. *Investiga... memoriam*: Vulg., Job 8: 8 ('search of their fathers'; lit., 'seek out the fathers' memory').

6. *Exemplum... Prophetas*: cf. Vulg., James 5: 10, 'exemplum accipite fratres laboris et patientiae prophetas' ('take, my brethren, the Prophets for an ensample of suffering adversitie, and of long patience').

7. *Rememoramini... priscos*: cf. Vulg., Heb. 10: 32, 'rememoramini autem pristinos dies' ('nowe call to remembrance the dayes that are passed').

7. [7]*Remember*: superscript enumeration of this clause, without a corresponding marginal note, suggests that the sequence was enumerated orally in delivery.

8. *lay*: 'apply or devote... to' (*OED sv* 39.c).

13. *the onely one storie*: Christ taught frequently from Old Testament *exempla*; Andrewes here fixes on the fact that to no other does Christ literally apply the imperative command 'Remember' (*'Memento'*).

17. *recidivation*: relapse into sin; apostasy (*OED sn* 1).

20. *Memento & fac*: Lat., 'remember and do'.

21. *Marie Magdalen's ointment*: Mark 14: 3–9; the subject and text of Andrewes's court Lent sermon in 1593 (*XCVI*, 285–98).

26. Μὴ καταβάτω μὴ ἐπιστρεψάτω: Gr., 'Mē katabatō mē ĕpistrepsatō' ('let him not come down, let him not return back'); Luke 17: 31.

26–27. *returne back*: although he does not use the term here, Andrewes's constant wordplay on 'back' ('look back', 'return back', etc.) dances around the epithet 'backsliding'; cf. *Pattern of Catechistical Doctrine*, 'backsliding is condemned... we are naturally like a bow, which being almost bent, and let go never so little, starts back' (p. 187).

p. 113, 3. *trifled*: dallied, delayed.

6–7. *despised... owne soule*: cf. Heb. 12: 5; Prov. 3: 11.

10. *Severè... Dei*: Lat., 'strictly to keep God's commandments'; cf. Vulg., Neh. 10: 29, 'ut facerent et custodirent universa mandata Domini Dei nostri' ('to observe and doe all the commandements of the Lorde our God'); also Exod. 16: 28, Ps. 119: 60.

14. *happly*: haply; by chance.

15. *feared*: frightened.

20. *tenor*: 'continuance, duration' (*OED sn* 2.a).

23. *Sequebantur a longè*: Lat., 'there follows behind'.

24–25. *Occasionem... amico*: Vulg., Prov. 18: 1 ('he seeketh occasions that wil depart from a frend', Douai-Rheims).

34. *as NINEVE did*: Jonah 3: 10.

38–39. *From Ur... to Canaan*: cf. p. 159, l. 15 and n.

p. 114, 3. *convenient*: pleasant, commodious.

4. *die by her flesh-pots*: Exod. 16: 3.

5. *graves of lust*: Num. 11: 34 (*LACT*).

6. *Stately city*: Ezek. 23: 31.

7. *desolate mountaines*: Ezek. 33: 28.

8. *restinesse*: restlessness.

15. *convulsion*: *OED* cites 1599 as the earliest usage meaning 'the action of wrenching', and 1585 for the 'involuntary contraction... of a muscle' (*sn* 1, 2).

22–23. *forsooke ... mercie*: cf. Jonah 2: 8. Although '*mercie*', or the power to save, is strictly speaking God's own, the diction here (from Jonah's prayer in the belly of the whale) highlights Andrewes's controversial point that God's mercy and grace is in a sense one's own, at least in the believer's freedom and ability to resist and reject it—a position opposite to Calvinism's insistence on the irresistibility of God's grace by the elect.

28–23. *Pharao ... nine times*: Pharaoh agreed and then refused to free the Israelites after each of the nine plagues (Exod. 7–12).

31–32. *Saul ... Judas ... Nero*: the periods of time during which these three were, respectively, a good king, a good disciple, and a good emperor.

33. *thirty yeare*: cf. Elizabeth, then in the thirty-sixth year of her reign.

p. 115, 1–2. *wracked in the haven*: shipwrecked in the harbour; the maritime imagery of these lines may allude to Elizabeth's deliverance from the Spanish Armada (1588).

7. *no whit*: no bit; not at all.

15–16. *delivered ... five Kings*: Gen. 14: 14–16.

17. *the five Cities*: pentapolis in the Dead Sea valley, including Sodom and Gomorrah, whose kings and people had initially been delivered from captivity by Abraham (cf. prev. n.); only Zoar, Lot's place of refuge, was spared from destruction (Gen. 19: 15–29).

20. *day of her visitation*: cf. Luke 19: 44; '*visitation*' here, as in the Old Testament prophets (cf. Jer. 51: 18), is a day of divine retribution upon the ungodly.

22–23. *daughters to attend her*: Gen. 19: 16.

28. *defection*: 'falling away from allegiance ... desertion' (*OED sn* 2).

33–34. *this forethinking ... faint proceeding*: the sense seems to be, 'this thinking to ourselves beforehand [i.e. assuming] that we are safely gone out of danger, this faint proceeding, this staying ... ', which fits the passage's pattern of anaphoric subordinate clauses ('this forethinking ... proceeding ... staying ... convulsion ... wavering').

39. *justifie*: confirm, corroborate by evidence; i.e. 'if they go back, their punishment will corroborate hers'.

p. 116, 13. *respite*: 'delay or extension of time', or 'an interval of rest' (*OED sn* I.1, 2).

13–14. *sodeine death ... pray against*: cf., from the Litany (*BCP*), 'From lightninges and tempestes, from plague, pestilence and famine, from battayle and murther, and from soudeine death, *Good Lorde delyver us*'; cf. Andrewes, *Pattern of Catechistical Doctrine*, 'so must we persevere according to our *quandiu*, that is, till we die, *usque ad mortem*, and not onely to natural but even to violent death' (p. 187).

16. *remorse of sinne*: cf. Andrewes, 'Propositions and Inferences to be made to the sick' (*c.* 1590): 'That, if His will had not been to shew mercie by this chastisement, He could & would have suddenly taken you away with a quick destruction; and not given you this time to bethink yourself, and to seek and sue to Him for grace' (*Manual of Directions for the Sick* (1648), 24–5).

20. *visitation of other men*: punning contrast to the earlier use of the word as punitive judgment (p. 115, l. 20); here, the pastoral visitation of the sick or distressed; cf. Order for the Visitation of the Sick (*BCP*), and Andrewes, *Manual of Directions for the Sick*.

26. *Josephus*: Flavius Josephus (*c.*37–*c.*100), Jewish historian and Roman citizen whose histories, written in Greek, have been a vital source for Christian accounts of the Apostolic decades.

27–28. Ἱστόρηκα ... *this day*: Josephus (cf. prev. n.), *Antiquities of the Jews*, i. 11 (*LACT*).

28. *A reed she was*: cf. 1 Kings 14: 15.
29. *melting water*: cf. Ps. 58: 7.
32. *verdure*: 'freshness... taste, savour' (*OED* II.4.a).
36. *the Heathen mans*: Herodotus (*c*.485–425 BCE), Greek historian.

p. 117, 1–2. *'Es...* GOD *better*: Herodotus (prev. n.) recounts how the Egyptian priest-king Sethos neglected his military duty, but, because of his subsequent faithful appeal to the god Hephaestus, was miraculously saved by a swarm of mice; hence 'at this day a stone statue of the Egyptian king stands in Hephaestus' temple with a mouse in his hand, and an inscription to this effect, "Look on me, and fear the gods" ' (*History*, ii. 141).

5–6. *Sent... ointment*: cf. p. 112, l. 21 and nn.

9. *their Quarters... stories*: quartered bodies of those executed for treason exhibited ('*sett up*') in public as admonitions ('stories'); cf. 'A Sermon Preached... the V. of November' (this edn.), p. 155, l. 22 and n.

9–10. *Ut pœna... Justi*: Lat., 'so that the punishment of the wicked be the wisdom of the just'.

11–12. *Ut lavet... peccatoris*: cf. Vulg. Ps. 57: 11 (juxt. Hebr.), 'laetabitur iustus cum viderit ultionem pedes suos lavabit in sanguinem impii' ('The righteous shall reioyce when he seeth the vengeance: he shall wash his feete in the blood of the wicked', Geneva, Ps. 58: 10).

15. *salt-petre*: saltpetre; sodium nitrate, the chief ingredient of gunpowder.

21. *Triacle... vipers*: treacle; 'antidote to venomous bites' (*OED* I.1.); cf. Bünting, *Itinerarium*, on the Dead Sea left on the site of Sodom, 'in this place the Serpent *Tyrus* (whereof they use to make Treacle) is found. It is a little Serpent about half a Cubit long, and a Finger thick, being of divers colours, and is so venomous, that where it biteth there is no remedy, unless by cutting off the Member: the Head of it is rough and hairy, and there seemeth to lye upon the Tongue of it, if it be angry, a fiery flame' (p. 64).

21. *aliena pericula*: Lat., 'another's peril'; from a proverbial adage; see 'Sacrilege a Snare' (this edn.), p. 89, l. 19 and n.

24. *savory*: 'pleasing to the taste'; also 'spiritually edifying' and 'of saintly repute or memory' (*OED sa* A.1, 2.b (a), (b)).

25–26. *Muria... Gregorie*: cf. Gregory the Great, *Homilia in Evang. LXX*, 1 (*PL*, 76.1189C), 'quia nimirum virtus boni operis perseverantia est, et voce Veritatis dicitur: Qui autem perseveraverit usque in finem, hic salvus erit'; ('because certainly the virtue of a good work is perseverance, and the voice of Truth has said, "he who perseveres to the end shall be saved" [Matt. 24.13]').

26–27. *Summer fruits*: quickly perishable soft fruits.

27. *Salt of the Covenant*: Lev. 2: 13; cf. also Andrewes, *Pattern of Catechistical Doctrine*, 'all other vertues are preserved by [perseverance], or (to use the Apostles phrase) seasoned with salt *[in marg: Col. 4.6.]*. As God set *David* over Israel by a covenant of salt, that is, by an everlasting covenant... to shew, that as the covenant is perpetual on Gods part, so ought the condition to be on ours, by perseverance' (p. 187).

28. *take winde*: 'to become tainted or corrupted by exposure to... air' (*OED* 'wind', *sn* II.8.a).

28–29. *Saint Augustine... virtutum*: Augustine seems not to have nominated perseverance thus; probably a mis-citation of Bernard of Clairvaux; cf. *Pattern of Catechistical Doctrine*, 'constancy and perseverance, is *virtutis apex*, the pitch and perfection of vertue, and as S. Bernard, *Perseverantia est unica filia summi Regis, finis virtutum, earumque consummatio*, perseverance is the onely daughter of the great King, the end and consumation of all vertues' (p. 187); attr. by modern scholars to Nicholas of Clairvaux, *Epistolae*, xlvi (*PL*, 196.1648A), 'Perseverantia est singularis filia summi regis, quae reliquarum virtutum conventum ad dominantis thalamum introducit'; cf. also next n.

30-31. *Perseverantia...coronatur*: Bernard of Clairvaux, *Epist. CIX*, 2 (*PL*, 182.252B), 'studete proinde perseverantiae, quae sola virtutum coronatur'; ('strive therefore for perseverance, which is the only crowned virtue').

33. *securitie*: assurance of salvation as one of the elect.

36. *tendere in anteriora*: Lat., 'to strive for things ahead'; cf. Vulg., Phil. 3: 13., 'quae quidem retro sunt obliviscens ad ea vero quae sunt in priora extendens me' ('I forget that which is behinde, and endevour my selfe unto that which is before'); Luther quotes the same verse when making a similar point, 'thus this pillar is truly a spice and the salt of wisdom; it admonishes us not to look back but to persevere, and, as Paul puts it, to "strain forward to what lies ahead"' (Luther, *Works*, iii. 300; *Werke*, xliii, 89-90).

39. *Vis...securitatem time*: Lat., 'Do you wish to be secure in fear? Fear security'; cf. Bernard, *Serm. de Diversis XIV*, 1 (*LACT*; *PL*, 183.574D), 'Et primus contra negligentiam timor exsurgit....Denique qui timet Deum, nihil negligit (Eccle. VII, 19), sed veretur omnia opera sua' ('and the first thing to rise up against negligence is fear.... Therefore, he who fears God, neglects nothing, but respects all of His works').

p. 118, 2. *Si permanseris*: Vulg., Rom. 11: 22 ('if thou continue').

2-3. *Noli...sed time*: Vulg., Rom. 11: 19 ('bee not hie minded, but feare', Geneva, Rom. 11: 20).

5. *make us keepe*: make us last (i.e. not putrefy; be preserved).

6-7. CHRIST's *twelve...one miscaried*: Judas Iscariot (Matt. 10: 2-4; Mark 14: 10).

7-8. *Et illum...intrare*: the image of wolves ravening the faithful flock is based on John 10: 12, Matt. 7: 15, and Acts 20: 29. The explicit application of the metaphor to Judas among the twelve quoted here is found in Ogerius Lucedii, *De Verbis Domini in Coena*, Serm. I, 3 (*PL*, 184.882B-C), 'Si lupus non timuit intrare in gregem Domini, unam de duodecim tam pauculo numero mactare et perdere; quid facturus est de grege commisso pastori?'; ('If the wolf did not fear to enter the flock of the Lord, one of the Twelve, such a small number to slay and destroy; what a responsibility it is to be made pastor of the flock?'). However, the works of Ogerius (1205-64, abbot of Locedio) were unpublished until *PL*; one must therefore assume a common source for this quotation, but it is unique in *PL*.

9. *Noah's eight...one fell*: Noah, his three sons, and their four wives (Gen. 6: 10, 7: 7); Noah's youngest son, Ham was cursed by Noah after the flood (Gen. 9: 25-7).

10. *Lot's foure*: himself, his wife, and two daughters (Gen. 19: 16).

11-12. *little after...of two*: tactfully vague allusion to Lot's incest with his daughters, who became pregnant by him (Gen. 19: 30-8); if 'one is *refused*' (i.e. morally culpable) in particular, perhaps Andrewes means Lot himself, or his eldest daughter whose idea it was to 'preserve seed of our father' by incest (Gen. 19: 32).

16-21. *Secondly...not be remembred*: perhaps the sermon's most emphatic anti-predestinarian statement; contrast Luther, who insisted that Lot's wife's punishment was only physical—'nevertheless her soul is saved'—not least 'since she has a splendid testimony of the life she has previously led' (Luther, *Works*, iii. 300; *Werke*, xliii. 89-90).

18. *estate*: her station in society, but also her spiritual state.

25–26. *Et non... respicientes*: Lat., lit., 'and they [who] go not out, and they [who] go out looking back'; highly compressed wordplay, clarified in the gloss that immediately follows; the sense is that those will die who either do not leave Sodom, or who leave it but look back.

26. *her*: Sodom.

27. *Lacus Asphaltites*: cf. Bünting, *Itinerarium*, 'Of the Lake, or Dead Sea, called Asphaltites', 'in the very same place where these Cities were burnt and destroyed, there is at this day to be seen a Lake about 36 Miles long. ... it boileth with Pitch and Brimstone, and in some places passeth by the name of the Salt Sea, and in others, the dead Sea, because of the noisome and venomous Air that riseth out of it, insomuch as the very Birds that fly over it fall down dead' (pp. 63–4); cf. also n. to p. 117, l. 21.

28. *Lot's Wive's salt stone*: cf. Bünting, *Itinerarium*, 'a little from *Zoar*, between this Lake and the Mountains of *Engedi*, the Pillar whereinto *Lot*'s Wife was turned, is yet to be seen shining like Salt' (p. 64).

30. *hard at*: next to; in front of.

34. *search*: penetrate.

35–36. *Saint Bernard) erubescere*: cf. Bernard, *Serm. de Diversis XXV*, 1 (*PL*, 183.605B), 'et excitans erubescere facit, et timere Deum'; ('and they were made to burn with shame, and to fear God'); cf. Andrewes, *Pattern of Catechistical Doctrine*, '*S. Bernard* saith, *Recordare præterita, & erubesce [sic]*, it will confound a man to remember what he hath done' (p. 187).

36. *contremiscere*: Lat., to tremble, fear.

37–38. *Stadium... dolichum*: a 'stadium' is a Greek measure or length of *c*.600 ft., the 'dolichum', a race of many stadia; cf. Plutarch, *The Philosophie* (*Moralia*), trans. P. Holland (1603), 'Dolichus, A long carriere or race, containing twelve, or (as some say) 24. Stadia' (sig. Z4z3ʳ). Cf. Andrewes on Heb. 12: 2 (Good Friday 1605), 'But, hold on our course till we finish it, even till we come to Him, who was not onely *Author* but *Finisher*, ... And so must we finish, not *stadium*, but *dolichum*' (*XCVI*, n.p., sig. 2M5ᵛ).

p. 119, 3. *except*: unless.

5. *Angel's... tuam*: Lat., lit., 'your life is protected', Andrewes's summary of the angel's injunction that Lot and his family flee Sodom (Gen. 19: 15).

6. *Non fecit tibi hoc*: cf. Vulg., Matt. 16: 22, 'non erit tibi hoc' ('this shall not be unto thee').

7–9. *Zoar... little one*: Gen. 19: 20, 22.

13. *meet*: apt, fitting; deservedly.

16. *Domine, Quid iste?*: cf. Vulg., John 21: 20, 'Domine quis est qui tradit te' ('Lorde, which is he that betrayeth thee?').

18. εὔθετος: Gr., ĕuthĕtŏs, 'fit', 'meet'; Luke 9: 62.

19. *leave... heart behind us*: proverbial; cf. Shakespeare, *Midsummer Night's Dream*, 'A foolish heart that I leave here behind' (III. iii. 320); but also Andrewes, *Seven Sermons* (1627), '*Nazianzen* and *Basil* were of that minde once, that by change of the place a man might goe from temptation: but afterward they recanted it, affirming; That it was impossible to avoyd temptation, yea, though he went out of the world, except he left his heart behinde him also' (p. 15).

20. *stay... stay*: wordplay (antanaclasis) on two senses of the word 'stay': 'remain' and 'halt'.

21. *writhe*: twist, turn back.

28. *perdet animam*: cf. Vulg., Luke 17: 33 (Christ's gloss on the exemplum of Lot's wife), 'quicumque quaesierit animam suam salvare perdet illam et qui perdiderit illam vivificabit eam' ('whosoever seeketh to save his life, shal lose it: and whosoever doth lose the same, shal quicken it', Douai-Rheims).

31. *to tender*: to hold dear; feel tenderly towards (*OED sv2* 3.a).

31. *Supra... irritus*: Lat., 'above all (i.e. the greatest) labour is lost labour'; cf. Tilley L9.

34–35. *joyning... clay*: Dan. 2: 32–3.

36–38. *Remember... the winde*: even by his usual standards of brevity, Andrewes uses here two extremely compressed biblical allusions to illustrate the social shame brought on those who fail to endure in following Christ: first, to the parable of the man mocked by his neighbours with the taunt, 'This man ("*Hic homo*") beganne to build, and was not able to finish' (Luke 14: 30); and second, Christ's sarcastic question to the curious who came to hear John the Baptist, 'What went ye out into the wildernesse to see?' (*Quid... videre?*) 'a reede shaken with the winde?' (Matt. 11: 7).

p. 120, 1–2. *falling... other fall*: cf. 1 Cor. 8: 9.

4. *Job's Wife... Ecebolius*: short catalogue of defectors from Judaeo-Christianity: Job's wife (Job 2: 9–10); Paul and Timothy's helper Demas (2 Tim. 4: 10); Ecebolius, Greek Christian turned Sophist tutor of Julian the Apostate (Roman emperor 360–3); cf. Andrewes, *Pattern of Catechistical Doctrine*, '*Demas*.... at the first was reputed so in the church, that Saint *Paul* joynes him with Saint *Luke*. But afterwards S. *Paul* saith, *Demas* hath forsaken me, having followed this present world' (p. 189).

9. *caveat*: warning.

16. *drunkard... his eyes*: proverbial; cf. Nicholas Breton, *A Dialogue* (1603), 'the Drunkard will swill till his eyes stare' (sig. C1ʳ).

17. *uncleane... loines*: physical decay through sexual promiscuity; cf. Andrewes on 'the sin of uncleannesse' (*Pattern of Catechistical Doctrine*): 'it is against a mans own body... both by defiling it... as also by weakning and decaying it... it brings rottennes to the bones, and breeds many lothsome diseases' (p. 437).

18–19. *Quis pudor... malo!*: cf. Thomas Cooke, *Episcopacie Asserted* (1641), 'as St. Hierome said in point of obedience, so may I say in matter of beneficence, quis pudor, quod nonpraestet fides, quod praestitit infidelitas' (p. 23); Jerome, *Epistolae*, lx. 5 (*PL*, 22.593).

26. *Alpha and Omega*: cf. Andrewes, *Pattern of Catechistical Doctrine*, 'because God is *Alpha* and *Omega*, the beginning and the end.... [w]heresoever our *Alpha* is placed, this must be our *Omega*, our eternity' (p. 187).

27. *thrise happy*: 'thrice' used vaguely and hyperbolically; 'very'.

29. *Consummatum est*: Vulg., John 19: 30 ('it is finished').

29–30. *Summa... colis*: Lat., 'the highest point of religion, is the imitation of that you worship'; a theological commonplace (cf. Augustine, *De Civitate Dei*, viii. 27; *PL*, 41.242), from Seneca (*Ep*. xcv), 'satis deos coluit, quisquis imitatus est' ('whosoever imitates them, is worshipping them [the gods] sufficiently').

31–32. *Verus... spe*: Lat., 'true love does not take strength from hope'.

35–38. *Reward... ever and ever*: cf. Rom. 6: 23.

37. αἰῶνες αἰώνων: Gr., 'aiōnes aiōnōn'; lit., 'ages of ages'; cf. Rev. 20: 10, 22: 5; cf. Lat. liturgical 'saecula saeculorum' ('world without end').

p. 121, 2. *wrath to come*: 1 Thess. 1: 10; cf. also Rev. 6: 7.

4. *finished my course*: cf. Andrewes, *Pattern of Catechistical Doctrine*, 'he that continueth to the end shall be saved, saith our Saviour. Upon which *S. Bernard*, not he that beginneth but he that persevereth to the end, this is the man that shall be saved' (p. 188).

5. *wanted*: lacked.

7. *prevented*: come before; anticipated.

12–13. *Blessed... CHRIST*: common apostolic benediction (blessing); cf. 2 Cor. 1: 13, Eph. 1: 3, 1 Pet. 1: 3.

13. *such a Prince*: Queen Elizabeth (see Headnote).

14–15. *Perseverance... virtus Reginarum*: Andrewes modulates into a fulsome concluding panegyric to the queen by recasting the sermon's key theological term into a royal attribute: by redeploying the patristic image of 'the Queen of vertues', introduced earlier in the sermon (p. 171, l. 22 and n.), '*Perseverance*' becomes less specifically the maintenance of a state of spiritual grace than Elizabeth's heroic political stability.

15–16. *like Zorobabel... Corner-stone*: Zerubbabel, royal governor who, with Joshua, began rebuilding the temple in Jerusalem after the Babylonian exile (Ezra 2: 2; Zech. 4: 6–10); hence, an OT type for Elizabeth, seen to have rebuilt the temple ('*layd the Corner-stone*') of Protestantism after England's Roman Catholic 'exile' under Mary Tudor; a biblical type for Elizabeth most familiar from the preface to the Geneva Bible ('whom God hath made as our Zerubbabel for the erecting of this moste excellent Temple, and to plant and maynteyn his holy worde'); cf. also William James's *A Sermon Preached before the Queenes Majestie at Hampton Court* (1578), a Lent sermon on Ezra 4: 1–3, which fully exploited it.

17. *a troublesome time*: the Elizabethan Settlement of religion in 1559, which restored Protestant worship with the *BCP* but only after a careful campaign in the Commons, and the fortuitous (for Elizabeth) deaths of key conservative bishops in the House of Lords; see Norman Jones, *Faith by Statute: Parliament and the Settlement of Religion, 1559* (1982).

18. *alluring... dangers*: '*proffers*' of marriage by Roman Catholic suitors, most seriously that of the Duc d'Alençon (1579); and the repeated, often real, threats of assassination, the most dramatic of which was the Babington Plot hatched by Mary, queen of Scots in (1586).

18. *head stone*: capping stone, the last stone put in place on the roof of a new building; Elizabeth therefore laid both the first stone ('*Corner-stone*', l. 14) and the last in the re-erection of the Church of England; thus Andrewes praises not only Elizabeth's initiative, but also her deep resistance to any change in the ecclesiastical polity after the settlement of 1559; cf. next n.

19–20. *Prophett's acclamation... an ending*: Andrewes's recounting of Zechariah's prophetic acclamation at Zerubbabel's laying of the cornerstone and headstone of the new Temple (Zech. 4: 6–9) is embellished with typological applications to Christ, who repeatedly identified himself as the fulfilment of Ps. 118: 22: 'Jesus saith unto them, Did ye never reade in the Scriptures, The stone which the builders rejected, the same is become the head of the corner?' (Matt. 21: 42; cf. Act. 4: 11.) This system of allusion thus typologically reaches from the Jewish temple, to Christ (the rejected but later exalted head of the church), and then to Elizabeth (rejected and imprisoned under Mary, but re-founder and defender of the true faith from her accession). For an extended application of this architectural imagery to Christ and King James, see Andrewes's sermon before James on Easter Day (also Accession Day) 1611 (*XCVI*, 435–46).

23-24. *a little one... shall live.* Lot took comfort that his refuge, Zoar, was small (Gen. 19: 20). Andrewes applies this in conventional fashion to the national pride in 'little' England, elect and favoured by God out of all proportion to her size.

24-25. *Cities... round about us*: further application of the text's imagery to contemporary politics, probably the 'combustion' of Roman Catholic advances by Spain in the Low Countries, by Spanish-aided rebels in Ireland, and by Henry IV's abjuration of Protestantism in exchange for Paris less than one year before (July 1593); hence Andrewes probably infers a 'recidivation' by Henry (and France) not unlike Lot's wife's, which in turn highlights Elizabeth's confessional 'perseverance'.

26. *Heathen... viri*: Cicero, *De Officiis*, I. xviii. 61, 'Vos enim, iuvenes, animum geritis muliebrem, illa virgo viri' ('For you, young man, show a womanish soul, you maiden a man's'); Cicero's praise of Cloelia (a Roman girl rewarded for her courage) as an exemplum of fortitude.

28-29. *He which begann... CHRIST*: Phil. 1: 7 (*LACT*).

32-33. *we... Remembrancers*: preachers; ministers; cf. pp. 111-12 and nn.

34. *qui ea... insidiatur*: Bernard, *Epist*. XXXII, 3 (*PL*, 182.138B), 'diabolum soli semper perseverantiae insidiari, quam solam virtutum novit coronari'; ('only perseverance is always attacked by the devil, because it is the only virtue to be crowned').

36. *this example*: metaphorically, Lot's wife (as enjoined by Christ in the text); literally, Elizabeth (as enjoined by Andrewes in his peroration).

38. *Ut hæc... condiat nos*: Lat., 'so that this column support us, and this salt season us'; from Augustine (see p. 110, ll. 34-36 and n.).

A SERMON PREACHED AT THE COURT, ON... GOOD-FRIDAY

Text. *XCVI* (1629; F_1, editor's copy), 333-48, collated with *XCVI* (1632; F_2, Bodl. Antiq. c.E.1632.2); some few variants also supplied from *XCVI* (1635; F_3; editor's copy) and *LACT*. Unusually, F_2 and F_3 contain some substantive improvements over F_1 for this sermon, most notably the substition of '*naile*' for the egregious '*netle*' (p. 196, l. 4), and a clearly necessary paragraph break at p. 200, l. 4, both of which suggest careful correction not usually found in F_2; F_1, however, remains the editor's choice for copy text because F_2 modernizes spellings which, in F_1, are clearly closer to the Elizabethan authorial originals; not corrected in F_2, however, were several glaring errors in marginal scriptural citations from F_1; correct citations are supplied and documented here from *LACT*.

Headnote. This is the first court sermon for Good Friday by Andrewes. Since his appointment as a royal chaplain in 1590, he had preached during the court Lent series on weekdays in mid-Lent, days reserved for lower clergy of rising distinction. In 1597 he was appointed to both Ash Wednesday and Good Friday, a clear mark of his growing prestige. The former of these days had for over a decade been taken by the august dean of St Paul's, Alexander Nowell, or the prominent bishop of Durham, Toby Matthew; Good Friday had since 1589 been supplied by Andrewes's Cambridge contemporary, Thomas Dove, dean of Norwich (McCullough, *Sermons at Court*, 'Calendar of Court Sermons'). This promotion in the Lent lists is probably linked to Andrewes's appointment as a prebendary of Westminster in the same year. The sermon was, therefore, a debut of sorts, and indeed set a remarkable precedent for richly imagistic, emotional sermons on the Passion that were informed (openly) by patristic and (tacitly) by Roman Catholic iconographic and meditative traditions (see Sources). This is the first surviving example in a court sermon of Andrewes's characteristic strategy of reviving pre-Reformation themes and images by presenting them afresh as grounded not in a liturgical tradition, but in scripture and the early Church Fathers. His choice and application of scriptural text engages—by clear implication—the pre-Reformation Good Friday practice of adoring the crucifix. But instead of commending meditation upon a physical crucifix (as countless pre-Reformation sermons had done), he metaphorically 'holds up' the verbal, scriptural, image of Christ on the cross. And he demands that his auditory 'regard' it not on his own, or his church's, authority, but rather that of Christ himself, as spoken through the prophet Zechariah.

Significantly, the court Good Friday sermon was returned to Thomas Dove from 1598 until 1604; perhaps Andrewes's handling of the Passion was too avant-garde. But with the accession of James, he returned to the same themes with a vengeance in court Passion sermons for 1604 and 1605. No three sermons by Andrewes are so similar, to the point of the latter two repeating verbatim many passages from 1597. All three take texts (Zech. 12: 10, Lam. 1: 12, Heb. 12: 2) in which the main verb is 'look upon', and the object of that looking is the crucified Christ. Separately and collectively they deserve much closer study as exemplars of the post-Reformation attempt to convey in words what Catholic art achieved in painted, sculpted, and theatrical art forms.

Theologically, this, like the other Good Friday sermons, contains clear statements by Andrewes on the doctrine of the Atonement (Christ's sacrificial satisfaction for human sin). Broadly speaking, they are rooted in an Anselmian understanding of Christ's satisfaction of God's justice as a judicial exchange of Christ's perfect life for sin. However, Andrewes emphatically restates the characteristically Protestant understanding of this formula in which Christ not only offers a perfect satisfaction (Anselm's view), but also suffers painful punishment. This view, usually described as 'penal substitution', can be found in Luther as well as Calvin, but Andrewes seems much closer in spirit and diction to Luther, who (like Andrewes here) strives to place God's penal justice in the context of love, not just wrath. Penal substitution theory has at its heart the language of sacrifice, which Andrewes relishes here. However, he does not (like most contemporary Protestants) separate Christ's atoning sacrifice from the eucharistic sacrifice. On the contrary, the crucified Christ is really present in the Holy Communion that was (unlike in Roman Catholic uses) celebrated on Good Friday. Finally, it must be noted that the very nature of Good Friday emphasizes only one particular aspect of soteriology—Christ's sacrifice—which gives unusual prominence to Anselmian and penal substitution theory here; for important qualifications to these elsewhere in Andrewes, see Further Reading.

Sources. This sermon invites close comparison with Bishop John Fisher's 'A Sermon Preached on Good Friday' (*c.*1520, printed 1578), in Cecilia A. Hatt (ed.), *English Works of John Fisher* (2002). Although there are striking similarities (documented in the notes), the editor is not convinced of direct influence *per se*. Both authors draw from a common inheritance of devotional writings on the crucified Christ, most significantly the sermons of Bernard of Clairvaux. For these, see Fisher, ed. Hatt, pp. 289–99, 324–49; and for the influence of the same sources on late medieval English poetry on the Passion, see Rosemary Woolf, *The English Religious Lyric in the Middle Ages* (1968). Although it is entirely possible that Andrewes knew and used these late medieval sources, it is equally possible that he worked directly with their antecedents in patristic authors. However, insofar as Fisher epitomizes late medieval treatments of the Passion, it is worth noting Andrewes's significant departures from it. These include far less emphasis on penitence and shame as the primary effect of meditating on the cross; and a focus not primarily on the physical, but the spiritual suffering of Christ. Furthermore, Andrewes clearly grafts onto these pre-Reformation sources some of Luther's famous early works, including the 'Meditation of Christ His Passion' (1519), printed in England in *Special and Chosen Sermons of D. Martin Luther* (1578), the 1518 *Duo Sermones de Passione*, and Luther's commentary on Ps. 22 from *Operationes in Psalmos*; Luther's Latin works are cited here from the Weimar *Werke* (1883). Finally, the sermon should be read in the context of several vernacular works written by English Catholics, that, if not direct sources, are part of a particular fashion in the 1590s, even among Protestant readers, for stylistically and emotionally heightened devotional prose and verse on the Passion, including Thomas Lodge's *Prosopopeia Containing the Teares of the Holy, Blessed, and Sanctified Marie, the Mother of God* (1596); and Robert Southwell, SJ, *Epistle of Comfort* (1589) and *St Peters Complaint* (1595).

Further Reading. J. W. Blench, *Preaching in England in the late Fifteenth and Sixteenth Centuries* (1964), 108–12, uses this sermon to exemplify Andrewes's mastery of what he calls the Elizabethan 'modern style' (that is, simply, the full naturalization of the rules of classical orations in the Christian humanist sermon), noting a particularly 'medieval fulness' in the subdivision of the sermon. Lossky, *Lancelot Andrewes*, 171–4, offers brief but insightful commentary. A. B. Chambers, '"Goodfriday, 1613. Riding Westward": Looking Back', *John Donne Journal*, 6 (1987), 185–201, juxtaposes the sermon with Donne's poem to offer an outstanding reading of both; his article is one of the best examples of how Andrewes's sermons can respond to fine literary analysis. Andrewes's other Good Friday court sermons, from 1604 and 1605, are *XCVI*, 349–82. Another version of 1604, preached at St Giles's Cripplegate (n.d.) with some significant variants, is found in *AS*, 639–43. For an introductory overview of Protestant atonement theory, see L. W. Grensted, *A Short History of the Doctrine of the Atonement* (1920), 191–221. For Andrewes's qualifications to Anselmian theory, see Lossky, *Lancelot Andrewes*, 181–6.

p 122, 6. *Respicient... transfixerunt*: not Vulg. ('et aspicient ad me quem confixerunt'), but instead closer to Lat. translations from Hebrew, as Trem. ('respicientque ad me quem transfixerunt'); Andrewes prefers, to the point of tacitly rejecting Vulg., the two verbs (respicere, transfigere) from the latter translation (cf. p. 124–25; pp. 131–32, and nn.).

7. *And they... have pierced*: Geneva and Bishops' Bibles.

9. *a like place*: a similar Christological prophecy.

11. *materiall*: substantive, apt.

17. *to preach* JESUS: Act. 8: 35.

20–21. *Holy Ghost... Passion*: conventional assertion that the Holy Spirit is the author of scripture; thus, the '*Holy Ghost*' offers proof ('warrant') of the last act of the Passion in the account 'reported' in John's gospel (the version appointed for communion on Good Friday, *BCP*).

21. *last act... Passion*: the piercing of Christ's side after his death by a Roman soldier (John 19: 34); in Roman Catholic meditative and iconographic tradition, the last of the Five Wounds of Christ.

26. *Psalme 22*: Andrewes invokes the pre-Reformation liturgical use of Ps. 22 (Vulg., Ps. 21). Its opening words, 'My God, my God, why hast thou forsaken me', are quoted by Christ on the cross (Matt. 27: 46). This is the first of many images shared between Ps. 22 and the Passion accounts in the Gospels which led the earliest commentators ('the ancient Writers'), particularly Augustine and Jerome, to expound it as a prophetic articulation of Christ's sufferings on the cross. This conventional view is summarized in the 'argument' to Ps. 22 in the Bishops' Bible: 'David first in the figure of Christe as one forsaken, cryeth to God the father, utteryng his crosse, affliction, humblenesse, and mockes geven of the people, governours, and priestes.' Many in Andrewes's auditory would also have made a connection between the Psalm's opening phrase in Vulg.—'Deus, Deus meus, *respice* in me'—and the same Latin verb in the sermon's text—'*Respicient* in Me'. Until 1552, Ps. 22 was literally 'the Psalme of the Passion' in England, appointed for Good Friday matins in all major Roman Catholic uses, and then for communion on Good Friday in Cranmer's first prayer book (1549); it was dropped in 1552 and not reinstated. It was also the first of the 'Psalms of the Passion' conventionally found in the *Horæ* or *Primer* of the pre-Reformation church in England (F. Procter and W. H. Frere, *A New History of the Book of Common Prayer* (1961), 20). Andrewes's reintroduction of it into a Good Friday service is a typical example of his nostalgic preference for many aspects of the earlier liturgies.

27. *front . . . this Psalme*: each Ps. has a prefatory title; see next n.

28–30. *Cervo matutino . . . chased*: variants of the title for Ps. 22 (Vulg. 21) were disputed from the earliest Christian times. Translations from the Septuagint (as Vulg.), read 'Pro adsumptione matutina' ('*For the morning enterprise*', Douai-Rheims), while those derived directly from the Hebrew (most English translations) read, 'Victori pro cervo matutino canticum' ('Psalm of victory for the morning hart'; sometimes also 'cerva matituna'). From patristic times, translators were aware of both readings, and applied the title to Christ leaping up (either like the morning itself, or a hart in the morning) in the Resurrection of Easter Sunday (Jerome, *Comment. in Osee*, ch. VI, v. 3; Augustine, *Enarr. in Psalm. XXI*). Less common until the Reformation were readings of the title (in addition to the Psalm itself) as an allegory of the Passion. Luther (*Operationes in Psalmos*), however, was emphatic: 'cervam autem absque dubio Christum passum appellat, quia Judaeis in die carnis suae captus et gentibus ad dilaniandum traditus est, sicut cerva a canibus venaticis capitur et venatoribus traditur excarnificanda' (*Werke*, v. 599); ('without doubt the suffering Christ is called a hart, because in the day his flesh was he was captured by the Jews and handed over to the Gentiles and ripped in pieces, like a hart is caught by hunting dogs and given over to torture'). This is reflected in the Bishops' Bible, 'To the chiefe musition of the mornyng hinde, a Psalme of David', glossed, 'David likeneth him selfe beyng in persecution to a hinde hunted with dogges in the mornyng'. Calvin (*In Librum Psalmorum*, 1557) avoids the issue entirely: 'haec inscriptio obscura est' (p. 94). Andrewes repeats ll. 28–31 almost verbatim in Good Friday 1605 (*XCVI*, 372).

p. 123, 6–7. *fore-part . . . respicient, &c*: Zech. 12: 10 in full reads: 'And I wil powre upon the house of David, and upon the inhabitants of Jerusalem the spirit of grace and of supplications, and they shall looke upon me whom they have pierced, and they shal mourne for him, as one mourneth for his onely sonne, and shall be in bitternesse for him, as one that is in bitternesse for his first borne'.

9. *Prophet . . . Apostle*: Zechariah and Paul, respectively.

10 ἀφορᾶν: Gr., 'aphŏran', 'to look'; fr. Heb. 12: 2, 'Looking vnto [ἀφορῶντες] Jesus the authour and finisher of our faith' (Andrewes's text for Good Friday 1605; *XCVI*, 365-82).

13. *spectacle*: 'a person... set before the public gaze as an object either of... contempt or... admiration' (OED *sn¹* 2.a & b); but cf. the use of the word later (p. 199, l. 12) to mean 'entertainment'; both are grounded in Andrewes's punning awareness of the etymological link between the text's main verb *respicere* ('to regard') and *specere* ('to behold'), the root of *spectaculum* ('spectacle').

15. *some time... unto it*: cf. Luther, 'Meditation', 'if one should... meditate rightly upon the passion of Christ, by the space of one day, or of one hower, yea on the space of a quarter of an hower, we should faithfully pronounce of him, that he hath done better, then if he had pined him selfe with fasting the space of a whole yeare' (p. 71).

16. *this very day*: Good Friday.

19. *Respicientes in Eum*: 'looking upon him'.

20-26. *lift up... before us*: the series of biblical allusions in this passage allows Andrewes a daring, but safe, flirtation with something close to what most Elizabethan Protestants would baulk at as adoration of the sacrament. Although the marginal note cites Christ's likening of himself to the brazen serpent raised up on a cross by Moses in the Wilderness (John 3: 14), Andrewes in fact adapts the corresponding OT passage (Num. 21: 8) which promises that physical beholding of the object on the cross brings salvation (*'that we may look upon Him and live'*). The New Testament application mentions only belief in, not looking upon, the crucified Christ for salvation (cf. also p. 129, ll. 21-26, and p. 133, ll. 13-17; repeated on Good Friday 1604, *XCVI*, 363). Andrewes is therefore also very careful to acknowledge the orthodox Protestant formula of reading scripture and preaching as valid means to 'look upon' Christ, but, unusually for the time, he adds as the final—and by implication, most important and neglected—means, which is beholding the *'holy Sacrament'* in which the Passion is 'so effectually represented before us'. Astutely, however, Andrewes's insistence on the heightened significance of communion on Good Friday ('if at any time, at this time to take place') could also be simultaneously interpreted as good Reformed practice. Mass was not celebrated on Good Friday in the Roman Catholic church; the priests instead received the reserved sacrament consecrated on Maundy Thursday. To avoid the idolatry perceived in the reservation of the sacrament, and to insist on the commemorative nature of the eucharist, Cranmer's prayer books enjoined the celebration of Holy Communion on Good Friday, as seems to have occurred immediately after this sermon (p. 134).

30. *Quem transfixerunt*: 'whom they have pierced'.

31. *Respicient in Eum*: 'they shall look upon him'.

36. *Saint John... that point*: John 19: 37 (cf. p. 122, ll. 20-24).

p. 123, 36-p. 124, 1. *Zacharie (here)... repeated it*: conventional assertion that Old Testament prophets (here, Zechariah, Daniel) had mystical knowledge of Christ as the fulfilment of their prophecies; cf. Andrewes, sermon for Easter 1610, 'the *faith* of this *Feast*, so ancient... began not with the *Christians*; the *Patriarchs* had it, as many hundred yeares before CHRIST, as we are after' (*XCVI*, 424).

3. *stile*: style; 'legal, official, or honorific title' (*OED sn* II.18.a).

8. *Occidetur*: Lat., lit., 'he shall fall', but usually 'be slain' or 'violently killed'.

28. *(as... after appeare)*: cf. pp. 135-36.

33. *Respicient... transfixus est*: 'look upon Him who is pierced'.

37. *in the handling*: in the interpretation of the text.

39–40. *transfixerunt... gradation*: 'gradation', literally defined as a gradual process through something, describes '*transfixerunt*' ('they have pierced through'), but also puns on the rhetorical trope *gradatio*, or 'climax', wherein the last word of one clause becomes the first in the next, two complex examples of which follow (see next nn.).

40. *fixerunt... confixerunt*: a *gradatio* (see prev. n.) of Lat. past participles proceeding from the root verb *figere* ('*fixerunt*', 'they have fixed'), through the derivatives '*suffixerunt*' ('they have fixed up, fastened'), and '*confixerunt*' ('they have fastened together'), all shown to be inferior to the climactic '*transfixerunt*' (l. 39); '*confixerunt*' is the Vulg. reading (see n. to p. 122, l. 6).

p. 125, 1–4. *Not, the whipps... his heart*: another more elaborate *gradatio* (see prev. nn), here through the Instruments and Five Wounds of the Passion to arrive at the climax of the spear and heart-piercing.

5. *trans... transcendent*: punning climax of the entire paragraph's rhetorical *gradatio*; the prefix '*trans*' ('through') most perfectly conveys the root sense of '*fixerunt*' ('shall pierce'); hence it is 'a *transcendent*', in Tomistic philosophy, an abstract quality of goodness, being, or unity that surpasses any of the Aristotelian ethical categories (*OED sa* B.1.a).

9. *his... divers parts*: 'its generality out of diverse parts'; i.e. is the sum of distinct parts.

12. *quicke*: living, alive.

24. *anima compatientis... at rebound*. Andrewes refines the distinction between Mary's suffering and Christ's by playing on the common etymological root of the English words 'passion', 'compassion', and 'patience' in the Latin noun *passio* ('suffering'), and its adjectival form *patiens*: Mary's was a 'compassionate soul', that is, her soul ('*anima*') was suffering (*-patientis*) in sympathy with (*com-*) Christ; his soul ('*anima*') was suffering ('*patientis*') alone. Mary's '*Compassion*', then is at one remove or '*rebound*' (grammatically and essentially) from Christ's. One further layer of wit here is that the English name for the rhetorical trope *antanaclasis*—the repetition of the same or similar words in different senses (cf. 'passion', 'compassion')—is 'rebound' (George Puttenham, *The Arte of English Poesie* (1589), 216–17).

26. *temper*: degree of hardness and flexibility in forged metal (usually applied to swords).

26. *dint*: stroke or blow of a weapon.

32. *The Apostle*: Paul.

33. *The Prophet*: David.

37. *all foure Evangelists*: Matthew, Mark, Luke, John; authors of the Gospels.

p. 126, 11. *Derelinqui à Deo*: 'forsaken by God'; cf. Matt. 27: 46.

14–17. *though not that... dangerous to define*: this cryptic aside seems to stress Christ's human suffering to the point of including in it a spiritual suffering so acute as to have approached despair, or even cursing God for forsaking him on the cross (Ps. 22: 1, Matt. 27: 46; see p. 185, l. 22 and n.). Andrewes of course rejects the latter possibility as 'blasphemy', but registers unease with any understanding of the Passion which diminishes its fully human suffering, both physical and spiritual, or which chooses to emphasize its physical pain at the expense of the moral pain of the world with which Christ was also afflicted; cf. Geneva gloss on Matt. 27: 46, 'this crying out is proper to his humanitie, which notwithstanding was voyde of sinne, but yet it felt the wrath of God, which is due to our sinnes'. Andrewes's anxiety about 'blasphemy' may reflect Luther's extensive consideration of the same (*Operationes in Psalmos*, Ps. 22: 2), which concludes, 'quod in nobis murmur et blasphemia est, in Christo per omnia simile' (Luther, *Werke*, v. 601–6); ('that which in us is murmuring and blasphemy, in Christ is all by way of comparison')—that is, it is only like blasphemy, because though Christ felt the human pains of dereliction, his divine nature was incapable of any sin that in natural men would be prompted by it. Andrewes returned to the idea in his sermon for Good Friday 1604 when considering Christ's agony in Gethsemane—'that houre, what his feelings were, it is dangerous to define: we know them not, we may be too bold to determine of them'—and commended the petition from the Greek liturgy for Good Friday, '*By thine unknowne Sorrowe and sufferings, felt by thee but not distinctly knowen by us, have mercie upon us and save us*' (*XCVI*, 354).

18. *despight*: despite; both feelings and acts of contempt, scorn.

22. *contumelious*: disgraceful, spiteful.

23. *pitch*: height, extreme.

28. *Eli, Eli &c*: Matt. 27: 46 and Mark 15: 34 record Christ's quotation of Ps. 22: 1 on the cross in Greek transliterations of the original in Hebrew and Aramaic (respectively); the bilingualism is preserved in subsequent translations; cf. Geneva, 'Jesus cryed with a loud voyce, saying, Eli, Eli, lama sabachthani? that is, My God, my God, why hast thou forsaken me?' (Matt. 27: 46).

35–36. *as they were*: as if they were.

p. 127, 7. *passioned*: *OED* (*sv* 2.) cites this as the last example of the verb in its obsolete sense 'afflicted'; but cf. Prospero to Ariel, 'Hast thou, which art but air, a touch, a feeling | Of their afflictions, and shall not myself, | One of their kind, that relish all as sharply | Passion as they, be kindlier moved than thou art?' (Shakespeare, *Tempest*, V. i. 21–3).

9. *Of the Persons*: the main arguments and images of pp. 127–28 are recapitulated, frequently verbatim, in Good Friday, 1604 (*XCVI*, 359).

9. *implied in the word*: third person plural subject 'they' is contained ('implied') within the Lat. verb '*transfixerunt*'.

14–17. *Souldiers... Pilate... Jewes*: Andrewes criticizes the casual blame of historical parties, especially the Jews, for the Passion, a popular and conventional characteristic of late medieval and early modern Christianity. Cf. the collects for Good Friday which assert believers' benefits from, but not guilt for, the crucifixion, and specifically petition for the conversion of 'all Jewes, Turkes, Infidels, and heretikes' (*BCP*); cf. also the Geneva gloss to Acts 2: 23: 'the fact [deed; the crucifixion] is sayde to bee theirs, by whose counsell and egging forwarde it is done'. Lossky (*Lancelot Andrewes*, 172–4) describes Andrewes here as unusual in his anticipation by hundreds of years of a modern concern over anti-Semitism in commemoration of the Passion. However, this was a unique hallmark of Luther's early writings, as in the opening argument of his 'Meditation': 'First, some doe so thinke upon the passion of Christ, that they are incensed with anger against the Jewes... and thus they are content, and thinke this to be sufficient' (p. 67); cf. also p. 128, ll. 22–27 and nn.

18. *Quest of Inquirie*: inquest; judicial investigation.

19. *inditeth*: indicts; accuses.

20. *by very construction*: by the grammatical construction itself (cf. l. 9 and n.).

30. *the Twelve men*: the jury.

37–38. *Quis ex... peccato?*: Vulg., John 8: 46 ('Which of you can rebuke me of sinne?', Geneva).

p. 128, 9. *stept between... the blow*: this is a striking summary of penal substitution theory (see Headnote). Andrewes repeats the claim almost verbatim on Good Friday 1604: 'it is we, that... should have been smitten with these sorrowes by the fierce *wrath* of GOD, had not he stept between the blow and us, and latched it in his owne body and soule, even the dint of the fiercenesse of the *wrath of* GOD' (*XCVI*, 359). The image is possibly derived from Ps. 106: 23, 'Therefore he minded to destroy them, had not Moses his chosen stand in the breach before him to turne away his wrath, least he shoulde destroy them'; cf. Bonaventure, *The Mystical Vine* (trans. anon., London, 1955), who applies the verse to Christ: 'Our Mediator "stood in the breach" before the Father to "turn away his wrath lest he should destroy us"' (p. 30). The specific imagery of 'the blow' does not seem to have entered English theological writings until Andrewes's use of it here, but can be found in Luther: 'ictus Dominus patitur' ('the Lord suffered the blow'; 'In Passione II', *Werke*, i. 341). Cf. Francis Meres, *Wits Common Wealth: The Second Part* (1634), 'hide our head, which is Christ, that taking the blowes vpon vs, wee may safegard the faith' (p. 172); Thomas Manton, *Sermons* (1693), 'Justice would have reached forth a deadly stroke to us, but Christ catched the blow' (p. 1154; also pp. 126, 651, 1013); and Robert South, *Twelve Sermons* (1698), 'when the Justice of God was lifting up the Sword of Vengeance over our Heads, Christ snatch'd us away from the blow, and substituted his Own Body in our room, to receive the whole stroke of that dreadful Retribution' (p. 489).

11–13. *polluted... pierced his heart*: elaborate parallel construction that counterpoints the traditional iconography of Christ's Five Wounds or *Arma Christi* (nailed hands and feet, thorn-crowned head, pierced side) with corresponding biblical and prayer-book phrases for the human sin that was their cause: 'Him... you have taken, with wicked handes you have crucified and slaine' (Acts 2: 23); 'Their feete are swifte to shead blood' (Rom. 3: 15); 'We have followed too much the devices and desires of our own hearts' (General Confession, Morning and Evening Prayer, *BCP*); cf. Luther, 'Meditiation', 'wherefore when thou considerest that his handes were pearsed with nayles, thinke that it was thy worke: when thou remembrest his crowne of thornes, perswade thy selfe that it was thy wicked cogitations, which caused it, &c.' (p. 69).

24. *we, are the cause thereof*: cf. Fisher, 'Sermon', 'Thy sinne was the cause of his death. Thy sinne gave him his deathes wound' (*English Works*, 309); and Luther, 'Meditation', 'resolve deepely in thy minde, and dout not a whit, that thou art he which so tormented Christ, forasmuch as thy sinnes were most certainly the cause thereof' (pp. 68–9).

25–26. *the Jewes... onely accessaries*: cf. Luther, 'Meditation', 'for albeit the wicked Jewes be now judged of God and dispersed, yet were they Ministers of thy transgressions, and thou for a certainty art he, which with thy sinnes hast crucified and slayne the sonne of God' (p. 70); cf. also p. 122, ll. 14–17 and n.

30. *bowells*: in premodern physiology, the interior of the body or viscera, thought to be the seat of the tender emotions, in particular, of mercy; cf. Andrewes, Gunpowder Anniversary sermon, 1612, 'of all parts, the *bowells* melt, relent, yeeld, yerne soonest. Consequently, the *mercies* from them, of all other, the most tender.... because they are not drie, but full of affection, and come cheerfully' (*XCVI*, 929–30).

36–37. *Quia non... est*: 'because not to look is to despise'.

p. 129, 5. *lay drawing on*: lay dying; cf. William Perkins, *Golden Chaine* (1600), 'the thiefe... was now dying and drawing on' (p. 785).

5–7. *Priest and Levite... looked on*: cf. Fisher, 'Sermon', 'If thou saw... thyne enimie thus mangled and wounded, it might styrre thee to take compassion upon him! If thou sawe any Jew or Sarazin thus tormented, it might move thee to pittie!' (*English Works*, 309).

14. *Yea* CHRIST... *inviteth us*: cf. Bernard, *In Cant. Cantic.* Serm. LXI, 7, 'Vult ergo videri, vult benignus dux devoti militis vultum et oculos in sua sustolli vulnera, ut illius ex hoc animum erigat, et exemplo sui reddat ad tolerandum fortiorem' (*PL*, 183.1074B); 'What He desires then, is to be seen; the Leader full of kindness and bounty desires that the countenance and the eyes of His devoted soldier should be fixed upon His wounds, to draw from them strength and encouragement, and to render him stronger to endure his sufferings, through the power of his example' (*Works*, trans. S. J. Eales (1896), iii. 370).

16–20. *ancient Writers... fierce wrath*: cf. Bernard, *Feria IV Hebd. Sanct. Sermo*, 11, 'De dolore vide quid dixerit: O vos omnes qui transitis per viam, attendite, et videte si est dolor sicut dolor meus' (*PL*, 183.268D); ('Of sorrow, see what He said, "O all you who pass by the way, behold and see if there is any sorrow like my sorrow"'); conventional also in late medieval writing; cf. Fisher, 'Sermon', 'thou maist here take matter inough of sorrow, for here our saviour pitiously cryeth and complayneth of his great sorrowes, saying, *O vos omnes*...' (p. 308); Andrewes took this verse as his text for his Good Friday sermon, 1604 (*XCVI*, 349–64).

27–33. *our danger... his request*: Last Judgement, 'the time' when God will look upon the unrepentant sinner and not heed any appeal to look instead upon the atoning Christ (*'respicere in Eum'*; 'to look upon Him'); also a characteristic inference for Andrewes, contrary to dominant Calvinist orthodoxy, that salvation or damnation is a choice that rests with the believer, not predestination by God; the image and argument is expanded in the sermon's peroration (pp. 135–36).

36. *iteration*: repetition.

37. *re-aspicient*: Lat., 'look again', showing the verb *respicere*'s formation from the root *aspicere* (to behold), plus the prefix *re-* ('back' or 'again').

38–39. *per actum elicitum... the Schoolmen*: Lat., 'by an elicited act', i.e. by an act of choice or will; a common category in Thomistic ('the Schoolmen') moral theology; cf. Aquinas, (*Summa* 1a 2æ.71, 6), 'A human act (*actus*) is human because it is voluntary, whether it is internal, e.g. to will or to choose (*a voluntate elicitus*); or external, e.g. to speak or to act'.

39–40. *Originall... facient se respicere*: in the Hebrew '*Originall*', 'hibitu', translated here into Lat., 'they shall make themselves to look' (*'facient se respicere'*), hence the verb form itself (a '*commending Conjugation*') stresses volition or causation on the part of the beholder; Andrewes seems to understand the Hebrew verb as the 'Hiphil', or causative active form; however, in the modern understanding of the text it is a simple active ('look into'); yet, Andrewes may have understood the immediately preceding conjunction 'waw' ('and') as a sign of a causative; in sum, the grammatical argument fits Andrewes's interpretative design, but is not accurate in light of modern biblical scholarship.

p. 130, 5–6. *as Pilate... Ecce Homo*: Pilate presented Christ to the mob saying, 'Behold the man' (*'Ecce Homo'*; John 19: 5); the Latin phrase was also used iconographically for paintings of the suffering Christ depicted alone immediately before the crucifixion.

7. *unreasonable creature*: an animal.

11–12. *those that be innocent... spectacle*: restated verbatim Good Friday 1604 (*XCVI*, 356–7).

12–14. *the Verse... Spirit of grace*: cf. p. 123, ll. 4–8, p. 129, ll. 16–20 and nn.

16–17. *the Centurion... SONNE of GOD*: cf. Fisher, 'Sermon', 'doubtlesse O thou christian soule, he that hunge for thy sake on the crosse, was verelie the sonne of God, as the noble Centurio[n] sayde' (p. 302).

24. *Onely begotten... High GOD*: composite of two common scriptural epithets for Jesus; cf. John 3: 16, Mark 5: 7.

25–26. *S. Augustine... amaritudo tanta!*: 'O the bitterness of my sins, for the taking away of which such a bitterness was necessary'; not Augustine, but cf. Bernard of Clairvaux, *In Dominica Palmarum*, Serm. I, 4., 'Væ tibi, amaritudo peccatorum nostrorum, propter quæ solvenda, tanta amaritudo necessaria est' (*PL*, 183.258A); ('Woe be to you that your sin is of such bitterness that it required such a bitterness to discharge it').

29–31. *looke in Eum... tender love*: cf. Luther, 'Meditation', 'but rather so by pearsing inwardly and contemplating his most loving hart, with how great love towards thee it is replenished, which brought him hereunto' (p. 72).

35. *Ego sum*: Vulg., John 18: 6 ('I am he').

36–38. *lay downe... for his friends*: cf. Fisher, 'Sermon', 'there can no more bee asked of any man then that.... No man can shewe greater charitie, then for to put hys owne life in jeopardie for his friendes' (p. 311).

36. *lay downe His life for us sinners*: cf. 1 Tim. 1: 15; Luke 5: 32.

p. 131, 6. *iteratis vicibus*: Lat., 'repeating by turns', 'over and over'.

11. *enured*: inured; accustomed to, through repetition, habit.

21–22. *which immediatly followeth... plange*: Zacc. 12: 10 (Vulg.) continues, 'et plangent eum planctu quasi super unigenitum' ('and they shall lament for him, as one mourneth for his onely sonne', Geneva); hence Andrewes's adapted imperative, '*Respice & plange*' ('look and lament').

26. *Respice & transfigere*: 'look and be pierced [lit., transfixed]'.

34. *Civill*: public; here, as at a state funeral (see next n.).

34–35. *a lamentation... for Josias*: Josiah, pious boy-king of Judah, killed in battle against the Egyptians, and buried with great pomp at Jerusalem (2 Chron. 35: 23–5); in Good Friday 1604 Andrewes treats this in slightly more detail, quoting much from these lines verbatim (*XCVI*, 357).

35. *Behold... JOSIAS is heere*: cf. Matt. 12: 41.

37. *without any fault of theirs*: Josiah ignored an embassage from the Egyptian pharaoh protesting that Josiah was not the enemy he sought; since Josiah attacked nonetheless, his death was not '*any fault of theirs* [the Egyptians]' (2 Chron. 35: 10–22).

38. *massacred*: mutilated, mangled (*OED sv* 3.); cf. the lamenting Virgin Mary in Lodge, *Prosopopeia*, 'What soul so sensles, that beholding a prince in his owne kingdome, amongst his owne subiects, massacred by his owne sonne, wil not grieue at it' (sigs. F2^{r-v}); and Southwell, *Marie Magdalens Funeral Teares* (1591), 'the Lord of the world, is thus darkened, massacred, and outragiously missused' (p. 22^v).

38–39. *for... our transgressions*: Isa. 53: 5.

p. 131, 39–p. 132, 1. *the dumbe... SONNE of GOD*: in the Gospel accounts, the inanimate parts of creation ('senselesse creatures') acknowledged the hideousness of the Passion: the sun was eclipsed (Matt. 27: 45), and 'the earth did quake, and the rocks rent' (Matt. 27: 51). Cf. Fisher, 'Sermon', 'But whereunto speake I of reasonable creatures, the unreasonable, and the unsensible creatures shewed a maner of sorrowe. The earth quaked. The mighty stones brast in sunder' (p. 309); and Donne, 'Good-friday, 1613. Riding Westward', 'It made his owne Lieutenant Nature shrinke, | It made his footstoole crack, and the Sunne winke' (ll. 19–20). Cf. also Andrewes, Good Friday 1604, 'all the *Creatures* in heaven and earth, seemed to hear this his mournfull *Complaint*, and in their kind, to shew their *regard* of it.... Shall the *Creature*, and not we?' (*XCVI*, 362).

1–2. *And we ... like effect*: cf. Luke 19: 40.

12. *a wreake*: 'an instance of taking vengeance or exacting retribution' (*OED sn* 2., citing this as the last example of the usage).

14. *mortifying or crucifying*: Pauline metaphors for 'killing' sinfulness; cf. Col. 3: 5; Gal. 5: 24.

18–19. *Respice, ne ... peccatum*: Lat., 'look, [so that] you may not look: Look upon Christ, [so that] you may not look upon sin'.

22. *what in us lieth*: 'what in us we are always potentially capable of'.

24. *list not wound sinne*: 'would rather not wound sin'.

30. *hable*: able.

33–35. *as the Fathers ... not forget us*: such patristic commentary on Isa. 49: 16 is in fact scarce; the source is Peter of Blois (Petrus Blesensis), *De Duodecim Utilitatibus Tribulationis* (*PL*, 207.996B), 'Unde ipse dicit: Non obliviscar tui; in manibus meis descripsi te, quando scilicet expandi in cruce pro amore tuo' ('wherefore he [Christ] himself says, I shall not forget you; you are written in my hands, since certainly they were stretched out upon the cross for the love of you'); Andrewes's copy of Blesensis, *Insignia Opera* (Paris, 1519), now lost, was left to PCCL (*LACT*, vol. xi, p. cxiv).

35–36. *the print ... Capitall letters*: cf. Fisher, 'Sermon', 'with this most precious blud was illumined the fyve greate Capital letters in this wonderful booke. I meane by these capital letters the great wounds of his body, in his handes, and in hys feete, and in his side' (p. 304).

36–37. C*HRIST pierced ... booke of love*: for the late medieval tradition of the crucified Christ as a book, see Headnote. Cf. Fisher, 'Sermon', 'I saye that a booke hath two boardes: the two boardes of this booke is the two partes of the crosse, for when the booke is opened and spread, the leaves be cowched upon the boardes. And so the blessid body of Christ was spred upon the crosse' (p. 303). Ultimately, the 'Christ as book' image derives from Rev. 5: 1 (Woolf, *English Religious Lyric*, 253 n. 2). Andrewes's 1605 repetition of it ('being spread and laid wide open on the *Crosse*, He is *Liber charitatis*', *XCVI*, sig. 2M 4^v) is marginally glossed as Hab. 2: 2 ('And the Lorde answered me, and sayde, Write the vision, and make it plaine vpon tables, that he may that readeth it'). The more specific conceit of Christ as a book 'of love' ('*liber charitatis*') is neither Patristic nor used by Fisher. But Luther (*In Passione II*) fulsomely treats Christ's wounds as 'full, clear, living letters and signs' ('satis claris, vivis, expressis litteris et signis') that are legible as love: 'quid significet sanguis inter flagella, spinas et clavos? summam caritatem' ('what does the blood from the whips, thorns and nails represent? the highest love') (*Werke*, i. 341). Cf. also Lodge, *Prosopopeia*, 'all these [wounds] are but stripes to stir you to love God ... books in which you reade his wisdome' (sig. B8^r).

38–39. *Quia Clavus ... vulnera*: Lat., 'because the piercing nail is to us an opening key that allows us [to see, to enter] his bowels through his wounds'; adaptation of Bernard of Clairvaux, *Serm. in Cant.*, Serm. LXI, 4., 'At clavis reserans, clavus penetrans factus est mihi, ut videam voluntatem Domini. Quidni videam per foramen? Clamat clavus, clamat vulnus, quod vere Deus sit in Christo mundum reconcilians sibi.

Ferrum pertransiit animam ejus, et appropinquavit cor illius, ut non jam non sciat compati infirmitatibus meis. Patet arcanum cordis per foramina corporis; patet magnum illud pietatis sacramentum, patent viscera misericordiae Dei nostri, in quibus visitavit nos oriens ex alto' (*PL*, 183.1072C–D); 'But the nails wherewith He was pierced have become for me, as it were, master keys, to open for me the treasury of the Lord's will. How can I do otherwise than see with clear vision through a cleft so broad? The nails cry aloud, that God was in Christ, reconciling the world unto Himself. The sword passed through his soul, and came near to His Heart, that He might so learn to have a fellow feeling with our infirmities. Through the clefts of His Body the secret of His Heart is laid open, and that great mystery of goodness, the lovingkindness and mercy of our God, in which the Dayspring from on high hath visited us, is manifested to our thankful gaze' (*Works*, iii. 368); cf. Woolf, *English Religious Lyric*, 'a parallel is often made between the love-wounded heart and the lance-wounded heart. In this tradition, Christ's wounded heart is a symbol and proof of His love' (p. 186); Andrewes repeats this Bernardine exemplum in Good Friday 1605 (*XCVI*, 363).

p. 133, 3. *Ecce... dilexit Eum*: 'behold how much he loved him'; cf. Vulg. John 11: 36 ('Ecce quomodo amabat eum').

5. *Ecce quomodo dilexit nos*: 'behold how much he loved us'; see prev. n.

5. *Water and Blood*: John 19: 34.

17. *Respice & crede*: Lat., 'look and believe'.

29. *Respice & Spera*: Lat., 'look and hope'.

33. *primitive felicitie*: original happiness (before the Fall).

33–36. *By the death... power of darknesse*: John and Paul explicitly equate Christ with the Passover lamb (John 1: 29; 1 Cor. 5: 7–8); the Israelites were freed from Egyptian slavery by their Passover (Exod. 12–13); typologically ('spiritually'), the Christian is freed from slavery to sin by Christ's Passion.

37. *death of the High Priest*: Andrewes adds to Christ's role as sacrificial victim that of sacrificing priest, thus completing the NT's most important symbolic economies of the salvation worked by the Passion: just as Christ the 'undefiled *Lambe*' has its type in the OT Passover lamb, Christ as 'Great High Priest' (Heb. 4: 14) fulfils another type, the OT Levitical priesthood; Christ as the consummation of both priest and victim is discussed extensively by Paul in Hebrews, on which Andrewes draws heavily here; Heb. 10: 1–25, with its attention to Christ as victim, was the Epistle appointed for communion on Good Friday (*BCP*).

p. 134, 8–10. *Augustine... blood*: Augustine, *In Joann. Evang. Tract. CXX*, 2, 'Vigilanti verbo Evangelista usus est, ut non diceret, Latus ejus percussit, aut vulneravit, aut quid aliud; sed, aperuit: ut illic quodammodo vitae ostium panderetur, unde Sacramenta Ecclesiae manaverunt' (*PL*, 35.1953); ('the Evangelist is careful using this word, so as not to say, his side was struck, or wounded, or anything else; but opened: by which means the door of life was thrown open, out of which the sacraments of the church flowed'); Andrewes makes an uncharacteristic error in confusing the Evangelist (John) with the Apostle (Paul).

10. *Respice & Recipe*: Lat., 'look and receive'.

12–13. *first words... Chapter*: Zech. 13: 1; the text itself does not connect the fountain prophesied here with the 'side of him whom they have pierced' (12: 10): 'In that day there shalbe a fountaine opened to the house of David... for sinne, and for uncleannesse'.

15–18. *Baptisme ... Body and Blood*: patristic and Roman Catholic commentaries are much closer to Andrewes's explicit glossing of the water and blood as the sacraments of eucharist and baptism. Augustine repeatedly interprets the event as the institution of the church and its sacraments (cf. ll. 8–10 and n.; also *In Joann. Evang. Tract. CXX*, 2; *Serm. de Temp. CCXVIII*, 14; and *Serm. de Script. V*, 3). The Rheims-Douai side-note to John 19: 34 is similarly explicit: 'And both bloud and water apart did flow forth, to shew us the fountaine of the two principal Sacraments ... Baptisme and the Eucharist, springing to life in the Church'. Geneva, however, glosses only a general purification by water and blood: 'Christ being dead upon the crosse, witnesseth by a double signe, that he onely is the true satisfaction, and the true washing for the beleevers'.

18–19. *we ... this day*: Holy Communion would have been celebrated immediately following Andrewes's sermon.

22. *suffer ... in vaine*: glimpse of the 'come and go' informality of worshippers attending different parts of services in early modern England, and of Andrewes's habitual criticism of worshippers who privileged sermon-going over public prayers and communion, even in the chapel royal; cf. the 'exhortation at certain times when the curate shall see the people negligent to come to the Holy Communion' (*BCP*); and 'Pattern of Catechistical Doctrine' (this edn.), pp. 27–28.

30. *Respice & Retribue*: Lat., 'look and render (give back)'.

31. *Quid retribuam*: Vulg., Ps. 115: 12, 'quid retribuam Domino pro omnibus quae retribuit mihi' ('What shal I render to our Lord, for al thinges that he hath rendred to me?, Douai-Rheims, Ps. 115: 3).

32–33. *others desired to see*: Matt. 13: 17.

34–35. *the Samaritan ... His goodnesse*: Luke 17: 15–16.

p. 135, 8. *respects*: deliberately multivalent, including the senses 'regard, consideration', 'discrimination, partiality, or favour in regard of persons or things', and 'heed, care, attention' (*OED sn* III.13.a, b, and c); but primarily a characteristic use by Andrewes of a verb as a concretized plural substantive—'*lookings*'.

9. *reflexed*: 'directed backwards' (*OED sppla* 2; the earliest cited usage of this sense is 1656); perhaps also with the sense of 'reflected, thrown back; due to, or caused by, reflection' (*OED sppla* 1), applied metaphorically to the believer's mind; cf. *The Problemes of Aristotle* (1595), 'why is it ... the hardest thing of all to know a mans selfe? ... is this because it cannot be done but by a reflexed action? And to reflect and looke vnto himselfe, is a token that we are separated from the flesh' (sig. G5^r).

10. *facient se respicere*: see p. 129, ll. 39–40 and n.

12. *to flesh ... heavy spectacle*: cf. Andrewes, Good Friday 1604, 'it should have our deepest consideration.... But if that cannot be had, (our nature is so heavy, and flesh & bloud so dull of apprehension in Spirituall things) yet at least wise, *some regard*' (*XCVI*, 363).

15. *to turne*: to translate.

18. *looke, ... looke upon it*: 'see to it, that they look upon it'.

19–22. *strange spectacle ... vanities*: 'public display forming an entertainment for those viewing it' (*OED sn* I.1); here, probably paying to attend public theatre or bloodsports, or court pageants and masques (contrast p. 123, l. 13 and n.).

27. *violenti rapiunt illud*: Vulg., Matt. 11: 12 ('and the violent take it by force', Geneva).

28. *Actum elicitum*: see p. 129, ll. 38–39 and n.

30. *facias, or fac facias*: Lat., 'you may do it, or make it be done'.

p. 136, 3–5. *Behold... Gentes terræ*: free reconstruction, from Geneva and the Vulg., not only of Rev. 1: 7 (in marg.), but also Matt. 24: 30—'et tunc parebit signum Filii hominis in caelo et tunc plangent omnes tribus terrae et videbunt Filium hominis venientum in nubibus caeli cum virtute multa et maiestate' ('And then shall appear the signe of man in heaven: and then shall all the Tribes of the earth mourne, and they shall see the sonne of man comming in the clouds of heaven, with power and glory')—and perhaps Gen. 22: 18—'et benedicentur in semine tuo omnes gentes terrae' ('and in thy seed shall all the nations of the earth be blessed').

10. *place and time shall be*: Last Judgement, when all will '*looke upon*' Christ as Judge (cf. p. 129, ll. 27–33 and n.); cf. also Southwell, *Epistle of Comfort*, 'O howe terrible will these woundes of Christe be, to the Sinagoge, when that shall be veryfyed in the daye of dome, *videbunt in quem transfixerunt*? They shall looke on him whom they haue persed?' (p. 193^v).

15. *awhit*: 'written together for *a whit* in 16–17th c.' (*OED*); a bit, at all.

15–16. *Respicientes... despiciet*: Lat., 'he shall look upon [those who] have looked upon [him], & look away from [those who] have looked away from him'.

27. *Donec totus... in cruce*: cf. Pseudo-Bernard, *Vitis Mystica* (*PL* 184.704B), 'Totus vobis figatur in corde, qui pro vobis totus fixus est in cruce' ('Let him be wholly fixed in your heart, who was for you wholly fixed on the cross'); itself a quotation of Augustine, *De Sancta Virginitate*. lv.56 (*PL* 40.428); quoted again by Andrewes, Good Friday 1605 (*XCVI*, 362); (sig. C5^v).

28. *saltem*: Lat., 'at least'.

30–33. PETER... *wept bitterly*: Luke 22: 61–2; cf. Southwell's devotion of 20 stanzas of apostrophe to Christ's convicting, but forgiving, eyes in *Saint Peters Complaint* (1595), which concludes, 'But O, how long demurre I on his eies, | Whose looke did pearce my heart with healing wound: | Launching impostumde [i.e., "lancing infected"] sore of perjurde lies, | Which these two issues of mine eyes hath found' (pp. 11–15).

p. 136, 39–**p. 137**, 2. *thy name... a Saviour*: see 'A Sermon Preached... the V. of November' (this edn.), p. 160, ll. 1–3 and n.; cf. Lodge's use of the same in the context of the Passion, 'looke on his name, it is wonderfull: (*Jesus*) by interpretation, a saviour' (*Prosopopeia*, sig. E4^v).

9. *compunction*: remorse; but punning on the Latin root *compungere*, to prick or puncture (i.e. the heart).

10–12. *pricked... warme within us?*: cf. Andrewes, Good Friday 1604, 'stay and see, whether he will *regard* us or no. Sure he will, and we shall feele our *hearts pricked* with sorrow, by consideration of the *cause in us*, our *Sinne*: And againe, *warme* within us, by consideration of the *cause in him*, his *Love*' (*XCVI*, 363).

17. *Nemo scit*: Lat., 'no one knows'; resonant NT phrase applied to both the unknowable time of Christ's Second Coming in judgement (Matt. 24: 36, Mark 13: 32), and the inscrutability of Christ's person to the unfaithful (Luke 10: 22, John 7: 27, 1 Cor. 2: 11); here gathering this sermon's stress on the need to look upon Christ and know him in this life, before meeting him in the next as a then unknown and terrible judge.

A SERMON ON ISAIAH 6.6–7 PREACHED AT ST. GILES' CRIPPLEGATE, 1 OCTOBER 1598

Text. *AS*, 515–22 (for this folio, see textual note to 'A Lecture on... the Creation of Eve'). Although its brevity (when compared to authorially prepared texts) is clear evidence that this sermon is a summary, scrutiny of its outline reveals a complete structure consistent with Andrewes's usual practice. Furthermore, as the annotations document, the diction is indisputably Andrewes's own, as are many of the arguments and examples which can also be found in texts from *XCVI. Sermons*. The text lacks the usual authorial apparatus of marginal divisions and citations, and the paragraph structure is idiosyncratic (perhaps randomly imposed by the compositor in the printing house). The editor, however, has decided against attempting any rearrangement of the main text or the introduction of additional marginalia in order to preserve this record of the hearer's reception of the sermon. The outline below summarizes the sermon's structure as it might have been signalled in the terms and enumeration of parts in an authorial quarto or *XCVI. Sermons*; numbers in bold are from ordinal numbers used in the text itself.

EXORDIUM (p. 138, ll. 6–19). Assertion of the eucharistic purging of sin.
DIVISION OF TEXT (p. 138, l. 16–p. 138, l. 7)
    I. The 'Element' (coal, eucharist, Christ)
    II. The 'Word' (Seraphin's address, priestly administration of eucharist)
SUMMARY ('OCCASION') OF TEXT (p. 139, l. 8–p. 140, l. 11)
    I. The prophet's 'vision'
    II. The prophet's 'confession'
[BODY OF SERMON]
    I. Outward action of sacraments
        1. The element itself (p. 140, ll. 11–24)
            i. has divine force of Christ
            ii. has two natures, 'natural' and 'divine'
        2. Christ's love a fire like the coal's (p. 140, ll. 25–31)
        3. Graces of Holy Ghost in sacraments (p. 140, l. 31–p. 142, l. 4)
            i. in 'water' of baptism for original sin
            ii. in 'fire' of eucharist for actual sins
        4. Administered by 'angels', the priests of the Church (p. 142, ll. 5–28)
        5. Administration of 'the Word' (p. 142, l. 29–p. 143, l. 41)
            i. best in a sacramental thing
            ii. inferiority of preaching
    II. The inward effect of sacramental action (p. 144, l. 1–p. 145, l. 11)
        1. Efficacy for 'taking away' original sin, and 'purging' actual sin
        2. Certainty of the same
        3. Speed of the same
SUMMARY (p. 145, l. 12–p. 145, l. 24)
APPLICATION to worship, and good works (p. 145, l. 25–end)

Ed. has emended 'tongues' to 'tongs', and 'Ceraphin' to 'Seraphin'; the former is an accepted early modern spelling, but could cause unnecessary confusion with modern 'tongues'; the latter is a typesetter's error or an idiosyncrasy in the copy text.

Headnote. This sermon was preached in Andrewes's routine course of duties as vicar of St Giles's Cripplegate on Sunday, 1 October 1598. It is one of four preached there about the eucharist, and preserved only in *AS* (pp. 515–21, 571–8, 594–600, 614–19). The dates of this and the others (4 Feb. 1598, 7 Oct. 1599, 2 Nov. 1600; all Sundays) suggest that it was Andrewes's custom to celebrate communion with sermon on the first Sunday of each month. This practice was highly unusual, and confirms Tyacke's view that the doubling of expenditure for communion wine at St Giles's during Andrewes's tenure there is a mark of his avant-garde commitment to sacrament-focused worship.

In the sixteenth century, eucharistic theology was one of the most controverted topics not just between Catholics and Protestants, but among Protestants themselves. Andrewes's own views on it have hitherto been inferred mostly from remarks made *passim* in *XCVI. Sermons*. Those remarks occur in brief invitations to receive communion, offered in the conclusions of sermons preached on the major feast days when celebration of communion was required by statute (Christmas, Easter, Whitsunday), but when the theme of the feast itself is the main subject of the sermon. That is, the eucharist is not the central topic of any of the sermons usually regarded as canonical. The significance of this sermon cannot be underestimated on two further counts. First, it is a remarkable example of how Andrewes expounded issues in a parochial setting that he would only gingerly touch in the more politically exposed court context. Second, the eucharistic theology argued here departs radically from late Elizabethan Calvinist orthodoxy. The sources evinced by the editor suggest that Andrewes was directly indebted to German Lutheranism a full generation after the date when most historians have assumed that any influence of Lutheran theology in England had disappeared under the tide of Swiss Calvinism.

Unlike the vast majority of earlier Tudor controversial writing on the eucharist, Andrewes's sermon is not against transubstantiation specifically, nor about the manner of Christ's presence generally. Instead, the real presence of Christ in the eucharist is for Andrewes a given, upon which he builds an even more radical (for his English context) argument for the efficacy of the sacrament. Insofar as Andrewes does address presence in this sermon, it is to assert that, like the hypostatic union of Christ's two natures (human and divine), the consecrated eucharistic elements similarly contain both their natural elements and the true body and blood of Christ (p. 141, l. 39–p. 142, l. 4; p. 143, ll. 2–7); crucially, that presence adheres in the elements themselves before reception, and independent of any cooperation by faith in the believer. Although Andrewes does not use the term here or elsewhere, this understanding of presence is that of 'consubstantiation'. From that assumption about presence, Andrewes expounds the belief that the eucharist itself remits sins. The Reformed English consensus, entirely congruent with Calvin, had been recently put in Book V of the *Laws of Ecclesiastical Polity* (1597) by Andrewes's acquaintance, Richard Hooker. In it, Hooker discussed eucharistic efficacy in terms of spiritual nourishment, not remission of sins (v. 67. 1; *FEWRH*, ii. 330–1). He insisted that Christ was present only by the faith of the believer, and 'not therefore to be sought for in the sacrament, but in the worthie receiver of the sacrament' (v. 67. 6; *FEWRH*, ii. 334–5). Roman Catholicism, while affirming transubstantiation, also insisted that worthy reception of the eucharist depended upon an anterior state of grace in the believer. That is, that the remission of sins was a prerequisite for reception—not a function of it—gained not just through baptism and faith (as for Calvin and Hooker), but also through the Catholic sacrament of penance and absolution. Andrewes thus occupies a position divorced from both Reformed (Calvinist) and Tridentine Roman Catholic doctrine. Instead, he is in accord with the Lutheran eucharistic theology consolidated in the 1570s by the leading German Lutheran theologian Martin Chemnitz (Kemnisius). The Council of Trent had responded to Luther's views on eucharistic remission of sins with an explicit canon (Session 13, number 5): 'Si quis dixerit, vel praecipuum functum sanctissime Eucharistiae esse remissionem peccatorum ... anathema sit' ('If anyone says that the primary function of the most blessed Eucharist is the remission of sins ... let him be anathema'). Andrewes argues in this sermon for precisely the position attacked by Trent, and does so in the terms used by Chemnitz (see Sources).

Andrewes's views on eucharistic efficacy also produce a sharp division between the sacramental functions of baptism and the eucharist. Much of this sermon is devoted to the argument that baptism remits original sin, while the eucharist remits sins committed after baptism ('actual' sins). This is foreign to Reformed doctrine, wherein baptism fully and finally remits both original and actual sin. As Calvin emphatically put it, 'nor is it to be supposed that... we must seek new remedies of expiation in other so-called sacraments, just as if the power of baptism had become obsolete' (*Institutes*, ii. 514). Even Hooker, who pushed at the boundaries of mainstream Calvinism by describing the sacraments as instruments of grace, comes nowhere near Andrewes here on either eucharistic presence or efficacy. And for many English Protestants in the 1590s, Richard Hooker was of course not the arbiter of orthodoxy, but rather William Perkins, for whom the eucharist was a nourishment and seal, instead of an instrument, of justification.

Sir John Harington, describing Andrewes's Elizabethan reputation, noted that 'scandall was taken of some, though not given by him, for his reverent speaking of the highest misterie of our faith, and heavenly foode the lords supper' (*Supplie or Addicion to the Catalogue of Bishops*, ed. R. H. Miller (1979), 140). This sermon shows why. A eucharistic theology like that offered by Andrewes here had probably not been pressed in any significant public forum since the Lutheran scruples of the early Elizabethan bishops Edmund Guest and Richard Cheyney successfully steered both the Order for Holy Communion and the 39 Articles toward clearer affirmations of the real presence in 1559 and 1563, respectively. In the latter instance, they were, with the queen's endorsement, able to suppress Article 29 ('Of the wicked which do not eate the body of Christe in the use of the Lordes Supper'). This article offended the Lutheran insistence that Christ was really present in the elements, regardless of the faith or spiritual state of the receiver—a position congruent with Andrewes's here. Perhaps significantly, the only person living at the date of Andrewes's sermon who had countenanced such a theology was Elizabeth Tudor herself.

Sources. Consensus on the Christian interpretation of Isaiah's vision, purgation, and commission as a prophet (Isa. 6), was established in the patristic commentaries of Jerome, Origen, Cyril of Alexandria, and Basil (*PL*, 24.92–5, 1101–44; *PG*, 70.102–8; *PG*, 30.512–17, respectively). All interpreted the vision christologically, with the coal from the altar an Old Testament type for the saving merits of Christ. None, however, interprets the vision as a prophecy or allegory of the eucharist. But the liturgies of both Basil and Chrysostom apply Isa. 6: 7 as words of administration at the eucharist, which Andrewes seizes upon as the precedent for his own explicitly eucharistic interpretation (p. 138, ll. 6–11 and n.).

Isa. 6: 7 had featured in the printed debate over the real presence and transubstantiation between Thomas Cranmer and Stephen Gardiner in 1550–1. The two opponents' arguments were collated and published by Cranmer as *An Aunswer... unto a craftie and sophisticall cavillation, devised by Stephen Gardiner* (1551; the new edition of 1580 is quoted here). Within a much larger debate, archbishop and bishop contested Chrysostom's use of Isa. 6: 7 in *Homily IX of Repentance* (hereafter *Hom. IX*, sometimes called 'De Eucharistia'; for a modern English trans., see *St John Chrysostom on Repentance and Almsgiving*, trans. G. G. Christo (1998), 126–30). In his first treatise, Cranmer confronted Roman Catholic use of Chrysostom's assertion (*Hom. IX*, 3) that the eucharistic bread and wine, like wax burned in a fire, was completely transformed at consecration. According to Cranmer, 'at these wordes of Chrisostome'—taken to prove transubstantiation—'the Papists do triumph'. He refuted this by quoting 'the very next sentence that followeth in Chrisostome (which craftely and maliciously they leave out)'. The 'next sentence' is an adaptation of Isa. 6: 7: 'Wherefore (sayth he) when ye come to these mysteries, do not thinke, that you receave by a man, the body of God, but that with tongues [tongs], you receave fier by the angelles Seraphin' (Cranmer, *Aunswer*, 334–5). This, to Cranmer, proved that Chrysostom spoke no more literally about a transubstantiation of the elements than he did when he asserted (from Isaiah) that a Seraph administered communion. As late as 1585, Cranmer's arguments from Chrysostom and Isa. 6: 7 were recycled (without acknowledgement) by Thomas Bilson in *The True Difference betweene Christian Subjection and Unchristian Rebellion* (pp. 800–2). Andrewes thus audaciously uses a text (Isa. 6.7) well known as a Protestant proof-text against the real presence as a text to argue for it. This may also colour his unapologetic explication (vs. Cranmer's dismissal) of priests as analogous to angels (p. 209).

Andrewes may also have been aware of the flurry of Swiss Reformed commentaries on Isaiah which use Isa. 6: 7 as a case study on the nature of sacraments. These have been used in the notes here for comparison with Andrewes's own interpretations: Martinus Borrhaius, *In Iesaiae Prophetae Oracula* (Basle, 1561); Heinrich Bullinger, *Isaias... expositus Homilii CXC* (Zürich, 1567); Heinrich Moller, *In Iesaiam Prophetam Commentarius* (Zürich, 1588); Wolfgang Musculus, *In Esaiam Prophetam Comentarii* (Basel, 1570); Huldrych Zwingli, 'Apologiam Complanationis Isaiae' (1529), in *Operum*, 3 vols. (Zurich, 1581), vol. iii. These exemplify the full range of eucharistic doctrines then debated within Swiss Protestantism as it increasingly defined itself against not just Roman Catholicism, but also Lutheranism.

But Andrewes's chief source seems not to be interpretations of his chosen biblical text as much as it is the sacramental theology expounded by Martin Chemnitz (1522–86) in his rebuttal of the Council of Trent, *Examinis Concilii Tridentini* (Frankfurt, 1574), and his major theological work, *De Duabus Naturis in Christo de Hypostatica Earum Unione* (Jena, 1591). The former is cited in the modern English translation by Frank Kramer, *Examination of the Council of Trent Part II* (1978); key terms and phrases are supplied in the original Latin parenthetically, with references, from the 1574 *Examinis*. None of the works cited here appears in the catalogue of Andrewes's library (which is acknowledged to be incomplete). However, his use of Chemnitz's *Examinis* in *Two Answers to Cardinal Perron* (1618, pub. 1629) is accepted (*LACT*, xi. 76–80). For comparison, the notes here also include pertinent quotations from the primary Roman Catholic response to Chemnitz and other leading reformers, Robert Bellarmine's *Disputationes... adversus huius temporis haereticos* (3 vols., Ingolstadt, 1591), a text Andrewes (like Hooker, who addresses it directly in the *Lawes*) must have known. Finally, references from other works by Andrewes are adduced here to show the consistency of his eucharistic theology; in particular, the Lutheran understanding of the sacraments put bluntly here throws into sharper relief more politic hints of the same from the Jacobean court sermons. Andrewes does not repeat, but also does not contradict, these positions in the three other communion sermons in *AS*, which focus not on remission of sin, but sacramental grace to resist sin, preparation for communion, and incorporation into the body of Christ through receiving the sacrament.

Further Reading. For Andrewes's sacramentalism, see Tyacke, 'Lancelot Andrewes'; and Lake, 'Lancelot Andrewes, John Buckeridge and Avant-Garde Conformity'. For Cranmer and Gardiner's polemics on the eucharist, see Diarmaid MacCulloch, *Thomas Cranmer* (1996), 461–92. For the spectrum of Continental Protestant eucharistic theology, see B. A. Gerrish, 'Gospel and Eucharist: John Calvin on the Lord's Supper', and 'Sign and Reality: The Lord's Supper in the Reformed Confessions', in Gerrish, *The Old Protestantism and the New* (1982), 106–30. The best (though not at all definitive) treatment of Andrewes's eucharistic theology is Lossky, *Lancelot Andrewes the Preacher*, *passim*. For Hooker, Perkins, and Andrewes's other English contemporaries on the same, see Bryan Spinks, *The Two Faces of Elizabethan Anglican Theology* (1999), and *Sacraments, Ceremonies and the Stuart Divines* (2002); and Voak, *Richard Hooker and Reformed Theology*. For Lutheranism and the Elizabethan Settlement, see William P. Haugaard, *Elizabeth and the English Reformation* (1970).

p. 138, 4–5. *Sed advolavit... &c.*: lit., 'But one of these two Seraphim flew to me, having in its hand a live coal; which had been taken with tongs from the altar. And it applied [it] to my mouth saying, &c. [Loe, this hath touched thy lips, & thine iniquitie shall be taken away, and thy sinne shalbe purged]' (Isa. 6: 6–7); the Latin departs significantly from Vulg., but is very close to Trem. ('sed advolans ad me unus ex istis Seraphim habens in manu sua prunam, quam forcipibus sumserat ab altari, Admovit ori meo dicens, [ecce, attingit hoc labia tua: jam amovetur iniquitas tua, & peccatum tuum expiatur].'); Andrewes may have used Trem. directly, or like him (and unlike Vulg.), translated the passage directly from the Hebrew.

6–9. *In the Liturgy... Seraphin*: in the Eastern liturgies of both Basil and John Chrysostom, the celebrant says after himself partaking of the bread and chalice, and then after administering it to the deacon, 'Lo, this hath touched my [thy] lips: and mine [thine] iniquity shall be taken away, and my [thy] sin purged' (*The Orthodox Liturgy*, SPCK (1939), 88–9; see also *The Divine Liturgy of... Chrysostom* (Oxford, 1995), 45); cf. also, in Chrysostom's Prayer of Oblation, 'thou by thy Holy Spirit having wrought the change... that they may be to them that partake thereof unto sobriety of soul, the remission of sins...' (*Orthodox Liturgy*, 74). Chemnitz probably has these same texts in mind when he claims, 'this our teaching introduces nothing new. There are prayers in all the liturgies of the ancients (*'omnibus... veterum liturgiis'*) that the receiving of the body and blood of Christ may result in the remission of all sin' (*Examination*, 240; *Examinis*, 82b).

11. *whole fruit... Isaiah*: cf. the same arguments and scriptural evidence in Andrewes's sermon at court, Whitsunday 1620: 'For, *Hic est omnis fructus* (saith *Esai*, and it is a ground with us,) *All the fruict we have, is the taking away of sin*'; and 'there is no people, under heaven, but have sense of these two [guilt and sin]; and no *religion* is, or ever was, but laboured to remove them both' (*XCVI*, 737).

14. *seale and signe*: language not in any English trans. of Matt. 26: 28, but typical of Reformed eucharistic theology; cf., from John Northbrooke's refutation of Roman Catholic sacramental theology, *Spiritus est vicarius Christi in terra* (1571): 'The sacrament is not the testament of Christ, but a seale or signe of it' (p. 69^v).

18. *Christ assureth... remission*: Christ's words at the institution of the eucharist, repeated by the priest at the consecration in the Roman Catholic mass, St Chrysostom's Eastern liturgy, and the *BCP* Order for Holy Communion (*BCP*): 'And he took the cup, and gave thankes, and gave it to them, saying, Drinke ye all of it: For this is my blood of the new Testament, which is shed for many for the remission of sins' (Matt. 26: 27–8); cf. Andrewes, sermon at court ('Of Absolution'), March 1600, 'there is also another power for the *Remission of sinnes*, in the institution of the holy *Eucharist*. The words are exceeding plain: *This is my bloud of the new Testament, for the Remission of sinnes*', and Christmas 1612, 'And, if yee seeke to be ridd of your sinnes, this was *broken*

for you, and this was *shed for you*, for that very end, for the *remission of sinns*' (*XCVI*, pt. II, p. 59; pt. I, p. 61), and 'A Sermon Preached... on Whit-Sunday' (this edn., p. 223, ll. 19–25); cf. Chemnitz, defending the eucharistic remission of sins, 'we do not do this on the basis of our own thinking (*speculatione*) or from rashness.... in the institution itself Christ expressly mentions the forgiveness of sins (*Christus expressis verbis nominat remissionem peccatorum*)' (*Examination*, 237; *Examinis*, 81b); cf. also Andrewes's inclusion of 'remission of sins', with a marginal gloss to Matt. 26: 28, in his catalogue of the properties of the eucharist in his prayer 'At the Offertory', *Preces*, 122; the Catholic position is summarized by Bellarmine (*Disputationes*, ii. 861D), 'effectum Eucharistiae praecipuum non esse remissionem peccatorum mortalium, sed nutritionem animae, & preservantionem à peccatis' ('the principle effect of the Eucharist is not the remission of moral sin, but nourishment of the soul, and preservation from sin'); cf. also Zwingli on Isa. 6: 7 (*Opera*, iii. 230^v), 'Vere quidem prophetae remitti peccata scimus: sed virtute numinis, non virtute signi' ('truly indeed we know that the prophet's sins were forgiven: but by the power of the divine will, not by the power of the signs').

20. *Sacrament... Element... word*: Andrewes divides the parts of the sermon into the two parts of the classic Augustinian definition of a sacrament as composed of a tangible thing ('Element') made spiritually efficacious by its conjunction with the holy '*word*'. Cf. Augustine, *In Johan. Tract. LXXX*, 3: 'Accedit verbum ad elementum, et fit Sacramentum' (*PL* 35. 1840); ('add the word to the element, and a sacrament is made'). The eucharistic theology of *BCP* placed the greatest priority upon the spiritual property of the sacrament (the '*word*')—itself determined not by any 'word' of the priest, but by the participation through faith of the individual believer—rather than the element itself. Cf. Bullinger (*Isaias... Homilii*, 34^r) on Isa. 6: 7: 'Carbo sacramentum est, cui & verbum coniungitur' ('the coal is a sacrament when it and the word are joined'); and Moller (*In Iesaiam*, 62^v) on the same: 'in primis observandum est, quod verbum coniunget cum sacramentis, absque; eo enim haec nihil sunt, nisi mortua elementa aut ociosa [*sic*, 'odiosa'?] ceremonia' ('first, it is observed that the word is joined with the sacraments; without it, they are nothing but dead elements or odious ceremonies'). In its assertion that the 'word' makes the divine actually present, Andrewes's is closer to Chemnitz (*De Duabus Naturis*, 48): 'Et Deus illis non adest inseparabiliter, sed ex pacto, iuxta Verbum: nam extra usum non sunt talia Sacramenta' ('And God is not there in them [the elements] inseparably, but by a pact with the Word; for without application [of the Word] they are not proper Sacraments').

25. *Seraphim... Priests*: an analogy explicit only in the Eastern liturgies, but cherished by Andrewes; cf. p. 142 and nn.

28–29. *wisdome... Eucharist*: patristic consensus accepted Christ as the coal or the altar, but did not apply this directly to the eucharist, although the conclusion is a logical one; cf. Cyril on Isa. 6: 7: "Χριστοῦ σύμβολον, ὃς δἰαήμᾶς, χαὶ ὑπὲρ ἡμῶν προδεχόμιδεν ἑαυτον τῷ θεῷ χαὶ πατρι" (*PG*, 70.107; 'This therefore was the symbol and representation of Christ, who for us and for our sake was himself made a sacrifice'); and Basil on the same: "Ταχα οὖν δημαίνει τὴν ἐν τῇ σαρχὶ τοῦ κυρίου" (*PG*, 30.513; 'perhaps therefore this signifies the future advent of the Lord in flesh').

p. 138, 29–p. 139, 2. *St. John... Christ Jesus*: Geneva cross-references John 12: 41 with Isa. 6: 9, but does not interpret the Prophet's vision as one of the Second Person of the Trinity (Christ); the gloss to Isa. 6: 1 identifies the 'Lord sitting upon a throne' only as 'God' enthroned as 'judge'. Reformed commentaries carefully control christological readings to avoid the implication of a bodily presence of Christ in the eucharistic elements.

Bullinger (*Isaias... Homiliis*, 31ᵛ) asserts that John 12: 41 refers to Isaiah's vision of Christ, but insists that the coal was a symbolic sacrament that showed externally—but did not itself effect internally or actually—the power of the Holy Spirit to remit sins ('Deus enim condonat & removat peccatum, sacramenta significant, & veritatem attestantur foris. Ignis autem significat spiritus sancti virtutum', p. 33ᵛ); ('God therefore forgives and takes away sin; the sacraments signify and attest to the truth externally'). Moller (*In Iesaiam*, 62ᵛ) posits the altar itself as Christ: 'ara vero significat Christum' ('the altar truly signifies Christ').

6. *by the element*: cf. Cyril on Isa. 6: 7: "Ἀνθρακιδῇ οὖν εὐμαλα παρεικαστέον τὸν Ἐμμανουήλ, ὃς εἰ καί γένοιτο πως ἐν τοις ἡμετέροις χείλειν, τράντυ τε καί τράντως ἀφαιρει τὰς, καί περιχαθαριεῖ τας ἀνομιας." (*PG*, 30.108; 'It is therefore correct to compare Emmanuel to this coal here, who if applied in this way to our lips, takes away all sin, and purges iniquity'); and contrast Hooker, 'we conformably teach, that the outward signe applyed, hathe of itselfe noe naturall efficacie towards Grace' (*Laws*, VI. vi. 11; *FEWRH*, iii. 87.27–8).

9–13. *The vision... Hosts*: paraphrase of Isa. 6: 1–2, 5; '*as a Judge ready to give Sentence*' is verbatim quotation of Geneva gloss.

15. *scaped*: escaped.

18. *last generall day*: the Day of Judgement ('*generall*' because it will apply to all).

18–20. *Wee shall... wicked*: cf. Matt. 25: 31–2.

27. *conversation*: one's habit of being; also spiritual being (OED *sn* 1).

31–33. *in vain... condemn us*: culpability for sins of omission as well as of commission is a traditional part of Christian moral theology; the *locus classicus* is Rom. 7: 15. Cf. *BCP*, General Confession at Morning and Evening Prayer: 'we have left undone those things which we ought to have done; we have done those things which we ought not to have done'. More generally, cf. Andrewes's 'An Act of Penitence with a Meditation on the Last Judgement', *Preces*, 164–8.

p. 140, 18–24. *two natures... heavenly part*: the insistence here on the two natures of the 'coal' (and by analogy the eucharistic elements, and the incarnate Christ) separates Andrewes from the Roman Catholic doctrine of transubstantiation.

25–31. *Secondly... bare us*: Andrewes exploits the conventional Protestant allowance of allegorical interpretation of the Song of Solomon. Cf. the Geneva glosses to 8: 6: 'The vehement love wherewith Christ loveth [the Church]' (headnote), and 'The spouse desireth Christ to be joyned in perpetuall love with him' (gloss). Significantly, he elaborates the 'Coles' as Christ's burning love for the Church, not vice versa (as the second gloss suggests).

31–32. *quia non... accendit*: 'Because he not only loves himself, but also inflames others'; cf. Gilbert Foliot, *Expositio in Cantica Canticorum*, 'Qui quidem ignis, semper ignis est, semper calefaciens, et in dilectione Dei cor semper accendens; aliquando ignis cum flamma, quando non solum ardet et accendit, immo lucet in opere, et quod intus agit, manifestat in re; ita quidem, quod aquae multae non possunt hanc charitatem extinguere' (*PL*, 202.1300C); ('whereby it is true that a fire, while it is ever a fire is [also] always an agent of enflaming. Even so, the heart is continually enflamed by the love of God. Now at last, it is a blazing fire (of passion), because it does not just burn and enflame, it shines forth in deed. And because it emits from within, it is therefore manifested in reality. It is for this reason that many waters cannot quench this love').

40–41. *Ananias... Baptized*: Musculus (*In Esaiam*, 151) also compares the efficacy of baptism, as epitomized by Ananias' instruction to Saul (Paul), to the efficacy of the coal from the altar. But he makes no distinction between original and actual sin, and insists that the ceremony is a sign of an already accomplished purgation by God's grace ('Opus hoc est gratiae Dei, cuius signum est baptismus'; 'this work is by the grace of God, the sign of which is baptism').

p. 141, 7. *tanquam furni*: Lat., 'as it were, by an oven'.

23–24. *fires... terrifie malefactors*: corporal punishment by branding hands, ears, or faces was routine for petty criminal offences.

32–39. *The love... actuall transgressions*: this obscures what were probably intended to be sharper parallelisms continuing the contrast between baptism's purging of original sin, and the eucharist's purging of 'actuall' sin after baptism.

33. *lively*: clearly, vividly.

34. *wee must come often*: cf. Andrewes, sermon at St Giles's ('Worshipping of Imaginations'), January 1592, where, criticizing the common practice of communion only once per year, he says, 'for sure, we should continue also in... the frequenting of it, if not so often as the Primitive Church did (which, either *thrise* in the *weeke*, or at the furthest *once*, did communicate) yet, as often as the Church doth celebrate; which (I thinke) should do better to celebrate more often' (*XCVI*, pt. II, p. 36); cf. Chemnitz, who, citing the same practice of the early church, argues 'on this basis people are to be taught, admonished, and exhorted to more diligent and frequent use of the Eucharist' (*Examination*, 330); for monthly communions at St Giles's under Andrewes, see Headnote, and Tyacke, 'Lancelot Andrewes', 14–15.

34–35. *purging... Apostle speaks*: Heb. 1: 3.

35. *si in luce*: lit., 'if in the light'; not a quotation from John 1: 7–9, but related to its metaphor of Christ as 'that true light, which lighteth every man that commeth into the world' (v. 9).

41. *hem... can heale*: cf. Chemnitz, 'Chysostom says: "If those who touched the hem of His garment were properly healed, how much more shall we be strengthened if we have Him in us whole ('*si totum illum in nobis habeamus*')?"' (*Examination*, 234; *Examinis*, 80b); Hooker uses the same example to argue against speculation about the mode of presence, 'if... that poore distressed woman comminge unto Christe for health could so constantlie resolve hir selfe, *May I but touch the skirt of his garment I shalbe whole*, what moveth us to argue of the maner how life should come by bread' (*Lawes*, v. 67. 12; *FEWRH*, ii. 342); see also p. 143, ll. 19–20 and n.

p. 142, 2–3. *here we have... Sacrifice it self*: the coal burned perpetually on the altar to burn ('touch') the sacrificial offering placed on it (historically, a lamb; typologically, 'Christ himselfe'); hence, a strong metaphorical statement of both a sacrificial eucharist and the real presence; cf. Andrewes, sermon at St Giles's ('Worshipping of Imaginations'), January 1592, 'the *bread, which we break is the partaking of* CHRIST'*s true bodie* (& not, of a *Signe, figure* or *remembrance* of it.)' (*XCVI*, pt. II, p. 35).

5–8. *office... called Angells*: Andrewes is indebted here to the Eastern liturgy's analogy between priests and angels as sacramental ministers; cf. the priest's prayer at the Entrance with the Holy Gospel, 'Master, Lord our God, you have set orders and armies of Angels and Archangels in heaven to minister to your glory; grant that, with our entrance, holy Angels may enter, concelebrating with us, and with us glorifying your goodness.' The idea (and iconography) also became rooted in Roman Catholicism; cf. Robert Parsons's *A Brief Discours* (1580), which cites Gregory the Great and Chrysostom to attest that 'the verye Angels of heaven doe come downe at that tyme, to adore that sacred Bodye.... As al the holy Fathers... dyd both beleve and teach' (sigs. 44^v–45^r); see next n.

9–10. *Malachi... of Hosts*: Andrewes here sides squarely with the Rheims translators; cf. Gregory Martin, '"because he is the angel of the Lord of hosts," which is also a wonderful dignity, so to be called; they [Protestants] after their cold manner of profane translation say, "Because he is the messenger of the Lord of hosts" ' (Fulke, *Defence*, in *Works*, i. 483). Cf. Andrewes, *Scala Coeli* (1611), 'Thus much they are to learne from hence, that the Priests are *Angeli Domini exercituum. Mal*.2.7.' (pp. 78^(r–v); also *LACT*, v. 355–6); cf. also the sharp clericalism of his claim at court, March 1600 ('Of Absolution'), that in every available means for remission of sins (baptism, eucharist, preaching, and prayer) 'is the person of the *Minister* required, and they cannot be dispatched without him' (*XCVI*, pt. II, p. 59).

18. *etiam... peccatum tuum*: lit., 'therefore Jehova has taken away your sin'; cf. Vulg., 2 Sam. 12: 13, 'Dominus quoque transtulit peccatum tuum'; ('the Lord also hath put away thy sinne').

19. *availeable*: 'capable of producing a desired result; of avail; efficacious' (*OED sa* I.1).

23–25. *for not hee... hold it*: cf. 39 Articles, article 26 ('Of the unworthynesse of the ministers, which hinder not the effect of the Sacraments'); but unusually, Andrewes emphasizes the efficacy and validity of the elements in their own right before administration, not their efficacy only when 'such as by fayth... ryghtly do receave' them; cf. Trem., gloss on the seraph (Isa. 6: 6), 'administer voluntatis Dei ad confirmandum Prophetam, ut sequentia ostendunt: nam non amplius hic verbo & sacramento in Propheta efficit per se ipsum, quam ministri Dei in Ecclesia: sed unus est spiritus qui operatur omnia in omnibus' ('an assistant to the will of God for the strengthening of the Prophet, from which the following are shown: he [the seraph] no more makes this word and sacrament efficacious in the Prophet, than the minister of God in the Church: but it is only the Spirit which works all in everything'); cf. also Bellarmine, responding to Cranmer's rebuttal of Gardiner (see Headnote), 'nam in priore manifesti sunt tropi, dum sacerdotum vocat Angelum Seraphicum, & corpus Domini ignem, & manum sacerdotis forcipem: neque negat accipi corpus Domini à sacerdote, sed negat illum eo tempore gerere se, ut homine, sed potius Angelico ministerio illum uti confirmat' (*Disputationes*, ii. 624D–625A); ('for in the first place they are manifest tropes, as long as the priest is called a seraphic angel, and the fire the body of the Lord, and the tongs the hand of the priest: and it does not deny accepting the Lord's body from the priest, but denies that he [the priest] conducts himself in his time as a man, but rather confirms that he acts with the power of a ministering angel').

32–33. *Leper... Christ*: Mark 1: 41 (also Matt. 8: 31, Luke 5: 13).

33–36. *but the Centurion... his lips*: characteristically sarcastic dismissal of ministry only by the word, which, in its original delivery, probably took the form of an imagined objection by an interlocutor ('but... eight verse'), with the tart reply in Andrewes's own voice ('so... lips'); Bullinger (*Isaias... Homilii*, 34^r) cites the Ethiopian eunuch, and another centurion, Cornelius (Acts 8, 10), as exemplars of purgation of sin by the ministry of the word alone in preaching, to argue (unlike Andrewes) that the sacraments work by the same means of grace through faith ('gratia Dei, per fidem') as preaching; cf. Gerrish, 'as Calvin thinks of [the sacraments], they are simply another form of the Word.... '[h]ence it is a mistake to ascribe to the sacraments some kind of secret powers, endowed with quasi-magical effect' ('Gospel and Eucharist', 110).

41. *Ghostly*: spiritual.

p. 143, 3. *aptare sibi corpus*: lit., 'take to himself a body'; cf. Vulg., Heb. 10: 5, 'corpus autem aptasti mihi'; ('a body hast thou ordeined me').

6. *Hypostasis of the Sun*: the relationship of light to the sun is a central metaphor for the hypostatic union of the divine and human natures in the person of Christ in Chemnitz, *De Duabus Naturis*, ch. VI, 'Quomodo ex similitudine unionis Lucis & Solis... doctrina illa, de hypostatica duarum in Christo naturarum unione... illustrari possit' ('How by the analogy of the union of light and the sun... this doctrine of the hypostatic union of Christ's two natures can be shown'). At Christmas 1612, Andrewes also uses '*hypostasis*' and the metaphor of light from the sun to argue first the consubstantial and coequal procession of the Son from the Father, and then to apply the same by analogy to the eucharist: 'there is a correspondencie, between the *Word*, and *His brightnesse*; and, between the *Sacrament*, and *His Character*. The *Word* giveth a *light*, and *His brightnesse* sheweth in it *ad horam*, and not much longer. The parts of the *Sacrament*, they are permanent, and sticke by us' (*XCVI*, 56–7); cf. next n.

7. *Sacrament... Earthly nature*: Andrewes applies the same analogy between Christ's nature and the sacraments at court, Christmas Day 1623: 'the blessed *Eucharist*, is (as I may say) a kind of *hypostaticall union* of the *Signe*, and the *thing signified*, so united together, as are the *two natures* of CHRIST' (*XCVI*, 157); Chemnitz devotes an entire chapter of *De Duabus Naturis* (ch. XXX) to defending eucharistic consubstantiation by the analogy of Christ's hypostatic union; Chemnitz's *Theses quaedam de Unione Duarum Naturam in Christo Hypostaticae... a clanculariis Sacramentariorum patronis sparsae* (Leipzig, n.d.) is a redaction of *De Duabus Naturis* specifically composed to combat, by assertion of the same analogy, 'sacramentarian' denials of the eucharistic real presence (pp. 3–12); for an excellent discussion of the sermon for Christmas 1623, including a tentative suggestion of Chemnitz's influence upon Andrewes in it, see Lossky, *Lancelot Andrewes*, 96–100; finally, compare Hooker's summary of 'the Lutherans interpretation' of the eucharistic bread, '*This is in it selfe before participation really and truly the naturall substance of my body by reason of the coexistence which my omnipotent bodie hath with the sanctified element of bread*' (*Lawes*, v. 67. 12; *FEWHR*, ii. 340).

9. *one bodily sacrament*: baptism; cf. p. 140, l. 31–p. 141, l. 14.

10–11. *By another... Sacrament*: Holy Communion; in his sermon at court, March 1600 ('Of Absolution'), Andrewes itemized baptism, eucharist, receiving the scriptures, and priests' prayers as 'tend[ing] to the *remission of sinnes*' (*XCVI*, pt. II, p. 59); for a more nuanced argument of both the reciprocity and the distinction between baptism and communion, see Andrewes's sermon for Whitsunday 1620 (*XCVI*, 735–44); on the latter, see Lossky, *Lancelot Andrewes*, 285–6; cf. Chemnitz, 'through Baptism we are reborn in Christ; having been reborn, we are nourished with the Word and the Eucharist; if we have fallen, we return through repentance and faith to the promise of grace... the Eucharist, which contains the basis for the remission of sins ("*quae continet fundamentum remissionis peccatorum*"), namely the body and blood of Christ, is not excluded also from this use' (*Examination*, 239; *Examinis*, 82b); Bellarmine (*Disputationes*, ii. 860D), marshals his erstwhile enemy Calvin (*Institutes*, IV. xvii. 40–2), 'ubi videtur negare, quod Lutherani dicunt, per Eucharistiam remitti peccata mortalia & requirere cum Catholicis, ut homo antè per poenitentiam justificetur, quàm ad Sacramentum accedat' ('where he is seen to negate that which the Lutherans say, that by the Eucharist moral sins are remitted, and to require with Catholics that a man be previously justified by penitence when he comes to the Sacrament').

19. *hemme of a garment*: cf. Matt. 9: 20–2 (also Luke 8: 44; cf. Mark 5: 27), and p. 141, l. 41 and n. The story of the woman with the issue of blood was another text disputed between English Protestants and the Rheims translators, but here Andrewes sits

between both Reformed and Catholic opinion. Martin objected that English Protestants wrenched the text to prove salvation *sola fide* with Christ's words to the woman, 'thy faith hath saved thee'. He preferred instead Rheims's 'thy faith hath healed thee', because 'that faith was of Christ's omnipotency only and power'. So whereas English Protestants invested saving power in the faith of the believer, the Rheimists seated that power in Christ—but Andrewes places it in the sacramental element itself (here, the 'garment') (Fulke, *Defence*, in *Works*, i. 425–6).

29. *Per... peccata*: lit., 'by mercy sins are purged'; Prov. 16: 6, but not. Vulg. ('misericordia et veritate redimitur iniquitas'); cf. Geneva, 'by mercy and trueth iniquitie shalbe forgiuen'.

31–33. *Whereas... his tongue*: contrast Andrewes's application of the purging of Isaiah's lips to preaching in his prayer 'Before Preaching': 'O Thou coal of double nature, which in the tongs didst touch the lips of the prophet and take away his iniquity: touch my lips, who am a sinner, and purge me of every stain and make me skill to shew forth thine oracles' (*Preces*, 258).

33. *Prophets eare*: cf. Andrewes, sermon for Gunpowder Day 1617, 'All our *holinesse*, is in hearing: All our *Service*, eare-service: that were in effect, as much as to say, all the body were *an eare*' (*XCVI*, 992).

34–35. *sermon... bodily element*: one of Andrewes's characteristic overturnings of the reformed priority given to preaching as a means to salvation, especially trenchant here for recommending not just prayer over preaching (cf. 'A Sermon Preached... Whit-Sunday', this edn., pp. 321–4), but the eucharist itself (*'bodily element'*).

39–40. *Sacrament... meete together*: cf. Andrewes, sermon for Christmas Day 1623, 'the *holy Eucharist* it selfe is called... a *Collection* or *gathering*.... For, at the celebration of it (though we gather to Prayer, and to Preaching, yet) that is the principall *gathering*, the *Church* hath' (*XCVI*, 157–8); cf. also 'A Sermon... on Christmas Day. Anno 1609' (this edn.), pp. 220–23.

p. 144, 8. *Adams figge leaves*: Gen. 3: 7.

9. *plaister*: healing remedy applied with a bandage; both Andrewes and Chemnitz are fond of medicinal metaphors for the eucharist; cf. Chemnitz, 'we may eat of that bread and drink of that cup as often as we recognize and feel that that medicine and remedy which our Good Samaritan pours into our wounds is useful' (*Examination*, 330), and Andrewes, sermon for Whitsunday 1620, 'His *bloud* is not onely *drinke, to nourish*; but *medicine, to purge*', and Christmas 1612, 'For, the medicine, which purgeth *ex proprietate*, His flesh and bloud goe to it' (*XCVI*, 744, 60); see also Hooker's peroration on the eucharist, 'it serveth as well for a medicine to heale our infirmities and purge our sinnes as for a sacrifice of thanksgiving' (*Lawes*, v. 67. 12; *FEWRH*, ii. 343); one suspects rhetorical flourish here, as its language of eucharistic remission is without precedent elsewhere in Hooker.

24–32. *Christ doth not... his own nature*: Andrewes distinguishes here between different understandings of the doctrine of the Atonement (the reconciliation of mankind to God through Christ's sacrifice). The first portion (*'Christ... for sinnes'*) restates the classic Western (Anselmian) understanding of Christ standing as a sacrificial substitute for the judgement due to mankind after the Fall. The subsequent qualification ('but offers... own nature') takes up a point emphasized by a smaller body of patristic opinion, most associated with the Greek father Athanasius, which held that in the Incarnation Christ not only humbled himself, but also elevated human nature; cf. 2 Pet. 1: 4, and Athanasius, 'He became man that we might be made divine'

(*De Incarnatione Verbi*, quoted in Lossky, *Lancelot Andrewes*, 186). This passage is a strikingly condensed summary of what Lossky finds most distinctive in Andrewes's theology: 'for Richard Hooker... the debate about justification finds its resolution in the notion of participation.... For Andrewes, the resolution of the conflict is placed in the perspective of the deification of man' (*Lancelot Andrewes*, 267–8).

p. 145, 2. *for a little... cried out*: 'for, a little before, he that [had] cried out'.

3. *Væ mihi*: Vulg., Isa. 6: 5 ('Wo[e] is me').

4. *Ecce ego, mitte me*: Vulg., Isa. 6: 8 ('Here am I, send me').

6–10. *participating... lives precious*: cf. Chemnitz, 'and so faith has in the use of the Eucharist a firm anchor of consolation, trust, and certainty concerning the forgiveness of sins. It also has an effectual remedy (*antidotum*) for raising up and supporting a feeble faith... against want of confidence, doubt, faintheartedness, and despair' (*Examination*, 239; *Examinis*, 82b).

31. *confession of sinfull men*: in the Order for Holy Communion, the 'generall confession' of sin made by the priest 'in the name of all those that are minded to receive the holy Communion' (*BCP*).

33. *confession of Angels... Hosts*: the 'Sanctus', the hymn beginning 'Holy, holy, holy'; from the fourth century sung at the conclusion of the preface to the eucharist, and based on a verse (Isa. 6: 3) preceding Andrewes's sermon text; an apt summary of the sermon's theme of participating as ministers or fellow-worshippers with the angels (cf. p. 142 and nn.).

A SERMON PREACHED... THE V. OF NOVEMBER. A.D. MDCVI.

Text. The copy text is the earliest witness, *XCVI* (1629; F_1), 889–900. Collation with F_2 provides no substantive variants. This is the first of ten Gunpowder Treason sermons preached by Andrewes at court between 1606 and 1618, collected in *XCVI*, 889–1008; and in *LACT*, iv. 202–405.

Headnote. The Gunpowder Plot had its roots in the desperation of a small number of extremist recusants impatient with non-violent attempts to win toleration in England. Led by Richard Catesby, Guido Fawkes, and Sir Thomas Percy, they stockpiled gunpowder and wood in a chamber underneath the Parliament House in Westminster that had been rented by Percy. Informed by a cryptic, anonymous letter to the Catholic-sympathizing Lord Mounteagle, the king and his counsellors apprehended Fawkes at the scene of the crime on Tuesday, 5 November. Fawkes proudly admitted to attempting to decimate the entire ruling order, including the royal family, at the state opening of Parliament that day. The government's apprehension, trial, and execution of the plotters was swift and violent, and grew to include a full-scale prosecution of the Jesuits in England as well. The Jesuits had featured little in the initial panic after the plot's discovery, but the Earl of Salisbury, Robert Cecil, worked desperately in the ensuing months to exploit every possibility of linking the plot with the long-hated Jesuit mission. Several Jesuits, including their superior in England, Henry Garnet, were apprehended and executed for treason in 1606. They had counselled the ringleaders against the plot, but their failure to notify the authorities of its existence (because of the seal of the confessional) condemned them. No event before the regicide in 1649 so marked the nation's psyche as did the Gunpowder Plot. The deliverance from it took its place next to the defeat of the Spanish Armada as evidence of England's—now Great Britain's—status as elect among nations, and as a focal point for anti-Catholic sentiment and policy. To commemorate this providential blessing, 5 November was declared by Parliament in January 1606 to be a feast day observed nationally by attendance at a special form of morning prayer (or, optionally, communion). This was promulgated by authority as *Prayers and Thanksgiving to be used by all the Kings Majesties loving Subjects, For the happy deliverance...from the... intended Massacre by Gunpowder, the 5 of November 1605* (1606). The service is based very closely on that commissioned by James at his accession for the annual commemoration of his deliverance from the 1600 Gowrie Conspiracy (5 August), which was itself derived from the service marking Queen Elizabeth's accession (17 November). Andrewes's sermon presented here was preached at the court's first official commemoration of the Gunpowder Treason on the first anniversary of its discovery; allusions within the text make it very clear that it was delivered immediately after the new state service had been sung in the full choral and ceremonial splendour of the Chapel Royal at Whitehall, in the presence of King James, Queen Anne, and Prince Henry. It manifests an intimate and sophisticated engagement with the special prayers and lessons appointed in the new liturgy (especially Psalms 35, 68, 69), and closely follows the official version of events as used in the prosecution of the plotters and the Jesuit priests. Several aspects, however, make it far more than a mere propaganda piece. Although Andrewes does continue the government's work of vehemently stigmatizing the Jesuit mission, he, unlike most preachers, does not allow anti-Jesuit satire to spill over into wholesale anti-Catholicism. Significantly, his prime objection to the Jesuits' role—their alleged celebration of mass and granting of absolution to the plotters—is predicated on Andrewes's acceptance of the Catholic mass and its priests as valid (and therefore horrifying to see the same used so inappropriately); there is no mention of the Pope (as Antichrist or not), nor of Roman Catholic doctrine. He recalls the horrors that might have befallen the assembly in unusually personal terms that betray the fact that he—consecrated a bishop on the day before the plot was to be carried out—was to have been among those 'so many baskets of heads, so many peeces of rent bodies' (p. 152). But he then turns to the perhaps unexpected topic of proper feasting. There is first a strong dose of criticism here, disguised as advice, for the new monarch who was already legendary for his bacchanalian carousing. But more generally, Andrewes here assays further themes to which his Gowrie and Gunpowder sermons would repeatedly return, such as the affirmation of the church's right to declare feast days and to endorse moderate bodily cheer and mirth, and an insistence upon the Christian obligation to turn joy and religious enthusiasm into good works. Together, these exemplify Andrewes's anti-puritanism and inform his later emphatic support of the 'Book of Sports' (1618). Finally, the sermon is striking for its encomium to choral music accompanied by instruments as it might have been performed in the Chapel Royal. The extended peroration on the 'Hosanna' and 'Benedictus' (Ps. 118: 26; Matt. 21: 9; p. 159-end), including its direct typological application to King James, suggests a cultural connection, if not influence, between it and settings of versions of the same text ('Hosanna to the Son of David') early in James's reign by Orlando Gibbons (1583–1625) and Thomas Weelkes (d. 1623). Assessing influence is vexed by lack of exact dating for either anthem. Weelkes was organist and choirmaster at Chichester, Andrewes's episcopal see since November 1605; Gibbons had been Gentleman of the Chapel Royal since

March 1604, and was thus probably in the choir on this and the other feast days on which Andrewes preached.

Sources. In addition to the state service of commemoration (see above), Andrewes's sermon is intimately linked with the arguments, and even diction, of the full range of regime propaganda marshalled against both the plotters and the Jesuits. Some of these would have been available to Andrewes in print, including the official account of the plot published almost immediately after it with *His Majesties Speech in this last Session of Parliament* (1605), and the first official pulpit account, William Barlow's *The Sermon Preached at Paules Crosse... after the Discoverie of this late Horrible Treason* (1606). But Andrewes is also conversant with the unprinted major arguments used by the prosecution at the plotters' and Jesuits' trials, which he might well have attended. The trial speeches and testimonies are collected in T. B. Howell, *A Complete Collection of State Trials*, 21 vols., vol. ii (1816).

Further Reading. The best account of the plot and trials is Antonia Fraser, *Faith and Treason: The Story of the Gunpowder Plot* (1996). For Gunpowder Day as holiday see David Cressy, *Bonfires and Bells: National Memory and the Protestant Calendar in Elizabethan and Jacobean England* (1989), ch. 9; and Cressy, 'The 5th of November Remembered', in Roy Porter (ed.), *Myths of the English* (Cambridge, 1992), 68–90. For Gunpowder Plot sermons, see Lori Anne Ferrell, *Government by Polemic: James I, the King's Preachers, and the Rhetorics of Conformity, 1603–1625* (1998), ch. 3; Lossky, *Lancelot Andrewes*, ch. 7; and McCullough, *Sermons at Court*, 116–25. For the literary influence of the plot, of which Andrewes's sermon is an important early example, see Stella Revard, 'Milton's Gunpowder Poems and Satan's Conspiracy', *Milton Studies*, 4 (1972), 63–77.

p. 146, 6–7. *A DOMINO... ea*: Vulg., Ps. 117: 23–4.

8–9. *This... in it*: Geneva.

8. *mervailous*: marvellous.

19. *fairely*: 'completely, full, quite' (*OED sadv.* 7).

21. *as sheepe... slaughter*: cf. Rom. 8: 36 (quoting Ps. 44: 22), Acts 8: 32 (quoting Isa. 53: 7); and the first collect in the Gunpowder service for Morning Prayer where the intended victims are 'by Popish treacherie appointed as sheepe to the slaughter' (*Prayers and Thankesgiving*, sig. D2^r).

p. 147, 1–2. *not eaten out, by them*: early example of 'eat out' meaning 'to destroy as a parasite or corrosive' (*OED* 'eat' 17.c); here, 'solemne Daies' prevent the corrosive destruction of 'memorable Acts', and 'by them' (the 'solemne Daies') the 'Acts' are 'kept still fresh'.

6. *Haman's bloudie lotts*: the Book of Esther recounts the court intrigue of Haman's plot against the counsellor Mordecai, his cousin (raised as his daughter), Queen Esther, and all the Jews, a plot foiled by the faithfulness of King Ahasuerus. The plotters 'cast Pur (that is a lot)' (Esther 3: 7) 'to know what moneth and day should be good to enterprise this thing, that it might have good successe: but God disappointed their lots and expectation' (Geneva gloss). An annual feast to commemorate the deliverance was thus declared (Esther 9: 19), 'as the Iewes do even to this day, calling it in the Persians language Purim, that is, the day of lots' (Geneva gloss). This was an irresistible source for Gowrie and Gunpowder sermons; Andrewes's sixth Gowrie sermon and tenth Gunpowder sermon are on texts from Esther that expand on the hinted connections here (*XCVI*, 830–43, 997–1008).

8–9. *Destroyer... Passe-over*: Exod. 12: 23 (*LACT*).

12–14. *by law... acknowledgement*: on 25 January 1606 the Commons passed to the Lords its bill for 'a publick Thanksgiving to be given to Almighty God, every Year, on the Fifth Day of *November*'; it received its second and third readings in the Lords on 28 and 30 January, and Andrewes was present (as bishop of Chichester) on all these days. See *Journals of the House of Commons, 1547–1628* (1803), 260; *Journals of the House of Lords* (1771), ii. 363–4. The resulting statute is in *Statutes of the Realm* (1819), 3 Jac. I.c.1, pp. 1067–8.

21. *this Psalme*: Ps. 118. Andrewes takes his text from one of the most familiar and resonant Psalms. Known traditionally as 'The Great Hallelujah', it was originally a song of praise by David for his deliverance from Saul, but from the Gospel authors onwards, parts were applied to the triumphant Christ; it was appointed to be read at Evening Prayer on Easter Day (*BCP*). Andrewes ranges very freely throughout the Psalm, not staying as close as usual to his chosen verses, to supply the sermon's complex thematic imagery.

23. *treatie*: 'treating of a subject in speech or writing' (*OED sn* 1.a).

30. *à posteriori*: Lat., 'from what comes after', i.e. empirically and inductively reasoned.

33. *this of David's*: in the historical sense of the Psalm, the circumstances of deliverance that prompted David to write the Psalm made 'his' day a day of God's '*Doing*'.

35. *gaudium erit plenum*: 'joy shall be full'.

36–37. *our Hosanna... Benedictus*: the cry of the multitude at Christ's triumphal entry to Jerusalem (Matt. 21: 9), which quotes Ps. 118: 26: 'Hosanna to the sonne of David: Blessed [Lat: *Benedictus*] is he that commeth in the Name of the Lord, Hosanna in the highest.' There is also the possibility of liturgical nostalgia in Andrewes's use of Latin here; in the pre-Reformation mass, the preface to the consecration reached a climax with the 'Sanctus' and 'Benedictus', both of which ended with the 'Hosanna' refrain (*Osanna in excelsis*); the 'Benedictus' was dropped in Cranmer's Order for Holy Communion (*BCP*).

p. 148, 1–2. *Is there any daies*: accepted early modern usage of 'is' for third person plural subjects.

3. *naturall and civill*: conditions in nature (i.e. the weather), and in human affairs.

5–6. *Poet... Father of daies*: Horace, *Odes* I. xxxiv. 5 (*LACT*), invokes 'Diespiter', archaic form of 'Jupiter', from Lat., 'dies Pater', '*Father of daies*'; cf. OT epithet for God, 'Ancient of days' (Dan. 7: 9, 13, 22).

12. יְהִי: Hebr., 'yehi'; 'let there be' (Gen. 1: 3, 6, 9, etc.).

12. *Sit*: Lat., 'let there be'.

12–13. *Lett... drie land*: cf. Gen. 1: 3, 6, 7, 9, 26 (*LACT*).

13. *Some, with Faciamus*: Andrewes pursues the distinction between days during which God created by simple command ('Let there be'), and those which involved his consultation and deliberation with the second person of the Trinity, Christ ('Let us make') in his 1592 lecture on the creation of Eve (this edn., pp. 100–101).

17. *letteth*: prevents, hinders.

24. *sensible*: 'perceptible to the inward mind or feelings' (*OED sa* I.2); but, modifying 'impression', also 'perceptible by the senses' (I.1.a).

28. *Faciamus diem hunc*: Lat., 'let us make this day'.

34. *shadow of death*: Ps. 23: 4.

37–38. *fiat... faciamus*: 'Let there be'; 'Let us make'.

p. 149, 1. *Hic est*: 'This is'.

3. *Dies Dominicus*: Lat., lit., 'the Dominical (i.e. Lord's) Day'; 'Sunday'.

3–4. *all... this verse*: much patristic thought had gone into justifying the translation of the Jewish Sabbath (Saturday) to the Christian Sunday; the debates were revived after the Reformation by more advanced Protestants' anxieties over proper Sabbath observance, the most extreme of whom, so-called 'judaizers', called for a return to Saturday worship. Andrewes also succinctly argues the orthodox case (citing as examples the Gunpowder and Gowrie commemorations) in his sermon for Easter 1618 (*XCVI*, 529), and at length in his 1619 *Speech... against the two judaicall opinions of Mr Traske* (in *OP*; also *LACT*, xi. 81–94).

5. παραβολή, *as Isaac*: Gr. 'parabŏlē', parable, analogy; from Heb. 11: 18–19: 'Of whom [Abraham] it was said, That, in Isaac shall thy seed be called: Accounting that God was able to raise him up, even from the dead: from whence also he received him in figure [παραβολή]'; for the interrupted sacrifice of Isaac, see Gen. 22: 1–18, and p. 228, ll. 24–28 and nn.

10. *dictante Spiritu*: 'dictated (declared) by the Spirit'.

11–12. *dies à Deo factus*: 'a day made by God'.

12–13. *former... diem Domini*: 'the Lord's doing makes [it] the day of the Lord', referring to Ps. 118: 23 ('this is the Lord's doing').

14. *Factum est*: 'it is done (or made)'.

15. *à Domino*: 'by the Lord'.

17. *goe to it*: *OED* (*sv* 64) cites 1735 as the earliest example of the colloquial sense here of 'to get to work'. However, Andrewes's use implies 'getting to' conjugal 'work'—the four aspects combining to make 'a *day of* GOD's *making*'—that bears comparison with Shakespeare's bitter use of the same phrase for lechery in *King Lear*: 'The wren goes to't and the small gilded fly | Does lecher in my sight. Let copulation thrive' (IV. vi. 111–12). The earliest recorded performance of *Lear* was at court, 26 December 1606.

21. *forepart of the Psalme*: Ps. 118: 5, 10–13, David's catalogue of persecutions suffered at the hands of his enemies.

34. *shrewd*: 'of evil nature, character, or influence' (*OED sa* 3.a); cf. Shakespeare, *Antony and Cleopatra*, IV. ix. 5: 'This last day was | A shrewd one to's.'

p. 150, 1. *denominates*: gives a name to.

13. *Usque ad miraculum*: 'even to the point of a miracle'; Andrewes's translation which follows ('so great, that *mervailous* withall') depends upon the common etymological roots of both 'mervailous/marvel' and 'miraculous/miracle' in Lat., *miror*, 'to wonder at'.

16. *A Domino... mirabile*: 'by God made and marvellous (miraculous)' (see prev. n.).

24–25. *right hand... passe*: Ps. 118: 15, 16.

32. *makes the odds*: compressed form of 'to make the odds even', i.e. to 'level inequalities, to adjust or do away with differences' (*OED sn* 1).

p. 151, 3. *compassing*: encompassing, encircling.

4–5. *undermining... under ground*: Andrewes here follows the government's assertion—promulgated in the first official account of the conspiracy, in Guy Fawkes's purported confession printed with it, and later in Coke's prosecution—of the existence of a tunnel dug under Parliament by the conspirators that was later abandoned for the rented basement room where the powder was eventually discovered (*His Majesties*

Speach, sig. E3ᵛ, H2ᵛ; *State Trials*, ii, col. 162). For the improbability of the tunnel, and the possibility that this was a detail added for 'literary' shock effect, see Fraser, *Faith and Treason*, 110–12, 204. The figurative sense of 'undermining' was also current; cf. John Bridges, *A Defence of the Government* (1587, p. 200), describing ministers who build on the church's foundation 'with all care: least sathan with his mynes secretly wrought, do undermine it'.

    8. *danger... discried*: cf. the prediction in the Mounteagle letter that the intended victims '*shall not see who hurts them*' (*His Majesties Speach*, sig. F3ᵛ).

    10. *He*: David (Ps. 118: 12).

    11. *brood of vipers*: Matt. 3: 7, 12: 34.

    11. *mordentes in silentio*: Lat., 'that sting in silence'.

    12. *the deadly blow*: a common pun in accounts of the plot, from the original enigmatic *double-entendre* in the Mounteagle letter: '*For though there be no apparance* [sic] *of any stirre, yet I say, they shall receive a terrible Blow this Parliament*' (*His Majesties Speach*, sig. F3ᵛ).

    15. *his three Estates*: nobility, clergy, and commons.

    19–25. *King David... kingdome*: every official account of the plot took particular care to enumerate in detail the estates and offices of the intended victims. Andrewes's contribution to the form here is to cast his list in the conceit of OT types: King James (*King David*); Queen Anne (*Queen Esther*); Prince Henry (*Salomon*); Prince Charles (*Nathan*); Lord Ellesmere, Lord Chancellor (*Jehosaphat*); the Earl of Dorset, Lord Treasurer (*Adoram*); the Earl of Salisbury, Principal Secretary (*Seraja*); Archbishop of Canterbury John Bancroft and Archbishop of York Matthew Hutton (*Sadoc and Abiathar*); the house of bishops (*twenty more, the chiefe of the Priests*); Chief Justice of the King's Bench John Popham (*Admo*); '*Joab his Generall*' has a less obvious equivalent, but is probably the Earl of Worcester, Master of the Horse, who also deputed as Earl Marshall; or perhaps alternatively, the Earl of Nottingham, Lord Admiral. The '*forty eight Worthies* or *Nobles*' are cognate for the House of Lords, and the 'Principall of all the *Tribes*' the House of Commons. The marginal list of sources needs to be supplemented with 2 Sam. 8: 17 and 1 Chron. 11: 20–47 (*LACT*). There is some confusion in the sources as to whether the 5-year old Charles, Duke of York (later Charles I) was present at the state opening of Parliament. Thomas Wyntour's confession included an account of plans to kidnap the Duke from his chamber at Whitehall during the mêlée caused by the explosion nearby, but Sir Edward Philips argued at the trial that the blast would have destroyed 'the whole royal issue male', leaving only the Princesses Elizabeth and Mary alive (*His Majesties Speach*, sig. I4ᵛ; *State Trials*, ii, col. 165).

    30. *Locusts... pitt*: cf., 'And so the earth as it were opened, should have sent forth of the bottome of the *Stygian* lake such sulphured smoke, furious flames, and fearefull thunder, as should have by their diabolicall *Domesday* destroyed and defaced... our present living Princes and people' (*His Majesties Speach*, sig. E3ᵛ).

    31–32. *Tragœdies... prodigiously impious*: cf., from Coke's prosecuting speech, 'It is a *sine exemplo*, beyond all examples, whether in fact or fiction, even of the tragick poets, who did beat their wits to represent the most fearful and horrible murders' (*State Trials*, ii, col. 167); although the allusions are not specific, Aeschylus and Seneca, authors of famously violent Greek and Roman tragedy, would have been typical examples to the early modern mind.

    31. *Heathen men*: ancient Greeks and Romans (see prev. n.).

33. *Hunnes... Turcilingi*: Germanic nations or tribes of northern Europe legendary for their savage attacks on the Eastern Roman Empire in the third to fifth centuries; cf. Coke's exclamation, 'O barbarous, and more than Scythian or Thracian cruelty!' (*State Trials*, ii, col. 176).

35. *barbarous... Beasts*: a *gradatio* from civilized, to barbarous, to beastly horror first deployed by King James in his speech to Parliament (*His Majesties Speach*, sig. B3ʳ); the official indictment of the plotters similarly accused them of the intention to kill in a manner 'most barbarously and more than beastly' (*State Trials*, ii, col. 161).

36–37. θηριτης *brutishnesse... imagine*: Gr., thērités ('savagery'); Aristotle, *Ethics*, VII. i. 1 (*LACT*): 'the states of moral character to be avoided are of three kinds—Vice, Unrestraint, and Bestiality (θηριτης)' (trans. H. Rackham, who notes that the Gr. combines the English senses 'brutality' and 'bestiality').

38. *havock*: havoc; destruction, devastation, particularly of quarry in a hunt.

40. *looke to paterne it*: 'seek a model for it'; cf. Coke's prosecuting declaration that 'this offense is such, as no man can express it, no example pattern it, no measure contain it' (*State Trials*, ii, col. 168).

41. *from the Devill*: from the outset the plot was described as Satan's work, the most sustained such effort being Bishop William Barlow's devotion of an entire section of the first post-plot sermon preached at Paul's Cross to Fawkes's '*hyperdiabolicall divelishnes*' (*The Sermon Preached at Paules Crosse, the tenth day of November* (1606), sig. C2ᵛ–D1ʳ). Sermon treatments of the plot as a doomed satanic rebellion, including this and others by Andrewes, had an enduring literary and political legacy; see Cressy, *Bonfires and Bells*, 151–2; and Revard, 'Milton's Gunpowder Poems'.

p. 152, 9–11. *Esau's crueltie... Ladies*: Gen. 32: 11; 2 Kings 25: 8–21; Esther 3: 13.

14. *Put to*: add up; *OED* cites 1605 as the last usage of this sense (*sv* 53.a).

28. *Hoc est... conculcare*: 'this is to trample upon Christ as well as Paul'.

33–34. *abomination... holy place*: Daniel's prophecy of the defiling of the Temple with idolatry (Dan. 9: 27) was applied by Christ as a portent of the Apocalypse (Matt. 24: 15; Mark 15: 14). Protestants often glossed this as the idol of the Roman Catholic mass, and Roman Catholics, conversely, as the Protestant abolition of the same (cf. Geneva and Douai-Rheims glosses on Matt. 24: 15). Andrewes retains the common use of 'his' as a genitive neuter (not masculine) pronoun that does not imply personification, i.e. '*his* [its] *abomination*' (*OED*, s poss. pron., B.3.c).

36–37. *yea... taken effect*: several plotters expressed some degree of repentance at their trials; Father Garnet maintained throughout his interrogation that he had always been horrified by the plot (Fraser, *Faith and Treason*, 224, 252).

40. *Neither root... left*: cf. Mal. 4: 1 ('the day commeth that... shall burne them vp, sayeth the Lorde of hostes, and shall leave them neither roote nor branche'), perhaps made current in this context by Thomas Wyntour's confession that the plot 'strake at the Roote, and would breed a confusion fit to beget new alterations' (*His Majesties Speach*, sig. I1ᵛ–2ʳ).

40–41. *Strangers... murtherers exalted*: the plotters' ('*murtherers*.') plans for the post-plot state were never very clear in their own minds, except for their own status as liberating Catholic heroes. According to Coke, the kidnapped Princess Elizabeth was to have been used initially as a puppet monarch. But Sir Edward Philips, Serjeant-at-Law, asserted the plotters' intention 'to ruinate the state of the commonwealth, and to bring in *strangers* [i.e. foreigners] to invade it', a speculation based on the plotters' hopes that an invasion force from Spain would join in the liberation of English Catholics (*State Trials*, ii, cols. 161, 165, 169–70).

p. 153, 2. *pitch*: highest point, summit, extremity.

3. *Undertaken... holy Sacrament*: the five main conspirators—Catesby, Wyntour, Wright, Fawkes, and Percy—swore to the secrecy of their plot on a primer in a Lambeth inn on 20 May 1604 and then attended mass celebrated in an adjoining room by the Jesuit, Father John Gerard. By his own account and the unvaried testimony of all the plotters, he knew nothing of the plot when he administered the sacrament (Fraser, *Faith and Treason*, 99).

4–6. *warranted... JESUS*: promulgation of the main points of the regime's assertion that the plot was 'warranted' by the Jesuits, as argued in all the trials; the prosecutors, like Andrewes here, savoured the irony of the order's name (cf. Phil. 2: 10); cf. Coke's scoff that the Jesuits 'use the reverence of religion, yea, even the most sacred and blessed name of Jesus, as a mantle to cover their impiety' (*State Trials*, ii, col. 171).

6–7. *these holy... Jesuites*: both the Jesuits generally, and their Superior ('*chiefe*') in England, Father' Henry' Garnet.

7–8. *absolution... well done*: the fugitive conspirators were confessed, absolved, and heard mass by the Jesuit Father Hart (alias Hammond) at Huddington Court, Worcestershire, on 7 November (Fraser, *Faith and Treason*, 223–4).

8–9. *justified... sanctified... glorified*: ironic application of the classic formula of salvation as justification, sanctification, and glorification, to the supposed Jesuit endorsement of the plot. Roman Catholics maintained salvation not merely by God's decree, but by the participation of the believer in that process through sanctifying good works. In Andrewes's parody, the Jesuits play God by decreeing the plot not only '*justified* as lawfull', but also as a 'meritorious' good work for which the plotters would be granted salvation, that is, '*glorified*' in heaven. Andrewes thus shows the 'failure' not only of the Gunpowder Plot, but also by implication, the equally flawed 'plot' of Roman Catholic soteriology. Cf. also Coke's prosecution claim that 'Catesby was resolved by the Jesuits, that the fact was both lawful and meritorious' (*State Trials*, ii, col. 175).

10. *long yer*: long ere.

11. *canonized... holy act*: '*canonized*' not in respect to persons declared saints, but the 'act' of regicide set up as canon (church) law.

11–12. *the Conclave*: locked (fr. Lat., *cum clave*, 'with a key') chamber in which Roman Catholic cardinals meet to elect a new pope; more generally, any meeting of the College of Cardinals in Rome; cf. John Donne's anti-Jesuit satire, *Ignatius His Conclave* (1611).

12. *Now... of it*: boast not only of the foiling of the plot, but also the trial and execution of the leading Jesuits in England; Coke branded the plot 'the Jesuits Treason' at Garnet's trial, and predicted, 'I conceive their fall to be near at hand, both by divinity and by philosophy... their time is at an end' (*State Trials*, ii, col. 237).

16–17. *rejecting this Stone*: King James, in the terms of Ps. 118: 22 (cf. also Matt. 21: 42, Mark 12: 10, 11; Luke 20: 17; Acts 4: 11; Eph. 2: 20; 1 Pet. 2: 4, 6), the '*Stone*' rejected by the '*builders*' of the plot; Andrewes devoted an entire sermon to the application of this verse to James and Christ when Accession Day and Easter Day coincided in 1611 (*XCVI*, 435–46); cf. p. 160, ll. 26–27 and n.

17–19. *favoured... blow him up*: technically, James, unlike Elizabeth, was never excommunicated by the Pope. Like the state prosecutors, Andrewes exploits extreme Jesuit statements that justified the killing of heretical sovereigns. Cf. the official indictment of the plotters, which claimed that the Jesuits persuaded them 'that our said sovereign lord the king, the nobility, and whole commonalty... (papists excepted) were heretics; and that all heretics were accursed and excommunicate; and that none heretic could be a king; and that it was lawful and meritorious to kill... the king, and all other heretics within this realm' (*State Trials*, ii, col. 160). Garnet, in fact, distanced himself from tyrranicide at his trial, even pressing the fact that James was legitimate and not excommunicate—obviously to no avail (Fraser, *Faith and Treason*, 104–5, 258). For Andrewes on regicide, see 'A Sermon Preached... the Fifth of August' (this edn.).

21. *shrining*: enshrining; an ironic appropriation of the Roman Catholic practice of venerating relics, to Protestant eyes an '*abomination*' in the church.

22. *missall*: a typically multi-layered pun: generally, relating to the mass; specifically, meaning both the liturgical book (the 'missal') used by the priest to say mass, and, derogatorily by Protestants, the Roman priest himself (cf. 'missal-priests', 'mass-priests'); finally, in the literal etymological sense of 'sent away, dismissed' (Lat., 'missus')–the plotters were 'dismissed' by the priests to 'send-off', or kill, their intended victims.

23. *orison*: prayer; rare in the singular (*OED sn* 1.b).

25. *qui legit... videt*: 'he who reads it understands it; nay, he who sees it [understands it]'.

26–27. GOD send... should: reverberation of the 'missal' pun (see n. above): 'May God cause ["send"] those who would have been victims of the Plot [those listening to the sermon] to learn the lesson they should from it'.

31. *factum fuisset... est?*: 'the [thing] that was to have been done... the [thing] that was done?'

31. *blowen over*: blown over; '(of storms or storm-clouds) to pass over a place without descending upon it; to pass away, come to an end; also *fig.* of misfortune, danger, etc.' (*OED sv¹* 12.c, citing 1617 as the earliest usage).

33–34. *snare... delivered*: Ps. 124: 7.

34–35. *both Houses*: of Parliament, Lords and Commons.

35. *haire... perished*: Luke 21: 18.

37–38. *little Benjamin... Juda &c.*: another OT conceit for the royal family and nobility (cf. p. 223 and n.), here from Psalm 68, one of the proper Psalms in the Gunpowder Treason commemoration service.

39. *Stone... corner*: see ll. 16–17; p. 160, ll. 27–30 and nn.

p. 154, 3–5. *A Dæmone... God's doing*: parody of Vulg., Ps. 117: 23 and Geneva Ps. 118: 23 (see p. 146, ll. 6–13 and nn.).

6. *ward*: watch, protection.

7–9. *satt... his limmes*: for God's bemused surveillance of rebellion by the forces ('*limmes*', 'limbs') of Satan, cf. Ps. 2: 4, 37: 13; for the literary influence of the motif in Gunpowder contexts, see Revard, 'Milton's Gunpowder Poems'.

9. *mercie... his workes*: Lam. 3: 22. King James opened his speech to Parliament on the discovery of the plot by invoking this verse: 'I must therefore begin with this old and most approoued Sentence of Divinitie, *Misericordia Dei supra omnia opera eius*. For Almighty God did not furnish so great matter to his glory by the Creation of this great World, as hee did by the Redemption of the same' (*His Majesties Speach*, sig. A4ᵛ). Andrewes took this as his text for his Gunpowder Treason sermon in 1612 (*XCVI*, 959–70).

15–16. *Leviathan... chaine*: Job 40: 20–1 (Geneva; AV, Job 41: 1–2); the biblical sea monster, or whale, whose power can only be controlled by God; traditionally identified with Satan (cf. Isa. 27: 1).

21. *goe... the lott*: in his speech at the plotters' trial Coke also saw Providence at work in the fact that 'God suffered their intended mischief to come so near the period; as not to be discerned, but within few hours before it should have been executed' (*State Trials*, ii, col. 182). The delayed discovery was as much Salisbury's, as it was God's, way of drawing the net as tightly as possible around the plotters and of maximizing public shock and indignation at the intended treason (Fraser, *Faith and Treason*, 156–8). For the biblical pun on 'lott', see p. 147, l. 6 and n.

24–28. *the hill... blow*: Andrewes conflates imagery from both the account of Fawkes's apprehension, and the arrested sacrifice of Isaac by Abraham (cf. p. 149, ll. 4–5 and n.). Fawkes was apprehended amidst 'Billets and Coales... Barrels of powder... to the number of thirtie sixe', holding 'three matches, and all other instruments fit for blowing up the powder ready upon him, which made him instantly confesse his owne guiltinesse' (*His Majesties Speach*, sig. G4^r).

29. *treacherie... like water*: Ps. 58: 7.

31. *arserunt... spinis*: not Vulg., but Andrewes's trans. of Ps. 118: 12 ('They... are extinct even as a fire among thorns'; *LACT*).

33–34. *priusquam... fire*: cf. Ps. 58: 9, Geneva translation and gloss: 'As raw flesh before your pots feele the fire of thornes: so let him cary them away as with a whirlewinde in his wrath'; 'As flesh is taken rawe out of the pot before the water seethe [boils]; so he desireth God to destroy their enterprises before they bring them to passe'.

34. *gate*: got, took.

36–37. *bewrayed... bewrayers*: 'revealed... revealers'.

37–39. *Eccl. 10... penns*: Eccles. 10: 20—'Curse not the king... for a bird of the aire shall carry the voyce, and that which hath wings shall tell the matter'—invites a serendipitous double pun: the anonymous letter interpreted by the king was written with a quill (*'feather'*) pen; the loyal recipient who showed it to the king was Mounteagle. Woodcuts of the plot's discovery would also depict the letter's delivery to the king by a descending eagle, punning not only on Mounteagle's name, but probably also alluding to the gift of prophetic interpretation in the descent of the Holy Spirit on King James (cf. Fraser, *Faith and Treason*, pl. opp. p. 157).

p. 154, 40–p. 155, 1. *This... His worke*: Ps. 64: 9.

5–11. *This... would doe it*: James's interpretation of the Mounteagle letter was hailed as miraculous divine inspiration (see prev. n.). Only days after the discovery Barlow told the crowd at Paul's Cross that the royal interpretation proved 'that in Kinges there is a divine inspiration' (*Sermon*, sig. E1^r). At the conspirators' trial Coke elaborated 'how the King was divinely illuminated by Almighty God, the only ruler of princes, like an Angel of God, to direct and point... to the very place... out of the dark words of the letter concerning the terrible blow' (*State Trials*, ii, col. 182).

8. קסם: Hebr., 'qesem'; divination, oracle.

9–10. *Joseph... riddle*: Gen. 41: 45 (*LACT*).

14. *reclaimed*: converted, reformed.

16. *even GOD... withall*: '*withall*' = preposition, syn. 'with'; hence, 'it was even God that they strove [struggled] with'.

16–18. *hidden... perished there*: led by Catesby, the surviving plotters tried unsuccessfully to raise an armed rebellion by recusants in Warwickshire and Staffordshire. In their last stand at Holbeach House, Staffordshire, on 8 November, four were shot and killed in the sheriff's ambush (Fraser, *Faith and Treason*, 171–2, 180–3, 186–7).

18–20. *perished... them thither*: Andrewes declares that the plotters killed at Holbeach were ushered directly to hell by Satan, following the logic that their souls must suffer the same fate as their treason ('as this I say did'): to 'perish eternally' with the diabolical maker 'who never left them'.

20–21. *cast... disfigured them*: the accidental igniting of gunpowder spread out to dry by a fireplace in Holbeach House maimed several of the fugitive plotters. This evident piece of poetic justice was not lost on the prosecuting regime. Barlow at Paul's Cross observed that God 'would not suffer them to bee taken, till they were fired out of the house, who woulde have fired us within a house: striking some of their eyes out with Gunne-powder, (the insturment of our death)' (*Sermon*, sig. E1^v). At their trial, Coke described 'the little blow at Holbeach' as another touch of miraculous providence since 'the powder taking fire and blowing up, scorched those who were nearest', but left them alive for trial (*State Trials*, ii, col. 182). Andrewes, especially in light of what follows, probably has this latter point in mind when calling the Holbeach plotters '*powdered*', meaning, 'to sprinkle the flesh of animals with salt or powdered spice, esp. for preserving' (*OED, sv^1*, 2.a; see also next note).

22. *their quarters... ours*: the plotters who survived to stand trial were hanged, drawn, and quartered (the statutory punishment for treason) on 30 and 31 January 1606; the bodies of Catesby and Percy, who had died at Holbeach, were exhumed for the same purpose. The decapitated heads were hung from the corners of the Parliament House that they had intended to destroy, and would still have been *in situ* at the time of Andrewes's sermon as emblems of the retributive justice he articulates here.

27. *as prints*: as handprints, fingerprints.

39–40. *Come... God is!*: Ps. 66: 4 (*LACT*).

p. 156, 1. *exalt... to see*: grisly allusion to the traitors' heads 'exalted' a few buildings away from the Chapel Royal on Parliament House (see p. 155, ll. 21–22 and n.).

2. *say to him*: to the Prophet, David.

7. *mirabile*: Lat., 'miraculous'.

12. *his full Christendome*: 'its full Christendome'), its proper name-giving as at baptism or christening (*OED* 'christendom', 4.b.(b)); cf. more extended treatment of 'full Christendome' in 'A Sermon Preached... the fifth of August', this edn., p. 183–84 and nn.

14–15. *When... that dreame*: Ps. 126: 1; with verses 2–4, the text of his court Gunpowder Treason sermon the following year (*XCVI*, 901–10).

16. *in a maze*: in amaze, = 'amazement', 'extreme astonishment, wonder' (*OED sn* 4).

22. *strangers... strange*: European powers, including Catholic ones, were carefully exempted from any officially sanctioned suspicion, and expressed unanimous shock and condemnation of the treason. See *His Majesties Speach*, sig. C3^r; *State Trials*, ii, col. 168; and Fraser, *Faith and Treason*, 193.

p. 157, 6. *to assay*: to try.

7. *Prophet*: David.

18. *Nehemia's promise... joy*: Neh. 8: 10.

27–28. *two words... tongues*: the two terms from his text under consideration, '*Exultemus & lætemur*' ('rejoice and be glad') in the three 'biblical' languages ('tongues') of Latin, Greek (ἀγαλλιάω and χαίρω), and Hebrew (בֶּן and שמה 'gil' and 'samah'), in all of which the former describes bodily expressions of joy, and the latter spiritual or emotional expressions of it.

p. 158, *constituere... altaris*: Vulg., Ps. 117: 27 (Ps. 118: 27, *LACT*).

4. *levin of malignitie*: cf. Matt. 13: 33, 1 Cor. 5: 8; 'leaven', literally yeast, but metaphorically in the NT, 'An agency which produces profound change by progressive inward operation' (*OED sn* 2.a).

5–7. *preaching... bells*: important early example of Andrewes's resistance to sermon-centred piety at James's court, and an anticipation of his regular use of Gunpowder Plot sermons there to commend more careful liturgical (including musical) observance of feast days; also perhaps a discrete attempt to qualify or correct the statute instituting the new feast day, which loosely enjoined 'the said Morning Prayer Preaching or other Service of God' on the day. After cautioning against 'onely *preaching*', he gracefully complements full choral service as the congregation in the Chapel Royal would have heard it immediately before he preached. Special choral anthems were composed for the festival, presumably for use in the Chapel Royal and cathedral churches; texts or parts of texts for seven survive; one of these (anon.) is a setting of part of Andrewes's text, Ps. 118: 24 (Ralph Daniel and Peter LeHuray, *The Sources of English Church Music 1549–1660*, 1972). Another anonymous Gunpowder verse anthem ('Hearken ye nations', Bodl. MS Rawl. Poet. 23) combines, like Andrewes here, lurid imagery of the plot with a paraphrase of Ps. 118: 23–4 ('This day our God from foe's bloodthirsty ire, | Hath sav'd as brands new taken from the fire | This day is the day Himself made | O rejoice and sing, and sing His praises with a cheerful voice'). There is debate about whether string bands, as well as organs, accompanied the pre-Restoration Chapel Royal choir, but Andrewes's allusion here ('with *instruments...* of the *Queer*) seems to suggest so. Bell-ringing had been part of the spontaneous celebrations on the day of the plot's discovery in 1605; although not mentioned in the 1606 statute, bell-ringing, along with bonfires, was one of the most distinctive features of parish observances of 5 November. See Cressy, *Bonfires and Bells*, 146; for the holiday legislation, see p. 147, ll. 12–14 and n.

8. *Hosanna in altissimis*: Matt. 21: 9 (*LACT*).

8. *key*: intensity of tone or style (a transferative sense of the literal musical meaning 'pitch' or 'tone').

9. *close*: secretive, covert.

10. *Shemei... David*: 2 Sam. 19: 16–21, 20: 1–2.

10. *fleering*: smiling obsequiously; cf. Juan de Santa Marâia (*sic*), trans. J.M., *Policie Unveiled* (1632): 'They come towards you with a fleering Countenance, but no sooner have you in their reach, but they snap at you' (p. 333).

11. *taken on*: put-on, false.

17–18. *you wott what*: 'you know what'.

18–19. *de fontibus... heart*: Ps. 68: 26 (the second proper Psalm appointed for the Gunpowder Treason commemoration service); Geneva and Bishops' Bible keep the more literal 'ye that are of the fountaine of Israel'; *BCP*, reproduced in the official service, reads 'Give thanks O Israel, unto God the Lord in the congregations: from the ground of the heart' (sig. B2ʳ).

24–30. *joy... Calve's feast*: daring critique of James's court's reputation for indecorous feasting and drunkenness, which had reached scandalous proportions during the visit of James's brother-in-law, Christian IV of Denmark, three months earlier (August 1606); Sir John Harington's account (*Letters and Epigrams*, ed. N. E. McClure (Philadelphia, 1930), 118–26) of the drunkenness and vomiting after the Gowrie day masque

(5 August) corroborates Andrewes's complaints; the latter had on the same morning preached his first Gowrie anniversary sermon (*XCVI* (4th edn., 1641), 1009–20).

34. *Aperite... Justitiæ*: Vulg., Ps. 117: 19; 'open me the gates of righteousness' (Ps. 118: 18, *BCP*).

35. *blessed... house of the Lord*: cf. Ps. 118: 26.

p. 159, 4. *endites us a versicle*: 'indites [composes] a versicle for us'; a short dialogue of sentences from scripture, usually from the Psalms, recited or sung responsively between minister and congregation (or choir) in a liturgy; Andrewes alludes to Ps. 118: 26 (see p. 147, l. 36 and n.). Although a short set of versicles (verses and responses) was retained in Cranmer's orders for Morning and Evening Prayer ('O Lord, open thou our lips', etc.), in Roman uses they were much more elaborate, and associated with processions on high festival days. Andrewes here revives that pre-Reformation, festival, processional sense of versicles by retrieving Ps. 118: 26 ('Blessed is he that commeth in the name of the Lord') as it was adapted by the crowds and children who hailed Christ's triumphal entry into Jerusalem and his arrival in the Temple (Matt. 21: 9, 15), thus safely commending in purely biblical terms a liturgical custom that had been proscribed at the Reformation. The Mattheian version was also used by Jacobean composers Orlando Gibbons and Thomas Weelkes for festival anthems probably sung in the Chapel Royal (see next n.).

6. *children... perfect*: Matt. 21:9, 16; but also in context of sung service in the Chapel Royal, a punning gesture to the choristers, the Children of the Chapel.

7–10. *summe... His name*: glosses the subject of the 'Benedictus' and 'Hosanna' (prev. n.) as King James, recently 'come unto us' from Scotland.

13. *tolletur à vobis*: 'it is taken from you'.

13. *worme... gourd*: Jonah 4: 6–7.

16. *exultate in tremore*: Vulg., Ps. 2: 11; lit., 'rejoice in fear'.

22. *neerly*: nearly; closely, intimately.

23–24. *God... wrought in us*: cf. 2 Thess. 2: 17.

27. *quickned*: inspired, enlivened.

29–34. *foure times... still*: recondite allusion to the four times in the scripture that the exclamation 'Hosanna' is spoken or transliterated. Ps. 118: 25 in English translations ('Help me now, O Lord: O Lord, send us now prosperity', *BCP*) is a literal rendering of 'Hosanna! Hosanna!' The Greek ὡσαννά ('hosanna') is a transliteration of 'the originall' Hebrew 'hosiah-na' (hence the observation that 'the *Evangelist* lett it alone'). Heb. 'ana' is a primary particle of incitement and entreaty ('oh!', as in Ps. 118: 25 'O Lord'; these are Andrewes's '*interjections*: all to make it passionate'). Andrewes's own rendering of Ps. 118: 25 ('*Now good Lord... yet still*') is closest to *BCP*.

36–37. JESUS...*for ever*: Heb. 13: 8 (*LACT*).

p. 159, 41–p. 160, 1. *saving... his name*: the Gr. Ἰησοῦς ('Jesus') is a transliteration of the Hebr., 'Jeshua', a later form of 'Joshua', which transliterated means 'Yahweh will save'; for Andrewes on the name of Jesus, cf. *XCVI*, 75, 473–4.

13. *shaddow... wings*: frequent metaphor for divine protection in the Psalms (cf. Ps. 17: 8, 57: 1, 63: 7), also used in the Gunpowder service, in the second collect for morning prayer: 'from all treasons and conspiracies, preserve [the royal family] in thy faith, feare and love, under the shadow of thy wings against all evill and wickednes'; also in the special prayer concluding the Litany: 'shield our gracious King under the

shadow of thy wings, that no mischievous attempt may come neere' (*Prayers and Thankesgiving*, sig. D3ᵛ, E3ᵛ).

14. *light ... countenance*: common Psalmic metaphor (cf. Ps. 4: 6, 44: 3, 90: 8).

15–16. *exultemus ... from within*: see p. 157, ll. 25–29 and n.

17–18. *Praysed ... His servants*: Ps. 35: 27 (*LACT*).

21. *Head ... corner*: Ps. 118: 22, applied to King James (see p. 153, l. 16; p. 160, ll. 27–29 and nn.).

24–25. *read, Blessed be he*: in Ps. 118: 26.

27. *that ... amongst us*: by repeating the third person masculine pronouns, Andrewes compresses the analogy between the triumphant Christ and King James: 'that [Jesus] would blesse [King James], and make [King James] blest, that, in [Jesus's] blessed Name, is come amonst us'.

28–29. *corner ... fall asunder*: Andrewes elaborates this architectural imagery in his sermon on this text for Easter and Accession day 1611, where he proliferates political, moral, and doctrinal equivalents for the two 'walls'; that which he clearly intends here is the union in the person of James both of the crowns of England and Scotland, and more generally, James's headship over both church and state. Cf. from the later sermon, 'that is, the two estates, *Civill* and *Ecclesiasticall*, which maketh the maine *Angle*, in every Government.... And, the happy combining of these two, is the strength of the *Head*, and the strength of the whole *Building*' (*XCVI*, 442–3).

29. *If otherwise ... not*: dramatic *aposiopesis* that registers both scruple and horror at articulating the possibility of the king's deposition, or worse.

31. *House of the Lord*: Ps. 134: 1 (*LACT*).

38–39. *Name ... foure yeares*: Ps. 118: 26; James acceeded to the English throne 25 March 1603.

p. 161, 3–4. *incense ... altar fast*: Ps. 118: 27 (*LACT*).

4–5. *dismisse you ... drinke*: morning prayer and sermon in the Chapel Royal immediately preceded the main meal of the day; thus Andrewes literally dismisses the congregation to go from his sermon to the ensuing feast in hall or presence chamber.

18. *this Day ... gladnesse*: a fine example of Andrewes's ability to compose new prayers almost entirely from small fragments and phrases of scripture, shown most extensively in the *Preces*; see Lossky, *Lancelot Andrewes*, 303–4 et sqq.

19. *glorious ... wonders*: Exod. 15: 11 (*LACT*).

A SERMON PREACHED ... ON CHRISTMAS DAY.
ANNO 1609

Text. [block orn.] | Two | Sermons preached | before the Kings Maiestie at | *Whitehall. Of the Birth of* | CHRIST | The one on Christmas | day ANNO 1609. | *The other on Christmas day* last ANNO 1610. | ¶ By the Bishop of *Elie* his Maiesties | Almoner. | [rule] | [block orn.] | [rule] | ¶ Imprinted at London by *Robert* | *Barker*, Printer to the Kings most Excel- | lent Maiestie. ANNO 1610. (*STC* 628, hereafter, Q_2). This printing of the sermon as the second of two consecutive Christmas sermons by Andrewes is a corrected edition of A SERMON PREACHED BE- | fore the Kings Maiestie | *at White-Hall,* | On Munday the 25. of De- | cember, Being Christmas day, | ANNO 1609. | ¶ By the Bishop of *Elie* His | *Maiesties Almoner.* | [block orn.] | [rule] | ¶ Imprinted at

London by *Robert | Barker*, Printer to the Kings | most Excellent Maiestie. (1610; *STC2* 619, hereafter Q_1). Both appeared by royal command (on the evidence of the King's Printer, and Chamberlain; for the latter, see Headnote). Significant variants shown in the apparatus include the addition of two clauses (p. 164, ll. 25–26; p. 175, ll. 21–22) in Q_2. That these were probably extant in the MS copy text for Q_1, but mistakenly skipped by its typesetter is suggested by the fact that in both instances the first word after the omitted text is the same as the last word before the omission, classic cases of typesetter's errors of anticipation. Also documented is the correction of several egregious spelling errors; more minute, but probably authorial, are subtle changes to punctuation throughout, which, almost without exception, clarify either grammar, parallelism, or the vocal inflection of words or clauses. Not recorded here are the numerous incidental variants, the large majority of which are from the typesetter's free manipulation in both quartos of double-letter and terminal-'e' spellings (e.g. 'bee/be', 'full/ful', 'fulnesse/fulnes') as well as 'and/&' to justify line margins. Also not recorded are several corrections by Q_2 of Q_1's inconsistent capitalization of personal pronouns for Christ and the Virgin Mary. The uniform improvement of Q_2 over Q_1 suggests that Q_2 was corrected by Andrewes or his amanuensis against the manuscript copy text used for Q_1. The 'importunitie' with which King James commanded the sermon into print (see Headnote) perhaps accounts for the poorer quality of Q_1. The editors of *XCVI* (F_1) used the inferior Q_1 as their copy text, evidenced most clearly by the absence of the two passages found only in Q_2. The only substantive variant readings common to F_1 and Q_2 are obvious errors from Q_1 that could have been corrected in F_1 by an attentive editor or typesetter without recourse to another copy text. Copy texts used for this edition are Bodl. Sermons 1(15) (Q_1); collated with Bodl. B20.23(3) Linc. (Q_2); and *XCVI* (1629, editor's copy; F_1).

Headnote. Contemporary accounts suggest that this was one of Andrewes's most popular sermons with the king and court. John Chamberlain reported to Dudley Carleton on 30 December that Andrewes 'preached at court on Christmas day with great applause, being not only *sui similis* ['like himself'], but more then himself by the report of the King and all his auditors. I am promised some notes of his sermon, and then your part is therein.' On 13 January he enthused to Sir Ralph Winwood, ambassador to the Hague, that 'I hope we shall have [Andrewes's] sermon upon the 4th to the Galatians 4th verse, preached on Christmas day last with great applause: the King with much importunitie had the copie delivered him on Tewsday last before his going toward Roiston, and sayes he will lay yt still under his pillow' (Chamberlain, *Letters*, i. 292, 295). 'The copie' may have been a manuscript from the author, but given Chamberlain's anticipation of print publication, might also have been an advance copy of Q_1 from the King's Printer. The reasons for the king's enthusiasm, and for the relative neglect of the sermon in modern times, may be the same. Stylistically Andrewes's prose here is at its most intensely Senecan, with syntax compressed to the shortest, most intense units possible. These characteristics were highly fashionable in early Jacobean prose, but foreign to modern taste. Similarly, the sermon's structure is relentlessly symmetrical, proceeding in a minute exegetical *gradatio* through the component parts of the biblical text and revealing only incrementally a sum of parts that is greater than the whole. The result is a dazzling *tour de force* of brevity and intensity that, although it lacks discursive narrative or pictorial imagery, is in its very form imitative of the subject of the sermon: the Incarnation paradox that an unbelievable 'fulness' is to be found in the Word, both written and Incarnate. Characteristically,

Andrewes concludes the sermon by calling the court to a bodily participation in the 'fulness' of the Incarnation not just through holiday 'pastime', but also incorporation into the body of Christ through liturgical worship, and, consummately, in the 'ful service' of the Eucharist. The sermon's theological themes of sonship, adoption, inheritance, and investiture would have had further contemporary application as the court prepared for the heir apparent, Prince Henry's investiture as Prince of Wales (May 1610), an event also anticipated by Ben Jonson's Twelfth Night masque, *Prince Henries Barriers*, performed twelve days after this sermon.

Sources. This sermon shows little direct debt, acknowledged or not, to specific patristic or contemporary sources, with only passing mention of Tertullian and Cyprian, and a fleeting—probably incorrect—allusion to Alcuin. It does, however, reflect the consensus of using Gal. 4: 4 as an orthodox proof text for the two natures of Christ, particularly to refute Gnostic denials of his humanity (revived, in Andrewes's view, by Anabaptists); cf. pp. 169–70 and nn.; and Jerome, *Comment. in Epist. ad Galatos* (*PL*, 26.372); Augustine, *Sermo LII*, iv. 10 (*PL*, 38.58); and Rabanus Maurus, *Ennar. in Epist. B. Pauli* (*PL*, 112.312–13). Andrewes also makes a conventional connection between Christ's circumcision and Paul's insistence that Christ was 'made under the Law' (cf. pp. 170–71 and nn.). Striking, however, is Andrewes's unusual treatment of the circumcision as a type or anticipation of the Passion, which seems to be the first such by a Protestant author in English. In Reformed thought, circumcision was treated either as a metaphor for mortification of the flesh (cf. *BCP*, collect for the Circumcision of Christ), or, following St Paul (Gal. 2), as a type of Christian baptism and an emblem of the Old Covenant abolished by the New. Circumcision as an anticipation of the Passion was, however, a commonplace in late medieval devotional writing, epitomized by the pseudo-Bonaventuran work translated by Nicholas Love as *The Mirrour of the Blessed Lyf of Jesu Christ*. This work insists on two of Andrewes's principal points about the feast, that 'the blessid name of Jesu . . . this day was openly declared', and 'that this day oure lord Jesu bygan to scheden his precious blood for our sake', hence, 'in these great festes and solempnites we schulde make moche merthe and be joyful' (*Mirrour*, ed. L. F. Powell (1907), 51–2). But closer to Andrewes's time, devotion to the Circumcision was a hallmark of Jesuits' writings, whose society was dedicated to the name given Christ at his circumcision, and the high altar in whose mother church, the Gesu in Rome, was dedicated in 1587 to the Circumcision. The Circumcision is one of the 'Mysteries of the Life of the Lord' appointed for meditation in the Second Week of Ignatius Loyola's *Spiritual Exercises* (ed. and trans. W. H. Longridge (1930), 168). The only anticipation found by this editor of Andrewes's treatment of that event in Christ's life as a type of the Passion is that of Robert Southwell, SJ, in 'His Circumcision' ('The head is launst to worke the bodies cure, | with angry salve it smarts to heal our wou[n]d', ll. 1–2), which appeared in *Moeoniae* (1595); such a treatment seems to have become fashionable in the 1630s with similar poems by Richard Crashaw, Christopher Harvey, George Wither, and Frances Quarles.

Further Reading. Lossky, *Lancelot Andrewes*, briefly discusses this as one of four sermons that best exemplify Andrewes's 'insistence on the genuine reality of the Incarnation' (pp. 34–40). Andrewes returns to this sermon's themes of the fullness of time and things in the person of Christ in his court sermon for Christmas 1623, on Eph. 1: 10 ('That, in the dispensation of the fullnesse of the times, He might gather together into one all things . . .'), *XCVI*, 148–58.

p. 162, 1-3. *before the Kings Majestie... 1609*: Andrewes's fourth Christmas sermon before James I, preached in the Chapel Royal at Whitehall, in the course of the sung morning service of Holy Communion, after the lessons and Creed, and immediately before the offertory and communion itself; the Christmas sermon and king's communion inaugurated the 'twelve days of Christmas', the social highpoint of the court calendar, marked throughout by feasting and plays (cf. p. 175 and nn.).

5. GALAT. *4. vers. 4,5*: from the Epistle for Holy Communion for the Sunday after Christmas Day (*BCP*), but here in the Geneva translation; quotation from the text in Latin is less integral to this sermon than others, and seems to be neither Vulg. nor Trem., but Andrewes's own translation from English; the sermon assumes familiarity with the whole lection (Gal. 4: 1-7), the Christmas Day Epistle (Heb. 1: 1-12), and the Collect shared by Christmas Day and the Sunday after Christmas Day: 'Almyghtye God, whiche haste geven us thy onlye begotten sonne to take our nature upon hym, and this daye to bee borne of a pure Vyrgyn; Graunte that we beyng regenerate, and made thy children by adoption and grace, maye dailye be renued by thy holy spirite, through the same our Lorde Jesus Christe who lyveth and reygneth &c.'.

16-17. *For we... this Feast*: 'Just as there are twelve months in the year, there are twelve days of Christmas'; by custom in the West, Christmastide extends for twelve days from Christmas Day (25 Dec.) to the Epiphany ('Twelfth Night', 6 Jan.).

20-23. *à Christi missâ... of Christ*: *apologia* for the English word 'Christmas' that renders pointless puritan objections to the Roman Catholic connotation of 'Christ's mass' by appealing only to scripture ('*God sent his Sonne*', v. 4; Lat., '*misit Deus Filium suum*', turned here into its more suggestive phrase, '*Christi missa*', '*sending of Christ*'); thus a fine example of Andrewes's ability to reclaim a contested part of pre-Reformation tradition through etymological legerdemain since 'Christmas' is in fact an unambiguous survival of the Old English 'Cristes mæsse', but Andrewes goes behind the sixth-century transferative sense of *missa* ('a sending') as the eucharist to reclaim its literal sense, as in '*God sent his Sonne*'; see next note.

21-23. *Tertullian... for one*: a historical-linguistic note that in pre-sixth-century Lat., 'missa' and 'remissa' were accepted gerundive forms of 'missio' and 'remissio' (for 'sending' and 'remitting'); hence, Tertullian and Cyprian exemplify early church writing that used those words literally, without any transferative application to the eucharist or 'mass'; cf. Tertullian, *Adversus Marcionem*, cap. XVII, 'Diximus de remissa peccatorum' (*PL*, 2.403D and ed. n.).

p. 163, 1. *Quando... temporis*: 'When the fulness of time came'; a literal Lat. rendering of Geneva (not Vulg., '*at ubi venit plenitudo temporis*').

p. 164, 2. *make a motion*: urge or bid.

23-24. *Ecce... Psal. 39.6*: Ps. 39: 5, 'Beholde, thou hast made my dayes as an hand breadth' (Geneva); Ps. 39: 6 (*BCP*); Trem. Ps. 39: 6, 'Ecce, palmares disposuisti dies meos'); not Vulg. (Ps. 38: 6: 'Ecce breves ['mensurabiles', juxt. LXX] posuisti dies meos').

24-31. *observation... our dayes*: neither ed. (nor *LACT*) can trace this allusion; the alleged source in Alcuin (in marg.) certainly seems an error; Andrewes's pupil at Westminster School, David Stokes, in his *Verus Christianus, or Directions for Private Devotions* (1668), paraphrases (without acknowledgement) this passage, '*dies palmaris*. David thought his to be such, that he could *span* them, (*Ps.* 39. 6.) measure them at his fingers ends: and so may we. Nature hath imprinted the memory of it there, that we should never forget it. For the *fingers* are longer and longer, to the top of the Middle. finger (which is the highest,) and then they go *lower and lower, with a descent that is more suddain*. And so doth our *Life* with a more violent, quick, and praecipitate descent, and perhaps without such degrees' (p. 58).

30. *full pitch*: full extent.

p. 165, 3. *Sunne... Meridian Line*: zenith; noon.

3–4. *moneth... Moone*: sun and moon are 'opposed' once each month (*'moneth'*), i.e. at 180° longitude from one another when viewed from the earth's surface.

4–5. *Yeare... Solstice*: one of two days in the year (12 Dec., 13 June, Old Style) when the sun is farthest from the equator; Andrewes probably intends the summer solstice, being the longest (*'full'*) day of the year (*cf.* OED 'solstice' 1.b).

5–6. *In man... verses before*: of full legal age; 'Then I say, that the heire as long as hee is a childe, differeth nothing from a servant, though to be Lord of all' (Gal. 4: 1).

14. *Misit Deus*: 'God sent'.

17. *missions*: 'sendings' (Lat. *'missio'*, fr. *'mittere'*, 'to send'; cf. p. 162, ll. 19–26 and nn.).

18–19. *some measure... Prophets*: God's partial revelation of his plan for salvation by 'sending' the Law to Moses and the promise of the Messiah through the Prophets; cf. ll. 32–37; p. 176, ll. 5–14, and nn.

19. *implements*: pun on literal sense of 'a filling' (Lat. *'implementum'*, fr. *'implere'*, 'to fill'), and transferative sense dominant in English, 'things that serve as equipment' (*OED sn* I.1).

25–26. *Quando... temporis*: '*When he came*, then it was *the fullness of time*'.

33. *in promise... prophecies*: conventional metaphors for the truths partially revealed in the Old Testament, but made fully manifest in the New; cf. 1. Cor. 10: 1–4, 6, 11; and Milton, *Paradise Lost*, xii. 300–4, which also relies upon Gal. 4: 4, 'So law appears imperfect, and but given | With purpose to resign them in full time | Up to a better Covenant, disciplined | From shadowy types to truth'.

p. 166, 5. *Nonage*: 'in one's minority' (*OED sn^1* 1.b).

5. *sub Pædagogo... ver. 24*: Gal. 3: 24, 'Wherefore that Lawe was our scholemaster [Vulg. and Trem., *'pedagogus noster'*] to bring us to Christ, that we might be made righteous by faith'.

6–7. ὑπὸ στοιχεῖα... *words before these*: Gal. 4: 3, 'Even so, we when wee were children, were in bondage under the rudiments [Gr., ὑπὸ στοιχεῖα, 'hupŏ stŏichĕia'] of the world.'.

16. *second verse... ὑποθεσμία*: Gal. 4: 2, 'But is under tutours and governours, until the time appointed [Gr., ὑποθεσμία, 'hupothĕsmiă'; *LACT*: 'προθέσμια', prŏthĕsmia'] of the Father'.

17–18. *Tempus præfinitum à Patre*: Gal. 4: 2 (Vulg.; see prev. n.).

18–21. *though the Father... appoint*: in law, sons whose deceased fathers had not specified an age of inheritance for them could claim their estate ('heritage') upon reaching their majority; inheritances for sons of living fathers waited upon their fathers' gift, death, and/or written wills.

22. προθέσμια: see to l. 16. n.

24. *full point*: final punctuation mark, full-stop ('period' in modern American usage).

35. *To have sit*: 'to have sat'; 'sit' as a past participle was common in Elizabethan usage (*OED* 'sit' 7.ϵ).

p. 167, 5–6. *So... the Text*: Gal. 4: 5.

7–8. *to disease*: to discomfort, to trouble.

11. *compassion... bowels*: see 'A Sermon Preached... on... Good-Friday' (this edn.), p. 128, l. 30 and n.

11. *else*: or else; otherwise.

15. *served our turnes*: served our needs.

22. *onely begotten Sonne*: familiar biblical epithet for Jesus (cf. John 1: 14, 18; 3: 16), also used in the Nicene Creed.

26. ἐξαπέστειλε: Gr., ĕxapestĕilĕ, 'sent' (Gal. 4: 4).

29. *some besides*: someone (or something) else.

30. *power of his might*: Eph. 6: 10.

31. *troad... our feete*: Rom. 16: 20.

32–33. *ostendit Deus... ostendit Deus*: '"God shows his love", but not, "Behold, how much love God shows"'; cf. Vulg. and Trem., 1 John 3: 1, 'videte qualem caritatem dedit nobis Pater' ('see what love the Father gives to us').

p. 168, 4. *His Sonne made*: Andrewes here begins a careful consideration of Christ's two natures, both human ('*made*') and divine ('as He was, *neither made, nor created*'); crucially for Andrewes, in a classically patristic sense, the two natures are logically antithetical but mystically unified in the incarnate second person of the Trinity. See Headnote and Further Reading, above; see also 'A Sermon Preached on Isaiah 6.6–7' (this edn.).

14–15. πλήρωμα χρόνον κένωμα Χριστοῦ: Gr., 'plērōma chrŏnōn kĕnōma Christou' ('the fulness of time [is the] emptiness of Christ'); Andrewes's own composite of key clauses from Gal. 4: 4 and Phil. 2: 7.

16. *Exinanivit seipsum*: Lat., 'he emptied himself' (Phil. 2: 7); cf. Vulg., 'sed semet ipsum exinanivit'; Douai-Rheims retained the Latinism, 'he exinanited himself'.

20. γενόμενον: Gr., 'gĕnŏmenon' (lit., 'having come from'; Geneva, 'made'); Gal. 4: 4.

24. γένεσθαι: Gr., 'gĕnesthai' ('to become'; 'to come into being').

26. *not to be sent alone*: 'not only to be sent'.

29. *Filium factum*: 'a son made'.

p. 169, 1–2. *Nusquam... upon Him*: Heb. 2: 16; a summary of the argument of the Epistle for Christmas Day (Heb. 1), which would have been sung immediately before Andrewes's sermon; also the text for Andrewes's first court Christmas sermon (1605; *XCVI*, 1–9).

3. *Domine... homo?*: Vulg., Ps. 143: 3.

4. *Homo... nihili*: Lat., 'man is like nothing'; cf. Vulg., Ps. 143: 4 ('homo vanitati similis factus est').

6–8. *did not abhorre... our sakes*: from the 'Te Deum' ('When thou tookest upon thee to deliver man: thou diddest not abhorre the Virgins wombe'), one of the canticles appointed for 'daily' Morning Prayer (*BCP*).

12. *behoofe*: advantage, benefit.

15–16. *as water... Anabaptist*: particularly heterodox brands of Anabaptism revived the ancient heresy that Christ's human nature was in fact feigned, not real, and that the Virgin was therefore only a '*pipe*' through which the exclusively divine Christ had passed; cf. John Boys, *An Exposition of the Dominical Epistles and Gospels... the Winter Part* (1610), '*Valentinus...* taught, Christ had not his body from *Mary* but that he brought it with him from heauen, and passed thorow the wombe of the virgin, as water thorow a conduit pipe: contrary to the text here; *made of a woman*' (p. 85); retailed by Tertullian, the image is ultimately from Irenaeus, *Against Heresies*, 'and there are some who say that [the Demiurge] also produced a Christ.... [a]nd that this was he who passed through Mary, as water passes through a pipe' (*LF*, iii. 21–2).

17. *Factum ... materiam*: Lat., '"Made from"; "from" indicates matter'; cf. Boys, *An Exposition* (see prev. n.), '*Ex muliere, non in muliere*: not in a woman, but of a woman. And the preposition *ex*, notes the matter, as an house is made of timber and stone; bread is made of wheat; wine, of grapes: and therefore Christ had the materials of his body from Mary'; a conventional patristic point; cf. Augustine, *Sermo LII*, iv. 10 (*PL*, 38.58), and Rabanus Maurus, *Ennar. in Epist. B. Pauli, in loc.* (*PL*, 112.312–13); see next n.

17. *She ministred the matter*: emphatic statement of the doctrine that Christ was 'born *of* the Virgin Mary' (Nicene Creed, emphasis added; see prev. n.); Andrewes is in full agreement with the second of the Thirty-Nine Articles, 'the Sonne...toke mans nature in the wombe of the blessed virgin, of her substaunce'; Protestant theologians were nervous, however, about crediting the Virgin with any degree of participation in the Incarnation that detracted from God as the sole author of salvation; Andrewes's emphasis on the Virgin's role here and in the ensuing paragraph, though orthodox, pushes reverence for the Virgin as far as was permissible in the prevailing Protestant climate of Jacobean England; his care here may be measured against the only slightly more daring descriptions of the Virgin's work in contemporary poems by John Donne, where Mary is 'Gods partner...and furnish'd thus | Halfe of that Sacrifice, which ransom'd us' ('Good Friday Riding Westward, 1613', ll. 14–15); and 'that faire blessed Mother-maid, | Whose flesh redeem'd us; That she-Cherubin, Which unlock'd Paradise, and made | One claime for innocence, and disseiz'd sinne, | Whose wombe was a strange heav'n for there | God cloath'd himselfe, and grew' ('The Litanie', ll. 37–42; wr. 1608).

18. *Flesh of her flesh*: cf. Gen. 2: 23 (which refers to Adam's flesh).

18. *Semen mulieris*: Lat., 'seed of a woman'; cf. Gen. 3: 15.

18. *Semen intimum substantiæ*: Lat., 'the innermost seed of the substance'.

21. *both twaine*: 'both of the two of'.

21–24. *God sent ... in the world*: cf. from Thirty-Nine Articles, no. 2, 'two whole and perfect natures, that is to say the God head and manhood, were joyned together in one person, never to be divided, whereof is one Christe, very GOD and very man'.

23. *before all worlds*: Nicene Creed, 'Christ...begotten of his Father before all worlds' (*BCP*).

24. *in the world*: cf. John 9: 5, 13: 1.

25. *that verse of the Psalme*: from Ps. 2, appointed in the Sarum Rite for mattins during the octave of Christmas (transferred to Morning Prayer on Easter Day in *BCP*).

32. *inter natos mulierum*: Vulg., Matt. 11: 11 ('among them that are borne of a woman').

36. *without*: unless.

38. *factum ex muliere*: Vulg., Gal. 4: 4 (lit., 'made of a woman').

p. 170, 3. *no originall soile*: no Original Sin; both Christ's true human nature, and his simultaneous freedom from Original Sin, is necessary in the orthodox understanding of the economy of salvation; cf. Heb. 4: 15, and the Proper Preface to Holy Communion on Christmas Day (*BCP*): 'Because thou didst give Jesus Christ, thine only Son, to be born as this day for us, who by the operation of the Holy Ghost, was made very man of the substance of the Virgin Mary his mother, and that without spot of sin, to make us clean from all sin'.

7. *lying in one belly*: proverbial for fraternity or similarity; cf. William Cowper, *The Mirrour of Mercie* (1615), 'yea in *Jacob* and *Esau* both gotten of one father borne of one mother, that lay together in one belly, their education was alike, their disposition unlike' (p. 60); and Andrewes, *The Wonderfull Combate* (1592), 'the nature of bread & stones are not much unlike, they come both out of one belly: that is to say, the earth' (p. 35^v).

9. *Surety*: guarantor, usually financial, in a legal agreement, liable for any default by the signatory.

10. *Chirographum contra nos*: Col. 2: 14; cf. Vulg., 'delens quod adversum nos erat chirografum decretis quod erat contrarium nobis'); ('wyping out the hand writing of decree that was against us, which was contrarie to us', Douai-Rheims).

28–29. *circumcised... whole lawe*: the Jewish rite of the circumcision of male children, performed eight days after birth, the mark of being bound by the Covenant of the Mosaic law (Gen. 17: 9–14); Jesus was circumcised eight days after birth (Luke 2: 21), thus making him 'a debter to the whole lawe'; calculating from the Nativity on 25 December, the Western church kept the Feast of the Circumcision on the eighth day of Christmastide, 1 Jan.; retained in the *BCP*; cf. Andrewes, *The Wonderfull Combate* (1592), 'Our Saviour Christ by his Nativitie took uppon him the shape of man; by his Circumcision,] he tooke upon him*, [*in marg*: '*Gal. 4.4.'] and submitted himselfe to the degree of a servant: by the first, hee made himselfe in case and able to performe the worke of our redemption; by the second, hee entred bound for the performing of it' (p. 1).

32–33. *tanquam... effundendi*: 'As earnest [money] for shedding all [of his] blood'.

37. *not sub lege... Capitali*: Lat., 'not under a pecuniary [financial] law, but a capital [law]'.

p. 171, 3–4. *factus sub lege... in Cruce*: 'made under the Law, and made on the cross'.

6–7. *then, He had his name... a Saviour*: like Christian baptism, Jewish circumcision included the naming of the child; Christ was named 'Jesus' at his circumcision (Luke 2: 21); for the name's etymological meaning 'Saviour', see 'A Sermon Preached... the V. of November' (this edn., p. 159, ll. 36–37 and n.); cf. Bede, *Hom. X*, 'In Die Festo Circumcisionis Domini' (*PL*, 94.53–8, esp. col. 56); cf. also Andrewes, *Preces*, 'Christ', in which the speaker twice petitions that he be made 'a partaker' by faith in the benefits of 'circumcision, firstfruits of blood'; and 'Creation, Providence and Redemption', which offers thanks for 'the circumcision, subjecting to the law | the firstfruits of blood | the lovely name of JESUS' (pp. 189–90, 212).

10. *of record*: recorded; legally binding.

13. *the Directive part*: the objective requirements ('directives') of the Mosaic law.

16. *the Principall*: financial metaphor; the 'principall' sum of a loan, exclusive of any further interest or penalty due.

19. *forfeiture*: rare use of the word meaning 'penalty for an offence' (*OED* 'forfeiture' 2.b); Milton's use of the same word in the same context is striking, where Christ 'durst upon his own head draw | The deadly forfeiture, and ransom set' (*Paradise Lost*, iii.220–1).

25–27. *Either... Sixe dayes a peece*: the division of the twelve days of Christmas (25 Dec.–6 Jan.) into successive six-day celebrations for the Incarnation of Christ and then his satisfaction of the Law seems to be Andrewes's own, and depends on the almost perfectly medial position in Christmastide of the Feast of the Circumcision (1 Jan.); see next n.

27. *severall moities*: although in general usage 'moieties' means 'parts' or 'portions', Andrewes presses here the specific etymological and legal sense of two exact halves (fr. Lat. *'medietatem'*, 'middle'; *OED* 'moiety' 1.a, 2.a). 'Severall moities' is technical legal language for two equal portions of an inheritance (*OED* 'several' *sa* II.9): the two six-day parts of Christmastide inherit or 'divide this *Solemnitie* betweene them'.

p. 172, 13. *stated*: 'to be settled in a position of safety; also to be settled in rank, dignity or inheritance' (*OED* 'state' *sv* 1, 2); cf. next nn.

14. *invested*: 'to establish (a person) in the possession of any office, position, property, etc.' (*OED sv* I.5); cf. prev. and next n.

18. *Seised*: to be legally put in possession of property, dignity, or inheritance (see prev. nn.).

19–21. *Onely... the former*: the rhetorical figure *antimetabole*—'where two or more words are repeated in inverted order' (Brian Vickers, *In Defence of Rhetoric* (Oxford, 1988), 492)—an ornament common in classical and vernacular prose and poetry, as well as in the style (*'Idiom'*) of 'the *Scriptures'*; cf. George Puttenham, *The Arte of English Poesie* (1589), 'ye have a figure which takes a couple of words to play with... and by making them chaunge and shift one into others place they do very pretily exchange and shift the sence' (sig. O5^r).

27. *ut ille... ut nos*: 'as by him... as by us'.

28–29. *Redeeming... buying backe*: calls attention to the literal etymological sense ('as the word giveth it') fr. Lat. *re-* (back, again) + *emere* (to buy).

32. *made away*: alienated, transferred, or given away for nothing; 'to make away' could also mean 'to put to death' (*OED* 'make' *sv* 84.a, c).

37. συγκεκλεισμένοι *Cap. 3.23*: Gal. ['*Cap(ut)*', 'chapter'] 3: 23, 'But before faith came, we were kept under the Law, as under a garison, and shut up [Gr. συγκεκλεισμένοι, 'sugkekleismenoi'] unto that faith, which should afterward be reveiled'.

p. 173, 11. *Non auro, nec argento*. Lat., 'neither gold nor silver'; cf. Vulg., 1 Pet. 1: 18 ('non corruptibilibus argento vel auro').

12. *pretioso sanguine*: Vulg., 1 Pet. 1: 19, '[by his] precious blood'; but also punning on the etymological root of Eng. 'precious' in Lat. 'pretium' ('price or value'), hence the following line, 'His precious blood, was the *price'*.

17. *suffer that*: suffer that which.

25–26. *Till then... under the Lawe*: Gal. 3: 5.

30–31. *old yeere... new estate*: a metaphorical distinction between the state of mankind before and after redemption by Christ, but also a pun anticipating both New Year's Day (1 Jan., also the Feast of the Circumcision; see p. 171, ll. 5–6 and n.), and the new year (1610) in which Prince Henry would come into his maturity and 'new estate' as Prince of Wales.

p. 174, 6. *peculiar*: 'special or exclusive characteristic' (*OED sn & a* B.I.3).

8–9. *our Fieri... ex muliere*: 'our "making" out of His "made of a woman"'.

9–10. *We made partakers... nature*: simple statement of a theological principle that sets Andrewes apart from mainstream Calvinism; influenced by Eastern patristic thought on the Incarnation, Andrewes stressed not only Christ's taking upon himself the corruption of human nature, but also his reciprocally giving back to redeemed

Christians the perfection of his divine nature; for this 'deification' of human nature, see 'A Sermon Preached on Isaiah 6.6–7' (this edn.), pp. 144–45 and n.

12. *Lex hominis*: Lat., 'the law of man'; cf. 'haec est lex hominis', Lat. trans. of 2 Kings 7: 19 found only in those from Hebrew (not Vulg.); cf. Jerome, *Dialogus contra Pelagianos* (*PL*, 23.557B), and Trem., 'haec est ratio hominis'; cf. ll. 16–17.

13. *gracious is the Prince...much*: in medieval and Renaissance schemes of the virtues, mercy was the defining attribute of God (Ps. 103: 8), and thus, by analogy, of earthly rulers, particularly of monarchs (Prov. 20: 28); cf. Shakespeare, *Measure for Measure* (performed at court on St Stephen's night, 26 Dec. 1604), II. ii. 59–63: 'No ceremony that to great ones longs, | Not the king's crown, nor the deputed sword, | The marshal's truncheon, nor the judge's robe, | Become them [rulers] with one half so good a grace | As mercy does.'

15. *scape*: escape.

16–17. *Non est...hæc*: 'this is not man's law'.

21. *orbe*: Lat., childless.

30. *strangers*: foreigners.

33. *So, in the next verse*: Gal. 3: 6.

33–34. *to give us seisin*: cited as an early example of the figurative sense of the act of giving a symbol of possession ('seisin') of something (*OED sn* 1.b); here, the Holy Spirit ('*Spirit of his Sonne*') is the given token that symbolizes or epitomizes 'the priviledge of the *Adoption*'.

34–35. *Jewes...Pater*: Hebrew and Latin, respectively, for 'father'.

p. 175, 2. *option*: earliest cited use of the word meaning 'a wish or desire' (*OED sn* 1.5).

17. *Plenitudo...plenitudinis*: Lat., 'In the fulness of time [is the] time of fulness'; a perfect *antimetabole* (see p. 172, ll. 19–20 and n.), and a good example of how Latin often affords Andrewes a diction far more concise than is possible in English.

26. *whether*: which(ever).

27–28. *fulness of Bread...pastime*: the social festivities of Christmastide; feasting ('*Bread*'), splendid clothing ('*braverie*'), plays, pageants, games and music ('*sport... pastime*'); contrast the separatist Henry Barrow, *Brief Discoverie of the False Church* (1590), 'Thus they celebrate the nativitie, circumcision, epiphanie & resurrection of Christ, with gay clothes, cleane houses, good cheare, the viole in the feast to stir up lust in stead of devotion, eating & drinking & rising up to play and daunce, after the maner of *Bacchus* in his feastes, with their Lords of misrule, commonly called Christmas lordes, a[l]mes, enterludes, nummeries, Sodomitish maskes, wassal cuppes, with thowsandes of abhominations, which chast & Christian heartes & eares abhor to heare or thinke of' (p. 81).

29. *apparance*: preparation (*OED*, last usage cited 1594).

33. *reversion*: 'the right of succeeding to, or next occupying, an estate' (*OED sn* I.1.b).

33. *goodly heritage*: inheritance; Ps. 16: 6.

34–35. *eate not...spirituall joy*: characteristic caution against social festivity overtaking the spiritual; cf. 'A Sermon Preached...the V. November' (this edn.), p. 158–59 and nn.

p. 176, 2. *Beatus...jubilationem*: Vulg., Ps. 88: 16.

7. *emptie ages*: those ages before the revelation of Christ in the Incarnation; in sermons for Easter 1610 and Christmas 1613, Andrewes addressed the prophetic anticipation of those feasts by Job and Abraham, respectively (*XCVI*, 423–46, 62–71).

10. *instantly*: urgently.

11. *Christmasse*: cf. p. 162, ll. 19–26 and n.

18. *Osculamini... the Babe*: for Ps. 2, see p. 169, l. 25 and n.; this Lat. trans. of Ps. 2: 12 occurs only in those from Hebrew, as Trem.; Vulg. reads 'aprehendite disciplinam' (lit., 'accept instruction'); the quotation not only plays on the touching seasonal image of paying reverence to the newborn Christ ('the first duetie enjoyned to us this day'), but also reinforces the theme of proper rejoicing—'Serve the Lorde in feare, and rejoice in trembling. Kisse the sonne [Lat., '*Osculamini filium*'], lest he be angry, and ye perish in the way, when his wrath shall suddenly burne' (Ps. 2: 11–12, Geneva).

20. *Corpus aptasti mihi*: cf. Vulg. (Heb. 10: 5), '*corpus autem aptasti mihi*' ('but a body hast thou ordeined me').

21. *our Shilo*: the holiest site in Judah, site of the altar and Ark of the Covenant before David's removal of them to Jerusalem; Gen. 49: 10 ('The scepter shall not depart from Judah... untill Shiloh come') was interpreted christologically, 'Which is Christ the Messiah, [the] giver of all prosperitie: who shall call the Gentiles to salvation' (Geneva gloss); cf. Andrewes, Christmas 1620, 'Silo's *comming should be expectatio* (say some, and some, *aggregatio*) *Gentium: All nations looke for Him; all be gathered to Him*' (*XCVI*, 133).

22. ἀπέστειλε: Gr., 'sent'.

24–26. *And... was conceived*: continuation of the list of subjects to whom thanks are due, begun in the preceding paragraph (l. 17); thus not only to Christ ('*Him* that *was sent*'), but also to God ('the *Father*') and the '*Holy Ghost*'; a recapitulation of the Nicene Creed's statements of the Son's relationship with the Father ('the onely begotten Sonne of God'), and the Holy Spirit ('incarnate by the holy Ghost').

26–27. *To the Father... Adoption*: catalogue of gifts to believers from the three persons of the Trinity for which thanks are respectively due (to God for sending the Son, to the Son for redemption, to the Holy Spirit for '*Adoption*'); for adoption as the particular act of the Holy Spirit in baptism, see Andrewes's sermon for Whitsunday, 1615 (*XCVI*, 674–85, esp. p. 684).

38–39. *Holy Eucharist... Thanksgiving*: Gr. εὐχαριστια ('eucharistia'; Eng.,'eucharist'; lit. 'thanksgiving')—since the early church (but not in the NT), a term for Holy Communion.

40. *Quid retribuam Domino?*: Vulg., Ps. 115: 12 ('What shall I give unto the Lord?').

40. *Calicem salutaris*: Vulg., Ps. 115: 13 (lit., 'I will take the cup of salvation'); see next n.

p. 177, 1–2. *cup... Eucharist*: Andrewes explicitly applies Ps. 116: 11–12 (Vulg., Ps. 115: 12–13) as a prophetic type of the Christian eucharist. Such an exposition was conventional in patristic sources (cf. Bernard of Clairvaux, *Serm. in Circumcisione Dom.*, 4: 'nos accessimus, et bibimus illum. Accepimus calicem salutaris'; 'we approach and drink Him [Christ]. We take the cup of salvation'; *PL*, 183. 138), was dominant in early modern Roman Catholic exegesis, and emphasized in the Douai-Rheims translation of the key phrase 'calicem salutaris' as 'the chalice of salvation'. Mainstream Protestant commentary—unlike Andrewes here—avoided the potential eucharistic connotations, either by carefully historicizing the allusion ('In the Law they used to make a banket, when they gave solemn thankes to God, and to take the cuppe and drinke in signe of thanksgiving'; Geneva gloss), or by focusing on the verse's secondary injunction to 'call upon the name of the Lord' in non-eucharistic worship such as prayer and preaching (cf. Calvin, *Institutes*, III. xx. 28). Cf. also 'A Sermon Preached... Whit-Sunday' (this edn.), p. 223, ll. 19–25 and nn.

5–6. *Testament-wise...Legacie*: as an inheritance ('*Legacie*') stipulated in a will (*Testament-wise*).

13. *12. dayes more*: the twelve days of Christmas (see p. 162, ll. 16–18, p. 171, ll. 25–27 and nn).

17. *not Jobs dies...emptie*: perhaps a summary of Job's complaints during his affliction by Satan (cf. Job 7: 1, 6, 16, and 17: 1); more likely is Job's waiting for his own 'fulness of time' for praising God to come (cf. Job 14: 13–14), in contrast to Andrewes's auditory who are gathered to celebrate the 'fulness' of Christmas in the eucharist; an anticipation of his next sermon at court, Easter 1610 (see p. 176, ll. 7–8 and n.).

34. *Not as heere...every one*: very discrete formulations of two of Andrewes's more avant-garde principles, the real presence of Christ in the eucharist ('heere He is, something'), and the deification of mankind through the Incarnation ('something in every one'); but limited (deliberately?) here by the primary emphasis on eucharist as 'thanksgiving'.

35. *omnia in omnibus*: Vulg., 1 Cor. 15: 28 ('all in all').

A SERMON PREACHED... THE FIFTH OF AUGUST

Text. [block orn.] A | SERMON | PREACHED | *before His Maiestie,* | On Sunday the fifth of August | last, at Holdenbie, | *By the Bishop of Elie, His* | Maiesties Almoner. | [block orn.] | [rule] | ¶ Imprinted at London by *Robert* | *Barker,* Printer to the Kings most | Excellent Maiestie. | ANNO DOM. 1610. (STC^2 612.5). Bibliographically one of the most complicated of Andrewes' printed works. The copy text chosen, STC^2 612.5 (= Q_2), is a resetting of a first printing earlier (or almost simultaneously) in the same year, STC^2 612 (= Q_1). However, quires from the two different settings were indiscriminately mixed in the printing house. For this edition eight copies were collated, all of which contained quires from both settings, but no two of which were alike in the way they were built up from Q_1 and Q_2 quires, although Q_2 quires predominate in all collated copies. The copies collated are: Bodleian Library, Oxford B 20.3(6), Linc.(= O_1), Gibson 265(5) (= O_2), Vet. A2 e.333 (= O_3), Vet. A2 e.430(5) (= O_4); All Souls Library, Oxford VX.2.12(3) (= *OAS*); British Library 3187.bb.17.(7.) (= *BL*); Cambridge University Library 8.24.14 (= CUL_1), E.12.9 (= CUL_2). *BL* and CUL_1 are reproduced on *EEBO* under *STC* 612.5 and 612, respectively; this collation shows that the distinction between *STC* numbers is almost entirely notional beyond their respective title pages. Both Q_1 and Q_2 have signatures A–I4 K3. STC^2 states that only quires A–E were reset for Q_2; however the present collation shows that G and I were also reset. The only settings therefore found in all collated copies of both editions are F, H, and K. Because of the uniform superiority of Q_2 readings, but the absence of any examined copy of Q_2 not contaminated with quires from Q_1, this edition presents a text reconstructed from Q_2 quires found in two different copies: O_1 (sigs. A–D) and *BL* (sigs. E, G, I). The quires common to both (F, H, and K) are set from O_1. Variant Q_1 readings shown in the apparatus are from *OAS* (sigs. A, C, G, I) and O_2 (sigs. B, D, E). From the evidence of the few substantive variants between Q_1 and Q_2, Andrewes's (or his secretary's) emendation and correction of the typesetters' errors in Q_1 would seem the most logical explanation for the resetting. The fact that so many sheets from Q_1

were reused in Q_2 argues against a reissue to meet public demand for additional copies, unless the occasion of such demand was taken as opportunity for correcting previous errors. The majority of variants are in the duplication or reduction of letters by the typesetter to make up lines, and are not recorded in the apparatus. These are overwhelmingly the addition or subtraction of terminal 'e's' (e.g. 'wee'/'we', 'Lawe'/'law'), but also terminal double consonants ('holinesse'/'holines', 'shall'/'shal'), '&' for 'and', and conventional contractions ('whō'/'whom'). Recorded here, however, are non-incidental changes in spelling, improvements in punctuation, and adjustments to word order and syntax, all of which clearly improve the text and can be assumed to be deliberate authorial (or secretarial) emendations. Q_2 introduced very few new errors for which a Q_1 reading is here preferred.

The sermon was set for a third time in 1620 as part of an octavo collection of eleven sermons all also issued separately in quarto between 1604 and 1620 (STC^2 624.5, hereafter, Z; for its contents and importance, see Introduction; the copy used here is CUL Syn. 7.61.221). On the evidence of the substantive variants between Q_1 and Q_2, Z took as its copy text a state of Q_2 having quires E and G of Q_1 but B, C, D, I of Q_2 (with F, H, and K being common to both quartos in the copies I have examined, and those sigs. of Z showing no new variants, only the state of A, where there are no substantive variants between the quartos, cannot be determined). Z was very poorly typeset, and introduces 15 substantive errors, including the omission (clearly by typesetting error) of 17 words of text (180, ll. 3–4; p. 186, l. 12). F_1 (pp. 795–813) in turn took Z as its copy text without correcting any of its grosser errors, including neither its omissions, nor the egregious attribution, by typesetter's inversion, of '92' extra verses (instead of '29') to Psalm 105 (p. 203, l. 25). In *LACT*, iv. 43–75.

Headnote. This is the third of nine surviving court sermons by Andrewes on the anniversary of the king's deliverance from an alleged assassination plot against him by the Earl of Gowrie and his brother Alexander near Perth on Tuesday 5 August 1600. The first, for 1606, appeared only in the fourth edition of *XCVI. Sermons* (1641); the last, for 1623, was prepared but not delivered (F_1, 876–85). In July 1603 the Privy Council ordered Archbishop Whitgift to institute the observance of the anniversary as a national day of thanksgiving in England, as was already the case in Scotland, 'by public assembly, prayer, and thanksgiving to God in all parish churches...by cessation from work and labour, and by all good and lawful means and signs of gladness', and special forms of morning prayer and holy communion (E. Cardwell, *Documentary Annals*, ii. 60). Although mentioned in neither the Privy Council document nor the resulting *Fourme of Prayer... [for] the fift of August*, commemorative sermons were immediately hallmarks of the new holiday. Politically, the Gowrie sermons, like the Gunpowder Plot sermons after 1605, were not only vital occasions for expressing loyalty to the crown, but early focal points for assertions of Stuart divine-right absolutism, of which Andrewes's are the most substantial, sophisticated, and uncompromising. At court, solemnization of the deliverance extended to James's institution of sermons on every Tuesday of the year. From the very day of the plot's discovery, its veracity was doubted. According to Thomas Plume, biographer of Andrewes's Westminster School pupil John Hacket (1592–1670), Andrewes 'once fell down upon his knees before *King James*, and besought his *Majesty* to spare his *customary* pains upon that day, that he might not mock *God* unless the thing were true: the *King* replied, Those people were much too blame who would never believe a Treason unless their *Prince* were actually murdered; but did assure him in the Faith of a Christian, and upon the *Word* of a King, their Treasonable attempt against him was too true' (Plume, 'An Account of... the Author', in Plume (ed.), *A Century of Sermons...by...John Hacket* (1675), p. viii). Andrewes's anxiety may explain his careful adherance to the official accounts of the plot (see Sources).

Andrewes's Gowrie sermons, long ignored because of their political content, epitomize the views of kingship violently overturned by the English Civil War. The sermon chosen for inclusion here is one of the best examples not only of Andrewes's high view of kingship, but also of the rhetorical and scholarly brilliance with which he could express it. Although on a topic less palatable to modern readers, the preacher's relentless pursuit of the fullest possible exegesis and application of his short text here is every bit as accomplished as his expositions on the Incarnation or Resurrection. The Gowrie sermon for 1610, the tenth anniversary of the plot, was given added urgency by the assassination of Henry IV of France in May of that year, and by Andrewes's continued involvement (by royal command) as a polemical writer in the controversy with Cardinal Robert Bellarmine over papal vs. regal authority, sparked by the Oath of Allegiance imposed upon Catholics in the wake of the Gunpowder Plot. The sermon can be read as an English précis of the key arguments made in Andrewes's Latin responses to Bellarmine, *Tortura Torti* (1609), and the larger *Responsio ad Apologiam Cardinalis Bellarmini* (1610), which was nearing completion at the time of this sermon, and would appear in print only three months later. The subject of the royal prerogative that had such a heated international currency is also related in the sermon to the tense domestic debates in the 1610 Parliament over subsidies and the legislative reform of royal privileges known as the Great Contract.

Typically, however, Andrewes uses the occasion of even an explicitly political sermon to address compelling issues of the nature of Christianity itself. Here, this is in the richly symbolic vocabulary of anointing, both the Christian ceremonies of which (baptismal christening and royal anointing at coronation), and the terms for it (through the Greek and Latin root *chrisma*) link Christ, kings ('God's anointed'), and all baptized Christians. The same image system also steeps the sermon in a characteristic reverence for liturgical ceremony that deftly avoids discredited 'popery' by using instead the vocabulary of Levitical priesthood and the Eastern (Byzantine) liturgies.

Sources. In this sermon, Andrewes shows an intimate knowledge of the details contained in official accounts of three sensational contemporary events—the Gowrie Conspiracy itself, the assassination of Henry IV, and the exccution of Henry's assassin. These are: *The Earle of Gowries Conspiracie against the Kings Majestie* (1603); *A True Report of the most execrable murder...upon the late French King Henrie the 4.* (1610); *The Copie of a Letter Written from Paris...Declaring the manner of execution of Francis Ravaillart* (1610); *The Terrible and Deserved Death of Francis Ravilliack* (1610). Andrewes is also sensitive to several points pursued by James I in *The Kings Majesties Speach to the Lords and Commons...the xxi of March* (1610). Moreover, as would be expected given his concurrent work on *Tortura Torti*, he engages directly here the most extreme Jesuit statements of resistance theory and regicide, most importantly Juan de Mariana, *De Rege et Regibus Institutione* (Toledo, 1599). Andrewes's own *Tortura* and *Responsio*, are here quoted from the exemplary *LACT* editions (vols. vii, viii).

Further Reading. For Gowrie court sermons, see McCullough, *Sermons at Court*, 116–19; the theological content of those by Andrewes is considered collectively with the Gunpowder Plot sermons by Lossky, *Lancelot Andrewes* (ch. 7), who addresses specifically the theology of anointing in this sermon (pp. 319–25). Ferrell, *Government by Polemic* (ch. 2), offers an astute reading of Jacobean Gowry and Gunpowder sermons, describing this as the 'apogee' of Andrewes's apologetics for James, and as containing a critique not just of papalism, but also of the intemperate anti-Catholicism of James's other preachers. For an outstanding survey of the general context of Stuart absolutism's debates with papalism, see Johann P. Sommerville, *Politics and Ideology in England 1603–1640* (1986), and, for more detail, his 'Jacobean Political Thought and the Controversy over the Oath of Allegiance' (Cambridge Ph.D. thesis, 1981). For the Great Contract, see Pauline Croft, *King James* (2003), 69–82.

p. 178, 1–3. *A Sermon... 1610*: adapted from title-page of Q_2 (see Text, above).

2–3. *fifth... Holdenbie*: Holdenby (sometimes 'Holmby') House, Northamptonshire, one of the great Elizabethan 'prodigy houses', built 1578–83 by Sir Christopher Hatton, sold by his heir to James I in 1608, and used annually thereafter during the summer royal progresses; also the site of Charles I's imprisonment in 1647. Holdenby's chapel, where the sermon was presumably preached, was modelled on those in the major London royal palaces. Such was the importance of paying respects to the king on Gowrie Day that the members of the Privy Council journeyed from London specially to attend this sermon. Queen Anne and Prince Henry, with their households, joined the king's court for the holiday, and must have attended the sermon with the king. William Lord Knollys reported to Lord Treasurer Salisbury from Holdenby on 7 August that 'the king & Queen & prince are all well thankes be to god & this 5. off August ys well passed over both with myrth & the best & aptest sermon ffor the daye that ever I heard by the bisshopp off Elye' (McCullough, *Sermons at Court*, 23–4, 119; PRO SP 14/57).

5. *1 CHRO.16.22*: Andrewes's quotations from his biblical text are complicated by the fact that (as he explains, p. 181, ll. 9–10; p. 202, ll. 33–34) 1 Chron. 16: 8–22 is a quotation of Ps. 105: 1–15, between which there are slight but important variations in diction in both Latin and English bibles and psalters. Andrewes prefers here the Vulg. and Geneva versions of both texts, thus giving at least four versions quoted. His choices are not random, but ideologically and aesthetically charged. For example, the prominence given in this sermon to the Vulg. itself (over the Protestant Latin translation by Tremellius sometimes used in other sermons) is explained by the former's consistent use of '*christos meos*' instead of Tremellius's '*unctos meos*' for 'mine anointed'—that single word ('*christos*') being the foundation of the entire sermon's analogy between Christ and kings. Vulg. texts are 1 Par. (= 1 Chron.) 16: 21–2 and Ps. 104: 14–15.

6. *Nolite... meos*: Vulg., 1 Par. 16: 22.

7. *Touch... Anointed*: Geneva.

13. *the 14. verse*: 1 Chron. 16: 14.

13. *Ipse... noster*: cf. Vulg., 1 Par. 16: 14 ('ipse Dominus Deus noster').

14. *challengeth*: claims.

16. *the verse before*: 1 Chron. 16: 21.

16. *Non reliquit hominem*: does not give leave to, does not allow; cf. Geneva, 'He suffered no man to do them wrong'.

18. *quicke of touch*: quick, eager to touch.

24. *a voyce... staying their handes*: for this dramatization, Andrewes employs the scenario of God's angel preventing the sacrifice of Isaac: 'But the Angel of the Lord called unto him from Heaven.... Lay not thine hand upon the childe' (Gen. 22: 11–12).

25–26. *Whom God... to touch*: parody of Matt. 19: 6, used as the declaration in the Solemnization of Matrimony (*BCP*), 'those whom God hath joined together, let no man put asunder.'

27–28. *Psalmist... your hearts*: v. 8 of Ps. 95, the 'Venite exultemus domino', said or sung daily in Morning Prayer (*BCP*).

27–28. *Hodie si vocem*: Vulg. (Ps. 94: 8).

29. *day... ten yeeres*: tenth anniversary of the Gowrie Conspiracy (5 Aug. 1600).

29–30. *same Person... place*: God in heaven.

p. 178, 30–p. 179, 1. *His Anointed... stand*: King James.

2. *Text, dixit... est*: 'the Text said so; the day was made so'.

3–4. *when... Ne perdas*: for his previous Gowrie sermon (1608; *XCVI*, 784–94), also at Holdenby, Andrewes preached on 1. Sam. 26: 8–9, which includes David's injunction against killing Saul, '*Ne perdas*' ('Destroy [him] not'), in Andrewes's own Latin trans. (cf. Vulg., 'ne interficias'; Trem., 'ne perimito').

5. *straiter*: stricter.

5. *larger compasse*: more extensive application and authority.

6–7. *Sed ecce... here*: parody of Matt. 12: 41(b) and 12: 42(b).

8. *Audivi... de cælo*: 'I heard a voice from heaven' (Rev. 14: 2, 13; but cf. also 2 Pet. 1: 17–18 and Mark 1: 11).

11–12. *Non alienæ... suæ*: 'not a voice from another instrument, but his divine response'.

14. *there... Destroy not*: cf. p. 264, l. 11 and n.

27. *first... Commandement*: Matt. 22: 38.

31–31. *Patriarchs... Law of Nature*: time in biblical history of the forefathers of Israel (Abraham, Isaac, and Jacob, including the latter's twelve sons, heads or 'Patriarchs' of the twelve tribes of Israel); therefore, the time before the Law was given to Moses, when God's people lived by the natural law of reason and conscience rather than a revealed code of law; for the 'Law of Nature' and Jacobean political theory, see Sommerville, *Politics and Ideology*, 12–17.

34–35. *phrase... fundamentall law*: Andrewes registers here a sensitivity to popular trends in language; *OED* records the first use of 'fundamental' meaning 'forming an essential or indispensable part of a system, institution, etc.' as 1601 (Shakespeare, *All's Well*, III. i. 2); on this term and concept, see J. H. Burns (ed.), with Mark Goldie, *The Cambridge History of Political Thought 1450–1700* (1991), 270.

37. *what Text*: what precedent, what proof-text.

p. 180, 10. *non tangendæ*: 'not to be touched'.

11. *couched*: expressed, set down in writing (*OED*, sv. I.14).

12. *de non tangendo*: 'for not touching'.

28. *Fathers... forbidden likewise*: most forcefully, Augustine, *Enarr. in Psalm. CIV*, cap. 9–10.

35. *keepe... from touching*: 'to keep kings from being touched'; but cf. p. 195, ll. 29–35.

35. *if it selfe*: if the text itself.

p. 181, 7. *the moode*: grammatically; the imperative mood.

9–11. *verse... them all*: Andrewes's text is from the Chronicler's account (cf. also 2 Sam. 6: 17–19) of David's great religious celebration for the return of the Ark of the Covenant to Jerusalem (1 Chron. 16: 1–43), which includes a festival psalm (vv. 8–36) adapted from Pss. 105: 1–15; 96; and 106: 1, 47–8. Andrewes's text (1 Chron. 16: 22) is therefore also 'a verse of a Psalme' (Ps. 105: 15). In Vulg., the Hebr. '*Halleluja*' (lit., 'praise the Lord', *BCP* 'praise ye the Lord') is used as a title for 19 or 20 Psalms (104–6, 110–18, 134–5, 145–6, 148–50; some versions also 147). One of Andrewes's authorities on the Pss. cited elsewhere in the sermon (p. 183, l. 21), *Psalmi Davidis Vulgata Editione*, ed. Génébrard (Paris, 1587), titles twenty 'Hallelujah psalms'.

12–15. *proclaimed... verses before*: 1 Chron. 16: 4–6 details David's appointment of Levite musician-priests, including their chief, Asaph, and the instrumentalist Benaiah, to lead the psalm-singing at the return of the Ark. '*Queere*' is the already almost obsolete Middle English form for 'quire' ('choir') consistently preferred by Andrewes.

20–21. *late heavie accident*: assassination of Henry IV of France (14 May 1610).

22. *wretches there... avow it*: Henry IV was assassinated by the fanatical Roman Catholic François Ravaillac; worse than actual regicides, Andrewes argues, are the 'other... wretches', principally extreme Jesuit theorists, who 'dare to avow' in print the deposition and even killing of heretical princes. Andrewes returns to these theorists, and the Roman Catholic hierarchy's tentative censorship of their arguments, in more detail later in the sermon.

26–28. *this day... Anointed*: ten years earlier, the Ruthven brothers ('two wicked Impes') were 'cut short' in their alleged attack on James ('the Lords *Anointed*').

31. *Non taliter... Nationi*: cf. Vulg. (Ps. 146: 20), 'non fecit similiter omni genti'; Trem. (Ps. 146: 20), 'non fecit ita ulli genti'.

32. *every King... gracious*: Henry IV of France.

p. 182, 4. *the Substantive*: a noun; early modern English grammars distinguished between 'noun adjectives' and 'noun substantives'; 'Mine anointed' is a 'noun adjective' (adjectival noun-phrase); Andrewes now 'seeks' the 'noun *substantive*' for it, e.g. 'Kings'.

7–8. *call... never christened*: false kings, those not properly to be called 'the Lord's anointed' ('*Christos Domini*'); also a multi-layered pun—at baptism, infants received the Holy Ghost and were given their 'Christian' names; the service was colloquially known as 'christening' from the pre-Reformation rite of signing the cross on the child's forehead with holy oil (chrism)—thus, Christ (Lat. 'Christos', fr. Gr. '$Χριστός$', 'the anointed one'), Christians, and kings ('*Christos Domini*') are all joined by the etymology and analogy of their several 'anointings'.

9. *Ecce... illic*: Vulg. (Mark 13: 21).

10–11. *these Christes here*: the 'annointed ones' mentioned in the text; Andrewes sets out here to determine whether the text refers to 'the Lord's annointed ones' in general, or to kings in particular.

16. *first world*: first age of biblical history (cf. p. 179, ll. 29–31 and n.).

17. *Princes... generations*: Eccles. 44: 7.

20. *Audi... inter nos*: cf. Vulg. (Gen. 23: 6), 'audi nos domine princeps Dei apud nos'; and Trem., 'audi nos domine mi, princeps Dei, tu inter nos'.

21–22. *Prince... Kings at once*: Gen. 14.

33–34. *Pater... Patriarches*: '*Patriarches*', from Lat. '*Pater*' ('father') and Gr. $ἀρχή$ ('archē', 'rule').

34–35. *unctos... Anointing at all*: Augustine, *Quaestiones in Hept. CLXXIII*: 'ut etiam ante unctionem sic appellarentur' (*PL*, 34.656); ('it was still so called [holy] before being anointed'); Augustine here discusses the Holy of Holies in the Temple, which was in essence and name holy even before ceremonial anointing; he does not, as Andrewes, make any application of this argument to priests or patriarchs.

p. 183, 3. *Fathers of their Countreys*: patriarchalism was one of the cornerstones of monarchical absolutism. Paternity was a particular keynote of James's and his bishops' view of kingship: the ecclesiastical canons of 1606 cited Adam and the other OT patriarchs as proof that patriarchal power (*potestas patria*) was the first expression of the regal power (*potestas regia*) vested in kings directly by God. James himself had stressed this principle in a speech to Parliament in March 1610. See Sommerville, *Politics and Ideology*, 27–33; and *The Kings Majesties Speach* (1610), sigs. A4^v, B2^{r-v}.

11. *old world... any Tables*: cf. p. 179, ll. 29–31; p. 182, ll. 16–29.

15–17. *Councels... Francford*: Andrewes cites the ecumenical ('general') Council of Ephesus (431), the Fourth Council of Toledo (633), and the Carolingian ('Westerne') Council of Frankfurt (794), all of which produced synodical letters or canons endorsing imperial power over matters ecclesiastical. Canon 75 of the Fourth Council of Toledo glossed 1 Chron. 16: 22 as referring explicitly to kings; Andrewes cited this against Bellarmine in *Tortura Torti* (p. 290).

18–21. *dispatch... of Kings*: Andrewes summarizes conciliar and patristic evidence by quoting the Frankfurt Council's citation of Jerome's commentary on Ps. 44: 7 (*BCP* Ps. 45: 7, 'thy God hath anointed thee with the oil of gladness above thy fellows'): 'Non enim B. Hieronymus & caeteri sanctae scriptur[ae] Tractatores, ha[n]c participationem unctionis, de adoptivis fratribus, sed de regib[us], qui Christi vocaba[n]tur, intellegi voluer[unt]' ('Indeed, St Jerome and other writers on the holy scriptures, understand this act of anointing to pertain to kings, who are called the "anointed ones", not to adopted brothers [in Christ]'). Andrewes quotes from his edition of the *Conciliorum Omnium* (5 vols., Venice, 1585), iii. 649, col. b (now PCCL 4.11.17 [III]).

19–20. *[in marg.] Append... 74*: Andrewes's documentation for his reference to 'the third generall Councel of *Ephesus*', citing *Conciliorum Omnium* (see prev. n.), i. 1097, 'Ad Tomum Quartum Appendix Tertia', i.e. an appendix to vol. iv of the acts of the Council of Ephesus (not vol. iv of the *Conciliorum*), which is an episcopal letter by Cyril of Alexandria asserting orthodox Christology against Nestorius; it is the source of other subsequent arguments in the sermon; for the Council of Toledo, *Conciliorum*, iii. 76 (*LACT*).

21. *Cajetan, and Genebrard*: Génébrard, *Psalmi Davidis* (Paris, 1587, p. 324), glosses 'christos meos' as 'reges & principes meos', and, like Andrewes above, asserts that the patriarchs and prophets were princes *avant la lettre*. Cajetan (Tomasso de Vio), *Psalmi Davidici* (Venice, 1530), however, does not equate 'christos' with kings, but only anointed patriarchs and prophets ('appellat patriarchas unctos & prophetas', p. 174^r). Andrewes's copy of the latter (Paris, 1540), is PCCL 3.16.7.

24. *to entercommon*: early example of the word meaning 'to share or participate with others, or mutually' (*OED sv* 4).

26. *without booke*: 'recited without book or from memory' (*OED*, 'without', *sprep* B.III.9.a), which may function here as a secondary pun on the primary sense of 'without authority' (cf. 'warrant', l. 13).

28. *appropriate to*: 'attached or belonging as an attribute, quality or right' (*OED*, *spple* A.4.b).

33. *the New... Old*: New and Old Testaments.

34–35. *Foure... Twelve times*: '*Mine Anoynted*' (1 Sam. 2: 35, 1 Chr. 16: 22, Ps. 105: 15, 132: 17); '*Thine anoynted*' (2 Chron. 6: 42, 84: 9, 89: 38, 89: 51; Ps. 132: 10); '*His Anointed*' (1 Sam. 2: 10, 12: 3, 12: 5; 2 Sam. 22: 51; Ps. 2: 2, 18: 50, 20: 6, 28: 8, Isa. 45: 1);

and 'GODS [or "the Lord's"] *Anoynted*' (1 Sam. 16: 6, 24: 7, 11; 26: 9, 11, 16, 23, 2 Sam. 1: 14, 16; 19: 21, 23: 1; Lam. 4: 20).

36–37. *Patriarchs... but one*: cf. p. 267, l. 11; p. 296, ll. 16–18, and nn.

39. *joyne issue*: take issue, disagree.

p. 184, 1. *cary it*: 'carry it'; win the debate.

9. *fellowship of the Prophets*: from the 'Te Deum' ('The goodly fellowship of the Prophets, praise thee'), one of the canticles appointed for daily Morning Prayer (*BCP*).

11–12. *corner... of the Maccab*: 2. Mac. 1: 10.

12. *full Christendome*: cf. p. 183 and n.; and 'A Sermon Preached... The V. of November', (this edn.) p. 156, ll. 12–17 and n.

15. *their... Translator*: Jerome, translator of Vulg., authorized by Rome.

15–17. *same... Christus ever*: Andrewes stretches a point here. Vulg. never uses '*unctus*' as a substantive ('anointed one'), whether for priests or kings; the only examples of 'anointed one' use 'christus' and refer to kings. For '*unctus*' as a participle describing priests, cf. Lev. 4: 3, 4: 16.

19–20. *from the rest*. 'apart from the rest'; i.e. 'it is given them' only, not to 'the rest'.

21–24. *They are... Anointed*: daring reworking of Heb. 1: 4, 5 ('Being made so much better then the Angels, as hee hath by inheritance obtained a more excellent Name then they. For unto which of the Angels said he at any time, Thou art my sonne, this day have I begotten thee?') which—exploiting the etymological link between Christ and the king as '*Christos meos*'—substitutes kings for Christ himself, and regal anointing for Christ's superiority to angels.

26. *stile*: title.

27. *denomination*: name.

33. *a reason... tangendo*: 'a reason for not touching'.

37. *slightly*: slightingly, lightly.

p. 185, 1. *free-hold*: tenure of an estate or office in perpetuity for an individual and his heirs (cf. 'stile', p. 184, l. 26 and n.).

3. *laide*: synonym for 'put in (a claim)' (*OED* 'lay' sv VIII.53.c); thus, 'there are two claims for whose the anointed are'.

6–7. *Pope... the Emperours*: papal coronation of Roman emperors, and their successors the Holy Roman Emperors, dated from Leo III's crowning of Charlemagne at Rome in 800. Anointing with chrism only became a part of the coronation liturgy in the later Middle Ages.

10. *depose... dispose of them*: typically arch summary of the major points disputed in the Oath of Allegiance controversy—the Pope's temporal power to '*depose*' kings and (according to the shrillest Jesuit theories) to absolve subjects from any guilt in killing ('*dispose*') deposed heretical princes.

14–15. *Touch not... who will*: sarcastic articulation of what Andrewes takes to be the papalist position: '"Touch not his": that is, not the Pope's kings: as for any others, it matters ("skilleth") not, anyone can touch them.'

16. *cleane marred*: completely disfigured.

18. *Non ens*: 'a non-entity' (*OED*); lit., a 'not being' (Lat. *non* + *pr. pple esse*, 'to be').

18. *in rerum naturâ*: Lat., lit., 'among natural things'; i.e. 'in the whole world'.

18–19. *That... till Moses*: the ceremony of anointing appears first in biblical history in God's instructions to Moses for the consecration of Aaron and his sons as priests (Exod. 28: 41).

19. *these... in the Text*: the Patriarchs.

30. *reteined... with us*: the English coronation rite included an elaborate anointing on the hands, breast, shoulders, arms and head, and was of particular symbolic importance to James. Andrewes, as Dean of Westminster, had participated intimately at James's English coronation (July 1603), assisting during the anointing by unfastening and fastening the king's tunic and holding the golden bowl of oil, arraying the king in pall, hose, and sandals for the crowning, and administering the cup at the king's communion. Throughout the ceremony and service he attended at the king's side as prompter. It has been assumed that Andrewes was responsible for much of the ceremony's liturgical medievalism, including the reversion to the pre-Reformation title of his office, 'Abbot of Westminster'. See Roy Strong, 'How James I was Crowned', *Country Life* (22 May 2003), 106–9; J. Wickham Legg, *Coronation Order of James I* (1902).

33–34. *Samuel... Salomon*: the high priests Samuel and Zadok ('*Sadoc*') anointed Saul and Solomon king, respectively (1 Sam. 10: 1; 1 Kings 1: 39–40).

36–39. *Sacrament... any Meos*: Andrewes here makes the conventional distinction between a sacrament—an act or form by which cooperation with the divine will and the recipient's disposition imparts effective divine grace (see 'character', p. 191, l. 21 and n.)—and a mere ceremony, which only confirms through symbolism a status quo, adding nothing not already possessed by the recipient. Because the minister of a sacrament does not influence the efficacy of the sacrament itself (cf. Thirty-Nine Articles, no. 26), it holds, in Andrewes's argument, that the lesser form of a ceremony affords even less room for claims of influence or proprietorship by the minister ('no interest in the *partie* by it').

p. 186, 2. *buzzed of... them*: central to Roman Catholic claims for the deposing power of popes was the belief that kings' power was originally seated in the people who had in turn transferred or 'translated' that power to kings. Protestant absolutists like Andrewes insisted that that power derived only and exclusively from God; he here parodies the Catholic position for making kings 'the people's anointed' ('*Christi populi*') and subject to ('helde of') them. See Somerville, *Politics and Ideology*, 21–2, 24–6, 59–64.

3–8. *Cardinall... Gods doing*: Cardinal Robert Bellarmine, SJ (1542–1621), chief opponent of James and Andrewes in the Oath of Allegiance controversy, made the original transference of power from people to kings (see prev. n.) central to his arguments for the papal deposing power. In his *Responsio*, nearing completion at the time he preached this sermon, Andrewes rounded fiercely on Bellarmine in similar terms for denying that the latter's *de Laicis* (1608) maintained the superiority of the people to kings. Andrewes argued that this position made a mockery of God's choice of David and Solomon as kings of Israel (*Responsio*, 421, 425–6).

9. *then*: probably an emphatic contraction (not recorded by *OED*) of the phrase 'or then', meaning 'or else, or otherwise'(*OED* '*then*', B.II.4.c).

15–16. *Pope saith... himselfe*: ironic allusion to papal claims to be *Vicarius Christi*, Christ's representative (lit. 'substitute') on earth.

17–18. *Christum Domini*: 'the Lord's anointed' (i.e. the king).

18. *fall to*: set about to.

22–23. *from beneath*: from the people.

24. *that is none*: that which is none.

27. *[in marg.] Chap. 4.14... Verse 29*: uses Vulg. numbering; Geneva = Dan. 4: 17, 25, 32.

29. *Sententia... Sanctorum*: 'the sentence of the watchers, and the speech of the holy ones'; cf. Dan. 4: 17 (see prev. n.).

32–33. *Primitive...favour them*: the early church ('*Primitive*' fr. Lat. *primus*, 'first'), *c.* first to third centuries, before Constantine's conversion and subsequent grant of protection to the church in the Roman Empire (313) where before it had been subject to imperial persecution.

33–36. *Cuius... old Irancæus*: cf. *Opus Eruditissimum Divi Irenaei* (Paris, 1567), 243, 'Cuius enim iussu homines nascuntur, huius iussu & reges constituntur'; Iranaeus, bishop of Lyons (*c.* 130–200), one of the earliest Greek Fathers, hence 'old *Irancæus*').

36–37. *Inde illis... Tertullian*: paraphrase of Tertullian of Carthage, *Apologeticus Adversus Gentes*, cap. XXX, 'Illius enim est ipse, cuius et coelum est et omnis creatura. Inde est imperator, unde est et homo antequam imperator; inde potestas illi, unde et spiritus' (*PL*, 1.441); ('for [the emperor] himself is His to whom heaven and every creature appertains. He gets his sceptre where he first got his humanity; his power where he got his breath of life'; *ANCL*, xi. 109–10).

p. 187, 1. *Diadema... Esai 62*: 'a royall diademe in the hand of thy God' (Isa. 62: 3); cf. Vulg. (Isa. 62: 5), 'diadema regni in manu Dei tui'.

15–16. *Christi... non legitur*: 'the Pope's anointed, Samuel's or Zadok's anointed; Judah's or Israel's anointed, one does not read of'; summary, with biblical examples, of Andrewes's two types of false proprietorship over kings (by priests, by the people); for Samuel and Zadok, cf. p. 274, l. 1 and n.; Judah and Israel became rival Jewish kingdoms after the death of Solomon.

17. *inferre*: derive by logic or reason; deduce, conclude.

17. *hand off*: early modern form of 'hands off!' (*OED* '*hand*' B.II.54).

25–26. *Uncti... Tangentes*: 'anointed'... 'touchers'.

26–27. *Christiani... Christi*: 'Christians'... 'anointed'.

29–31. *contradiction... towards them*: Korah's challenge ('contradiction', fr. Lat., 'contra' + 'dicere', 'to speak against') to Moses over the hegemony of the Aaronic priesthood, on the grounds that all people were equally holy, was the first lay rebellion against the clerisy in the OT (Num. 16; 26: 9 11). God's punishment of the rebels by their being swallowed up in the earth, followed by a plague to smite a further 14,000 sympathizers, made it a stock warning against opponents of a hierarchical clerisy, such as presbyterians ('the new paritie'), '*Anabaptists*', and puritans ('those that pricke [gallop] fast towards them'). Cf. Hooker, *Lawes*, vi. I. 4 (*FEWRH*, iii. 3–4).

33. *peculiar*: particular.

34. *designeth*: signifies, symbolizes.

p. 188, 8. *reade*: translate.

9–10. *Hebrew... Christos meos*: Hebr. *māšîach* ('messiah') means 'anointed one'; for the Greek and Latin, see n. to p. 182, ll. 7–8.

11. *farre more forcible*: a strikingly unashamed preference for Vulg. and LXX.

11–12. *old writers... Unctos*: the early translators of the Bible (both LXX and Vulg.) all declined ('uniformely forbore') to translate ('to turne') '*Unctos*' instead of '*Christos*' in 1 Cor. 16: 22 and Ps. 105: 15. Andrewes maintains a significant silence on the fact that Trem.'s Protestant Latin Bible uniformly uses 'unctos' instead of 'christos'.

18. *Synonymi*: 'synonyms' (Lat. transliteration of Gr., meaning 'the same name').

20. *Heire of all*: Heb. 1: 2.

22–23. *vouchsafe... vouchsafe*: plays with two senses, i.e. 'those whome God and Christ [*permit or allow*] to take into the charge of any their kingdomes, [to] them, they [*confer or bestow*]' their owne names (*OED*, sv II.5.b, and I.1, respectively).

26–27. *Chrisme... sacred signature*: chrism is oil fragranced with balsam; in Eastern and Roman Catholic liturgical use it is consecrated by a patriarch or bishop and used for the ritual signing with the cross at baptism, the reconciliation of apostates and converts, the consecration of churches and altars, and anointing royalty at their coronations. Chrismation was not retained in any rites of the *BCP* (but cf. its anomalous survival in James's coronation rite; see p. 185, ll. 30–3 and n.). Lossky suspects in this passage an allusion to episcopal consecration of chrism (cf. p. 188, ll. 29–31), and, in the phrase 'sacred signature' (p. 188, ll. 25–8) a reference 'to the formula used in the rite of chrismation... in the Byzantine tradition: "The Seal of the gift of the Holy Spirit"' (*Lancelot Andrewes*, 321). This is strongly supported by Andrewes's own statement to the French Cardinal Perron: '*Chrisme* (indeed) is very ancient, yet never but as a ceremony, which though we retaine not, yet the invocation of the grace of the Holy Ghost, we doe' (*OP*, pt. II, p. '12', *vere* 13; *LACT*, xi. 26).

27–35. *Holy oyle... applied*: flurry of details in God's instructions to Moses for the use of holy oil in the Jewish Tabernacle ('Sanctuary'), Exod. 30: 22–33.

28–29. *[in marg.]* **Psal. 89.21*: *BCP*; Geneva Ps. 89: 20.

36–37. *Sacri apices... Divalis iussio... Sacra vestigia*: Lat., 'Holy writs... Sacred commands... Holy steps'.

p. 189, 8. *Uzza so found it*: Uzzah, struck dead for touching the Ark of the Covenant to steady it when the oxen bearing it stumbled (2 Sam. 6: 3–7).

10–11. *in Commune Sanctorum*: Lat., 'in the communion of saints', one of the articles of the Apostles' Creed (*BCP*), asserting the spiritual union between Christ and all members of the church in earth and heaven; hence, a statement of equality among believers in the mystical body of Christ.

11. *Omnes... Reges Christi*: 'all saints are not "Christs", but kings are "Christs"'.

11–12. *We cannot... Christs*: reversal of Geneva gloss on 'anointed' (1 Chron. 16: 22), 'mine elect people and them whome I have sanctified'.

14. *[in marg] Psal. 45.8*: Vulg., Ps. 44: 8; *BCP* and Geneva, Ps. 45: 7.

19. *Chrisma Christi*: 'the anointing [or chrism] of Christ'.

21. *Dii and Christi*: '"Gods" and "Christs"'; cf. Ps. 82: 6, 1 Chron. 16: 22.

27. *Holie... Christ himselfe*: historically, innermost compartment of the Jewish Tabernacle or Temple, where the Ark of the Covenant rested, and site of the annual high priestly sacrifice on the Day of Atonement; in Christian terms, type or figure for 'Christ himselfe', whose death and resurrection was a full and final atonement for sin (Heb. 9).

34. *unchristed*: depending on the degree of Andrewes's punning in delivery, this could be pronounced 'un-christed', with the sense and sound of 'un-christened', or 'un-chrīsted', as in 'un-Christ-ed'.

36–37. *They... their pennes*: the print war over the papal deposing power touched off by the Oath of Allegiance was one of the largest pan-European debates of the seventeenth century. For a bibliography of English contributions, see Peter Milward, *Religious Controversies of the Jacobean Age* (1978); for continental involvment, see bibliography in C. H. McIlwain (ed.), *Political Works of James I* (1918).

p. 189, 37–p. 190, 11. *Because... touch it not*: Andrewes had acknowledged the power of the church to excommunicate even kings, but insisted that that power rested only with the church in council, not popes, and, crucially, that it did not extend to any right of subjects to depose an excommunicate sovereign (*Tortura*, 55–7). For a summary of the papalist position attacked here, see Sommerville, *Politics and Ideology*, 195–9.

2. *pitch*: all editions before F_1 read 'picke', but historical usage of the the two alternate readings convinces ed. that 'pitch' is a valid correction of an error in Q_{1-2} and O. OED cites no modern use of 'pick on, upon', in the now familiar sense of 'to single out for attention or adverse criticism' before 1875 ('*pick*' *v 1* VII.15). To 'pitch', however, was common in early modern English and better fits the sense of this line: 'to fix, settle, or place in thought... to come to a conclusion about' (*v 1* II.14).

3. *gratia gratum faciens*: 'grace freely made'.

4. *gratia gratis data*: 'grace freely given'.

8–9. *De iustâ abdicatione*: Jean Boucher, *De Justa Henrici Tertii Abdicatione Francorum Regno* (Paris, 1589), infamous open appeal for the deposition of Henry III of France; when the latter was assassinated before Boucher's book was finished, the author concluded it instead with praise for the assassin; cf. Frederic Baumgartner, *Radical Reactionaries: The Political Thought of the French Catholic League* (Geneva, 1975).

9. *make a holy league*: the 'Sainte Ligue' or 'Catholic League' founded 1576, refounded 1584, to crush Protestant interests in France; cf. prev. n.

9. *touch him*: murder him.

9. *blow him up*: as planned in the Gunpowder Plot (1605).

10. *cost Christendome deare*: cf. Andrewes (*Tortura*, 57), 'absit autem, ut tantarum calamitatum Ecclesia causa sit' ('from this comes one of the greatest calamities of the church').

10–11. *Noli me tangere*: 'touch me not' (John 20: 17).

15. *Cyrus*: king of Persia 558–530 BCE; as conqueror of Babylon, hailed by the captive Jewish nation there as God's agent for their liberation, and called 'messiah' ('annointed one', cf. p. 277, l. 8 and n.) by Isa. (45: 1); for Cyrus as proof of the divine right of even heathen kings, cf. Cyril of Alexandria's letter from the Council of Ephesus (*Conciliorum Omnium*, i. 1097, cap. 1).

19–20. *those of Juda*: southern Israelite kingdom, seat of David and Solomon who united it with Israel in the north; after the division of the kingdoms following Solomon's death, Judah kept purer religious rites.

22. *orthodox*: 'correct, right', with respect to theology and doctrine (*OED sa* A.2); not an epithet for the Eastern Orthodox (Greek) Church (*OED sa* 4); the ensuing list of Eastern emperors, however, might suggest a very early anticipation of the latter sense.

22–23. *Constantius... Heraclius*: emperors of the Eastern (Byzantine) Roman Empire, fourth to seventh centuries, all associated, in varying degrees, with unorthodoxy, heresy, or persecution of Christians.

28. *Julian... flat Pagan*: 'The Apostate', Roman emperor who renounced Christianity for paganism in 361.

30. *quia deerant vires*: Lat., lit., 'because the forces were lacking'; Catholic resistance theory argued that early Christians refrained from rebellion against impious rulers only because they lacked the military means to do so.

32–33. *acclamations... Christiani sumus*: Jovian, captain of Julian's bodyguard, was proclaimed emperor by them upon the latter's death in 363. Their acclamation paraphrased here probably derives from the Greek church historian Socrates' account as available in the histories of the early church collected and translated in Cassiodorus, *Historia Tripertita*: 'Cumque vox omnium communiter proclamasset, dicentium se quoque esse Christianus, suscepit imperium' (*PL*, 69.063); ('And with one voice they proclaimed that he who took upon himself the imperial power must be a Christian.')

35. *twelve Patriarchs*: twelve sons of Jacob, fathers of the tribes of Israel; Andrewes draws here on Jacob's prophecies to them of their characters (Gen. 49).

38. *might be Roboam*: recondite piece of humour which compares Issachar, dubiously characterized by Jacob as 'a strong asse, couching downe betweene t[w]o burdens' (Gen. 49: 14) with Rehoboam, King of Judah, who proved himself 'none of the wisest' by responding to an appeal for leniency from King Jeroboam of Israel with the charge, 'And now whereas my father did lade you with a heavy yoke, I wil adde to your yoke' (1 Kings 12: 11).

p. 191 6–7. *termed... ten times*: David's persistence in calling Saul 'Gods *Anointed*'; references are those from 1 & 2 Sam. in n. to p. 271, ll. 5–7.

12. *inunctus*: 'not anointed', 'unanointed'.

15. *Ranger... Forrest*: forest warden or gamekeeper; also the official title of keepers of royal forests (*OED sn¹* 2.a); suggested here by 'Nimrod the mightie hunter' (Gen. 10: 9).

20. *Reges... in perpetuum*: Lat., lit., 'he places kings in the throne forever'; cf. Job 36: 7, 'non aufert a iusto oculos suos et reges in solio conlocat in perpetuum'; ('He shal not take away his eyes from the just man, and he placeth kinges in the throne for ever, and there they are extolled', Douai-Rheims).

25. *sent*: scent.

27. *qui currunt... sui*: Lat., lit., 'who run after the scent of their prince's ointment'; cf. Vulg. (Cant. 1: 2–3).

p. 192 3–4. *Non occides... perdas*: '"Kill not" or "Destroy not"'.

5. *sillily*: 'in a foolish, absurd, or senseless manner'; pre-dates the earliest citation for its sense (1627) (*OED, sadv.* 2).

7–8. *Verse before... nocere*: ostensibly 1 Chron. 16: 21, but actually the cognate Ps. 104: 14, from Augustine's exposition of the latter, 'non permisit hominem nocere eis' (*Enarr. in Ps. CIV*, 9; *PL*, 37); cf. Vulg. (Ps. 104: 14, juxt. LXX), 'non reliquit hominem nocere eis'; Vulg. (Ps. 104: 14, juxt. Hebr.), 'non dimisit hominem ut noceret eis'; Vulg. (1 Par. 16: 21), 'non dimisit quemquam calumniari eos'; and Trem. (1 Chron. 16: 21), 'non permisit cuiquam opprimere eos'.

10. נגע *properly plaga*: with different vowel markings, the same Hebr. word can mean 'to touch' ('naga'), or 'a wound' ('nega'), the latter of which = Lat., 'plaga' ('a blow or wound').

11. *Qui tangit & angit*: Lat., 'which touches and torments'.

16–17. *ut in transitu prosint*. Lat., 'that they are good in passing'.

24. *simple*: simple-minded; naive.

25. *immediate*: unmediated.

25. *mediate*: mediated; done with or through another thing.

28. *sorcerie*: James was famously convinced of the reality of witchcraft, oversaw persecutions of witches in Scotland, and wrote his *Daemonologie* (1597) against sceptics. The official account of the Gowrie Conspiracy alleged that the Earl carried a 'parchment bagge, full of magicall characters, and words of inchantment, wherein it seemed that he had put his confidence', and that this was 'an infamie which hath followed

and spotted the race of this house, for many discents' (*Earl of Gowries Conspiracie*, sig. C3ʳ).

33–34. *non est... Philosopher*: 'there is not action except by contact'; paraphrase of Aristotle's definition of motion or change (*Physica*, iii. 2).

36. *cominus... eminus*: Lat., 'hand to hand'... 'from a distance'.

37. *Nolite sic tangere*: Lat., 'touch not like this'.

p. 193, 6. *Et qui... pungit*: Lat., 'and he who vexes them that God anoints'.

10. *tactus dolore cordis*: Lat., 'touched with the grief of the heart'.

11–12. *the verse... calumniari*: 'hee suffered no man to speak ill of them'; cf. Vulg. (1 Par. 16: 21).

13. *calumnia*: Lat., calumny, slander.

16. *Shimeis tongue*: Shimei publicly cursed David, for which he was later executed by Solomon (2 Sam. 16: 5–13; 1 Kings 2: 36–46).

16–17. *Jacobs hand*: Gen. 31: 29.

18–19. *foot of... Emperours*: a disputed point in the Oath of Allegiance controversy was the truth of the legend that Pope Alexander III trod upon the neck of Holy Roman Emperor Frederick Barbarossa (cf. King James, *Premonition*, in C. H. McIlwain (ed.), *The Political Works of James I* (Cambridge, Mass., 1918), 165). But this is also an unusually pictorial image for Andrewes, and is probably directly influenced by the woodcut from Foxe's *Actes and Monuments* which adds to its earlier German exemplar Ps. 91: 13 as a legend, a verse which Andrewes proceeds to quote (see next nn.). For this iconographic tradition, see John King, *Tudor Royal Iconography* (1989), figs. 36, 37, 50, 51.

20. *Nolite calcare*: Lat., 'tread not upon'.

21–22. *Super aspidem & Basiliscum*: Vulg. (Ps. 90: 13, juxt. LXX), 'super aspidem et basiliscum ambulabis et conculcabis leonem et draconem'; ('Thou shalt walke upon the lyon and aspe: the yong lyon and the dragon shalt thou treade under feete', Geneva). Andrewes, like the illustrator Foxe's *Actes and Monuments* (see prev. nn.), cites Ps. 91: 13 as if it were a Roman Catholic emblem for the deposition of princes. The dragon and lion were also the heraldic supporters of the Tudor royal arms. Thus, in the preacher's view, they are 'trodden upon' by the Pope's excommunication of Elizabeth I. In the royal closet in Holdenby's chapel, James listened to this sermon sitting in a window framed by royal lions and surmounted by the Tudor royal arms (McCullough, *Sermons at Court*, 24).

23. *undecent... familiar touch*: this is very likely an oblique criticism of the indiscreet physical affection shown between James and his male favourites. The closest of these, Robert Carr (later Earl of Somerset) was approaching the height of his intimacy with the king at the time of this sermon. Andrewes was perhaps one of the few clergy who could venture such a caution; according to Thomas Fuller, his 'gravity in a manner awing *King James*, who refrained from that mirth and liberty, in the presence of this Prelate, which otherwise he assumed to himself' (*Church-History of Britain* (1655), XI. i. 46).

25–29. *Magdalen... tangere*: text and subject of Andrewes's sermon before the king on Easter, 1621 (*XCVI* 543–52).

33. *Regalia*: royal powers and privileges.

p. 193, 38–p. 194, 1. *if... long after*: probably Charles V of Spain and Holy Roman Emperor, d. 1558, one year after abdication and retirement to a monastery.

2–6. *licencious touching... evils*: Andrewes touches here the vexed Parliament of 1610, on summer recess at the time of the sermon but in protracted negotiations with the king over the exchange of sensitive royal prerogatives for cash grants from Parliament, a bargain known as 'The Great Contract'. The insistence of the Commons on negotiating with the sovereign on matters of prerogative infuriated James, who would have agreed entirely with Andrewes's inference here that these were 'light and loose *touchings*'. Andrewes's refusal to pursue the point ('I list not dilate it') is typical of his avoidance (in pulpit and after 1616 in Council) of state matters that did not directly influence the church. He may also have been cautious after Samuel Harsnett's defence of the royal prerogative in a court sermon on 11 March 1610 had been rounded upon in the Commons (Sommerville, *Politics and Ideology*, 132).

8. *that touch himselfe*: that Satan might touch Job himself (in addition to the things belonging to Job).

9. *touch him home*: touch him to the quick; but punning on the point that Satan vexes his victims indirectly by persecuting their homes and families.

10. *directly*: 'immediately'; also 'unambiguously'.

10–15. *Pharaoh... Lords Anointed*: Gen. 12: 10–20. Andrewes's strong statement that queens are 'one and the same person' with their kings (based on the Pauline concept of 'one flesh' in marriage, 1 Cor. 6: 16) makes unavoidable an application here to James and Queen Anne. The choice of the story of the disrepute brought on Abram's house by Sara's infidelity with Pharoah is almost certainly a warning against the disrepute brought on James's house by rumours of Anne's Catholicism and sympathetic correspondence with the Pope (for whom Pharoah was a common biblical type in Protestant polemic).

17–18. *esse... fore... in being... to be*: Lat., *esse*, present infinitive ('*in being*'); Lat., *fore*, future infinitive ('*to be*').

22. *whole race Royall*: allusion to royal progeny with particular resonance after the investiture of Henry as Prince of Wales during parliamentary session in June, part of James and Lord Treasurer Salisbury's charm offensive to win support for the Great Contract; cf. Croft, *King James*, 77–8.

24. *set to*: placed against; defends against.

26. *not, Ne tangite... tangere*: 'Not, "Touch not", but, "Have not the will to touch"'.

28. *voluntas tangendi*: Lat., 'the will of touching'.

35–36. *velle tangere*: Lat., 'to wish to touch'.

37. *two Eunuches, Esth. 2*: Bigthan and Teresh, eunuchs (court officers) who plotted the assassination of King Ahasuerus (Esth. 2), subjects of Andrewes's 1616 Gowrie sermon, where they are portrayed more fully as biblical types of the Gowrie brothers (*XCVI*, 844–58).

p. 195, 6–7. *They... touched not any*: the Gunpowder plotters were, famously, foiled before they could execute their treason. See 'A Sermon Preached... the V. November' (this edn.).

19–20. *sortiuntur... delicti*: Lat., '[they] are held to the reckoning of this crime'.

29–35. *given... others life*: such a stinging denunciation of regicide perpetrated by other princes would have been impossible in a sermon preached to Elizabeth I, who was ultimately responsible for the execution of James's mother, Mary Queen of Scots (1587). Andrewes's position here echoes James's own vehement warnings to Elizabeth that she not set a precedent for regal regicide (cf. Croft, *King James*, 22). The biblical precedents cited here—'the two *Abimelechs*' as well as '*Pharao*'—reflect contemporary belief that Gen. 12: 10–20, 20: 1–14, and 26: 7–11 record separate historical events (which modern scholars take to be literary variations of one another) in which a foreign king (Pharoah in the first, Abimelech in the latter two) is rebuked in a dream for 'touching' the wife (Sarah, Rebecca) of a patriarch (Abraham, Isaac) disguised as the latter's sister. These *exemplas*' unusual argument that the wives of patriarchs were themselves God's anointed encourages retrospective application of them to Mary Queen of Scots and Elizabeth I ('each to spare, and to save the others life').

36. *no let*: no allowance.

p. 196, 2–3. *holy religious... martyrs*: sarcastic catalogue of Roman Catholic apologists for papal deposing power and regicide; the last category, martyrs, derives from the most extreme Jesuit view, articulated most infamously by Mariana, that killing a heretical prince could be meritorious for salvation, and thus worth dying for; Andrewes may have in mind the most famous rebuke to the Jesuit doctrine of martyrdom, John Donne's *Pseudo-Martyr*, which had appeared in Jan. 1610.

8. *whole Law... Commandements*: Judaic law as set down in the Mosaic books of Exod., Lev., Num., and Deut., of which 'the ten Commandements' (Exod. 20: 1–17) is a summary.

10. *assay*: attempt.

17. *idem velle, & nolle*: Lat., 'the same willingness and the same unwillingness'.

22. *casteth*: 'to form by throwing up, to raise (a mound, bank, earthwork)' (*OED*, sv. IV.30).

23–24. *Cherubims two... other*: in Solomon's Temple, two carved-gilt cherubims stood over the Ark of the Covenant in the Holy of Holies (1 Kings 6: 23–7).

29. *Hemistichion*: transliteration of the Gr. ημιστίχιον ('half-line'), usually found in English in the Latin form 'hemistichium' or 'hemistich'.

p. 196, 38–p. 197, 1. *fearefull examples... away*: King Henry III of France, assassinated 1589; King Henry IV of France, assassinated 1610.

5–6. *Ishbosheth... his bed*: 2 Sam. 4: 5–11.

13–14. *Baanah... Bigthan... Zimri*: 2 Sam. 4: 10–11, Esth. 2: 21, 1 Kings 16: 8–10.

15–16. *Religion... till now*: cf. how Henry IV's assassin, Ravaillac, 'was brought out of... the prison... the knife (wherewith he killed the King) chained to the other hand, so openly to be seene, that the lest childe there present might behold it'. During the ensuing torture, Ravaillac purportedly declared that his motive 'was, because the King tollerated two Religions in his Kingdome' (*Terrible and Deserved Death*, 3, 10).

p. 197, 39–p. 198, 2. *whereby... owne Kings*: the semi-official English account of the assassin Ravaillac's trial and execution asserted that a Paris Jesuit was complicit in the plot, and made an explicit connection between the crime and Jesuit propaganda: 'they doe well finde, that the damnable Maximes which have bene insinuated these 20. yeeres by seditious Bookes, and Preachings, in derogation of the sacrednesse and authority of Princes, have bene a chiefe occasion of this mischiefe. A point which all Princes had neede neerely to regard' (*Copie of a Letter*, 5).

5–6. *booke is condemned*: Andrewes's account of the attempts to censure or censor Mariana's *De Rege*, though polemical, is accurate, and reveals just how well informed he and the court were on matters unfolding in France in the wake of Henry's assassination. On 6 July 1610 the Jesuit General, Aquaviva, tried to quell heated anti-Jesuit passions in France, where the Parlement had ordered the public burning of

Mariana's book in June, by sending to his French members a decree forbidding the teaching of tyrannicide or regicide. For a text of the decree and discussion of its context, see Guenter Lewy, *Constitutionalism and Statecraft... the Political Philosophy of Juan de Mariana, S.J.* (Geneva, 1960), 142, 167.

7–8. *eleven yeeres... authorized*: Mariana's *De Rege* was first published in 1599 with the approval of his Spanish Jesuit superiors (Lewy, *Constitutionalism*, 140).

8. *eight whole yeeres*: cf. nn. to ll. 14–34.

11. *Index expurgatorius*: the *Index Librorum Prohibitorum* ('Index of Prohibited Books'), was a list, first issued by the Congregation of the Inquisition under Pope Paul IV in 1557, of books forbidden for reading by members of the Roman Church; a subsidiary list, the *Index Expurgatorius*, defined those books which could be read only after passages offensive to Roman doctrine or morals had been deleted ('expurgated').

13–18. *censured... a tale*: rumours of any Jesuit 'Censure' of Mariana before 1610 were in fact 'but a tale'. The source of what Andrewes sceptically retails here may have been Aquaviva's request to Mariana in 1600 that he tone down praise of the assassin of Henry III in the book's second edition (which appeared 1605), for the sake of mollifying anti-Jesuit feeling in France. The resulting changes to the text were slight, and Aquaviva only demurred at the subsequent protests of his French members (Lewy, *Constitutionalism*, 140–1).

19–20. *Why... Esaus hands*: Andrewes compares the censure of Mariana coming only after the assassination of Henry IV to Isaac's not realizing that his son Jacob had pretended to be his brother Esau until Isaac had given him Esau's birthright (Gen. 27: 22–3).

22–34. *condemned?... where we were before*: Andrewes must have seen a copy or summary of Aquaviva's July decree (cf. prev. nn.). Although it purported to be a statement against regicide, it did contain loopholes that Andrewes polemically exposes here. As in his engagement with Bellarmine, he points out the circularity of the papal arguments for the deposing power. First, that popes could declare any king a heretic (and thus a usurper), and hence call for his deposition. Secondly, both Bellarmine and Aquaviva deny private authority for tyrannicide but leave open the possibility of some public (papal) authority for it. In both cases, the pope held an arbitrary power to define whether a king was a king or not. Technically speaking, Catholic resistance theorists disapproved of killing a king—but once excommunicated and deposed by pope or commonwealth, and thus no longer a king, he could be killed as a usurping tyrant if he persisted in exercising regal power. Cf. Lewy, *Constitutionalism*, 135, 142, 167; Andrewes, *Responsio*, p. xviii; and Somerville, *Politics and Ideology*, 198.

27–28. *Non hoc... expedire*: Lat., 'not at this time, but when he shall judge it expedient'.

30–31. *private man... authoritie*: one of the loopholes in Aquaviva's decree (see prev. nn.).

p. 199, 6. *Mitte manum, & tange*: Lat., 'put forth the hand, and touch' (cf. Job 1: 11).

7. *Nolite... Christos eius*: Lat., 'touch not his anointed'.

24–29. *not lay... will of God*: the official English account of the assassination of Henry IV stressed Henry's disregard of warnings for his safety: 'hee (not believing Predictions) sayd, that it was an offence to God to give credit unto them, and that having God for his guarde hee feared no man', and he travelled on the fatal day 'without suffering any of his Guard to follow him, being very confident' (*True Report*, 8–9). James's lifelong aversion to crowds and fear of regicide was further fuelled by reports of new Jesuit plots on his own life in the wake of the French assassination (Sommerville, *Politics and Ideology*, 198), and Andrewes here deftly inverts Henry's purported trust in Providence in order to urge or justify James's greater caution.

26–29. *Non... Tertullian*: Tertullian, *De Exhortatione Castitatis*, cap. II (*PL*, 2.915).

31. *without*: unless.

36–37. *mittere se deorsum*: Lat., 'that casts himself down'; cf. Vulg. (Matt. 4: 6).

p. 200, 11. *lists*: 'a limit, bound, boundary' (*OED* sn *3*, II.8.a).

15. *Morte morietur*: Lat., lit., 'he shall die the death'.

21. *Vitæ alienæ... suæ*: Lat., 'he is master of another's life who cares not for his own'.

22. *Contemptor suæ*: Lat., 'disregardful of his own'.

22–23. *Comprehensor æternæ*: 'possessor of eternity'.

30–31. *hanc talem... pestem*: Virgil, *Aenied*, iii. 620 (*LACT*); the narrator's interjection in the description of the Cyclops, 'keep such a plague away from earth!' (trans. Mandelbaum, 1971).

31. *ne velint*: Lat., 'they would not'.

32. *ne possint*: Lat., 'they could not'.

36. *tangibiles*: Lat., 'touchable'.

37. *tangendi*: Lat., 'touched'.

p. 201, 12. *Maranathas*: 'accursed ones'; from Gr., μαραναθά, 'The Lord is come', used as a Christian valediction; but in some Greek texts and the early English translations of 1 Cor. 16: 22 confused by Paul's use of the word immediately following the curse, 'anathema' ('Yf any man love not the Lorde Jesus Christe, the same be Anathema maranatha.', Bishops' Bible); 'anathema maranatha' was thus mistakenly used as 'an intensified form of *anathema*' (*OED*) in its sense of a person or persons accursed; Andrewes seems to be unique in using '*Maranathas*', instead of 'anathemas' as a substantive.

21. *Nolo tangi*: Lat., 'I will not have them touched'.

24–25. *verse next before*: 1 Chron. 16: 21.

26. *Put to... Corripuit*: Andrewes uses the Geneva trans., 'but rebuked Kings for their sakes' (cf. Bishops', 'yea he reproved kinges'). But for his back-translation of the verb into Lat. ('*Corripuit*'), he again quotes not Vulg. (1 Par. 16: 21) '*increpuit*' ('rebuked'), but its cognate (Ps. 104: 14, juxt. Hebr. and LXX), ' et corripuit pro eis reges'. '*Corripuit*' in a transferative sense also means 'rebuked', but in its literal sense, 'seized' or 'snatched', imports more violent force into the ensuing passages on corporal and capital punishment. '[W]ee' is here a formal first person singular.

27. *twitch*: 'a jerk; a pluck; a snatch'; both noun and verb forms in this paragraph have connotations of sudden and violent punishment, including capital punishment by hanging (cf. *OED sv¹* 3.c).

28–29. *Tangentes tangentur... corripientur*: Lat., 'those who touch shall be touched... those who touch shall be snatched'.

34. *kindly*: natural, fitting.

36. *kinde*: way, manner.

p. 202, 7. *Pincers... Lead*: cf. 'with Tongues [tongs] and Iron Pincers, made extreame hott... the appointed Executioners, pinched and seared the Dugges of his Breastes, the brawnes of his Armes and Thighes, with the calves of his Legges, and other fleshy partes of his Body, cutting out Colloppes of Flesh, and burned them before his face.... they put upon his navell a rundle of clay, very hard, with a hole in the midst, and into the same hole powred they moulten lead, till it was filled' (*Terrible and Deserved Death*, 10).

11–12. *as the first was*: Pharaoh.

21. *those two*: the Gowrie brothers.

24. *keepe*: guard, protect.

26. *miscarie withall?*: 'is killed nonetheless?'

28–29. *Corripuit...permisit nocere*: Lat., 'he cut [them] short...he did not permit [them] to harm [them]'.

35. *Psalme...twentie*: cf. p. 181, ll. 9–11 and n.

p. 203, 9. *his Arke...allied*: Andrewes earlier in the sermon made the conventional analogy between the Ark and Christ's body (cf. p. 189, ll. 25–8); here he uses the same scriptural metaphor to insist on the Protestant (and Eastern) principle that monarchs ('*His Anointed*') are the rightful supreme governors of the church ('his Arke').

25–30. *29 verses...96. psal.*: for the composite psalm sung in 1 Chron. 16, cf. n. to p. 181, ll. 9–11. Andrewes here attaches significance to the fact that the portion from Ps. 105 stops at its v. 15 before continuing with Ps. 96.

p. 204, 8–9. *Red sea...fire*: Exod. 14; Dan. 3: 27.

10–11. *throat...throwen downe*: as in previous Gowrie sermons, Andrewes follows the king's version of events, according to which Alexander Ruthven 'put his right hand to his sword...he with his left hand claspt the King by the throate, with two or three of his fingers in his majesties mouth, to have stayed him from crying....with struggling and wrastling' (*Earle of Gowries Conspiracie*, sig. C1^{r-v}).

22. *sword...twitched them*: the Earl and his brother were stabbed to death by the king's retainers.

23–24. *Pharao's tactus...for ever*: Andrewes alludes to God's curse of 'Pharaoh and his house with great plagues' (Gen. 12: 17) as an analogue for the act of the Scottish Parliament that abolished the name and title of Ruthven and Gowrie, and ordered the levelling of the castle where the conspiracy was carried out (*ODNB*, *sn* Ruthven, John).

25. *severally, a severall*: 'separately, a separate'.

p. 205, 1–2. *till hee smoked*: gruesome allusion, by way of a v. from the Ps., to Ravaillac's torture with 'scalding Oyle, Rosen, Pitch, & Brimstone, melted together' as well as 'molten lead' (*Terrible and Deserved Death*, 10).

6–11. *sitting...his harme*: Henry IV was stabbed through the open window of his coach while passing through a crowded Paris street, and was accompanied by three dukes (*True Report*, 9–10).

11–15. *But Ours...Him*: Alexander Ruthven allegedly led James to a remote 'little study' guarded by an armed servant, Andrew Henderson, then left to bring his brother the Earl there as the third party to the planned assassination. James was not literally 'left alone', except in the sense of being separated from his own retainers, Henderson being always present (*Earl of Gowries Conspiracie*, sig. B3^r–4^v, D3^r–4^r).

19–22. *one...stayed his hand*: the role of Ruthven's servant, Andrew Henderson, is one of several discrepancies in the official accounts. In the narrative, Henderson remained passive during Ruthven's assault, only having opened the window for the king to shout from before his master's return. Henderson's deposition before the privy counsellors (appended to the published narrative), however, gives him an active saving role: 'the deponer [Henderson] pulled the garter out of maister *Alexander* his hand... pulled the maisters hand from his Highnesse mouth, and opened the window: & then his Majestie cried out thereat'; upon arriving home afterwards, 'the deponers wife enquiring of him, what the fray meaned? The deponer answered, that the Kings Majestie would have beene twice sticked, had not he relieved him' (*Earl of Gowries Conspiracie*, sig. D3^v–4^r). In no part of the published account does Henderson either 'rebuke' or 'stay' Ruthven's hand, much less anticipate Andrewes's sermon by speaking 'this very Text'.

27. *yeerely...yea daily*: the Gowrie plot anniversary was observed by statue 'yeerely' in Scotland and England, and 'weekely' at court by sermons on every Tuesday of the year; 'daily' is perhaps more metaphorical, or an allusion to the *BCP* versicle 'O Lord save the king' in daily Morning and Evening Prayer.

33–34. *scattered...their hearts*: from the 'Magnificat' ('He hath scattered the proud in the imagination of their hearts'), sung daily at Evening Prayer (*BCP*).

38. *[in marg.] Psal. 89.38, 44, 45*: The phrases quoted ('But thou...to the ground') are Andrewes's free adaptations of Ps. 89: 37–8, 43–4 (*BCP*); although the language is closest to *BCP*, the v. numbering is Geneva and Bishops'.

40. *Præceptum flebile*: Lat., 'a mournful precept'.

40–41. *Præceptum...Cantabile*: Lat., 'precept in song'; cf. Ps. 118: 54 (Vulg., juxt. LXX), 'carmina erant mihi præcepta tua'.

p. 206, 6. *Nolentes*: Lat., 'not willing'.

11. *Decennalia*: Lat., tenth anniversary celebrations.

A SERMON PREACHED...ON...WHIT-SUNDAY

Text. *XCVI*, F_1 (1629, ed.'s copy), 710–21; collated with F_2 (1632, Bodl. Antiq. c.E.1632.2), and F_3 (1635, ed.'s copy). Like all of Andrewes's surviving court sermons for Whitsunday, there are no witnesses, manuscript or print, before F_1. With the exception of the egregious misnumbering of three verses in the biblical text prefacing the sermon, the setting of F_1 is exemplary. F_2 supplies only ten corrections of spelling and capitalization.

Headnote. For Andrewes, Whitsunday was the culmination of the church's liturgical year: the saving work of Christ was begun in the incarnation at Christmas, won in the crucifixion and resurrection at Easter, and perfected and sealed with the sending of the Holy Ghost at Pentecost. The sermon presented here is the eleventh of fourteen surviving Whitsunday sermons preached to the court of James I between 1606 and 1621; a fifteenth was written for 1622 but not delivered (*XCVI*, 595–768).

The sermon for 1618 epitomizes Andrewes's dominant doctrinal concerns presented throughout the series: the assertion of the Western church's post-Nicene belief in the distinct personhood of the Holy Spirit that proceeds from both the Father and the Son; and the integral role of the Spirit in the economy of salvation. But the treatment of complex Trinitarian doctrine is firmly subordinate to Andrewes's pastoral and rhetorical application of these assertions to the practical divinity of salvation. The final phrase of his text here—'shall be saved', '*salvabitur*' (Acts 2: 21)—is the target at which the entire sermon aims, and the preacher treats the preceding verses of his text as directions for how to achieve that goal. Characteristically, one key word from the text—*effundam*, 'I shall pour out'—is refracted throughout the sermon like light through a prism. The wordplay on it evolves with calibrated precision from the opening's light-hearted punning on the apostles' rumoured drunkenness at Pentecost, through the 'pouring' of the Holy Spirit's gifts, the 'pouring down' of hellfire at Doomsday, the 'pouring out' of the soul in prayer, and, climactically, the 'effusion' of Christ's blood in the eucharist. The thematic imagery that begins in the vulgar wine of drunkenness is transfigured into the ineffable 'cup of salvation'. En route, Andrewes delivers a sustained discussion, unique in his sermon oeuvre, of eschatology, as well as one of his most unapologetic attacks on the Jacobean cult of the sermon. The result is a masterful example of Andrewes's ability to apply the general tenets of Christian soteriology to the controverted realities of the Jacobean church.

The very word order of Joel's prophecy quoted in Acts allows Andrewes to amplify an argument that appears more briefly throughout his career: preaching, while necessary and vital, is a means to salvation categorically inferior to prayer (by which he means not only private devotion, but also corporate liturgical prayer, and its consummation, the eucharist). In a stroke of metadramatic genius, he preaches a sermon against sermons on a text from the first sermon by St Peter, itself on a text from a sermon by Joel. The tradition of conformist attacks on the godly enthusiasm for preaching was one well established by three of Andrewes's most intimate associates in Elizabeth's reign: John Whitgift (in the 1570s Admonition Controversy with Thomas Cartwright), Richard Hooker (in his *Laws of Ecclesiastical Polity*, written in response to the puritan Walter Travers), and Richard Bancroft (who carried this work into James's reign with restraints on popular preaching in the Canons of 1606). Andrewes himself had also had first-hand experience in 1590 with the most radical exponent of popular preaching, the separatist Henry Barrow. Barrow's transcript of Andrewes's third and final attempt to argue him into conformity before his execution for sedition is a barbed summary of many of the points made here against private inspiration and congregational independence.

The prompt for Andrewes's 1618 criticisms of nonconformity, however, is clearly the crisis sparked in 1617 by James's attempts to impose English ceremonial worship, episcopal confirmation, and the observance of major feastdays (including Whitsunday) on the Scottish kirk. Andrewes had been one of the stars in James's clerical entourage taken to Scotland the previous spring. In the chapel royal at Holyrood on Whitsunday 1617 Andrewes had delivered a sermon also extolling episcopal authority and the restraint of preaching; his unusually frequent references to it in this sermon underscore the regime's commitment to the controverted 'Five Articles' that would be pushed through the kirk's General Assembly at Perth in August. The sermon, however, also includes an oblique but sharp criticism of James himself—its frank condemnation of the privileging of preaching over liturgy in James's English chapel royal indicts the Supreme Governor himself for the same slighting of '*invocation*' in favour of '*prophesying*' with which the Scots and English nonconformists stood accused.

Source.   For this sermon's pneumatology, Andrewes cites as his principal patristic source Ambrose, *De Spiritu Sancto*, and Didymus ('the Blind') of Alexandria, *De Spiritu Sancto*. The latter was known in its Latin translation by Didymus' pupil, Jerome, in whose works it was printed in the early modern period. For his treatment of his text's apocalyptic themes, Andrewes only alludes to a generalized patristic consensus, but several sources are readily identifiable. The only systematic patristic commentary on Acts is that of John Chrysostom, *Commentaria in Actorum Apostolorum*, widely available in Latin editions of the *Opera*, and in Greek. Jerome's *Commentaria in Joelem* also treats the prophecy quoted here in the text from Acts. A further important source is Jerome's use of Acts 2: 16–21 to refute the Montanist heresy in *Epistolæ XLI*

Ad Marcellam. Since Andrewes does not quote directly from these latter sources, they are quoted here in English translations.

Further Reading. Andrewes's sermons for Whitsunday have not received the same critical attention as the Easter and Christmas sermons popularized by the Oxford Movement and T. S. Eliot. A case for their crucial importance to understanding Andrewes's theology is convincingly made by Lossky, *Lancelot Andrewes*, 208–88. For Lossky, this sermon in particular is a key statement by Andrewes on the major point of doctrinal division between the Eastern and Western churches: the procession (or not) of the Holy Ghost from both the Father and the Son (the '*Filioque*') (pp. 244–7). For the context and influence of Andrewes's court-pulpit campaign against excessive preaching, see Eric J. Carlson, 'The Boring of the Ear: Shaping the Pastoral Vision of Preaching in England, 1540–1640', in Larissa Taylor (ed.), *Preachers and People in the Reformations and Early Modern Period* (2001), 249–96; McCullough, 'Making Dead Men Speak'; and McCullough, *Sermons at Court*, 155–67. For Andrewes and Henry Barrow, see *The Writings of John Greenwood... with the Joint Writings of Henry Barrow and John Greenwood, 1587–1590*, ed. Leland Carlson (1962), 140–62). For the Scottish context, see Pauline Croft, *James VI & I* (2003), 165–7; and Maurice Lee, Jr., *Government by Pen* (1980), 155–94.

p. 207, 2. *Greenwich*: early Tudor palace of Greenwich, favourite seat for the Jacobean court during Whitsuntide; in 1623, James would commission Andrewes, as Dean of the Chapel, '"to cause Greenwich Chapel to be new repaired and gilded, being much decayed, as not having been new furnished since Queen Mary's days"' (McCullough, *Sermons at Court*, 32).

4. *Whit-Sunday*: feast of Pentecost, commemorating the descent of the Holy Ghost upon the Apostles fifty days after the Resurrection; in importance as a holy day, second only to Easter; the English name, dominant since Anglo-Saxon times over the Graeco-Latin 'Pentecost', means literally 'White-Sunday', believed to allude to the white robes once worn by those baptized on the feast day (*OED*).

7. *Sed hoc... &c*: Vulg., as are Andrewes's frequent Latin quotations of key phrases from his text *passim*; the complete passage is:

> 16 sed hoc est quod dictum est per prophetam Johel
> 17 et erit in novissimis diebus dicit Dominus effundam de Spiritu meo super omnem carnem et prophetabunt filii vestri et filiae vestrae et iuvenes vestri visiones videbunt et seniores vestri somnia somniabunt
> 18 et quidem super servos meos et super ancillas meas in diebus illis effundam de Spiritu meo et prophetabunt
> 19 et dabo prodigia in caelo sursum et signa in terra deorsum sanguinem et ignem et vaporem fumi
> 20 sol convertetur in tenebras et luna in sanguinem antequam veniat dies Domini magnus et manifestus
> 21 et erit omnis quicumque invocaverit nomen Domini salvus erit

8–20. *But... shalbe saved*: Geneva, but omitting the clause 'in those daies' that follows '*powre out my* Spirit' in v. 18; vv. 17–21 quote Joel 2: 28–32.

22–23. *first Whitson-Sermon... Whit-Sunday*: Andrewes's text is from St Peter's sermon to the crowds at Pentecost immediately following the descent of the Holy Ghost upon the Apostles in a rushing wind and tongues of fire (Acts 2: 1–15).

24–25. CHRIST... *out of Esai*: on Whitsunday 1617 Andrewes had preached before the king at Holyrood House in Edinburgh on Luke 4: 18–19, Christ's quotation of Isa. 61: 1–2 (*XCVI*, 698).

25–27. *Both... present occasion*: oblique criticism of preaching that either ignored Prayer Book holy days when choosing texts for sermons, or strayed into private or political speculation instead of close biblical exegesis; Andrewes's criticism was more forceful in presbyterian Scotland the previous year (see prev. n.) when he archly noted that Christ preached on Isaiah 'to teach us thereby... to keep us within; not to flie out, or preach much, either without, or besides the booke' (*XCVI*, 698).

27. *lewd surmise*: malicious rumour.

28. *gift of tongues... heaven*: Acts 2: 3–4.

p. 208, 5–8. *Well... out it comes*: colloquial expansion of Acts 2: 13 ('And others mocked, and said, They are full of newe wine').

5. *Well fare*: 'a genuine expression of good wishes (= "May it go well with", "good luck to") or [as here] employed ironically' (*OED*).

7. *outlandish*: *OED* (*sa* 1.b) cites this as the first of only two uses of the word as an absolute adjective (i.e. without a modified noun), here meaning 'foreign (language)'.

9–10. *grande Miraculum... ludibrium*: 'great miracle... great laughing-stock'.

10. *Mysterie*: 'religious truth known only from divine revelation... doctrine of the faith involving difficulties which human reason is incapable of solving' (*OED, sn¹* I.2); here the revelation, and associated doctrines, of the Holy Spirit.

17. *prayes audience*: asks for attention.

18–21. *they misse... answering*: cf. Chrysostom, *Comm. on the Acts*, Homily V: 'but [St Peter] did not insist upon this to the letter; for there was nothing of the kind about them; the others said it only in mockery. Hence we learn that on unessential points one must not spend many words' (*LF*, xi. 32).

19. *to be gone*: *OED* ('gone' *ppl a* 1) 'lost, ruined, undone'; here, drunk.

20. *before nine... morning*: 'but the third hour of the day' (Acts 2: 15).

27. *habemus... propheticum*: Vulg. (2 Pet. 1: 19); 'We have also a most sure worde of the Prophets'.

35–36. *De Spiritu meo... Effundam... Dicit Dominus... Super omnem carnem*: Vulg. (Acts 2: 17), '"Of my spirit"... "I shall send"... "Says the Lord"... "Upon all flesh"'.

p. 209, 2. *salvabitur*: 'he shall be saved' (Vulg., 'salvus erit').

4. *accessorie*: 'additional, extra' (*OED, sa* A.1.a, citing 1618 as the first usage).

7. *prophetabunt*: Vulg. (Acts 2: 18); 'they shall prophesy'.

8. *Memorandum*: 'an injunction to remember something' (*OED, sn* 3.).

9. *Great Day of the* LORD: Judgement Day, the Last Day.

9. *from the matter*: away from, unrelated to the matter.

9–10. *more then needs*: more than is necessary.

16. *the Day*: Pentecost (Whitsunday).

18. *with the Rabbins*: rabbinical tradition interpreted prophecies like Joel's as predicting the coming of the Messiah.

20–21. *having done... this day*: 'Having done his "*errand*" on earth, Christ ascended to heaven, and sent the "*Spirit*" down to do its errand today.'

21–22. *His first*: his first '*errand*'.

26. *memorie of it*: memorial, or commemoration, of Pentecost.

30. *OF ... powred first*: this section (pp. 209–10) is a dense doctrinal definition of the nature of the Holy Spirit and its relationship to the two other Persons of the Trinity (Father and Son). In the four numbered paragraphs Andrewes asserts the orthodox Western view that the Holy Spirit is (1) a distinct Person of the Trinity, (2) a Person that proceeds (from the Father and the Son), (3) that the third Person is nothing less than God, and (4) that only a portion of the Spirit is poured out upon mankind.

30. *De Spiritu meo*: Vulg. (Acts 2: 18); 'of my Spirit'.

31. *honour ... owne Day*: feast day in honour of the Holy Spirit.

33–34. *Nicene Creed ... Prophets*: Nicene Creed, said at Holy Communion (*BCP*), includes the article, 'And I believe in the Holy Ghost, the Lord and giver of life, who proceedeth from the Father and the Son, who with the Father and Son together is worshipped and glorified, who spake by the prophets'.

37. *natura rationalis*: Lat., 'a rational nature'.

37. *determinate*: 'clearly defined or individualized' (*OED sa* B.1.a).

p. 210, 1. *Fusus à Fusore*: Lat., 'poured out by the Pourer'.

2. *natura rationalis determinata*: Lat., 'defined as a rational being'.

5. *behoves*: 'it is incumbent upon or necessary for (a person) *to do* (something)' (*OED sv* 4.a).

6–7. *No Person ... so farre*: cf. Ambrose, *De Spirito Sancto* I. vii.82, 'de quo Angelo Scriptura hoc dicit? de qua Dominatione? de qua Potestate? Cujus inveniemus Angeli virtutem per plurimos esse diffusam? Angeli enim ad paucos mittebantur, Spiritus autem sanctus populis infundebatur' (*PL*, 16.724B); ('of what angel does the Scripture say this? of what Dominion? of what Power? The strength of which angel do we find diffused over many? Angels were sent to few, but the Holy Spirit was poured out over entire peoples').

6. *participate*: 'made to share' (*OED sppl.a.* 1).

9–10. *Ambrose ... Heirom's Master*: cf. Sources; with the exception of p. 210, ll. 6–7 (see n.), no exact parallels in Andrewes's diction or argument to this point can be found in these sources; ensuing arguments (below, *passim*) are, however, directly indebted to them.

11–12. *It is not ... all flesh*: cf. Ambrose, *De Spiritu Sancto*, I. viii.92, 'non Spiritum ait, sed de Spiritu; neque enim nos capere possumus plenitudinem Spiritus sancti, sed tantum accipimus, quantum de suo arbiter nostri pro sua voluntate diviserit' (*PL*, 16.726C–D); ('he does not say "Spirit", but "of the Spirit"; nor are we able to receive the fulness of the Holy Spirit, but we receive as much of it as our Lord by his will shall mete out').

12–13. *And parts ... gifts and graces*: anxious insistence on the complete indivisibility and divinity of the Holy Spirit by distinguishing between the fallacious idea of the Spirit itself being literally divided into 'parts' among the faithful, and the emanation from it of '*gifts* and *graces*'.

14. *Beames ... streames*: cf. Ambrose, *De Spiritu Sancto*, I. XIV–XVI for the Holy Spirit as *lumen* ('light') and *flumen* ('a stream').

17. *Spirit ... last yeare*: cf. p. 207, ll. 24–6 and n.; on Luke 4: 18 ('The Spirit of the Lord is upon Me'), Andrewes had commented that 'the comming of the *Spirit*, in the Text heer upon CHRIST, was the cause of the comming of the *Spirit*, this day, upon the Apostles' (*XCVI*, 699).

21. *He came in fire*: Acts 2: 3.

29. *streight*: straightway, immediately.

29. *CHRIST's glorifying ... day*: the sending of the Holy Ghost was the completion of the work of salvation that had begun with Christ's incarnation; thus Whitsunday ('this

very day'), even more than the Resurrection or Ascension, is the culmination of '*CHRIST's glorifying*'; cf. Lossky, *Lancelot Andrewes*, 208–15.

p. 210, 35–p. 211, 1. *the Translators... Joël*: Hebr. 'moreh' (from verbs meaning either 'to fear' or 'to pour') can, with different vowel markings, mean both 'teacher' and 'early (first) rain'; repeated several times in Joel 2: 23; cf. Geneva, 'rejoyce in the Lorde your God: for he hath given you the *rayne of righteousnes*, he wil cause to come downe for you the rayne, even the first raine, and the latter raine in the first moneth', and Douai-Rheims, 'be joyful in the Lord your God: because he hath given you a *doctor of justice*, and he wil make the early and the late showre to descend to you as in the beginning' (italics added); the point had been archly disputed by William Fulke and Gregory Martin (Fulke, *A Defence*, in *Works*, i. 574–5).

6. *phialls... of GOD*: Rev. 16: 1.

8. *aspergam... this day*: Lat., 'I shall sprinkle', referring here to baptism; Whitsunday, with Easter Eve, was one of the traditional days in the early church for the baptism of catechumens.

9. *largesse*: bountifulness, generosity.

11. *copiosa sanguinis effusio*: Lat., 'a copious effusion of blood'.

12. *copiosa Flaminus effusio*: Lat., 'a copious effusion of wind'.

14. *copiosa redemptio*: 'copious redemption'; cf. Ps. 129: 7 (Vulg.), 'quia apud Dominum misericordia et copiosa apud eum redemptio'; ('for with the Lord there is mercy, and with him is plenteous redemption', Ps. 130: 7).

14. *effundam copiose*: Lat., 'I shall pour out copiously'.

16. *effluet... effundam*: Lat., '[he] pours out... I shall pour out'.

16. *Sic oportet impleri*: cf. Luke 22: 37 (Vulg.), 'dico enim vobis quoniam adhuc hoc quod scriptum est oportet impleri in me'; ('For I say unto you, That yet the same which is written, must be perfourmed in me').

18. *goe on our owne heads*: 'out of one's own thought, device, or will; of one's own accord, spontaneously' (*OED* 'head' n^1 IV.33).

20–21. CHRIST... *last yeare*: cf. p. 207, ll. 24–6, p. 210, l. 17 and nn.; Andrewes's 1617 treatment of Christ's anointing and sending sternly defended the episcopal ordination of priests and deacons (*XCVI*, 702–3).

24. *Ecce ego, mitte me*: Vulg. (Isa. 6: 8), 'Here am I, send me'.

30. *shut the heaven*: cf. Matt. 23: 13, Luke 4: 25, Rev. 11: 6.

31. *strikes... the vessell*: does not open the vessel (e.g. a jar) by breaking it at the neck.

36. *assignations*: allottings, apportionments (*OED*).

p. 212, 2. *Singulis prout vult*: Vulg. (1 Cor. 12: 11); ('severally [individually] as he will').

4. *Dicit Dominus*: Lat., 'God says'.

6–7. *Dominum nostrum... CHRIST*: Nicene Creed (*BCP*): 'I believe... in one Lord Jesu Christ'.

12. *dedit... Domino meo*: 'The Lord gave to my Lord'.

14. *one spiration*: one breathing (breath).

18. *Quis... Quid... à Quo*: 'Who... What... by Whom'.

18–19. *Father... the HOLY GHOST*: summary of the orthodox Western doctrine that the Holy Spirit proceeds from both the Father and the Son (*a Patre Filioque*); for this passage as evidence of Andrewes's differing from Western Scholasticism on this point, see Lossky, *Lancelot Andrewes*, 244–7.

20. *two natures of Christ*: divine and human.

20–21. *Effundam is fundam ex*: Lat., *ex* ('out of') + *fundam* (ppl. *fundere*, 'to pour').

26. *quills*: 'a small pipe or tube; esp. a small water-pipe'; or, 'a tap or faucet' (*OED sn¹* 2.a., b).

28. *à Quo... ex Quo*: 'By Whom'... 'From Whom'.

38. *kindly*: 'naturally belonging to or connected with a person or thing; own, proper, suitable' (*OED sa* I.1.c).

p. 213, 4. *gramen... fœnum*: 'grass'... 'hay'.

5–6. *caro... flesh*: Rom. 8: 3 (*LACT*).

13. *Verbum caro factum*: Vulg. (John 1: 14); ('the Word made flesh').

13. *symbolisme*: 'practice of representing things by symbols, or of giving a symbolic character to objects or acts; the systematic use of symbols; hence, symbols collectively or generally' (*OED*); *OED* cites the earliest use of the word as 1654; all other examples are from the nineteenth century and later; Andrewes has imported the word into English by transliterating Gr. and Lat. *symbolismus* (cf. also next n.).

13–15. *gate... in rem*: '*symbolisme*' (cf. prev. n.) of Hosea's image of a '*gate of hope*'; the 'incarnation' opened a door of hope ('*in spem*', 'in hope') for the sending of the Holy Ghost that became reality ('*in rem*', 'in thing') at Pentecost; witty rearticulation of Andrewes's insistence that Christ's 'errand' on earth (p. 209, l. 20) was only complete with the sending of the Holy Ghost at Pentecost.

15. *remembred*: reminded.

17. *saliens... æternam*: cf. Vulg. (John 4: 14), 'fons aquæ salientis in vitam æternam'; ('a well of water, springing up into everlasting life').

21. *fundam in... fundam super*: 'poured into'... 'poured upon'.

25. *parted*: divided, disposed.

26. *comedite*: Lat., 'eat'.

28. *in Baptisme... washed*: cf., 'we beseech thee... look upon these children, sanctify them and wash them with thy Holy Ghost' (*BCP*, second collect at Public Baptism).

30. *nosthrills*: nostrils.

30. *wrest*: wrist.

33. ἔξωθεν: Gr., 'ĕxōthĕn'; 'externally', 'from without'.

35. ἄνωθεν: Gr., 'anōthĕn'; 'from above'.

36. *phansie*: fancy; 'a supposition resting on no solid grounds; an arbitrary notion' (*OED sn* A.6).

13, 39–p. 214, 1. *outward cæremonie... oyle*: cf. 'A Sermon Preached... the Fifth of August' (this edn.), p. 185 and nn.

1. *induing [induemini]*: to clothe; from the Lat. *induere* (*OED sv* IV.6), hence '*[induemini]* putting some robe... upon'.

2. *ensigne*: 'badge or symbol of dignity or office...; = Lat., *insignia*' (*OED, sn* 4).

3. *Baptisme... so done*: the minister was not only to sprinkle water 'upon' the child's head, but also to make the sign of the cross (cf. 'ensigne', above) on its forehead (*BCP*).

4. *Dove... upon* CHRIST: recapitulation of Andrewes, Whitsunday 1617: 'For, if [the Spirit] be *super*, we be *sub*. That we be carefull then to preserve Him in his *super*, to keepe him in his due place (that is) *above*. In signe whereof, the *Dove* hovered aloft over CHRIST, and *came downe upon Him*' (*XCVI*, 703); cf. also Andrewes, Whitsunday 1615, on the baptism of Christ (Luke 3: 21–2; *XCVI*, 674–85); for baptismal themes in the Whitsun sermons more generally, see Lossky, *Lancelot Andrewes*, 225–31.

5. *their new offices*: as Apostles.

7. *evill brook*: ill abide.

8–9. *hands of fellowship... imposition*: cf. Gal. 2: 9, 'And when James, and Cephas, and John, knew of the grace that was given unto me... they gave to me and to Barnabas the right hands of felowship, that we should preach unto the Gentiles'; in presbyterian and nonconformist traditions, 'giving the right hand of fellowship' (a handshake) was a sign of admission to communion or of commissioning a minister, thus to Andrewes a perversion of the laying-on of hands in episcopal ordination.

10–11. *no sub... last yeare*: cf. Andrewes, Whitsunday 1617: 'That *above*? Nay any *above*? Nay, they inferior to none. That *above*, and they *under*? Nay *under* no *Spirit*: no *super*, they. Of all Prepositions, they indure not that, not *Super*: all æquall, all even at least.' (*XCVI*, 703).

13. *Confusion will come*: prediction of anarchy ('*Confusion*') in a church not ordered by episcopal authority (and, by implication, in a nation at large that rejects royal authority over its church); the primary target here is Scotland's looked-for submission to the Five Articles of Perth (see Headnote), but criticism of English nonconformity is of course also implied.

15–17. *Jewe's-flesh... omni*: under the Old Covenant, the Jewish nation claimed special status as God's chosen people ('*Non taliter omni*', Vulg. Ps. 147: 20, 'not so with other [nations]'); hence, they monopolized ('*engrossed*') the Spirit; under the New Covenant in Christ they are equall with '*any other*' (cf. Gal. 2: 23–9).

23–24. *Non est distinctio*: Lat., 'there is no difference'.

31–32. *strangers... first covenant*: foreigners ('strangers') to God's Covenant with Abraham (cf. ll. 15–17 and n.).

32–33. *And... in it*: the God of Israel was acknowledged by non-Jews as well as Jews; cf., the repenting king and people of Nineveh (Jonah 3), Ruth, and Cyrus of Persia (Isa. 45: 1–7).

36–37. *Notus in Judæâ* DEUS: Vulg. (Ps. 75: 2); 'God is knowen in Judah' (Ps. 76: 1).

p. 215, 1. *promiscuè*: Lat., promiscuously, freely.

4. *super servos meos*: Vulg. (Acts 2: 18); 'upon my servants'.

6. *give in*: 'to hand in, to deliver (an account, return, etc.) to the person officially appointed to receive it' (*OED*, sv 59.e).

7. *Quicunque invocaverit*: Vulg. (Acts 2: 21); 'whoseover shall call upon'.

9–10. *By which... Christians, too*: 'One notes that Jews and Muslims are excluded to the extent that, like hypocritical Christians, they consciously reject Christ' (Lossky, *Lancelot Andrewes*, 255 n. 143).

14. *Utquid effusio hæc?*: Lat., 'To what end this effusion?'

16. *Utquid perditio hæc?*: Vulg. (Matt. 26: 8); 'What needed this waste?'

18. *salvabitur*: Lat., 'shall be saved'; cf. Vulg. (Acts 2: 21).

20–22. *Spirit... spiritualizing it*: epigrammatic summary of one of the most distinctive aspects of Andrewes's soteriology; in contrast to mainstream Calvinism's insistence upon the total depravity of human nature that must wait for glorification only in heaven, Andrewes insists upon a gradual process of 'deification' of human nature through cooperation with grace in this life; cf. Lossky, *Lancelot Andrewes*, 186, 256–64.

p. 216, 3. *the empty caske*: language itself; cf. Andrewes, Whitsunday 1608 on Acts 2: 4 (*XCVI*, 608–16); and his lectures on Gen. 2: 19–20 (*AS*, 204–16).

6–7. *That saying... de excelso*: key phrases from Isa. 32: 14–15 (immediately translated by Andrewes) are in fact not 'much used' by the patristic authors most cited by him (cf. only Jerome, *Commentaria in Isaiam*, *PL*, 24.360–2); perhaps a recollection of the appointment of the passage in ancient breviaries and missals for the ferial days between the Ascension and Pentecost, when the church did '*but grope*' in the '*darke*' in the days between Christ's departure from earth and the sending of the Holy Spirit.

12–13. *usuall terme... Epistles through*: cf. Paul on the gift of 'prophecy' or preaching, 1 Cor. 12: 10, Eph. 3: 8, 1 Thess. 5: 20, 1 Tim. 4: 14.

15. *Agabus... daughters*: Acts 21: 9–10 (*LACT*); Jerome similarly dismisses NT prophets Agabus and Philip's daughters as insufficient evidence of a continued prophetic tradition after Pentecost (*Epistola XLI*, 2).

15. *Saint John*: St John the Divine, author of Revelation.

23. *quomodo Prædicabunt*: Lat., 'how shall they preach?' (Rom. 10: 15); cf. Vulg., 'quomodo vero praedicabunt'.

38–39. *Oracles of* GOD: ROM. 3: 2 (*lact*).

p. 217, 4. *We... their sonnes*: not Jews ('*sonnes*'), but Gentiles ('*servants*'); reflects current prosecution by Andrewes and others in Star Chamber of 'Judaizers', extreme Protestants who, like some in apostolic times, insisted upon the observance by Christians of Mosaic law; the most prominent of these in England, John Traske, was sentenced in June, only weeks after this sermon; Andrewes himself had given the prosecuting speech, which began, 'It is a good worke to make a *Jew* a *Christian*: but to make *Christen men Jewes*, hath ever been holden a foule act, and severely to be punished' ('A Speech delivered in the Starr-Chamber against... *M*. TRASKE', *OP*, 65; *LACT*, xi. 84).

9. *Quid... triticum*: Vulg. (Jer. 23: 28; *LACT*); 'what is the chaffe to the wheate'.

12. *transeant*: 'they pass away'.

15–21. *libertie... to prophecie*: denunciation of preaching by any other than ordained and licensed ministers; orthodox Jacobean opinion was anxious over even the private 'opening of Scriptures' by godly women in their own households; cf. Gervase Markham's 1615 warning against wives 'drawing a contempt upon the ordinary Ministrie, and thinking nothing lawefull but the fantazies of their owne inventions, usurping to themselves a power of preaching and interpreting the holy word, to which onely they ought to be but hearers and beleevers' (quoted in Christine Peters, *Patterns of Piety: Women, Gender and Religion in Late Medieval and Early Modern England* (Cambridge, 2003), 323); Andrewes's sternly Pauline position here ('*nolo mulieres*', lit., 'I do not wish women') might be contrasted with his encomium to Mary Magdalen as 'apostle to the apostles' ('A Sermon Preached... on Easter Day', this edn., p. 226, ll. 33–35; and more fully in the succeeding year's sermon, *XCVI*, 556–7). In the early church, Montanus (*c*.170) was joined in his heretical apocalyptic prophesying by 'those demented women Priscilla and Maximilla' (Jerome, *Epistola XLI*, 4, *LF* NS, vi. 56); '*Anabaptists*', persecuted by mainstream Protestant and Roman churches, were influential among nonconformists in Tudor and Jacobean England (cf. George H. Williams, *The Radical Reformation*, 3rd edn. (1992), ch. 30.3); radical separatists, including Anabaptists, held valid the personal interpretation of scripture and preaching by laymen (but not women); cf. congregationalist Henry Barrow, 'this exercise of prophecie belongeth to the whole church, and ought not to be shut up in this maner amongst the priests only, the people being shut out either to speake or heare' (*Writings of Henry Barrow*, 529; for Barrow against preaching by women, p. 532).

24. *musto pleni*: Vulg. (Act. 2: 13); 'full of newe wine'.

24. *cerebro vacui*: in the first instance, this is a Lat. commonplace meaning 'empty in the head' (cf. Thomas Linacre's 1525 *Rudimenta Grammaticus*, sig. B1ʳ, where it appears as an example of 'nownes construed with an ablatyve case'). But cf. also Matt. 5: 22 ('And whosoever sayth unto his brother, Raca, shalbe worthy to be punished by Councill. And whosoever shall say, Foole, shalbe worthy to be punished with hellfire'), and Edward Leigh's commentary, 'Ex Syriaco *Raka* vanus, cerebro vacuus à radice evacuare, fundere, effundere' (*Annotations upon all the New Testament* (1650), 12). Leigh's etymology of the Hebrew derogatory epithet 'Raka' suggests yet another level of punning by Andrewes on his text's key-word *effundere* (to pour out): drunkards (unlike the Apostles) pour too much liquour into, and pour out all sense from, their heads. Leigh, an intimate of James Ussher, with whom Andrewes was on cordial terms, edited Andrewes's *Learned Discourse of Ceremonies* (1656; *LACT*, vol. vi).

26. *humor*: moisture or fluid, but with punning reference to the four physiological humours believed to determine health and temperament.

27. *must*: new wine.

29. *phrensie*: frenzy; 'wild folly, distraction, craziness' (*OED*, 'frenzy' *n* 2).

37. *Cyclopian Church*: like the one-eyed Cyclops Polyphemus (Homer, *Odyssey*, ix; cf. next n.), a body monstrously dominated by one organ, here the mouth ('where all were *speakers*'); the first use of the word cited by *OED* is 1641 (in a parliamentary sermon by Joseph Symonds, an English minister in Rotterdam, that defends precisely the kind of Dutch-influenced Protestantism that Andrewes here parodies); cf. also Andrewes, Gunpowder 1617, 'All our *holinesse*, is in hearing: All our *Service*, eare-service: that were in effect, as much as to say, all the body were *an eare*' (*XCVI*, 992).

37. Ἀκούει οὐδεὶς οὐδὲν οὐδένος (*in marg.*): Gr., 'akŏuĕi ŏudĕis ŏudĕn ŏudĕnos'; 'no one hears nothing from no one'; example in Greek of Andrewes's fondness for the rhetorical figure *polyptoton*, the repetition of different forms of the same word (here, Gr. οὐδέν, 'nothing', or 'no one'), probably punning on the name taken by Ulysses to fool Polyphemus, Οὖτίς ('Nobody').

p. 218, 7. *the quicunque...invocaverit*: 'the "whosoever" ("whosoever shall call")'; Vulg. (Acts 2: 21).

9. *shippers of Holland*: Dutch mariners or skippers; 'shippers' is itself from Middle Dutch, 'schippers' (*OED*); parody directed at both the class (uneducated tradesmen) and stereotyped religion ('*Anabaptist*', p. 217, l. 19) of Dutch Protestants; the Dutch were England's greatest marine trading partners, as well as England's (especially London's) largest religious refugee population, most of which was strictly Calvinist, but also included many radical separatists.

10. *all that be Prophets*: 1 Cor. 14: 31 (*LACT*).

16–19. *with the Apostle...them all*: 1 Cor. 12: 4–6 (*LACT*).

23. *gifts for men*: Ps. 68: 18 (*LACT*).

23–24. *Misit...last yeare*: cf. p. 211, ll. 20–1 and n.

24. *vocavit...Talenta dedit*: Vulg. (Matt. 25: 14–15); '"He called"..."He gave gifts"'.

28–31. *take not...be subject*: another denunciation of lay preaching and private religious enthusiasm; the '*Spirits*' to whom all are '*subject*' are earthly superiors, both the clerical hierarchy and, ultimately, the king (cf. also next n.).

p.218, 37–p. 219, 1. *dreame...Prophets rise still*: Montanist heresy (cf. p. 217, ll. 14–21 and n.); Montanus believed that God had 'descended by the Holy Spirit' upon him and that as a result he 'possessed a fulness of knowledge such as was never claimed by Paul' (Jerome, *Epistola XLI*, 4); cf. on this and the matter of superior '*Spirits*' (prev. n.), Andrewes's 1590 exchange with Henry Barrow (*Writings of John Greenwood*, 141):

> ANDREWES: But the spirits of men must be subject unto men, will you not subject your spirit to the judgment of men?
> BARROW: The spirit of the prophets must be subject to the prophets, yet must the prophets judg by the word of God....
> ANDREWES: This savoreth of a pryvat spyrit.
> BARROW: This is the spirit of Christ and his apostles, and moste publique they submitted theire doctrines to the triall of all men by the word. So do I.
> ANDREWES: What, are you an apostle?
> BARROW: No, but I have the spirit of the apostles.

4–16. *No (saith Joël)... His Name*: Andrewes here rebuts post-millenarian views, like those of the Montanists in the early church and early modern Anabaptists, that the Second Coming of Christ would be preceded by a 1,000-year period of renewed prophecy and conversion (Rev. 20). Post-millenarians held that Joel's prophecy quoted by St Peter predicted a latter-day outpouring of the Holy Spirit like that at Pentecost as a herald of the Millennium. Andrewes, however, follows the orthodox consensus established by Jerome and Augustine which interprets the Millennium metaphorically as the Kingdom of God on earth that was the church established on the day of Pentecost. Jerome's proof text against Montanist apocalyptic fervour was Andrewes's here (Acts 2: 14–18), wherein Joel's prophecy is held to be fulfilled by Pentecost itself, and is not the prediction of a further future event preceding a literal Millennium: 'If... Peter... said that the prophecy and promise of the Lord were then and there fulfilled, how can we claim another fulfilment for ourselves?' (*Epistola XLI*, 2; *NPNCF*, vi. 55). Augustine also insisted that the so-called 'last days' began at Pentecost. Also using St Peter's quotation of Joel, Augustine declares, 'there were last days even then.... we, like the Apostles, are living in last times' (*Epistola CLXXXXIX*, 24). Cf. also Augustine, *Civitate Dei* (*The City of God*), xx.

5. *presently*: immediately.

13–14. *dies... novissimorum*: 'the last day of the last [days]'.

17–18. *A second... saved*: cf. Chrysostom, *Comm. on the Acts*, Hom. V, 'for if these things are the prelude of that day, it follows that the extreme of danger is impending. But what next? He again lets them take breath, adding, "And it shall come to pass, that whosoever shall call upon the name of the Lord, shall be saved"' (*NPNCF*, xi. 32).

24–27. *And last... prepare for it*: cf. Chrysostom, *Comm. on the Acts*, Hom. V: 'at the same time the Apostle strikes fear into them, by reminding them of the darkness which had lately occurred [at the Crucifixion], and reminding them of things to come.... these things are the prelude of a certain and dreadful day. Do you see how he made their souls to quake and melt within them, and turned their laughter into pleading for acquittal?' (*NPNCF*, xi. 32).

24. *per modum stimuli*: Lat., lit., 'by means of a goad'; e.g. 'by stirring up', 'by prompting'.

24–25. *Ut... terrorem hunc*: Lat., 'so that knowing this terror'; cf. Vulg. (2 Cor. 5: 11), 'scientes ergo timorem Domini'; ('knowing therefore that terrour of the Lord').

32. *dies servi*: 'the day of the servant'.

39. *Quid... novissimo*: Vulg. (Jer. 5: 31).

p. 220, 1. *great dayes*: 'a feast- or fast-day of high importance' (*OED* 'great' IV.20.c).

4–5. *quis potest... chapter*: Joel 2: 11 (*LACT*).

9. *Ecce Signa*: Lat., 'behold the signs'.

11. *Hebrew... smoke*: Judges 20: 40 (*LACT*).

11. *palmizare*: Lat., 'to grow like a palm tree'?; evidently Andrewes's own coinage; Andrewes contrasts a fiery portent (that will flare up and then fade) with the eternal fire that awaits the damned after Doomsday; the imagery seems indebted to the popular natural history of palm trees derived from Pliny, which praises the tree's physical attribute of uprightness, and associates its longevity with the Phoenix, the legendary bird that rises from its own ashes; cf. *Batman uppon Bartholome* (1582), 'boughs of palme... reare themselves upward, & be alway greene, & never bend downward'; and 'when this Palme is so olde, that it fayleth all for age: then oft it quickneth and springeth again of it selfe. Therefore men suppose, that *Phoenix*... hath the name of this Palme in *Arabia*. For he dieth and quickneth, and liveth oft... as *Plinios* sayth there' (fo. 309ʳ).

23–26. *all flesh... world over*: a similar composite of classical Roman (cf. next n.) and Christian belief in the ominous significance of eclipses is Shakespeare's comparison of the 'portentous figure' of Hamlet's Ghost to the 'disasters in the sun' and the moon 'sick almost to doomsday with eclipse' after Caesar's assassination, which, 'As harbingers preceding still the fates | And prologue to the omen coming on, | Have heaven and earth together demonstrated | Unto our climatures and countrymen' (*Hamlet*, ed. Harold Jenkins, I. i. 112–28; these lines appear only in the second quarto of 1604); cf. also *King Lear* (I. ii).

25. *dies atri*: Lat., lit., dark days; in the Roman calendar, days on which the Republic had suffered great misfortunes.

29. *who... abide it?*: Joel 2: 11 (*LACT*).

32. *day... White Sunn*: cf. p. 207, l. 4 and n.

39. *or with this*: or with Doomsday.

p. 221, 17. *Queer*: near-obsolete form of '*quire*' ('*choir*'), consistently preferred by Andrewes.

19–20. *Oratorie of Prayer... of preaching*: punning exploitation of the etymological link between the Lat. verb *orare* ('to pray'; hence, *Oratorie* as '*Prayer*') and the Lat. noun *oratoria* ('oratory'; hence rhetorical public speaking as in '*preaching*').

21–22. *The other... worth*: nominally conforming ministers often truncated or entirely omitted prayer book liturgies and the appointed readings from scripture in order to allow more time for preaching. Directly influenced by Andrewes's thinking, Charles in 1629 required all sermons to be preached only after prayer book service had been read, and outlawed afternoon sermons. See Carlson, 'Boring the Ear', in Taylor (ed.), *Preachers and People*, 287; McCullough, *Sermons at Court*, 164; McCullough, 'Making Dead Men Speak', 411.

25–26. *gratia gratis data... gratis data... gratum faciens*: Lat., 'grace freely given'... 'freely given'... 'giving thanks'.

30. *conceit*: 'personal or private opinion' (*OED sn* II.4).

32. *challenges between them*: 'a summons to fight, esp. to single combat or duel' (*OED sn* 7); contrast Andrewes's slightly more positive comparison of the contest between prayer and preaching on Easter 1620 ('A Sermon Preached... on Easter Day', this edn., p. 242).

33. *prerogatives*: 'natural or divinely-given advantage or privilege' (*OED sn* 2).

35. *effundam Spiritum meum*: Lat., 'I will pour out my Spirit'; cf. Vulg. (Acts. 2: 17), 'effundam de Spiritu meo' ('I will powre out of my Spirit').

39. *auricular profession*: cf. Andrewes, 'A Sermon Preached... on Easter Day', this edn., p. 242, ll. 2–4.

39. *sedentarie*: 'requiring continuance in a sitting posture' (*OED sa* A.1.a), i.e. sitting to hear a sermon.

p. 222, 1. *heare... two Anthems*: in the Chapel Royal, the choral anthems sung before and after the sermon; see McCullough, *Sermons at Court*, 155, 162–3.

3. *suffer*: predominantly here 'to be the object of an action, be acted upon, be passive', or 'to submit patiently too' (*OED sv* I.4, 5), as in 'our selves, meerly *passive* in it' (l. 1); but also probably with punning reference to being 'subjected to... something evil or painful' (*OED* I.2), i.e. a bad sermon.

6–7. *quicunque prophetiam audiverit*: Lat., 'whosoever shall hear the preacher'; parody of Acts 2: 21 ('whosoever shall call on the name of the Lord').

10–11. *Domine... prophetavimus*: Lat., 'Lord, in thy name, we have prophesied'; cf. Vulg. (Matt. 7: 22), 'Domine nonne in nomine tuo prophetavimus' ('Lord, by thy name have we not prophecied?').

12. *Nescio vos*: Vulg. (Luke 13: 25 and 27); 'I know thee not'; Christ's damning response to hypocritical followers.

13. *faine*: 'glad, rejoiced, well-pleased' (*OED sa* 1).

15–16. *pertaines... our duty*: prayer.

18–19. *to invocate*: to pray; cf. the forensic examination of 'invocation' in 'Pattern of Catechistical Doctrine' (this edn., pp. 11–21).

19–20. *de Spiritu... carnem*: Vulg. (Acts 2: 17); 'of my Spirit upon all flesh'.

21. *quicunque prophetaverit*: 'whosoever shall preach'; another parody of Acts 2: 21 (cf. ll. 6–7 and n.).

22–23. πᾶς ὃς ἂν... *Rom.X.XIII*: Gr., 'pas hŏs an'; lit., 'all who ever', i.e. 'all who' or 'whosoever'; cf. Acts 2: 21 ('*Peter*, heer'), '*Whosoever* shall call... shalbe saved'; also Rom. 10: 13 ('*Paul*'), 'For *whoseover* shall call... shalbe saved'.

24–25. *invocaverint... closest to salvabitur*: cf. Chrysostom, *Comm. on the Acts*, Hom. V, 'for in the invocation is the salvation' (*NPNCF*, xi. 34).

24. ἐχόμενον σωτηρίας: Gr., 'ĕchŏmĕnŏn sōtēriās'; 'having salvation', in the sense of contiguity or relation, i.e. invocation 'is [like, or as much as to say] having salvation'; cf. Pauline descriptions of Christ 'in whom we have redemption' (ἐν ᾧ ἔχομεν τὴν ἀπολύτρωσιν, Eph. 1: 7).

30. *last cast*: 'at the last shift, in extremities, near to death or ruin' (*OED*, 'cast' *v* I.4.b).

31–33. *called upon... mouthes*: conventional deathbed piety called upon the dying to pray to the last, either vocally, or, when unable to do so, to make gestures of invocation; cf. John Buckeridge's account of Andrewes's own death, 'and when he could pray no longer *voce*, with his voice, yet *oculis & manibus*, by lifting up his *eyes* and *hands* he prayed still: and when *nec manus, nex vox officium faciunt*; both voice, and eyes and hands failed in their office; then *Corde*, with his *heart*, he still prayed, untill it pleased GOD to receive his blessed soule to himselfe' (*A Sermon Preached at the Funeral*, app. to *XCVI*, 22).

33. *Dying... for it*: dying, we ask others to pray for us.

33. *suffer*: allow.

p. 222, 37–p. 223, 5. *no faith...saved*: careful negotiation of competing emphases in Protestant and Roman Catholic soteriology: *sola fide* (by faith alone) vs. with the merit of works (living a good *'life'*); Andrewes characteristically says that both are necessary, *'faith'* validated by *'depart[ing] from iniquitie'*; cf. 'A Sermon Preached at St Maries Hospital' (this edn., Headnote and nn. *passim*).

2–3. *putt these...to it*: cf. Chrysostom, *Comm. on the Acts*, Hom. V, 'invoke: not any how, for it is written, "Not every one that saith unto Me, Lord, Lord:" but with inward earnest affection, with a life more than commonly good, with the confidence which is meet' (*NPNCF*, xi. 34).

3. *recedit ab iniquitate*: Lat., '[he] withdraws from iniquity'; cf. Vulg. (2 Tim. 2: 19), 'et discedat ab iniquitate omnis qui nominat nomen Domini'; ('let every one that calleth on the Name of Christ, depart from iniquitie').

4. *Sureties...assure him*: Joel (Joel 2: 32), Peter (Acts 2: 21) and Paul (Rom. 10: 13) as guarantors ('Sureties') that anyone who *'calleth upon Him...shalbe saved'*.

8–10. *signes heer...the Pouder-treason*: compares the intended effects of the Gunpowder Plot to Joel's apocalyptic vision; Andrewes carried in his mind a vivid terror of the plot (cf. 'A Sermon Preached...on the V. of November' (this edn.), pp. 146, 151–2); by 1618, mainstream Calvinists invoked it in pulpit opposition to the Spanish Match and endorsement of military intervention against Spain in the Palatinate; Andrewes conversely deploys its memory to argue for a pacifist foreign policy and the curtailment of preaching; see David Cressy, *Bonfires and Bells* (1989), ch. 9; and Lori Anne Ferrell, *Government by Polemic* (1998), ch. 3.

14–16. *fire...quenched*: Mark 9: 43–6, 48 (*LACT*).

17. *Qui...salvus erit*: Vulg. (Acts 2: 21); 'He who calls [prays], shall be saved'.

21–22. *Accipiam...invocabo*: Vulg. (Ps. 115: 13); 'I will take the cup of salvation, and call upon the Name of the Lord' (Ps. 116: 13); historically, 'in the Law they used to make a banket, when they gave solemne thankes to God, and to take the cuppe and drinke in signe of thanksgiving' (Geneva gloss); Andrewes, following patristic and pre-Reformation liturgical usage, applies the text to the eucharist; Ps. 115 (116) was appointed in the Sarum Rite for mass on Maundy Thursday, when Christ prayed in Gethsemane, 'Father, if thou wilt, take away this cuppe from mee' (Luke 22: 42), and then resolved after his betrayal, 'shall I not drinke of the cuppe which my Father hath given me?' (John 18: 11).

24–25. *Quicunque...salvus erit*: Lat., 'Whosoever shall take the cup of salvation and call upon the name of the Lord, shall be saved'; adaptation of Acts 2: 21, and a striking example of Andrewes's avant-garde attribution of saving power to the eucharistic elements themselves (cf. 'A Sermon on Isaiah 6.6–7', this edn., Headnote and *passim*).

25. *Another effundam*: another 'pouring out'; both Christ's blood on his cross, and the sacramental wine poured out at the Holy Communion, which was celebrated immediately following the sermon.

29. *doubt*: suspect, judge.

31–32. *a voice...in GOD's eares*: Gen. 4: 10 (*LACT*); cf. Andrewes's lecture (19 Aug. 1599) on Abel's blood (Gen. 4: 10), *AS*, 422–8.

32–33. *cup of blessing*: 1 Cor. 10: 16 (*LACT*).

36. *remission...purchase*: Matt. 26: 28 (*LACT*).

37. *salvation...Day of the LORD*: Joel 2: 31 (*LACT*).

38. *import*: 'to be of consequence or importance to; to relate to, have to do with; to concern' (*OED sv* II.7).

39. *shalbe saved*: Acts 2: 21; pronounced *'shalbe savéd'*.

p. 224, 1–2. *to yeeld... His benefits*: Ps. 116: 12 (*LACT*).

3–5. *As the former... our thanksgiving*: just as the '*Cup of Salvation*' drowns sin, so does the cup of '*thanksgiving*'; deployment of Cranmer's more reformed language of the eucharist as a 'sacrifice of praise and thanksgiving' (*BCP*), thus carefully qualifying (but also carefully not denying) the previous paragraph's less reformed emphasis on the real presence of Christ's sacrificial blood in the eucharist.

6. *His saving health*: Ps. 67: 2.

8–9. *per... hoc Spiritu*: Lat., 'by this blood, for this Spirit'.

9–11. *render... effundam too*: punning language that flirts with an assertion of the Real Presence; literally refers to the priest's 'pouring out' of the wine before consecration, and then the distribution of it afterwards to the communicants with the words 'The blood of our Lord Jesus Christ which was shed for thee' (*BCP*); but allusion to the historical Passion ('*bloud, that was powred out*'), and the conflation of both under the epithet 'a reall *effundam*' blurs the distinction.

A SERMON PREACHED... ON EASTER DAY

Text.   A SERMON | PREACHED AT | White-hall, on Easter day | *the* 16. *of April*. | 1620. | *By the Bishop of Winchester*. | [device: McK.300] | [rule] | LONDON, | Printed by ROBERT BARKER, | and IOHN BILL, Printers to the | Kings most Excellent Maiestie. | M. DC. XX. (*STC2* 611, hereafter *Q*). Although *Q* was issued separately, some copies were also bound as part 4 of a ten-sermon collection, without general title-page, in the same year (*The copie of the sermon preached on Good-Friday, STC2* 624.5). A fair manuscript copy of the sermon, in the hand of Andrewes's amanuensis Samuel Wright, survives in Trinity College, Cambridge MS B.14.22, fos. 34^v–47^v (Peter Beal, *Index of English Literary Manuscripts*, vol. i, pt. 1; 1980, 'AndL12'; hereafter *MS*). Corrections and additions in the hands of both Wright and Andrewes in *MS* provide rare evidence of Andrewes's practice of composition and revision (cf. Introduction). *MS* is substantially the same text as *Q*, and is gracefully copied complete with marginal citations and outline numbers, as well as ornamental flourishes in the same format as the quartos printed in Andrewes's lifetime. *MS* lacks only a title and date, commencing with the sermon text. However, significant variants (additions, deletions, and some reorganization of paragraph structure) between *MS* and *Q* suggest that at least one further fair copy preceded that used to set *Q*. Arguments for choice of copy-text could be made for *MS*, *Q*, and, perhaps least strongly, the posthumous F_1. Ed. has chosen *Q* on the grounds of its status as the last text produced during Andrewes's lifetime, and because presenting it here allows the most efficient comparison with both *MS* and F_1. Some readings from the latter are here preferred as obvious corrections of typesetting errors in *Q*. All substantive variant readings from *MS* are recorded in the apparatus. Passages in *Q* that appear as marginal and interlined superscript additions and corrections in *MS*, as well as deleted readings, are also documented; those not specified as being in the author's own hand are by Wright. Variants in punctuation, italicization, and capitalization between *MS* and *Q* were too numerous to record, and most could be the result of compositors' or printing house style. Only those judged by ed. to be authorial, or substantive enough to change grammatical sense or oral delivery are recorded. The sermon appeared in *XCVI* (F_1) as 'Sermon XIV of the Resurrection' (pp. 531–42). F_1 was set from *Q*, committing only four new typographical errors (two of these being in marginal citations of scripture) and omitting four words. Included in *LACT*, iii. 3–22 (from F_2); and Story (ed.), *Sermons*, 192–217 (from *Q*, without collation of *MS*).

Headnote. This is the fourteenth of eighteen Easter sermons preached by Andrewes at court between 1606 and 1624 (the last was prepared but not delivered) and printed in F_1 (pp. 383–590). It is a magisterial example of Andrewes's mature 'solemn sermon' style. In it he applies the intense economy of his minute exegetical method to the dramatic sweep of an entire biblical narrative, the appearance of Christ to Mary Magdalen on the morning of the Resurrection. The sermon was originally conceived to address John 20: 11–17, but Andrewes left this pericope's final verse ('Touch me not, for I am not yet ascended to my father') for his Easter text at court in two subsequent years (cf. p. 225, l. 24 and n.). The fact that verse 17 is very clearly included in his *divisio* (p. 227, ll. 11–15), argues very strongly that the truncation of the sermon occurred only in delivery, and that all of the surviving states are faithful reconstructions of what was actually preached from the pulpit on the day (cf. Appendix 1 and its Headnote).

Several organizing structures overlap and interlock effortlessly in this sermon, like the sophisticated main and subplot structure in a Shakespeare play. These include not only the dominant narrative progression from verse to verse, but also the *dramatis personae* (Mary, angels, Christ), and ten 'characters' of love epitomized in Latin epigrams. The formal sophistication of the piece has made it an exemplary text for structuralist literary analysis. Historiographically, it contains in its peroration a key pronouncement by Andrewes on the increasingly divisive Jacobean debate over the relative efficacy of preaching and the sacraments. Thematically, its highly emotive charting—through the experience of a female protagonist—of the progress from death and grief to recognition and redemption bears comparison with Shakespeare's late plays *Cymbeline*, *Pericles*, and *The Winter's Tale*. The sermon self-consciously exploits theatrical imagery, diction, and forms, which should encourage comparison with the English mystery cycles' dramatizations of the scene of Mary Magdalen at the tomb. These derive from the medieval liturgical enactments of this Gospel passage (the 'Quem Quaeritis'). Some of these plays (most clearly the Digby 'St Mary Magdalene' and the 'Shrewsbury Fragment' play of the same name) show the direct influence of the homily attributed to Origen which Andrewes also exploits here (cf. Sources, below, and Rosemary Woolf, *The English Mystery Plays* (1972), 8–9, 333–5). The theatrical spirit of the sermon is suggestively captured by David Scott in his free adaptation of the recognition scene (this edn., pp. 240–42) as a play-text in *Sacred Tongues: The Golden Age of Spiritual Writing* (2001), 30–3.

Sources. Of the sermons included in this edition, this is the most profoundly indebted to patristic sources. This debt reaches far beyond mere quotation or adaptation, and is a fine example of Renaissance *imitatio*, the complete internalization by an author of model texts to produce a work that is both a homage to them and an original surpassing of them. Andrewes's handling of his biblical text at once sequentially, thematically, and by *dramatis personæ* is rooted in his response to homilies by Origen, Gregory the Great, Augustine, Ambrose, and 'Bernard' (actually Nicholas) of Clairvaux. The freedom with which he quotes and paraphrases these authors, as well as the absence of all but Ambrose from the posthumous catalogues of his library, makes the identification of specific editions used unlikely and of limited use here. The dominant source is the *Homilia de Beata Maria Magdalena*, probably an early medieval text, but traditionally attributed to Origen, and known in the early modern period (like most of the Alexandrine father's works) in Latin translation. The homily had an independent print history in England, appearing first in Latin in 1505, and in English in 1555 and 1565 (*STC2* 18846, 18847, 18848). I have quoted from the standard early modern Latin edition by Erasmus, *Origenis Adamanti... Opera* (Basel, 1571; the homily appears in the separately paginated '*Pars secunda*'). This homily inspires not only the majority of the sermon's thematic imagery, but also its extended use of quasi-theatrical devices like dramatic irony and prosopopoeia. Also influential for numerous substantive theological points, in order of importance, are number XXV of Gregory the Great's *Homiliæ in Evangelia XL* (on John 20: 11–18), number CXXI of Augustine's *In Joannem Evangelium Tractatus CXXIV* (on John 20: 10–29), and the *Sermo in Festo Beatæ Mariæ Magdalenæ*, until modern times attributed to and printed with the works of Bernard, but now attributed to Nicholas, of Clairvaux. Andrewes also draws on sections 156–61 of Ambrose's *Expositio Evangelii Secundum Lucam*. Andrewes's debt to these sources is far greater than his own citations in *Q*, or even the more thorough annotating work of the *LACT*, suggests. Close comparison of them with Andrewes's text confirms the *LACT* editors' complaint that Andrewes often quoted his patristic sources very loosely from memory. Moreover, the witness of *MS* shows the confusion in Andrewes's own mind about his sources, citing the wrong Father even after changing his mind more than once (cf. p. 240, ll. 26 and n.).

Further Reading. *MS* is described by P. J. Klemp, '"Betwixt the Hammer and the Anvil": Lancelot Andrewes's Revision Techniques in the Manuscript of His 1620 Easter Sermon', *Papers of the Bibliographical Society of America*, 89 (1995), 149–82. Klemp's descriptions are sound, but his analysis of that evidence is (perhaps necessarily) subjective. An outstanding literary analysis is Stanley Fish, 'Structuralist Homiletics', *Modern Language Notes*, 91 (1976), 1208–21. Theological features in the sermon are addressed in Lossky, *Lancelot Andrewes*, ch. 5, *passim*. For prayer vs. preaching, cf. Lake, 'Lancelot Andrewes, John Buckeridge'; and McCullough, *Sermons at Court*, 155–67. For the pseudo-origen and Ovidian sources, see Debora Shuger, *The Renaissance Bible* (California, 1994), 170–6.

p. 225, 1–2. *A Sermon... 1620*: adapted from title-page of *Q* (see Text); although using *Q* as copy text, Story uses title from F_1, perpetuating the Laudian error of the king's presence at the sermon (cf. next n.).

1. AT *White-hall... 1620*: in June 1620 John Chamberlain sent Dudley Carleton a printed copy of the sermon (*Q*) noting that it had been 'preached on Easterday last to the Lords and rest of the houshold at court, which was so much commended that the King wold needs have him set yt out' (*Letters*, ii. 309). This confirms that, as was customary, Andrewes as Dean of the Chapel Royal preached the early morning Easter sermon before the lords and household; the later sermon before the king was preached by the Lord Almoner (Bishop George Mountaigne). F_1 uniformly—and on this evidence, incorrectly—titled all of Andrewes's Jacobean court sermons as 'preached before the King'. Cf. McCullough, *Sermons at Court*, 150–54, and prev. n.

5. *Maria autem... &c*: Vulg.

21–22. *But... your God*: the Geneva and Authorized versions are very close in diction; Andrewes uses readings unique to each, which suggests that he set the text from memory, mixing the two. Not a proper in *BCP*.

23. *This last... touched*: Andrewes returned to the first part of John 20: 17 ('*Touch me not*') as the text of his court Easter sermon in 1621 (*XCVI*, 543–52), and the final part ('*For I am not yet ascended... to my God and your God*') for the same place and feast in 1622 (*XCVI*, 553–65). Cf. also the aside at p. 351, l. 2 . It is surprising that a preacher as seasoned as Andrewes, and known for the exactitude with which he prepared his sermons before preaching, would so misjudge the time required for delivery. Still, I find it difficult to accept Klemp's conclusion that *MS* was written before delivery ('Revision Techniques', 153, n. 14).

25. *abroad*: outside; in the wider world.

26. *Verbum... suo*: lit., 'the word of a day in its day', i.e. a text appropriate for the day. Andrewes plays here with a literal translation of the Hebrew in 1 Kings 8: 59; Geneva translates 'alway as the matter requireth', with gloss, 'Ebr [Hebrew]. the thing of a day in his day'.

28. *expresse for it*: specific about it.

p. 226, 6. *Evangel*: the Gospel; a favourite pun on the etymological Greek senses of both 'good message' (Gospel) and 'good messenger' ('a good Angel'). Cf. Andrewes's imagined announcement by Gabriel to the shepherds: 'I am *Angelus Evangelizans*, an Angell with a Gospell, one that comes with no *bad newes*' (*XCVI*, 35); also Gregory, *Hom. XXV*, 3: '*Latina lingua angelus nuntius dicitur*' (*PL*, 76.1191B); and, more exactly, Augustine, *Tractatus in Joannem CXXI*, 1: 'An, quoniam qui graece Angeli decuntur, latine sunt nuntii, isto modo Christi Evangelium velut a capite usque ad pedes, ab initio usque in finem significabant esse nuntiandum?' (*PL*, 35.1956). ('Is it because those that in Greek are called "angels" in Latin are "messengers" that they in this way signified that Christ's Gospel is to be announced from "the head to the feet", from the beginning to the end?')

9–11. *first birth... Shepherds*: cf. prev. n. Andrewes preached three Nativity sermons at court (1610, 1618, 1619) on the angels' annunciation to the shepherds (Luke 2: 10–14): *XCVI*, 33–43, 108–28.

12. *spred abroad... world*: cf. Acts 1: 8.

15. *a sinful woman*: Andrewes accepts the Western tradition that conflated Mary of Magdala (John 20) with the reformed prostitute (Luke 7: 36–50) and Mary, the sister of Martha (Luke 10: 39). Eastern tradition, and modern scholars, differentiate between the three.

18–19. *by a woman... both*: cf. Gregory, *Hom. XXV*, 6 (*LACT*): 'Ecce humani generis culpa ibi absciditur unde processit. Quia enim in paradiso mulier viro propinavit mortem, a sepulcro mulier viris annuntiat vitam; et dicta sui vivificatoris narrat, quae mortiferi serpentis verba narraverat' (*PL*, 76.1194). ('Behold, the sin of humankind was taken away from whence it came. Just as in Paradise the woman brought death to the man, from the sepulchre a woman announced life to men; and her words told of being made alive, just as the telling of the serpent's words told of being made dead.') Ambrose writes similarly in *Exp. Evang. Sec. Lucam*, 156 (*PL*, 15.1843B).

24. *two great leaves*: 'parts of a door, gate, or shutter' (*OED* 'leaf', I.12.b).

27. *peccatrix*: Lat., sinner (female); cf. p. 227, l. 23 and n.

30. *non obstante*: notwithstanding (lit., 'being no hindrance'). From a legal phrase used in royal patents granting a benefit *non obstante aliquo statuto in contrarium* ('notwithstanding any statute to the contrary'). Andrewes's use of the phrase as an adverb (vs. a noun) pre-dates the earliest such use (1646) in *OED*.

34. *Apostle... to the Apostles*: the epithet *apostolorum apostola* ('apostle to the apostles') to describe Mary Magdalen was a patristic commonplace; cf. Rabanus Maurus (*PL*, 112.1488A), Peter Damian (*PL*, 144.820B), and Peter Abelard (*PL*, 178l 485A, B). One of the earliest, though less epigrammatic, articulations of the idea is in one of Andrewes's primary sources, Gregory, *Hom. XXV*, 10 (*LACT*): 'apostolis, eius videlicet nuntiis, ipsa nuntiaret' (*PL*, 76.1196B); ('it was she who announced the news to the apostles who were themselves his messengers').

p. 227, 4–5. *goes along... all*: lit., 'Mary appears in *"all"* the verses'; but also, in the sense of *dramatis personae*, 'she interacts, or is in company with, all the other characters ('*Parties*', l. 60)'; cf. *OED* ('go', B.VII.73.b).

14. *ascendo*: 'I ascend'.

16. *use*: application; conventional from the phrase 'doctrines and uses' to describe that part of the sermon that applied 'doctrine' to everyday moral 'use'.

23. *fælix peccatrix*: 'happy sinner'; cf. Rabanus Maurus, *De vita Mariae Magdalenae et Martha*: 'O beata peccatrix, et ardentissima Christi amatrix' ('O blessed sinner, and most ardent lover of Christ' (*PL*, 112.1480B).

30. *sustulerunt*: 'they have taken away'.

p. 228, 1–2. *Defectus fidei... Origen*: paraphrase rather than quotation; cf. Origen, *Opera*, 453: 'Sed quomodo errabat quæ sic pro te dolebat, & sic te amabat? Certè si errabat, in dubitanter dico quòd ipsa errare se ignorabat, & sic error non procedebat ab errore, sed ab amore & dolore. Igitur misericors & juste iudex, amor quem habebat in te, & dolor quem habebat in te, excuset eam apud te, si fortè erret de te: nec attendas ad mulieris errore[m], sed ad discipulæ amorem, quæ non pro errore, sed pro dolore, & amore plorabat'; ('But how did she err who so grieved for thee, and so loved thee? Certainly if she erred, I can say without doubt that she did not know she erred, and that that same error proceeded not from error but from love and grief. Therefore, o merciful and just judge, for the love she had of you, and the grief she had for you, forgive her if perhaps she errs: nor mark the woman's error, but the disciple's love, which was not out of error, but of grief and love'); Andrewes quotes more directly from the passage again below (p. 233, ll. 26–7).

4. *proofe... Him living*: Luke 7: 37, John 12: 3.

7. *last... yet darke*: Mark 15: 40, 16: 1–3; John 20: 1.

18–19. *Amor... monumentum*: 'Love stands beside the tomb.' The first of ten summary Latin epigrams that punctuate Andrewes's enumeration of the 'ten... arguments of her great love' (ll. 10–11). Although not patristic quotations, they do seem to be inspired by similar summary ejaculations to a quasi-personified 'Amor' in Origen and Gregory, or late medieval pseudo-Bernardine devotional texts.

24–26. *Their going... behind them*: cf. Origen, *Opera*, 451: 'Ó Maria... quid cordis erat tibi, ut sola stares ad monumentum discipulis abeuntibus? Tu ante illos venisti, & cum illus rediisti, & post illos remansisti. Cur hoc fecisti? Sapiebas plus illis, aut diligebas plus quàm illi, quia non timebas ut illi?' ('O Mary... what heart was in you such that you stood alone at the sepulchre when the disciples had gone away? You came before them, you returned with them, and you lingered after them. Why did you do this? Are you wiser than they, or do you love more than they, or fear less than they?')

26–27. *Fortior... Augustine*: Augustine, *In Joann. Evang. Tract. CXXI* (*LACT*): 'Viris enim redeuntibus, infirmiorem sexum in eodem loco fortior figebat affectus' (*PL*, 35.1955); ('The men, however, went away; the weaker sex was fixed in the same place by a stronger affection').

28. *thence*: from there.

31. *Amor... recedentibus*: 'Love remains, all others are gone away'; cf. Origen, *Opera*, 450, 'Amor faciebat eam stare' ('Love made her to stand').

32. *give over*: give way; yield.

33. *stood... wept*: Andrewes follows Origen (*Opera*, 450) in moralizing the two verbs 'stood' and 'wept': 'videamus si possumus, cur staret, videamus & cur ploraret. Prosit nobis & illius stare, prosit & illius plorare'; ('Let us see if we can why "she stood", and why "she wept". We can profit from this "to stand" and this "to weep" ').

34. *a good*: 'in good earnest'; cf. Shakespeare, *Two Gent.* (*c*.1590?), IV. iv. 162: 'I made her weep agood'.

p. 229, 3. *misse*: absence.

5. *Amor amarè flens*: 'Love bitterly trickling down'.

6–7. *ever and anon*: over and over again.

9. *character*: 'feature, trait, characteristic' (*OED sn* II.8.a). Andrewes's gloss, 'comes from the same root', however, is a suggestive anticipation of the much later eighteenth-century sense, 'one of the distinguishing features of a species or genus' (*OED* II.8.b). Cf. p. 239, ll. 22–3.

10. *dilectio... from diligo*: Lat. *diligo* ('diligere'), 'to love', root of the *n* derivations *dilectio* ('love') and *diligentia* ('diligence').

10–11. *Amor diligentiam diligens*: 'Love loving diligence'.

12. *give over*: give up, cease.

15. *But... looked in, (too.)*: Gregory, *Hom. XXV*, 2: 'Certe jam monumentum vacuum viderat, jam sublatum Dominum nuntiaverat' (*PL*, 76. 1189); ('Of course she had already seen that the sepulchre was empty, had already reported that the Lord had been taken away'); and Augustine, *In Joann. Evang. Tract. CXXI*, 1: 'Cur hoc fecerit nescio. Non enim nesciebat non ibi esse jam quem quaerebat; quandoquidem inde sublatum et discipulis ipsa nuntiaverat' (*PL*, 35.1956); ('Why she did this I do not know. For she was not unaware that he whom she sought was not there, because she was the one who had reported to the disciples that he had been carried away').

16. *suspect... eyes*: Augustine, *In Joann. Evang. Tract. CXXI*, 1: 'Utrum quod nimium dolebat, nec suis nec illorum oculis facile putabat esse credendum?' (*PL*, 35.1956); ('Whether because she grieved immoderately, or because she would not so easily believe either her eyes or theirs?'). *LACT* suggests Augustine's homily as the source for p. 000, ll. 131–3 (cf. next n.), but this seems a misplaced reference for the present allusion.

18–21. *Thus we... find it, then*: cf. Gregory, *Hom. XXV*, 2 (*LACT*): 'Sed amanti semel aspexisse non sufficit, quia vis amoris intentionem multiplicat inquisitionis. Quaesivit ergo prius, et minime invenit; perseveravit ut quaereret, unde et contigit ut inveniret.' ('But it is not enough for a lover to have searched once, since the strength of love increases the fervency of the search. Therefore she sought once before, and found nothing; she persevered in searching, and thus laid hold of the thing she sought.')

21. *Amor... ubi quæsivit*: 'Love seeks where it has sought'.

24. *multum*: 'many'; 'number'.

24. *Ut prosit... Origen*: cf. p. 228, l. 33 and n.

26. *doubt*: suspect.

26. *juxta mensam*: 'by the table'; also 'by the altar'; an allusion to the Last Supper (cf. Matt. 26: 17–30), and, by extension, to the Holy Communion (celebrated immediately following Andrewes's sermon).

28. *stiffe-joynted... to seeke*: cf. Origen, *Opera*, 454: 'Et ne fortè erecta cervice repellas eum à te, humiliando inclina te.' ('And lest you repel him [Christ] with a strong proud neck, humbly incline yourself to him.') That Andrewes adjusts the metaphor from 'neck' to 'joints' suggests a secondary reference to the obligation to kneel to receive Holy Communion, a point he frequently and stridently argued in his court sermons (cf. in particular, Easter 1614; *XCVI*, 469–80).

31. *sutable*: suitable; accordant, correspondent (*OED sa a.* 2).

35. *lien*: layed, lain.

p. 230, 3. *by degrees*: incrementally, in stages; also punning on the 'degrees' (ranks) in the cosmic hierarchy ('*His Angels*, before *Him*').

4. *vulgar*: common, inferior.

7. *habit*: attire.

7. *site*: 'position occupied by some specified thing' (*OED sn^2* 1.a).

12. *this day*: the day of Christ's Resurrection; the first Easter day.

14. *But... place is blessed*: Origen (*Opera*, 452) includes an extended lament in the voice of Mary Magdalen in which she praises the blessedness of Christ's tomb. Cf. also ll. 19–20 and nn.

17. *auspicium*: auspicious portent.

18–19. *Quid gloriosius... Angelorum*: 'What is more glorious than an angel? what more vile than the worm? He who made the worms' place, also made the angels"; paraphrase of Augustine, *In Joann. Evang. Tract. I*, 13: 'Quid praeclarius angelo in creaturis? quid extremius vermiculo in creaturis? Per quem factus est angelus, per ipsum factus est et vermiculus: sed angelus dignus coelo, vermiculus terra. Qui creavit, ipse disposuit.' (*PL*, 35.1385); ('What is more excellent than an angel among creatures? What worse than a worm among creatures? He by whom the angel is made, by the same is the worm made: but the angel is fit for heaven, the worm for the earth. He who made, also puts in order.')

19–20. *That... place for Angels*: Augustine extends his argument (cf. prev. n.) to exclaim upon the paradox that Christ, superior even to angels, nonetheless in his incarnation made himself lower than the worm, thus defying God's order in Creation ('Ecce quid fieri voluit propter te'; 'Behold what he was willing to do for you'). Andrewes, influenced by Origen (cf. n. to l. 14), adapts that paradox to the tomb itself.

22–23. *Easter day colour*: white is traditionally the colour of joy, and thus liturgically associated with Easter. Cf. Andrewes, Easter 1608: '*white* is the colour of gladnesse .... so, this day, the *Angells* were all *in white*, to teach us thereby, with what *affection*, with how great *Joy*, and gladnesse, we are to celebrate and solemnize this Feast' (*XCVI*, 409).

25. *represent*: 'to present (oneself or another person) to or before a person'; also, 'to show, exhibit, or display to the eye' (*OED sv.^{1}* 1.a, 4.a).

25. *Fuller*: one who fulls (cleanses, whitens, thickens) cloth.

28–29. *Heaven mourned... white*: Andrewes made the same contrast between Good Friday and Easter colours in his sermon for Easter 1608 (*XCVI*, 409).

31–32. *in albis... found Christ*: 'allusion to the practice of the early Church according to which the newly baptized ("them that found Christ") who had just been baptized at Easter kept for eight days the white robes of their baptism' (Lossky, *Lancelot Andrewes*, 156).

p. 230, 34–p. 231, 1. *grave... place of rest*: Cf. Origen, *Opera*, 452: 'Hoc ergo sepulchru[m] non deseram, quia ita mori erit co[n]solatio mea, & in morte mea erit requies mea'; ('Therefore I shall not desert this sepulchre, because thus to die shall be to me a consolation, and in my death shall be my rest').

2. *Psalme of the resurrection*: Ps. 16, appointed for Easter Eve in pre-Reformation Sarum Rite.

3. *rest in hope*: cf. Ps. 16: 9.

3. *members... head*: cf. Geneva gloss to Ps. 16: 10 ('neither wilt thou suffer thine holy one to see corruption'): 'This is chiefly meant of Christ by whose resurrection all his members have immortalitie.'

4–5. *rest... Sabbath eternall*: the Sabbath was the seventh day of the week, set aside by God as a day of rest from all labour to commemorate his rest after the six days of Creation (Exod. 16: 22–30). Andrewes quotes here from Paul's attempt to explain (not entirely clearly) how the Jewish Sabbath applied to Christians. Like most commentators, Andrewes interprets Paul's Sabbath as a figure for 'the everlasting rest, wherein we begin to live to God, after that the race of this life ceaseth' (Heb. 4: 3, Geneva gloss). Augustine (*City of God*, xxii. 30) was one of the first metaphorically to expound the 'perpetual Sabbath' as *'eternall'* rest in heaven. Cf. Edmund Spenser, *Faerie Queene*, 'Mutabilitie', VIII. ii. 7–9: 'But thence-forth all shall rest eternally | With Him that is the God of Sabbaoth hight: | O that great Sabbaoth God, graunt me that Sabaoths sight' (pr. 1609).

6. *at the head... feet*: Gregory and Augustine puzzle why the angels are so seated (*PL*, 76.1191B; 35.1956).

10–11. *Arke... two Cherubims*: Gregory, *Hom. XXV*, 3: 'Unde et duo cherubim quae propitiatorium tegunt ses invicem aspiciunt versis vultibus in propitiatorium.... Quid vero per propitiatorium nisi incarnatus Dominus figuratur?' (*PL* 76.1191C); ('And the two cherubim which covered the mercy-seat looked at one another with their faces turned toward the mercy-seat.... Truly, what does the mercy-seat represent but the incarnate Lord?'). Cf. Exod. 25: 19–20.

15. *In mysterie they referre it thus*: 'symbolically the Church Fathers interpret it thus'.

18–20. *In principio... there, another*: Gregory, *Hom. XXV*, 3 (*LACT*): 'Quasi ad caput sedet angelus, cum per apostolum Joannem praedicatur quia *in principio erat Verbum, et Verbum erat apud Deum, et Deus erat Verbum*. Et quasi ad pedes sedet angelus, cum dicit: *Verbum caro factum est, et habitavit in nobis*' (*PL*, 76.1191B); ('In a sense, one angel sits at the head when the apostle John preaches that "in the beginning was the Word, and the Word was with God, and the Word was God". And in a sense an angel sits at the feet when [John] says, "The Word was made flesh and dwelt among us"'); cf. John 1: 1, 14.

21. *queere*: the already near-obsolete form of 'choir' (*OED*) preferred by Andrewes.

25. *go... in white*: the linen winding sheet or shroud in which all corpses were buried; cf. David Cressy, *Birth, Marriage & Death... in Tudor and Stuart England* (1997), 430–2.

26–27. *they guard... resurrection*: the existence of guardian angels was a controverted point, asserted by the Eastern and Roman churches, scorned by Calvin, and avoided as suspect by most English Protestants. The ex-Jesuit John Salkeld published and dedicated to James I *A Treatise of Angels* (1613), which argued forcefully on patristic grounds for their existence. His florilegium of Latin and Greek patristic sources (pp. 259–80) includes no argument that angels 'guard our bodies' after death. Perhaps this is an extension of the Roman Catholic burial rite's 'in paradisum deducant te angeli', evoked, for example, by Horatio's 'And flights of angels sing thee to thy rest' (*Hamlet*, v. ii. 313); cf. Benjamin Camfield, *A Theological Discourse of Angels* (1678), 'after the separation of Body and Soul asunder, they are careful and diligent in their attendance to Lodg the departed Spirit safely in its Rest and Happiness' (p. 98).

28. *of the Angels*: from the angels.

32–33. *with us... Head-angels*: in places of social precedence; i.e. in positions of honour at the 'head' of a table.

p. 232, 1–2. *Ne... Desinat*: Horace, *Ars Poetica* (*LACT*): 'Which in some swarthy fish uncomely ends' (l. 5, trans. Ben Jonson, ed. G. Parfitt, 1975); from a parody of a bad portrait painter's placing a human head on an animal's lower body.

2. *a blacke... a white*: Andrewes again flirts with the boundaries of Protestantism's strictly scripture-based views of angels (cf. p. 232, ll. 26–7 and n.). Andrewes's image here hints at medieval iconography for Doomsday, where good ('white') and bad ('blacke') angels wrestle over the souls of the departed, which in turn was based on plentiful patristic arguments like Didymus of Alexandria's 'good and holy men have for their keepers Angels of light: the bad, angels of darkenesse' (quoted in Salkeld, *Treatise of Angels*, 259–60). Cf. Calvin's dismissal of 'the vulgar imagination... that two angels, a good and a bad, as a kind of genii, are assigned to each individual' (*Institutes*, i. 147).

7–8. *dumb shew... dialogue*: a striking group of theatrical metaphors (cf. Headnote). Common in medieval and early modern drama, a 'dumb show' presented action without dialogue. Andrewes's extension of the image to an 'apparition' that 'vanished away' also recalls the elaborate theophanies in court masques and Shakespearian romance, such as the harpies' banquet in *The Tempest*, Jupiter's descent in *Cymbeline*, and Queen Katherine's angelic vision in *All Is True* (*Henry VIII*). But with 'dialogue, too'—the combination of 'sight and voice' ('*visio & vox*')—the scene at the tomb supersedes fantastic dumb show by making real the interaction between earthly and heavenly protagonists.

10–11. *And... no more she had*: Augustine, *In Joann. Evang. Tract.* CXXI, 1: 'Ita enim dixerunt, *Quid ploras*? ac si dicerent, Noli plorare' (*PL*, 35.1956); ('Indeed, that they said "Why do you weep?" was as much as to say, "Weep not"').

12. *piæ... cæcæ*: 'pious tears, but blind'.

12–14. *imagining... grave emptie*: Gregory, *Hom.* XXV, 1 (*LACT*): 'Exquirebat quem non invenerat, flebat inquirendo' (*PL*, 76.1189C); ('She sought for him whom she had not found; she wept as she searched').

17. *conceit*: conception, understanding.

19. *Our ploras... quid*: 'our "you weep" never has a "why"'; i.e. 'Our weeping never has a reason'.

23. *elench*: 'a syllogism in refutation of a proposition that has been syllogistically defended'; generally, a 'fallacy' (*OED*, sn 1.a., b).

23–24. *à non... causâ*: 'putting a wrong cause for a [true] cause'.

25. *sustulerunt*: 'they have taken'.

30–33. *But that... dead body*: Augustine, *In Joann. Evang. Tract.* CXXI, 1 (*LACT*): '*Dominum meum*: Dominum suum vocans corpus exanime Domini sui' (*PL*, 35.1956); ('"My Lord": calling her Lord, the lifeless body of her Lord').

p. 233, 4–6. *His body... to her*: Origen, *Opera*, 450: 'Prima fuit causa doloris, quia vivum perdiderat: sed de hoc dolore aliquantulum consolationem habebat, quia mortuum se retinere credebat: nunc autem de isto dolore consolari non poterat, quia corpus defuncti non inveniebat'; ('The first cause of her sorrow was that she had lost the [living] man: but of this sorrow she had some degree of comfort because she believed that she would still have him dead: now however she has not even that comfort, because she cannot find his dead body').

7. *offices of love*: 'duties of love'; a common epithet; cf. William Perkins, *Golden Chaine* (1600), 637, 'The office of love is onely to have compassion'; and Shakespeare, *Merry Wives* (1597), 'I profess requital... in the simple office of love' (IV. ii. 3–4)

7–8. *Etiam... amor*: 'even at the sight of a cadaver love revives'; Origen, *Opera*, 450: 'Metuebat ne amor magistri sui in pectore suo frigesceret, si corpus eius non inveniret, quo viso recalesceret'; ('She feared that the love of her master would grow cold in her breast, if she did not find his body, by the sight of which [her love] would warm again').

10–12. *S. Augustine... nothing at all*: Augustine, *In Joann. Evang. Tract. CXXI*, 1 (*LACT*): 'amplius dolentes quod fuerat de monumento ablatus, quam quod fuerat in ligno occisus' (*PL*, 35.1955); ('grieving more for his having been taken from the tomb, than for having been slain on a tree').

11. *sublatus de monumento*: 'carried from the tomb'.

11. *occisus in ligno*: 'killed on a tree [lit., wood]'.

12. *Right*: precisely, quite (*OED sadv.* II.5).

13. *cleane*: completely.

14. *nescio ubi*: 'I know not where'.

18–19. *So that... comfort*: Augustine, *In Joann. Evang. Tract. CXXI*, 1 (*LACT*): 'quia nesciebat quo iret ad consolandum dolorem' (*PL*, 35.1956); ('because she did not know where to go for comfort to her grief').

19. *nescio ubi... right*: Andrewes's sharp dramatic focus on Mary's '*nescio ubi*' is a condensation of her extended first person lament in Origen's homily that reaches a panicked climax with: 'Si juxta monumentum maneo, ego illum non invenio: si à monumento recessero, nescio infelix quò vadam, nescio ubi eum quæram' (*Opera*, 452); ('If I stay next to the sepulchre I do not find him; if I go from the sepulchre, I know not, wretch, where I shall go; I know not where I shall seek him').

24–25. *Non credens... sublatum*: 'Not believing he was risen, she believed he was taken away.' MS and *Q*'s attribution of this to Augustine (omitted in F_1) cannot be confirmed in his works or in Andrewes's other primary sources.

26–27. *Shee erred... errour too*: cf. p. 228, l. 1 and n.

32. *scandall*: lit., 'a grossly discreditable circumstance, event, or condition of things' (*OED sn* 3.b), but recalling Gal. 5: 12, 'τὸ σκανδαλον τοῦ σταυροῦ' ('the scandal of the crosse', Rheims; *OED sn* 1.b).

32–34. *opprobrious... own Him*: cf. Phil. 2: 8.

p. 234, 4. *Amor... scandalizatus*: 'Love that is not scandalized at [his] scandal'.

9–10. *Angels... at all*: Origen, *Opera*, 452: 'Denique ego non quæro angelos, sed eum qui fecit me & angelos. Non quæro angelos, sed meum & angelorum dominum'; ('Furthermore, I do not seek angels, but him who made me and angels. I do not seek angels, but the lord of me and angels').

10. *extasie*: trance or stupor; following Origen, Andrewes intends the Greek etymological sense of 'being out of one's self' (cf. next n.).

11. *Domine... Bernard*: a good example of Andrewes quoting from memory and not checking his sources. Not Bernard, but Origen, *Opera*, 453 (the speaker addresses Christ): 'Ideoque forsitan non cognoscit te, quia non est in sese, sed propter te est extra

se.' ('She therefore does not know you, because she is not in herself, but because of you she is out of herself.').

11–12. *Amor extasin patiens*: 'Love in an ecstasy'.

17. *quid ploras?*: 'Why do you weep?'

18–22. *If . . . maner comfort*: Origen, *Opera*, 452 (cf. p. 233, ll. 18–19 and n.).

23. *Amor . . . renuens consolari*: 'Love refusing comfort for loss'.

29. *break . . . sports*: 'interrupt none of our accustomed pastimes for it'.

p. 235, 4. *touched . . . string*: 'to say something apt or telling about' (*OED*, sv 19.b), with metaphorical pun on 'to strike the strings' (*OED*, 9.a)—as on an angelic harp.

8. *sit*: sat; common early modern form of the past participle (*OED*, sv, A.7.ϵ).

10. *supersedeas*: punning on the fig. meaning, 'something which stops, stays, or checks' (*OED*), and the literal etymological one, 'to sit above' (cf. prev. n.).

10. *comes in place*: 'to come to be . . . to come into notice, appear' (*OED*, sn¹, V.21.a); a very late example of the phrase, the last usage of which cited by *OED* is 1579. The context suggests further punning on the senses of 'place' as position in social scale (III.9.a), the physical space occupied by right of social position (IV.13.a), and official position or office itself (IV.14.a).

13. *Christus adest*: 'Christ is there'.

14. *Adest Christus . . . Augustine*: 'Christ is there, nor is he ever far from those who seek him'; probably a misattribution to Augustine. Andrewes seems to have conflated Ambrose—*Exp. Evang. Sec. Luc.* 161: 'Adest Christus, quemadmodum quaeritur?' (*PL*, 15.1844C); ('Christ is there, why is she seeking like this?')—with Origen, *Opera*, 454: 'ploret unusquisque ad Jesum, & quaerat fideliter Jesum, quia non celavit se quaerenti peccatrici'; ('Let everyone weep to Jesus, and faithfully seek Jesus, who hides not himself from the seeking sinner').

15–17. *this case . . . we see*: cf. Origen, prev. n.

22. *happly*: perchance.

23. *to try*: to test; cf. Origen, *Opera*, 453, 'Dulcis magister, ad quid quæso provocas spiritum huius mulieris? ad quid commoves animam eius?' ('Sweet master, why do you torment the spirit of this woman? why do you vex her soul?')

26. *the Apostle*: Paul.

27–28. *O . . . & tu*: 'O if thou hadst known, even you'; the beginning of Christ's lament over Jerusalem (Luke 19: 42).

28. *standeth us in hand*: 'to behove, concern' (*OED* 'stand', B.II.47.b).

31. *comming in presence*: appearing ceremonially, also in the sense of appearing in a place designated for such an appearance (cf. *OED* 'presence' 2.b, c, d); Andrewes's scene-setting evokes the customary practice of subjects (here, angels) rising or making an obeisance upon the king's (Christ's) entry into the Presence Chamber. Cf. '*comes in place*', p. 235, l. 10.

p. 236, 3. *misknew*: 'not to recognize (a person)' (*OED* sv 4, citing no examples between 1570 and 1840).

6. *dressed it*: 'to till, cultivate, prune, or tend (a field, garden, or plant); to treat with manure, etc.' (*OED* sv 13.c).

8. ἑτέρᾳ μορφῇ: Gr., 'hetera morphē', 'in a different form'.

13–14. *Saint Gregorie . . . erravit*: 'indeed, in erring she did not err'; cf. Gregory, *Hom. XXV*, 4 (*LACT*): 'Forsitan nec errando haec mulier erravit' (*PL*, 76.1192C); ('as it happened, this woman did not err in erring').

18. *false semblant*: 'deceitful countenance'; perhaps also the allegorical figure Faux Semblant from Jean de Meun's *Roman de la Rose*.

20. *Paradise... His planting*: the orthodox point that Christ, as the creating Word, executed his Father's will at the Creation; cf. Gen. 2: 8 ('And the Lord God planted a Garden eastward in Eden'), on which Andrewes preached in 1591, alluding to Christ's later appearance to Mary Magdalen: 'so here is resembled unto us the name of a Gardiner to plant an Orchard for us and our use: to which end Christ represented and shewed himself in that shape and form... for it was he that trimmed up this Garden of Paradise for us' (*AS*, 156).

23. *Paul... Apollo*: 1 Cor. 3: 6 (*LACT*).

25-29. *gardens... eternall life*: Origen, *Opera*, 453: 'Etenim Jesus est & hortulanus, quia ipse seminat omne semen bonum in horto animæ tuæ, & in cordibus fidelium suorum. Ipse omne holus plantat bonum, & rigat in animabus sanctorum'; ('For indeed Jesus is also a gardener for he plants all the seeds of goodness in the garden of our souls, and in the hearts of his faithful. He also plants all good herbs and waters them in the souls of the saints'); cf. also Gregory, *Hom. XXV*, 4: 'Forsitan nec errando haec mulir erravit, quae Jesum hortulanum credidit. An non spiritaliter hortunlaus erat, qui in ejus pectore per amoris sui semina virtutum virentia plantabat?' (*PL*, 76.1192C); ('Perchance this woman did not err in her error of believing that Jesus was a gardener. Was he not a spiritual gardener to her, who planted in her breast by love the seed of fruitful virtue?')

27. *noysome*: 'harmful, injurious, noxious' (*OED sa* 1).

27. *unsavoury*: of plants, 'not attractive to the taste' (*OED sa* 1).

p. 237, 8. *resembling*: likening.

12. *opere & veritate*: 'in deed and in truth' (1 John. 3: 18).

19. *quickens*: vivifies, enlivens.

19-20. *Quem quæris... quem quæris*: 'He whom you seek asks of you, "Whom do you seek?"'; cf. Origen, *Opera*, 453 (*LACT*): 'Ecce Jesus venit ad te, & quem quæris quærit à te: Mulier quid ploras?' ('Behold Jesus comes to you, and he whom you seek asks of you, "Woman, why weepest thou?"')

21-22. *Si quæris... Augustine*: 'If you seek [him], why do you not recognize [him]? If you recognize, why do you seek?'; actually Origen, *Opera*, 453 (*LACT*), 'O Maria si quaeris Jesum, cur non cognoscis Jesum? et si cognoscis Jesum, quid quaeris Jesum?' ('O Mary, if you seek Jesus, why do you not recognize Jesus? and if you recognize Jesus, why do you seek Jesus?')

p. 238, 4-7. *Thus say... no hope*: cf. Gregory, *Hom. XXV*, 7: 'Citius enim a morte voluit resurgere, ne nostra diu anima in infidelitatis morte remaneret' (*PL*, 76.1194B); ('He therefore willed to rise quickly from the dead, so that our souls would not remain long in the death of unbelief'); also 1 Thess. 4: 13, Geneva gloss: 'We must take heed that we do not immoderately bewaile the dead, that is, as they use to do which thinke that they are utterly perished'.

13. *wipes... all eyes*: Rev. 7: 17, 21: 4.

14-15. *30 Psalme... sackcloth*: Ps. 30: 11 (*LACT*); appointed for Easter Eve in the Sarum Rite.

18. *in kinde*: appropriate, fitting.

28. χαίρετε: Gr., 'chairete', 'Greetings', 'Hello'; stressing the etymological sense 'be glad', or '*Rejoice*'; cf. Geneva, 'God save you'; AV, 'All hail' (Matt. 28: 9).

31–33. *last Easter... cause for it*: the previous Easter (1619) King James lay dangerously ill at Newmarket, and many feared that his death was imminent; Andrewes was summoned to preach his prepared Easter court sermon at his bedside, and his place at court was taken by John Donne (McCullough, *Sermons at Court*, 151; Donne, *Sermons*, ii. 197–212).

34. *kindly*: appropriate to its nature.

p. 239, 1–2. *She... word from her*: Origen, *Opera*, 453, comments similarly on the other verb in the clause, *posuisti* ('you have laid him'): 'Dixerat autem Apostolis primò ubi posuerunt eum: hoc idem postmodum dixit angelis, ubi posuerunt eum: & nunc tibi dixit de te: ubi posuisti eum. Multum dulcescit verbum hoc in corde eius, quod sic abundat in ore eius'; ('For she had said first to the Apostles, "Where have they laid him?" Then she said the same afterwards to the angels, "Where have they laid him?" And now she says to you—of yourself—"Where have you laid him?" This word is so dear to her heart that it is always in her mouth').

1–2. *sustulerunt... sustulisti... si tu sustulisti*: 'they have taken away... you have taken away... if you have taken away'.

3–5. *But, to Christ... the fact*: Origen, *Opera*, 453, 'Angelis dixit, Tulerunt & posuerunt: & non dixit, Tulistis & posuistis'; ('to the angels she said "*they* have taken", and "*they* have laid": and does not say [to them, as to you], "*you* have taken", and "*you* have laid"').

6. *corses*: corpses.

9–11. *Bernard... circa Te*: another confusion of Bernard for Origen, *Opera*, 453: 'Igitur misericors & juste judex, amor quem habebat in te, & dolor quem habebat pro te, excuset eam apud te, si fortè erret de te'; ('therefore merciful and just Judge, for the love she had toward you, for the sorrow she had for you, excuse her before you, even if perhaps she errs about you').

12–13. *any error... sustulisti*: in Origen, the speaker asks that Christ forgive Mary for failing to recognize him (cf. prev. n.), not (as here) for her false accusation of carrying away Christ's body.

15. *Prophetat & nescit*: 'she prophesies and yet knows not'.

16. *si tu*: 'if you'.

17–18. *For, quod... Himselfe*: Origen, *Opera*, 453: 'Tu enim virtute tua surrexeras, & quod de te factum fuerat tu ipse feceras'; ('For you rose by your own power, and what was done to you, you yourselfe did it').

18–20. *His taking... owne glorie*: cf. Petrus Chrysologus, *Sermo LXXX*: 'est istud causa, non casus; mysterium, non eventus; ordo, non culpa' (*PL*, 52.0425A); ('this here is a cause, not a chance; a mystery, not an accident; an arrangement, not a fault').

22–23. *Characters... ten*: cf. p. 228, ll. 10–12; p. 229, l. 9 and nn.

24. *si tu sustulisti eum*: 'if you have taken him away'.

24–28. *which Him?... names Him*: Nicholas of Clairvaux (attr. Bernard), *Serm. in Fest. B. Maria Magd*, 9 (*LACT*): 'Quem eum, Maria? Cum de nullo feceris mentionem, ad quem relationem facias? Putasne quod in omnium cordibus versetur ita memoria dilecti tui...?' (*PL*, 185.220B); ('Which "him", Mary? Make you no mention of what relationship you have? Can you not because the memory of your loved one has distracted your mind...?')

29. *Solæcismus amoris*: 'solecism [ungrammatical speech] of love'.

29–30. *loves owne Dialect*: this striking phrase seems to be Andrewes's own, but cf. Bernard, *Sermones in Cantica Canticorum LXXIX*, 1, 'lingua amoris ei qui non amat, barbara erit' (*PL*, 183.1163c); ('the language of love to one who does not love shall be barbarous'). The phrase is also used by Dr Joseph Beaumont in his allegorical epic *Psyche, or, Loves Mysterie (1648)*: '*Jesus* whose Ear is always ope to them | Who speak *Loves Dialect*, straight heard her Crie' (xix. xxxiii.2–3). Beaumont (1616–99) was an ardent Laudian, friend of Richard Crashaw (author of an elegy to Andrewes), and son-in-law and client of Andrewes's former chaplain, Matthew Wren. He was also author of a lyric similar in subject and tone to Andrewes's sermon (and/or Origen's Magdalen homily), '*EASTER Dialogue. S. Joh. 20.13*' (*Complete Poems*, ed. Grosart, 2 vols. (1880), ii. 250–1).

33. *Amor... ignorare*: 'Love which thinks that no one should be unaware of that which it thinks on.' Of the sermon's ten summary Latin tags, this owes the strongest debt to a patristic source; cf. Gregory, *Hom. XXV*, 5: 'Sed vis amoris hoc agere solet in animo, ut quem ipse semper cogitat, nullum alium ignorare credat' (*PL*, 76.1192C); ('But the strength of love often makes the soul believe that no one else could be ignorant of the one it thinks about').

34. *ego tollam*: 'I shall take'.

p. 239, 35–p. 240, 3. *Alas... doe it, though*: Nicholas of Clairvaux (attr. Bernard), *Serm. in Fest. B. Maria Magd.*, 9 (*LACT*): 'Mira res! Hominem perfectae aetatis; virum cujus corpori vix centum librae sufficiunt unguentorum, tenerrima mulier portabis et tolles? Ardens et affecta locutio, quae de puritatis amore refusa, promittit quod implere non potest' (*PL*, 185.0220B); ('Wondrous thing! A grown man; a man whose body had been covered with up to a hundred pounds of spices. You, a delicate woman, will take and carry away? Ardent and loving speech, which out of the sincerity of love undertakes that which it cannot do').

3–5. *O mulier... woman*: Origen, *Opera*, 454: 'Ò mirabilis mulieris audacia. Ò mulier non mulier. Et si ancilla ostiaria interrogaverit te quid factura es? Ego eum tollam. Ò ineffabilis huius mulieris amor, ô mirabilis mulieris audacia, ô mulier non mulier: nullum locum excipit, nullum anteponit, sine timore dicit, absolutè promittit, Dicito mihi ubi posuisti eum, & ego eum tollam' ('O wonderful woman for audacity! O woman not a woman! And if the young woman at the gate asked you what you were going to do? "I will take him up." O unspeakable love of this woman! O wonderful woman for audacity! O woman not a woman! She excepts no place, she yields to nothing, she speaks without fear, she absolutely promises, "Tell me where you have laid him, and I will take him up"').

5. *lustie*: 'healthy, strong' (*OED sa* 5.a).

6. νοῦν ὑπὲρ ἰσχὺν: Gr., 'noun huper ischon' ('courage above strength').

8. *assay*: attempt, challenge.

8–9. *& nihil... difficultatis*: 'and it is ashamed of nothing unless it be to call something difficult'.

10. *Affectus... propriarum*: 'affection without an awareness of its proper strength'.

11. *dilexit multùm*: 'she loved much'.

15. *magnes amoris amor*: 'love is the lodestone of love'; cf. *XCVI*, p. 381.

26. *Recognosce... recognosceris*: as *LACT* noted, the exact quotation is Gregory, *Hom XXV*, 5: 'Recognosce eum, a quo recognosceris' (*PL*, 76.1192D); ('Recognize him by whom you are recognized'). But Andrewes may be forgiven recalling (*in marg.*) Augustine, *In Joann. Evang. Tract. CXXI*, 2: 'nisi quia tunc conversa corpore, quod non erat, putavit, nunc corde conversa, quod erat agnovit?' (*PL*, 35.1957); ('what else but that having turned her body, she thought he was what he was not, and now, having turned her heart, she recognized what he was').

p. 241, 1–6. *A cloude... scatters it*: Origen, *Opera*, 453: 'Mulier ista, quia densa nube doloris obtecta non videbat solem, qui mane surgens radiabat per fenestras eius, & per aures corporis sui, iam intrabat domum cordis sui'; ('This woman was covered with such a thick cloud of sorrow that she could not see the sun, which, rising in the morning, shines through her windows and the ears of her body, and now interred into the house of her heart').

10. *to her hands*: ready for her, without exertion on her part (*OED*, sn II.34.c).

13–14. *Contrariorum... exultavit*: 'The opposite effect results from the application of an opposite. If she wept for his taking away, she rejoiced for his resurrection.' Not an identifiable quotation. Among Andrewes's sources, Origen and Gregory stress the sweet irony of the plot reversal more directly than Augustine (next n.). The first sentence is a common medical tag, attributed to Hippocrates, for the healing of one condition by the application of an opposite, e.g. an antidote (cf. *PL*, 49.435).

14–15. *If sad... restoring againe*: cf. Origen, *Opera*, 454: 'O mutatio dexterae excelsi. Conversus est dolor magnus in gaudium magnum, mutatae sunt lachrymae doloris in lachrymas amoris'; ('O change of the right hand of the Most High. Changed is great sadness into great joy; changed are the tears of sadness into tears of love').

19–20. *Well now... living soule*: Gregory, *Hom. XXV*, 10: 'Viventem reperit, quem mortuum quaesivit' (*PL*, 76.1196B); ('She found him alive whom she sought dead').

20–22. *quickening... as dead*: Origen, *Opera*, 454: 'Tunc revixit spiritus eius, & reversus est sensus eius'; ('Then her spirits revived, and her senses returned').

27. *made her all greene*: 'full of vitality', 'of tender age, youthful' (*OED* 'green' *a* II.6, 7); hence, emblematic of her spiritual revivification. Perhaps also, in light of Mary Magdalen's past as a prostitute now transformed to new spiritual life by Christ, a witty appropriation of the bawdy phrase 'to give a woman a green gown' (i.e. by rolling amorously on the grass); cf. Antony Munday, 'he was so bold as to give her a greene gowne when I fear me she lost the flower of her chastity' (*OED* I.1.g).

33–34. *aures... mihi*: 'mine ears thou hast opened'.

35. *With the Philosophers... wisedome*: hearing was, since Aristotle, conventionally thought the superior of the five senses; cf. Louise Vigne, *The Five Senses: Studies in a Literary Tradition* (1975), 79–84.

36. *meet*: 'suitable, fit, proper' (*OED sa* A.3).

p. 242, 1. *voce quàm visu*: 'the voice, more than the sight'.

2. *sicut... sic vidimus*: '"as we have heard"... "so we have seen"'.

5–6. *Hodie si vocem*: 'today if ye will hear his voice'.

7–8. *this day... both*: with Christmas and Whitsunday, Easter was one of the only days on which Holy Communion was required to be celebrated, hence offering the rare ministration of both sermon and sacrament together.

19. *make use of them*: even on high feast days many attended sermon, but either left before communion, or stayed and did not receive. Cf. *BCP*, Holy Communion, 'exhortation... to come to the Holy Communion'.

19. *I shall not... verse*: not in *MS*, which, however, does conclude with the ensuing final paragraph as in *Q*; cf. p. 225, l. 23 and n.

21. *fond fashion... Sacraments*: cf. Headnote.

34–36. *holy mysteries... bodies hereafter*: cf. *BCP*, Holy Communion, final '*exhortation*': 'he hath instituted and ordained holy mysteries, as pledges of his love, and continual remembrance of his death, to our great and endless comfort'.

APPENDIX 1: A SERMON PREACHED AT THE SPITTLE... APRIL. 10. 1588

Text. St Paul's Cathedral MS 38F22.01 (see below), hereafter *SPMS*, fos. 51^r–67^r. The text presented here is a conservative transcription of the manuscript which preserves its orthography and spelling. Conventional contractions are expanded in square brackets. Scribal overstrikes are preserved, and interlinear additions and corrections are enclosed by ^carets^. Folio numbers (added in the MS in a modern hand) are inserted in the text in boldface square brackets.

SPMS contents and description. *SPMS* was unknown to modern scholars until discovered in 2004 by Dr Mary Morrissey. It is a small (258 × 175 mm) vellum-bound volume of 67 leaves titled (on its cover in a contemporary hand) '1588 | 4. Sermons viz: | Dr Bright on good Fryday 5 Apr: 1588 at P: Crosse | Etc.'. Its contents are as follows: 'A sermon preached at Paules crosse on Good=fridaye *Aprilis* 5. 1588. By M[aster] Bright' (1^r–16^v); 'A sermon preached at the Spittell one mundaye in Easter week *Aprilis 8* 1588. By M[aster] *Doct: Bisse*' (fos. 17^r–34^r); 'A sermon preached at the Spittell one Tewesdaye in Easter weeke 1588 *Aprilis 9* by M[aster] Doctor Powell' (fos. 35^r–50^r); and 'A sermon preached at the spittle by M[aster] Andrewes the wednesday in Easter weeke. *April. 10. 1588*' (fos. 51^r–67^r). The front paste-down bears the bookplate of 'The Earl of Westmoreland 1856' and a nineteenth-century St Paul's bookplate.

The volume was compiled exclusively for the texts it contains, and is not an occasional miscellany. There are no leaves without text, and each is carefully pricked in pencil for lineation, and all margins are double-ruled with red ink. The entire volume is written in the same fair secretary hand, with italic script used for most patristic and biblical quotations. There is no marginal apparatus or later marginalia. All texts in *SPMS* are clearly copies of anterior witnesses, evidenced by the fact that all of the scribal corrections in it are incidental copying errors, rather than substantive emendations. Uniformity of orthography and spelling across these texts by four different preachers (e.g. the idiosyncratic preference throughout of 'one' for 'on', and 'to' for 'too') possibly suggests that the original witnesses were not prepared by their authors, but by a single recorder who took the sermons down as they were preached. However, the amount of verbal and structural detail shared by *XCVI* and *A1* seems too great to be entirely possible even by a skilled recorder. Yet, several passages contain unambiguous instances of temporal verisimilitude, the most striking of which is Powell's admission, 'I shold now enter into the mattere it selfe but I am warned by those that stand behind me that the tyme is past, which will not suffer me to enter into it and my strength will not hold out' (fo. 45^v)—obviously a remark to be found only in a transcript of the text as delivered, rather than as prepared.

The editor, after consultation with Dr Morrissey, would suggest that the texts in *SPMS* might derive from transcripts of the sermons—as they had been actually delivered—made (after delivery) by their authors. This would most probably have been done for the use of the rehearser, Dr Thomas Holland, whose job it would have been to summarize on the Sunday after Easter the previous three sermons and then to preach his own sermon about them. A Jacobean Spital preacher, Thomas Goff acknowledged what must have been common practice, his 'courteous imparting of my notes to him [the rehearser] many dayes before' to assist the latter's work (*Deliverance from the Grave* (1627), sigs. A2^{r-v}; the editor is grateful to Dr Morrissey for this reference). That preachers were capable of preparing, after the fact, very exact transcripts of what they had said from the pulpit is demonstrated in the Jacobean cases of John Burgess and John Donne, both of whom were required to produce, after delivery, texts of exactly what they had preached for them to be scrutinized by the authorities (see McCullough, *Sermons at Court*, 141–7, and Donne, *Sermons*, vii. 39–42). The theory that these texts were prepared for Holland's use might be further suggested by the fact that only Holland's rehearsal sermon is missing from *A1*; however the marginal note to Bisse's sermon about Holland's (fo. 29^v) casts some doubt on this theory. Perhaps *A1* is a copy of what was prepared originally for Holland but then desired by another party. What can be positively concluded, however, on the evidence of the two texts of the Andrewes sermon (discussed below), is that *A1* preserves the 1588 Spital sermons as they were preached, not as they might have been prepared to be preached.

The Sermons Other than Andrewes's. The Good Friday sermon for Paul's Cross (fos. 1^r–16^v) is by 'M[aster] Bright' ('D[octor] Bright' on the front cover)—probably Arthur Bright, MA (Cantab) 1576, DD 1589, Rector of Castle Camps, Cambs. (1585–90), and subsequently Rector of St Botolph's Bishopsgate and prebend of St Paul's (1590; d. 1618) (Venn)—is on Rev. 5: 6–10 (the adoration of the Lamb by the 24 Elders). It is a workmanlike moralization of the vision. It is striking, however, for its forceful appeal to uniformity in worship ('some stand either altogeather, or to much for preachinge agaynst prayer, some contrariwise stand altogeather for ~~preach~~ prayer and are to much agaynst preachinge, some will have all preaching & no prayer, some will have all prayer and no preachinge', fo. 10^r). In particular, Bright decries the lack of uniformity in ceremonial gesture, 'yet now adayes it is taken for a token that a man hath well p[ro]fited in hearinge the word of God if he can be present at preachinge & prayers & shew no outward signe of reverence, no vncoveringe of the head, no knelinge, no standinge vp... many will come into the church even vp to the pulpitt & so depart agayne never vncoveringe ther heads, others will be vncovered at sermon yet covered at prayers' (fo. 10^v). On both matters, Bright presses the same points in the same terms as Andrewes in his catechistical lectures in Cambridge (1585) and throughout his later career (cf. 'Pattern of Catechistical Doctrine', this edn., pp. 31–48). The sermon also contains an *apologia* for Psalm-singing in churches, and suggests that a collection for the redemption of captives was taken at the sermon (fos. 11^r, 15^v).

'M[aster] D[octor] Bisse'—probably Dr Philip Bisse, Archdeacon of Taunton (d. 1613, Foster)—preached on Easter Monday on Matt. 13: 27–30 (the parable of the tares). Clearly aimed at the presbyterian *classis* movement and puritanism more generally, his sermon is a forceful rejection of those who 'forsake & leave the church... or seeke such a purityc of the church as that all these evils might be ridde out of it' (fo. 18^r). Bisse argued that the presence of the wicked within the church militant was a fact of its life from the time of the Apostles (citing Judas), and that it was Christ's business alone—at Judgement—to separate the wheat from the tares. Bisse admitted that there were various sorts of wickedness sown by Satan in the Church of England, but anatomized these to show what lessons the godly could learn from their negative example. *Passim*, he refuted accusations by Catholics that justification *sola fide* led to a dearth of works of charity (fos. 27^{r-v}), called for a greater commitment to clerical residency and frequent preaching (fos. 29^r–30^v), decried the sin of simony (fos. 30^v–31^r), and made the conventional appeals to City charity for the poor and the redemption of captives (fos. 26^r–27^r).

'M[aster] Doctor Powell'—either Dr William Powell, formerly rector of All Hallows Bread Street, and then Archdeacon of Bath; or Dr David Powell (d. 1598), canon of St Asaph (Foster, *ODNB*)—took as his text for Easter Tuesday James 1: 26–7, the famous apostolic definition of true religion as works of charity. Powell did little to control the text's potential applicability against *sola fideism*. Indeed, on this infamously controverted point he said only, 'every one shalbe encoraged to doe good, and lett vs never stand to dispute with the papists concerninge meritts and good workes, let me have care to serve God and to doe good to my breathren, and then if the lord shall give me salvation what is that to me, whether he give it me for desart or for of his free mercye these are but triffles, & are not to be stood one, lett vs goe one in good workes' (fo. 50ʳ). Significantly, of the two preceding sermons, it is Powell's that Andrewes singles out for special commendation (main text, p. 66, l. 37; *A1*, p. 261, ll. 9–10). On the spiritual as well as the social benefits of good works, Powell's conclusion is strikingly similar to Andrewes's: 'wherby we consecrate & vowe our selves in Godlines to God, to serve him in holines, and in righteousnes to our neighboures wherin lastly we have p[ro]mises in this life, and also of the ioyes of the life to come, here is the matter forme efficient and finall cause of religion' (fo. 46ᵛ).

Andrewes's Sermon. A nineteenth-century hand has entered in the right margin of the first page of Andrewes's text (fo. 51ʳ), 'Note. A remarkable circumstance this being the original Sermon differs materialy from the one in print. See Bp. Andrews Sermons pt. 2. page 1.' The text of *A1* does indeed depart significantly from that of *XCVI* (hereafter, references to this text are by line number as presented in this edition). But the differences are in matter cut or condensed from the latter in the former, not in the presence of anything substantially different between the two. It is this editor's summary judgement that *XCVI* gives the text as it was prepared to be preached, and that *A1* is a transcript of what Andrewes was actually heard to say on the day, when, presumably because of pressures of time, he made cuts during delivery.

In the first instance, *A1* contains nothing not in the structure and argument of *XCVI*, except for minor variations in exempla and diction which are entirely consistent with the delivery of a prepared text from memory. Thus, for example, *XCVI*'s 'So hath the *King* of *Kings* His *Lawes* and *Statutes*, His *Precepts* and *Commissions* by authority delegate' (p. 42, ll. 3–4) was recorded in *A1* (p. 244, ll. 4–5) as, 'so the lord of lords hath his lawes & statutes *Rom. 7*. his p[re]cepts and commissions.' The epithet '*King* of *Kings*' is replaced by a logical cognate ('lord of lords'); the scriptural reference to Romans is articulated where in the printed text it sits silently in the margin; and the qualifying prepositional phrase 'by authority delegate' is forgotten. Many passages in *A1* preserve the same arguments as *XCVI*, but do so in drastically abbreviated form. One section (*A1* p. 259, ll. 8–38) contains the same exempla as *XCVI* (p. 62, l. 1–p. 63, l. 2), but in a completely different order. Often what is lost in this category of changes (condensations and rearrangements of *XCVI*) is the verbal play for which Andrewes is famous. For example, although the key terms 'venture' and 'assurance' are present in *A1* (p. 253), lost through abbreviation is *XCVI*'s rich thematic wordplay on the same mercantile terminology (p. 53). Also notable are the frequent instances of *A1* occluding what in *XCVI* are sharp changes of topic signalled in print by paragraph breaks. Compare, for example, *A1* (p. 258, ll. 15–19),

> we must glory of nothing for that we have nothing or o[ur] owne, neither must we trust any thing, for that we have nothing of o[ur]selves, let vs trust in god that

giveth all things to every one to enioy, for it is the great goodnes of god that not only giveth vs all things to have them, but it is the same goodnes of god that giveth vs to enioy them...

with *XCVI* (p. 61, ll. 6–10),

we must *glorie* of nothing, for that we have nothing *of our owne*; neither must we *trust* any thing, for that we have *nothing of our owne*.
That giveth us all things to enjoy:] Not onely to *have*, but to *enjoy*. For, so to have them, that we have no *joy* of them...

A1 not only misses the paragraph break, but runs the argument of the two into a single sentence, presumably because the preacher did not, as in the prepared text, clearly begin a new argument by re-quoting the relevant portion of his scriptural text ('*That giveth us all things to enjoy*'). These changes of abbreviation could reflect any combination of three things: (1) the 'filter' of a note-taker; (2) abbreviation by Andrewes during delivery because of time constraints; or (3) a hasty post-delivery reconstruction by Andrewes. Similarly, any of these might also have resulted in the absence in *A1* of the more nuanced wordplay and unusual diction in *XCVI* (compare the absence in *A1* of the majority of unique usages documented above in the Headnote to the *XCVI* text).

As a final point on the minor departures between *A1* and *XCVI*, it should be noted that very occasionally *A1* contains exempla not found in *XCVI*. These are, however, minor additions that only elaborate points already present in *XCVI*, and which probably simply occurred to the preacher on the spot. The best examples of this are the addition (*A1*, pp. 247–8) of Philip of Macedon and Philip of Spain as further anecdotal evidence of military commanders who hire mercenaries (*XCVI*, p. 45, l. 40), and the detailed application in *A1* (p. 262) of the papal bull *Regnans in Excelsis* and the assassination of William of Orange as examples of papal treachery. These are only obliquely touched in *XCVI* (p. 71).

The most significant differences between the two texts, however, are in the passages completely absent from (rather than merely condensed in) *A1*. These fall into three categories. First, there is a consistent omission throughout *A1* of summary recapitulations of arguments found at the end of paragraphs in *XCVI*. These are documented in Appendix 2. Second, there are three drastic omissions of entire sections from the latter portion of the *XCVI* text (p. 65, l. 16–p. 66, l. 4; p. 69, l. 14–p. 71, l. 11; p. 73, l. 8–p. 79, l. 33), and, third, what is essentially a recomposition of the sermon's conclusion.

That the major cuts come in the last third of the sermon suggests that Andrewes abandoned them because of the constraint of time when in the pulpit. Powell had found himself in a similar situation (see above), but Andrewes perhaps tacitly abbreviated his sermon rather than (as Powell) admitting vocally that he was being tapped on the back and urged to bring matters to an end. The first cut (*XCVI*, 65–6) simply reduces the number of exempla used to define 'what is it to *do good*?' However, the choice of these, rather than others, may have been ideologically prompted. The missing matter includes the sermon's most stinging rebuke of City magnates' patronage of puritanism in its sarcastic warning that such persons should not dare to criticize lazy clergy as long as they themselves were lazy with their riches.

That the two other passages missing in *A1* were intended for delivery, and not added in a later revision, is strongly suggested by the fact that the *divisios* of both sermons include them. The first omission (*XCVI*, 69–71), on the 'quality' of good works, should follow logically from the preceding treatment of the 'quantity' of good works, as advertised in both *divisios* as the second part of the second 'affirmative' charge to do good works (*XCVI*, p. 41, ll. 21–4; *A1*, p. 244, ll. 7–10). In the body of *A1*, however, Andrewes departs from his *divisio* by first withholding the discussion of the 'quantity' of works (*XCVI*, p. 68, l. 3–p. 69, l. 14) and completely excising the discussion of their 'quality' (p. 69, l. 14–p. 71, l. 11). *A1* instead contains only the application of works to 'the church' (*XCVI*, p. 71, l. 12–p. 73, l. 7); *A1*, p. 261, l. 37–p. 262, l. 40), and then inserts the now repositioned passages on the 'quantity' of works (*XCVI*, p. 68, l. 3–p. 69, l. 14; *A1*, p. 262, l. 40–p. 263, l. 32).

Immediately after the repositioned material on works' 'quantity' comes the largest omission in *A1* (of *XCVI*, p. 73, l. 8–p. 72, l. 33). This eliminates the entire concluding portion of the sermon which had been announced in both *divisios*: the '*reason*' (*XCVI*) or '*occasion*' (*A1*) of doing good works, that laying up the '*foundation*' of good works leads to 'the *end*' of obtaining '*eternall life*' (*XCVI*, p. 41, ll. 25–27; *A1*, p. 244, ll. 10–12). That is, *A1* omits discussion of the third and final verse of the preacher's announced and divided text (1 Tim. 6: 19). As suggested, the omission of the final part of a sermon strongly suggests the preacher's need to abbreviate because of time running short. But it is also certainly significant that the portion cut is by far the most theologically avant-garde, and thus controversial, part of the prepared (*XCVI*) text. Without this, *A1* reads like a far more conventional exhortation to good works as a duty of the faithful, and loses entirely the more radical arguments which hint at the role of works in the economy of salvation. Andrewes may indeed have run out of time, having planned to elaborate a position on works even more avant-garde than that ventured by Powell. But Andrewes might also have chosen on the day to keep mum, especially if Powell's remarks on the Tuesday had raised eyebrows, or worse.

The conclusions of the two texts are similar, but reflect the changes Andrewes seems to have had to make between the version preserved in *XCVI*, and that in *A1*. The controlling conceit of both is the fear of hearing the apostle's 'charge' not in this life, or from a preacher, but from Christ himself at Judgement. However, the final paragraph of *A1* differs entirely from that of *XCVI* because it packs into its short space the images and arguments of works as a 'foundation' for life in heaven—precisely the material treated *in extenso* in the body of the *XCVI* text but cut in delivery. This new conclusion, therefore, was either a chance to make points, however briefly, that time had not allowed; or, it was a case of having deliberately saved potentially controversial language for the relative safety of the very few last minutes before leaving the pulpit. The absence of a concluding prayer in *A1* is most likely either because the note-taker stopped when the sermon did, or, if the text was prepared by Andrewes for the rehearser, because it was not an integral part of the sermon itself and therefore not of importance for his rehearsal purposes.

INDEX OF BIBLICAL TEXTS

This index includes scriptural citations in the lectures and sermons themselves, as well as scriptural sources mentioned in the introduction or cited in the commentary. References to Psalms cited or quoted in the Vulgate retain their unique numbering and are noted with (V). Scriptural texts of the sermons in this edition are given in italics.

Genesis
 1–3:13   348
 1:3   101, 353, 393
 1:6   353, 393
 1:7   350, 393
 1:9   393
 1:12   350
 1:14   148
 1:16   350
 1:22   350
 1:24   350
 1:26   148, 350, 393
 1:27   100, 349
 1:28   351
 1:29–31   350
 2:3   16, 33, 34, 299, 300
 2:6   100
 2:7   349
 2:8   458
 2:15   33
 2:16–17   349
 2:17   330
 2:18   100–7 passim, 348–53 passim
 2:19–20   101, 440
 2:23   409
 3:7   389
 3:15   169, 231, 352, 409
 4:10   294, 446
 4:16   295
 4:23   312
 6:2   107
 6:10   361
 7:7   361
 9:25–7   361
 10:9   191, 426
 11:1–9   293
 11:31   355
 12:1   355
 12:10–20   428, 429
 12:17   202, 432
 14   419
 14:14–16   359
 14:17–24   338
 14:20   87
 17:9–14   410
 18:2   24
 18:23   152
 18:25   152
 19:1–29   355
 19:5   294
 19:14   355
 19:15   362
 19:15–29   359
 19:16   359, 361
 19:17   109
 19:20   362, 365
 19:22   362
 19:24   212, 294
 19:26   112
 19:27   25
 19:30–8   361
 19:32   361
 20:1–14   429
 22:1–18   394
 22:1   23
 22:7   154
 22:11   12, 417
 22:18   378
 23:6   182, 419
 24:13   25
 24:26   24
 24:33   24
 25:30–4   309
 26:7–11   429
 26:11   200
 26:16   182
 27:22–3   430
 28:20   13
 31:24   193
 31:40   294
 32:6   49
 32:11   396
 35:22   190
 38:16   190
 40:22   343
 41:4   63, 90
 41:5   399
 41:38   155
 43:7   334
 48:22   182
 49:5–7   190
 49:10   176
 49:14   190

Exodus
 1:10   93
 1:16   152
 3:5   22
 7–12   359
 8   114, 318
 8:19   150
 10:12–20   344
 10:24   85
 12:2   149
 12:3   147
 12–13   376
 12:23   393
 12:27   24
 14   432
 15:11   403
 16:2–3   288
 16:3   110, 358
 16:13   110
 16:22–30   454
 16:28   358
 16:32–4   339
 17:1–10   339
 17:3   288
 17:4   16
 17:9   187
 17:11   25
 19:12   189, 200
 20:1–17   429
 20:2–3   285
 20:4–5   290, 291
 20:8–10   296
 20:10   300
 22:6   152
 25:17   274
 25:18–21   325

INDEX OF BIBLICAL TEXTS

25:19–20   454
25:19   231
25:23–30   357
30:22–33   424
31:29   427
32:6   158
33:10   25
33:11   30
33:17   240
34:27   334
34:33   216
35   68
36:13   296
49   426
49:10   413
49:14   426

Leviticus
2:13   360
4:3   421
4:16   421
5   88
5:15   343
6:9   141
7:16   87
13:46   351
19:30   22, 38
20:7   86
24:20   295
26:2   22, 38
27   87
27:30–3   340

Numbers
3:26   32
10:10   157
11:18   110
11:24–9   346
11:29   218
11:34   358
13:34   48
14:2–3   288
14:4   110
14:42   356
16   346, 423
16:3   187
16:21   201
16:24   201
16:31   93
18   90
18:19   341
18:21   88
18:26   343
21:8–9   129
21:8   369
23:10   25

23:15   26
23:18   26
23:25   43
24:11   309
26:9–11   423

Deuteronomy
4:13–14   35, 300
4:32   155
5:15   299–300
5:31   35
8:14–17   288
9:18   25
11:5   24
15:4   73
15:11   75
16:10   87
16:11   157
17:20   51
18:1–9   337
26:13   87
27:10   295
27:24   192
28:47   324
29:19   50
32:2   210
32:7   112, 357
32:32   109
33:8   86
33:19   40

Joshua
7   345
7:26   93
21:19–26   343
23:12–13   107

Judges
4:7   32
9:15   45
17:7–8   97
17:10   97
20:40   444

1. Samuel
2:10   420
2:15   48
2:35   420
2:36   97
8:22   14
9:21   46
10:1   422
10:9–10   191
12:3–4   183
12:3   420
12:5   420

12:23   16
13:14   18, 312
16:6   421
16:14   191
18:27   353
19:14   32
19:33   311
20:3   154
20:18   32
20:27   48
20:29   32
22:9   97
22:22   128
24:7   421
24:11   421
25:17   50
25:36   49
26:8–9   418
26:9   190, 421
26:11   421
26:16   421
26:19   179
26:23   421

2. Samuel
1:10   195
1:13   195
1:14   421
1:16   421
1:20   157
1:21   195
3   336
3:7   50
4:5–11   429
4:10–11   429
4:12   202
6:3–7   424
6:14–23   314
6:17–19   418
6:22   22
7:2   83
7:19   174
8:17   395
11:21   111
12:5   130
12:7   130
12:13   142, 387
15:25   14
16:5–13   427
17:7   104
18:3   151
19:16–21   401
19:21   183, 190, 421
20:1–2   401
20:24   151
22:3   317

INDEX OF BIBLICAL TEXTS

22:51 420
23 151
23:1 421

1. Kings
1:39-40 422
2:36-46 427
2:46 202
6:23-7 429
8:54 25
8:59 225, 450
10:11 318
10:22 318
11:26-40 336
12:11 426
12:25 343
12:31 97
13:33 346
14:15 360
16:8-10 429
17:1-16 328
19:18 23, 292
20:12 129
21 309
21:7 48
22:27 50

2. Kings
2:12 67, 322
7:19 412
11:16 93
13:14 322
14:9 49
22:8 43
25:8-21 396

1. Chronicles
11.20-47 395
13:10 189
16:1-43 418
16:1 203
16:4-6 419
16:5 203
16:8-36 418
16:8-22 417
16:14 417
16:15 183
16:21 417, 426, 427, 431
16:22 178-206 *passim*,
 417-33 *passim*
16:28 182
16:37 203
16:42 203
26:4 83
26:15 97, 346
26:18 97, 346

26:27-8 83
28:29 336
29:7 83
29:8 83
29:14 73, 90, 326
29:23 187

2. Chronicles
6:13 24
6:42 183, 420
13:5 121
13:6-12 343
15:3 96
20:12 12, 286
23:13 25
24:4-22 343
24:7 343
29:29 24
29:31 16
31:4 87, 92
31:6 92
31:10 97
33:16 16
35:10-22 374
35:23-5 374
84:9 420
89:38 420
89:51 420

Ezra
2:2 364
4:1-3 364
4:5 45
9:5 25
10:32 340

Nehemiah
1:11 71
8:4-5 26
8:9-10 157
8:10 400
10:33 88
13:4-11 343
13:6 91
13:10 96

Esther
2 428
2:21 194, 429
2:23 202
3:7 392
3:13 396
4:14 71
6:6 45
9:19 392
9:26 147

Job
1, 2 14
1:9 62
1:11 192, 430
1:18 152
1:19 152
1:21 60, 317, 318
2:4 78
2:5 192
3:3 148
3:6 148
6:15 114
7:1 414
7:6 414
7:7 111, 357
7:16-17 414
8:8 111, 112, 357, 358
8:9 111, 357
8:14 57
9:11 235
10:9 111, 357
14:13-14 414
16:10 216
19:5 331
19:9 22, 292
20:20 57
22:15 317
24:7 318
27:8 58
29:21 30
31:16 323
31:24 53
35:23 142
36:7 187, 191, 426
40:20-1 399
41:24 128

Psalms
1:3 160
2 409
2:4 398
2:7 169
2:11-12 413
2:11 159, 402
2:12 176
2:20 420
4:6 403
7:8 42
10:4 314
14:4 96
15:4 32
16 454
16:6 412
16:8 136
16:9 158, 231, 454
16:10 454

17:8   402
18:2   314
18:44   158
18:50   420
19:1   18
20:6   199, 420
21:2(V)   295
21:4   187
21:13   155
22   368
22:1   370, 371
22:2   371
22:16   124
23:4   393
24:1   60
25:1   11
25:21   12
27:4   13
28:5   129
28:8   420
29:9   19
30:11   458
34:3   27
35   391
35:13   16
35:14   17
35:27   403
37:3   63
37:5   59
37:6   105
37:7   352
37:13   398
39:3   143
39:5   406
39:6   406
40:6   241
40:7   176
40:9   17, 23
42:4   32
44:3   403
44:7(V)   420
44:8(V)   424
44:22   392
45:7   424
45:8   189
47:8   188
48:8   242
49:16   54
50:15   17
50:23   16
55:17   18
57:1   402
57:10   17
57:11(V)   360
58:7   360, 399
58:8   154

58:9   399
58:10   117, 360
62:8   11
62:10   47
63:7   402
64:3-4   125
64:8   154
64:9   399
65:11   148
66:4   400
66:14   17
66:18   223
67:2   214, 447
68   391, 398
68:18   442
68:26-8   153
68:26   158, 401
68:28   13
69   391
69:26   126
71:8   119
71:16   17
71:23   158
72:18   150
75:2(V)   440
76:1   214, 440
77:20   339
78:18   14
78:25-9   318
78:27   14
78:29   61
78:30   14
78:31   14
78:57   110
82:5   51
82:6(V)   314
82:6   186, 424
83:18   350
84:2   23
84:4(V)   285
85:3   12
85:4   12
86:17   154
88:9   25
88:16(V)   412
89:15   176
89:20   424
89:21   187, 188
89:23   12
89:37-8   433
89:38   205
89:43-4   433
89:44-5   205
89:48   330
90:4   76
90:8   403

90:13(V)   427
91:3   92
91:11   199
91:13   427
91:16   79
95   292
95:1   17
95:5   292
95:6   24
95:7   242
95:8   418
96   419, 432
101:5   48
103:8   412
104   182
104-6   419
104:14(V)   426, 431
105:1-15   417, 419
105:15   152, 419, 420, 423, 432
106:1   419
106:4, 6-7(V)   351
106:23   372
106:47-8   419
108:1   18
109:27   155
109:29   155
110:1   212, 216
110-18   419
111:1   17
111:4   146
115(V)   446
115:1   67
115:12 (V)   288, 377, 413
115:13(V)   413, 446
115:16   60
116:11-12   413
116:12-13   176
116:12   16, 134, 447
116:13   134, 223, 446
116:15   230
117:19(V)   402
117:23-4(V)   392, 398
117:27(V)   401
118   393
118:1-4   150, 161
118:3   156
118:5   394
118:6   151
118:8-9   150, 154
118:8   154
118:10-13   149, 394
118:11   151, 154
118:12   151, 395, 399
118:13   151
118:15-16   150, 394

INDEX OF BIBLICAL TEXTS

118:15 150
118:17 146, 149
118:19 157, 158
118:22 153, 364, 397, 403
118:23–4 146–61 *passim*,
   392–403 *passim*
118:25 159, 402
118:26 391, 393, 402, 403
118:27 403
118:54(V) 433
119:18 275
119:36 275
119:54 202, 205
119:60 358
119:63 32
119:73 13
119:79: 32
119:118 30, 295
119:132 136
119:164 18
119:165 42
119:175 18
121:1 25
122:1 27
122:6 16
123:1 25
125 13
125:1 160
124:7 398
126:1–4 400
126:1 156
126:2 156
127(V) 293
127:3 318
129:7(V) 438
130:7 211, 438
132:4 38
132:10 420
132:17 420
133:1 19
134–5 419
134:1 403
135:2 25
135:15 52
136:4 161
136:12 161
136:23–4 161
137:4 327
137:6 16
137:7 152
141:2 25
142:2 11
142:5 323
143:3 408
143:4 408
144:3 169

144:5 176, 205
144:15 61
145–6 419
146:3 330
146:20 419
147 419
147:1 19
147:12 17
147:20 61, 181, 214, 440
148–50 419
148 288
149:1 17
150 288

Proverbs
1:24 23
3:9 85
3:11 358
3:16 315
3:28 69
5:3–4 93
5:15 64
5:22 95
6:13 30
6:17 27
7:23 93
8:17 23
11:28 52
12:18 193
12:23 30
13:10 313
14:4 96, 338
14:9 30
15:13 324
15:14 29
16:6 143, 389
16:10 155
17:19 49
17:24 30
18:1 113, 358
18:5 30
18:10 13, 59, 286
18:11 52
19:12 275
20:17 93
20:25 82–99 *passim*,
   334–47 *passim*
20:28 412
23:4–5 53
23:31–2 93
25:4 144
25:12 30
25:21 145
27:1 159
27:24 53
29:18 96, 216

30:8–9 311
30:8 13
30:9 47
30:13 48
30:15 90, 321

Ecclesiastes
1:1 291
1:9 111
4:9–11 103
4:10 351
4:17 291
5:1 22, 30, 31
6:2–3 61
7:4 29
7:19 361
9:7–8 331
9:8 230
9:11 60
10:19 45
10:20 154, 399
11:8 111, 357
44:7 419

Song of Solomon (Canticles)
1:2–3 426
1:4 191
3:1 29
8:6 140, 385

Isaiah
1:25 141
2:9 23
5:27 29, 294
6 381
6:1 384, 385
6:3 86, 390
6:5 145, 385, 390
6:6[–7] 138–45 *passim*,
   378–90 *passim*, 408,
   412, 446
6:8 145, 211, 390, 438
6:9–10 30
7:9 109, 356
9:3 175
9:7 174
9:15 98, 347
12:14–16 216
14:16 156
23:3 40
23:8 40
24:13 16
27:1 399
32:14–15 440
32:17 295
36:6 58

38:21 144
40:6 213
40:8 51
40:24 343
43:1–3 xxx
43:18 129
44:22 144
45:1 183, 190
45:1–7 440
45:1 185, 420
46:9 112, 357
49:16 132
51:8 94
51:21 217
53:5 374
53:6 128
53:7 392
53:8 323
53:10 124
56:7 158, 351
56:11 89
58:1 43
58:13 86
59:1 58
61:1–2 436
62:3 187, 423
62:5(V) 423
62:6 111
64:1 176
65:12 23
65:24 16

Jeremiah
1:1 280
2:10 155
4:31 70
5:9 325
5:29 325
5:31 219, 443
6:10 51
6:13 141
6:16 112, 358
8:4 109, 355
23:28 441
23:29 143
30:16 95
31:12 236
31:15 152
31:22 156

Lamentations
1:12 129, 366
3:22 398
4:20 183, 190, 421

Ezekiel
3:18 98
3:20 98
9:4 120
11:3 48
13:17–18 309
18:24 118
22:18 141
23:31 358
28:12 40
28:14 71
33:28 358
33:31 26
36:31 139
47:3–5 175
48:14 90

Daniel
2:32–3 110, 363
3:17–18 13
3:27 153, 432
4:14 186
4:17 422
4:22 186
4:24 21, 290
4:25 422
4:29 186
4:32 422
5:1–4 343
5:24–5 93
5:26 199
7:9 393
7:13 393
7:22 393
9:16 12
9:26 123, 124
9:27 152, 396

Hosea
2:15 226
4:4 50
4:5 49
5:12 94
6:4 114
6:5 50
6:6 296
7:5 158
7:7 96
9:8 96
11:4 103

Joel
2:11 444
2:23 211, 438
2:28–32 435

2:30 152
2:31 446
2:32 446

Amos
1:1 280
6:13 52
8:5 318
8:12 114

Jonah
1:2–3 309
2:8 359
3 440
3:10 358
4:6–7 328, 402
4:7 103

Micah
2:1 53

Nahum
1:3 345

Habbakuk
1:4 48
2:2 375
2:10 30
3:13 183

Zephaniah
1:7 30
1:9 323
3:3 48

Haggai
1:4 83, 336
1:6 95
2:8 317
2:9 60
2:16–17 95

Zechariah
4:6–10 364
4:10 150
9:11 134
11:12 97
12:10 122–37 *passim*, 366, 367–78 *passim*
12:11 131
13:1 134, 140, 376

Malachi
1:8 31, 295
1:14 31, 295

INDEX OF BIBLICAL TEXTS

2:3   158
2:7   142, 387
3:8   89
3:11 95
4:1   396

Wisdom
1:12   80, 330
11:17 164

Ecclesiasticus
21:14 29
21:17 29
44:7   314

2. Maccabees
1:10   421

Matthew
2:16   152
2:25   111
2:27   33
3:7   395
3:8   xxx
3:10   345
3:11   208
4:1   351
4:6   199, 431
4:9   22, 23
5:15   21
5:22   442
5:44   16
6   55
6:9–13 275
6:11   318
6:13   318
6:19   330
6:19–20 317, 345
6:20   326
7:4–7 329
7:6   86
7:7   16
7:15   361
7:22   222, 335, 445
7:24–5 279
7:27   77
8:8   142
8:9   23, 27
8:31   387
9:13   32, 296
9:20–2 388
9:20   142
9:33   156
9:37   65
10:2–4 361
10:4   104
10:22 378
10:24 310
11:7   119, 363
11:8   338
11:11 409
11:12 135, 377
11:14 40
11:15 40
11:28 109, 355
11:29 45, 310
12:34 395
12:41–2 418
12:41 374
12:42 64
12:45 120
13:3–12 328
13:17 377
13:20 114
13:22 54
13:27–30 463
13:29 152
13:33 309, 401
13:37–40 328
16:18 9, 283
16:22 119, 362
17:5   174
18:6   120
18:23–35 327
19:6   418
19:8   299
19:21 327
19:35–6 286
20:22 13
20:28 173
21:9   159, 160, 391, 393, 401, 402
21:15 402
21:16 402
21:42 364, 397
22   90
22:1–14 352
22:12 28
22:21 92, 339
22:36–40 301
22:37–8 343
22:38 418
23:13 438
24:8   220
24:13 360
24:15 86, 152, 153, 396
24:20 36
24:28 96
24:30 378
24:36 378
25   287, 288, 289, 290
25:12 292
25:14–15 442
25:14 218
25:15 211
25:21 177
25:27 327
25:31–46 322
25:31–2 385
25:41 31, 295
26:7   231
26:8   440
26:14–16 345
26:15 310, 346
26:17–30 452
26:27 289, 383
26:28 134, 177, 383, 384, 446
26:33 110, 356
26:36–44 351
26:38 125
26:39 13, 25
26:40–56 293
26:40 29
26:53 130
27:5   345
27:24 128
27:45 374
27:46 126, 368, 370, 371
27:49 126
27:51 374
27:54 130
28:9   238, 458
28:13 227
28:19 42

Mark
1:11   418
1:41   387
2:12   156
2:16   152
3:32   26
5:7   374
5:13   14
5:20   20
9:29   152
9:43–6 446
9:48   446
12:10–11 397
12:25 351
13:21 182, 419
13:32 278
13:36 29
14:3–9 358
14:4   83, 327

14:4–6   336
14:10   361
14:33   126
14:34   125
15:14   396
15:34   371
15:40   451
16:1–3   451
16:9   225
16:12   236

Luke
1:68   317
1:69   314
1:78   317
2:1   339
2:10–14 450
2:12   xxxvii
2:13   231, 350
2:14   18, 289
2:21   171, 410
2:23–4   339
2:26   183
2:55   125
3:22   213
4:18–19 436
4:18   210, 437
4:20   30
4:21   146
4:25   438
5:13   387
5:14   20
5:17   26
5:26   156
5:32   374
6:24   76
6:38   328
7:36–50 450
7:37   226, 451
7:47   227
8:18   30
8:44   388
9:62   119, 362
10:1   104
10:16   30, 295
10:17–20 315
10:24   176
10:32   129
10:39   26, 450
11:8   15
12   55
12:15–21 316
12:18   323
12:19   64
12:20   56
12:22   316

12:47   27, 317
12:48   68
13:25   445
13:26   222
13:27   445
14:24   23
14:30   119, 362
15:13   91, 343
16:1–13 327
16:14   51
16:19–31 319
16:19   64
16:20–5 328
16:22–4 326
16:24   68
16:25   306
17   354
17:5   13
17:11–19 289
17:15–16 377
17:18   108
17:28   24
17:31   358
17:32 xxxiv, 108–21
         passim, 353–65 *passim*
17:33   363
18:2   15
18:11   312
18:13   25
19:8–9   319
19:38   160
19:40   375
19:42   235
19:44   235, 359
20:17   397
21:18   398
21:28   136
22:3–6   345
22:31   12
22:37   211, 438
22:41   25
22:42   446
22:44   126
22:61–2 378
22:61   136
23:14–15 127
24:16   236, 241
24:17   238
24:32   29, 137, 145, 242
24:35   242

John
1:1   454
1:3   101
1:7–9   386
1:7   141

1:14   168, 171, 408, 439,
         454
1:16   177, 212
1:18   408
1:24   212
1:29   376
1:42   32
1:45   32
2:20   86
3:14   123, 369
3:16   374, 408
3:27   318
4:14   213, 439
5:26   317
6:35   320
7:6   164
7:27   378
7:39   210
8:4   345
8:14   344
8:44   151
8:46   127, 371
9:5   409
10:8   228, 229
10:11–17 225–42 *passim*,
         447–61 *passim*
10:12   361
10:18   130
11:35   355
11:36   133, 376
11:41   25
12:3–8   327
12:3   231, 451
12:4–8   343
12:6   345
12:8   72
12:13   160
12:15   160
12:23   165
12:27   126
12:41   140, 384, 385
12:48   331
13:1   409
13:29   64, 97
15:3   143
15:4   109, 355
15:13   130
16:7   102, 350
16:12   147
17:1   25
17:15   12
17:17   86
18:6   130, 374
18:11   446
19:5   373
19:11   186

INDEX OF BIBLICAL TEXTS 475

19:30 363
19:34 367, 376, 377
19:37 122, 135, 369
19:39 240
20:1 451
20:10–29 449
20:11–17 447–61 *passim*
20:11–18 449
20:22 213
20:25 142
20:28 133
21:20 119, 362
22:17 425
22:42 13

Acts

1:5 210
1:7 166
1:8 450
1:12 301
1:18–19 344
2 301
2:1 28
2:1–15 435
2:3–4 436
2:3 214, 437
2:4 440
2:5 214
2:11 216
2:13 xxxvii, 436, 441
2:15 436
2:16–21 207–224 *passim*, 433–47 *passim*
2:21 433
2:23 371, 372
2:31 216
2:33 213
2:34 216
2:37 131, 137
2:46 324
3:19 142
4:11 364, 397
4:24 28
4:35 87
5:1–10 343
5:1–5 345
5:3 89, 95, 345
5:10 93
5:17–28 308
7:51 293
8:6 28
8:9 45
8:19 46
8:20 70
8:22 143
8:27–39 279
8:32 392
8:34 122
8:35 367
11:29 88
13:8 32
13:16 30
13:33 226
13:41 156
14:15–17 318
15:9 214
16:14 30, 314
17:27 235
19:35 308
20:7 28, 37
20:9 26, 29
20:24 145
20:29 361
20:35 19, 324
20:36 25
21:9–10 441
21:16 355
22:16 141
24:1–26 311
24:17 88
24:26 46
27:30–32 200
28:4 347
28:24 99

Romans

1:8 110
2:5 79
3:2 441
3:8 152
3:15 372
6:17 324
6:23 116, 363
7 42, 464
7:14 172
7:15 385
7:18 110
8:3 439
8:11 317
8:17 174
8:21 117
8:29 169
8:32 133
8:36 392
10:12 214
10:13 275, 445, 446
10:14 222
10:15 216, 441
11:4 292
11:19 361
11:22 109, 118, 356, 361
12:1 330
12:3 50
12:6 324
12:11 145
12:13 71
12:19 145
13:7 90, 92
16:20 408
16:27 289

1. Corinthians

1:3 330
2:2 124
2:11 378
3:6 458
3:11 77
3:13 216
4:7 318
5:7–8 376
5:8 309, 401
6:5 195
6:16 428
6:20 22, 26
7:1 104, 351, 352
7:5 21
7:25–40 352
7:28 105
7:35 105
7:36 104
8:9 363
9:8 345
9:9 212
9:10 96
9:13 87, 92
10:1–4 407
10:5 158
10:6 407
10:12 109, 355
10:13 12
10:14 49, 313
10:15 144
10:16 446
11:3 231
11:4 23, 24
11:10 31
11:22 28, 38
11:26 123
11:28 11
11:33 27, 32
12 211
12:4–6 442
12:7 51
12:10–14 6
12:10 6, 441
12:11 6, 212, 279, 438
12:13 177
12:29 218

14:23 26
14:25 26
14:31 218, 442
14:32 218
14:34 217
15:22 349
15:28 177, 414
15:32 151
15:45 241, 349
15:58 76
16:1 88
16:2 37
16:22 431

2. Corinthians
1:9 317
1:13 364
4:4 339
4:15 16, 70
5:1 76
5:11 219, 443
5:18 142
5:21 171
6:2 177
8:20 97
9:6 75, 97, 323
9:7 323, 331
9:8 69
9:12 97
10:5 50
11:20 85
12:8 14, 15

Galatians
1:16 51
2 405
2:9 214, 440
2:10 9
2:23–9 440
3:1 123
3:3 119
3:5 411
3:6 412
3:23 411
3:24 407
3:28 104
4:1–7 406
4:1 407
4:2 407
4:3 407
4:4 328
4:4–5 162–77 *passim*, 403–14 *passim*
4:7 60, 61
5:3 170

5:7 121
5:12 456
5:15 98
5:24 281, 375
6:6 71

Ephesians
1:3 364
1:4 86
1:7 445
1:10 405
1:18 68
1:23 177
2:12 167, 172
2:14–15 37
2:14 214
2:20 77, 397
3:8 441
3:14 25
3:17 328
3:18 77, 329
4:13 164
4:30 177
5 86
5:2 318
5:6 28
5:22–33 349
5:25 100
5:26 86
6:10 408

Philippians
1:7 365
1:18 311
2:7 22, 168, 291, 408
2:8 22, 292, 456
2:10 292, 397
3:10 242
3:13 117, 361
4:10 97
4:11 17
4:12 83

Colossians
1:10 69
1:23 77
2:9 167, 212, 231
2:14 170, 171, 410
3:5 52, 281, 375
4:6 360

1. Thessalonians
1:10 363
4:3 86
4:13 238, 458

5:6–7 294
5:7 28
5:12 50
5:20 441

2. Thessalonians
1:7–8 330
2:1 330
2:16 330
2:17 402

1. Timothy
1 8
1:3–4 309
1:7 49
1:9 170
1:15 374
1:17 331
2:2 203
2:8 25
2:14 352
3:2 97
3:7 106
4:5 86
4:8 33
4:10 317
4:14 441
6:8 318
6:10 125
6:13 330
6:17–19 40–81 *passim*, 307–31 *passim*
6:19 466
6:20 320

2. Timothy
1:9 300
2:2 16
2:19 222, 446
2:26 92
3:4 49, 313
3:9 7
4:7 121
4:8 329
4:16 110, 356

Titus
2:10 26
2:14 318
3:8 323
3:11 7

Hebrews
1:1–12 406
1:2 174, 423

INDEX OF BIBLICAL TEXTS 477

1:3   174, 386
1:4–5   184, 421
1:6   231
1:12   330
2:1   111, 169, 357
2:10   174, 351
2:16   169, 408
3:14   328
4:3   454
4:9   231
4:14   376
4:15   409
5:1   343
5:5   281
5:14   7
6:6   127
8:20–1   xxx
9   424
9:5   274
10:1–25   376
10:5   143, 387, 413
10:27   311
10:29   134, 208
10:32   112, 358
11:9   76
11:18–19   394
11:19   149
11:25   63, 319
12.2   123, 362, 366, 369
12:5   358
12:10   189
12:22   31, 339
12:24   223
12:25   31
13:4   86
13:5   17
13:8   402
13:22   325

James
  1:5   62
  1:11   56
  1:14   106

1:17   59, 213, 288
1:22   xxii, xxxvi
1:23–4   111
1:26–7   305–6, 464
1:27   66, 321
2:6   48
2:14–17   321
4:3   14
4:4   316
5:10   24, 112, 358
5:13   12
5:15   15, 21

1. Peter
  1:3   364
  1:12   31, 295
  1:18–19   173
  1:18   411
  1:19   134, 411
  1:24   314
  2:4   397
  2:6   397
  2:15   67, 322
  2:18   28, 293
  3:5   24
  3:18   144
  5:8   344
  12:3   131

2. Peter
  1:4   174, 389
  1:17–18   418
  1:19   208, 436
  2:20   5
  3:8   328
  3:18   13
  3:19   5

1. John
  3:1   167, 408
  3:17   54
  3:18   458
  5:14   13, 286

5:16   15
5:18   206

Jude
  6   51
  10   49
  11   187

Revelation
  1:1   142
  1:7   136, 378
  1:8   120
  1:10   37, 301
  1:15   293
  3:15   141
  3:16   339
  4:10–11   28
  4:10   22
  5:1   375
  5:6–10   463
  5:13   289
  6:7   363
  6:16   136
  7:9   230
  7:12   18
  7:17   458
  9:3   151
  10:6   177
  11:6   438
  12:4   96
  12:9–10   331
  14:2   418
  14:13   230, 418
  16:1   438
  19:6   293
  19:10   122, 216
  20   443
  20:6   231
  20:10   363
  21:4   458
  21:14   328
  22:1   212
  22:5   363

GENERAL INDEX

This index covers only the editorial matter (Introduction and Commentary) in this edition. Biblical persons, events and places are not included (for these, use Biblical Index).

Abbot, George xxviii, lx, 349
Abelard, Peter 451
Abraham ben Ezra 333
absolutism 415, 417, 422; *see also* James VI & I; patriarchalism
Addison, Joseph xliii
adoption, *see* Holy Spirit
Aeschylus 395
Alanus de Insulis 326
Alcuin 405, 406
Alençon, Francis, duc d' 364
allegory 282, 385
almsgiving xvii, xxiii, 290, 304, 327–8, 463, 464
Alvey, John 332–3
Ambrose lvi, 283
   De Cain et Abel 287
   De Spiritu Sancto 434, 437
   Expositio Evang. Sec. Lucam 448–9, 450, 457
Ames, William 294
Anabaptists 299, 405, 408–9, 423, 441, 443
'analogy of faith' 324, 351
Andradius (Dieguus Payva Dandrada) 277, 278, 279, 280, 283, 285
Andrewes, Joan (mother of Lancelot) xv, lviii
Andrewes, Lancelot
  LIFE
   childhood and education xv, lviii
   ordination xv, lviii
   college catechist xv–xvi, lviii
   London preferments xvi–xviii, lviii
   prebend of Southwell lviii
   royal chaplain xxi, lviii
   canon of Westminster xxiii, lix, 365
   dean of Westminster xxiii, lix, 422
   bishop of Chichester xiii, xxiii, lix, 391
   lord high almoner xxiii, xxviii, xxix, lix, lx
   translator of Authorized Version xxvii–xxviii, lix
   bishop of Ely xxvii, xviii
   privy councillor xxviii, lix, 428
   dean of the Chapel Royal xxix, lix, 435, 449
   bishop of Winchester lix, xxix
   illness and death xxix–xxx, lx
   will l n., lx
   library of 295, 382, 448, lx; *see also* Cambridge, Pembroke College Library
  WORKS—GENERAL
   manuscripts xv, xvii, xviii n., xxiv, xxxviii n., li–ii, 347, 404, 433, 447–8, 449, 450, 462–6
   quarto texts xlix–x, liv
   sermons printed by royal command xxv, xxxviii, xlix
   XCVI Sermons xii–xiii, xv, xvii–xx *passim* xxi, xxiii, xxiv, xxv, xxxviii n., xlv, xlviii, xlix, li, lii, liii–iv
   Library of Anglo-Catholic Theology (*LACT*) xiii–xiv, l, lii, liii, liv, lv, 448, 449; *see also* Wilson, J. P.; Bliss, James
   Ash Wednesday sermons xxiv
   Christmas sermons xiv, xxiv–xxv, xxvi
   Easter sermons xxiv, xxvi, 448
   Good Friday sermons 365–6, 367
   Gowrie Plot sermons xxvi–xxvii, liii, 415–16, 432
   Gunpowder Plot sermons xxvi–xxvii, 390–2, 415
   Whitsunday sermons 433, 435, 439
  WORKS—INDIVIDUAL, EXCLUDING *XCVI SERMONS*
   ΑΠΟΣΠΑΣΜΑΤΙΑ SACRA xviii–xix, l, 347–8, 378–9, 446, 458
   Concio ad Clerum pro gradu Doctoris xx, 272
   Concio . . . in discessu Palatini 272
   De Decemis 333
   De Usuris 324
   Learned Discourse on Ceremonies 442
   Manual . . . for the Sick xviii, 359
   Morall Law Expounded 276–303 *passim*
   'Notes on the Book of Common Prayer' 292
   Opuscula Quædam Posthuma xx, xxxviii
   Pattern of Catechistical Doctrine (1650) xv–xvi, l, 276–303 *passim*, 355, 356, 358, 359, 360, 362, 363, 364

GENERAL INDEX

Patterne of Catechisticall Doctrine
   (1630-42) 276-303 *passim*, 297, 321
Preces Privatae (ed. Brightman) xvi, xliii,
   274, 285, 384, 385, 389, 410
Private Devotions (1647) 272
Responsio ad ... Bellarmini lix, 416, 430
Scala Coeli 285, 387
Seven Sermons (1627) 272, 362
Seventeen Sermons on the Nativity (1887) xiv
Speech Against ... Traske 298, 394, 441
Tortura Torti lix, 416, 420, 425
Two Answers to Cardinal Perron 382, 424
The Wonderfull Combate (1592) 272, 410

WORKS—FROM *XCVI SERMONS*
'Of Absolution' 383, 387, 388
Ash Wednesday 1593 302
Christmas 1605 408
Christmas 1607 xxii, 279
Christmas 1609 389
Christmas 1610 450
Christmas 1612 383-4, 388, 389
Christmas 1613 412
Christmas 1618 xxxvi, 450
Christmas 1619 450
Christmas 1620 413
Christmas 1622 xiv
Christmas 1623 388, 389, 405
Easter 1608 453
Easter 1610 369, 412, 414
Easter 1611 300, 364, 397, 403
Easter 1614 293, 453
Easter 1615 302
Easter 1618 298, 394
Easter 1621 427, 441, 450
Easter 1622 450
Good Friday 1604 369, 371, 372, 375, 377, 378
Good Friday 1605 321, 362, 368, 369, 375, 376, 378
Gowrie 1606 402
Gowrie 1609 418
Gowrie 1616 392, 428
Gunpowder 1607 400
Gunpowder 1612 372, 398
Gunpowder 1617 293, 294, 389, 442
Gunpowder 1618 392
Lent 1591 339
Lent 1592 336
Lent 1593 358
Lent 1596 306, 319
Whitsunday 1608 440
Whitsunday 1615 413, 439
Whitsunday 1617 436, 437, 439, 440
Whitsunday 1620 383, 388, 389
'Worshipping of Imaginations' 386

Andrewes, Thomas (father of Lancelot) xv, lviii, 305
angels 437, 450, 453, 455
   analogous to priests 382, 384, 386, 390
   'guardian' 454-5
anointing xxvii, 416, 417, 421
   at baptism 419
   of bishops 346
   of kings 419, 421
Anne of Denmark, queen of England 391, 395, 417, 428
Annunciation, the 300
Anselm 366, 389
anti-Calvinism lx, 333, 348, 353; *see also* predestination; perseverance
anti-Catholicism 417
Aquaviva, Claudio 429-30
Aquinas, Thomas 280, 282, 373
Arboreus, Johannes 334
Archer, Ian 306, 307
Aristotle xxxi, lvii, 300, 307, 461
   Ethics 396
   The Problems of Aristotle (1595) 377
   Physica 427
Arius, Arians 284
Ark of the Covenant 274, 325
Armada, the Spanish (1588) xvi, 274, 275, 304, 317, 325, 343, 359, 391
Ascentiontide 441
Athanasius 389-90
atheism 278, 338-9
Atonement, the 366, 367, 372, 389-90
Aubrey, John xxxix n., xli, 294, 301
Augustine lvi, 293, 295, 302, 306, 307, 320, 354, 360, 365, 368, 456, 457; *see also* Prosper of Aquitaine
   Contra Epist. Manichaei 279
   Contra Julianum 283
   Contra Max. Episc. Arian. 350
   De Bono Conjugali 348, 352
   De Civitate Dei 363, 443
   De Doctrina xxxi, 280, 281, 324
   De Genesi ad Litteram 348, 350, 351
   De Grat. et Lib. Arb. 300
   De Virginitate 378
   Enarr. in Psalmos 286, 290, 293, 317, 357, 368, 418, 426
   Epistolae 283, 286, 443
   In Joann. Evang. Tract. 287, 288, 349, 376, 377, 384
   In Joann. Evang. Tract. CXXI (on Mary Magdalen) 448-56 *passim*, 460, 461
   Quaestiones in Hept. 419-20
   Retractionem 318
   Scala Paradisi, see Bernard of Clairvaux

GENERAL INDEX

Sermones de Scripturis 286, 287, 308, 309, 310, 311, 312, 314, 315, 316, 321, 326–7, 330, 341, 345, 377, 405, 409
Sermones de Temp. 288, 290, 377

B., R., (*trans.*) 354
Babington Plot 312, 364
Bacon, Sir Francis xxviii, xxxiii, xl n., 357
Bach, J. S. xxxix
Badger, George 276
Badger, Richard xii, l n., liii, 331
Badger, Thomas 331
Bancroft, Richard xvi, xxviii, lix, 310, 332, 334, 338, 342, 395, 434
baptism 381, 386, 388, 438, 439, 453; *see also* Holy Spirit
   instituted at crucifixion 377
   names given at 400, 410, 419
Barker, Charles l n.
Barker, Robert (King's Printer) xxv, l, 403, 404, 414, 447
Barker, Robert (jr.) l n.
Barlow, William 392, 396, 399, 400
Baro, Peter 353
Barrett, William 353
Barrow, Henry lviii, 297, 299, 332, 412, 434, 435, 441, 443
Bartholomaeus, Anglicus 322, 444
Basil lvi, 302, 362, 381, 383
   De Spiritu Sancto 284
   Epistolae 283, 287
   Homiliae 319
Bateman *or* Batman, Stephen, *see* Bartholomaeus, Anglicus
Baumgartner, Frederic 425
Baynes, Ralph 333, 336
Beal, Peter li
Becon, Thomas 350
Bede, the Venerable 284–5, 410
Bedel, William 282
Bellarmine, Robert xxviii, lii, lix, 416, 420, 422, 430
   de Laicis 422
   Disputationes 278, 280, 382, 384, 387, 388
Bennett, Kate xli n., 294, 301
Bernard of Clairvaux lvi, 354, 360–1, 364, 366, 456, 459, *see also* Pseudo-Bernard; Nicholas of Clairvaux
   Epistolae 365
   In Cant. Cantic. 373, 375, 459–60
   Scala Paradisi 281
   Sermones 288, 289, 290, 294, 361, 362, 373, 413
Beaumont, Joseph 460
Bible lvi, 346

The Bible in English Database lv, lvi
Bishops 368
Douai-Rheims xxviii, lvi, lvii, 278, 290, 291, 306, 324, 328–9, 330, 387, 388–9, 396, 407, 413, 438
Geneva lvi, 438
   glosses 330, 331, 338, 356, 370–1, 371, 377, 384, 385, 392, 396, 399, 413, 424, 446, 454, 458
   preface 364
interpretation of xxxiii–iv, 278–85; *see also* allegory; 'analogy of faith'; type, typology
trans. Tremellius 348–9, 367, 383, 387, 406, 407, 408, 412, 417
Vulgate xliv, 349, 367, 406, 407, 408, 417, 423
Bibliotheca Teubneriana Latina lvii
Bill, John 447
Bilson, Thomas 382
bishops 285, 320, 328, 333, 334, 335, 337, 342, 345, 424, 431, 440
Bisse, Philip (?) 304, 305, 309, 317, 319–20, 321, 322, 323, 325, 326, 462–3
Blench, J. W. 367
Bliss, James lii, lv
Boas, F. S. 343
Bodin, Jean 292
Bonaventure 372
Book of Common Prayer 301, 333, 369, 424; *see also* liturgy
   (1549) 292, 368
   (1552) 293, 368
   (1559) 273, 293, 364
   appointed ('proper') lessons 354, 367, 393, 406, 407, 450
Borrhaius, Martinus 382
Boucher, Jean 425
Boys, John 408–9, 409
Brennus 344
Bridges, John 395
Brigden, Susan 307
Bright, Arthur (?) 304, 305, 462–3
Brightman, F. E. xvi n., xxxix n., 274
Buckeridge, John lix, 276, 298, 331
   ed., Andrewes, *XCVI Sermons* xii, xiii, xiv, xv, xvii, xviii, xli, xlviii, xlix, l
   funeral sermon for Andrewes xi n., li, 445
Bullinger, Heinrich 382, 384, 385, 387
Bünting, Heinrich 354, 360, 362
Burchardus Wormaciensis 341
Burgess, John 463
Burns, J. H. 418
Burton, Henry lx, 297, 299, 299–300, 300, 301

Caesarius of Arles 356
Cajetan (Thomas de Vio) 282, 283, 333, 420
Calvin, John lvii, 306, 315, 353, 366, 380, 387, 454
  In Librum Psalmorum 368
  Institutes 381, 388, 413, 455
Calvinism, Calvinists xiii, xvii, xix, xx, xxii, 359, 373, 380, 411, 442, 446; *see also* anti-Calvinism
Cambridge 301, 334
  colleges 343–4
  Emmanuel College 301
  Pembroke Hall (later College) xv, xvii, xxviii, lviii, 277
  library lvi–vii, 277, 295, 375, 420
  Regius Professor of Divinity, *see* Whitaker, William
  St. Mary's church 294, 331
  Trinity College xxxix n.
  library li, 272, 447
  University xx, 274, 278, 304, 331–3, 335, 345, 353
  Vice-Chancellor, *see*, Preston, Thomas
Cambyses, king of Persia 344
Camfield, Benjamin 455
Campion, Edmund 306, 320
Cano, *or* Canus, Melchior 280
canons 283, 295, 380, 420; *see also* Church of England; Councils, church
Cardwell, E. 415
Carey, John xlvii n.
Carleton, Sir Dudley xxv, 404, 449
Carlson, Eric J. 435, 444
Carlson, Leland 435
Carr, Sir Robert, later earl of Somerset 427
Cartwright, Thomas xx, 434
Casaubon, Isaac xxviii
Cassiodorus 426
Catesby, Richard 390, 396, 397, 399
Catholic League, the 425
Cecil, Sir Robert, later earl of Salisbury lix, 390, 395, 399, 417, 428
Cecil, Sir William, later lord Burghley 337
Cerularius of Constantinople 284
Chaderton, William lviii
Chamberlain, John xxv, xxviii, xlii n., 404, 449
Chambers, A. B. 367
Chambers, D. D. C. lvii n.
Chapel Royal (institution) xii, xxi, xxxix n., 391–2, 401, 402, 445; *see also* worship
  Children of the Chapel 402
chapels royal (buildings) xxi, xxix, 311, 377
  Greenwich lx, 435
  Hampton Court xxxix n., 353
  Holyrood xxix, 434, 436
  Whitehall lx, 391, 400, 403, 406, 447

Chapman, George 294
Charlemagne, emperor 421
Charles I, king of England and Scotland xii, xxix, xxx, xlvii, lx, 297, 395, 417, 444
Charles II, king of England and Scotland 347
Charles V, king of Spain 427
Charlwood, John 272
Chemnitz, Martin (Kemnisius) xx, lvii, 380
  De Duabus Naturis in Christo 382, 384, 388
  Examinis Concilii Tridentini 382, 383, 384, 386, 388, 389, 390
Cheyney, Edmund 381
Chillingworth, William 282
chrism 424
chrismation, *see* anointing
Christian IV, king of Denmark 401
Christmas, Christmastide 406, 410–11, 412, 413, 414, 461; *see also* liturgy
Chrysostom l, lvi, 286, 289, 293, 302, 306, 317, 348
  Commentary on the Acts 434, 436, 443, 445, 446
  Commentary on the Psalms 315
  De Virginitate 351
  Divine Liturgy 383
  Homilies 280, 287, 288, 289, 290, 294, 302, 329, 351, 381–2
  On the Incomprehensible Nature of God 290
Church, the 279
  'militant' and 'triumphant' 275, 325, 463
  excommunication 425
Church of England, *see also* Book of Common Prayer; laity
  Articles of Religion (1571, 'Thirty-nine Articles') 329, 381, 387, 409, 422
  Book of Homilies 297, 328
  canons (1606) 273, 420, 434
  lands and tithes xx–xxi, xxiii, 332–3, 334–47 *passim*
  Ordinal 346
  Royal Injunctions (1559) xv, 272
  royal supremacy 275, 432, 440, 442
churches (buildings) 291, 336, 337, 347; *see also* worship; liturgy
Cicero xxii, xxxi, lvii, 307, 311, 333, 354
  De Officiis 365
  De Senectute 346
  Pro Cnaeo Plancio 288
  Pro Sext. Rosc. 295
  Tusculan Disputations 345
  Verrine Orations 311
circumcision 410
  of Christ 405
clergy 330
  attire 346
  celibacy 352

non-residence 336–7, 343, 463
pluralism 336–7
'seminary' or 'missionary' priests 325, 355
simony 325–6, 463
Cliffe, J. T., 334
Coke, Sir Edward 394, 395, 396, 397, 399, 400
Collinson, Patrick 307, 313, 335, 342
confession xviii
Constantius, Byzantine emperor 425
Cooke, Thomas 363
Corpus Juris Civilis 341
Councils, church 279, 283–4, 341, 425; *see also* canons
    Basle 283–4
    Carthage 295
    Constance 283–4
    Constantinople 284
    Ephesus 420, 425
    Ferrara 283
    Florence 283–4
    Frankfurt 420
    Nicaea 284
    Toledo (4th) 420
    Trent 278, 280, 301, 380, 382
    Conciliorum Omnium (Venice, 1585) 420, 425
Court of Augmentations 335
Cowper, William (bp.) 410
Coxe, H. O. 274
Cranmer, Thomas 274, 287, 289, 292, 337, 338, 346, 381–2, 387, 447; *see also* Book of Common Prayer
Crashaw, Richard 405, 460
Crassus, M. Licinius 344
Cressy, David 392, 396, 401, 446, 454
Croft, Pauline 417, 428, 435
Cromwell, Thomas 335
Crooke, Andrew 347
Crowley, Robert 355
Crick, Richard 296
crucifix xxiii, lx, 366
Cyprian xliv, 318, 405, 406
Cyril of Alexandria 381, 384, 385, 420, 425

Damasus 284
Davies, Horton xlvii n.
'deification', *see* 'divinization'
Deventer 310
Devereux, Robert 3rd earl of Essex lix
Didymus Alexandrinus ('The Blind') 350, 434, 455
Dionysus the Great 283
'divinization' *or* 'deification' 389–90, 411–12, 414
divorce 299

Doerkson, Daniel xlvii n.
Dohna, baron von 310
Donne, John xxxv, xlvii, 348
    'Goodfriday, 1613. Riding Westward' 367, 373–4, 409
    Ignatius His Conclave 397
    'The Litany' 409
    Pseudo-Martyr 429
    sermons xxxix n., 355, 459, 463
Dorman, Marianne xiii
Dove, Thomas 365, 366
Downame, John 333, 347
drama xv, xxi, xxxvii, xlviii, lii, 343, 344, 377, 394, 395, 406, 412, 448, 449, 451, 455; *see also individual dramatists*; masques
Drant, Thomas 304, 305, 306, 315, 317
Dryden, John xliii
Dudley, Robert, earl of Leicester 304, 310, 335
Dun, Henry 312
Duppa, Brian lix
Dutch, *see* Low Countries

Early English Books Online lv
Easter 300, 304, 453, 461
Eastern Church 283, 284, 411–12, 425, 450
    liturgies 371, 381, 383, 384, 386, 416, 424
Ecebolus 363
Edward II, king of England 316
Edward VI, king of England 322, 336, 337
Egerton, Thomas, baron Ellesmere 395
Eikon Basilike 347
Ekins, Nicholas 347
ἐκκλεσια ('ecclesia') 302
election xix, 356; *see also* predestination; perseverance
Eliot, T. S. xi n., xii, xiii–xiv, xxiv–xxv, xxx–xxxi, xlv, xlvi–vii, xlviii, 435
Elizabeth I, queen of England xxi, 275, 310, 311, 312, 332, 337, 354, 381, 397, 428–9
    court xx–xxi, 335, 336
    excommunication 325, 427, 465
    Privy Council 275, 304, 309, 337
    in sermons xxiii, 353–4, 307, 316–17, 322, 336, 353–4, 359, 364–5
    'To the Troops at Tilbury' 354
Elizabeth, princess; later queen of Bohemia 395, 396
Ely (bishopric) 337
Erasmus, Desiderius 342, 449
eucharist 285, 289, 302–3, 378–90, 405, 414, 434; *see also* liturgy; Hooker, Richard
    adoration 369
    administered to infants 285
    consubstantiation 380, 388

eucharist (cont)
  ευχαριστια ('thanksgiving') 413, 447
  frequency xviii, 379, 386
  the mass xliv, 391, 393, 396, 397, 398, 406, 446
  participation xxii
  real presence xiv, xxxvi, 289, 380, 384–5, 386, 388, 447
  reservation 369
  remits sins xix–xx, 380, 383–4, 385, 388, 389, 446
  sacrifice 293–4, 366, 376
  transubstantiation xxviii, 380, 381–2, 385
execution (for treason) 360, 400, 431–2
ex officio oath 313

Fall, the 348, 352
Familists 299
Fane, John 11th earl of Westmorland 462
Farindon, Antony 293
fasting 290
Fathers, the lvi–vii, 279, 282, 283, 349, 366, 448–9, 454
Fawkes, Guido *or* Guy 390, 394, 396, 397, 399
Fawne, Lawrence 347
feast days xxiii, xxvi, 391, 401, 436, 444,
feasting xxv, xxxviii, 391, 401–2, 403, 406, 412, 453
Ferrell, Lori Anne xxvi, 392, 417, 446
Fincham, Kenneth xxix n., xlviii n., 346
Fish, Stanley xxxii n., 449
Fisher, John 366–7, 372, 373, 374, 375
Fitzgerald, William 278
Five Wounds of Christ ('*Arma Christi*') 367, 370, 372, 375
Florus, L. Annaeus 333, 344
Foliot, Gilbert 385
Foxe, John xvii
  Actes and Monuments 302, 328, 335, 337, 338, 427
Fraser, Antonia 392, 395, 397, 398, 399, 400
Frederick I ('Barbarossa'), emperor 427
friars 345
Fulgentius 275
Fulke, William xxviii, lviii, 277, 306
  A Defence 283, 289, 290, 292, 302, 338, 387, 389, 438
  A Discoverie 284
  A Rejoynder 324
  A Sermon ... within the Tower 285
Fuller, Thomas 427

Gardiner, Stephen 381–2, 387
Garnet, Henry 390, 396
Garrett, William 277
Génébrard, Gilbert 419, 420

Gerard, John 397
Gerrish, B. A. 383, 387
Gibbons, Orlando 391–2, 402
Gill, Stephen xlvi n.
Gnostics, Gnosticism 405; *see also* Valentinus
Godwin, Francis 326
Goff, Thomas 462
Goldie, Mark 418
Good Friday 303, 304; *see also* liturgy
Goodrich, Thomas 338
Gowries, *see* Ruthven
Gowrie Plot
  annual commemoration 300, 415, 417, 418, 433
  The Earle of Gowries Conspiracie (1603) 416, 426–7, 432–3
grace 425, 444
  irresistibility 359
Greek Church, *see* Eastern Church
Green, Ian 278
Gregory the Great lvi, 315, 451
  Epistolae 316
  Moralia 287
  Homilia in Evang. 288, 360
  Homilia in Evang. XL (on Mary Magdalen) 448–55 *passim*, 457, 458, 460, 461
Gregory Nazianzen 362
Grensted, L. W. 367
Greville, Sir Fulke lix
Grotius, Hugo xxviii, 279
Guest, Edmund 381
Guibbory, Achsah xxi n.
Guigi V, Prior 281
Gunpowder Plot xxiii, xxviii, 416, 425, 428, 446
  annual commemoration 300, 391, 393
Gwalter, Rudolf 356

Hacket, John lix, 415–16
Hall, Joseph 307
Harding, Thomas 321
Harington, Sir John xl, xli, 381, 401–2
Harsnett, Samuel 428
Hastings, Henry, earl of Huntington xvi, lviii
Hart (*alias* Hammond), Fr. 397
Harvey, Christopher 405
Hatt, Cecilia 366
Hatton, Sir Christopher 417
Haugaard, William P. 383
Heal, Felicity 334, 337, 337–8
Heathen, the, *see* Cicero
Hebb, Andrew 331
Heirom, *see* Jerome
Hellowes, Sir Edmund 326
Henry III, king of England 316

Henry VII, king of England 275
Henry VIII, king of England 275, 303, 325, 335–6, 338
Henry III, king of France 310, 425, 429
Henry IV, king of France xxvi, 365, 416, 419, 429; *see also* Ravaillac
  A True Report [of the assassination of] (1610) 416, 430, 432
Henry, prince of Wales (*d.* 1612) xxv, xl n., 391, 395, 405, 411, 417, 428
Heraclius, Byzantine emperor 425
Herbert, George xxiii, xli–iii, lix
hermeticism 352
Herodotus lvii, 333, 354, 360
Hewison, Paul xiii, xvi n., xxvi n.
Heylyn, Peter 273, 274, 298, 302
Hilary of Poitiers 279, 282
Hill, Christopher 334
Hodgkinson, Richard 347
Holbeach House (Staffs.) 400
Holdenby ('Holmby') House (Northants.) 417, 418, 427
Holgate, Robert 338
Holinshead, Raphael 317
Holland, Philemon 292, 362
Holland, Thomas 304, 462
Holy Spirit, *see also* Whitsunday
  adoption through 413
  author of scripture 367
  gifts of 279
  'person' of, defined 437
  procession 433, 435, 437, 438
Homer lvii, 333
  Iliad 334, 346
  Odyssey 442
Hooker, Richard lix, 297, 302, 383, 390, 434
  Lawes of Ecclesiasticall Polity xvi, 291, 293, 300, 301, 302, 303, 308, 382, 423, 434
  on the eucharist 380, 381, 385, 386, 388, 389
Hooper, John 302
Horace lvii, 393, 455
Hosius, Stanislaus 321
Howard, Charles, earl of Nottingham 395
Howard, lady Frances lix
Howell, T. B. 392
Huddington Court (Worcs.) 397
humanism xxii, lv
Hutton, Matthew 395
Hutten, Ulrich von 336
Huysmans, Joris-Karl xlvii

Ignatius Loyola 405
images 291, 292, 301, 335
imitatio 448

Incarnation, the 389–90, 404–5, 410, 411–12, 414, 437, 439, 453, 454
  Christ's two natures 408–9, 438
  'hypostatic union' 380, 388
  human participation xxii, xxv
  and words xxxvi
Index Librorum Prohibitorum, Index Expurgatorius 430
Instruments of the Passion 370
Ireland 343, 365
Irenaeus lvi, 280, 282, 409, 423
Isaacson, Henry xvii n., xviii n., 276, 277, 348
Isidore 286, 301
Islam 278, 279, 440

Jackson, John 276
James VI and I, king of Scotland and England xxv, xxviii, xli, 297, 366, 395, 399, 404, 417, 427, 428, 430–1, 454, 459
  Accession Day 300, 364
  'Book of Sports' 297, 391
  coronation lix, 422, 424
  court xii, xvii, xxiii, xxix, 401, 406, 412, 415, 417, 427, 428, 433, 434, 449, 459
  Daemonologie (1597) 426
  death lx
  Gowrie Plot 415–17, 419
  Great Contract (1610) 416, 417, 428, 428
  Hampton Court Conference (1604) lix
  His Majesties Speach (1605) 392, 394–5, 395, 396, 398, 399, 400
  The Kings Majesties Speach (1610) 416, 420
  Oath of Allegiance lix, 416, 421, 422, 424, 427
  Premonition (1609) 427
  Privy Council 415, 417, 428
  royal prerogative xxvi, 416
  Scottish progress (1617) xli, lix
  in sermons 397, 403
  Spanish Match xxix, lx, 446
James, William 364
Jerome lvi, 283, 296, 302, 349, 381, 420, 421, 434, 437; *see also* Didymus Alexandrinus
  Chronicon 284
  Commentaries 405, 324, 441, 434, 368
  Dialogus contra Pelagianos 412
  Epistolae 363, 435, 441, 443
Jesuits xxviii, 306, 397, 405
  and Gunpowder Plot 390, 391, 392, 397–8
  and regicide 397–8, 416, 419, 429, 431; *see also* Mariana
Jesus, Name of 378, 402, 405, 406; *see also* Circumcision, of Christ
Jewel, John 306, 321

GENERAL INDEX

Jones, Norman 364
Jonson, Benjamin xxxi, 301, 405, 455
Josephus, Flavius lvii, 333, 343, 344, 354, 359
Jovian, Roman emperor 425
Juan de Santa Maráia 401
Judaism, 'the Jews' 278, 279, 371, 372, 440; *see also* 'Rabbis, the'
'judaizers' 394, 441
Julian ('the Apostate') 363, 425
Justinian, Roman emperor 341
Justinus, M. Junianus 333, 344
Juvenal lvii, 333, 341

Katherine of Aragon, queen of England 325
Keble, John xlvi n.
Kemnisius *or* Kemnitius, Martinus, *see* Chemnitz, Martin
King, John 427
Klemp, P. J. xiii n. xlviii n., li, 272, 449, 450
Knolles, Richard 292
Knollys, Sir Francis 332, 334, 335, 336, 337
Knollys, Lettice, countess of Leicester lviii
Knollys, William, baron Wallingford, later earl of Banbury 417
Knox, John 342, 345
Kramer, Frank 382
Kyd, Thomas xv

lay patrons 337, 341, 343-4
Lake, Peter xii n., xix n., xxix n., xlviii n., 302, 335, 382, 449
Lanquet, Thomas 355
Lanyer, Amelia 352
Last Judgement 309, 322, 331, 373, 378, 385, 434, 436, 443-4, 455, 463, 466; *see also* post-millenarianism
Latimer, Hugh 302
Laud, William xli, xlii, xlvii 276, 297, 333, 337, 344, 347
    ed., Andrewes, *XCVI Sermons* and *Opuscula Posthuma* xii, xiii, xiv, xv, xvii, xviii, xli, xlviii, xlix, l, 276, 331, 449
Laudians, Laudianism 276, 291, 293, 297, 298, 302, 303, 347-8, 460
'Law of Nature', *see* natural law
lawyers 313, 343, 345; *see also* Westminster Hall
lectures xviii, xx
Lee, Maurice, Jr. 435
Legg, J. Wickham 422
Leigh, Edward 280, 442
Lever, Thomas 335
Levi ben Ghershom 333
Lewy, Guenter 430
Liberius 284
Linacre, Thomas 442

Lindsay, David 302
liturgy xx, 289, 366, 416; *see also* sermons
  ORDERS and SERVICES; *see also* Eastern Church; Sarum Rite
  Holy Communion 274, 275, 286, 289, 292-3, 377, 381, 383, 384, 390, 393, 406, 437, 446, 452, 461
  Morning Prayer 274, 286, 292, 329, 402, 408, 409, 418, 421
  Evening Prayer 308, 402
  Matrimony 351-2, 418
  Baptism 439
  Burial 455
  Litany 354, 359
  Visitation of the Sick 359
  Christmas 406, 409
  Circumcision of Christ 411, 412
  Good Friday 287, 366, 367, 368, 369, 371, 376
  Gowrie Conspiracy Anniversary 391, 415
  Gunpowder Plot Anniversary 391, 392, 401, 402-3
  Accession Days 391
  consecration of bishops 346
  consecration of churches 345
  coronation 421, 422, 424
  LITURGICAL TEXTS
  Apostles' Creed 424
  confessions 350, 372, 385, 390
  Doxology 289
  Benedictus 391, 393, 402
  Gloria in Excelsis 289
  Gloria Patri xxxiii, 289
  Nicene Creed 413, 437, 438
  Sanctus 390, 393
  Te Deum 408, 421
  Magnificat 329
  Venite 292, 418
  versicles 402, 433
Lloyd, Lodowick 336
Lodge, Thomas xv
  Prosopopeia 367, 374, 375, 378
London, City of; *see also* Westminster
  All-Hallows- by-the-Tower xv, lviii
  Bridewell Hospital 326
  Christ's Hospital 304, 319, 322, 326
  Globe Theatre xxx
  Lambeth 397
  Lord Mayor and Aldermen xvi, lviii 274, 275, 304, 307, 308, 311, 314, 320, 323, 330
  Merchant Taylors' School xv, lviii
  Peasants' Revolt 314
  Recorder 304
  Rehearsal Sermon 303, 304, 462-3
  St. Giles Cripplegate lviii, 379

GENERAL INDEX

Andrewes's sermons at xvii–xix, xxii, 274, 277, 285, 295, 348, 350, 367, 378–90, 386
St. Mary's Hospital, sermons at xvi–xvii, xliii–iv, lvii, 303–7, 322, 328, 462–6
St. Paul's Cathedral xvii, lviii
   Andrewes's sermons at xvii–xix, 274, 277, 285, 299, 299, 348
   Paul's Cross 303, 332, 396, 399, 400, 462, 463
St. Saviour's, Southwark (Southwark Cathedral) xxx, lx
Spital, *see* St. Mary's Hospital
'Stranger' Churches 326, 442
Tower of London xv
Trinity House 305
Winchester House xxx, lx
Lossky, Nicholas xix n., xxii, xxvi, xlviii n., 354, 367, 371, 383, 388, 390, 392, 403, 405, 416–17, 424, 435, 438, 439, 440, 449, 453
Love, Nicholas 405
Low Countries 317, 343, 365, 442; *see also* Deventer
Luther, Martin xx, l, lvii, 353, 361, 366
   Lectures on Genesis 348, 349, 350, 351
   on the Passion 367, 369, 371, 372, 375
   Operationes in Psalmos 368
   Theses 322
Lutheran churches, Lutheranism xx, 283, 380, 381, 383, 388
Lyly, John xviii, xl, 305

MacCulloch, Diarmaid xlviii n., 293, 334, 354, 382
McCullough, Peter xii n., xiv n., xxi n., xxiii n., xxix n., xxxi n., xxxvi n., xlvii n., 278, 354, 392, 416, 417, 427, 435, 444, 449, 459, 463
McCutcheon, Elizabeth xlviii
McIlwain, C. H. 424
Mack, Peter xxxi n., 305, 307, 308, 328
Manton, Thomas 313, 372
Marcus, Leah 354
Mariana, Juan de lvii, 416, 429, 430
   De Rege 416, 429–30
Markham, Gervase 441
Marlowe, Christopher 353
Marprelate Controversy 304, 320, 332
marriage 348–53 *passim*
Martin, Gregory xxviii, 292, 338, 387, 389, 438; *see also* Bible, Douai-Rheims
Marvell, Andrew 352
Mary, princess (*d.* 1607) 395
Mary, queen of Scots 312, 342, 364, 428–9

Mary I, queen of England xv, 333, 335, 364, 435
   martyrs under 337
Mary, the Virgin 409
masques 401–2, 405, 455
Matthew, Toby (bp.) 365
Mattingly, Garrett 310
Mawe, Leonard lx
Maximilla, *see* Montanus
Melancthon, Phillip 334
Merbeck, John 292
Mercier, Jean 333
Meres, Francis 372
merchants, *see also* monopolies 305, 307, 315, 320, 324, 326, 327, 330, 343
Meun, Jean de 458
Migne, J. P. lvii
Miller, George xii, liii
Miller, R. H. 381
Milton, John xvii, xix n.
   Accedence Commenc't Grammar 291
   Doctrine ... of Divorce 299
   Lycidas 344
   Paradise Lost 350, 407, 410
   Sonnet XIII 333
Milward, Peter 306, 424
Mishle Shelomoh ben David 333
Mitchell, W. Fraser xlii n., xlvii n.
Moller, Heinrich 382, 384, 385
monopolies 324
Monothelites 284
Montagu, Richard lx
Montanus, Montanist heresy 434–5, 441, 442–3
Morrissey, Mary xxxi n., lii, 462
Moseley, Humphrey 347–8
Mountaigne, George 449
Mounteagle, Lord, *see* Parker, William
Mozley, James B. xiii n., xxvi n., xlv–vi
Mulcaster, Richard xv, lviii
Munday, Anthony 461
Musculus, Wolfgang lvii, 306, 316, 382, 385–6
music, *see* worship

Nash, Thomas (1588–1648) 336
Nashe, Thomas (1567–1601) xviii, xl, 305
natural law 308, 418
Nazianzen, *see* Gregory Nazianzin
Neale, Sir John 335, 337
Nestorius 420
Newman, J. H. xiii, xlvi
Nicholas of Clairvaux 361
   Sermo in Festo B. Mariæ Magdalenæ 448–9, 459, 460
Nicolson, Adam xxviii n.

Noel, Henry xl
non-conformists, 'sectarians' 280, 299, 354, 355, 440; *see also* Anabaptists, Familists
Norton, Glyn P. xxxiv n.
Norton, Roger 276
Nowell, Alexander 365

Oecumenius 302
Ogerius Lucedii 361
Origen lvi, 279, 282, 349, 381, 451,
    De Oratione 285
    (attr.) *Homilia de B. Maria Magdalena* 448–9, 451, 452, 453, 454, 455, 456, 457, 458, 459, 460, 461
Orsisius 291
Orthodox Church, *see* Eastern Church
Ovid lvii, 356
Owen, Trevor xxvi, xlii n., xlvii n.
Oxford English Dictionary, Andrewes and 305
    cited as first or unique usage 312, 313, 324, 412, 436
    cited as last usage 371, 375
    usages which predate first citations 285, 295, 299, 309, 310, 323, 358, 377, 394, 398, 425, 426, 439, 442, 450, 452
    usages which postdate last citations 313, 396, 412, 457
    usages not found in 355, 422
    other citations of 285, 324
Oxford Movement xiii–xiv, xlv–vi, lii n., 435
Oxford University
    Bodleian Library lv, 272
    colleges 343–4
    Jesus College lviii
    Lincoln College xxxix n.
    Magdalen College xlvi n.
    Regius Professor of Divinity, *see* Holland, Thomas

Pakeman, Daniel 347
Palatinate 446
Parisius 301
Parker, Kenneth 297
Parker, William, baron Mounteagle 390, 395, 399
parliament 276, 333, 334, 336, 391, 395, 398, 416, 428; *see also* James VI & I; Westminster
    Scottish 432
Parry, Graham xviii n.
Parsons, Robert 320, 386
patriarchalism xxvii, 420
Patrologia Latina Database lv
Peck, Linda Levy xii n.
Pentecost, *see* Whitsunday
Perault *alias* Peraldus, Guillaume 301
Percy, Sir Thomas 390, 397

Perkins, William 372, 381, 383, 456
Perron, Jacques Davy, du 242
perseverance xxii–xxiii, 353, 355, 361, 364
Peter of Blois (Petrus Blesensis) 375
Peter Comestor 300
Peter Damian 451
Peter Lombard 350
Peters, Christine 348, 352, 441
Petrus Chrysologus 459
Philip of Macedon 310, 465
Philip II, king of Spain 310, 465
Philips, Sir Edward 395, 396
Phillips, Edward 327
Philpott, John 335
Pierce, Thomas xviii, 347, 356
Pliny 322; *see also* Bartholomaeus, Anglicus
Plume, Thomas 415–16
Plutarch 292, 344, 362
Pole, Reginald 329
Poliziano, Prosper 300
pope 397
    as 'Antichrist' 391
    as 'Christ's vicar' 422
    spiritual power 425
    temporal power xxvi, xxviii, xliii, 279, 284, 421, 422, 424, 427, 429, 430
popes
    Alexander III 427
    Eugenius IV 284
    Honorius I
    Leo III 421
    Leo X 284
    Paul IV 430
    Pius V 325
Popham, Sir John 395
Porter, H. C. 334
post-millenarianism 443
Potter, Lois 348
Powell, David (?) *or* William (?) 304, 305, 305–6, 316, 319, 320, 321, 323, 325, 326, 328, 462, 464, 465, 466
Prayer, prayers 285–90, 403
    at death 445
    before sermon xxii, 272–4, 331, 389
    bidding 272–4
    concluding sermons xxxii
    Lord's, the 275
    to saints xxviii
preachers, duties of 357, 365
preaching, *see* sermons
predestination xxii–xxiii 306, 329, 350, 353, 361, 373; *see also* perseverance
presbyterianism, presbyterians xx–xxi, 304, 307, 313, 332–4, 338, 342, 346, 423, 463
    Dedham Classis 296–7, 299
Preston, Thomas 344

priesthood
    'of the believer' 346
    Levitical *or* Aaronic 340, 376, 416, 419, 423
    ordination 440
Primerose, David 300
Primus, J. H. 296
Priscilla, *see* Montanus
Procter, Francis and W. G. Frere, *New History of the BCP* 274, 368
Prosper of Aquitaine 287, 289
Prynne, William 302
Pseudo-Bernard 378, 451
Pseudo-Bonaventure, *see* Love, Nicholas
Puckering, Sir John 272
'puritans', 'puritanism' xvi, xx, xxvii, xxix, xxx, xl, 301, 320, 332–3, 345, 391, 406, 423, 434, 463, 465; *see also* presbyterians nonconformists
Pusey, E. B. xlvi n.
Puttenham, George 411

Quarles, Francis 405
Quintilian xxxi

Rabanus Maurus 405, 409, 451
'Rabbis, the'; rabbinical scholarship 333, 335, 336, 339, 436
Rackham, H. 396
Randall, Catherine xxxiv n.
Ravaillac, Francis 416, 419, 429
    The Copie of a Letter [concerning the execution of] (1610) 416, 429
    The Terrible and Deserved Death [of] (1610) 416, 429, 431–2
Read, Sophie xliii
regicide 325, 416, 428, 429
Reisner, Noam xxxvi n.
relics 398
resistance theory 416, 425, 430
Revard, Stella 392, 396, 398
Rheimists, Rheims New Testament, *see* Bible, Douai-Rheims
rhetorical tropes and figures
    antanaclasis 370
    antimetabole 411, 412
    aposiopesis 403
    asyndeton xxxiii
    gradatio 370, 404
    metaphor 281
    periphrasis xxxiii
    polyptoton 442
    simile xxxiv
    vituperatio lvii
    'wordplay' ('puns', *paranomasia*) xliii–iv
Richard II, king of England 316

Ricks, Christopher xlvii n.
Ridley, Nicholas 302, 338
Roover, Raymond de 327
Royal Society, the xliii
Royston (Cambs.) xxv, 404
Royston, Richard 347
Ruthven, Alexander 415, 419, 428, 432
Ruthven, John, earl of Gowrie 415, 419, 426–7, 428, 432

sabbath, *see* worship
Sacks, David Harris 324
Sackville, Thomas, earl of Dorset 395
sacrament 422
saints 325
Salisbury (bishopric) 337
Salkeld, John 454, 455
Sandes, Henry 296–7, 299
Sandys, Edwin (bp.) 304, 305
Sandys, Sir Edwin xv
Sarum, Use of, *or* Sarum Rite 287–8, 292–3, 346, 409, 446, 454, 458
Satan 331, 396, 398, 399, 428
Scotland, Church of xxix, xli, 342, 434, 436
    'Five Articles of Perth' 434, 440
Scott, David xlii n., 448
Seneca xlii, lvii, 333, 395, 404
    Epistolae 294, 342, 363
Seneca the Elder 311
sermons 294; *see also* lectures
    by women and laymen 441, 442
    court Lent series xxi, 353, 354, 365–6
    delivery (performance) xxxviii–xl
    'doctrine and uses' xli, 451
    frequency and length xxii, xxx, 320, 346
    importance relative to prayer and liturgy 293, 377, 387, 389, 400, 434, 435, 442, 444–5, 448, 461, 463
    parts of xxxi–iii, xxxviii
        division xxxii, 307, 308, 384
    rules for composition xxxiii
    study required for xxxvii, 339
Shakespeare, William xii n., xxvii, xliii, 305, 448
    All Is True (*Henry VIII*) 455
    All's Well That Ends Well 418
    Antony & Cleopatra 394
    Cymbeline 313, 355, 448, 455
    Hamlet 321, 444, 455
    1 Henry IV xxii
    2 Henry IV 312
    Henry V 315
    King Lear 394, 444
    Measure for Measure 412
    Merry Wives of Windsor 456
    Midsummer Night's Dream 362
    Othello 323

Shakespeare, William (*cont*)
  Sonnet 72 336
  Tempest 371, 448, 455
  Winter's Tale xlvii, 448
  Two Gentlemen of Verona 452
Sharpe, Kevin 334
Shuger, Debora xii n., xlviii n., 449
Sidney, Sir Philip xxxi
sin; *see also* baptism; eucharist
  of 'omission' and 'commission' 385
  Original 409
  'original' and 'actual' 381, 386
Smith, Nigel 352
Socrates (historian) 425–6
sodomy 355
sola fide 306, 329, 446, 463, 464; *see also* works
Solomon ben Isaac 333
Somerset, Edward, earl of Worcester 395
Sommerville, Johann 417, 418, 420, 422, 425, 428, 430
South, Robert 372
Southwell, Robert,
  Epistle of Comfort 367, 378
  Marie Magdalens Funeral Teares 374
  Moeoniae 405
  St Peter's Complaint 367, 378
Sparke, Michael 276
Spenser, Edmund xv, xxxix
  The Faerie Queene xxxi, 353, 454
Spinks, Bryan 383
Stanwood, Paul G. xviii n.
Stapleton, Thomas 277, 279, 281, 282, 284–5, 285
Star Chamber 441
Steward, Richard 303
Stokes, David 274, 406–7
Story, G. M. xiii, xxiv, xxvi n., xlvii n., xlix, l, li, liii, liv, lv, 448, 449
Stow, John 304, 314, 316
Strabo, Walafridus 341
Straw, Jack 314
Strong, Roy 422
Strype, John 334
Suarez, Francisco 303
sumptuary laws 313
Symonds, Joseph 442

Tacitus xlii
Tertullian xliv, lvi, 405, 406, 409, 423, 431
Theodoret 302
Theophilus of Antioch 302
Thomason Tracts 331
Tractarians, *see* Oxford Movement
Traske, John 298–9, 441
Travers, Walter 334, 434
Tremellius, John Imanuel, *see* Bible

Trent, Council of, *see* councils
Trevor-Roper, Hugh xvii n.
Trinity, the 413, 437
Turner, Christopher xlii n.
Twelve Tables, the 342
Tyacke, Nicholas xvi n., xix n., xlviii n., 278, 291, 295, 302, 334, 348, 353, 354, 379, 382, 386
Tyler, Wat 314
types, typology 364, 376, 381, 386, 391, 395, 406, 413, 424, 428

Ussher, James 442

Valentinus 408–9
Vane, Lady 335
Vickers, Brian xxxi n., xxxiii n., xxxiv n., xxxviii, 411
Vigne, Louise 461
Virgil 333
  Aeneid 337, 339, 431
Voak, Nigel 300, 383

Walsingham, Sir Francis xv, xvii, lviii, lix
Walworth, William 314
Warner, John 303, 331
Warren, Jason Scott xli n.
Waser, Caspar 339
Webber, Joan xxxiv n.
Weelkes, Thomas 391, 402
Welsby, Paul xiv n., 357
Westminster
  Hall 316
  Parliament House 390, 394, 400
  School xxiii, xlii, 274, 406, 415
  Whitehall 395
  Whitehall Preaching Place xxi
Weston, Hugh 302
Whetstone, George 312
Whitaker, William 278, 279–38 *passim*
White, Francis 297
White, John 307
White, John (bp.) 302
Whitgift, John xx, xxi, 337, 345, 354, 415
  'Against Farming of Tithes' 332, 334, 338, 347
  An Answere to ... An Admonition 293, 434
Whitsunday 301, 435, 461
William of Orange (*d*. 1584) 325, 465
Williams, John 302
Williamson, George xxxv n., xl n., xlii
Wilson, J. P. xxiv, lii, lv
Wilson, Thomas 342
Winwood, Sir Ralph 404
witchcraft 426–7
Wither, George 405

woman, nature of xix, 348–53 *passim*
Woods, Susanne 352
Woolf, Rosemary 366, 375, 376, 448
Wordsworth, William xlv–vi
works
    duty xxii, xxx, xli, 391
    efficacy xvii, xxxvi, 305–6, 320–1, 327–9, 397, 446, 464, 465–6
  worship 349
    behaviour at 377
    music 391, 401, 419, 445, 463
    physical gestures in xvi, 291–96, 310, 453, 463
    the sabbath (Sunday) xvi, 296–301, 394, 454
Wren, Matthew lx, 460
Wright, Christopher 397
Wright, Samuel li, 447
writs of prohibition 313
Wyntour, Thomas 395, 396, 397

Zwingli, Huldrych 382, 384